Shelley Fenno Quinn

. . .

Developing Zeami

THE NOH ACTOR'S ATTUNEMENT IN PRACTICE

University of Hawai'i Press
Honolulu

© 2005 University of Hawai'i Press
Printed in the United States of America

10   09   08   07   06   05   6   5   4   3   2   1

LIBRARY OF CONGRESS CATALOGING-IN-PUBLICATION DATA
Quinn, Shelley Fenno.
Developing Zeami : The noh actor's attunement in practice / Shelley Fenno Quinn.
    p.   cm.
Includes bibliographical references and index.
ISBN 0-8248-1827-X (hardcover : alk. paper)
ISBN 0-8248-2968-9 (pbk. : alk. paper)
1. Zeami, 1363–1443—criticism and interpretation.   2. Nåo.   I. Title.

PL792.S4Z837 2005
895.6'22—dc22

2004027786

University of Hawai'i Press books are printed on acid-free paper and meet the
guidelines for permanence and durability of the Council on Library Resources.

Book design and composition by Diane Gleba Hall

Printed by The Maple-Vail Book Manufacturing Group

To my mother,
Marilyn Whitcomb Fenno,
and the memory of my father,
Ross V. Fenno

•   •   •

Contents

. . .

Contents
. . .

Acknowledgments

．　．　．

This book has been long in the making. The list of those who have been generous with their guidance and support is even longer, and I only wish I had the space to name them all. I am deeply indebted to my teachers in the Department of East Asian Languages and Cultures, Indiana University, including my late adviser, Prof. Kenneth K. Yasuda, and two other wonderful mentors, Profs. Jurgis Elisonas and Sumie Amikura Jones. I also want to thank my cohorts in the graduate program there, Drs. Fumiko Togasaki, David Slawson, and Barbara Arnn, for their friendship and their example. When I was a visiting graduate student at Dōshisha University in Kyoto, my adviser, Prof. Yoshiki Mukai, and my tutor, Prof. Hideo Inada, were such attentive guides as I made my initial forays into Zeami's writings. My sincere thanks to them as well.

I am very grateful for the support of scholars at the Hōsei University Institute of Nōgaku Studies in Tokyo for hosting me three times as a visiting researcher in the 1990s and for facilitating my work in Tokyo in innumerable ways. Special thanks to Emeritus Prof. Akira Omote, whose annotated editions of Zeami's treatises have greatly enriched my understanding. Prof. Haruo Nishino, the institute director, and Prof. Reiko Yamanaka of the institute faculty have been unstintingly generous with their time and advice. I am also grateful to Prof. Mikio Takemoto, director of the Waseda

University Tsubouchi Memorial Theatre Museum, for kindly sharing his research on the newly discovered transcription of Zeami's *Sandō*. Moreover, I want to thank Prof. Akiko Miyake of Yokohama National University for her generous support of my research projects.

I have benefited much from collaborations with colleagues at The Ohio State University. To mention only a few, my thanks to Profs. Naomi Fukumori and Charles J. Quinn, Jr., in early Japanese texts, Chan Park and Mark Bender in folklore and performance, and Thomas P. Kasulis in comparative studies. I also want to thank other scholars who have supported my work: Profs. Yan-shuan Lao, Xiaomei Chen, Diane Birckbichler, Galal Walker, Bradley Richardson, Mari Noda, Maureen Donovan, and James Huffman. Working with graduate students here has given me wonderful opportunities to grow, and I am especially grateful to Noriko T. Reider, Shinko Kagaya, Todd S. Squires, Leo Shing Chi Yip, and Minae Savas for many fruitful discussions.

It has been a privilege to train in noh acting and noh flute under professional performers over the years. The late Yasuo Yagi, *shite-kata* of the Kanze School of Noh, was my first teacher. Intensely devoted to his art, he opened up a whole new world to me, and I will be forever grateful to him and his family. I owe a great debt to my first flute teacher, Mr. Masanori Hoashi (Morita School), and his wife, Yōko, whose friendship and understanding of noh traditions and Japanese cultural practices in general have been an inspiration. I am most fortunate in my current teachers, Mr. Hiroyuki Matsuda of the Morita School in Tokyo, and Mr. Tomotaka Sekine, Kanze School, and his wife, Yoshie. Their training has enriched my research immeasurably, as has the friendship and support of fellow learners, especially Ms. Eiko Kobayashi and Ms. Fusae Andō.

Sincere thanks to the Japan Foundation, the Japan-United States Educational Commission (Fulbright Commission), and The Ohio State University Seed Grant program for funding that supported completion of the first two parts of this book. I wish to express my gratitude to the College of Humanities and the Department of East Asian Languages and Literatures (DEALL) for graciously granting me a subvention. My thanks to Prof. J. Marshall Unger, then chair of DEALL, for supporting the application. Special thanks to Tōshiba International Foundation (TIFO) for additional subvention support for a paperback edition. I am grateful to Brent and Noriko T. Reider also for their generous donation to DEALL, part of which I have used for copyright permission fees.

Dr. Kate Nakai, editor of *Monumenta Nipponica*, has kindly granted permission to append an expanded version of my English translation of *Sandō*, which originally appeared as "How to Write a Noh Play: Zeami's *Sandō*," *Monumenta Nipponica* (spring 1993): 53–88. I thank Hōsei University Institute of Nōgaku Studies for allowing me to reproduce three images from Zeami's treatise *Nikyoku santai ningyō zu*. My sincere thanks also to Mitsui Bunko in Tokyo for permitting publication of two images of masks in its collection, and to Mr. Yoshihiro Maejima, Prof. Shōzō Masuda, and the Yoshikoshi Sutajio for permission to publish their photographs of performances. As my research assistant, Ms. Minae Savas has been a great help with copyright negotiations. My thanks to the East Asian Studies Center, The Ohio State University, for funding her position.

Ms. Patricia Crosby, executive editor at University of Hawai'i Press, could not have been more generous with her encouragement, her advice, and her patience. My sincere thanks also to Ms. Cheri Dunn, managing editor, for her professionalism and support. I am very fortunate in my copy editor, Ms. Susan L. B. Corrado, who has been impeccably attentive to those devilish details. The suggestions of my two anonymous reviewers have been very helpful, truly going beyond the call of duty. I am deeply saddened that Ms. Sharon Yamamoto, the first editor with whom I worked at University of Hawai'i Press, is not here to thank.

I am very grateful to my family—Marilyn, Doris, Lynn, Gwen, Carol, Charles, Chick, the Maxwell and O'Hagan clans—for believing in me and waiting so patiently for this book to reach completion. Chick, a special thanks for being there. I wish Ross, Marie, and Patti could be with us too. I do not know how to thank my mother, who is a wonderful role model and a loving presence in my life in countless ways. Nor can I count the ways that I am grateful to my husband, Charles J. Quinn, Jr., for his loving support, his good humor, and his inspiration.

Developing Zeami

· · ·

Introduction

. . .

Z eami Motokiyo (1363?–1443?), actor, playwright, and theorist of the noh theatre, is widely acclaimed today as one of the most innovative thinkers in the history of the stage. He has long enjoyed recognition as a seminal playwright of noh, an art that depicts the life of the emotions in a synthesis of dramatic, musical, and choreographed elements. Along with this activity as a playwright, he produced twenty-one critical writings over four decades that record his efforts to discern what worked best with audiences. These treatises contain a nuanced and comprehensive phenomenology of the stage informed by a lifetime of artistic practice. Intended as instructions for his successors on how to get ahead in the competitive business of performing, they reflect a growing awareness on his part of the greater efficacy of a multisensory and open theatrical form for engaging the interest of audiences.

Unlike his plays, which have been performed continuously since his own lifetime, his critical corpus began to be published and made available to the general public only in 1908 and 1909. In the last century, his treatises have taken on a new life as fruitful objects of inquiry for scholars and practitioners of theatre and performance around the world. As Gerould has noted, "Like all the most enduring theories, Zeami's treatises exist both within their own historical period and also independently of the theatre practice that gave rise to them."[1] Gerould also rightly cautions that one must tread carefully when ascribing universal appeal across time and cultural context, and it is not the intent of this volume to take such a facile approach. At the same time, Zeami's treatises continue to offer a wealth of insights to audiences beyond the specific concerns of one theatrical tradition, on issues ranging from the nature of dramatic illusion and audience interest, to tactics for composing successful plays, to issues of somaticity and bodily training.

This book is an interpretive study of Zeami's treatises that addresses all of these areas as it traces the development of his ideas on how best to cultivate attunement between performer and audience. I have titled it *Developing Zeami* because it takes the position that an understanding of his ideas is best gained by reconstructing their development as a process. For example, one of Zeami's accomplishments as a playwright that is often mentioned is the honing of a certain dramatic prototype, referred to today as *mugen* (dream) noh. This type of play was designed to foster the engagement of the audience in co-creation of the story, or so I will argue. While the importance of *mugen* noh as "product" should not be underestimated, for its full import to be understood it needs to be situated in the larger context of what kind of performance Zeami wanted to promote. How did *mugen* noh contribute to the larger aim of a successful performance? What Huxley and Witts state in their reader on modern performance is no less true in the case of Zeami's dramaturgy: "Performance means process as well as final artefact, and an engagement with process is essential to any full understanding of the form."[2] Indeed, for Zeami the prototypical form that a drama should take was the by-product of the process that he wished to promote onstage. For these reasons, this volume will situate Zeami's precepts on composing in the larger context of his theories about dramatic representation and the elicitation of audience interest.

Needless to say, tracking the development of Zeami's ideas means that they must first be examined within the particular ecology of *sarugaku* (the earlier name for noh) in Muromachi Japan (1336–1573), where they emerged in response to a nexus of local variables. Many concepts that are key to understanding Zeami's drama theory, among them the aesthetic ideal of *yūgen* (mystery and depth/grace) and that of *hana* (the flower), are referred to throughout his critical corpus, but their meaning, too, changes over time. Any clear understanding of his mature theory of the stage depends on examining the kinds of performance variables and tensions that these core ideas were intended to address as Zeami struggled to reinvent his art. That is, to understand the underlying rationales for his theory of how to engage audiences, it is crucial to also examine how it changed and why. In so doing, we become better able to explore how certain aspects of his ideas about performance may speak to us today.

Zeami's Developing "Flower"

Zeami's own term for successful attunement between performers and audience is *hana* (flower). One further way to characterize the aim of this volume is as the pursuit of Zeami's deepening understanding of the variables that allow this flower to bloom. In its most fundamental sense, it may be defined as "simply that which [creates a sense of] novelty in the mind the of the spectator."[3] He holds to this conception throughout his critical writings. He is certainly not the first to employ the metaphor of the flower to underscore the link between beauty and mutability. However, in his critical treatises there is an added dimension to this image because he uses it to allude to all manner of stage effects/affects as experienced by the spectator. Therefore, the flower is not a thing intrinsic to any particular object or aspect of a performance. Rather, it is a total effect created by whatever happens to work for particular audiences in particular performances. A seemingly simple metaphor, it turns out to be enormously complex, for it signals his commitment to negotiating all the variables that may affect what the spectator perceives and feels.

Those variables may be outside of the performers' direct control, such as the season, the time of day, the weather, the physical setting (outdoors/indoors; town/country), as well as the social mix of the audience. They include the age and physical appeal of the performers as well as how effectively they perform. Moreover, the flower is premised not only on the playwright's creation or the performer's proficiency in the execution of requisite techniques such as chanting, dancing, and the representation of characters, but on the combined effect of these various layers as they are synthesized in the mind of the spectator. Zeami also uses the flower as a metaphor for the art of the actor. An actor who possesses the flower is one who has cultivated both the sensibility and the technical versatility to read his audience and to adjust his performance accordingly. Certainly one important concern motivating all of his pedagogical writings is developing the capacity in his disciples to thus read their audiences.

In the quotation from *Kaden* (Transmission of the flower) above, Zeami states that the impression of novelty in the mind of the spectator implies the presence of the flower. Novelty does not refer to bizarre or aberrant subject matter in a play or its performance, but on the manner in which one performs: "When [two people are] executing the same vocal music or acting, the skilled one will have special interest. The unskilled one will [simply execute techniques] the way he has learned [them], so there will be no sense of novelty."[4] What is more, the difference arises from the skilled actor's ability to invest his techniques with the nuances of his feeling. The techniques themselves may be routine enough, but his ability to exploit them to create interest and this sense of novelty will make him stand out.

The flower, a sensation of interest aroused in the audience, and this sense of novelty are both aspects of the same "mind" (kokoro), Zeami observes. Moreover, such effects depend on cultivating the capacity to avoid slipping into the rut of habit. "Know first of all that the flower consists in not dwelling [in one style]. When you avoid dwelling [in one style], and you shift [freely] into other styles, this will [create a sense of] novelty."[5] It is because flowers fade that their blossoming arouses a sense of novelty. So it goes with styles of performance, he adds. If the actor slips into habitual repetition of only one style, he will become too predictable to inspire a sense of novelty.

As Zeami's ideas and observations about performance mature, he develops further insights into how the playwright and the performer can foster the optimal conditions for creating the effects of the flower. Over time, his treatises provide an increasingly philosophical slant on the concept as his understanding of the nature of attunement deepens. In a treatise titled *Kakyō* (Mirror of the flower; 1424), he likens the relation between the character the actor plays and the underlying state of mind of the actor to that between a marionette and its strings.[6] The marionette seems to have a life of its own while all its strings are intact and working properly. However, when a string breaks, then the fictionality of the puppet is revealed. The dramatic illusion is destroyed as we are reminded that the puppet had depended for its effects on the manipulator working the strings. Similarly in *sarugaku*, techniques of imitation are fabrications made possible by the mind (kokoro) of the actor. Zeami cautions that just as in the case of the strings of a puppet, the workings of the actor's mind must remain invisible to the audience in order to be effective. In his theory of the stage, he thus comes increasingly to attribute the locus of stage effects to the ground rather

4

than the figure—that is, to the actor's underlying capacity to manipulate material as he senses and reacts to audiences rather that to any intrinsic appeal of the content of that material in isolation from its use.

A performer who has internalized techniques to the extent that he can consciously apply them in order to create moving effects may be called skillful, but ultimately the most moving effects depend on the actor going beyond the acquisition and conscious application of techniques. Zeami states that ultimate effects with audiences are possible only after there is no conscious willing on the part of the actor. Extrapolating on his puppet metaphor above, the superbly accomplished manipulator must himself forget that the marionette has strings. Once the striving for effects is something that is not part of the actor's conscious orientation, then optimal attunement with an audience becomes possible. Although Zeami makes a distinction between the mind and the techniques of the actor and holds that the highest grade of the flower emanates from the mind of the actor, this is a cultivated mind that grows in concord with the acquisition of bodily techniques.

Building the Foundation: *Nikyoku santai* (The "Two Modes and Three Styles")

The primary stages of such training of the actor should follow guidelines in abidance with a particular configuration of performance that Zeami refers to as *nikyoku santai* (the "two modes and three styles"; hereafter referred to as *nikyoku santai*). Another way to characterize this volume is as tracking Zeami's development of this concept of performance and its ramifications for his deepening philosophy of attunement. In a nutshell, *nikyoku santai* was originally the outgrowth of his efforts to reorient the relationship of the elements of song and dance with techniques of imitation. *Nikyoku*, which has also been translated variously as the "two arts," "two elements," or "two media," refers to the activities of dancing and chanting. A more liberal and telling gloss for "dance and chant" might be "movement and vocalization." *Nikyoku* also forms part of another term that is important in Zeami's critical theory, *buga nikyoku* (two modes of expression, dance, and chant). He expected the actor in training to internalize these two modes prior to acquiring skills more specific to the playing of roles. In this way, techniques of representation were applied to the actor's preexisting foundation, composed of musical and choreographic techniques. I have translated *nikyoku* as "two modes" to emphasize Zeami's idea that all stage action should unfold via these two forms of expression.

The "three styles" refer to three types of representation, translated here as the "venerable style" (*rōtai*), "feminine style" (*nyotai*), and "martial style" (*guntai*). Whereas early in his career Zeami delineates nine types of characters that are suitable as subjects for imitation, the three styles are a later refinement more suggestive of human prototypes. As their labels imply, the venerable style holds for elderly characters, the feminine style for female ones, and the martial style for warriors. Zeami comes to treat all other possible roles as derivatives of these three styles.[7] As noted above, he considered the two modes to be the prerequisites for training in the techniques of representation embodied in the three styles. The novice actor should first internalize basic techniques of dancing and chanting, and only then should he train in the three styles. That is, representational techniques should be executed via the primary media, dance and chant.

Indexing the Flower in Three Parts

This volume examines *nikyoku santai* as an index of the flower as it develops in three domains, and each domain is the focus of one of its parts. Part 1 concentrates on Zeami's formulation of *nikyoku santai* in conjunction with a rethinking of what kind of representational style was most effective for eliciting audience empathy. It is at the heart of what I consider to be his shift from a style of representation informed by the action to a kind of poiesis, or poetically based representation. I argue that the shift was prompted by his deepening insights into patterns of human reception on two fronts. First, he came increasingly to recognize that the best way to captivate an audience was to leave space for their active involvement in signifying practices. The surest way to create such space was to abandon a representational style based on verisimilitude and to instead construct a multisensory flow of images for each spectator to synthesize on the basis of his own receptivity and imaginative engagement. This is the first sense in which I intend the term "poiesis" here. That is, I mean it in the broader sense of *creation* by an audience in response to what is happening onstage.

The second sense in which I apply the term has to do with this increased reliance on language in engaging the audience. Part 2 explores Zeami's dramaturgy, in which *nikyoku santai* becomes a kind of organizing principle of the dramatic action. The configuration evolved in tandem with the increased importance of texts that rely on poetic tropes and narrative to create a style of play that fosters a kind of echo chamber of allusions. I will argue that *nikyoku santai*, in this domain as well, was central to the fostering of a multimedia stage event effective in eliciting the imaginative engagement of audiences—key to invoking the flower.

Part 3 will examine the ramifications of installing *nikyoku santai* at the heart of the actor's training program as Zeami depicts it in his mature treatises on training. In *Kyūi* (Nine levels), an undated treatise believed to have been written late in his career, Zeami discusses nine levels of artistry that are intended as developmental guidelines for the actor to follow as he strives to develop the capacity to consistently elicit interest and a sense of novelty despite the vicissitudes of performance. The aforementioned style of acting, in which the actor's intentions are hidden even from himself, would correspond to the uppermost of the nine levels. The two modes and three styles are positioned at the entry levels of training. One thing that becomes clear from this paradigm is that Zeami considered the process of acquiring this bodily training in *nikyoku santai* as conducive to cultivating the capacity to achieve attunement with audiences. This final segment of the volume will thus explore the idea that inculcation of *nikyoku santai* in training was not only important for the creation of the role, but also for the creation of the actor. In the following I will discuss in a bit more detail some of the major issues addressed in each of the three parts.

Part 1: A Shift in Representational Styles

Part 1 begins by examining the cultural backdrop of Zeami's troupe's performances in order to reconstruct his rationale for creating the *nikyoku santai* configuration. I argue that the initial impetus may well have been tactical, growing out of a concern that his own style of *sarugaku*, based in the Yamato region of what is today Nara Prefecture, was not keeping up with the competition from the troupes based in the Ōmi area, north of the capital of Kyoto. The Ōmi troupes were recognized as having a high *yūgen* quotient in their art, which met with the approval of potential patrons of the Kyoto establishment such as the third Muromachi shogun, Ashikaga Yoshimitsu (1358–1408).

Yūgen (variously translated as "mystery and depth" or "grace") will be familiar to students of medieval Japan as a much precedented critical term at the heart of various discourses on Japanese poetry, such as the thirty-one-syllable *waka* and the linked verse form known as *renga*. It was also to become central to Zeami's treatises, as well as to those of the major theorist and playwright of *sarugaku* in the succeeding generation, Konparu Zenchiku (1405–1470?), in the domain of *sarugaku*. I argue that the first step in this process was the necessity that Zeami felt to increase the prevalence of musical elements such as singing and dancing (aka the *yūgen* elements) in his style of *sarugaku* in order to keep up with the competition and maximize possibilities for powerful patrons.

In his earliest characterizations of the quality as embodied in the competition, Zeami speaks of the prevalence of singing and dancing that characterizes the rival Ōmi style as having *yūgen*. The Yamato style, on the other hand, was better known for its mimetic scenes, as well as for its excellence in the performance of demonic roles. The *sarugaku* style that Zeami inherited from his father seems to have placed greater weight on mimetic techniques aspiring to lifelike semblance than on less directly representational elements such as singing and dancing. Such mimetic moves were often performed in scenes that aspired to credible semblances of "real life" for audience consumption. Moreover, the Yamato style was known for its excellence in the performance of demonic roles, which, within the framework of a representational style that claimed to imitate real life, could aspire to the *yūgen* elements of dancing and singing only at the expense of dramatic credibility.

Song and dance had been part of *sarugaku* traditions prior to Zeami's generation, but evidence suggests that they coexisted rather loosely with mimetic elements in the infrastructure of a play. There are records of song-and-dance routines performed with little vestige of a dramatic framework. Rather, such routines seem to have been based on the more direct appeal of their sensuousness and pageantry. Within the frame of dramatic representation, song and dance seem to have functioned primarily as musical highlights in the plot action—that is, as performances within performances. Those elements were inserted into the plot action as developments in the story. This is how Zeami describes their function in plays of his father's generation, at least.

Both Zeami's plays and his critical writings indicate that he deliberately worked to shift this balance. In his later years he moves the emphasis away from this mimetic stance in favor of a performing art that is organized around these elements of the chanted line and dance. Virtually no attempt is made to persuade us that what is happening onstage approximates "real life." On the contrary, he comes to use dance and chant in ways that served to undermine all claims to realistic imitation and to defuse all semblances of the kind of closure that plot-driven action tends to foster. I argue that he did this by redefining the relations of a play's parts. Whereas mimetic elements and musical or choreographic ones had been only loosely aligned in older plays, by means of the *nikyoku santai* configuration, Zeami fused those elements into necessarily coexisting ones in the very exposition of a play.

That is, he resituated dance and song at the heart of a performance such that they figured not only in the dramatic fiction, but were two inexpendable modes in the dramatic diction. He thereby greatly enhanced the importance of the musical and choreographic elements both in performance and in the overall infrastructure of a play. Moreover, these innovations offered him a basis on which to shift to a representational style keyed to the portrayal of the inner life of a character. The enhanced presence of dancing and singing sufficed to reframe the nature of the dramatic illusion in his style of *sarugaku*. Two of the staple characters in his style of *sarugaku*, warriors and demons, could now dance and sing without fear of violating the dramatic illusion since the very presence of the two modes sufficed to undermine any claim to realistic imitation. In Zeami's mature style of performance, no attempt is made to disguise the sign system as such.

Yūgen as an Emergent Property: Some Hints from the Poets

In part 1, the case is made that Zeami's quest to intensify the *yūgen* elements in Yamato *sarugaku* was a catalyst for thus assigning chanted poetry and dance more central roles in the dramatic action. What is more, I make the case that Zeami gleaned some important hints on how to invoke such emotional qualities on the basis of precepts set down by a prominent poet of the period, Nijō Yoshimoto (1320–1388), in his pedagogical writings on composing *renga*. When Zeami and his father, Kan'ami Kiyotsugu (1333–1384), were able to secure the patronage of Yoshimitsu, it enabled Zeami to become acquainted with the leading members of the intelligentsia of the day. Yoshimoto tutored the shogun in poetic composition and served as an influential arbiter of taste in the shogunal circle. It is likely that he would have inculcated his aesthetic preferences in Yoshimitsu, and it is equally likely that Yoshimitsu's aesthetic preferences would not have been lost on Kan'ami and Zeami. We also know that Zeami was in contact with Yoshimoto and participated at least twice in *renga* composing sessions with him. Moreover, Yoshimoto's lavish praise of the boy Zeami's abilities as a versifier is preserved in a letter written by Yoshimoto in 1376.[8]

Yoshimoto was a seminal figure in the formation of a theory of the *renga*. He considered evocation of the *yūgen* quality as the ultimate accomplishment in *renga* composition. In his treatises he associates *yūgen* with aristocratic grace and polish, a beauty of form that reflected a cultivation of the poetic sensibility. I argue that Zeami may have taken his clue for how to implement *yūgen* qualities from Yoshimoto's precepts concerning *kakari* effects in *renga*, sonorous overtones that emerge in the flow of the recited lines. Drawing on some of the points first set down by Fujiwara no Shunzei and his son Teika in their critical writings on *waka* composition, Yoshimoto points out that the impression the poetic line creates has much to do with the context of its delivery. In this regard the temporal consideration of promoting a sense of polished linguistic flow across the linked verses of a *renga* composition is more central to the creation of an impression that the material has *yūgen* than is the propositional content of the material distinct from the context of the poetic composition.

I argue that Zeami set about implementing the *kakari* dynamic in the three-dimensional contexts of the *sarugaku* stage. His major means of replicating a polished flow onstage was the intensification of chanted and danced elements. These elements in turn contributed to the tenor of the representation, making it possible for the impression created by ostensibly non-*yūgen* subjects such as demons to be mellowed by the modes of delivery. As Zeami continued to strive for an intensification of these elements in his quest for heightened *yūgen* effects, and with reference points from poetic traditions, he arrived at a new understanding of the nature of how to move audiences. Whereas his early writings reflect a search for *yūgen* effects on the basis of the content of the characters and materials used in plays, gradually his focus shifts to the aural and visual modalities through which a play is performed. And in his mature theory, he comes to locate the ultimate source of *yūgen* effects in the underlying sensibility of the actor himself, the informing, embodied intelligence that mediates all stage techniques.

In part 1 I conclude that Zeami's first motivation for integrating *yūgen* elements into his art may well have been motivated by the pressure to cultivate patrons, but that in his efforts to effect that integration he came to reevaluate some of the basic premises of his style of *sarugaku*. He moved away from the traditional emphasis on lifelike semblances as he came to realize, through his stage practice, that *how* material is rendered has everything to do with *how* it is perceived by an audience. In his thinking, *yūgen* came to be less a noematic content than a property that emerges in the process of a perceived performance. With this realization came an intensified awareness of the integral role of elements such as poetry, dance, and music in establishing a mood that serves as an envelope for actual techniques of representation.

Part 2: The Literary Turn

Part 1 explores *nikyoku santai* as the logical outcome of this evolving understanding that the creation or co-creation of meaning onstage is less referential than it is constitutive. Part 2 argues that the shift that occurs in Zeami's understanding of the nature of dramatic representation in turn becomes a catalyst for the development of his style of dramaturgy. He developed a dramatic prototype that assumed the ultimate interpretive act to be that of each spectator as he experienced the multiple media of text, song, dance, and representation unfolding onstage. Meaning then was an emergent property that did not reside in any one element of a prototype, or of a performance, but ultimately in the act of reception itself. As Gadamer has observed, "The text brings an object into language, but that it achieves this is ultimately the work of the interpreter. Both have a share in it."[9] I believe that as Zeami's ideas on representation evolve, he comes to a similar realization.

Over time, Zeami's critical writings suggest a deepening understanding that the nonverbal and the verbal do not enjoy transferability. Language is not a simulacrum of reality, and a representation that struck an audience as "real" did not depend on somehow mirroring reality. Gradually he abandons concern for reproducing physical resemblances, similar to what Diamond in another tradition has called the "conventional iconicity" by which "theatre laminates body to character."[10] I will attempt to show that the increased centrality that Zeami assigned to narrative exposition freed him from the constraints of trying to make objects (and events) seem real onstage by virtue of their literal duplication. It allowed him to organize a performance more in congruence with the figurative language of a literary text, which formed the context for interpreting what was happening onstage.

This part of the volume will explore how his deepening understanding of the expressive potential of language to reconstitute what we perceive as "reality" seems to have been a primary motivating factor in the shift in Zeami's ideas on representation. His texts exploit the power of the word to create imaginary worlds beyond the constraints of the realistic representation of scenes. An increased use of the narrative voice was one corollary to the increased presence of chanted language and dance as the modes of the exposition.[11] While employing dialogue and monologue as framing devices for establishing the dramatic setting and orienting us to events in the dramatic present, he added substantial narrative passages that retold a story at the heart of the drama. I hope to demonstrate that in his plays we do not watch characters enact events so much as we watch them collaborate in enacting a textual narrative. As White has written, "language is never a set of empty forms waiting to be filled . . . or attached to preexistent referents in the world." Rather, it is already "freighted with figurative, tropological, and generic contents before it is actualized in any given utterance."[12] We will track the growth of a similar sense of the freighted nature of language and its integral role in the creation of Zeami's poetic of the stage.

Of Zeami's twenty-one critical writings, one is devoted entirely to this aspect of his art. Titled *Sandō* (lit. "The three paths"; trans. here as The three techniques; 1423), it sets down the steps that the playwright should take to write plays that are commensurate with the configuration of the *nikyoku santai. Sandō* describes composition as a threefold process. First, the playwright must choose a protagonist whose image lends itself to poetic modes of expression, including song and dance. Second, he must structure the play in such a way that there are two climactic points in the development of the action, the first bringing the linguistic and sonic appeal of the chant to the fore, the second highlighting danced expression. The third step is the actual composition of the lines, which includes a range of prosodic concerns as well as the apt choice of poetic allusions. Language should also be chosen for its sonic possibilities.

Along with an analysis of Zeami's ideas on playwriting in general, which is the central concern of part 2, an updated, annotated translation of the *Sandō* text is attached as appendix 1. Recently there has been a major development in *Sandō* scholarship in Japan, the discovery of a traced reproduction of a no longer extant transcription of the *Sandō* manuscript. The transcription was part of a collection of Zeami's critical treatises that had been housed in the Matsunoya Bunko (Matsunoya Library) in Tokyo, a collection belonging to a Tokyo banker, Yasuda Zenjirō (1838–1921). The manuscripts are known as the Matsunoya Bunko *bon* (Matsunoya Library manuscripts).[13]

These manuscripts, which had been held in high repute as the best manuscripts available, burned at the time of the Great Kantō Earthquake of 1923. The historiographer Yoshida Tōgo (1864–1918) published his own edited copy of the Matsunoya Bunko *bon* in a print edition in 1909 titled *Nōgaku koten Zeami jūrokubu shū* (The *Nōgaku* classics: Zeami's collection of sixteen [writings]). These edited manuscripts are known as the Yoshida *bon*, and it is the Yoshida recension of the *Sandō* manuscript that has served as the primary textual basis for subsequent exegeses of the treatise.[14]

The traced reproduction of the Matsunoya Bunko manuscript of *Sandō* has been recently discovered in the Yoshida family holdings (Yoshida Bunko) and has been examined by Takemoto Mikio, scholar and expert on the textual traditions of noh, who writes that certain of its passages differ from the Yoshida recension and offer fresh perspectives on the *Sandō* text and on the process of textual interpretation of Zeami's treatises more generally.[15] In my notes to the English translation of *Sandō* I have tried to point out where the traced reproduction of the Matsunoya Bunko *bon* differs significantly from the manuscript on which my own English translation of *Sandō* is based, the Yoshida *bon*.[16]

Turning to the content of the treatise, *Sandō* sets down the ground rules for a dramatic model that has come to be labeled in modern times as *mugen nō* (dream noh/phantasmal noh). Plays that follow the *mugen* format typically feature a protagonist *(shite)* who is a supernatural being and who appears initially in the first act with his or her true identity disguised. He or she will begin to tell a story to a listener, the supporting actor *(waki)*, from an ostensibly detached stance. However, as the story unfolds that distance begins to dissolve. The *waki*'s curiosity begins to be redirected from the contents of the narrative to the identity of the narrator. In a two-act play, the *shite* will exit between acts and then return in his or her true identity. In the second act the *shite* participates unreservedly in reenacting the salient points of the story. Some plays in this group have the *shite* of the second act appear in the *waki*'s dream, which is one justification for this modern classification of "dream" noh. The classification has in turn influenced how many modern scholars of noh have chosen to organize their ideas.

In his study of *mugen* noh, Tashiro comments on how the narrative voice works to frame experience in this type of drama: "The story told by the *shite* of a *mugen* play frequently touches on events that occurred after the *shite's* death, and the teller goes back and forth freely between first and third person perspective."[17] He goes on to qualify this by commenting that writing the lines in this way suggests an underlying assumption that "the *shite* is essentially a narrator."[18] The point of view of the *shite* is thus extremely fluid. The *shite*, as well as the chorus, an important presence in all noh plays, and, sometimes, the *waki*, may weave back and forth between multiple perspectives. The *shite* may speak as his mortal self or as the retrospective interpreter of the events leading up to or following his own death, or he may weave back and forth between these stances. This weaving is especially complex when the *shite* plays the role of ghost. Noh ghosts are about memory, situated beyond, or after, the actual events. More important than the events themselves in such plays is the lingering emotional residues of the ghost's story.

As Yasuda has pointed out, a noh performance creates an "aura of mental and emotional echoes,"[19] and this is especially the case when the play follows the organization principles of a *mugen* noh. It may be likened to an echo chamber of allusions in which a familiar story is reenacted with reference to earlier versions of the tale or by drawing on thematically related material from the poetic traditions. In *Sandō*, Zeami refers to one exemplary play that was seminal in the development of the *mugen* format. Its title, *Takasago*, is a place-name, a reference to the setting for the first act of the play, Takasago Bay in Harima Province. (The title was *Aioi*, Wedded pines, in Zeami's time.) The play tells the legend of two pine trees as depicted in the first imperial anthology of *waka* poems, *Kokin waka shū* (Collection of *waka* poems, ancient and modern), while drawing extensively as well on a medieval interpretive commentary about that canonical work titled *Kokin waka shū jo kikigaki (Sanryūshō)* (Lecture notes on the "Preface" to the *Kokin shū* [Selected comments by the three schools]). *Takasago* belongs to the classification of plays about Shinto deities *(kami)*, known as *kami nō*. Such plays fill the obligatory function of establishing the appropriate celebratory atmosphere early in a day's program. Part 2 will offer an analysis of *Takasago* to discover whether Zeami practices his own precepts as set down in *Sandō*. We will explore an "echo chamber" in a celebratory key. A translation of *Takasago* is provided in appendix 2 to this volume.

In a tradition far removed from Zeami's, but surely where there are some affinities, William James complained to his brother Henry in a 1907 letter about the latter's obstinate indirectness. Whereas William likes to "say a thing in one sentence as straight and explicit as it can be," he is critical of Henry's style, which he characterizes thus.

> To avoid naming it straight, but by dint of breathing and sighing all round and round it, to arouse in the reader . . . the illusion of a solid object, made (like the "ghost" at the Polytechnic) wholly out of impalpable materials, air, and the prismatic interferences of light, ingeniously focused by mirrors upon empty space.[20]

According to one commentator, what troubled William about his brother was that he "had no respect for objects as they might be claimed to exist independently of the act of the mind that summoned them to appear."[21] At the risk of conflating two very different worlds, it seems to me that Zeami's choice to move away from mimesis toward poiesis reflects a similar understanding of the power of performed language to create worlds that are felt as real.

As noted above, the term "*mugen* noh" is a latter-day coinage, not a classification that is problematized as such by Zeami, so one must be careful to avoid an anachronistic treatment.[22] That is, it is safe to say that Zeami did not set out to create *mugen* noh as we know it. Instead, I want to make the case that the *mugen* play (subsequently named as such) was the outgrowth of his efforts to organize performances in ways that would best serve to articulate the *nikyoku santai* configuration as a process of performance. *Nikyoku santai*, in turn, grew out of his intuitions on how to invoke the flower in performance. The *mugen* style is open-ended, keyed to tapping the power of memory to fill in what is not actually represented onstage. I want to make the case that Zeami seems to have developed his style guided by an intuition that the more such interpretive faculties in the audience are solicited and engaged in a performance, the higher the likelihood that they will be moved by it.

Part 3: *Nikyoku santai* and the Training of the Actor

The third and final part of this volume traces the ramifications that the *nikyoku santai* configuration had on Zeami's deepening understanding of the optimal training of the actor. *Nikyoku santai* comes to be situated at the entry levels of Zeami's orthodox training program, a program designed to refine and attune the actor's sensibilities vis-à-vis audiences. In his most mature works on this subject, the configuration becomes the starting point in an incremental training program for the body and the mind. The approach I take in part 3 diverges from that in the earlier parts in one important sense. Prior to the third part, the focus is on Zeami's efforts to open the stage event up to poiesis to better foster opportunities for imaginative engagement on the part of spectators. However, in part 3, I make the case that Zeami's training program assumed certain underlying principles of performance that were of universal validity and that assumed certain patterns of reception common to all audience members. That is, he developed a set of ideas about the nurturing of the flower that assumed underlying principles of perception and attunement. By cultivating mastery of these principles, the actor could come to sustain a high level of interest despite the inevitable existence of many unpredictable variables and individual tastes. Taking *nikyoku santai* as its starting point, this section looks at some of these principles in a selection of Zeami's mature writings on training. It begins with principles for cultivating the ability to perform with optimal timing and pacing, and then principles ensuring that a certain progression from auditory to visual media is implemented in performance. *Nikyoku santai* assures a certain ordering of the elements of performance, but it is the performer who must implement these elements based on his intuitions. The emphasis in this section will be *how* the actor should apply such intuitions.

Finally, the focus will shift to the efficacy of *nikyoku santai* as a set of guidelines formative of the optimal state of mind of the performer. As noted above, in his later work Zeami takes the position that the actor will experience his deepest attunement with audiences in those moments when he is detached from self-conscious striving for effects. He refers to the ideal state of mind in which this occurs as *mushin* (no-mind), which he further describes as a condition in which the actors' intentions are hidden even from themselves. *Mushin* is one of a number of terms from Buddhist and Taoist discourses that Zeami alludes to with increasing frequency later in life to frame his discussions about the phenomenon of performing. No study of his mature theory of the stage can afford to overlook the parallels that he deliberately draws with some basic tenets in those discourses concerning human somaticity and attunement.

His later treatises such as *Yūgaku shudōfū ken* (Views on modes of training in the arts of entertainment; undated), *Kyūi*, and *Shūgyoku tokuka* (Gathering gems, achieving the flower; 1428) suggest that Zeami saw the ideal mental readiness of a master actor to consist in the kind of non-dual, non-differentiated wisdom on the basis of which one realizes that distinctions between subjective ego and objective things are merely illusions produced by the discriminatory faculties of ego-consciousness. The ideal state of mind of the actor is like the enlightened Buddhist mind—the mirror that reflects everything without discriminatory thinking or subjective judgment. The actor, too, should train to achieve this mirror-like state, because it helps him to be free of subjective thinking that stands to obstruct his ability to react spontaneously with his surroundings. With these points in mind, chapter 7 reviews some very basic precepts of Buddhism and Taoism to which Zeami seems to turn for models within which to thus frame his own thinking about training.

Finally, I make the case that Zeami's *nikyoku santai* offered the actor a path of assiduous practice to follow in order to cultivate such attunement. The idea that such cultivation of the body in training is transformative—conducive of a new mode of being that is removed from everyday ego consciousness—is also fundamental to Buddhist meditational practices. Philosopher Yuasa Yasuo has noticed Zeami's emphasis on making the body shape the mind. He points out that Zeami seems to have reversed the quotidian notion that the body should adhere to conceptual or intellectual understanding. Rather, the flower can be achieved only when one has acquired "the correct bodily mode, for only then can the correct mental mode be opened up."[23] Zeami's flower takes on such ontological grounding in his mature theory. He seems to have shared a view common to Buddhist meditation-based pedagogies—that self-cultivation of the body can lead to a higher epistemological perspective and that such a perspective, in turn, is "correlative with the ontological status of reality."[24] Although this is a rather sweeping statement, such a worldview on Zeami's part would account for the sanguine stance he takes in his critical writings on the existence of universals of human experience.

Once he had developed *nikyoku santai* and put it in place as the heart of the actor's training program, I believe Zeami began to see that configuration as a basis for fostering a new somatic awareness in the actor. He posed *nikyoku santai* as a set of incremental steps that could, through the bodily training they impose, work to induce in him the kind of transformation in ego-consciousness needed to achieve optimal oneness with audiences. The final chapter of this volume examines this hypothesis with reference to some of Zeami's mature critical writings on training. To my knowledge, no one has yet explored the possible significance that *nikyoku santai* played in

Zeami's theory of somatic transformation and in his late views of the cultivation of the flower. I want to make the case that when he established *nikyoku santai* as a set of norms for the actor to embody, it also became possible for Zeami to develop a theory of the flower that went beyond those same norms. The volume ends with a discussion of the seasoned actor who has outgrown the formative stages dictated by *nikyoku santai* and has achieved ultimate freedom as an artist.

Back in the *Yūgen* Again

It is my hope that this book will be of interest both to general readers and specialists with interests in a range of areas, from theatre and performance studies, to Japanese studies, to somatic and religious studies. This is ambitious, but so is tracking Zeami's flower; the trail winds through all of this terrain. When it comes to the latter two domains, somatics and religious studies, a disclaimer is in order. I come to these fields as an amateur and tread with trepidation. Buddhologists will find little that is new about Buddhism here, for instance, but I hope that my discussion of Zeami's use of Buddhist frameworks in his elucidations of performance and training will offer points of interest.

Thanks to the work of Mark J. Nearman, J. Thomas Rimer and Yamazaki Masakazu, and others, a large portion of Zeami's treatises is now available in English. Given this fact, and given the scale of Zeami's contributions, it is a bit surprising that few book-length studies in English have been produced on the subject of what his critical theories have to offer.[25] I believe that a study of such length is most efficacious for situating key concepts in Zeami's theory in the context of their use and that doing so is important for a comprehensive understanding of his thought.

One example of a key concept that profits from a contextualized analysis would be *yūgen*. Much fruitful research has already been done in English scholarship over the past fifty years on the question of what *yūgen* signifies in Zeami's writings. Here I will mention only a few of the many contributions. Ueda argued in 1967 that it was a beauty "not merely of appearance but of spirit; it is the beauty manifesting itself outwards."[26] Shortly thereafter, Tsubaki also provided a balanced overview of the concept in medieval aesthetics in which he argues for *yūgen* as a "beauty of gentle gracefulness," which unified elements from aristocratic and warrior cultures.[27] Nearman has discussed the quality in relation to acting: "In Zeami's treatises, it would appear to refer to the effect created when an actor holds his audience by sustaining his vigor (stage energy) through his concentration while displaying an outer restraint and gracefulness in execution."[28] Goff has written of *yūgen* similarly as a composite effect of restraint and intensity, only in the realm of Zeami's views on representation styles. She notes that he considered aristocratic women commendable subjects because the quality of *yūgen* was ensured in them, and when *yūgen* was "combined with their intense emotional suffering, [it] provided the perfect sort of dramatic, or aesthetic tension."[29] Scholars in religious studies also have commented on *yūgen*. For LaFleur, "*Yūgen* moves beyond the text to reveal, through the tranquility it captures, the presence of nirvana in the midst of samsara . . . in the concrete actions of the characters on stage."[30] Thornhill maintains that Zeami's notion of *yūgen* is quite different from the concept in medieval *waka* in that it "becomes a specific style of performance," rather than representing "the phenomenon of inner depth."[31] Most recently, Brown has argued for a micropolitical reading of Zeami's *yūgen* as symbolic capital in the complex game of attracting patrons.[32]

All of these insights, though not necessarily congruent with each other, aid our understanding of what *yūgen* meant in Zeami's art. So one must ask how this one concept can inspire such multiple readings. I think that tracing the development of these many ideas in context helps to answer this question, and I hope to do so. I argue that initially Zeami's reasons for touting the *yūgen* quality indeed seem to have been politically motivated. Then as he sets about implementing *yūgen* in *sarugaku*, his interest becomes focused on importing subject matter (court ladies) assumed to be endowed with the quality. He ascribes the *yūgen* quality to some objects and not to others on the basis of their perceived referential content. He looks upon gentle and strong subjects as incompatible, the former enjoying the *yūgen* cachet, the latter not. Then his focus shifted from the *what* of such content to the *how* of its representation. By adroit use of chanted and danced elements, the impression created by the representation of even a strong character may be "softened," that is, "*yūgen*-ized." This performance-based realization much in mind, Zeami proceeds to hone the *nikyoku santai* configuration, which functions as a type of insurance making the presence of *yūgen* mandatory in all representation of characters, even demonic ones.

In his later thought, Zeami's interest in *yūgen* effects seems to shift away from issues of representation to training. He sets *nikyoku santai* at the foundation of a training program. Again *nikyoku santai* functions as a kind of insurance, this time making the embodiment of *yūgen* elements mandatory in the development of the actor. Rather, he shifts the locus of *yūgen* effects to the cultivated mindfulness of the actor and away from specific roles or specific elements of performance. By his late treatises, such as *Kyūi*, he makes fewer references to the quality of *yūgen*, and it no longer seems to be a topic that he singles out for the reader's attention. Far from suggesting that he places less importance on *yūgen* at this stage, I will argue that cultivation of *yūgen* is so ensured by his established training regimen that there is no longer a need to problematize it in his treatises. If the novice actor follows the training program, then, when he brings sufficient innate ability to the task, he will come to embody the quality naturally. In such fashion, the meaning of *yūgen* changes according to its use. This is true for other key concepts as well.

Reconstructing Zeami's ideas from a developmental perspective has one further advantage that I have tried to pursue. As in the case above concerning the evolution of his thinking on *yūgen*, a number of Zeami's insights seem to have been prompted or instilled by his experience of the stage. They are things he gleaned on the basis of emergent properties of performance and training rather than from starting as abstract concepts to be applied to those domains. To get at the emergent quality of his thinking on performance, it is important to watch it develop.

I recall many years ago reading the following statement by Keene in reference to one of Zeami's most challenging treatises, *Kyūi*: "Zeami's descriptions are elusive but there can be no doubt that he knew exactly what he meant."[33] With the hubris of a fledgling graduate student, I thought, "Now, that's a truism." At this point, I have struggled with these texts long enough to appreciate the truth (and the elegance) of that remark. Anyone who has read Zeami's treatises knows that there is one insurmountable problem for modern readers—they assume a readership steeped in medieval *sarugaku* performance. We are not supposed to be reading these documents at all. Zeami intended them exclusively for his own disciples. They are often cryptic. He concocts vocabulary whenever it suits him, and in his late works he makes liberal allusions to Buddhist and Confucian texts that pose their own challenges. As a reader, one must confront the unsettling likelihood that there's a whole lot of poiesis going on. One can never be sure exactly what these texts "mean." Of course, this is true for any text, since we know that each act of reading is an act of interpretation— but especially for these texts.

Such heightened indeterminacy is amply reflected in the glosses provided by the annotators of the Japanese language editions, as well as in the English translations available. Interpretations differ on a routine basis. In *Developing Zeami*, my tack has been to try to convey some part of this polyvalence by sharing the differing interpretations in the notes whenever possible.

Abbreviations

. . .

NKBT 40   *Yōkyokū shū*, I. Ed. Yokomichi Mario and Omote Akira. Nihon
            Koten Bungaku Taikei 40. Tokyo: Iwanami, 1960.

NKBT 65   *Karon shū, nōgakuron shū*. Ed. Hisamatsu Sen'ichi and Nishio
            Minoru. Nihon Koten Bungaku Taikei 65. Tokyo: Iwanami, 1961.

NKBT 66   *Rengaron shū, hairon shū*. Ed. Kidō Saizō and Imoto Nōichi. Nihon
            Koten Bungaku Taikei 66. Tokyo: Iwanami, 1961.

NKBZ 51   *Rengaron shū, nōgakuron shū, hairon shū*. Ed. Ijichi Tetsuo, Omote
            Akira, and Kuriyama Riichi. Nihon Koten Bungaku Zenshū 51.
            Tokyo: Shōgakukan, 1973.

Nose, vol. 1   Nose Asaji. *Zeami jūrokubushū hyōshaku*. Vol. 1. Tokyo: Iwanami,
               1940.

Nose, vol. 2   Nose Asaji. *Zeami jūrokubushū hyōshaku*. Vol. 2. Tokyo: Iwanami,
               1944.

NSTS   *Zeami, Zenchiku, Gei no Shisō, Michi no Shisō* 1. Nihon Shisō
            Taikei Shinsōhan. New Printing (Iwanami, 1995). Ed. Omote Akira
            and Katō Shūichi. Nihon Shisō Taikei. Tokyo: Iwanami, 1974.

SNKBZ 88   *Rengaron shū, nōgakuron shū, hairon shū.* Ed. Okuda Isamu, Omote Akira, Horikiri Minoru, Fukumoto Ichirō. Shinpen Nihon Koten Bungaku Zenshū 88. Tokyo: Shōgakukan, 2001.

SNKS, vol. 1   Itō Masayoshi, ed., *Yōkyoku shū,* Shinchō Nihon Koten Shūsei. Tokyo: Shinchōsha, 1983.

SNKS, vol. 2   Itō Masayoshi, ed., *Yōkyoku shū,* Shinchō Nihon Koten Shūsei. Tokyo: Shinchōsha, 1986.

SNKS, vol. 3   Itō Masayoshi, ed., *Yōkyoku shū,* Shinchō Nihon Koten Shūsei 72–74. Tokyo: Shinchōsha, 1988.

Tanaka   Tanaka Yutaka, ed. *Zeami geijutsuron shū.* Shinchō Nihon Koten Shūsei. Tokyo: Shinchōsha, 1976.

• • •

PART I

Zeami's Shift in Representational Styles

I

. . .

The Social Context of Zeami's Secret Treatises

eami Motokiyo[1] occupied a very humble place in the scheme of things as the son of a *sarugaku* actor, a calling thought by some to be fit for beggars.[2] Yet even performers had some prospects for upward mobility in medieval Kyoto. The salons of the Muromachi *bakufu* were a gathering place for artists and intellectuals from all walks of life, members of the military and aristocratic elites, and commoners too, provided they were accomplished in the arts. The ranks of the shogun's attendants included artists and arbiters of taste whose pedigrees were their skills in such métiers as tea, painting, and *waka* and *renga* composition. The Ashikaga were enthusiastic supporters of *sarugaku* as well as the rival form of popular entertainment, *dengaku* (lit. "field music"), and initially it seems to have been Ashikaga patronage that spurred Zeami and his father Kan'ami[3] to rethink their style of *sarugaku*.

In 1375, when Zeami was approximately twelve years old,[4] he came to the attention of the third Ashikaga shogun, Yoshimitsu. This took place at Imagumano in Kyoto, where Yoshimitsu made it known that he wished Zeami's father to dance the sacred role of the old man-cum-deity, Okina, in *Shikisanban*, the auspicious ritual piece that would normally open a day's program.[5] Shortly thereafter, Yoshimitsu offered Kan'ami and Zeami his patronage.[6]

Kan'ami and Zeami derived their livelihood from affiliation with a particular *za* (troupe). In medieval Japan, the *za* functioned as the fundamental organizational unit of *sarugaku* actors and musicians who earned their living by performing together.[7] Kan'ami and Zeami belonged to the Yūzaki *za*, one of four major *za* based in Yamato Province.[8] We know that the Yamato *za* were affiliated with both the complex of Kasuga Shrine and Kōfukuji Temple, located in the city of Nara, and the Tōnomine complex of Myōrakuji Temple and Danzan Shrine, on a mountain south of the city. It is believed that the primary affiliation for the Yamato *za* was with Tōnomine, where they participated in performances held as part of the Yuima-e (annual reading of the *Vimalakīrti-nirdeśa-sūtra*) in the tenth month.[9]

Members of the Yamato *za* were also obliged to perform annually at *takigi sarugaku* (*sarugaku* in firelight), held in the second month in conjunction with religious services of the Kasuga and Kōfukuji complex.[10] There were numerous *za* throughout the Nara and Kyoto areas. Along with the four *za* of the Nara, or Yamato, area (*yoza*), six *za* based in Ōmi (present-day Shiga Prefecture, northeast of Kyoto) appear to have thrived.[11] Relations between the *za* were openly competitive, each vying with the others for celebrity and support. It was also common to host *tachiai* (joint) performances, in which different *za* would openly compete for audience approval.

Another type of venue in which actors might appear was the *kanjin sarugaku* (subscription *sarugaku*), open-air performances of a large scale held to raise funds for a cause, sometimes religious, or sometimes simply to provide actors with personal income. Actors needed permission and sponsorship by influential people to stage such events. People of all backgrounds were able to attend provided that they could pay an entrance fee. Records show that *dengaku* subscription performances were also popular, especially from the period of the Northern and Southern courts (1336–1392) into the early fifteenth century, but subsequent to that, participation of members of the *sarugaku za* of Yamato grew conspicuous.[12] De Poorter has pointed out that these subscription performances were an important venue for *sarugaku* performers because they offered them the opportunity to catch the eye of powerful potential patrons.[13]

Performers also supplemented their incomes by touring throughout the outlying areas of Kyoto and Nara, and these tours were the major means of assuring widespread popularity for the art. For Kan'ami and Zeami, such a tour to the Kyoto area from their base in Nara offered them the opportunity to secure the patronage of the utmost political authority of the time, Ashikaga

Yoshimitsu. As a result of winning Yoshimitsu's patronage, Kan'ami and Zeami broadened their base of activity from the temple grounds and the provincial circuit to the shogunal palace and mansions of elite audiences in the Kyoto capital. This was not simply a question of adding new patrons to their list, but of a qualitative shift from predominantly religious contexts to more secular ones. As Zeami's biographers frequently note, the shift is reflected in the events that took place at Imagumano. This was the shogun's first viewing of *sarugaku*, and it was suggested by Yoshimitsu's attendant that on this occasion Kan'ami should be cast in the role of the old-man deity, Okina, in the play *Shikisanban*.

Shikisanban (or *Okina*, as it is named today) is thought to be the oldest play in the *sarugaku* repertoire, dating back to the Heian period (794–1185). By Zeami's generation, it was the practice of his *za* to stage it as a sequence of three dances, each performed by a different character. The central dance is that of the old man, Okina. He is traditionally thought of as a being possessed of divine energy. His dance played the ritualistic function of praying for the peace and tranquility of the realm.[14] The actor who performed the role was thought to be possessed by the spirit of Okina when the Okina mask was placed on his face. It is believed that the primary function of *sarugaku za* throughout the latter part of the Kamakura period (1185–1333) was to perform *Shikisanban* at religious functions. By Kan'ami and Zeami's time, the element of entertainment had gained ascendancy in *sarugaku*, but still *Shikisanban* retained its sacrosanct place in the repertoire. It was performed routinely at the head of a program of plays to establish the appropriately auspicious mood.

Not just any actor qualified to perform the role of Okina. In Kan'ami's day, the part was reserved for the most venerable member of the *za*.[15] Yoshimitsu's request that the middle-aged Kan'ami perform the role amounted to a new precedent in the practices of the *za*. The erstwhile custom of casting the most venerable performer as Okina seems to have been ignored in shogunal performances thereafter.[16] The fact that Kan'ami's reputation had preceded him to reach the ears of the shogun, as well as Zeami's own high praise of his father's artistic accomplishments, indicates that Kan'ami, then at the prime of his career, was a star performer in the Yūzaki *za*. It thus appears to have been Kan'ami's merits as an entertainer, not to mention the promise of the young Zeami, that attracted Yoshimitsu's interest. Very probably the shogun was sexually attracted to Zeami as well, but there is no definitive documentation of this.[17]

As mentioned above, access to the shogunal circles allowed Kan'ami and Zeami to become acquainted with the cultural elite of the day. The court aristocrat and poet-critic of *renga*, Nijō Yoshimoto, appears to have taken Zeami under his wing. His praise of Zeami's talents is preserved in a letter that he wrote in 1376, after having met Zeami for what is thought to be the first time. The letter verges on the fulsome. If his words are to be taken at face value, Yoshimoto was not only impressed with the adolescent's gifts as a *sarugaku* performer and a poet, but he thought that Zeami also had an aptitude for the courtly sport of *kemari* (football).[18] It is interesting to note that Yoshimoto's letter praises Zeami's *waka* and *renga* verses on the grounds that they have interesting artistic effects (*kakari*) and a style having *yūgen*. As we will see, *kakari* and *yūgen* were also aesthetic concepts that Zeami was later to apply extensively in his efforts to strengthen poetic elements in *sarugaku* to please Kyoto patrons. We know that Zeami was invited to participate in a *renga* composing session at Yoshimoto's residence in 1378 as well and that his contributions there were also praised highly.[19]

There can be no doubt that as both a playwright and writer of secret treatises Zeami was influenced by Yoshimoto. Part 1 will go into some detail concerning the influence that Yoshimoto's pedagogical writings seem to have had on Zeami's ideas about how the highly touted *yūgen* quality might be incorporated into *sarugaku*. But prior to such a comparison in chapter 2 of their specific precepts, here I will briefly address the enormous impact that exposure to Yoshimoto and other artists must have had on Zeami's general understanding of literary composition and the part it might play in *sarugaku* practice.

The Literary Turn of *Sarugaku*

As Zeami's plays demonstrate, he was able to acquire an education in the classics, assumedly through shogunal patronage and the exposure to literary texts that it availed. It is clear from his writings that he was conversant with a range of such texts, from vernacular works in the tradition of belles lettres to Chinese writings of Buddhist and Confucian provenance. In the case of a professional performer of *sarugaku*, this seems to have been unprecedented. In his critical treatises, Zeami speaks of the composition of plays by the *sarugaku* performers themselves as if it were a routine matter, although evidence suggests that the preservation of texts on the part of performers was hardly an established practice prior to Kan'ami's generation. To date, there are no extant texts of complete plays that predate Kan'ami.[20] According to Takemoto's estimate, existing documents, all related to Zeami's sphere of activity (*Zeami kankei no shoshiryō*), provide evidence that a repertoire of about fifty pieces existed, but this includes the titles of plays that are no longer extant, as well as fragments of pieces composed solely to be chanted (*utaimono*).[21] Takemoto believes that plays in this early period were readily dismantled and their parts recycled into new compositions, making it extremely difficult to reconstruct the earliest avatars.[22]

Researchers frequently allude to an extant chronicle of a performance held as part of a festival at the Kasuga Wakamiya in Nara on 10 II Jōwa 5 (1349; era name also read Teiwa) as the earliest evidence that a *sarugaku* repertoire did in fact exist. Both *sarugaku* and *dengaku* were performed by amateur shrine attendants on this occasion. The female attendants had been instructed by *sarugaku* players, and the male attendants by *dengaku* players.[23] The women (*miko*) opened the program with *Shikisanban*, followed by performances glossed as "Norikiyo ga Toba-dono nite jisshu no uta yomite aru tokoro" (Norikiyo [the priest Saigyō] composes ten verses at the residence of Emperor Toba), and "Izumi Shikibu no itawari o Murasaki Shikibu no toburaitaru koto" (Murasaki Shikibu visits Izumi Shikibu when she is ill). The extant records list the names of the participants and the casting. What is especially significant is that the glosses for each play reflect the existence of dramatic content. The editors of Iwanami Kōza surmise that scripts for these pieces probably existed,[24] although they have been lost.

Zeami says frustratingly little in his treatises about the texts of plays that predated Kan'ami. We do know that Ōmi and Yamato *sarugaku* as well as *dengaku* troupes had repertoires and that they borrowed freely from the repertoires of rivals. In *Sandō*, his treatise on composing, Zeami mentions a number of such plays. For instance, he alludes to the character of the Rokujō lady from *Genji monogatari* (Tale of Genji) reworked into the lead role of a play associated with the Ōmi style of *sarugaku*, *Aoi no Ue* (Lady Aoi), as replete with *yūgen* potential. Plays originating in the *dengaku* repertoire such as *Shiokumi* (Scooping salt water) and *Sano no Funabashi* (Floating bridge at Sano) are also mentioned. However, it is not clear whether texts of these plays actually existed during the period when Kan'ami was active.[25]

In 1999, Yashima Sachiko of the Kokuritsu Komonjo Kan (National Institute of Paleography) announced the discovery of a *sarugaku* program dated 9, 10 II Ōei 34 (1427). This document has proven to be the oldest

extant record of a complete program put on by *sarugaku* professionals. It
includes fifteen play titles along with the names of the lead performers for
all plays.[26] Yashima discovered it on the reverse side of a diary kept by Jinson
(1430–1508), an abbot at the Kōfukuji complex in Nara. Jinson, the son of
the regent and renowned literatus Ichijō Kanera (1402–1481), took up his
tenure as abbot of the subtemple Ichijōin in 1441 and became the superintendent (*bettō*) of Kōfukuji in 1456. The program was actually written
down by a predecessor, Kyōgaku (1395–1473), who had been the superintendent of Kōfukuji at the time of the performance. The paper that he
wrote it on was subsequently recycled in Jinson's diary.

The program mentions the appearance of an actor from the rival Konparu group on the ninth and then provides a full accounting of the titles of
the plays and the lead actors for the tenth, when the Kanze group (Zeami's
direct affiliates) turned out. Three actors from the Kanze group shared the
program: Zeami's son, Jūrō Motomasa (Kanze Motomasa, ?–1432), his
nephew, Saburō Motoshige (hereafter referred to as On'ami, 1398–1467),
and Jūnijirō (b. ca. 1383?), a disciple of the Kanze actor Jūnigorō Yasutsugu
(1353–1434).[27] The performance was held at the invitation of Kyōgaku at
his quarters, the Ichijōin subtemple. It was a traditional custom to extend
such an invitation to the *sarugaku* players during the annual religious services known as Shunigatsu-e, held at the Kōfukuji complex from the first to
the fourteenth day of the second month.[28] Some of the titles mentioned are
quite surprising because they seem to correspond to extant plays whose
primary attractions are spectacular staging or technical virtuosity rather
than poetic lyricism such as Zeami advocated. Until the discovery of this
program, many scholars had assumed that plays that draw heavily on spectacle were more characteristic of late Muromachi styles that postdated
Zeami. Two examples of such plays would be *Shuten dōji* (Wine-tippling boy;
presently titled Ōeyama [Mount Ōe]), in which the warrior Minamoto no
Yorimitsu (Raikō) seeks out a carnivorous, wine-loving demon on Mount
Ōe in Tanba Province. Raikō drinks with the demon and then slays it once
it has lapsed into a drunken stupor. The other play, *Shōjō*, set in China, is
about a mythical creature (*shōjō*) resembling an orangutan who resides in
the sea and loves to drink wine. The play features his colorful dance and
his gift of a bottomless barrel of magical wine to a local wine merchant to
reward him for his filial piety.[29]

The discovery of this program makes it clear that plays contrastive with
those that Zeami advocates actually coexisted with those that he prefers to

acknowledge in his treatises. It is also evidence that by Zeami's time plays had established titles rather than rubrics encapsulating their content, such as those used on the performance program of 1349 introduced above. Whether those plays in the newly discovered 1427 program, which Zeami does not mention in his critical writings, had actually taken on a textual form by this time is not clear. However, we do know that producing play scripts had become an integral part of Zeami's routine by this date.

It is very difficult to come to any conclusions about what the earliest plays must have been like given the limited evidence available. Zeami's treatises such as *Sandō* and *Zeshi rokujū igo Sarugaku dangi* (Zeami's talks on *sarugaku* after reaching sixty; hereafter referred to as *Sarugaku dangi*), conversations transcribed by Zeami's son, Shichirō Motoyoshi, provide far more detailed information on the plays that were in the *sarugaku* and *dengaku* repertoires than any other source. At the same time, however, it is highly likely that any play mentioned by Zeami has been revised by him. This makes it challenging to ascertain with any certainty what the compositional styles of his predecessors or even his contemporaries might have been.

During Kan'ami's prime, collaboration between *sarugaku* performers and poets seems to have been common, the performers composing the music and the poets the lines of the plays.[30] This would seem to be further evidence that composing plays had not been standard procedure for the *sarugaku* performers themselves and that some performers did not have the ability to compose texts on their own. Omote also notes the participation of poets who attended the shogun, such as Ebina no Naamidabutsu (Naami, ?–1381) and Rin'ami (Tamarin, dates unknown), in such collaborative efforts, which must have served to upgrade the literary quality of *sarugaku* plays significantly.[31] We know that Zeami was acquainted with these poets from a reference in his treatise titled *Go on* (The five vocal sounds; undated) to a piece of chant titled *Kaidō kudari* (Journey to the eastern provinces). He mentions that the lines were composed by Rin'ami and the music by Naami and Kan'ami.[32] In *Sarugaku dangi* Zeami also mentions the play *Shii no shōshō* (Junior captain of the imperial guards, fourth rank), now titled *Kayoi Komachi* (Komachi of the frequent visits), which dramatizes a legend connected with the beautiful Heian poet Ono no Komachi and a suitor, the Fukakusa junior captain. He had journeyed to her residence ninety-nine nights in the hope that if he kept his vow to do so for one hundred nights in succession, then Komachi would agree to meet him. Instead, he died on the ninety-ninth night. In the play they come back as ghosts and

reenact the events of the legend. He tries to prevent her spirit from reaching Buddhist enlightenment, but at the end of the play they both do so. The
play was originally composed by a Buddhist preacher/performer (*shōdōshi*)
in the Yamato area but was later revised by Kan'ami and then revised again
either by Kan'ami or Zeami.[33]

Perhaps these attributions in *Sarugaku dangi* reflect a shift in Zeami's
attitudes toward authorship. The entire passage includes a list of plays that
was previously recorded in *Sandō*, which is dated 1423, seven years before
the date affixed to *Sarugaku dangi*. As Motoyoshi notes, the list is the same
except that authors' names have been added in *Sarugaku dangi*. Both tracts
adhere to the necessity of adapting plays in accordance with the changing
times, but it is interesting to speculate on whether the inclusion of details
about authorship in the later document reflects a growing sense of proprietary rights over the texts as objects as well as an increased sense of agency
on the part of practitioners concerning the production of their own scripts.

In sum, as far as Kan'ami's generation of *sarugaku* is concerned, it seems
very likely that performers did not conceive of plays as texts to be preserved
in written form. De Poorter makes this point also: "It is even questionable
whether [plays] were ever written down. In the event that these old plays
were composed by the players themselves, they must surely have been very
simple." She shares O'Neill's doubts concerning whether *sarugaku* players
in this early period would have been literate enough to produce literary
texts. She also provides two examples from *Sarugaku dangi* of actors who
were probably illiterate.[34] But of one thing there can be little doubt—at
least later in his life, Zeami came to have a strong proprietary sense concerning the texts that he was composing. A number of them copied in his
hand remain,[35] and he discusses the lines and chanting styles for specific
texts in several of his treatises. It seems likely that his access to Yoshimoto,
Rin'ami, Naami, and others had not only allowed him to develop literary
skills, but to develop a sense of textuality that was uncommon for *sarugaku*
performers prior to his time. The importance that he placed on revising and
preserving texts seems to have set a precedent in the history of *sarugaku*.
In the generations to follow, their preservation became the normal practice,
and it also became customary for *sarugaku* texts to be composed by the
performers themselves.

Zeami's literary turn is also manifested in the fact that he chose to write
secret treatises at all. To date, no pedagogical writings on *sarugaku* by performers that precede Zeami are available.[36] It is fair to say that he is seminal

as well in the formation of the tradition of critical writings on *sarugaku*. Perhaps one inspiration for writing down his precepts was Yoshimoto, who had produced a number of pedagogical treatises on *renga*. For Yoshimoto, who was schooled as well in the prolific critical tradition of the *waka*, the activity of writing poetic criticism could not have entailed much of an epistemological leap. But for Zeami to take it into his head to set down the principles of his craft must have been no simple matter.

Ong has observed that oral culture "has nothing corresponding to how-to-do-it manuals for the trades"[37] because such manuals are predicated on analytical categories that depend on writing to "structure knowledge at a distance from lived experience."[38] It is necessary for the kind of interiorization that writing enables to be in place. Perhaps what makes Zeami's treatises seem accessible to us today is that they are thoroughly informed by the experiential knowledge of a practicing performer. At the same time, his critical theories bear witness to an unprecedented level of interiorization that came with his literary enfranchisement. More about these critical writings below.

The Efficacy of Writing Critical Treatises

Zeami's extant secret transmissions number twenty-one.[39] Because he did not date all of them, their exact chronology cannot be ascertained, but to some extent it is possible to reconstruct their order based on analysis of the texts themselves. Scholars frequently divide Zeami's career and his critical treatises into early, middle, and late periods, each of them corresponding to the tenure of third, fourth, and sixth shoguns of the Muromachi *bakufu*: Yoshimitsu, who was shogun from 1368–1394; Yoshimochi (1386–1428), who served from 1394–1423; and Yoshinori (1394–1441), from 1429–1441. As the criterion for defining the development of Zeami's ideas, of course such categories are somewhat arbitrary. The dividing line between the middle and late periods is particularly fuzzy since Zeami's composition of a number of undated treatises seems to span the middle and late years.[40] Yet it cannot be denied that Zeami's fate hung on the whims of the Ashikaga and that his relations with them had a direct bearing on production of critical treatises.

Yoshimitsu's patronage of Zeami lasted from approximately 1374 until Yoshimitsu's death in 1408. Those years saw the death of Kan'ami (d. 1384) and the birth of two sons, Jūrō Motomasa (?–1432) and Shichirō Motoyoshi (dates unknown). It is likely that Zeami had adopted his nephew, On'ami, but perhaps decided not to make him his successor when his own son Motomasa was born. This would be one possible explanation for the seeming lack of closeness between Zeami and his nephew in later years. Although On'ami did in fact become the third troupe head in the Kanze lineage, Zeami never acknowledges this in his treatises.[41] It was routine for *sarugaku* actors to pass their art on to their children, who would succeed them. When Kan'ami died, it left Zeami not only with the task of representing their style of *sarugaku* in his own lifetime, but also of passing on the art to the next generation, namely to his own offspring and to disciples of particular promise.

The ten years after his father's death may not have been easy for Zeami. There are no records of performances by him. Rather, the *sarugaku* performer who records show had strong shogunal support belonged to the Hie *za* in Ōmi and was known as Inuō or Dōami (?–1413), and was apparently closer to Kan'ami in age. In 1382, for instance, he performed at Kitano Tenmangū Shrine in Kyoto to a capacity crowd.[42] In 1389, records show that Inuō was included in a shogunal pilgrimage to Itsukushima Shrine on Hiroshima Bay and had lavish gifts bestowed on him by the various daimyō (regional barons) who hosted the entourage, apparently in order to please the shogun.[43] Inuō continued to enjoy the shogun's patronage until Yoshimitsu's death.

In 1408, Yoshimitsu entertained Emperor Go-Komatsu (1377–1433) at his Kitayama residence, where the emperor stayed for approximately twenty days. During this time three *sarugaku* performances took place. Records list Inuō as appearing twice, but no mention is made of Zeami.[44] Zeami praises Inuō highly in *Sarugaku dangi*, crediting him with mastery of a *yūgen* style of performance, about which more will be said in the ensuing chapter. Along with what seems to have been a genuine admiration for Inuō's gifts, Zeami must have felt inspired to incorporate Inuō's *yūgen* style into the Yamato style for extrinsic reasons as well. This is a point that I will develop in chapter 2.

The secret treatise played an important part in that process of educating successors and passing on innovations, such as those that would intensify *yūgen* elements in Yamato *sarugaku*. By 1400, Zeami had written the first three chapters of his first treatise, which will be referred to in this volume as *Kaden*.[45] Those chapters are as follows.

1. *Fūshikaden* daiichi, "Nenrai keiko jōjō" (Manifested images of the transmission of the flower, chapter 1: "Items concerning training over the years"): a discussion of how training in *sarugaku* should proceed in incremental stages based on the actor's age group.
2. *Fūshikaden* daini, "Monomane jōjō" (Manifested images of the transmission of the flower, chapter 2: "Items concerning imitation [of characters]"): enumeration of nine types of characters and strategies for representing them.
3. *Fūshikaden* daisan, "Mondō jōjō" (Manifested images of the transmission of the flower, chapter 3: "Question and answer on various matters"): comprehensive inquiry into the best strategies for getting through to audiences, including discussions of optimal timing, relations between movement and text, and the various qualities to be invoked in performance.[46]

Zeami's ostensible motive for writing the early chapters of *Kaden* was the preservation of his late father's insights, as he states in the colophon to chapter 3, but underlying that must have been the purpose of instilling his own precepts in his successors. These first chapters of *Kaden* comprise all of his critical writings that can be traced with certainty to his early years. In addition to them, there is a fourth chapter titled *Fūshikaden* daishi, "Shingi" (Manifested images of the transmission of the flower chapter 4: "Divine matters"), which situates the *sarugaku* lineage in mythic creation narratives. It is undated. Omote suggests that it was originally intended as an addendum to the first three chapters, but there is no clear proof of this.[47] He also thinks that it may have been introduced as a chapter in its own right when the tract titled *Ōgi* (Initiation into the secrets) was added as the fifth chapter of *Kaden*.[48]

One of the oldest manuscripts of *Ōgi*, a late Muromachi copy named Sōsetsu *shomei bon*, has a colophon dated 1402. Because all of the other important transcriptions lack this information, scholars speculate that 1402 is not a reliable date and that *Ōgi* may well have been written later.[49] Indeed, *Ōgi* addresses concerns that do not appear in the earlier chapters of *Kaden*, such as the differences between Zeami's style of Yamato *sarugaku* and the rival styles of Ōmi *sarugaku* and of *dengaku*. *Ōgi* sounds the new note that the actor must become conversant in all of these rival styles and that universal acclaim depends on his ability to remain versatile on such a scale. Zeami also cautions that the actor should not despair if he falls out of favor in the capital, but should continue to cultivate a broad base in the countryside as well. If he does this, then his art will not atrophy and he will preserve the possibility of a revival in his fortunes as an artist.[50] An awareness of such vicissitudes in Ōgi would seem to suggest a date of composition a bit later than that recorded in its colophon.

Zeami began to experience such vicissitudes only after the death of Yoshimitsu in 1408. Yoshimochi had become shogun in 1394, but it was not until Yoshimitsu's death that his son's own tastes in entertainment were clearly demonstrated. Like his father, Yoshimochi was an active patron of the performing arts, but he seems to have favored the rival art of *dengaku* over *sarugaku*. (*Dengaku* had been the favored art of Yoshimochi's forefathers, notably the first Ashikaga shogun, Takauji [1305–1358].) Although Zeami and his sons still received Yoshimochi's patronage, the *dengaku* performer Zōami (dates unknown) appears to have been his favorite. During the decade from 1412 to 1422, for instance, *dengaku* performances in the Kyoto area outnumbered *sarugaku* performances by approximately two to one.[51] Moreover, Yoshimochi sponsored Zōami in *sarugaku* performances every year throughout this period.[52]

Zeami's production of critical treatises proliferated during the years of Yoshimochi's rule, after what is estimated to be a hiatus of sixteen years. We know that he completed a revised version of the seventh chapter of *Kaden* in 1418. Titled *Kaden daishichi*, "Besshi kuden" (Transmission of the flower, chapter seven: "Special oral transmissions"), it addresses tactics for achieving the true flower (*makoto no hana*) — that is, the ongoing ability to arouse interest in audiences by successfully adapting to all manner of variables. It is likely that this seventh chapter originally existed as an independent treatise. It has two variant manuscripts that are believed to be approximately ten years apart. According to the colophon of the 1418 manuscript, Zeami gave the earlier draft to his younger brother, Shirō (dates unknown). The date on the earlier manuscript is illegible. Omote and Takemoto estimate that the tract was composed sometime around 1408. The later manuscript was intended for someone by the name of Mototsugu, which is believed to be a childhood name of Zeami's son, Motomasa.[53]

As of this time, Zeami's critical writings increased dramatically. A treatise on musical composition titled *Ongyoku kuden* (Secret teachings on vocal music) is dated 1419, followed in 1420 by *Shikadō* (Path to achieving the flower), an important writing on various aspects of performance and training. *Nikyoku santai ningyō zu* (Sketches of the human figures [appropriate] for the two modes and the three styles [an illustrated description of acting styles]), is dated 1421. Then in 1423 he completed *Sandō*, on composing plays. Another of his most important treatises, *Kakyō*, a comprehensive theoretical discourse on principles of acting and audience interest, was completed in 1424 (although it is thought the larger portion of it had been composed by 1418).[54]

The immediate motive for this burst of productivity is not attested, but it seems suggestive of changing circumstances. During this period of productivity, assumedly both of Zeami's own sons would have entered their second decade of life and would be taking on positions of responsibility in the troupe. Zeami must have felt increased pressure to prepare them to succeed in the very competitive business of retaining patronage. Unable to offer them security, he could at least provide them and other promising performers of his group with pointers on how to excel. Zeami's frequent injunctions to secrecy in his treatises surely reflect such a concern.

Yet it was not until a period subsequent to this proliferation of writing that records show Zeami and his offspring truly confronting adverse circumstances. Whereas Yoshimochi continued to support the Zeami group, albeit not as enthusiastically as he supported Zōami, the sixth shogun, Yoshinori, who took office in 1429, showed clear signs of hostility toward Zeami and Motomasa. From 1429 onward, Zeami endured a succession of misfortunes, many of them connected with Yoshinori's seeming disfavor. For instance, in 1424 Zeami had been appointed *gakutō* (music director) at Daigoji Temple, south of Kyoto. This was a post proffered by a temple on a troupe's foremost actor, which thus gave that actor the right to perform there.[55] In 1430, Zeami's nephew performed at Daigoji on the recommendation of the shogun, which would seem to indicate that Yoshinori saw to it that On'ami replaced Zeami as *gakutō*.

Zeami's stiffest competition during this period was On'ami, his own nephew (and possible adoptive son). The records reflect that Yoshinori consistently favored On'ami over Zeami. Yoshinori became shogun in the third month of 1429. In the fourth month of that year, On'ami performed for Yoshinori at his residence, the Muromachi-*dono*, and received generous remuneration from the daimyō in attendance. He appeared there in the seventh month as well. There is no record of Zeami or Motomasa being present on either occasion.[56] In the first month of 1429, upon Yoshinori's urging, retired emperor Go-Komatsu hosted a performance by On'ami, and in the fifth month of the same year Yoshinori refused to allow plans for Go-Komatsu to similarly host performances of Zeami and Motomasa.[57]

It is interesting that just prior to these setbacks, Zeami composed treatises expressive of some of his most profound insights on his art. In 1428, five months after the death of Yoshimochi, he completed the major treatise titled *Shūgyoku tokuka*, which is a comprehensive work on how to optimize attunement with audiences. Three months earlier he had composed the treatise *Rikugi* (Six poetic modes), a discourse on how his ideas on nine levels of artistry (*kyūi*) available to the actor interface with the six poetic modes at the heart of critical theory of the *waka. Rikugi*'s discussion follows up on his composition of a separate, undated, and unnamed treatise that latter-day annotators have named *Kyūi*, which presents his mature views on these nine levels of an actor's art and how the actor should train in a prescribed sequence of steps. It is estimated that *Kyūi* must have been composed shortly before these dated treatises. Another undated and originally untitled treatise, subsequently named *Goi* (The five levels), is thought to have been composed around this time as well. *Goi* concentrates on a second taxonomy consisting of five types of affect that the accomplished actor can instill in a performance. All of these treatises show a deepening understanding on Zeami's part of a philosophy of attunement underlying the "flower." And yet it seems that it was On'ami's flower that was more attuned to the changed times.

The colophons on *Shūgyoku tokuka* and *Rikugi* clarify that they are transmissions destined for Konparu dayū Ujinobu, better known today as Konparu Zenchiku (1405–1470?). Zenchiku was the grandson of the actor Konparu Gon no kami and was also Zeami's son-in-law. As the heir to the headship of the Enman'i (or Emai) *za*, which came to be called the Konparu *za* in Zenchiku's generation, he was not of the same lineage as Zeami in a strict sense, but one might argue that he became the closest thing to Zeami's spiritual heir as well as being a gifted playwright and composer of critical treatises in his own right.

During the tenure of Yoshinori, Zeami probably produced four additional treatises. *Shudōsho* (Writings on the path of training; 1430) is dedicated to his *za*, with no specific names listed. It exhorts the members to work together in harmony and describes the roles that the various players should fulfill, such as that of the star member of the troupe in relation to the other supporting actors, and those of the comedic *kyōgen* actors and musicians. Omote is persuaded that Zeami wrote his two late treatises on vocal styles and themes around this time as well. They have subsequently been given the titles *Go ongyoku jōjō* (Items concerning the five [themes] of vocal music) and *Go on*. Zeami appended no colophons to these texts. Finally, Zeami's son Motoyoshi pulled together the notes of his father's narratives and precepts into *Sarugaku dangi*, the longest of the critical writings and an important chronicle of performers and performance practices starting with Kan'ami's generation. Toward the end of this compendium, Motoyoshi declares his intent to leave the *sarugaku* profession.

> [Trusting] that on the other hand
> the sacred Law of Buddha
> will protect my parents,
> I will retire from the art,
> please do not detain me![58]

He did indeed retire and take Buddhist vows. His reasons remain a mystery.

Then in 1432 Motomasa died mysteriously of unknown causes while on a tour in the Ise area. Zeami remained inconsolable over the loss of his heir, and in what is believed to be his last treatise, *Kyakuraika* (Flower of returning; 1433), he gives voice to his fear that the prospects of his troupe are dim. He admits that he had pinned all of his hopes on Motomasa, and upon his death there was nothing left to do but to write down the secrets for some nameless person(s) of the future.

> Because of his early death I have expressed it in paper and ink so that
> there may not be people in later ages who know only this title. . . .
> If such people appear, it will be Zea[mi]'s memento for [these] later
> generations.[59]

In *Kyakuraika* the seriousness of Zeami's commitment to his art becomes very clear (although the precepts therein seem very cryptic). Whereas he does mention Zenchiku as someone with prospects, he does not say a word about On'ami, which seems strange when one considers that On'ami was at his prime and seems to have been a very popular performer. In the fourth month of 1433, On'ami was the featured performer at a three-day *kanjin sarugaku* attended by the shogun and many other dignitaries. This event was most probably a celebration of On'ami's succession to the position of head of the Kanze troupe.[60]

In 1434, when Zeami was approximately seventy-one years of age, he was exiled to Sado Island by Yoshinori. The reason for such a measure is not known. One speculation is that it had to do with his opposition to On'ami's status as heir to the Kanze line. Did he refuse to share the secret transmissions with On'ami, perhaps? We do not know with certainty whether he ever returned from exile either, but it is possible that he was pardoned after Yoshinori's assassination in 1441 and that he lived out his remaining years in the care of his daughter and son-in-law, Zenchiku.[61]

The year of Zeami's death is also uncertain, although we know that it was on the eighth day of the eighth month. This information became available when it was discovered that Zeami's posthumous name was on a register of payments made to a Sōtō temple, Fuganji by name, in present-day Nara Prefecture. The subsequent passing of his wife, "Juchin," is also recorded in this register.[62] According to Ōtomo, Zeami's affiliation with Fuganji was probably a long-standing one. The cleric who founded this temple, Ryōdō Shinkaku, was from the same village as Kan'ami—Yūzaki— and they had grown up together. Ōtomo writes that Zeami joined Fuganji and received schooling as a monk there while at the same time pursuing his *sarugaku* calling. This would have been when he was in his early twenties, right around the time that his father passed away.[63]

2

. . .

Developing Zeami's Representational Style

T he question of how an actor should perform in role is one that recurs in Zeami's pedagogical writings over a period of decades. *Monomane* is the term that he uses to refer to the representation of characters. In his earliest critical writings, he identifies *monomane* as the hallmark of his performance tradition, Yamato *sarugaku*. His early use of the term seems to correspond best to the notion of mimicry, referring to techniques for creating copies of particular types of characters. However, as his thoughts about the chemistry of *sarukagu* performance evolve, so does this concept. Part of his growing understanding of how best to engage audiences, *monomane* comes to be reintegrated into a larger configuration of performance in which characters are depicted by means of such elements as poetic composition, instrumental and vocal music, and dance. Zeami's reworking of the concept is an integral part of a larger shift away from a representational style that conveys a story through lifelike reproduction of human behavior to dramatic enactment in which the emotional life of a character or his story is made the subject for mimesis.

Tracing the evolution of his thinking on *monomane* is one way to plot Zeami's move away from the more realistic style that he inherited from the generation of Yamato *sarugaku* performers toward a new poetic of the stage. At the same time, it will also help us to see that his style of drama never abandoned *monomane* traditions entirely. It was the rapprochement that he effected between the old and the new that formed the scaffolding for his innovations as a theorist and a playwright. We begin with a discussion of his earliest descriptions of *monomane* in the second chapter of *Kaden*. From that time, it is evident that for both practical and artistic reasons *monomane* cannot be discussed in isolation from Zeami's drive to intensify the presence of singing and dancing in plays. A case will be made that the initial impetus to import more musical elements into his style of play may well have been that a rival *sarugaku* troupe enjoyed a reputation for *yūgen* elegance on the basis of its musical appeal. Zeami's treatises suggest that general acceptance of a connection between musical pageantry and *yūgen* effects was already established when, as a young boy, he took up the *sarugaku* calling. We will next examine several stages of innovation on the part of Yamato *sarugaku* playwrights, all of them leading to the increased presence of musical and choreographic elements. We will reconstruct some of the turning points along the way, such as the importation of aspects of the *kusemai*, a rival performing art, by Zeami's father, Kan'ami, and Zeami's own efforts to incorporate instrumental dance, the erstwhile signature of the aforementioned rival style that had enjoyed the *yūgen* reputation.

All of this will provide the background needed to follow Zeami's rationale for developing the performance configuration that was to become central to both his theory and his practice of *sarugaku*, the two modes (chant and dance) and the three styles (the venerable, feminine, and martial styles). The final portion of this chapter will be devoted to its development, which amounted to a redefinition of *monomane* whereby lifelike duplication of originals was no longer apropos since there were no originals available. Instead, *monomane* techniques come to be reworked and introduced into the new ecology of poetic text, chanting, dance, and instrumental music to create the much more abstract style of representation that has come down to us today as Zeami's style.

Early *Monomane*: The Nine Character Types

In the earliest chronicle of what role-play was like in Yamato *sarugaku*, which is found in the second chapter of his treatise, *Kaden*, Zeami enumerates nine character types in the repertoire. His opening statement in that chapter underscores the fundamental importance of *monomane* techniques in this early stage of his art: "It is difficult to describe the [character] types of [the] *monomane* [repertoire] fully in writing. Be that as it may, they are crucial to this path, so you should take utmost care to train [in all] the types."[1] He then enumerates nine such character types. The following is a synopsis of his descriptions for each.

1. **The Woman:** this style includes figures such as the court lady, the dancing girl, or the madwoman. Style of dress is crucial. Demeanor should be gentle.

2. **The Old Person:** this style features graceful and dignified deportment. Dance is important: like an old tree that puts forth flowers. Bent posture is to be avoided.

3. **The Maskless Character:** since the role is that of an ordinary male character, it should be easy to play, but this is not necessarily so. One must not attempt to imitate the facial attributes of the character. Only comportment and general image should be emulated.

4. **The Mad Person (*monogurui*):** this is the most interesting type of role. There are two types: A) madness rooted in the character's own suffering; B) madness produced in the character due to possession by a spirit. Type A is preferable to type B. Deranged behavior should grow out of the character's psychic affliction. Never cast a female character as the victim of possession by a warring or demonic spirit. Costuming for a mad person can be more colorful than usual, for example, the character might carry a sprig of flowers in season.

5. **The Buddhist Priest:** there are few characters of this type. High-ranking priests should be dignified and noble. A traveling priest of lesser rank should create an impression of religious devoutness.

6. **The Warring Being:** even when played well, this character is of little intrinsic interest, except for prominent figures from the war between the Minamoto and Taira clans. However, if courtly elements are incorporated into the performance, then such characters can be of supreme interest.

7. **The Deity:** this type of role-play is in a demonic style. However, deities may also be performed in a style that features dance, whereas demons may not. Since there is no such thing as a model to emulate, costuming becomes very important.

8. **The Demon:** this is a specialty of the Yamato troupes. Of the two types of demons, the true demon from hell and the angry or possessed spirit, it is the latter type that should be emulated. In essence, the

demon is a frightening being, but one should not emulate that quality too faithfully because frightening an audience is diametrically
opposed to interesting an audience. Make the movement detailed in
articulation.

9. **The Chinese Person:** costuming is an important part of construct-
ing the role. It should be out of the ordinary and then will seem
vaguely Chinese.

Each entry describes the style of imitation considered optimal for rendering a certain character type as believable as possible to an audience.
Zeami's instructions concentrate on the general demeanor, costuming, and
comportment that are suitable for each. It is clear that he is not aspiring to
verisimilitude per se, given that three of the nine character types are supernatural beings. Rather, the actor should imitate selectively, basing his judgments on the associative images and the expectations about a character type
that he supposes the spectators to have.

According to Zeami, some characters should be mimicked in more detail
than others. In fact, he prefaces this listing with advice on when and when
not to be lifelike: "Generally speaking, the essence [of *monomane*] is to
resemble all aspects closely without exception. However, also be aware
that [resemblance] should be strong or weak depending on the subject."[2] If,
in playing the role of a Chinese, there is some touch that seems Chinese,
then no further attention to actual Chinese models is necessary, for
instance. Moreover, he specifies that the appearance and comportment of
members of the court or military aristocracy should be imitated in detail,
as should other high-ranking persons. Activities that involve artistic sensibilities (versifying or playing musical instruments) should also be reproduced in detail. On the other hand, the humble callings of farmers and
rustics should not be imitated in any detail, unless the subject is a traditional
one in poetry, such as a woodcutter, grass cutter, charcoal burner, or salt
gatherer. Ordinary women should not be emulated with much realism, but
the comportment of aristocratic women should be imitated impeccably.

Zeami's descriptions reflect a marked bias in favor of elegant aristocratic types of characters over forceful ones. In fact, several of the nine categories suggest subcategories that contrast the two. For instance, he remarks
that characters belonging to the *shura* category tend to lack interest. The
shura is the ghost of a warrior who, guilty of the sin of taking human life, is
destined for purgatory in the afterlife. This purgatory, called the *shuradō*

(path of the *shura*), is one of the six transmigratory modes of existence in the Buddhist cosmology. In his *Kaden* description, Zeami does not name specific plays, and there is very little known about plays predating him that featured *shura*.

If we take the warrior plays that Zeami composed later in his career as examples, typically the ghost returns to this world because of some attachment to it that remains unresolved. The ghost appears to a priest (today cast as the *waki*, or side actor) and appeals to the priest to aid him in finding release from his suffering. In *Kaden*, Zeami credits characters of the *shura* category with little of interest, with the exception of famous characters from the Genpei War (1180–1185) between the Taira and Minamoto clans. In such plays, one can incorporate qualities of courtly elegance, which give them interest. Judging from his own corpus of plays, Zeami was drawn to the losing side, the Taira warriors, who were, despite their warrior pedigrees, well versed in poetry, music, and other artistic endeavors associated with courtly culture.

There are two contrastive approaches to portraying the Shintō deity as well. Depending on the deity in question, an angry, demonic style of execution may be appropriate. However, in the contrasting style, dance may be appropriate. Finally, Zeami is adamant that in the style he calls most interesting—that of the mad person—spirit possession should not violate the femininity of a female victim or the masculinity of a male one. He seems to be attempting to move away from material that calls for a strong show of force on the part of a female character since such behavior would violate her original feminine image. When the source of her madness is spirit possession by a warring being or demon, then her behavior will seem demon-like rather than feminine. He stresses that such scenarios should be avoided. Instead, he advocates that a woman's madness be prompted by loss of a child, abandonment by a spouse, or death of a spouse. The form that her madness takes should be feminine, that is, it should be received by the audience as being in character.

In speaking of the traditional specialty of his Yamato school, the demon, Zeami stipulates two types: those beings that are truly hell-dwellers and those beings who are originally human but who suffer from possession by evil spirits. (Elsewhere, he refers to the former as having the heart and form of a demon, the latter as having the form of a demon but a human heart.) One should play only the latter type, and, still then, a demon play will lack interest unless the actor is superbly skilled. Zeami further states that this is so because a demon is by its nature strong and fierce, and a performance inspiring fear in an audience cannot also inspire interest. To make the performance of a demonic role interesting is like making a flower blossom on a rock.

This earliest description of the types of characters in the *monomane* repertory reflects a preoccupation with two different groups of characters: genteel, elegant ones and strong, rough ones. Zeami's description of variant styles of *monomane* techniques for the warrior ghost, madwoman, deity, and demon evidences such an awareness. A pattern emerges as to how the plays of these two strains should be executed as well. He suggests dance as an option for characters belonging to the elegant strain, but not for those belonging to the rough strain. He seems to draw a line between those character types whose identities lend themselves to singing and dancing and those who do not. He states that dance is a crucial element in performing an old-man role, for instance. In the woman category, he expressly mentions two types of characters who are professional performers of the *kusemai* and *shirabyōshi,* two performance arts having danced elements. Singing and dancing will seem in character for such figures. In the case of a warrior's ghost, the role-play may call for demonic comportment or for dance moves. Dance moves are appropriate for renowned warriors of the Genpei War. It was the aristocratic warriors of the Taira whose image lent itself best to danced expression. Zeami seems to be saying that demonic comportment is not intrinsically interesting, but a warrior with courtly sensibilities, expressed through dance, has redeeming features.

In the deity category, too, angry figures in a demonic style do not dance, but there are other kinds of deities, by implication not fierce, for which danced expression is appropriate. We may conclude that angry, demonic deities were not considered compatible with the activity of dancing. Dance is not mentioned in connection with characters in the demon category either, although Zeami says that detailed execution of foot and hand movement on the part of a demon with human origins can have redeeming interest.

Zeami's first major statement on *monomane* techniques thus reflects a concern with including scenes with singing and dancing in his plays. At this early stage, the allotment of these elements to a character seems to have depended on the identity of that character and the plausibility of performing such elements in the larger context of the drama. The gentler, or more genteel, the character, the more compatible and credible danced elements were perceived to be. The more demonic the behavior, the less compatible those same elements became.

In his discussion here of the representative character types, Zeami explicitly identifies the demon role as the signature of Yamato *sarugaku*, but it is clear that both the demonic and the martial modes were of less interest to him than the gentler role types, such as madwomen and venerable characters. It is also clear that one reason he was attracted to such gentle characters was that dancing and singing were considered dramatically credible modes of behavior for them, whereas allotting such elements to rougher or more violent characters risked violating dramatic credibility. For decades Zeami would pursue this interest in intensifying sung and danced elements in Yamato *sarugaku*. It was a motivating force in his development of the dramatic prototype of the two-part dream play, to be explored in part 2 of this volume. It would also have a major impact on his theory of acting, as we will explore further here. Next we will examine some of the early reasons for his strong attraction to danced and sung elements despite all indications that they were not the traditional strengths of his troupe.

Ōmi versus Yamato *Sarugaku*: *Kakari* and the *Yūgen* Quotient

SEARCHING FOR YŪGEN: EMULATING THE ŌMI STYLE

In the fifth chapter of *Kaden*, Zeami continues to single out *monomane* techniques as the defining attribute of his style of *sarugaku*. Moreover, he contrasts this style with that of rival troupes based in the Ōmi area (present-day Shiga Prefecture).[3] At the close of this chapter, he credits his father as the inspiration for the contents (as well as for that of the preceding four chapters).[4] If this attribution is taken at face value, then the following passage from chapter 5 may be assumed to reflect the state of the Yamato and Ōmi styles of *sarugaku* in Kan'ami's lifetime.

> In Ōmi they attach primary importance to the dimension of graceful beauty (*yūgen*), making imitation (*monomane*) secondary, and making artistic effect (*kakari*) the basis. In Yamato, we attach primary importance to imitation (*monomane*), expanding our repertoire to all types [of characters], yet aspiring to a style of graceful beauty (*yūgen*).[5]

Performers of both styles strived to create elements having a cultivated grace (*yūgen*) in their performances. However, the Ōmi performers attempted to evoke that quality directly through the appropriate artistic atmosphere *(kakari)*, whereas the Yamato performers aspired to imitating a range of characters while at the same time evoking a graceful atmosphere.

Yūgen is a much precedented term in the vocabulary of medieval aesthetics, and more will be said about its place in the poetic canon in the following chapter. Zeami is not explicit here about the kinds of stage effects that he associated with the term. Elsewhere, he does describe the quality as it should be manifested onstage. In the treatise *Kakyō* he identifies *yūgen* with "simply a form that is beautiful and gentle,"[6] and in the treatise *Shikadō* he likens the *yūgen* quality to a swan holding a flower in its beak.[7] A surface serenity and aristocratic beauty seem to have been at the core of his conception.

The first matter of note in the quotation above is that Zeami characterizes his own Yamato style as more representational, that is, more committed to representing characters. One may infer, then, that the Yamato style was weighted more heavily toward depicting a character in the context of a dramatic fiction. In contrast, the Ōmi style appears to have been more presentational, based on the evocation of an elegant atmosphere, with little regard for sustaining a dramatic fiction. The second point is that in the Yamato style, *monomane* elements coexisted with *yūgen* elements but were not considered as directly related to the evocation of that quality as was the element of *kakari*. In fact, the quotation above suggests that the Yamato style at times aspired to the *yūgen* atmosphere despite the presence of *monomane* elements that were not particularly conducive to creating that mood.

We also know from the passage quoted above that Zeami considered the element of *kakari* to be integral to the evocation of the *yūgen* quality. What did *kakari* consist of? Judging from his description in *Kaden* as well as other treatises, the effects of *kakari*—the key to *yūgen* in the Ōmi style—resided in the musical and choreographic elements of a performance. Annotations for the term *kakari* as employed in the quotation above differ somewhat, however. In the two oldest editions consulted, Nose Asaji's *Zeami jūrokubushū hyōshaku* and the Nihon Koten Bungaku Taikei edition edited by Nishio Minoru, no explicit connection is made between musical elements and the evocation of *kakari*. Nose glosses *kakari* as *"fūshi fuzei no utsukushisa,"* "beauty of visual appeal and bodily deportment."[8] Nishio equates it with *"fuzei no bi,"* "a beauty of bodily deportment."[9]

More recent annotators have attempted to be more specific on the chemistry of *kakari*. Tanaka Yutaka defines it as *tsuzukegara,* which may be

glossed as "the way of connecting [the parts of a sequence to each other]."
He points out that the term originates in the critical writings on *waka* and
renga, in which it refers to the effects evoked by how the words are connected to each other. On Zeami's usage of the term he states,

> Zeami refers to the overall image [of the performer] that emerges on
> the basis of that sequence of movement having to do [equally] with
> [all the elements], including chant, dance, vigorous moves, etc.[10]

In Tanaka's view, then, *kakari* is an overall effect growing out of the interrelation of multiple elements as they unfold in performance.

The Nihon Shisō Taikei annotation for the term *kakari* in the *Kaden*
passage above corroborates a connection between singing and the creation
of mood. As in Tanaka's annotation, it also adds movement to the equation:
"In concrete terms, it is a beauty of movement based on a fusion of chant
and dance."[11] This interpretation echoes an annotation by the same author,
Omote Akira, which was originally published a year earlier. He states, "In
concrete terms, it seems to be performance that abounds in the sense of
fluidity created by combined chant and dance."[12]

Zeami reiterates the connection between music and the eliciting of
yūgen in his treatise *Sarugaku dangi* as well. Written approximately twenty-
eight years after the second chapter of *Kaden*, *Sarugaku dangi* is a record of
the mature Zeami's perspectives on the art as set down by his son,
Motoyoshi. In the passage below, he forges an explicit link between singing
and *kakari*. (The translation for *kakari* in the following is "artistic effect.")

> As for the acting technique of Ōmi [Sarugaku], [the actors] do not
> in the least try to win admiration by standing still [unexpectedly].
> They only consider plenty of artistic effect as being essential. In the
> final part of the second act they all stand and sing [together], and
> then swiftly leave the stage.[13]

This passage links the artistic effect *(kakari)* of the Ōmi style to a musical
finale in which singing takes precedence over dynamic stage business. And,
as Zeami earlier noted in the second chapter of *Kaden*, the Ōmi style
depended on this *kakari* factor in the evocation of *yūgen*. In the Ōmi style,
at least, there appears to have been a close connection between singing and
the promotion of artistic effects associated with *yūgen*. Although both

Omote and Tanaka describe *kakari* as artistic effect derived from dance as well, Zeami draws no explicit link between *kakari* and choreography in either of the citations above. Such links must be sought elsewhere in his corpus, as we will do in the ensuing section.

THE INFLUENCE OF ŌMI PRECEDENTS
ON YAMATO CHOREOGRAPHY

Zeami's descriptions of the Ōmi style introduced in the prior section suggest that one key to *yūgen* effects was music and singing. In other of his treatises, there is evidence that the Ōmi style of performance provided a model for Zeami and his father to emulate in order to intensify *yūgen* effects on another front as well, and that is dance. In *Sarugaku dangi*, Zeami credits the Ōmi *sarugaku* player Inuō with a major innovation on Ōmi *sarugaku*, performance of the "celestial maiden dance" *(tennyo no mai)*. He attributes the dance to Inuō with "[h]e also danced the heavenly maiden, lightly and quickly, just like a bird drifting at the mercy of the wind."[14] In his late treatise titled *Kyakuraika*, he goes into more detail.

> The dance of the celestial maiden forms the basis for danced expression. Having been brought into our art [from outside], it is [now] the main dance. Inuō of Ōmi was skilled [at it]. For this reason, there are those who say, "The dance of the celestial maiden is the foundation style of Ōmi *sarugaku*."[15]

In *Sarugaku dangi*, Zeami makes it clear that the celestial dance was a feature of the Ōmi style prior to its incorporation into Yamato *sarugaku*. He also claims the credit for its adaptation into the latter: "Kan'a did not perform the heavenly maiden. But, as he said to Motokiyo in his last will that he should dance it, Zeshi started to dance it in Yamato [Sarugaku]."[16] (Kan'a refers to Kan'ami, Zeshi to Zeami.)

When the *Kaden* passage above contrasting the Ōmi and Yamato styles was written, the dance of the celestial maiden was probably still the exclusive purview of Ōmi *sarugaku*, serving as one element of that style that was associated by performers and audiences with the creation of a *yūgen* mood. The fact that it was Kan'ami's dying wish that Zeami introduce the celestial dance into Yamato *sarugaku* and that he did indeed do so suggests that both father and son recognized the desirability of intensifying the danced elements in a play. Presumably, both also saw a connection between dance and the artistic effects of *kakari*, that most crucial prerequisite to the evocation of *yūgen*.

In his study of the impact of the *tennyo no mai* on *sarugaku*, Takemoto argues that when Zeami introduced the *tennyo no mai* art into Yamato *sarugaku*, it made it possible to incorporate an extended dance section for the first time. As evidence, Takemoto notes that the oldest plays of Yamato *sarugaku* lack such a dance section in the second act.[17] He argues persuasively that the *tennyo no mai* was the ancestor of a group of dances that came to hold a central place in the noh performance tradition. These are instrumental pieces in which drums and flute follow one basic cycle of prototypical measures (*ryo-chū-kan keishiki*), with periodic variations. Tempo and tone will vary across this group of dances, but the instrumental

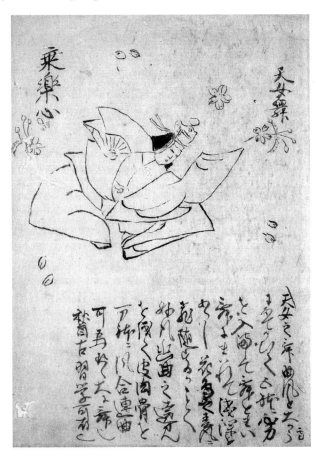

Figure 1 *Tennyo no mai* (Dance of the celestial maiden) from Zeami's treatise *Nikyoku santai ningyō zu*. The caption in the upper left says, "In the spirit of mounting the music." This copy of Zeami's manuscript dates to 1441. Believed to be in the hand of Zeami's son-in-law, Konparu Zenchiku. (Courtesy of Hōsei University Institute of Nōgaku Studies, Tokyo.)

prototype remains the same. Any of these dances are typically situated in the climactic, concluding section of a play.

With the incorporation of the *tennyo no mai* into Yamato *sarugaku*, it would seem that Zeami was able to add a new dimension to its *monomane*-based representational style: an extended dance section. If the *tennyo no mai* is, in fact, the ancestor of this group of instrumental pieces, then it would have added a structural component composed of instrumentation and dance, which would not necessarily have been contingent on such dramatic constraints as acting out the lines or developing the dramatic action.

This intensification of the role of dance and instrumental music may well have been spurred by Zeami's desire to intensify the presence of those artistic effects that were associated with *yūgen* in the Ōmi style, and for which the Ōmi players enjoyed accolades. Yet it is important to note that he never abandoned the Yamato trademark, *monomane*, in the hope of achieving the cachet of *yūgen*. Instead, as we will see, he struggled to have his *monomane* and his *yūgen*, too.

The Impact of the *Kusemai* on Yamato *Sarugaku*

Zeami's incorporation of the *tennyo no mai* into Yamato *sarugaku* was not the first innovation intended to intensify musical and danced elements in that style. Long before that, Kan'ami had effected one seminal change in the Yamato style that reflects such a shift in emphasis in role-playing: the introduction and adaptation of components from the then popular *kusemai*, a form of sung and danced entertainment, into Yamato *sarugaku*. As we shall see, the inception of the *kusemai* into the *sarugaku* art had provided a kind of base on which Zeami could build as he strived to intensify the presence of chanted and danced elements.

References to the *kusemai* art form can be traced as far back as the middle of the fourteenth century, although its origins are unclear.[18] It is generally accepted in Japanese scholarship that the *kusemai* was strongly influenced by an earlier art form composed of dance and song called the *shirabyōshi*, and Zeami speaks of both of these arts and their influence on *sarugaku* in his treatises. The *shirabyōshi* art was enormously popular in the late Heian and early Kamakura periods. The dancers, who were also referred to as *shirabyōshi*, were usually women who would appear costumed as men.

The *kusemai* dancers were of both sexes. The picture of a *kusemai* dancer in an illustrated scroll titled *Shichijūichiban shokunin uta awase* (Poetry contest of seventy-one artisans; ca. 1500) depicts a man in the traditional outfit of an upright hat (*eboshi*), wide trousers (*hakama*), and a wide-sleeved over robe (*suikan*). This was also the typical costume of a *shirabyōshi* performer. The figure is also equipped with a fan in his right hand and at his side a shoulder drum, accoutrements shared by the *shirabyōshi*.[19] By Zeami's time, the female performers of the *kusemai* seem to have gained ascendancy over their male counterparts. This is reflected in the discussion in his treatise *Sandō* of the character type of the *kusemai* dancer as portrayed in *sarugaku*. The *kusemai* prototype is introduced in a section devoted to compositional principles for *sarugaku* plays having female protagonists.

Much of what we know about the *kusemai* of the late fourteenth and early fifteenth centuries is based on Zeami's descriptions of it in his treatises. In *Go on*, for instance, he provides a brief overview of the various styles of *kusemai* performance.

> The professional *kusemai* groups are the Kamidō, Shimodō, Nishino-take, Tenjiku, and the Kagajo.[20] (My deceased father trained with Otozuru of this [last] group.) It is said that the Kagajo women are the artistic descendants of the female *kusemai* dancer Hyakuman, from the Nara area. All the [major] dancers of the *kusemai* have died out, and, if not for the style derivative of the Kaga women's *kusemai*, nothing would remain. The *kusemai* performed on the floats at the Gion Festival belongs to this line.[21]

KUSEMAI INFLUENCE ON THE VOCAL MUSIC
OF YAMATO SARUGAKU

Kan'ami's adaptation of the *kusemai* into Yamato *sarugaku* had profound ramifications on the musical structure of the traditional chant. In many of his critical treatises, Zeami comes back to this point. In *Ongyoku kuden* he devotes a section to "Knowing How to Distinguish between *Kusemai* Chant and Plain Chant [*tada ongyoku*]." He states,

> As for the *kusemai*, because it originated as its own art, it is as different from plain chant as black is from white. Thus, it is written with the Chinese character [meaning "not straight" or "tune"] and the character [meaning "dance"].[22] Although in the broad sense it can be said to be vocal music, you should understand from the [attribution

of] Chinese characters that it is a different kind of vocal expression. As for the difference, the substance [tai] of kusemai is its rhythm. In plain chant, the substance is the voice, and the rhythm its function [yū]. . . . One performs [kusemai] by standing and singing. The vocal music arises [as a function of] the visual appeal.[23]

In the earliest stage of adaptation, the kusemai chant was distinguishable from the chanting style that had been standard in Yamato sarugaku (tada utai, plain chant). The former stressed the rhythm and the latter the qualities of the voice. What Zeami means by "the voice" is developed later in Sarugaku dangi, which describes the plain chant more specifically as "having melody as its basis" (Tada utai wa, fushi o hon ni su).[24]

As the kusemai art form was further adapted to suit the context of sarugaku, Kan'ami modified its original music. Zeami describes this in the following passage.

> Ever since my deceased father danced the kusemai [titled] Shirahige in sarugaku, [the kusemai] has become our music also. Although Shirahige, Yura no minato, and Jigoku no kusemai are all in the sarugaku repertoire, they are basically similar to the specialists' kusemai. Moreover, Kaidō kudari and Saikoku kudari are compositions by Tamarin set to music by Naami and Kan'ami (my deceased father). These kusemai tunes are softer [in mood] than the specialists' kusemai.[25]

In Ongyoku kuden Zeami notes that this softening of the kusemai involved the mixing of the original kusemai music with the popular verse form called kouta, which he considered the orthodox chanting style of sarugaku. He goes so far as to state that this new mixed style of kusemai and kouta could be referred to as "the Yamato style of vocal music."[26]

STAGES OF ADAPTATION OF THE KUSEMAI INTO YAMATO SARUGAKU

Judging from kusemai texts preserved in Zeami's writings, kusemai performers took the stance of narrators rather than of dramatis personae. Kan'ami and Zeami would transmogrify such independent narratives into components within the larger dramatic framework of plays. At the same time, however, sarugaku performers also adopted the tradition of performing kusemai as chanted narratives in their own right. Such independent pieces were

considered particularly appropriate for indoor gatherings held by influential patrons, such as banquets at the residences of court aristocrats or
members of the warrior elite.[27]

The pieces named in the quotation above, for instance, all originated
as independent pieces. *Shirahige* tells the legend of the founding of the
Tendai complex, Enryakuji, located on Mount Hiei, northeast of Kyoto.
The narrative appears to be based on the eighteenth book of the epic tale
Taiheiki (The record of the great peace; fourteenth century).[28] The second
kusemai mentioned above, *Yura no minato* (Port at Yura), treats matters of
the heart. Kan'ami's compilation tells the story of a woman who, estranged
from her unfaithful husband, abandons her home and takes to the road. She
is deceived by a man she encounters and is sold into prostitution. The narrative concludes with her lament at having to spend her final years alone
in a brothel in distant Kakegawa (a town in modern Shizuoka Prefecture).[29]
In the late treatise, *Go on*, Zeami comments that *Yura no minato* marked
the beginning of a *kusemai* style that had *yūgen*. It is not clear what he
meant by this comment. Takemoto speculates that the language of the
original *kusemai* tended to favor a descriptive style with few poetic devices.
By contrast, Kan'ami's composition, *Yura no minato*, has passages that are
akin to the stylistics of *waka* poetry, and this is why Zeami credits it as a
piece having *yūgen*.[30]

According to Zeami in the passage from *Go on* quoted above, the new,
softened style was best represented by the pieces *Kaidō kudari* (Coastal
journey to the east; another title for *Tōgoku kudari* [Journey to the eastern
provinces]) and *Saikoku kudari* (Journey to the western provinces). The
lines of *Kaidō kudari* were composed by the noted *renga* poet Rin'ami. As
mentioned earlier, Rin'ami was one of a group of individuals employed by
the shogun (in this case Yoshimitsu) as arbiters of taste on a range of artistic matters.[31] *Kaidō kudari* is an extended *michiyuki* (travel song) composed
on the basis of a series of allusions to poetic place-names. It traces the lonely
journey of the captured Taira warrior Morihisa from Kyoto to Kamakura in
eastern Japan.[32] *Saikoku kudari*, too, was composed by Rin'ami, and the
lines were put to music by Kan'ami. It is an account of the flight westward
of the Heike clan after they are driven out of the Kyoto capital by the Genji
forces in the Genpei War.[33] Both of these are thought to have been composed for the *sarugaku* repertoire as autonomous *kusemai* pieces. *Kaidō
kudari* has since been imported into a play about Morihisa (*Morihisa*), which
is attributed to Zeami's son Motomasa.

Jigoku no kusemai is devoted to the enumeration of the sufferings to be endured in four of the six transmigratory paths of Buddhism: hell (*jigoku*), the realm of hungry beings (*gaki*), the realm of beasts (*chikushō*), and the realm of warrior ghosts (*shura* or *ashura*). In *Go on* Zeami attributes the composition of the lines to an unidentified individual named Yamamoto.[34] Although *Jigoku no kusemai* is also believed to have been an autonomous piece originally, it has a rather involved history that reflects the process of adaptation that the *kusemai* underwent as it grew to be an integral part of the structural framework of a play. Today, such a *kusemai* segment situated within a play is known as the *kuse* section. In both *Sandō* and *Sarugaku dangi*, Zeami discusses the composition of a *kuse* section in terms of its structural parts, and more will be said about this later in this volume.

According to *Go on*, *Jigoku no kusemai* was at one time embedded in the play titled *Hyakuman*.[35] This earlier version of the play still known today by the same title is not extant. However, it is thought to follow roughly the same story line as the revised version of the play that has come down to us. The famed *kusemai* dancer Hyakuman is maddened by grief at the disappearance of her child. She wanders to Seiryōji Temple in western Kyoto to attend an annual prayer service to the Buddha Amida. In the hopes of finding her child and curing her own madness, she dances as a prayer offering.

In an earlier version of the play, she performs the *Jigoku no kusemai*. However, *Jigoku no kusemai* was subsequently replaced by a new *kuse* section depicting Hyakuman's state of mind while searching for her child. This revised *kuse* narrates her distressed progress from the Nara area to Seiryōji, which is the setting of the play. Her dance accompanies this recapitulation of her wanderings. Her child, who is in the crowd at Seiryōji, recognizes Hyakuman as she dances, and they are reunited. In *Sarugaku dangi*, Zeami claims credit for the authorship of *Hyakuman*, and therefore this revision of the contents of the *kuse* is assumed to be his.[36] The piece *Jigoku no kusemai* was later imported into the play *Utaura* (Soothsaying by verse), a play by Motomasa about a shaman who is reunited with his young son.[37]

As an independent narrative, *Jigoku no kusemai* had constituted a kind of performance within a performance whose content was not related to the drama of Hyakuman's story. Zeami revised the content of the *kusemai* to be part of the story portrayed, rather than an isolated content functioning purely as a performance within a performance. To be sure, casting a famous *kusemai* performer such as Hyakuman to perform *Jigoku no kusemai* was one way to assure the centrality of the elements of singing and dancing. However, as Itō Masayoshi has noted, such a scenario did not meet Zeami's ideal for plays featuring a madwoman as he articulates it in the second chapter of *Kaden*. There he states that it is preferable for madness to be depicted as the outgrowth of a character's suffering rather than as behavior driven by such an outside force as possession by a spirit.[38] Whereas the revised version of the *kuse* does spell out the link between Hyakuman's personal loss and her mad behavior, the earlier version featuring the *Jigoku no kusemai* does not. Zeami's revision introduces a dramatic motivation for Hyakuman's plying of her trade that is embedded in the larger story.

As Omote has noted, importing a *kusemai*-style narrative into the structure of a *sarugaku* play was an innovation with important repercussions.

> Even though it was called "dance," danced elements in the *kusemai* were sparse, and it was vocal music that made telling a story its primary aim. Its style was prose, abounding in epic qualities. It was in Zeami's generation that [composers] came to notice this advantage to the *kusemai*, and produced scripts that situated the *kusemai* at the center of a play, using it to narrate the subject matter [of the play]. One must not forget that the incorporation of the *kusemai* into *sarugaku* not only magnified the musical effects exponentially, but also greatly influenced how noh plays would be composed.[39]

This important facet of the adapted *kusemai* will be addressed with more concreteness in part 2 of this volume.

THE ADAPTED *KUSEMAI* AND ITS RELATION TO *YŪGEN*

In several spots in his treatises, Zeami refers to the potential of the softened style of *kusemai* for eliciting the *yūgen* quality. For instance, in a discussion of the kind of chanted pieces that are appropriate on less formal occasions at private residences, he notes that the program need not be restricted to celebratory pieces.

> One may perform a piece suitable to the mood in a smooth, effort-less style having the artistic effect [*kakari*] and the style of *yūgen*. The *kouta bushi kusemai* that is currently popular should be appropriate.[40]

Kouta bushi kusemai refers to this new mixed style.

By the time that Zeami composed the early chapters of *Kaden*, the incorporation of the *kusemai* into Yamato *sarugaku* had already been accomplished. After he delineates the differences between the Ōmi and Yamato styles in the fifth chapter of *Kaden*, he names two of the earliest plays in the Yamato repertoire to incorporate the *kusemai* and makes a connection between his father's performance of these plays and the quality of *yūgen*.

> The Yamato style is recognized for its various roles that are based on *monomane* and lively language [*giri*],[41] or strong costumes, or angry comportment, and such accomplishments are indeed our specialties. But, when my late father was in his prime, he had mastered all styles, including characters such as [in the plays] *Shizuka ga mai no nō* (The plays with Shizuka's dance) and *Saga no dainenbutsu no onna monogurui* (Madwoman at the Saga Dainenbutsu), and hence earned universal praise and admiration. This was a style of peerless *yūgen*.[42]

Zeami makes the remarks above to underscore the point that the actor must train in all types of roles. The two plays mentioned are cited as examples that are contrastive with rough or angry role-playing in the old Yamato *sarugaku* repertoire. The distinction between rough/strong and elegant/gentle types of characters, first evident in the discussion of the nine types of characters, is apparent here as well.

The first play is believed to be the original version of the play *Yoshino Shizuka*, which features Minamoto no Yoshitsune's lover, the *shirabyōshi* dancer Shizuka (Shizuka Gozen). In the extant version, Shizuka, who is renowned as a particularly fine dancer, performs for a group of warriors sent by shogun Yoritomo to capture Yoshitsune. She agrees to do so in order to stall for time while Yoshitsune flees the scene.[43] *Saga no dainenbutsu no onna monogurui* was later reworked into the play *Hyakuman*, whose revisions are discussed above. Little is known about the contents of *Saga no dainenbutsu no onna monogurui*, but it is generally surmised to treat the mad Hyakuman's visit to Seiryōji Temple, which is located in Saga, west of the capital, at the time of the annual Dainenbutsu, a large-scale prayer gathering dedicated to invocation of the Buddha Amida's name.

Throughout his treatises Zeami credits female characters with possessing more of the *yūgen* atmosphere than other types of characters, so the fact that these two plays feature women would seem to be one reason for singling them out as having a *yūgen* style. Nevertheless, his attribution of this quality cannot always be construed unequivocally as a function of the identities of the characters represented. For instance, in the later work *Go on* he attributes the quality of *yūgen* to the vocal music of two pieces, *Yura no minato* and *Kaidō kudari*.[44] Although the *yūgen* overtones of the former might be accounted for by the subject matter, a woman's story, *Kaidō kudari* has nothing to do with female characters. It would seem that this particular piece must depend on other elements for its *yūgen* effects.

In his treatise *Fushizuke shidai* (How to compose the music; undated), Zeami provides some hints about variables that might be conducive to *yūgen* effects besides the identity of the characters represented. He is discussing the artistic strength of the new blended vocal style, referred to below as *kouta bushi kusemai*.

> Nowadays we have what is called *kouta bushi kusemai*, and one often hears the *kusemai* performed in the style of plain chant. This is a style that is smooth and has *yūgen*. It is [a type of] *kusemai*, but the music cannot really be called that of the original *kusemai*. The musical phrasing does not correspond [to the original *kusemai*]. However, the artistic effect *[kakari]* of the progressions from one word to the next, or one verse to the next, is good, and the music sounds interesting, so nowadays music should be composed to adhere to this style *[fūtei]*.[45]

Why does this new style of *kusemai* have *yūgen*? Zeami is not explicit on this point. It is clear from the rest of his remarks here that he sees the manner in which the lines of a play are delivered as important to sustaining the *yūgen* mood. Here, as in his discussion of Ōmi *sarugaku* in chapter 5 of *Kaden*, he associates the evocation of *yūgen* with the idea of artistic effect, or *kakari*. However, in this case the meaning of the term *kakari* signals something more specific than an atmosphere promoted by singing and dancing. It refers to the affect inspired by the progressions from one word or verse to the next.

This usage of the term *kakari* is reminiscent of Nijō Yoshimoto's usage of the term in reference to the poetics of *renga*, a point that we will return to in the ensuing chapter. Although *Fushizuke shidai* is undated, it is generally believed to be a product of Zeami's middle period.[46] The quotation above suggests a growing awareness in his middle years that the flow of the lines of a play were integral to fostering the graceful effects of *yūgen*, no matter what the subject matter.

Monomane Reoriented

If Kan'ami and Zeami were in agreement that the incorporation of danced and chanted elements into Yamato *sarugaku* was key to promoting an atmosphere of *yūgen*, then why did they not proceed to do so for all types of *monomane* from as early on as the first three chapters of *Kaden*? What was keeping them from emulating the more successful style of Ōmi *sarugaku* when playing all types of roles? The impasse seems to have been rooted in the nature of the early *monomane*, the Yamato trademark. As long as the Yamato style was predicated on the lifelike semblance of certain characters, the number of character types for whom the casting of dancing and singing was appropriate without stretching dramatic credibility was severely constrained. The enumeration of the nine *monomane* character types in chapter 2 of *Kaden* demonstrates that judgments about the suitability of danced and chanted elements was indeed based on the identity of the character. Gentle ones were thought suitable; forceful ones were not.

Zeami elaborates on the distinction between gentle characters and forceful or strong ones in the sixth chapter of *Kaden*.[47] He holds that the qualities of strength and *yūgen* exist in the content or substance of these subjects themselves. A rather lengthy enumeration of which subjects belong to either category then follows. Entities possessing *yūgen* include court ladies, female entertainers, beautiful women, handsome men, and, in the plant world, flowering plants. As for strong entities, he lists warriors, barbarians, demons, deities, and, in the plant world, the pine and the cedar. *Yūgen*-style subjects should be presented as such, strong subjects also presented as strong. If the actor mimics these objects faithfully, then the appropriate atmospheres will appear of themselves, he states.[48]

What, then, was to be done about some of the staple characters of the traditional Yamato repertoire, such as warriors and demons? If Zeami was to remain true to the Yamato *sarugaku* emphasis on *monomane*, then how was he to incorporate the *yūgen* elements of singing and dancing into plays representing such characters? It would seem that he had two choices: either to abandon the strong characters of the Yamato tradition or to violate dramatic credibility by the creation of dancing warriors and singing demons.

One solution proposed by Zeami was to downplay the degree of mimicry required in the playing of rough roles. As we have seen, as early as chapter 2 of *Kaden* he advises that elegant character types should be imitated more faithfully than inelegant ones. Moreover, in chapter 6 of the same he echoes that sentiment. He reminds us that *sarugaku* is an art that assigns the audience the top priority. When the audience includes individuals who put much stock in the evocation of the *yūgen* quality,

> If [the object of representation] is on the strong side, then even if you diverge a bit from truthful resemblance [*sukoshi monomane ni hazururu tomo*], you should play up the graceful [*yūgen*] side.[49]

A second solution was to avoid rough characters in the first place. In the ensuing section of the sixth chapter of *Kaden*, he stresses this idea.

> For the main material of a *sarugaku* play, you should choose a figure that has grace [*yūgen*] and, what is more, in composing, you should strive for a conception [*kokoro*] and language [*kotoba*] that are elegant.[50]

Also in *Sandō*, his treatise on composing plays, Zeami cites material about three aristocratic females, Rokujō, Yūgao, and Ukifune from *Tale of Genji*, as ideal manifestations of the *yūgen* quality.[51] He mentions these three characters in order to make the point that the type of character the playwright chooses to write about is a primary determinant of whether the play will be conducive to an atmosphere of *yūgen*.

> Generally speaking, our art takes form in dance and chant. However celebrated an ancient or artist, if the personage is not the type to perform these two modes of acting, then visional affect [stage effects] cannot materialize. Make sure you ponder and appreciate this well.[52]

Yet these expedients did not solve the basic problem of what to do with the warriors and demons. To eliminate them from the repertory would have been a radical departure from Yamato precedents, and perhaps this is why he never does abandon such characters.

Zeami is the author of more extant plays featuring warriors than any other *sarugaku* playwright. Moreover, plays by him such as *Nomori* (Keeper of the fields) and *Nue* (Chimera), which feature demonic protagonists, are thought to have been composed toward the end of his life. We shall see that rather than abandoning such rough characters, he revamped them by re-orienting the relation between *monomane* and the *yūgen* elements of singing and dancing in the overall configuration of a performance.

The most succinct account of the transformation that occurs in Zeami's construal of *monomane* is recorded in *Sarugaku dangi*. There he makes a statement that constitutes a radical departure from his earliest remarks in *Kaden* about the primacy of *monomane* in Yamato *sarugaku*.

> The art of theatrical entertainment is entirely [based on] imitation [*monomane*], but as *sarugaku* is *kagura*, the two elements of dancing and singing should be called its basic arts.[53]

The immediate context for these remarks is his discussion of the origins of the *sarugaku* art. He claims lineage to the art of *kagura*, dance and chanted performances that evolved in association with Shintō practices, stating that one of the oldest and most hallowed entries in the *sarugaku* repertoire, *Shikisanban*, descends from *kagura*. Moreover, he reinforces the primacy of singing and dancing by reference to a second authoritative source, the "Great Preface" of the Chinese classic *Shijing* (*Shih-ching*, Book of poetry).

> It was also said in ancient times: "To express one's aspiration is called poetry." This must be the source of all music. Therefore, how could one call someone who does not perform [skillfully] the two elements of dancing and singing a perfect performer?[54]

Zeami seems to be drawing on these hallowed precedents to provide a rationale for a style of *sarugaku* that places a new emphasis on the chanted word and dance while, at the same time, remaining faithful to his *monomane* roots. Importantly, this allusion to the *Shijing* valorizes music and dance by situating them in the larger context of poetic expression, although the type of verse form that he specifies in his paraphrase of the Chinese classic is the *uta* (referred to in this study as *waka*), the thirty-one mora verse form composed in vernacular Japanese.[55]

A SHIFT IN THE FUNCTION OF DANCING AND CHANTING IN PLAYING A ROLE

The "two elements of dancing and chanting" (*buga nikyoku*) mentioned in the passage above is a term that does not occur in the *Kaden* account of the nine role types of *monomane*, but comes to hold a central place in the treatises of Zeami's middle years. In the ensuing paragraph of *Sarugaku dangi*, he pursues the importance of singing and dancing by citing *Sandō*.

> In the *Sandō* it is said: "[Those who have attained] the level of supreme accomplishment have elegant beauty in dancing and singing as their basic style and they have to be equally good in the three characters.[56]

The "elegant beauty" referred to here is a translation of the term *yūgen*. Again he is making a connection between dance and chant and the elicitation of *yūgen*. However, his stipulation of how those elements are to be employed in order to evoke the quality strikes a new note. The original nine character types of *Kaden* have here been condensed to three characters (*santai*): the old man, the woman, and the warrior. Furthermore, dance and chant have come to comprise the elements of expression that the actor employs to play all three role types. The prerequisites for any skillful performance have become fluency in dancing and chanting and the ability to be "equally good in [playing] the three characters."

In the ensuing passage of *Sarugaku dangi*, Zeami continues to recapitulate statements he had made in earlier treatises. He begins by alluding to the earlier differentiation that he makes in chapter 5 of *Kaden* between the Ōmi and Yamato styles (as well as that of *dengaku*), but with clear-cut deviations from the original thought.

> In the *Kaden* it is said: "In Yamato [Sarugaku], Ōmi [Sarugaku] and Dengaku the styles are different. But the real master may not be lacking in even one of the styles. . . . Styles and patterns are different and individual, but the flower that looks attractive is not missing in Yamato [Sarugaku], Ōmi [Sarugaku] and Dengaku.[57]

The point he seems to be making here is the same point he made in the original statement in *Kaden*. The actor should be conversant with a variety of styles in order to retain his freshness and ability to adapt his style to particular audiences. However, in the original passage in *Kaden*, Zeami contrasts the Ōmi and Yamato styles, whereas in the *Sarugaku dangi* quotation above he stresses what they have in common. Although styles may differ, "the flower that looks attractive is not missing" in any of them. What all have in common is not necessarily the particular attributes of the styles themselves, but some other quality that they share. Zeami reinforces this synthetic approach in another passage in which he names the two *dengaku* actors Itchū (dates unknown) and Kiami (dates unknown), his father Kan'ami, and the Ōmi sarugaku player Inuō as the ancestors of the *sarugaku* art.

Finally, he addresses the question of the actor's training: how to proceed to acquire the ability to elicit an atmosphere of *yūgen* across the optimal variety of styles. He states,

> First one has to [begin] with the basic style, and gradually pass on [to all the styles]. I never learned [to play] the demon. After long experience in the two elements and the three characters, and a long time of practice, I am now performing the illusion of it.[58]

This passage suggests an added dimension in his discussion of how *monomane* elements should interface with chanted and danced elements in the course of an actor's training. The "basic style" refers to the aforementioned acting style premised on the "elegant" modalities of singing and dancing. Imitation of the three basic characters proceeds after the basic elements are mastered. (Hereafter, the two elements of singing and dancing will be referred to as the "two modes [of dance and chant]"; the three characters will be referred to as the "three styles [of *monomane*].")

Thorough training in *nikyoku santai* provided Zeami with the wherewithal to perform the "illusion of a demon" rather than performing the demon character itself. As we shall see, between the imitation of a demon and the imitation of its illusion lies the shift in his concept of *monomane*.[59] The development of this new configuration was a major breakthrough in his efforts to incorporate singing and dancing into plays featuring all types of characters. In the following section, we will explore the configuration in more detail.

DEVELOPMENT OF THE BASICS: *NIKYOKU SANTAI* (THE TWO MODES AND THE THREE STYLES)

In the treatises of Zeami's middle period, the nine characters disappear and the three styles of *monomane* (*santai*) take their place. The concept of the *nikyoku santai* is discussed in some detail in the following of his critical treatises, which span an eight-year period: *Shikadō, Nikyoku santai ningyō zu, Kakyō*, and *Shūgyoku tokuka*.[60] He discusses the impact of the configuration on a range of aspects, from the composing of a play (*Sandō*), to the training of the actor (*Shikadō/Shūgyoku tokuka*), to the execution of representational techniques (*Nikyoku santai ningyō zu/Kakyō/Shūgyoku tokuka*). We shall reserve the discussion of compositional techniques for the following portion of this volume, which is devoted to *Sandō*, and concentrate here on techniques of representation.

Zeami devotes one segment of his critical treatise *Kakyō* to describing the kinds of *monomane* that are called for in representing aged characters, women, and angry or rough *[ikareru koto]* characters. The caption for the segment is "First thoroughly become the figure [imitated]; then resemble [him or her] in your acting." He further explains that "becoming the figure" involves taking on the overall physical configuration (*sugata*) of the type of character: "First you should take on the configuration, and execute the dance, the vigorous movement, or the vocal music from within those contours."[61]

For instance, the elderly character should be stooped and unsteady on his or her feet and should point and pull back the arms with reserve. In the feminine style, the actor should keep his torso slightly more erect, point and pull back the arms with more elevation, move his whole body gently, keeping forcefulness out of his conception and carrying himself in a willowy way. In the angry style, the actor should bring forcefulness to the conception, take a strong bodily stance, and then execute vigorous movement.

Zeami does not use the term "three styles" in this passage, nor does he specify the identity of the angry or rough type of character. As is noted in the SNKBZ 88 annotation,[62] he typically employs the term for angry or rough—*ikareru*—to describe demonic behavior. By his treatise *Shikadō*, the term "martial style" (*guntai*) has crystallized and replaces the descriptive term *ikareru* in characterizing the third major type of *monomane*. By *Sandō*, the demonic style has been relegated to the status of a derivative of this newly coined "martial style." There is evidence that the *Kakyō* passage reflects the early stages of his thinking on the three styles. At the close of that treatise he states that he started the document when in his forties. This means that it was composed over a period of approximately twenty years. We know that the first fourteen of the eighteen segments comprising *Kakyō* existed as of 1418 because Zeami makes reference to them in another treatise, *Kashu no uchinukigaki*. All of this would indicate that this passage was composed prior to his full development of the *santai* prototypes.[63]

In the treatise titled *Nikyoku santai ningyō zu*, completed in 1421, Zeami discusses the characteristics of these three styles more abstractly, with increased attention to the actor's internalization of a role. The text is organized around illustrations of the basic figures and their characteristic postures. Each role is encapsulated in a phrase that both guides the actor's concentration on the role and sets the standard for the atmosphere that he should project. In the venerable style, the protagonist, an elderly person, should project a sense of "a serene heart and a distant gaze."[64] He likens this stage presence to an ancient tree in bloom. The woman played in the feminine style should "make her heart her form, abandoning forcefulness."[65] He calls this the foundation style for (evoking) yūgen. The warrior featured in the martial style, on the other hand, should "make forcefulness his form, [but] pulverize his heart."[66]

"Pulverizing the heart" is a translation of kokoro o kudaku, "kudaku" originally meaning "break down" or "be pulverized." The derivation for the word given in Iwanami kogo jiten is a useful reference point here: "to break down a tightly organized entity to a degree of minuteness at which it loses its original function."[67] In Zeami's parlance, the word seems to mean the breaking down of a uniform show of force characteristic of a warrior, to allow for a more detailed exposition of what is in his mind.[68] NSTS annotates the phrase along such lines: "For the purpose of expressing strength, [the actor] makes energy-packed physical movement his focus, while, inversely, he works his heart with delicacy to give interest."[69]

The style of the demon is treated as peripheral in this new configuration, referred to in Nikyoku santai ningyō zu as a derivative of the martial style. However, Zeami goes into quite some detail describing this derivative style. He posits two subcategories of demonic roles that echo his original distinction in chapter 2 of Kaden between human and nonhuman (true) demons. The former he calls the demon in "the style of pulverized movement" (saidōfū) and the latter the demon in the "style of forceful movement" (rikidōfū). Since the saidōfū type has "the form of a demon, but the heart of a human being," one should not put much force into one's actions, but should "break down the movement in a detailed way."[70] As in the martial style above, forceful movement is rendered less so by enhanced attention to detailed articulation. He continues, "Do not put force into mind or body, for lightness of the body is [the essence of] the saidō character."[71] He points out that vigorous moves (hataraki, or vigorous sequences of choreographed movement to instrumental accompaniment) have this saidō style as their basis. The actor may in certain cases play in the spirit of the saidō style for the madwoman and a range of other characters, young and old. Zeami closes the segment on an allusion to a precept in Kakyō: "When the Torso Moves with Emphasis, the Foot Steps with Calmness; When the Foot Steps with Emphasis, the Torso Moves with Calmness."

This principle is expressed in *Kakyō* as follows.

> When the torso and the foot move exactly alike, [the acting] appears crude. When [the actor] "robs" his foot [of emphasis] while using his body [with emphatic vigor], [the acting] is not crude even though [the character] appears to rage. When [the actor] moves his body calmly while stamping his foot with emphasis, [the acting] will not seem crude, because the body is [kept] calm even though the sound of the foot is loud. In effect, when what is seen and what is heard are not concordant, there is a feeling of interest [generated in the audience] by [the actor] creating a harmony between the two principles.[72]

Perhaps the lack of concordance between elements is more conducive to eliciting the interpretive powers of the audience as well. The object of imitation is not a fait accompli served up to the audience. Rather, it poses an anomaly that asks for imaginative engagement to be resolved. The original Japanese for this passage does not specify the actor as the agent who creates harmony between two principles. Therefore, it is also possible to attribute at least part of the effecting of this harmony to the workings of the spectatorial imagination.

On the forceful (*rikidō*) style, Zeami states,

> Since this is a style whose movement has forcefulness as its substance, it will not have refinement. Since the heart too is that of a demon, all of the visional affect [stage effects] will be ferocious, and interesting images will be few. However, if you have already performed a sequence of pieces and exhausted a number of [acting] styles, a one-time rendering [of the *rikidō* style] in the final phase [of a program] may have the provisional effect of surprising the eye and stirring the emotions. However, there should be no repeat performance. Understand this.[73]

He allows that the *rikidō* style can have the appeal of novelty if performed just once at the end of a day's program, but he has not swerved from his fundamental position, first set down in *Kaden*, that ferocity is incompatible with the arousal of interest.

69

Nikyoku santai ningyō zu also includes a discussion of the erstwhile specialty of Ōmi *sarugaku*, the *tennyo no mai* (dance of the celestial maiden).
This is Zeami's first critical treatise to mention the adaptation of this dance
into Yamato *sarugaku*. The caption beside the sample drawing of the
celestial maiden character states that the dance should involve "a spirit of
mounting the music" (*jōgakushin*), which is explicated in the NSTS
notation as "a spirit of mounting the rhythm and dancing" (*ongaku ni notte
mau kokoro*).[74] Zeami describes it with, "Concentrate on the musical style,
invest your whole body with spiritual strength, dance the dance, be danced
by the dance." He further states that since the celestial maiden is not
human, strictly speaking, performance of that character is outside the
parameters of the three styles, but still it is a feminine style.[75] In this way
the treatise first sets down the basic precepts for the three core styles of

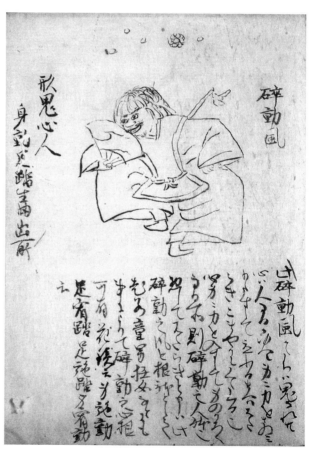

Figure 2 Demon in the
saidō style, having the
form of a demon but a
human heart. This is the
style of demonic depiction
that Zeami favored. Here
he describes it as one in
which neither body nor
mind is vested with forcefulness, with the result
that lightness of the body
(movement) becomes a
defining attribute. This
copy of Zeami's manu-
script dates to 1441 and is
attributed to Zeami's son-
in-law, Konparu Zenchiku.
(Courtesy of Hōsei
University Institute of
Nōgaku Studies, Tokyo.)

monomane, followed by discussions of the *saidō/rikidō* styles of demonic performance and the style of the celestial maiden. Whereas Zeami treats demonic role-play as derivative of the martial style, he speaks of the celestial maiden as a distinct style having points of resemblance with the feminine style.

From the actor's standpoint, the three styles of *monomane* involve the merging of inner conception and external configuration. As described above in *Kakyō*, each of the three has a prototypical configuration, a stage presence articulated by the visual elements of the actor's physical presence and movement and the aural ones of music and chant. Moreover, as noted in *Nikyoku santai ningyō zu*, the physical presence of the actor coexists with his inner concentration on the essential quality of the prototype he is playing. Imitation no longer centers on the imitation of surface likenesses.

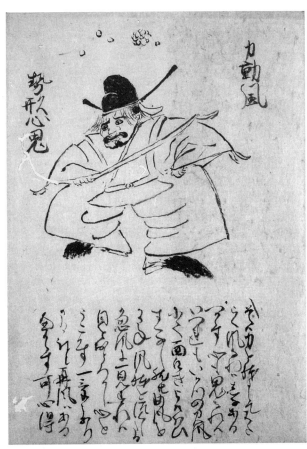

Figure 3 Demon in the *rikidō* style, having the force, form, and heart of a demon. This demon is holding a whip rather than a fan. His Chinese-style headdress, hunting robe, wide-brimmed trousers, and mask, which is similar to the close-mouthed grimace of the *kobeshimi* mask, suggest the costuming of demonic characters today, such as the *shite* in Act 2 of *Ukai* or of *Taisan pukun*. Zeami's treatises disparage this style. Copy of *Nikyoku santai ningyō zu* attributed to Konparu Zenchiku. (Courtesy of Hōsei University Institute of Nōgaku Studies, Tokyo)

Figure 4 *Shite* in the second act of *Ukai* (Cormorant fisherman), composed by Enami Saemon Gorō and revised by Zeami. The play is about the ghost of a cormorant fisherman (*shite* in the first act) who suffers in hell as a consequence of a lifetime spent in violation of the Buddhist prohibition against taking life. He was murdered in retribution for practicing his sinful calling in waters where it was strictly prohibited. He asks a traveling priest (*waki*) to pray for him and offers him lodging when no one else will do so. The *shite* in the second act is a demon from hell, sent to pardon the fisherman and help him reach salvation in recompense for his kindness to the priest. The demon's costume and mask (*kobeshimi*) resemble those of the demon in the *rikidō* style pictured in Zeami's treatise *Nikyoku santai ningyō zu* (p. 71). Actor: Sekine Tomotaka, Kanze school. (Courtesy of the photographer, Maejima Yoshihiro)

Compared to the description of the nine character types, the descriptions in these two treatises shed little light on how each prototype should dress or comport himself in a role. Physical description of character types is replaced by accounts of how the prototypes should move onstage. The *sugata* (configuration) for each seems to represent a physical posture suggestive of a physical prototype, but not imitative of the behavior of a character. That is, each prototype is depicted in terms of physical deportment rather than representational function. In the physical articulation of each style of *monomane*, choreographic concerns are more pronounced than dramatic ones. Zeami's primary objective here seems to be accounting for the integration of imitative *monomane* techniques with the coexisting elements of dance/vigorous moves and vocal music. The playing of a role is predicated on the embodiment of physical contours that are then filled in by means of such visual and aural expression.

THE ACTOR'S TRAINING IN *NIKYOKU SANTAI*

The relation of dance and chant to mimetic elements is clarified in Zeami's treatise titled *Shikadō*, which actually presents the earliest discussion of the configuration of *nikyoku santai*. As mentioned above, in that tract he concentrates on the training process to which the actor should adhere in order to gain mastery of *nikyoku santai*.

> Imitate the human configuration proper to an old man, to a woman, and to a forceful being. Master these three to the fullest, and then apply the two modes of dance and chant learned from childhood to the [articulation] of all types [of roles]. In our art, there is no other training than this. Any other types of performance are a natural function of the *nikyoku santai*, and you should wait for them to develop of themselves naturally.[76]

The child should concentrate on cultivating a basic mastery of the two modes, refraining from practice of the role-play techniques particular to the three styles. Then he should embark on training in the three styles when he has reached adolescence and after he has mastered the basics of dance and chant. From among the three styles, first he should concentrate on the venerable style and second on the feminine style. The martial style should be reserved for last. There is no explicit mention of the demon, erstwhile staple of the Yamato style, in this abridged enumeration.

Although the same configuration is under discussion in all of the treatises noted above, the process of playing a role as set forth in *Kakyō* and *Nikyoku santai ningyō zu* and the process of training to play a role articulated in *Shikadō* are reversed. In the playing of a role, the first thing required of the actor is a certain state of mind and bodily posture evocative of the style of character that he is playing. Next, he should employ dancing and chanting in the articulation of the role. However, the training process is the reverse. The novice should not even attempt to concentrate on role-specific techniques until he has acquired basic skills in the two modes.

In *Nikyoku santai ningyō zu*, Zeami elaborates on the reasons for postponing the acquisition of *monomane* techniques that he introduces a year earlier in *Shikadō*. The context for his remarks is the training of the child actor.

> The child's image is the most fundamental style of *yūgen*. Its techniques are dance and chant. When you study these two modes with extreme care, dance and chant will fuse into one conception and one style; you will become a master capable of art that is sure and long-lived. Then later, after you have made the transition from [the style] of the child to the three styles [of adulthood], when you perform the two modes, the visional affect [stage effects] of *yūgen* should be manifested naturally in the three styles.[77]

This is a process that is viable regardless of whether the subject matter is that most acclaimed to have *yūgen* attributes—the feminine style—or whether it belongs to the other two styles, whose subject matter lent itself less to *yūgen* effects. Zeami is putting forth a process of performance in which musical and bodily expression form the basis for the creation of *yūgen* in performance, whether or not the object of representation is one that audiences will be predisposed to classify as graceful.

Through the techniques of dance and chant, a residue of the childish beauty that he credits with *yūgen* may linger in the adult's stage persona. Dance and chant provide the primary modalities through which the actor may express himself; they also provide the actor with the means of imbuing a role with *yūgen* effects deriving from his own person. This new paradigm goes beyond the notion that the mimetic content of a role (graceful vs. rough) is the sole factor dictating whether an actor's performance will create an impression of *yūgen*. The gracefulness of the actor's physical presence, which he brings to bear at a premimetic level, also has an impact on his "*yūgen* quotient" when performing any role.

Zeami's most mature analysis of the two modes and the three styles and their relation to *monomane* comes in *Shūgyoku tokuka*. It will be recalled that this is a document that he composed in 1428 for his son-in-law, the *sarugaku* actor and composer Konparu Zenchiku. It is organized as a series of questions and answers. The issue of *monomane* comes up in relation to a question that he has not discussed in his earlier treatises.

> Practitioners of various arts each acquire their own personal magnitude [*gaibun*]. Are there things in particular about this personal magnitude that should be understood?[78]

Zeami's response is lengthy and moves through several phases. First he alludes to another of his critical treatises, *Kyūi*, devoted to the description of nine levels of artistry among actors. This treatise will be explored in more detail further on, but a brief synopsis of the levels is apropos here. The uppermost three levels are populated by the masters; from the top, they are the style of the wondrous flower (*myōkafū*), the style of the profound flower (*chōshinkafū*), and the style of the serene flower (*kankafū*). The middle three levels are the entry levels for the novice actor, consisting of the style of the correct flower (*shōkafū*), below that the style of expanding energy (*kōshōfū*), and below that the style of early beauty (*senmonfū*). The bottom three levels are for those actors who have either failed to master the basic skills of the art (*nikyoku santai*) or actors who are supremely skilled but occasionally descend to the bottom levels for the sake of novelty. It should be mentioned that these are abstract descriptions of an actor's stage style that do not address role-play techniques per se.

Zeami grants that each of these levels reflects on the actor's personal magnitude but that knowing one's personal magnitude involves more than pinpointing what level one has achieved in this taxonomy.

> Everyone thinks this is as far as it goes, and they do not understand how to cross over into [to comprehend] true personal magnitude. If you do not enter into true *monomane*, then you will not achieve personal magnitude.[79]

This insight suggests a universal paradox of acting: the actor can know himself by how well he can portray the other. To know the caliber of an actor, it is necessary to assess how completely he can become the role he is playing.

Zeami subsequently recapitulates the core concepts for the three styles, which are familiar from *Nikyoku santai ningyō zu*, but he also supplements the original precepts. To the core concept of the venerable style, "[a] serene heart and a distant gaze," he adds that the style calls for a stage presence that "evokes the misted over vision of an old person, who cannot see the distance clearly."[80] Furthermore, he states,

> If you execute the bodily posture and the feeling [in accordance with this core conception], and then perform the two modes, and act out the role of the character so as to be in complete accordance with this [core conception] also, it should constitute the personal magnitude [belonging to] the venerable style.[81]

He is also clear that the same type of physical and mental concentration on a core conception holds for the playing of feminine and martial styles as well. He goes into considerable detail about how this may be accomplished in the martial style. The actor should apply the core conception for this style, to "make forcefulness his form, [but] pulverize his heart," when executing the following.

> Since the martial style depicts *shura* ghosts for the most part, the [sequence of vigorous movements called] *hataraki* should involve carrying a bow; apply your body in striking patterns, retreating patterns, in blocking blows, parrying blows; bear in mind that you should stamp lightly. Well then, make your person calm when you perform, and you should be very careful that your acting does not cross into the realm of roughness.[82]

All of the above should serve to create the desirable kind of stage presence for the martial style.

The ensuing passage warns of what happens when the actor attempts to play a role without taking heed of the physical and mental foci provided by these core conceptions. For instance, when acting in the feminine style,

[y]our average woman does not think to try to resemble a woman. A woman is born as such. An aristocrat will behave as one, and a serving woman will adhere to her station. It is each [individual] acting as herself that constitutes comportment expressive of her personal magnitude. [When the actor] deliberately contrives to beautify his person and consciously aims at possessing *yūgen*, he is unlikely to succeed. (Understanding [the nature of] *yūgen* is a matter of great importance.)[83]

When an actor slips into this pitfall of trying to arbitrarily impose surface attributes without directing adequate attention to the underlying nature of the role, he becomes vulnerable to criticism. Referring to criticism of the actor on the part of audiences, Zeami remarks, "If they say, 'His [performance is] rough,' then [the actor] will [lapse into] doing nothing. Then, if they say, 'Why isn't he doing anything?' then his acting will get rough."[84] In short, the actor lacks ballast. He continues,

Thus, since the feminine image is most difficult for a male figure to emulate, I have set down this basic standard, "Make your form your heart and abandon forcefulness"; a stage image that has become one with that [standard] in body and mind—this constitutes personal magnitude in the feminine style. Just trying to imitate a woman without taking [these points] into consideration will not result in the personal magnitude [proper to] the feminine style. The [conscious] imitation of a woman does not a woman make.[85]

He elaborates on this point by reintroducing two terms that are discussed in some detail in the earlier *Shikadō: mushufū* (a style lacking mastery) and *ushufū* (a style having mastery).[86] To acquire "a style having mastery," the actor must first of all have native ability. In itself, however, this is not enough. On top of this, the actor must train carefully by emulating his teacher. First he must acquire skills in dancing and chanting, and he must do so to the extent that both body and mind achieve a level of ease in performance at which their execution seems like second nature. If he simply mimics the patterns that he learns without internalizing them completely, then the actor may appear to have mastered the techniques but will never develop into the bearer of a style that has expressive power.

In *Shikadō*, Zeami states that both talent and training are necessary for mastery. He appears to allude to this earlier treatise in his discussion of *monomane* techniques in *Shūgyoku tokuka* in order to drive home the idea that the imitation of any of the three *monomane* prototypes is not something that the actor can make up arbitrarily. There are prescribed steps that the novice must follow—parameters that he must submit to in the imitation of a character.

After discussing the three styles at some length, Zeami touches on two additional types of characters and how they should be acted. The first is the madwoman. In his earliest discussion of *monomane* techniques in the second chapter of *Kaden*, he calls the madwoman one of the most interesting character types. However, in subsequent discussions of *nikyoku santai* that predate *Shūgyoku tokuka*, she is hardly mentioned. Kitagawa notes that there are a number of parallels between *Shūgyoku tokuka* and the second chapter of *Kaden* and suggests that *Shūgyoku tokuka* reflects a desire on Zeami's part late in life to revert from the otherworldly emphasis of plays featuring ghosts to a more this-worldly orientation.[87]

This revival of emphasis on the madwoman role seems to corroborate such an idea. Moreover, it is consistent with Zeami's trajectory as a playwright. In a listing of representative plays in his middle treatise, *Sandō*, there is no madwoman category singled out. Moreover, some of his greatest works on that theme, such as *Hanagatami* (Basket of flowers) and *Hanjo* (Lady Han), are not mentioned until the later treatise, *Go on*, which scholars generally assume means that he had not yet written them at the time of *Sandō*. Zeami's interest in plays on the madwoman motif seems to have revived later in life. Yet it is important to note that the new gestalt of dance, chant, and mimetic elements that he had developed by that time made the actual performance style of the madwoman play quite a different thing than it had been in Kan'ami's generation.

In *Shūgyoku tokuka* Zeami describes the appeal of the madwoman character. He states that madness affords a dramatic basis for demonstrativeness on the part of a female character who otherwise would tend not to be demonstrative. In her right mind, a woman will characteristically avoid the public eye. In a fit of madness, however, she will more readily abandon herself to singing and dancing. In this way, she puts her beauty and sensibilities more on display than she would do normally, creating an image that is "more interesting than any other." He stipulates that this is a very challenging role that requires the utmost skill of the actor.[88]

Figure 5 *Shite* of *Hanagatami* (Basket of flowers), a madness piece by Zeami. The *shite* is mistress to an imperial prince who is proclaimed emperor and must depart immediately for the capital to take up his duties, leaving her behind. He sends her a letter with this news and, as a sign of his feelings for her, leaves her a flower basket he had used in his daily devotions. This photograph captures the moment when she has just received the letter and basket. Distraught about her loss, the *shite* then sets off with the basket for the capital to seek out the emperor; when she encounters his entourage, he recognizes her thanks to the basket. Contrary to her fear that she is just one woman among many and will be forgotten, he is true to her, and she becomes his consort. Actor: Kanze Hisao. (Photographed by Yoshikoshi Tatsuo.)

Finally, Zeami turns to his old bugaboo, the demonic character. He is stricter about the playing of the *rikidō* style of demon here than in the earlier *Nikyoku santai ningyō zu*, in which it is listed as one possible style. In *Shūgyoku tokuka* he simply dismisses it as one not performed by his school. *Shūgyoku tokuka* does not add much new information on the nature of demonic role-play. Zeami reiterates the idea from *Kaden* that there are no models to follow in real life. Then he specifies that the personal magnitude needed to play such a role effectively involves the actor's ability to "concentrate on a general image but distance himself from the principles that make for roughness; to soften his movement by detail[ed articulation]; and to fool the eye of the spectator."[89]

Annotators concur that "fooling the eye of the spectator" involves creating the impression of a demonic presence out of a vacuum (since there are no real models). However, given the nature of the *saidō* style of demon, described by Zeami as a being that preserves a demonic facade but is not truly demonic, it seems that another interpretation for "fooling the eye of the spectator" might be possible. That is, on the one hand, the actor plays to the audience's basic predilections about what a demonic being should be like, but, on the other hand, he portrays a character whose mental workings are not demonic at all. Zeami does not explain what he means, but the statement is reminiscent of his remark quoted earlier from *Sarugaku dangi* to the effect that after long years of practice, he does not play the demonic character, but he does play the illusion of one.

This section will conclude with an excerpt from the final passage of *Shūgyoku tokuka* because it underscores how far Zeami's understanding of representational techniques has evolved but, at the same time, remained constant. Although he devoted a career to intensifying the presence of such "elegant" elements as singing and dancing in the style of his troupe, drawing freely from rival arts in the process, he concludes *Shūgyoku tokuka* with a passage about *monomane* that leaves no doubt that he continues to consider it the ultimate standard for an actor to meet.

> As stated in *Mengzi* [*Meng-tzu*, The sayings of Mencius; 372?–289? B.C.E.], "To do something is not difficult; to do something *well* is difficult." Imitating generally poses no major difficulties, and projecting a visional affect [*kenpū*] having composure does not fall into the category of "difficult to do." Those who gain renown for truly

becoming one with the thing [represented] are few. This is [what may be meant by] the difficulty of doing something well.[90]

Early on in his thinking—in his description of the nine character types, for instance—the term *monomane* is used to describe the first activity mentioned in the passage above, "imitating" characters. However, in this passage, *monomane* has come to involve something beyond that, and beyond a graceful stage presence. Rather, it builds on and subsumes these elements. Zeami is admonishing the novice actor that reliance on reproducing surface behavior is spurious and will not allow him to get inside the character. Rather, to "truly become one" with the object represented, one must engage body and mind in the training program based on acquisition of the two modes and the three styles. Such a program offers guidelines for cultivating the "personal magnitude" (*gaibun*) needed to truly internalize a role, that is, to be capable of "true *monomane*" (*makoto no monomane*).[91]

In Conclusion

Zeami's formulation of the configuration of *nikyoku santai* provided him with a theoretical and practical means of incorporating dance and chant into all types of plays, those featuring elegant and rough characters alike. As long as singing and dancing were allotted a place in the dramatic fiction, constrained by the identity of the protagonist, those elements were viable only for a limited set of plays. Those plays featuring strong characters such as warriors or demons were necessarily excluded. By recasting those elements as the modalities by means of which an actor executes a role, he freed them from the confines of the dramatic fiction and reassigned them a crucial role in the dramatic diction. In so doing, he also shifted the orientation of *monomane* away from the original concept of a set of techniques for endowing a character with lifelike characteristics to a set of techniques for outlining the emotional tenor of a character.

   This chapter has argued that the pressure Zeami felt to incorporate the elements popularly associated with the elegance of *yūgen*—dance and song—into Yamato *sarugaku* proved to be the irritant in the oyster, the catalyst for his efforts to mold a new poetic of the stage. That is, it remained the irritant to the extent that he refused to forego the traditional emphasis on strong roles in Yamato *sarugaku*. His development of the configuration of *nikyoku santai* represents the culmination of his efforts to preserve dramatic scenarios while at the same time incorporating musical and danced elements. Within this new paradigm, even dancing warriors come to have credibility.

So far, our focus has been Zeami's reorientation of the relation between *monomane* techniques and the elements of dance and chant. By developing the configuration of *nikyoku santai*, he transformed musical, choreographic, and mimetic elements into coexistent staples of a representational style encompassing all categories of plays and all types of material. The increasingly abstract nature of the core *monomane* concepts that he develops goes hand in hand with an increasing reliance on the power of the performed text. By themselves, the three styles of *monomane* are cryptic. Performed language comes to play an increased role in filling out contours only suggested by the *monomane* itself. The following chapter will trace how Zeami's initial quest to intensify *yūgen* effects across plays led him to new insights into the role of the interpretive powers of the spectator in the creation of meaning, and the role of performed language in fostering such interpretation.

3

. . .

Fierce Moons, Gentle Demons

FROM ENDS TO MEANS

> Generally speaking, the essence [of *monomane*] is to resemble all aspects closely without exception. However, also be aware that [resemblance] should be strong or weak depending on the subject.

Throughout his lifetime, Zeami never abandoned the idea that his art should have a representational dimension beyond the pageantry of sung and danced entertainment. What is more, he never totally abandoned the representation of strong characters whose images were generally not associated with the idealized elegance of *yūgen*. We will see that his efforts to reconcile the gentle and strong strains of *monomane* were ongoing. Concerning strong and weak resemblance, he never strayed from the precept quoted above, but his ideas about where the locus of *yūgen* effects lay and the process involved in imbuing a character with that quality were to change markedly.

As we saw in the last chapter, Zeami developed a new configuration of performance, *nikyoku santai*, in which chant and choreographed movement became the avenues through which all types of roles were to be imitated. This new paradigm was perhaps most effective in treating cases for which weak resemblance was in order. It was most useful when the preconceived image of a character that the actor anticipated in his audience was most incongruous with the *yūgen* quality that he sought to elicit. *Nikyoku santai* puts in place a process for fostering "elegant" stage effects, even when working with the seemingly least elegant of materials.

The configuration was the product of Zeami's investigations into how visual, aural, and mimetic expression could best be integrated in ways that would prime an audience to attribute the quality of *yūgen* to a performance. The development of this configuration reflects a shift in Zeami's thinking on how to elicit *yūgen* effects. He came to locate such effects less in the referential content that performers and audiences were predisposed to ascribe to the object of representation and more in the modalities through which the representation took shape, and the impact that they had in performance. This chapter will trace this shift in Zeami's conception of *yūgen* and how it might be implemented. While it will concentrate primarily on his critical treatises on *sarugaku*, there will be one detour into the critical treatises on *renga* by Nijō Yoshimoto. I hope to demonstrate that principles of poetic composition espoused by Yoshimoto helped Zeami to see the expressive potential of performed language in his own art. It also helped him to recognize ways in which such principles might be extrapolated to suit the three-dimensional space of the stage. These realizations were instrumental to Zeami's shift.

Entering the Realm of *Yūgen*

Zeami's most comprehensive statement about how *yūgen* can be fostered comes in a segment of *Kakyō* titled "Entering into the Realm of *Yūgen*" (*Yūgen no sakai ni iru koto*). He talks about how the quality can be evoked at a number of levels: physical demeanor, language, music, dance, the three styles of *monomane*, and the angry stage presence, such as that of a demon. The passage begins with the most concrete embodiment of the *yūgen* ideal: the aristocratic personage. It concludes with the least likely exemplar, the demonic figure. In between, it addresses the modes of expression available to the *sarugaku* actor onstage: chanted language, dance, *monomane*. This sequence of aspects also reproduces the building blocks of the actor's technique, ranging from the atmosphere of his person, to linguistic and vocal elements, to choreographed elements, and finally to mimetic ones.

Zeami opens his discussion by appealing to the universality of the aesthetic ideal of *yūgen* across the arts. The opening rubric reflects such breadth, for "the realm of *yūgen*" is an expression recognizable from *waka* and *renga* criticism. (This point will be pursued below.) Moreover, he singles out *yūgen* as the most esteemed of styles in the art of *sarugaku*, a noteworthy shift away from his distinction in chapter 5 of *Kaden* between the *yūgen* style of Ōmi *sarugaku* and the *monomane*-based style of Yamato *sarugaku*. In this *Kakyō* passage, Zeami seems to be speaking for all *sarugaku* artists rather than for his particular troupe, and it is clear that he no longer thinks of *monomane* as the element more central to the Yamato style.

Entering the Realm of Yūgen

Concerning the style having *yūgen*, in various arts, the uppermost sphere of accomplishment depends on having *yūgen*. Especially in this art, a style having *yūgen* is considered of utmost importance. First, there is a style of *yūgen* that is commonly seen, and spectators appreciate this alone [as *yūgen*], but an actor who [truly] possesses *yūgen* is not easy to come by. This is because the flavor of *yūgen* is not truly understood. Thus, there are no actors who enter that realm.[1]

Zeami does not explain what he means by "a style of *yūgen* that is commonly seen," but evidently he is drawing a contrast between that which both actors and spectators commonly appreciate as *yūgen* and what he considers to be the true *yūgen*.[2] Zeami seems to be acknowledging that *yūgen* is widely construed as beauty accessible to the eye, but he also seems to be suggesting that "true" *yūgen* is more than meets the eye. Perhaps he is critical here of actors who attempt to derive *yūgen* effects by realistically emulating the appearance of elegant characters without recourse to the two modes and the feminine style that he advocated. As noted in chapter 2, this is a tendency that he condemns in *Shūgyoku tokuka*. In any case, it is evident that he conceived of the evocation of the quality as something more complex than most performers or audiences realized.[3]

Next Zeami moves into his actual description of how *yūgen* is best embodied in the human form.

Now then, where might it be that the realm of *yūgen* can truly be found? First, looking out in the world and the types of people in it, the court aristocrat has bearing of a high refinement and facial features that are incomparable.[4] This might be said to constitute a level having *yūgen*. If so, then the basic substance of *yūgen* is simply a form that is beautiful and gentle. *Yūgen* of person consists of a human form that is serene.[5]

He then turns to the various levels of performance.

Furthermore, your language should be graceful; study and inquire with great care into how the highborn and the high ranking are accustomed to choose their words, and when even the most casual of your utterances is graceful, this will be language [conducive to] *yūgen*.

Also, as concerns music, when the linking of the musical phrases *[fushikakari]* flows beautifully[6] and sounds supple,[7] this will be music [conducive to] *yūgen*.

As for dance, train very, very well, and make the artistic effect of your person *[ninnai no kakari]* beautiful, with a feeling of composure about you;[8] provided that there are points of interest to the eye,[9] this will be dance [conducive to] *yūgen*.

Also, as concerns *monomane*, if the artistic effect of the images *[sugata-kakari]* [fostered by] the three styles is beautiful, this will [be conducive to] *yūgen*.

Also, for an angry presence, such as that of a demon, even when your bearing[10] tends slightly toward the *rikidō* style, if you do not forget beautiful artistic effect *[kakari]*, and if you [follow the teachings], "Work the Mind Ten-Tenths . . ." and "When the Torso Moves with Emphasis, the Foot Steps with Calmness . . . ,"[11] and if your person is beautiful, this will be [conducive to] *yūgen* in [the style of] a demon.[12]

Perhaps the first point to stress is that Zeami's discussion above of the multiple elements through which the *yūgen* quality may be elicited replicates the phenomenological layers involved in playing a role. In the context of the actor's training, the first four—physical bearing, manner of speaking, musical phrasing, and dance—are to some extent pre-mimetic elements that are crucial to our perception of the actor's stage presence, regardless of what role he is playing. Only after the actor has trained in these four modalities should he build on them by training in actual representational techniques. The two final examples, concerning the three styles and the derivative angry style, are the sole ones to deal directly with role-play per se.

The second point worthy of mention is that his discussion of each element concentrates more on the "how" of the rendering than it does on "what" is rendered. His discussion of aristocratic bearing does not touch on what activities the aristocratic model should carry out, but on the kind of atmosphere s/he should bring to any activity. Similarly, in his discussion of language, what gets said is not as much in focus as the tenor of the utterance: the polish that it should possess. He does not prioritize types of music or dance either. Rather, he stresses supple flow of the music and serene bearing in general. His advice on the three styles of *monomane* is not addressed to the playing of specific roles. Each style can elicit *yūgen* effects as long as it is rendered *in a way* that has artistic effect, or *kakari*. The same is true for playing the demon role. Even when the "content" of a demonic role is somewhat ferocious, if the actor's form has beauty, the impression of ferocity will be tempered by a sense of that beauty.

Zeami's characterization of "how" each element should be performed is consistent across role types: beautiful, having composure, gentle, flowing, serene. These are attributes that he urges the actor to bring to the playing of any role. The actor's person, the most basic level of expression manifested to the audience, should embody these qualities. He enlists the flower metaphor to bring home his point.

> Although various character types differ, when [any of them] has the look of a beautiful flower, it will be always the same flower. That flower is one's physical stage presence. To show one's image (*sugata*) to best effect [depends on the workings of] one's mind (*kokoro*).[13]

The actor's person is the foundation—the ground out of which all techniques are initiated. Moreover, his physical presence affects how we perceive his performance of techniques. For this reason, the actor's training must involve the polishing of his person. Then the passage ends on less tangible ground, the workings of the actor's mind.

Whereas "the flower" of *yūgen* is the beauty of the human form (no matter what the role), Zeami calls the actor's mind "the seed" of *yūgen*. For him, mind is a dynamic entity. He characterizes it as a set of sensibilities that the actor must cultivate, involving:

1. Firmly grasping these principles [articulated above].
2. Studying poetry in order to promote elegance *[yūgen]* of language.
3. Studying elegant styles of dress in order to acquire beauty *[yūgen]* of form.
4. Ability to sustain the "one artistic effect" *[hitokakari]* of appearing beautiful across all the various *monomane* character types.[14]

Performing a role in the *yūgen* style thus involves a multiple layering of elements, and these layers build on each other. Mind is the ultimate ground against which all other elements figure. Out of that ground, the actor's physical presence materializes. His diction arises out of the physical context of his presence. Vocalization materializes as part of diction. As we shall discuss below, choreographed movement is grounded in the voice. As noted earlier in the discussion of *nikyoku santai*, role-play is mediated by all of the aforementioned layers. The actor's performance of a role may be best diagrammed as a pyramid, one layer building on the next.

Renga Antecedents: Nijō Yoshimoto on *Yūgen* and *Kakari*

A final pattern that emerges in Zeami's discussion of *yūgen* is the connection between the evocation of that quality and the phenomenon of *kakari*. As we have seen, the connection between *yūgen* and *kakari* is not a new one in Zeami's critical thinking. However, in this narrative above, his use of the term clearly diverges from that suggested in the *Kaden* passage delineating the Ōmi *sarugaku* style of performance. In the latter discussion, the elements conducive to *kakari* seem to be singing and, perhaps, dancing, and these elements are treated as compatible with gentle roles but not with strong ones. Here, however, he expressly mentions the importance of *kakari* in performance of all three styles of *monomane* and demonic types of characters. He goes so far as to say that there is one type of *kakari* (*hitokakari*) that is elicited in playing all of the different *monomane* roles. Clearly the term cannot be reduced to the presence of one or two elements in a performance. Rather, it seems to refer to the effects that emerge on the basis of the larger flow of a performance, no matter what the identity of the protagonist.

Zeami's developing conception of the *kakari* principle seems strongly influenced by Yoshimoto's ideas on *kakari* as they apply to the composition of linked verse (*renga*). Given that Yoshimoto was an influential arbiter of taste in the shogun's circle, it is not surprising to find evidence that Zeami incorporated some of Yoshimoto's ideas on *kakari* and *yūgen* as his dramatic theory developed. Not only was it a sound tactical move, but, as it will be argued below, Yoshimoto's theories about linguistic composition inspired Zeami to rethink the possible role of the utterance in nurturing the desired artistic effects onstage. Thus a brief overview of Yoshimoto's ideas as expressed in his critical writings will be useful for understanding the increasing importance of *kakari* in Zeami's conception of *yūgen* and the impact that this had on his acting theory in general. Yoshimoto speaks of the evocation of the *yūgen* quality as the ultimate accomplishment in *renga* composition. The following passage from Yoshimoto's critical treatise *Kyū-shū mondō* (Kyushu dialogues; 1376) sets down some of his basic premises.

> First, the most important thing in *renga* is the mind (*kokoro*). Strive day and night for seasonal images that have truth, for they should be [of the kind] to strike the listener [as reflecting] things just as they are. When [the poet] simply relies on how the words [in the previous verse] sound, then the poetic spirit will receive less attention, and thus the verses composed on that occasion will not make a deep impression. The spirit should be strong and the words gentle. In compositions these days, usually the spirit is weak and the language strong.[15]

In his commentary to this passage, Nose reviews two major conceptions of the critical term *kokoro* in the poetic tradition: as the idea or conception of the poem itself, or as the artistic sensibility that informs the composition of the poem. He notes that Yoshimoto is using *kokoro* here in its latter sense. The poet's mind, which includes his readiness and sensibility, is the most important factor in composing. Closely related to this notion of *kokoro* is that of the poetic sensibility or poetic spirit (*iji*), to which Yoshimoto attributes the effectiveness of a *renga* composition. He holds that *iji* is a communal sensibility that will be shared by poets who have achieved mastery of the art.[16] In this passage, it seems that he introduces the *iji* concept to remind the novice that words do not have intrinsic merit in isolation from their use. Rather, the ability to judge how to use them effectively is far more important, and such judgments depend on the *iji* of the poet—which will determine his ability to factor in multiple variables based on context.[17]

Kakari (aural affect) is one such variable that Yoshimoto considers of

paramount importance. The *kakari* of a verse in recitation may alter one's
impression of it, which in turn will have an impact on whether it strikes the
listener as having the quality of *yūgen*. The following passage continues that
from *Kyūshū mondō* cited above, in which Yoshimoto warns that over-
reliance on particular words or phrases for their own sake will impoverish
the poetic spirit. Next he states that it may diminish the expressive potential of *kakari*, the sonic flow, as well.

> What is more, *kakari* [aural affect] may receive less attention. Take
> the utterance of a gracious person with skill in the art and that of an
> unpolished, unversed person. Even if they utter the same words,
> they will seem separate things. In the end, *renga* is something that
> presupposes entry into the realm of *yūgen*. The honorable Shunzei
> said as much about the practice of *waka* [composition].[18]

How an utterance is rendered will be a determining factor in our perception
of its message, which, in turn, will influence its perceived *yūgen* quotient.

To optimize such *kakari* effects, no matter what the subject matter the
poet chooses, he should employ graceful language. Moreover, one acquires
such grace of language through practice.

> When one's practice from the beginning is based on rough verses,
> one's [choice of] words will be poor. If one learns based on [language
> having] *yūgen*, even a person lacking natural aptitude can acquire a
> [certain] style. While at the beginning stages, one should concen-
> trate on composing smoothly flowing verses that are graceful and
> mild, with little ornamentation; avoid complexity and preserve
> lightness of tone.[19]

Although Yoshimoto warns that *renga* poets must be wary about adopting
waka techniques without adapting them to the contexts of the *renga* genre,
he urges novice *renga* poets to use the first three imperial *waka* anthologies,
as well as such classical works as *Genji monogatari* and *Ise monogatari*, to
guide them in cultivating a style that has graceful diction.

In the critical treatise *Jūmon saihishō* (Notes on the utmost secrets in ten
questions; 1383), Yoshimoto warns against vulgar language: "Vulgar language
[*zoku naru kotoba*] is first of all what sounds low-class, rough, and coarse; it
sounds sordid. Language possessing *yūgen* sounds fresh and smooth."[20] It is

not so much what the subject matter consists of as the polish of its diction that determines whether language will sound vulgar or not. Yoshimoto refers to the combined effect of the *kokoro* (poetic mind) and the language as the *sugata* (configuration) of a poem, a term with precedents in *waka* criticism. On the subject of the *sugata*, he states,

> The *sugata* consists of the language. However, it is difficult to specify what is good and what is bad. What is good and what is bad emerges solely on the basis of how the verse is composed.[21]

In Yoshimoto's conception, training in the acquisition of a smooth and polished style of diction also has an impact on the cultivation of poetic sensibility *(iji)*. In this respect, Yoshimoto's ideas about training resemble those of Zeami. In the early stages of training, the performer should concentrate on internalizing techniques by the emulation of models. Such internalization in turn has a formative influence on the poetic sensibility. In other words, acquisition of technique also assumes cultivation of poetic sensibility. Whereas the novice cultivates such sensibility in the process of mastering technique, the master poet (or actor) applies techniques on the basis of his artistic sensibility, which is the combined effect of his ability and his training.

Moreover, Yoshimoto is adamant that the key to *yūgen* effects is not what subject matter the poet chooses, but the poet's ability to create verses that strike the listeners as flowing gracefully, no matter what the subject matter. The poet cannot expect to create *yūgen* effects simply by virtue of stock images evocative of elegance. It is the *how* of the mimesis rather than its propositional content per se that is key to arousing interest. In *Jūmon saihishō*, Yoshimoto compares a good composition to the skill of brewing tea. He draws on the metaphor of fragrance, stating that good tea may possess a fine fragrance, but it must be prepared just right for the fragrance to emerge fully. So it is with *renga* composition. The material for the composition may have promise, but if it is not handled properly, then it will not take on a beauty of configuration.[22]

That the quality of a verse is not determined simply by the caliber of its imagery or allusions in isolation from their treatment in specific contexts is also underscored in Yoshimoto's advice on how the poet should handle patently inelegant subject matter. Material generally acknowledged to lack grace and beauty should not be treated in language that also lacks those attributes. As in *sarugaku*, the stock example of such material in *renga* is the demon, a being whose image is distantly removed from the elegant beauty associated with the *yūgen* ideal. He explains that the demon is a kind of unorthodox subject matter that is not normally employed in *renga* composition. However, he continues by stating,

> It depends on the occasion. Unorthodox material can be a surprise attraction. An unskilled poet will have great difficulty composing [such a verse]. Just because it is a fierce entity does not mean that the verse should be rough. A person with graceful speech will make it sound like the ultimate in *yūgen*. A person with gruff speech will soon make it seem demon-like. Pay very careful attention to this. There can be fierce moons and blossoms. There can also be gentle demons. It does not depend on the thing [itself]. It depends on the skill *[kotsu]* of the composer.[23]

Just as in Zeami's earlier discussion about a *yūgen* style of demon in *sarugaku*, for Yoshimoto, how material is treated is a more important factor in reception than how that material may be classified in the abstract. It should also be noted that both Zeami and Yoshimoto allow for the occasional usage of demonic material for the sake of novelty, but insist that demonic material is unorthodox.[24]

Kakari is Yoshimoto's term for the aural overtones that contribute to the creation of "fierce moons and flowers" or "gentle demons." It is the *kakari* factor that is at the root of the phenomenon alluded to by Yoshimoto in the quotation above—the fact that the same words may seem very different depending on how they are spoken. In his treatise titled *Renga jūyō* (Ten aspects of renga; 1379), he stresses the vital role of kakari elements.

> In *renga*, *kakari* [aural effects] and *sugata* [configuration] should be considered most important. No matter how novel the material, if its configuration and aural effects are poor, then it will arouse no interest. It will be like a beautiful woman dressed in a burlap smock. A graceful *yūgen* presence should be put first.[25]

The term *kakari* is closely linked with sonorousness throughout Yoshimoto's treatises. His usage includes the artistic effects created in linking, as well as the beauty of vocal resonance and of the overtones and mood that such

resonance promotes.[26] For instance, Yoshimoto states, "When the preceding verse is strong, then your link should have strong diction; when the
preceding verse is delicate, then your link should have delicate diction. In
sum, *kakari* in *renga* is a matter of the words."[27]

Yoshimoto is not just referring to the phrasing of a poem, but to how it
sounds when it is recited. A *renga* poem is premised on progression from one
verse to the next. The objective of the poet is not to establish thematic or
tonal consistency of the whole poem when composing individual verses.
Rather, the life of a *renga* exists in crossing the selvedges between adjacent
verses.[28] The opening verse (*hokku*) is in three lines of 5, 7, and 5 syllables.
From there the poem progresses in alternating verses of 7-7 and 5-7-5, and
the focus of interest is how each verse relates to the adjacent verses; verses
are composed alternately by one of a group of contributing poets. The principles of linking are complex and beyond the scope of this study, but in addition to the progression of associative images called for in the composing of
a *renga*, the poets must be aware of how their links sound. Recitation forms
the medium through which verses are communicated and appreciated.
Kakari is a principle that addresses this sonorousness created by the progressions in the poem. It is a principle of performance closely linked to how
language unfolds in time.

Zeami's Evolving Ideas on *Kakari*

Internal evidence provided by Zeami's critical writings points to influence
from Yoshimoto on the question of how the *yūgen* quality might be best
invoked in performance. I believe that Zeami stole a page from Yoshimoto's
book when he came to advocate the fundamental role of the *kakari* dynamic
in that process. That influence is most readily discernible in Zeami's discussions of the creation of aural effects in the rendering of the lines of a play.
In his treatise *Ongyoku kuden*, he identifies two levels of expertise that are
necessary for vocal music to have interest.[29] The first level involves the
expertise of the composer of the lines, which includes understanding the
nature of the music and making the transitions between the words beautiful.
The second level involves the expertise of the singer, who should affix the
modulation and make the distinctions between words clear in his singing.[30]
Zeami then outlines what the process of composing the modulation should
involve, and *kakari* is introduced as one element to be considered.

> *Kakari* [emerges] on the basis of the words and phrasing; make the
> [vocalization of] each mora[31] correct, and make the linking of the
> words in the transitions between the verses smooth and pleasing to
> the ear, in a way that flows gracefully.[32]

Miyake Akiko gives the following interpretation of Zeami's usage of *kakari*:
"Upon apprehending that mood is created when the resonance of accent
and meter flow beautifully, [Zeami] defines *kakari* as that flow itself, or the
mood produced by that flow."[33] Miyake also attributes this awareness on
Zeami's part to the influence of Yoshimoto's *renga* theory. She also makes
the point that for Zeami it was also important that the semantic content of
the lines not be sacrificed to enhance their musicality. Nose's commentary
stresses harmony between those two elements. What the singer had to do
was to "harmonize the mood of the chant with the words comprising the
lines, 'translating' the [linguistic] beauty of the words into the musical
beauty [of the chant]."[34]

After defining these two levels of mastery, Zeami states that interesting
effects depend on combining the two. He then provides more details about
how *kakari* should relate to the other elements in performance.

> The modulation *[fushi]* corresponds to the overall patterns, *kakari* to
> the transitions between words and phrases, expressiveness *[kyoku]* to
> the mind *[kokoro]*.[35]

Whereas the patterns of modulation provide the structural options available to the chanter, expressiveness is an intangible that emerges. Elsewhere, Zeami defines *kyoku* as the "flower" arising out of the modulation.[36]

Kakari addresses the more concrete and processual aspect of chanting—
how the thing is rendered. The NSTS annotation for this passage tells us
that "the *kakari* arises from transitions between the words, and the expressiveness arises from the workings of the mind."[37] Nose's annotation speaks
of expressiveness as "a design pattern" arising from the *kakari*, something
beyond the structure, corresponding to the spirit of the vocal music.[38]
Kakari would seem to be that element that is felt to bridge the gap between
the formal aspects of the chanted line and the overall mood that materializes in performance.

Elsewhere in his treatises, Zeami makes observations about the nature
of *kakari* in its aural aspect that also suggest he saw the element as an

emergent one. Like Yoshimoto, he describes *kakari* as a kind of property that arises via the performance of a text, not as a property inhering to any particular referential aspect of a text. In fact, the resonances produced by the linking or the musicality of the words could at times take on a life of their own that could alter or temper our impression of the referential meaning of the language of the text or its mimetic content. For example, in *Sarugaku dangi*, Zeami mentions the importance of *kakari* in altering the effect of the lines. In a section devoted to the differences between vocal music of the *kusemai* and the *kouta* style that had characterized the earlier chant of Yamato, he states,

> Only the artistic effect *[kakari]* is [important in music]. The music of Yamato [Sarugaku] in ancient times did not have so much artistic effect, and so distortions of the words were often heard. If the artistic effect *[kakari]* is good, the distortions are hidden.[39]

Distortions here refer to dialectal differences at variance with the aristocratic style of speech that Zeami advocated for the sake of elegantly pleasing overtones.

In an ensuing section of *Sarugaku dangi*, he offers an example of the efficacy of *kakari*. The discussion opens with a pun on the term *fushi* (modulation), which can also mean the joint of a bamboo. "Just as with a bamboo joint, that which is called *fushi* has its bad points."[40] Assumedly, Zeami is referring to the fact that a bamboo joint can be knotty and difficult to handle, as is true for modulation as well. He continues,

> The artistic effect *[kakari]* is the basis [of music]. To stop abruptly and then draw out, or to shorten before prolonging [the note], is all [for the sake of] the artistic effect. Well then, if one reconsiders what artistic effect actually is, it is something like [saying] bear-tiger-leopard.[41]

The annotation for "bear-tiger-leopard" in this translation by De Poorter quotes Zeami's own citation and explanation of this Chinese allusion as it is recorded in *Kakyō*. It goes,

> "Bear, tiger and leopard are skins used as targets for the bow: tiger is for the Emperor, leopard for the dukes, bear for the great officers."

> Therefore, one should say tiger-leopard-bear but for euphony's sake one says it in the other order.[42]

Zeami uses this allusion to make his point that sonic appeal should sometimes take precedence over linguistic precision in the chanting of the lines of a play. As indicated in his statement above quoted from *Ongyoku kuden*, *fushi* corresponds to the structural parameters of the chant, whereas *kakari* refers to the effects created through the linking of the *fushi*.

This instantiation of the *kakari* dynamic at the level of aural effects is one thread that runs throughout Zeami's critical corpus. Both the idea that how the lines are linked should have an impact on the overall mood of the message and that such mood is instrumental to the evocation of *yūgen* have precedents in Yoshimoto's *renga* criticism, as we have seen. Returning to the passage on *yūgen* in *Kakyō*, one is reminded that one of Zeami's references to the dynamic of *kakari* in his description of *yūgen* effects there refers to this application of the principle to aural contexts. It is in his statement about music: "when the linking of the musical phrases flows beautifully and sounds supple, this will be music [conducive to] *yūgen*." The original for the phrase "linking of the musical phrases" is *fushigakari*, a compound that combines "*fushi*" and "*kakari*" (the initial "k" voiced in assimilation to the surrounding vowels [final "i" in *fushi*, first "a" in *kakari*]). While use of the word *kakari* connotes the linkages made between phrases, as noted in the NSTS annotation for the term, it is also possible to construe it as "the mood arising from the modulation of the musical phrases."[43] I think both meanings hold here.

The remaining usages in the passage on *yūgen* are not as neatly explained in terms of aurality, however. It will be recalled that Zeami uses the term in the *Kakyō* passage on *yūgen* to describe the artistic effects that dancing can promote ("make the artistic effect [*kakari*] of your person beautiful"). Moreover, the images of the actor's appearance in his playing of the three styles of *monomane* should have *kakari* that is beautiful. Clearly, this, too, is premised on more than just aural appeal, as is Zeami's advice on playing demonic roles ("do not forget beautiful artistic effect"). What, then, does Zeami mean when he uses the term *kakari* in reference to visual effects?

In our initial discussion of *kakari* as Zeami used it to describe Ōmi *sarugaku*, we established that the term referred to the ambiance created by the interconnective flow of the elements in a performance. Whereas the NSTS annotators interpreted those elements to be singing and dancing in the case of the Ōmi style, Tanaka gave the term a more comprehensive interpretation.

> Zeami refers to the overall image [of the performer] that emerges on the basis of the sequence of movement having to do [equally] with all [of the elements] including chant, dance, vigorous moves, etc.[44]

This annotation is arguably too broad to describe Ōmi *sarugaku* prior to Zeami's generation, but it is very useful for understanding his usage of the term in *Kakyō*, as well as usages in his later treatises. The connections that Zeami makes between *kakari* and *monomane* role types in the *Kakyō* passage on *yūgen* have just been introduced here as applications of the linking principles of *kakari* to eliciting effects in the visual dimension. However, it would be more accurate to refer to them as visual manifestations of a composite of elements of a range suggested by Tanaka in the quotation above. As Zeami's theory of performance develops, he refers increasingly to *kakari* as a mood invoked in the mind of the spectator on the basis of a combination of aural and visual modalities.

Of particular concern to him is the kind of resonances that can be induced on the basis of the interplay between sound (both chanted and instrumental music) and the actor's physical stage presence. As early as *Kaden* he notes the effects that the combined impact of diction and resonance in the chant can have on the visual image projected by the actor. For example, in chapter 6 of that treatise he discusses different types of plays.[45] Along with the ideal play, which is replete with linguistic nuances coming from allusive techniques, there is a simpler type of play, which does not depend as much on detailed linguistic exposition or elaboration but should embody "straightforward dancing and chanting, with stage gestures that are executed with smooth fluency." To perform such a play in a style having detailed elaboration is not appropriate. Striving for precedented language and visual overtones is something that applies to noh plays that call for interesting verbal exchanges [*giri*][46] and climactic points (in the action). When it comes to straightforward works, "even when an elegant [*yūgen*] figure chants stiff-sounding words, if the aural effects [*kakari*] of the chant are solidly upheld, then [the result] should be acceptable."[47] The effects created by the flow of the musical phrases thus compensate for specific elocutions that lack the supple grace that an elegant character is supposed to have.

"Straightforward" (*sugu naru*) is a term Zeami uses with regularity to describe plays that derive their effects principally from music and dance rather than from detailed mimetic elements.[48] Here he is saying that in such plays the aural effects created by how the language is chanted can take precedence over the tenor of the individual words. This point was already made above with reference to the impact that the sonic elements of the chanted medium can have on the audience's perception of the message of the chant. But in this passage, Zeami extends the sphere of that impact to include the audience's visual perception of the actor's stage presence. He goes on to say, "In fact, this should be understood as the basic nature of noh."[49]

The following precept, also from the sixth chapter of *Kaden*, is further evidence of Zeami's sensitivity to the potential for the spectatorial imagination to synthesize aural and visual modalities.

> In the slightest resonances of the words, ones such as *"nabiki," "fusu," "kaeru,"* and *"yoru"* are gentle, so it is as if they promote visual overtones (*yosei*) of themselves. Ones such as *"otsuru," "kuzururu," "yabururu,"* and *"marubu"* resonate strength, so the stage gestures should also be strong.[50]

The context for this observation is a discussion of the relative attributes of strong and *yūgen*-style characters. Zeami is cautioning the playwright to avoid strong-sounding language when depicting a graceful subject. Ostensibly this passage preserves his early distinction between the classifications of strong and gentle. On the one hand, it seems to support the notion that gentleness or strength is a preexistent property inhering in the object of representation. However, this passage also contains a tacit admission that the promotion of strong or gentle effects is dependent on the performance context. The playwright's choice of diction, the actor's style of utterance, and, of course, how the chant is received by the spectator are crucial factors in determining that context. Here, too, Zeami demonstrates an awareness that the tenor of the chanted language can have an effect on the overall impression created by the *monomane* action that accompanies it.

He expresses a similar sentiment earlier on in the sixth chapter of *Kaden*. He is discussing how to compose a play.

> Simply take words from Japanese and Chinese poetry [*shiika*] that sound graceful and are easily understandable. When graceful language

is matched to the movements, strangely, the human form[51] will, of itself, take on the air[52] of *yūgen*. Stiff-sounding language does not go well with stage action. However, stiff, obscure words too can have a place. They can be suitable, depending on [the identity] of the main character. Consider whether [the material] is Chinese or Japanese in origin. Just remember that low, vulgar language and stage style will result in noh of poor quality.[53]

Zeami is describing a style of dramaturgy that assumes the centrality of allusive techniques. He cautions the playwright to choose precedents that are easy and familiar so that they will be readily understandable when delivered orally in a performance. He allows for a certain degree of verisimilitude in that language should be allotted with the character of the protagonist in mind. If the protagonist is Chinese, for instance, then the stiffer, less lyrical air of Chinese compounds may be acceptable. However, he stops short of advocating mimetic accuracy when it comes to coarse material. Coarse language should be avoided in all cases because it will spoil the aesthetic atmosphere onstage. It should be noted that Zeami's objection to the coarse or vulgar (*zoku naru*) is reminiscent of Yoshimoto's condemnation of the same in his critical writings on *renga*. For both, the qualities of *zoku* and *yūgen* were diametrically opposed. In the realm of *sarugaku*, just as coarse language can spoil the impression that a character makes onstage, elegant language, such as apt choices of precedented usages from poetry, can enhance the *yūgen* quotient that audiences ascribe to the physical presence of the actor.

The diction of a play is therefore one modality that influences the mood of a performance and our impression of the characters and the action. The mode of vocalization of the lines will have an effect not only on our impression of their content, but also on our impression of the actor who is performing them. Reception of visual elements also will be predicated on their perceived relation to the total configuration of a performance. How we perceive a dance, for instance, will be determined by the appearance of the dancer and by the linguistic and/or musical elements that sustain the dancer's stage presence, as well as by the spectator's ability to integrate these elements into a meaningful whole. As early as chapter 3 of *Kaden*, Zeami advises that the actor's physical movement (moving his torso, his arms, and his legs), should be executed on the basis of the *fushi* (modulation) and the *kakari* (aural effects).[54] In *Kakyō*, he writes quite extensively on the importance of vocal and/or instrumental music as the ground out of which dance should figure.

> If dance does not arise from the music, then it will not [inspire] feeling. That point at which the fragrance of the actor's *issei* chant[55] carries over into the dance should have wondrous power. Also, when the dance concludes, there is a level at which [the feeling aroused by the dance] is resolved in the [ensuing] music.[56]

He is speaking of the selvedges at the beginning and conclusion of a dance section of a play. At the beginning, the mood of the preceding chant should be felt in the dance. At the conclusion, the ensuing music should heighten the impact of the dance. One element should carry over into and provide a context for the other. Ultimately, what comes across to an audience is the combined effect.

The role of *kakari* in Zeami's concept of this interrelation of music and movement grows more precise over time as Zeami comes to place increasing importance on the principle. In *Sarugaku dangi*, for instance, he says the following about *kakari* (artistic effect).

> [In a performance] everything is [based on] artistic effect. Even acting that seems to be without artistic effect will be interesting through some [special] artistic effect. If the artistic effect is good, the bad points are not noticed so much. If it is beautiful, even poor gestures are not ugly. [But] if it is bad, elaborate gestures look all the worse.[57]

The NSTS annotation interprets the meaning of this passage to be that individual choreographed patterns may lack artistic flavor (*omomuki*) but can take on individual interest by virtue of their contextualization in the larger flow of the performance. Although Zeami does not refer to music per se, his words do reveal that *kakari* is to be sought in how movement is executed in conjunction with other elements.

After this general statement about *kakari* in *Sarugaku dangi*, Zeami appends a series of anecdotes about how certain choreographed moves or parts of plays should be executed. The first anecdote involves instructions on how a performer should move his eyes.

To glance slightly sideways in a dance can be very interesting.' [But] one should not do it too much to the left. One should glance slightly sideways to the right. At each verse of five seven, five seven syllables [of the song], one should make a movement with the eyes.[58]

The ensuing anecdote regards the execution of the final lines of the play known today as *Matsukaze*. The ghosts of two fisher girls appear to a traveling priest at Suma Bay (in the area of present-day Kōbe). They share their obsession with the memory of Heian aristocrat Ariwara no Yukihira (818–893), whom they had fallen in love with when he had been exiled there.

Matsukaze is one of the oldest examples of a work composed on the madness (*monogurui*) motif. It will be recalled that Zeami ranked madwomen as the most interesting of the nine original *monomane* character types. Madness afflicts one of the two sisters, the ghost of Matsuzake (the *shite*), whose longing for Yukihira becomes so intense that she mistakes a pine tree for him. The lines quoted below involve the segment in which the two ghosts take their leave of the priest at the end of the play.

> In the play *Matsukaze, Murasame*, if one approaches [the supporting actor] at the passage "Please pray for the repose of our souls!" the acting will become slow-motioned. [Therefore] it is more interesting to hold on [without moving] up to "pray for the repose of our souls," to approach [him] at the words "We take our leave," and to go back when saying "and go back." When one goes back at "pines is" in "Only the wind in the pines is left," it is not interesting at all. One has to go back at "left." Such passages in particular will not be interesting if the meaning [of the words] and the acting[59] do not correspond.[60]

In contrast to the discussion of *monomane* types in *Kaden*, chapter 2, in which the objective of playing a role was to bring out lifelike resemblance, here technique seems to be predicated on matching the actor's movement with the chanted lines. At this late point in Zeami's drama theory, the chanted line has become an integral part of portraying roles. Moreover, what Zeami seems to consider as *kakari* here is the mood experienced on the basis of the perceived interplay of the *shite*'s acting and the lines of the play.

This account of how one should act the role of Matsukaze's ghost underscores the fact that in Zeami's developing conception, mimetic elements, too, had come to be finely tuned to the chanting of the lines. The *shite's* sense of timing—for instance, at what point in the text he should approach the supporting actor or withdraw—has everything to do with how that action is perceived by the audience. The *Matsukaze* anecdote, which is introduced as an example of *kakari* effects, is just one example of how Zeami saw the *kakari* principle operating in the combined effect of the sonic and semantic appeal of the lines and the actor's *monomane*-based techniques.

Let us return to the notion introduced briefly in the last chapter that performing a role involves layering elements in a configuration reminiscent of the shape of a pyramid. Such mimetic action as described in *Matsukaze* would correspond to the tip of the pyramid—the uppermost layer—sustained and mediated by the multiple interplay of the underlying layers. At the same time, Zeami's characterization in *Kakyō* of *yūgen* effects in the three styles ("if the artistic effect of the images [*sugata kakari*] [fostered by] the three styles is beautiful, this will be conducive to *yūgen*") seems to encompass more than just the tip of the pyramid. That is, the specific mimetic techniques must be seen in relation to the larger composite of underlying elements.

The word "image," my translation of *sugata*, may also be rendered as "configuration" or "contour." As noted above, Yoshimoto uses the term to refer to the overall image fostered by the combined effects of poetic sensibility and diction. Zeami, too, seems to employ the word to refer to the overall image arising from a composite of elements. However, in Zeami's trade, poetic sensibility and diction were part of a larger gestalt of the stage. In addition to the actor's underlying sensibility, and the impact of language, he had to contend with the physical realities of a theatrical art. In his parlance, *sugata* also seems to embrace the visual dimension. His usage of *sugata* in the *Kakyō* passage seems to refer to a visual presence that is more all embracing than particular techniques. At the same time, it is more than the surface beauty of the actor alone. The images for the three styles must each inspire a beauty of *sugata-kakari*, that is, a beauty of overall image and artistic effect. As we have seen, this is a multilayered proposition. And *sugata-kakari* is necessarily the product of co-creation between performers and the ultimate perceivers, the members of the audience, who must bring their own sensibilities into play to integrate these multiple media in their own minds and derive meaning from them.

Kakari Embodied: Skin, Muscle, and Bone

In *Shikadō*, Zeami employs the metaphor of skin, muscle, and bone to articulate the interrelation between some of these layers of performance. He
relates skin, muscle, and bone each to an aspect of the actor's artistry. Bone
corresponds to the actor's expression of his native ability, which makes
itself felt naturally in performance. Muscle is defined as the appeal created
by the accomplished performance of dance and chant. Skin refers to the
beauty and ease of the actor's image onstage upon having developed the
"muscle" and "bone" layers. He further states that the skin level corresponds to visual affects, the muscle level to aural effects, and the bone
level to effects that speak to the mind (*kokoro*) of the spectator.[61]

The sign of the performer accomplished at the bone level is that no
matter how carefully members of the audience mull over his performance
in retrospect, no weak points come to mind. At the muscle level, no matter how the spectator tries, the actor never seems to have run out of fresh
resources onstage. At the skin level, no matter what, the actor seems to
have the *yūgen* quality. Zeami laments that actors who are even aware of
such levels do not exist. He credits his own insights to his father Kan'ami's
teachings. As for what he has seen of recent performers, "they just exercise
[the level] of the skin a bit. And that is not true 'skin.' Furthermore, they
only emulate [fine performers] at the level of the skin."[62]

It is noteworthy that Zeami identifies the physical manifestation of
yūgen in the person of the actor as the uppermost layer in this larger paradigm of performance. However, it is clear from what he says that this layer
cannot be fully realized unless the bone and muscle layers are already in
place. He seems to be saying that *yugen* to be *yūgen* must coexist with
underlying properties. His statement that "[s]kin refers to an image that has
been carried to the utmost of ease and beauty once the [bone and the flesh]
have been developed"[63] is evidence of this. One cannot simply imitate the
appearance of a master actor and expect to thus emulate his artistic effects.

This metaphor of skin, flesh, and bone is an attempt to articulate the
interrelations between the psychic and physical aspects of the actor's art.
In his interpretation of Zeami's metaphor, Tanaka observes that the relations between the three layers are both incremental and synchronic. The
"true skin" can be actualized only via the other layers. However, those layers
each retain their own integrity. The relation between them is not simply
analogous to "ascending a ladder from the bone toward the skin." "Each has

its own individual meaning, mutually working in close conjunction [with the others]."[64] According to Tanaka, Zeami construed the skin category to be of a different order than the bone or the muscle. Whereas bone and muscle involve artistic form, the skin level is a kind of artistic "resonance of the spirit, or an overtone," which becomes manifest in moments when the actor has perfected a beauty of form at the other two levels. He continues, "[T]he skin [corresponds to] the image (sugata) of yūgen, or it may be thought of as an unparalleled explanation of [the phenomenon] called kakari."[65]

As discussed above in the segment on the paradigm of nikyoku santai, Zeami describes monomane techniques as having three aspects. The actor begins with a basic bodily stance and a concomitant state of concentration centering on a core concept for each of the three styles. Then the actor applies himself to specific danced, chanted, and, finally, mimetic techniques. If we relate these phases to the bone-muscle-skin paradigm, then, at the bone level we have the actor's capacity to take on the psychophysical configuration of the role. At the muscle level we have his execution of technique, chant, dance, and, most probably, mimetic action as well.[66] At the skin level we have the beautified image of the actor's resulting stage presence expressed as an emergent atmosphere perceptible to audiences. That stage presence has no life distinct from a flow of underlying properties but is not tantamount to them. Indeed, it seems that in his writing of Shikadō, Zeami had developed a theoretical framework for articulating how the actor might strive to foster the kakari dynamic in his person.

The Demon Revamped

Let us return to the Kakyō narrative on yūgen that opened this chapter. After introducing the three styles of monomane, Zeami next moves to the demonic style. It, too, should be a composite of polished surface sustained by movement and sound and, underlying these elements, a psychophysical stance on the part of the actor. Again he makes reference to the importance of a beautified stage presence having artistic effect (kakari). Unlike the rather tacit instructions for the three styles, he makes explicit reference to two techniques on which the actor should rely in endowing a demon with yūgen. The second of the two, "When the Torso Moves with Emphasis, the Foot Steps with Calmness; when the Foot Steps with Emphasis, the Torso Moves with Calmness," has already been introduced. It will be recalled that

Zeami states, "[W]hen what is seen and what is heard are not concordant, there is a feeling of interest [generated in the audience]."[67] The lack of concordance comes from the fact that when the actor's torso is moving in a way that emulates demonic deportment, he refrains from stamping his feet. When he stamps in demonic fashion, he keeps his torso serene.

The first technique that Zeami mentions here is explained elsewhere in *Kakyō* under the rubric "Work the Mind Ten-Tenths, Work the Body Seven-Tenths." When an actor is learning the techniques of his art, he will first emulate his teacher, executing his movement as completely as possible. However, with experience he will learn to temper his movement in accordance with what he feels. Zeami goes on,

> When [the actor] uses greater reserve in the working of his body than [he does in the working of] his mind, . . . his body will [then] become [for the spectator] the causal agent [for interpretation] and the spirit [of the character portrayed] will become the effect, [with the result that] there will be a feeling of interest [generated in the audience].[68]

Zeami first introduces the principle of causal agent and effect in *Shikadō*, in which he compares the causal agent to a flower, the effect to its fragrance; the causal agent is like the moon, the effect like its light. By exercising restraint, the actor creates space beyond what is palpable. Nearman, the translator of this passage, offers the following interpretation.

> In terms of acting, "to create the moon" would be a metaphor for the creating of a stage effect that would project and maintain sufficient intensity that the viewer would be able to "see" the glow of it as he would see "the moonlight." Even when an actor performing in this manner appears to be "doing nothing" on stage, that is, not moving or speaking, the tension created between the inner state of the actor and the outer restraint will still project a "spirit."[69]

Nearman continues with the observation that "this projected 'spirit' will appear to the spectator as the feelings and emotions of the character portrayed." One might add that another result of leaving some degree of a message implicit is to enhance the role of the audience member in the process of interpreting the meaning of what is happening onstage. The "projected spirit" of the actor may serve as an enticement to the interpretive faculties of the spectators, and the play itself may offer signposts for such interpretation. However, ultimately such an open-ended mode of communication relies on the active imaginative engagement of each spectator.

In the seventh chapter of *Kaden* also, Zeami offers instructions on how to play a demonic role. The heading for the section is "Concerning All Noh [Acting], One Important Thing to Keep in Mind." It goes,

> For example, when you perform in an angry style, you should not forget [to keep] your mind gentle. No matter how angry [your style], this will be your means of avoiding roughness. Keeping your mind gentle when [performing] an angry [style] is the way to assure novelty. Moreover, when performing the role [*monomane*] of an elegant [*yūgen*] character, you should not forget the principle of strength. This is how to avoid dwelling in any [one] aspect, whether dance, vigorous movement, *monomane*, or any other.[70]

This passage brings an important theme in Zeami's writings into relief, the connection between novelty and "the flower"—that which it takes to captivate an audience. When a performer limits himself routinely to certain styles or techniques, then his art becomes predictable. In Zeami's dramatic theory, the evocation of the flower depends on novelty. The experience of novelty depends, at least in part, on what, for the audience, is unpredictable. He considers the ability not to dwell in any one aspect as crucial to evoking a sense of novelty in the minds of the audience. In order to assure the capacity for eliciting such a sense, he advocates that the actor cultivate a state of mind that counterbalances his physical expression. This will introduce a kind of suggestive complexity that will arouse the imaginative involvement of the audience more than will the single-minded demonstration of one emotion.

What does this passage reflect about Zeami's views on dramatic imitation, or *monomane?* Preparing for a role obviously involves training of the mind as well as training in techniques of imitation. This passage serves as further evidence that his concept of *monomane* has moved away from advocacy of lifelike semblances for their own sake. Instead, he has commenced to formulate a training program that from the performer's perspective assumes a character to be a creative fabrication based on combined mind and technique. Moreover, the success of *monomane* would seem to depend less on faithful imitation of a character in any realistic sense than on the actor's ability to construct that character in accordance with more general strategies for engaging audience interest. The principle of novelty at the presentational level takes precedence over any commitment to mimetic realism at the representational level.

Strong and Weak Reoriented

As Zeami's thinking developed on the question of how *monomane* techniques could best be employed to evoke the *yūgen* mood, increasingly he came to write of *yūgen* as a process rather than a static attribute. We see a shift in his attribution of *yūgen* effects that may be likened to a shift between figure and ground. Figure refers to the qualities attributed to the identity of the object of imitation; ground refers to the actor's sensibility, which modulates the various elements of a performance to achieve *yūgen* effects. When Zeami makes this shift, then the old distinctions between strong and weak roles become more permeable. "Strong" or "weak" cease to be qualities that form an inalienable part of a character's identity. Rather, they are treated as distinctions rooted in how the actor performs. In the sixth chapter of *Kaden*, Zeami states,

> Thus, the strong and the *yūgen*-like are not separate things; that *monomane* which is faithful is strong, and the rough is that which departs from [faithful] *monomane*.[71]

His focus has shifted from the content of the representation to the presentational style of the actor.

It is significant that as Zeami's ideas on demons develop, he comes to stress the importance of music as one mode of this presentational style. In *Sandō*, for instance, he states,

> It is on the basis of the musical texture that the visional affect [visual stage effects] of the vigorous moves will take a flowering form. You should ponder the style of musical expression carefully before you write.[72]

In a letter that he wrote at the end of his life to his son-in-law, Konparu Zenchiku, Zeami also asserts a connection between demonic role-play and the aural dimension. He warns Zenchiku away from playing nonhuman demons, as they are an aberrant style, but concedes that it is acceptable to play the human type if one limits energetic expression to the aural dimension of vocalization.[73]

Going with the Flow

The demon is perhaps the best litmus test for measuring the profound shift in Zeami's ideas about the nature of dramatic illusion. Whereas the early chapters of *Kaden* assume that the locus of dramatic effects is the credible depiction of qualities inherent in the object of imitation, Zeami's later writings ascribe those effects to the interworkings of aural, visual, and mimetic modalities. Whereas *Kaden* posits strong, demonic roles and gentle, *yūgen* ones as mutually exclusive categories, in the later writings the actor undergoes the same process of training for both types. By first acquiring fluency in the basic modes of expression, dance, and chant, he brings that fluency to bear in the acquisition of skills in the three styles and their derivatives, such as demonic roles. Thus the effects of music, chant, and choreographed movement form the ground for the business of playing any role.

By altering the modes of depiction through the intensification of musical and choreographic elements and the concurrent simplification of *monomane* techniques, Zeami effectively preserves the semblance of a demonic presence, but not the substance—that is, a frightening, violent being. In fact, he does away with the concept of substance altogether, if substance is construed as an autonomous essence that exists onstage independent of our perception of it. He came to ascribe *yūgen* effects more to the actor's ability to manipulate multiple media in order to foster an impression of *yūgen* rather than to the received attributes of certain characters or materials isolated from their performative contexts. He came to realize that medium and message were inextricably related.

Zeami's adaptation of the *kakari* dynamic into *sarugaku* reflects this growing awareness that *yūgen* properties were not embedded in the subject matter but were emergent in the flow of a performance. This flow was to be induced by the interplay of multiple media. This interplay was subject to the modulating consciousness of the performer and, ultimately, synthesized into a meaningful whole by the spectator. The actualization of *kakari* effects was dependent on the synthesizing function of the spectatorial imagination. The term "resonance" has meaning only when there is an audience to resonate. If the actor's concentration is felt in the three-tenths of his performance that are intangible, then it is the audience that must feel it and interpret it. In Zeami's later theory of acting, the actor's mind forms the ground out of which an interplay of linguistic, vocal, kinetic, and visual elements find expression, but the "meaning" of this interplay of elements is something that the spectator must create.

Central to the argument presented in this chapter is that Zeami's developing theory of the stage owes much to the critical theory on *renga* of Yoshimoto. Although it is not known whether the young Zeami was actually introduced to any of Yoshimoto's critical writings, we do know that he was introduced to the man and composed *renga* together with him. Furthermore, a comparison of ideas set forth in their respective critical treatises is itself persuasive evidence of influence. Yoshimoto's view of *yūgen* as a kind of supple and polished elegance whose evocation depended more on the atmosphere invoked in the overall flow of the poem in recitation than on any a priori "elegance quotient" enjoyed by particular subject matter provided Zeami with important clues to how *yūgen* effects might be similarly invoked in his own art. Yoshimoto argued that *kakari*, the mood invoked by the smooth flow of integrated parts, was instrumental to invoking *yūgen* consistently across all kinds of subject matter. So powerful was this dynamic that even demons might appear gentle. I have argued here that Zeami took that principle and extrapolated on it. He discovered that in the context of a stage art, the smooth flow of danced and chanted elements could similarly alter the mood projected by a demon or by any other material outside of the received categories of elegance.

One point that becomes evident upon examination of the development of Zeami's ideas about the effects that can be created through the interplay of various modalities is that the language of a text becomes an increasingly important element in conveying information to an audience. Both aural and visual modalities are premised on the linguistic medium. The interrelation of linguistic and sonic facets of the chant, the chanted lines as a premise for the actor's dance and *monomane* techniques—the text is at the root of these principles. Even dances not matched to the chanted line but solely to the instruments (such as those believed to descend from the *tennyo no mai* dance of Ōmi *sarugaku*) are situated at a point in the play at which they have been amply contextualized by the preceding chanted sections.

Yashima Masaharu makes a similar point about the increased centrality of language that accompanied Zeami's condensation of the nine types of *monomane* into the three styles and his advocacy of a training program in which the two modes preceded inculcation in the three styles. He, too, points out that Yoshimoto's ideas about *kakari* appear to have aided Zeami in hitting upon the basis for expressing a kind of stage dynamic that "transcended *monomane*."

> At the same time that this shift brought increased depth to the acting itself, it also provided a leading clue to how poetic structure could be realized that Zeami was to follow in writing the works of his middle years. By incorporating the element known as *kakari*, Zeami was able, in the noh of his middle years, to commit the resonance [*yojō*] of language to the flesh, thereby accomplishing a form based on poetry.[74]

This increased importance that Zeami places on the expressive potential of poetic verse may well have been inspired by his exposure to Yoshimoto. At the same time, the growing centrality of chanted narrative was Kan'ami's legacy. As discussed in chapter 2, the incorporation of the *kusemai* into the original Yamato vocal style seems to have been one major factor behind the creation of a vocal style capable of sustaining an extended narrative. The enhanced rhythmicality of the new Yamato style of vocal music seems to have been conducive to the matching of movement to the chanted line and to the musical and choreographed enactment of a story line in general. As text thus came to occupy a more central place in a performance as a result of these various contributing factors, a subtle shift in the actor's orientation to his role occurred. To be sure, he continued to function as a character, but role-play did not involve imitating behavioral attributes so much as it did textual ones. For the actor, performance also came to involve serving as the focal point for the narrative line and its poetic tropes. All acting is mediated by language, and much of that language is figurative.

In his study titled *Nō, kyōgen no gei* (The art in noh and *kyōgen*), Dōmoto addresses the demands made on noh audiences to integrate text and stage action and derive their interpretations thereby. His remarks are directed to contemporary noh performance, but they reflect Zeami's legacy. He notes that to the extant that it is the function of the actor to physically embody a character in the play, the actor is constrained to speak by means of his body. From there, the spectator must do his or her part in realizing the overall import of the performance. The spectator must be receptive to the "physical language" (*nikutai gengo*) emoted in the bodily interpretation by this important facet of performance, the actor. But it is up to the spectator to amplify the actor's interpretation by transferring it to the lines of the text.[75]

The performance configuration of *nikyoku santai* was seminal in the creation of the kind of open, multimedia stage event to which Dōmoto alludes. Its implementation was to assure that noh would remain a dramatic art that depended for its effects on the active engagement of audiences in the interpretation of the events unfolding onstage. The ensuing part of this volume will explore what compositional principles Zeami put in place for assuring that both plays and performances subscribe to this kind of interactive format.

PART II

· · ·

Zeami's Literary Turn

4

. . .

Composing the Text

Although there are few extant records to suggest that *sarugaku* performers practiced the art of composing their own plays prior to Kan'ami's generation, Zeami's critical treatises assume that the actor must also be a playwright. In the third chapter of *Kaden*, which unfolds as a series of questions and answers between mentor and learner, the learner asks what the best tactics are for outshining rival troupes that are performing on the same program. The response goes,

> This is important. First, you should have a good number of plays [in your repertoire],[1] and you should change your style of noh to contrast with your competitors. This is what I meant when, in the Preface, I said, "Become somewhat versed in the way of *waka*."[2] In this art, when the actor is separate from the composer, then no matter how skilled [the actor], he cannot act [freely] in accordance with his own intuitions *[kokoro no mama narazu]*. When a composition is his own, the words and action will [already] be a part of him. So, if one who has the ability to perform noh [also] has skill in Japanese [verse], the composing of *sarugaku* plays should be simple. This is the lifeblood of our art.[3]

This precept situates composing in the larger context of the exigencies of performance, underscoring a pragmatic stance that runs through Zeami's critical treatises. His fundamental concern here and elsewhere is providing his successors with the skills needed to be successful performers, and composing is framed as one such skill. We have seen that he placed the utmost importance on the ability of the actor to be versatile. Both in his early discussion of the nine subjects of *monomane* and in his subsequent treatment of the three styles and their derivatives, he stresses the point that it is necessary to master all acting styles in order to preserve the capacity to inspire audiences with a sense of novelty. In turn, he thought of novelty as the key to success onstage. His advice above on composing is therefore analogous to his precept on versatility in acting. Novelty depends on effectively varying the mood established by a competitor's performance. When an actor has a diversified repertoire of his own authorship, he has the wherewithal to adjust his performance fluently and spontaneously to suit every circumstance.

Along with thus exhorting the novice playwright to be flexible, in the passage above Zeami is urging cultivation of literary skill. Taken from his earliest writings, this statement reveals that already he has linked such skill in the production of *sarugaku* texts with the art of composing poetry. However, it is not until Zeami's middle years that he actually articulates in concrete detail how poetry and other styles of language should be employed in composing plays. In *Kakyō*, for example, he reminds his disciples of the centrality of language, stating, "All the styles of *monomane* are visually and aurally dependent on the nature of the utterances."[4] In the sixth chapter of *Kaden*, another text believed to have been written in his middle period, Zeami makes a statement about how the chanted lines should fit into the larger configuration of a performance that reflects the growing importance he places on the existence of the chanted word.

> As a general rule, it is on the basis of the meaning that all stage action should come into being. That which manifests the meaning is words. For that reason, vocal music constitutes the causal agent, and acting, its effect. Therefore, the natural order is for bodily movement to arise out of the vocal music. It is backward to perform the vocal music on the basis of the bodily expression.[5]

This progression from auditory to visual modes of expression will be familiar from the preceding chapter as one of the basic principles underlying the evocation of artistic effect, or *kakari*, in Zeami's mature theory of acting. The aural dimension provides the context for the performance of elements having visual appeal. In this passage, he further observes that it is by training in accordance with this progression from auditory to visual that the actor can cultivate the ability to perform the chant and the dance as one seamless entity. This capacity to convey the two as one is the mark of the most skilled of performers. He also urges the playwright to abide by this progression as well, making sure to keep the potential for visual effects onstage the first thing in his mind as he composes.[6]

Zeami's *Sandō*: Composing Staged Poetry

SANDŌ AND THE *NIKYOKU SANTAI*

Zeami's most explicit and concrete discussion of how a text should be composed comes in his treatise *Sandō*. Of his twenty-one treatises, *Sandō* is the only one to concentrate exclusively on the subject of composing plays. Indeed, it is the first extant primer produced by a *sarugaku* professional to discuss that craft. Composed in 1423, one year prior to his completion of *Kakyō* and three years after *Shikadō*, it shows the same preoccupation with developing strategies for the intensification of the *yūgen* quality in Yamato *sarugaku*. The performance configuration of *nikyoku santai* allowed for a primacy of music, poetry, and dance that was in accord with this goal. In part 1, we traced Zeami's implementation of *nikyoku santai* into the Yamato acting style. This involved enveloping *monomane* techniques in musical and choreographic elements that could temper the overall mood of the representation of a character. In *Sandō*, he sets down the ground rules for implementing the same *nikyoku santai* in the composition of a play.

This treatise can be characterized as a primer for composing a prototypical play in two acts and five sequences, each of the five described in terms of their musical structure and diction, as well as their dramatic components. Each sequence, in turn, has component parts that are defined in terms of their musical and prosodic properties. After setting down the ground rules for an infrastructure composed of danced and chanted elements, *Sandō* delineates how these elements can be put to work in performing the three basic styles of representation: the venerable style, martial style, and feminine style. The prototypical play that Zeami introduces in most detail as his exemplar in *Sandō* is *Takasago* (originally *Aioi*, The wedded pines), which features deities played in the venerable style.[7] This is followed by precepts on composing plays in the martial style, for which he advocates the ghosts of warriors as protagonists. In a subsequent enumeration of desirable characters in the feminine style, he singles out as ideal the ghosts of aristocratic women such as the Rokujō lady, Yūgao, and Ukifune from the Heian classic *Genji monogatari*. Finally, he introduces roles that he classifies as derivative of these three protostyles, such as those of mad people, priestlike entertainers known as *hōka*, and the erstwhile Yamato specialty, demons. The *nikyoku santai* is implemented through a compositional process having three stages. It begins with the playwright's choice of subject matter, followed by his structuring of the action, and finally his composing of the lines.

SANDŌ AND MUGEN NOH

Zeami played a seminal role in the development of a dramatic prototype referred to today as *mugen* (dream) noh. Modern scholars have imposed two classifications on the noh repertoire: "present-time" plays (*genzai nō*) and "dream" plays. These classifications are based on the identity of the principal character (*shite*) of the play. The "present-time" play derives its name from the fact that the *shite* is cast as a living person.[8] *Mugen* plays, on the other hand, feature supernatural protagonists such as ghosts, Shintō deities, the spirits of plants, or demons. As we know, the appellation *mugen* stems from one possible interpretation of the frame for the action in plays of this category: the *shite* is appearing to the side actor (known today as the *waki*) as in a dream. However, this is not necessarily spelled out explicitly in the lines of a play and is frequently left to the spectator's interpretation.

Zeami's preference for *mugen* plays is well demonstrated in *Sandō*. The three styles are introduced with reference to exemplary characters that are all deities or ghosts. Moreover, of the twenty-nine representative plays listed by Zeami (Segment 3.5), only seven have protagonists who are living persons. Yet given that the term *mugen nō* was not in Zeami's critical vocabulary, it would be erroneous to argue that he had the honing of a *mugen nō* prototype in mind when he set about implementing the configuration of *nikyoku santai* into Yamato *sarugaku*. What modern scholars have classified as *mugen nō* may be more aptly described as the outgrowth of Zeami's original program, to create a highly poetic, multisensory stage event that did not depend for its coherence on the representation of the story. Rather, by means of poetry, music, and dance, the play alludes to a story that will be familiar to audiences. Terasaki has argued eloquently that there is a tendency in the stylistics of noh for literary devices to be used to invite a rhetorical reading. As she puts it, "The text's discursive tendency shows that the narrative constantly constructs double meanings by using intertextual devices, thus moving away from descriptions and representation." Part 2 of this volume will explore how Zeami's development of *nikyoku santai* assures a place for such figurative play of language as Terasaki describes all the while that a dramatic framework is preserved.[9]

Zeami's discussion of the language of a text concentrates on how to adapt a range of themes and techniques from *waka* and *renga*. At the same time, the text he describes encompasses a mix of linguistic registers. It includes more colloquial, dialogic passages and narrative tracts such as those that typify the *kuse* section of a play, as well as passages in verse. The text is an allusive web of imagery whose effectiveness depends in large part on the spectator's prior familiarity with the subject matter of the play. In discussing the first of the three techniques advocated in *Sandō*—the choice of material—Zeami cautions that the audience should already be familiar with the *shite* and his/her story. This precept suggests that he considered the techniques of composing a text to be premised on the horizons of expectation that the playwright could anticipate on the part of his audiences. It also reflects the importance he placed on activating the imaginative participation of the spectator as a prerequisite for capturing interest.

The Centrality of Linguistic Elements in Zeami's Prototypical Play

The centrality of language in the *Sandō* configuration becomes clear when one examines how the acting and the lines complement each other. The actors' presence on stage is not devoted wholly to the mimetic representation of a story in the model plays listed in *Sandō*. It often complements or represents the imagery suggested by the lines of the play. Or, typically, the emotional life of a character is depicted metaphorically by means of lines that serve the dual purpose of also providing exposition of the story. For instance, in Zeami's play titled *Takasago (Aioi)*, which serves as his exemplar in *Sandō* (and will be explored in detail further on), the following passage occurs immediately after the entrance of the *shite* and the *shite*'s companion (*tsure*), playing the roles of an elderly couple.

Year after passing year,	*Sugikoshi yoyo wa*
unknown the snowy number	*shirayuki no*
Piling, piling up,	*Tsumori tsumorite*
As hoary cranes	*oi no tsuru no*
Remain in their roost	*Negura ni nokoru*
beneath the dawn moon,	*ariyake no*
oft awakening	*Haru no shimoyo no*
in the frosty spring night,	*okii ni mo*
the wind in the pines	*Matsukaze o nomi*
the sole accustomed sound.	*kikinarete*
Our hearts companions,	*Kokoro o tomo to*
on a mat of sedge	*sugamushiro no*
we share our thoughts,	*omoi o noboru*
that is all.	*bakari nari.*

The setting of the opening act is the grounds of a shrine near the Takasago shore. The lines of this recitative, while on one level serving as description of the setting, also forge a metaphoric link between the couple that appears there and the aged cranes nesting in their roost at dawn on a frosty spring morning. In her study of the poet Shinkei (1406–1475), Ramirez-Christensen observes that in *renga*, distance between a person and his or her environment is often bridged by the method of analogy.

> Indeed, if one were to distill all the manifold ways of linking one verse to the next, it will be seen that they are all based on the rhetoric of the metaphor. The method recalls the operation of poetry in the Heian lyrical narrative, where metonymical details in the setting turn to metaphors in the poems composed by the characters.[10]

Zeami's poetic turn reflects his grasp of such stylistic techniques from the classics. He often invokes metaphoric associations, but as a playwright he goes one step further, transposing the literary metaphor into its visual embodiment on the *sarugaku* stage. In this scene, the spectator is asked to draw the analogy while contemplating the physical presence of the elderly couple. Inasmuch as they are introduced as participants in the scene, they can be said to enjoy a metonymic relation to the setting. Yet there is little mimetic stage business or dialogue that reveals their relation to it. According to the modern staging, one carries a broom and the other a rake, as if prepared to sweep the grounds of the shrine. They remain in a standing position, facing each other as they chant these lines. Indeed, mimetic elements suffice to suggest no more than human silhouettes whose colorations must come from elsewhere.

When the lovely image of the aged cranes is introduced, it, too, may be taken as a descriptive detail in the scene. However, when the crane image is seen in relation to the physical presence of the elderly pair onstage, then the juxtaposition makes a metaphoric dimension possible as well. A traditional symbol of longevity, the cranes also elicit a mood of pristine loneliness and gentle attunement in this context, qualities that are attributable to the elderly couple as well. This is just one instance in which the poetic dimension potentially reveals more about the characters than does the mimetic one. The very sparseness of mimetically motivated clues to the true nature of the two is cause for the canny spectator to look for other bases of interpretation, such as this kind of metaphoric trope.[11]

The compositional corollary for the configuration of *nikyoku santai* as set forth in *Sandō* assures a representational style that leaves open the possibility for such poetic connotation. This, in turn, had strong ramifications on the spectator's role in interpreting a noh performance. The diverse elements—poetry, vocal and instrumental music, choreographed movement—make for a very porous style of representation. They build on a text that is nuanced and particular in the expression of a character's emotional tenor, and at the same time on an acting style that is abstract and generic in its physical representation of that character. Mediating these codependent levels of the textual and the mimetic are the sonic and choreographic elements. While *Sandō* offers concrete guidelines on how these multiple media of a noh performance can be best arranged to guide the imaginative participation of the spectator, it stops short of legislating the conclusions that the spectator should reach. Aided only by prior familiarity with the story, Zeami's ideal spectator is left to synthesize these many elements in accordance with his own lights and sensibilities.

Sandō: The Three Techniques of Composing

Sandō is composed of thirteen segments that can be grouped in three major sections. The content of the treatise may be laid out as follows.

Section 1: The three techniques *(sandō)*
Segment 1: introduction
Segment 2: [technique of the] material *(shu)*
Segment 3: [technique of] structuring *(saku)*
Segment 4: [technique of] writing *(sho)*

Section 2: The three styles *(santai)*
Segment 1: venerable style *(rōtai)*
Segment 2: feminine style *(nyotai)*
Segment 3: martial style *(guntai)*

Section 3: miscellaneous
Segment 1: role of the *hōka* entertainer
Segment 2: role of the demon in the style of *saidō* movement
Segment 3: the ear-opening and the eye-opening
Segment 4: noh plays written for the juvenile actor
Segment 5: revision of plays
Segment 6: the centrality of *yūgen*

In the first section, Zeami introduces his three techniques of noh composition in the abstract. In the second section, he then applies those techniques to specific categories of plays, elaborating on how the basic compositional scheme may be adjusted to best portray each of the three prototypical identities for the *shite:* the old person, the woman, and the warrior. Section three addresses variations on the three prototypes as well as a miscellany of concerns that arise primarily from the gap between the ideal models that Zeami introduces in the earlier sections and the actual state of *sarugaku* in his time.

In the following analysis of the three techniques put forth in *Sandō*, how Zeami systematically goes about intensifying the presence of the two modes of dance and chant as mediating layers between text and stage action will be explored. The first of the three techniques, that of the material, cautions that the *shite* of a noh play should be the type of character to have musical and poetic ability. The second technique, structuring, advocates a dramatic model that derives its coherence from prosodic and rhythmic progressions rather than plot development. The third technique, writing, shows how language may be used to complement the musical structure without sacrificing its own richness of nuance. We will now look at each of these techniques in more detail.

THE TECHNIQUE OF THE MATERIAL

"Material" is my translation for the word *tane* or, in its Chinese *on* reading, *shu*. A more literal translation of the term is "seed" or "kernel," referring to the source material out of which the playwright can compose his play. In the section on the material, Zeami concentrates on the type of personage that is most effective as the *shite* of a noh play. Choosing characters whose identities and stories were readily associated with singing and dancing was one major means of ensuring the potential for the evocation of *yūgen* onstage. Although, as he states at the conclusion of *Sandō*, Zeami expected the actor to evoke the quality of *yūgen* whatever role he played, his chance of success was significantly enhanced when the character was generously endowed with the palpable grace of person and image associated with *yūgen*. Therefore, the playwright's choice of an appropriate *shite* aids the actor by laying the groundwork for the modalities associated with that quality.

Zeami introduces four types of personages that are suitable as noh *shite*: figures that perform *kagura*, men associated with the arts, women associated with the arts, and *hōka* entertainers. All four types enjoy some established link with performance contexts. *Kagura* is a generic term for song and dance performed in the context of Shintō-related rituals. Adaptation of the *kagura* performer into noh thus readily met Zeami's stipulation that the *shite* be familiarly associated with dance and chant. In the second category Zeami cites the historical figures Ariwara no Narihira (825–880), Ōtomo no Kuronishi (fl. 885–897), and the fictional character Hikaru Genji. All three of these figures enjoy the cachet of the courtier and the requisite skills in poetry, music, and dance. In contrast, the women performers span the social classes. Ise (877?–940?; also known as Ise no Go) and Ono no Komachi (fl. ca. 833–857) were Heian aristocrats widely known for their skill in the composition of *waka*, but Giō, Gijo (or Ginyo), and Shizuka, historical or quasi-historical figures depicted in medieval martial tales such as *Heike monogatari* (The tale of the Heike) and *Gikeiki* (Chronicle of Yoshitsune), were *shirabyōshi* dancers and commoners. It will be recalled that the *shirabyōshi* and the *kusemai* were two popular genres of entertainment that drew on singing and dancing.

The *hōka* was a type of popular medieval entertainer who was male. They, too, were recognized for their skills in singing, dancing, and playing instruments. According to Morita, from among the miscellany that made up the *hōka*'s repertoire, their specialty was showing off the dexterity of their hands by juggling objects such as a kind of bamboo rattle called a *kokiriko*, with magic tricks and acrobatics added.[12] The origins of the *hōka* tradition are unclear, but juggling was one of the features of *sangaku*,[13] the miscellany of different arts that migrated to Japan from China by the Nara period (710-784) and is believed to be one precursor to *sarugaku*. In the Muromachi period many *hōka* dressed as lay Buddhist monks, ostensibly to make Buddhist teachings more accessible to the populace through their art. Both of these aspects of the medieval *hōka*'s image—his track record as a performer and his Buddhist affiliation—are preserved in noh versions of the *hōka*. The protagonist of Kan'ami's play *Jinen Koji* is this type of character.

Zeami's plays on Shintō-related themes, such as *Takasago*, are usually in the celebratory mood and feature a Shintō deity who first appears disguised as an old man (Zeami's venerable style) to relate a myth that celebrates an auspicious theme of a public nature. In the second act, the deity then appears in true form to dance. In Zeami's prototypical program of plays— god or *waki* plays, as they will be referred to hereafter—were to be performed in the early phase of a program to set an auspicious tone. Often they celebrate the bounty of the realm and the benevolence of its rule. Although the narrative portions may relate past events, the apparition of a Shintō deity suggests a perpetual present, the root of its auspiciousness. This is the type of play that Zeami concentrates on in his structural prescriptions in *Sandō*.

Although Zeami applied the same basic five-*dan* template to the depiction of characters belonging to the other two styles of role-play, women and warriors, the outcome was often quite different. Female characters in plays following this scheme were not necessarily ghosts, but, as mentioned above, the three female protagonists that he cites as exemplars of a style evocative of *yūgen* in *Sandō* are ghostly characters: Ukifune, the Rokujō lady, and Yūgao from *Genji monogatari*. Some of his most recognized plays, such as *Izutsu* and *Higaki*, also have ghosts as their protagonists. In *Izutsu*, for instance, the ghost of a young woman, the wife of Heian poet Ariwara no Narihira, appears at his grave in the deserted grounds of a temple one autumn night to express her longing for her dead husband. In the martial style, moreover, Zeami invariably casts his protagonists as the ghosts of dead warriors. In the warrior play *Tadanori*, for instance, the ghost of the dead Taira warrior appears at the site of the battlefield on which he died. He reveals that his soul cannot rest because shortly after his death, the compilers of an imperial anthology included one of his poems but failed to attribute it to him by name.[14]

Figure 6 Ghost of the Rokujō lady from *Genji monogatari*, the lead role in the play *Nonomiya* (Shrine in the fields). *Nonomiya* is often attributed to Konparu Zenchiku. Rokujō shares her memories of Genji's visit to the shrine to see her after their affair had ended. She also relives the shame she had experienced when attendants of her rival, Genji's wife, Aoi no Ue, had pushed Rokujō's carriage out of the way and usurped her viewing spot at the Kamo Festival. In the tale, this incident had triggered her deadly attack on Aoi no Ue. In *Sandō*, Zeami mentions that aristocratic females such as the Rokujō lady are optimal for inducing the *yūgen* mood. Actor: Kanze Hisao, Kanze school, wearing a *zō-onna* mask by Zekan (d. 1616). (Courtesy of Professor Masuda Shōzō.)

In plays such as these, which do not follow the development of a plot in a linear fashion, the existence of an original source is doubly important in assuring coherence. The exposition of the story often occurs in fragments allotted at points in the text calculated to best bring out optimal stage effects, sometimes with little attention paid to maintaining a sequential plot line. For example, it is not unusual for a ghostly protagonist to recount and simultaneously reenact her own death, as in the play *Ama*, or for the events following the death of the protagonist to be presented prior to reenactment of the actual death scene, as in the play *Sanemori*.[15] In *Sarugaku dangi*, Zeami goes so far as to advocate that the natural sequence of a narrative be altered if it risks becoming too long-winded.[16]

In *Sandō*, he stresses that only the playwright of consummate skill can succeed at composing a play that he has made up entirely. When the story is a fiction of the playwright, Zeami cautions that the setting at least should hold points of reference familiar to the audience. Of the nine examples of protagonists that Zeami lists by name under the rubric of men and women skilled in the arts, only one, Hyakuman, lacks extant literary precedents. Narihira was the supposed author of *Ise monogatari*, a collection of fictional poem-tales that center on the life of a Heian courtier-poet. The work is episodic, many of the segments devoted to the amours of the protagonist. The protagonist of *Ise monogatari*, although never referred to by name, was generally believed to be Narihira himself, who had come to epitomize the image of the poet-paramour by the medieval period.[17] Hikaru Genji, the fictional hero of *Genji monogatari*, was equally esteemed for his elegant sensibilities. Like *Ise monogatari*, *Genji monogatari* portrays the complex of amorous relations cultivated by the hero. These two classical works have been used as the sources for numerous plays.[18]

According to the conservative estimates that prevail today in noh scholarship,[19] Zeami is credited with certain authorship of only one of the plays of the *Ise* group, *Izutsu*. None of the *Genji* group is generally attributed to him, although a good number, such as *Aoi no Ue* (Lady Aoi) and *Ukifune*, are thought to have undergone his revisions. To ascertain how he actually handles source material from the outset, it is more revealing to turn to his warrior plays, which draw on *Heike monogatari*, the epic chronicling the fall of the Taira clan in the Genpei War.

All of the six plays that Zeami lists as exemplars in Segment 2.3 of *Sandō* are taken from the Heike story, and he claims five of them as his own. Konishi suggests that the reason Zeami favored *Heike monogatari* to the Heian-period classic *Genji monogatari* was that the former was much more familiar to contemporary audiences. Whereas *Genji* was a literary work, various versions of *Heike* were originally performed as recited narratives throughout the medieval years. Access to the *Genji* was restricted to the cultural elite, but traditions of oral recitation made the *Heike* tales accessible to everyone.[20] On the basis of this empirical evidence, at least, Zeami showed a preference for the popular narrative over the canonical literary work, perhaps underscoring the importance he placed on building rapport with all kinds of audiences.

Zeami's warrior plays provide hints that he was far from advocating slavish attention to the details of the original source. To be true to the source meant that the playwright should preserve the image of the kernel personage and the basic action of the story. For example, in his play *Tadanori*, he interweaves two discrete episodes of the original *Heike monogatari* to arrive at the compound image of the *shite* as both poet and warrior.[21] Moreover, he combines tales about a single protagonist from various types of sources. Yonekura notes that the second act of the warrior play *Sanemori* is taken from *Heike monogatari*, whereas the first half is inspired by the reported appearance in 1414 of the warrior Sanemori's ghost. Yonekura surmises that Zeami used that contemporary sensation in order to give the standard tale of Sanemori a touch of novelty and a more direct appeal to the audience.[22] As demonstrated in these plays, then, the ideal material should be both familiar and novel.

THE TECHNIQUE OF STRUCTURING

The second phase of the compositional process, the technique of structuring *(saku)*, involves determining the nature and sequence of the vocal, choreographic, and mimetic elements of the play. While remaining true to the spirit of the original material, the playwright proceeds to adapt it to a five-step developmental sequence. Zeami devotes most of this segment (1.3) to introducing the component parts of each step, along with the underlying principle that should guide all compositional choices. He refers to that organizing principle as *jo-ha-kyū*.

Nogami has described *jo-ha-kyū* as "the grammar of expression" in noh, a term referring to an overarching sense of timing on the basis of which the parts of a play are articulated on stage.[23] The terms *jo*, *ha*, and *kyū* first appear in the critical literature of the genre of court music called *gagaku*. In *gagaku*, they are not used together as one compound. Rather, each is used

Figure 7 *Shite* (Act 2) of Zeami's warrior play, *Kiyotsune*. One of the exemplary warrior plays that Zeami lists in *Sandō*. The ghost of the young warrior-aristocrat Taira no Kiyotsune appears to his stricken wife in the capital to try to make her understand why he chose to take his own life. He laments the defeat of his clan and finally draws his sword in a reenactment of his own spiritual battle in warrior purgatory. Actor: Sekine Tomotaka, Kanze school (performance variant: *Koi no netori*), wearing a *chūjō* mask by Kawachi (d. ca. 1645). (Photographed by Yoshikoshi Ken.)

separately to refer to a particular portion of a *gagaku* piece, and not all portions are necessarily included in any one piece. The *jo* portion refers to an opening instrumental section that does not have a set rhythmic scheme and progresses calmly and smoothly. The *ha* portion has a set rhythmic pattern that proceeds at a measured pace. The *kyū* portion also adheres to a set rhythmic pattern and follows a slightly faster tempo. When *bugaku,* classical court dance, is performed to the *gagaku* instrumentation, the *jo* phase accompanies the entry of the dancers and the *ha* and *kyū* portions accompany the dance.[24]

Zeami does not mention the relation of *jo-ha-kyū* to *gagaku* precedents in his critical writings, and one cannot but wonder whether he was more directly influenced by *renga* poetics.[25] Yoshimoto applies the principle of *jo-ha-kyū* in his critical treatise *Tsukuba mondō* (Tsukuba dialogues; 1372) (in which he mentions *gagaku* antecedents but does not describe them).[26] It is possible that Zeami's understanding of the principle came more directly through his contact with Yoshimoto. Perhaps he saw the critical concept from poetics as having promise for unifying poetic elements in *sarugaku* plays as well. In any case, Zeami's conception, which comes to pervade his theory of noh at all levels, appears to be largely his own. He uses *jo-ha-kyū* to address the optimal interrelation between the phases of progressions at multiple levels.

The phases are linked in much the same way as the movements of a sonata. *Jo,* literally meaning "opening" or "preface," constitutes the introductory phase, which should be straightforward and unadorned. *Ha* signals the developmental phase of the progression. The word *ha* denotes to "break," and Zeami uses it in the sense that this second phase breaks down or elaborates on what has been more simply presented in the earlier *jo* section. That is, the *ha* phase should be more varied, as is suitable for more detailed and fuller treatment of what was presented in *jo.* The *kyū* phase should be upbeat and should move rapidly to a close, as is fit for the finale.

Zeami's earliest discussions of the principle occur in the third chapter of *Kaden,* in *Kashu no uchinukigaki,* and in *Kakyō,* in which he discusses it in relation to how the plays in a day's program should be arranged.[27] Whereas the *waki* play belongs to the *jo* phase of the program, the ensuing warrior play combines elements of *jo* and *ha.* The heart of the *ha* phase comes with the woman play, the third entry in the program. In the *Kakyō* passage, Zeami cautions that when a program follows the normal scheme of four to five plays, then the last play should be the beginning of the *kyū* phase. If *kyū* starts any earlier, then it ceases to fulfill its purpose as a brisk finale, he warns.[28] More will be said about the arrangement of the program in the ensuing chapter.

As Zeami's critical theory develops, the *jo-ha-kyū* paradigm comes to have increasingly broad applications. In *Sandō*, for the first time he applies it to explain how the five component sequences of a play should interrelate, as will be introduced below. By his late treatise *Shūgyoku tokuka*, he has come to apply it to all elements of a performance. For instance, he states,

> The order of the plays [in a program] and the internal structure of each should adhere to *jo-ha-kyū*. Moreover, the interest of any danced or aural [element] is attributable to the fulfillment of *jo-ha-kyū*. In the one gesture of turning a sleeve, in the resonance of one stamp, there is *jo-ha-kyū*.[29]

Judging from the contents of *Sandō*, Zeami saw the playwright's first task as ensuring that the structure of his play allowed for the fulfillment of the *jo-ha-kyū* progression in performance. Moreover, the playwright had to determine just what overall proportions of *jo-ha-kyū* were appropriate to the depiction of his chosen protagonist. As noted above, he saw the prototypical play as being composed of five stages or sequences, called *dan*. The first *dan* corresponds to the *jo* phase of the play, the next three *dan* to the *ha* phase, and the final *dan* to *kyū*. Each stage holds a characteristic pattern of component parts, although numerous variations on those parts are possible. In this segment (1.3) on the technique of structuring, Zeami restricts his list to those that are most basic to each *dan*. The resulting configuration is outlined in the following table.

The *shite* normally does not appear until *Dan* II, and *Dan* I is performed exclusively by the figure cast in the other role type that is not expendable—that of the side actor *(waki)*. In *mugen noh*, the *waki* is rarely himself the focal point of the dramatic interest. He functions to draw out the *shite*, divulging only enough of his own identity to elicit responsiveness on the part of his interlocutor. The *waki* frequently takes the identity of a traveling priest who visits the scene of the action out of no particular motive other than impartial curiosity. Although on occasion a *waki* may have a personal motive for going to the site, usually he does not have a prior acquaintance with the *shite*. The *waki* may be cast in other identities as well, such as that of a Shintō priest, a retainer to a prominent individual, or simply an

Outline of Noh Structure

Phase	*Dan*	Component Parts	Role Type
Jo	I	Introductory chant* (*shidai*)	*waki*
		Name-saying speech	
		One long passage of chant (traveling chant: *michiyuki*)	
Ha	II	Entry chant (*issei*)	*shite*
		[Recitative (*sashi*)	*shite*]**
		One long passage of chant (*hito-utai*) (Typically, one high-range chant [*sageuta*] and one low-range chant [*ageuta*])	
Ha	III	Spoken exchange (*mondō*)	*shite*/*waki*
		[Heightened exchange (*kakeai*)	*shite*/*waki*]**
		One long passage of chant (High-range chant)	chorus***
Ha	IV	*Kuse* section or	*shite*/chorus
		Plain chant (*tada utai*)	
Kyū	V	Dance or vigorous moves	*shite*
		Hayabushi match or	
		Kiribyōshi match	*shite*/chorus

* In Zeami's day, the sequence of the introductory chant and the name-saying speech was usually reversed. See translation, Segment 1.3.
** Components not expressly mentioned by Zeami in Segment 1.3.
*** It is not known exactly when the chorus crystallized as its own entity in a *sarugaku* performance. In Zeami's time, the *waki* and his entourage chanted the choral sections.

unnamed person who happens to be at the scene. The casting depends on the nature of the *shite* and the source material. The *waki* always plays a living person and is invariably male. In Zeami's time, the specific categories of roles for actors, such as *shite*, *waki*, or *tsure*, had not yet crystallized. But the distinction between the main actor and the secondary ones was clear.[30]

In the first *dan*, the *waki*'s primary role is to introduce the setting and establish the tone of the play. The conventional entry music for the *waki* is a passage of verse called the *shidai* (introductory chant), which, as Yasuda observes, must suggest "the affective theme of the entire play."[31] The introductory chant usually does not broach the specifics of the *shite*'s story. Rather, its content is often enigmatic, "with overtones suggesting some as yet unrevealed significance. Its significance to the *shite*'s story becomes clear as that story unfolds."[32]

The ensuing name-saying speech[33] usually entails a simple self-introduction by the *waki* and a brief statement of purpose. Normally, he is en route to the spot at which he is destined to encounter the *shite*, and the recitative is apt to make a cryptic allusion to the connection between that site and the *shite*'s background story. In Zeami's stylistic prototype, the *jo* phase concludes with a passage of poetic description, called the traveling chant (*michiyuki*) today. Typically it enumerates familiar landmarks that the *waki* is passing in the narrative, and its conclusion signifies that he has reached his destination. In today's staging, he retires to downstage left, where he ordinarily remains seated for the duration of the play.

The *shite* enters in *Dan* II, or the first segment of the *ha* phase. A noh play may have one or two acts. In a one-act play, the *shite* appears from the first in his or her original form, although alterations of costume may be made in the course of the act. In the two-act play, the *shite* appears in disguise in the first act but assumes his or her actual identity in the second.[34] In *Dan* II the *shite* typically enters on the poetic verse called the *issei* (entry chant). Like the entry lines of the *shidai*, the *issei* characteristically avoids direct reference to the identity of the *shite* or the nature of the story. It is often a visual description of the surrounding scene in which are embedded hints to the identity of the *shite*.[35] Frequently, the *issei* is followed by or interspersed with recitative (*sashi*) that often further amplifies the *shite*'s state of mind (although Zeami does not mention recitative here in his initial summary of a play's structure).

Although *Dan* II is devoted almost entirely to the self-absorbed reflections of the *shite*, little regarding his or her identity is revealed directly. The *waki*'s curiosity in the *shite* has been aroused, however, and in *Dan* III, corresponding to the second leg of the *ha* phase, the two finally enter into conversation, which begins in a spoken exchange (*mondō*; originally *mondai*), then moves into a heightened exchange (*kakeai*). The *shite* ordinarily answers the *waki*'s queries regarding some legend attached to the locale without letting on directly that he or she has any connection with it. The *dan* then climaxes in a high-range chant *(ageuta)* rendered by the chorus.

In Zeami's time, the chorus had not evolved into its present form. It was the actor cast in what later came to be called the *waki* role who served as leader of the chorus, and it was the secondary actors *(waki no shite)* who composed the rest of the chorus. Today, the leader of the chorus, and all its members, too, are trained to perform as *shite*, not as *waki*. It is also unclear whether in Zeami's time the secondary actors charged with the choral parts appeared in role as attendants to the *waki (wakizure*, as they later came to be called) or simply appeared as members of the chorus.[36]

Despite such divergences, the chorus has always formed an integral part of the exposition of a play. Choral narrative is used in multiple ways, its versatility a key to its effectiveness. It may render an impartial account of either past or present events, or just as suitably describe the emotive quality of a moment, or weave back and forth freely between these two perspectives. Numbering today anywhere from six to ten (usually eight), its members remain seated at stage left for the duration of the play. As is true of the *waki*, the chorus supports the *shite*'s performance, but unlike the *waki*, it never participates directly in the action. It may, however, take the voice of a character (most often the *shite*) to convey thoughts or feelings or to narrate events.

Miyake Kōichi notes that the choral section positioned at the end of *Dan* III typically functions to sustain the *shite*'s expression of emotion. Today, typically such expression steadily builds throughout the spoken exchange and the heightened exchange until it reaches a level that exceeds his ability to express himself in words. At this juncture, the chorus steps in to give further voice to the *shite*'s emotions while the *shite* confirms them in his movements.[37]

In the fourth *dan*, which corresponds to the concluding part of the *ha* phase, the *waki* has fulfilled his function of eliciting information from the *shite* and consequently fades somewhat into the background. The choral participation then intensifies. Whether *Dan* IV features a *kuse* section or the older form of chant standard to *sarugaku*, which Zeami calls *tada utai*, it is musically the most complex and colorful segment of the noh.[38] The distinction Zeami makes between the *kuse* section and *tada utai* is an important one in the history of the evolution of the noh. As previously mentioned, Zeami's father Kan'ami studied the performance of *kusemai* and subsequently adapted it to *sarugaku*. It is thought that the original *kusemai* consisted of straight, third-person narrative that concluded with a simple dance.[39] On the other hand, extended narratives appear to have been atypical in *sarugaku* up until the incorporation of the *kusemai*. The type of chant originally used in *sarugaku*—*tada utai*—was in the *kouta* style. *Kouta* (short song) was a contemporaneous form of popular song. It is believed that some time well prior to Zeami's critical writings, *kouta* had been imported into *sarugaku* without major revisions in its musical structure.[40]

The *kusemai* was modified considerably with its importation into noh, but it retained its narrative framework. Today the *kuse* section of a play normally constitutes the most complete and concentrated recapitulation of the story material. In warrior plays and frequently in woman plays, the chorus narrates the *kuse* while the *shite* dances. Takemoto has observed that Zeami's method as a playwright was "to maintain the semblance of a play built on dialogue, while at the same time setting out to transform noh into a form of musical drama by incorporating component parts that were not based on dialogue but on singing."[41] The insertion of a sustained narrative such as the *kusemai* would be one example of how Zeami implemented such a transformation. In a discussion of the significance of adding *kusemai* elements, Miyake Akiko points out that it also added a new narrative dimension to the chanting.

> One attribute [of the original *kusemai*] was a chanted narrative of considerable length and structural integrity, which made it possible to treat epic content such as that found in large-scale temple or shrine chronicles.[42]

Miyake speculates that the innovation may have been a primary contributing factor to Kan'ami's and Zeami's success at securing the patronage of the shogun Yoshimitsu.

Although today *kusemai* and *kouta* music have blended to the point that they are almost indistinguishable, in Zeami's time they were still thought of as discrete. We know that in *Ongyoku kuden* he characterizes the *kouta* style as taking melody as its basis, whereas the *kusemai* style makes the beat primary.[43] Not only does the original *kusemai* seem to have been a means of expanding the narrative components in the text of a noh play, but also a means to intensify rhythmical ones in its performance. It became possible to integrate storytelling and danced components and to assign them a foundational role in the infrastructure of Zeami's prototypical play.

The model Zeami describes in the technique of structuring is technically the prototype for a play whose protagonist is a deity. Elsewhere he describes this as the most straightforward and basic style.[44] His *waki* plays (god plays) are usually organized in two acts. The first act typically concludes with the fourth *dan*, at which point the *shite* reveals his true identity and exits to change costume. He reenters in his true identity for the second act, which constitutes the *kyū* phase of the play and the final *dan*.[45] In *Dan* V, either a formal dance or a choreographed pattern of vigorous moves (*hataraki*) is performed. The dance section is the visual culmination of all that has preceded and is supported primarily by the instrumental ensemble (*hayashi*).

The *hayashi* has always been an integral element of a noh performance. It consists of three or four musicians. Musicians playing the noh flute (*nōkan*), the shoulder drum (*kotsuzumi*), and the hip drum (*ōtsuzumi*) appear in all performances today. Depending on the play, a stick drum (*taiko*) may also be added to create more vivid effects. Although Zeami makes no direct reference in *Sandō* to the *hayashi*, he does briefly address the role of the musicians in the later treatise *Shudōsho*.[46] In that document, he stresses that the musicians should try to adhere to the *shite*'s interpretation. Regarding the drumming, for instance, he states, "Adjust to the mind/intent [*kokoro*] of the actor and perform with the two modes [of dance and chant] as your standard."[47] He urges the flute player to be guided by the "fragrance of the voice of the actor" in modulating his own pitch.[48] The *hayashi* is seated upstage and is active throughout the performance. Today, as a rule, it is silent during those segments that consist of intoned speech, as well as during most of the interlude of a two-act play. However, during the dance, which typically comes in the fifth *dan* of a play, its importance is particularly conspicuous because the chorus is mostly silent throughout most of this section.

The formal dances (*mai*) and vigorous moves (*hataraki*) make up the two major classifications of choreographed movement that are matched to the instruments.[49] Today, the vigorous moves tend to be much briefer than the formal dances and are not as finely matched to the flute instrumentation. Most plays employ one or the other of the two types of movement. Arguably, the distinction that Zeami made between gentle and strong in the formative years of *sarugaku* is reflected today in the staging of the two types of choreography. Plays featuring gentle *shite*, in the venerable or feminine style, tend to include formal dances, whereas warriors, demons, or rambunctious deities are more likely to perform sequences of vigorous moves.

After Zeami discusses matters pertaining to the dance in *Dan* V, he broaches the subject of the ensuing chanted section. As recorded on the table above, the chant of the fifth *dan* features heightened rhythmic patterns that Zeami calls the *hayabushi* and the *kiribyōshi*. His cursory reference to them assumes prior knowledge of noh chanting and provides just one example of the difficulties that the modern reader encounters when attempting to decipher instructions intended for a noh professional of the fifteenth century. Today there are basically two types of rhythmic orientations in noh: that which is strictly congruent with the drumming patterns (*hyōshi ai*) and that which is rendered simultaneously with the drumming patterns but is not strictly congruent with them (*hyōshi awazu*).[50] In the congruent case, there are three basic patterns for matching the vocal line to the instrumental line. The standard vocal line is twelve morae, consisting of an upper hemistich of seven morae and a lower one of five. By contrast, the core instrumental unit is an eight-beat measure. In today's prototype of the standard rhythmic pattern, called *hiranori*, the twelve morae are matched to those eight beats in a syncopated pattern. However, variations on this prototype are also common. *Hiranori* is by far the predominant rhythmic scheme. Of the component parts that Zeami enumerates, the introductory chant, traveling chant, high-range chant, low-range chant, and the final part of the *kuse* section (the *kuse* itself) all conform to this rhythm.[51]

The *hayabushi* match, or *chūnori* as it is called today, is one of two basic rhythmic alternatives to the *hiranori* match. Instead of twelve morae, sixteen morae are matched to eight beats, resulting in a brisker, more regular rhythm. The second alternative, the *kiribyōshi* match, known today as *ōnori*, consists of eight morae matched to the eight beats. Unlike the syncopated pattern of the *hiranori*, one mora is matched to one beat, and the decrease in the number of morae in a line from twelve to eight has the effect of prolonging syllable duration. Whereas the *hayabushi* (*chūnori*) match is primarily used at the close of warrior or demon plays, often in conjunction with vigorous moves, the *kiribyōshi* (*ōnori*) match more frequently appears in the concluding section of woman or *waki* plays.[52]

Having now looked over the component parts of a play as laid out in the table above, it should be clear that the overall contours of the action in Zeami's prototypical play are destined to draw the audience gradually into the *shite*'s story. In the *jo* phase the relatively objective observations of an outsider (the *waki*) are in the foreground. In the early parts of *ha*, the *shite* also takes the stance of an outsider narrating the tale. Through the spoken exchange *(mondō)* and heightened exchange *(kakeai)* of the second *dan* of *ha* (*Dan* III of the play), we become familiarized with the tale and drawn into it more deeply; and the more we are drawn in, the more the *shite* lets on about himself. As the *shite* becomes more communicative and, in the third *dan* of *ha*, reveals a knowledge of the story too intimate to be that of a passive observer, the focal point of audience interest shifts from the story itself to the identity of the *shite* telling it. This narrative suspense mounts, along with the musical tension, to bring the *shite*'s intimation or open admission of his identity at the end of *ha*. From that point, his narration is transformed into reenactment of his own story; his final apparition, in true form, and his dance bring his revelation to its culmination.

It is important to remember, however, that Zeami intended his five-*dan* scheme merely as a working model. He reminds the playwright (Segment 1.3) that the number may be altered in accordance with the magnitude of the material or the type of play in question. He reserves instructions on the actual content of the lines of the noh for the ensuing segment on the technique of writing (1.4). However, in Segment 1.3 he does mention that the basic building block for each *dan* is the line of twelve morae and that the playwright must arrive at the desired apportionment of the five *dan* by manipulating the number of lines in each.

THE TECHNIQUE OF WRITING

Once the playwright has decided on the dance, chant, and *monomane* that are appropriate for his chosen subject matter and has assigned each of these elements a place in the five-*dan* scheme, then he is ready to enter into the third phase of the compositional process, the technique of writing. It consists of a threefold process that embraces both poetic and musical phrasing. In the introductory segment of *Sandō*, Zeami describes this as the "gathering" of words, the "adding of modulation," and the linking of the lines. Segment 1.4 concentrates on the apt choice of language.

The reference to "gathering" is a key to Zeami's conception of poetic composition. He means that the playwright, rather than composing his own lines from scratch, should quite literally gather lines from famous poems. The incorporation of language from well-known older poems into a new poem is a technique with precedents in *waka* poetry called *honkadori* (allusive variation). *Honkadori* is one device for investing a new composition with multiple readings that go beyond the actual lines of a poem. Brower articulates the principle in the following.

Sometimes the allusion was an echoing of a recognizable few words of the original composition, sometimes a famous poetic conceit or conception identified with a particular older poem. The result was a complex superposition of the new poem upon the old, so that the meaning and atmosphere of both were simultaneously apprehended, whether blended, harmonized, or contrasted.[53]

Shirane has noted that the technique of *honkadori* may be viewed as an intertextual exercise in which a poem is read "primarily in relationship to earlier texts and literary conventions, as an 'open' text in which each word or phrase refers, not to a fixed referent (a given scene), but to other signs and signifiers."[54] Shirane, citing the work of Riffaterre, observes that when the mimetic reading of a poem (for its representational content) proves to be of only limited significance, then the informed reader will attempt to read the poem semiotically, or intertextually, as a text referring to various subtexts or signs.

The immediate context for Shirane's points is the *waka* poetics of Fujiwara no Shunzei (1114–1204), but they may be extrapolated to Zeami's adaptation of the intertextual techniques into noh. Not only did it reflect Zeami's concern with creating an art that would be apprized highly by literate audiences, but it was integral to the stylistic turn that he implemented: away from a stage art that could be read only mimetically toward an "open" poetry of the stage that could be read at multiple levels by audiences. As Takemoto has pointed out, there is no evidence that such allusive techniques were practiced in script composition by *sarugaku* performers prior to Zeami.[55] This principle, so established an element in the stylistics of noh now, must have been much less familiar to Zeami's peers in the trade. Perhaps its newness was the reason that Zeami provided rather detailed instructions on it in Segment 1.4 of *Sandō*, which concentrates on how *honkadori* can be implemented.

Through techniques of allusion, such as the *honka* (foundation poem) and the original source (*honzetsu;* lit. "foundation story"), the playwright can create meanings and moods that go beyond explicit referential content. The two techniques do differ, however, in the scale of their application in *sarugaku* composition. The *honzetsu* typically provides the source material on which the composition as a whole is based, the *shite*'s identity, and the outline of the plot coming from it. The *honkadori* technique tends to play a more subsidiary role as a means of adumbrating themes and highlighting points in the narrative. The entry chant (*issei*) of the *shite* in *Takasago*, the *waki* play by Zeami that is the focus of the latter portion of part 2 of this volume, offers a clear example of how allusion to a well-known, older poem can enrich the poetic import. In *Takasago*, the old man (*shite*) and the old woman (*tsure*) enter on the following entry chant.

At Takasago	Takasago no
spring breezes in the pines	matsu no harukaze
deepen into dusk,	fukikurete
The bell too is echoing	Onoe no kane mo
from the hill above.	hibiku nari.[56]

This chant contains an allusion to a poem by Ōe no Masafusa (1041–1111) that reads,

At Takasago	Takasago no
there upon the hill above	onoe no kane no
the bell sounds,	oto su nari
With the dawn	Akatsuki kakete
will frost have settled in?	shimo ya okuran.[57]

From Masafusa's poem Zeami borrows the place-name of Takasago, which is also the setting of the first act of his play. He also adopts the image of the bell sounding from the nearby hill. These two images are just enough to conjure an associative link with the older poem. The effect is not only to heighten the interest of the setting by linking it with poetic precedents, but also to reinforce our sense of a connection between the *shite* and the setting of the play. Beyond the surface similarities in imagery, however, the two poems contrast in tone. The seasonal shift from the wintry frost of Masafusa's poem to the soft spring breeze of the entry chant (*issei*) alters the entire mood of the newer poem. For poet Baba Akiko this shift from a wintry backdrop to the gentle mood of spring serves to bring out the loneliness of age all the more poignantly.[58]

In the case of both *honkadori* and *honzetsu* techniques, if the playwright violates the horizons of expectation concerning the original story, then the superposition will create dissonance, not resonance. In this regard, Zeami cautions the playwright to give special attention to the theme of the poem he chooses and to ascertain if its associations are in keeping with the

emotive quality he wishes to invoke. He specifies five themes as lending
themselves to adaptation into *sarugaku* texts: auspiciousness (*shūgen*),
yūgen, passionate love (*koi*), personal grievance (*shukkai*), and desolation
(*bōoku*). In *sarugaku*, the theme of auspiciousness (*shūgen*) is most characteristic of the *waki* play that opens a program.[59] Its subjects include rejoicing
for the peace, order, and prosperity of the realm as well as the longevity of
its rulers and subjects.

In two of his late treatises, *Go on* and *Go ongyoku jōjō*,[60] Zeami cites as
exemplars poems from the seventh book of the first imperial anthology
Kokin waka shū and thus forges an explicit link between the treatment of
auspicious material in *sarugaku* and precedented material in the world of
waka composing. The seventh book is devoted to poems on celebratory
themes (*Ga no uta*), consisting largely of poems presented to the guests of
honor at celebrations honoring their longevity (fortieth year, fiftieth, six-
tieth, etc.).[61] In *Go ongyoku jōjō*, for instance, Zeami gives the following
poem by Priest Sosei, which is introduced in the *Kokin waka shū* headnote
as a poem that Sosei composed on behalf of a woman for the celebration to
mark her father's fortieth year.

the crane beneath the	*Yorozuyo o*
pine offered in jubilee	*matsu ni zo kimi o*
they tell how much I	*iwai tsuru*
hope to dwell eternally	*chitose no kage ni*
in the shelter of your love.	*suman to omoeba.*[62]

This poem is one of five that Zeami introduces in *Go ongyoku jōjō*, each as
an exemplar for one of the five themes. Each poem employs the image of a
different type of tree. The received connection between the pine tree—
whose needles do not fall but remain green—and longevity is one that
Zeami does indeed exploit as a playwright, most notably in the *waki* play
such as the one mentioned here, *Takasago*. More will be said about *Takasago*
in the following chapter.

Zeami's earliest reference to *bōoku* is in contradistinction to the *shūgen*
mood. It occurs in his treatise *Ongyoku kuden*, in which he introduces *shūgen* and *bōoku* as the two modes of chanting in *sarugaku*. He explains that
the six lowest tones of the musical scale were appropriate for expressing the
sadness or pathos characteristic of *bōoku*, and the upper six lent themselves to expressing happiness, or the *shūgen* mood. He also discusses the

desired breathing and vocal control called for by the two.[63] The locus classicus for the term *bōoku* is surmised to be the "Great Preface" to the *Shijing*. This work includes the following statement: "The tones of a ruined state are filled with lament and brooding; its people are in difficulty."[64] "Ruined state" may be read *bōkoku* in Japanese. *Bōoku* is thought to be a deliberately corrupted pronunciation of *bōkoku*, done in order to avoid direct utterance of this inauspicious word. Zeami seems to be capitalizing on the cachet of this well-circulated teaching from the Confucian classics to provide an illustrious precedent and pretext for his own discussion of chanting styles. The NSTS annotation for the term notes that a tendency to reinterpret the meaning of *bōoku* developed in the late Muromachi period, based on the fact that it has a homonym meaning the "atmosphere inspired by a humble, secluded dwelling evocative of pathos *(monoaware na wabizumai).*" The Chinese characters for this dwelling usage came to be used to write *bōoku* in its desolation usage as well.[65]

Although *Sandō* gives no specific examples on this theme, in *Ongyoku kuden*, Zeami quotes a passage from the play *Sekidera Komachi* (Komachi at Sekidera) as evocative of *bōoku*.[66] The play treats Ono no Komachi as a destitute old woman reflecting on the art of poetry and on happier days in the past.[67] Her opening lines are quoted in *Ongyoku kuden*, and a translated excerpt from that quotation is recorded below. It does seem more a harbinger of the late Muromachi understanding of the word than a reflection of the more overtly political message in *Shijing*.

> Days go by without a single bowl of food;
> Whom can I ask for one?
> At night my tattered rags fail to cover me,
> But there is no way to patch the rents.
> Each passing rain
> Ages the crimson of the flowers;
> The willows are tricked by the wind,
> And their green gradually droops.
> Man has no second chance at youth;
> He grows old. The aged song thrush
> Warbles again when spring has come,
> But time does not revert to the past.
> Oh, how I yearn for the days that are gone!
> What would I do to recapture the past![68]

Whereas in *Sandō* the *bōoku* category is included in an enumeration of five types of thematic content suitable for importation into *sarugaku* plays, Zeami ceases to identify *bōoku* as its own classification in his late critical works. Instead he concentrates on the delineation of five vocal styles, each with its own characteristic themes and mood. In Go ongyoku jōjō, for instance, he enumerates the five themes of *shūgen*, *yūkyoku* (*yūgen* piece), *renbo* (passionate longing), *aishō* (lamentation), and *rangyoku* (piece having seasoned fluency). The term *bōoku* is mentioned in conjunction with the theme of *aishō*, which is a precedented poetic theme in *waka* treating death and mourning. Zeami does state that the scope of the tree metaphor most apropos to this classification includes both its *bōoku* and *aishō* facets: a grove of trees buried in the winter snows. So it seems that in his late treatises Zeami came to treat the *bōoku* theme as part of the larger *aishō* classification.

The theme of *shukkai* (modern Japanese *jukkai*) treats personal disappointments or grievances. By the twelfth century, *shukkai* had started to appear as a formal theme in *waka*.[69] Although Zeami makes no reference to specific plays that incorporate this theme, it seems particularly appropriate for those such as *Kinuta* (The fulling block) or *Kayoi Komachi*, in which the *shite* returns to this world as a ghost expressly to vent his or her resentment.[70] *Shukkai* is not included in Zeami's later classification of the five types of vocal music.

The concept of *yūgen* is a cornerstone of Zeami's dramatic theory, of course, and is ideally palpable at every level of a performance. In its broadest sense, a tone of *yūgen* should underlie the performance of all five of the themes that he enumerates in the segment on the technique of writing (1.4). However, as a specific poetic theme, he is referring to those poems that have subject matter whose content is to be taken as overtly endowed with gracefulness. That is, the term *yūgen* can be used to refer either to an aesthetic effect or, metonymically, to the subject matter that is credited with creating that effect. In this context, it refers to such subject matter.[71]

The *yūgen* theme overlaps one of the five types of vocal music set down in both Go ongyoku jōjō and Go on, the style labeled *yūkyoku* (lit. "*yūgen* piece"). Zeami names the cherry tree as the embodiment of this style and cites the following poem by Fujiwara no Shunzei as a model.

Will I ever view again   *Mata ya min*
cherry blossoms blooming   *Katano no mino no*

at Katano?   *sakuragari*
Snowy petals falling   *hana no yuki chiru*
in the spring dawn   *haru no akebono.*[72]

The next theme, *renbo*, recurs as a classification of vocal music in Go *ongyoku jōjō* and Go *on*. In those later treatises, Zeami introduces passionate love as a deepening of the *yūgen* theme. He states that it shares the gentle grace of the *yūgen* mood but that it has an added layer of pathos, a sharper edge, which he compares to the autumnal maple leaves. As his exemplar, he cites the following *waka* by Fujiwara no Ietaka (1158–1237).

Lower crimson leaves   *Shita momiji*
are falling on the mountain   *katsu chiru yama no*
in the evening shower.   *yū shigure*
Dampened is the stag perhaps   *nurete ya shika no*
who all alone is calling   *hitori naku ran.*[73]

The theme is manifested in noh as stories of unrequited love or separation. In Go *ongyoku jōjō*, *Hanjo* and *Matsukaze* are mentioned as representative plays.[74]

Zeami says nothing about restricting the above poetic themes to specific categories of plays, nor does he offer any strictures on combining poems of differing themes in one play. He does not seem to suffer qualms about employing the same poem or poems in more than one play, for the texts themselves demonstrate how frequently allusion to one and the same poem recurs in different plays.[75] He is more fastidious about certain other aspects of allusive techniques, however. Because the allusion depends for its effectiveness on prior familiarity with the poem on the part of the audience, he cautions the playwright to limit himself to those poems that are certain to be recognized. Moreover, he stipulates that the playwright refer to the setting of the action. Particularly when that setting is one familiar to the audience, allusions to it should be incorporated into the part(s) of the *ha* phase that hold the climactic moments. Reference to a famous site (*utamakura*) was a stock technique among *waka* poets for the evocation of intertextual readings. Kamens aptly characterizes the function of such place-names in *waka* in his study of the subject as "foundations for poem designs, or as loci of reference and reliance in the elaborative associative schemes which poets forge among poems."[76] It is no coincidence that many of the noted places and historical sites that Zeami mentions in his plays are locations traditionally invoked by *waka* poets, each having its own web of associations. As a student of the poets, Zeami exploited such place-names by staging them.

Finally, Zeami states emphatically that "fine words" and "well-known verses" be assigned to the *shite*. The remark in *Sandō* echoes a more explicit statement made in the earlier *Kaden:* "Important words should not be introduced into a section having no direct connection with the lines or the stage action of the *shite*."[77] As with every other component of a play, poetic language should be contrived to bring the *shite* into the foreground. To allot distinctive lines to the *waki* or any other role can only distract attention from this core concern in Zeami's style of dramaturgy.

Although *Sandō* is Zeami's most definitive and coherent statement on playwriting, other of his secret treatises also contain noteworthy pointers on that aspect of noh. Two segments of the sixth chapter of *Kaden* are devoted to playwriting, as well as a portion of the late treatise *Sarugaku dangi*. Some of the ideas introduced in these two sources are developed more fully in *Sandō*, but others provide reference points that enrich a reading of that work. For instance, in *Kaden*, Zeami applies the principle of progression from the aural to the visual modes to the concrete stage action, explaining that all movement onstage must grow out of the lines. Or, in *Sarugaku dangi*, he notes that poetic language is not effective if it is too obscure or too intellectually complex for ready reception through the ear. For more on composition, the reader is referred to those treatises.[78]

THE EAR-OPENING AND THE EYE-OPENING

Although Zeami introduces most of his major theoretical points in the first section of *Sandō*, which has been the focus for the preceding analysis, he reserves one important set of instructions on the organizing principles of a play for the last section. In Segment 3.3 of *Sandō* he goes into further detail about how to apply the three techniques of the material, structuring, and writing in keeping with the *jo-ha-kyū* progression around which the play's component parts should be organized. He characterizes that progression as having two climactic points that should further guide the playwright. These points reflect the development of the musical elements of the play. The first, called the ear-opening (*kaimon*), is induced by the chant; the second, called the eye-opening (*kaigen*), is induced in the course of the dance.

The ear-opening corresponds to that phase of a performance in which the content of the story and the expressiveness of its rendering combine to instill a deep impression in the spectator. The overall flow of the lines should build to this point. The eye-opening is that point at which the emotive quality revealed to the ear is consummated in visual form. Zeami leaves the playwright to position these two climaxes where he sees fit, specifying only that the eye-opening occur somewhere in the formal dance or the vigorous moves and that both occur somewhere in the *ha* or *kyū* phases. More important than the specific positioning of the two, which will vary somewhat with each play, is the sequence they should follow. The ear-opening must precede the eye-opening. That the progression from audio to visual modes is key to the actor's evocation of *kakari* effects onstage is a principle already familiar from part 1 of this volume. However, Zeami's discussion of the principle with explicit reference to playwriting occurs for the first time here in *Sandō*.

The terms *kaimon* and *kaigen* are also newly introduced here. Whereas the ear-opening depends on the skill the of the playwright, the eye-opening depends on the actor, Zeami says. However, the playwright must make room for such a climax in the infrastructure of the play. Zeami's inclusion of this segment in *Sandō* underscores the importance he places on the spectator's imaginative engagement in the process of a performance.

YŪGEN

The final segment of *Sandō* exhorts the playwright to set his aspirations on a style of performance having *yūgen*. Zeami talks first about actors who enjoy this quality in their performances: the *dengaku* performer Itchū, Kan'ami, and the Ōmi *sarugaku* performer Inuō. "All three made the *yūgen* elements of dance and chant the foundation of their styles and were masters of each of the three styles." Zeami contrasts these players with others who specialize in warrior or demonic roles. Their fame will not last. Upon the first reading, one might easily assume that he is defining *yūgen* here in the earlier way, as a property inherent in certain objects and not others, with elegant and inelegant objects following into two separate, a priori classifications. However, such cannot be the case since one of the three styles he is recommending as the key to *yūgen* effects is that of the warrior. By implication, then, he is saying that the warrior role, too, can be evocative of *yūgen*.

The gist of his statement seems to be that *yūgen* is not traceable to one particular style of acting. It is dependent on the artistic scale of the actor and his capacity to rise to the occasion by promoting a sense of freshness in the minds of the audience. Yet Zeami's ensuing statement reflects that the ultimate source of *yūgen* effects is not freshness per se: "When it comes to the grade of supreme effect in the style having a true foundation of *yūgen*, the visional affect [stage effects] appears to remain unchanged no matter what the era."[79] It is something that transcends styles, eras, and audiences both in the town and the country. Zeami also notes, "You should make material that promises *yūgen* effects the foundation of your style when you compose."[80] So it seems that *yūgen* effects are not constituted in the text either, although a well-crafted text enhances the possibilities for invoking the *yūgen* quality in performance.

In the end, it is impossible to situate what Zeami describes as *yūgen* in any particular location. Rather, it is an interactional phenomenon that is realized on the basis of a cluster of variables surrounding the sensibility and skill of the performer, the nature of the performance space, the proclivities of the audience, and so on. This is not to say that the compositional model set down in *Sandō* is entirely subject to the contingencies of each particular performance and audience. While on the one hand Zeami's prototypical play is intended to open up the stage event to the signifying capacities of particular audiences and to leave room for individual interpretation, on the other hand, the performer does not relinquish his germinal role in the creation of a moving performance.

Zeami seems to assume that there are principles of performance that will tend to elicit results, no matter how eclectic one's audience. Linguistic, musical, choreographic, and mimetic elements are the tools of the performer. These elements must be grounded in the performer's mindfulness and his intuitions about how to best adapt to particular audiences. The responsibility for anticipating preconditions for inducing the eye-opening thus lies with the performer. In his late treatises, Zeami argues for embodied factors of universal application that underlie the actor's ability to read audiences. We will explore some of them in the final part of this volume. But first, the chapter that follows will focus on the play that Zeami gives as his exemplar in *Sandō*—*Takasago*—in order to explore whether he actually practices his own precepts on composing plays, and if so, how he applies them to composing on the *shūgen* theme.

5

. . .

Zeami's Theory in Practice

AN ANALYSIS OF THE *WAKI* PLAY *TAKASAGO*

Sandō is Zeami's primer on the techniques for creating noh plays on the basis of the two modes and the three styles, and its most concrete discussions involve plays featuring the venerable style. In the segment on the martial style (2.3) he does specify that the warrior play should be constructed in five *dan*, but he qualifies this by stating that because "the image of the warrior depends on the authentic source, the mode of writing cannot be uniformly prescribed." His description of the feminine style in the prior segment (2.2) is even more general. He stresses the centrality of dance and chant in plays of that group but fails to put forth an overall model for their implementation. Rather, he gives piecemeal structural stipulations that are subordinated to descriptions of desirable types of kernel figures. In contrast, his prescriptions for the venerable style are very specific. In Segment 1.3 of *Sandō*, on structuring a play, this type serves as his exemplar, and in Segment 2.1, which is devoted to the venerable style, Zeami describes his prototype for a two-act play in the most detail.

He notes that the role of the old man is most suited to plays belonging to the *waki* classification. It will be recalled that *waki* literally means "side," and the term *waki sarugaku* refers to the play in the program that is "beside," or immediately after, the ritual opener, *Shikisanban*, which was then standard to the beginning of a noh program. Therefore, in its original usage, this

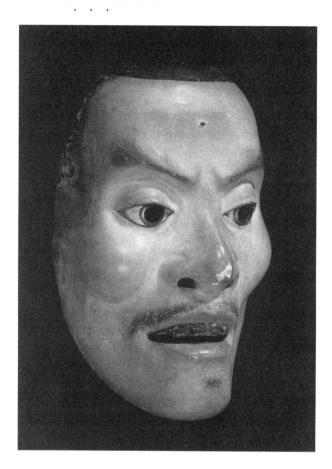

Figure 8 *Ayakashi* mask. Attributed to the Yamato artist Chigusa (14th–15th c.). This type of mask was first employed to represent young, vigorous Shintō deities such as the Sumiyoshi deity in Act 2 of *Takasago*. Today it is more commonly used for male ghosts, both warriors and common people. It was passed down in the Kongō troupe, and legend has it that the mask's features resemble those of Emperor Kanmu (737–806). (Courtesy of Mitsui Bunko, Tokyo.)

classification was the first full play of the day to follow *Shikisanban*. Defining characteristics of Zeami's *waki* play are that it has a deity as its protagonist and treats auspicious material. The protagonist typically appears in the guise of an old man in the lengthier first act, to reappear in his true identity in the concluding act. Indeed, this is the structural model that Zeami outlines in both Segments 1.3 and 2.1.[1]

Of the representative plays in the venerable style that he enumerates in segment 3.5, four belong to the *waki* category: *Yawata* (*Yumi Yawata*, The bow of Yawata), *Aioi* (*Takasago*), *Yōrō* (Longevity springs), and *Oimatsu* (Aged pine). Plays of this classification tend to feature public themes and devote less attention to nuanced depictions of the emotions such as are found in plays classified in the other two stylistic groupings introduced in *Sandō*—warrior and woman plays. Zeami did, however, choose to introduce

the *waki* plays in the greatest detail in *Sandō,* and for that reason examining a *waki* play here seems the most efficacious way to explore how he practices his own precepts as set down in that treatise. Of the four exemplary
waki plays mentioned by Zeami, the second in the list, *Aioi* (today titled
Takasago) is the play to which he alludes in the course of his discussion on
how to compose a play based on the venerable style (Segment 2.1). This
chapter will explore how he applies the techniques of material, structuring,
and composing in the context of this play.

This emphasis on *waki* plays also sheds light on Zeami's developing
conception of the ideal scheme of a performance, as well as on his thinking on how to train a playwright. For these reasons, before moving to analysis of *Takasago* itself, we will explore some of the factors underlying the
emphasis Zeami places in *Sandō* on composing plays belonging to the *waki*
category. A good starting point for exploring these issues is an enigma
posed by *Sandō*. Whereas the culminating segment of that transmission is
devoted to the advocacy of a style of performance having *yūgen,* Zeami does
not attribute this quality to *waki* plays.[2] If the kind of artistic effect that
plays of the *waki* classification are supposed to foster is not directly associated with what he then considered the ultimate stage effect, the atmosphere
of *yūgen,* then why does he concentrate on precepts for composing *waki*
plays in *Sandō?* Why does he not choose to highlight those plays that he
associates with *yūgen*—plays about women?

In order to discover Zeami's rationale for devoting so much of *Sandō* to
the ostensibly non-*yūgen* style of the *waki* play, it is important to examine
how he treats the *waki* play in relation to the other plays in a program, such
as those that he credits with *yūgen* effects. Each play is part of the larger
whole of the program. He not only construed the configuration of the two
modes and three styles as a guiding principle for the playwright as he plotted
the infrastructure of individual plays, but he also saw it as having bearing
on the interface between different types of plays in a program. With the
introduction of this configuration into the compositional process, all classifications of plays were made to adhere to a basic style composed of danced
and chanted elements, but from that baseline the three styles of representation (venerable, martial, and feminine) and their derivatives might
vary. Moreover, in Zeami's view, each of these styles was appropriate for a
certain place in a day's program of plays, a point that we will now explore
in more detail. Doing so will also afford us another glimpse at the shift in
his thinking on how to best create the atmosphere of *yūgen* onstage: that

its evocation is part of a larger process involving the cumulative chemistry produced as the larger program of plays unfolds.

The Function of the *Waki* Play in a Program

Some of Zeami's most revealing statements in his transmissions about the role he thought the *waki* play should fulfill in a program of plays occur in the course of his discussions related to the paradigm of *jo-ha-kyū*. In Segment 1.3 of *Sandō*, for instance, he assigns the *waki* play to the *jo* phase of a day's program. In *Kashu no uchinukigaki*, a very brief transmission written five years prior to *Sandō*, he offers the following, more detailed characterization of the play in the *jo* phase of a performance program, that is, the *waki* play.

> Since *jo* constitutes the beginning, it means that it is the foundation. As such, it has a configuration that is correct and "up front."[3] In *sarugaku*, the *waki* play corresponds to the *jo* phase [of a program]. The play should be straightforward[4] without too much detail; it should be auspicious, and should have overtones [kakari] that flow correctly.[5] The acting [waza] should consist entirely of chant and dance. Chant and dance are the most basic elements[6] in this calling. Therefore, noh plays situated in the *jo* phase should be based on chant and dance.[7]

The *waki* play fulfills an introductory function in a day's program and, as such, should progress smoothly, without embellishment. It should be auspicious in tone. Of particular interest is the connection that Zeami makes between a correct, straightforward compositional style and the predominance of the two modes of dance and chant. The *waki* play, based on the foundation elements of dance and chant, should, in turn, form the foundation of the day's program.

In the third chapter of *Kaden*, written eighteen years prior to the passage above from *Kashu no uchinukigaki*, he makes similar reference to the basic attributes of *waki* plays, stating,

> First, in the case of *waki* noh, [the play] should have a truly authentic[8] foundation story, and should have refinement, but it should not be that detailed; the music and movement should be staged in the usual way, and it should be performed with smoothness and ease.[9]

The first [play in a program] should be auspicious. No matter how
fine a *waki* play may be, it must not lack auspicious [elements]. Even
if the play is a bit second-rate, if it is auspicious, there shouldn't be
a problem. This is because it [occupies] the *jo* [position]. When it
comes to the second and the third plays [in a program], you should
make them the finest plays, with stage action that shows off your
strengths. Since the last [play][10] occupies the *kyū* [position], [here]
especially you should pick up the pace and insert [technically impres-
sive] moves.[11]

Although the general import of these two passages, written eighteen years
apart, does not differ significantly, there is one telling contrast in emphasis. "Music and movement" are treated as important components of performance in the older *Kaden* passage, but the idea expressed in *Kashu no
uchinukigaki* that "chant and dance are the most basic elements" (*kabu wa
kono michi no hontai naru beshi*) had not yet crystallized in the earlier writing.[12] This theory evolved in Zeami's middle years with his development of
the two modes and three styles configuration. *Kashu no uchinukigaki* may be
regarded as a precursor of the more fully developed discussion of that configuration, elaborated for the first time two years later in *Shikadō*.

The notion that a *waki* play should draw on source material and should
be executed in a smooth and uncomplicated way is consistent across the two
documents. Zeami's idea that a play does not need to be a masterpiece as
long as it is auspicious in mood seems to continue on into his middle
period. In the sixth chapter of *Kaden*, undated but probably written between 1408 and 1412, he characterizes plays that are superior and plays that
are second best.

As for noh of fine caliber, when a play has an authentic foundation
story, stage action having novelty, climactic points, and the artistic
effect [*kakari*][13] of *yūgen*, then it may be assigned to the first level.
When a play has stage action that does not inspire [a sense of] novelty, but [the play] does not have glaring flaws either, and it flows in
a straightforward manner and has points that inspire interest, then
it may be assigned to the second level.[14]

The first ranking of plays, having novelty, interesting stage action, and the
"artistic effect [*kakari*] of *yūgen*," seems to overlap with his provisions for

waki plays in one attribute only, the exploitation of an "authentic foundation story." However, the second-rate play, conspicuous neither for its flaws nor its strengths but straightforward and solid, seems to correspond more closely to his description of the *waki* play in *Kashu no uchinukigaki*.

Further on in the passage from *Kashu no uchinukigaki* he states the following about plays that should follow the *waki* play in a day's program.

> The second play [in the program] should have stage action[15] that differs from that of *waki sarugaku*; the foundation story should be authentic, and [the play] should have strength as well as refinement. This [classification] has stage action that differs from *waki* noh, but it should not yet get [too] detailed, and since it is not [yet] the time to exert all of your skill, this too is still part of the *jo* [phase].[16]
>
> As of the third play, [the program] moves into the *ha* [phase]. [The Chinese character for] *ha* [破] [also] is used to write ヤブル [lit. "to break"].[17] This means that the straightforward, correct form of the foundation style that makes up the *jo* phase moves into a more detailed [style]. *Jo* consists of the thing in its unaltered state; *ha* consists of softening and adding explanation to that. This being the case, in the third play, the moves should be more detailed, with stage action that has *monomane* [elements]. This should be the most important play of the day.[18]

In the prototypical program, the second play of the day should be in the martial style—a warrior play. It should not yet have the detail typical of the feminine or gentle style of the play slated to follow as the third entry in the program. That which is straightforward in plays belonging to the *jo* phase should be broken down, softened, and elaborated in the third play of the day. Annotators of the passage *"wa shite chū suru shaku no gi"* (consists of softening and adding explanation), concur that it refers to making the material more readily understandable. As noted in NSTS, the phrase connotes the idea of annotations in Japanese affixed to Chinese classics and Buddhist sources in Chinese to make their content more accessible, or "softer," to Japanese readers.[19] The idea that the third play in the program should have exposition that is more detailed than what has preceded is reiterated in the ensuing portion of this same passage of *Kashu no uchinukigaki*, quoted in its entirety below. I have underlined the relevant passage.

In the fourth play, it is particularly desirable to have stage action such as that in *giri* noh,[20] [which exploits the verbal dimension] in question and answer or argumentation; or such as that in tearful *sarugaku*.[21] The fourth and fifth plays still belong to the *ha* [phase].

Kyū refers to the finale. Since this is the parting phase [of the program], it constitutes the last of the stage action.[22] The overall image of the *ha* [phase] involves the breaking down of the *jo* [phase], the detailed rendering of various elements,[23] and the full showing of things.[24] *Kyū* is that phase in which the [effects of the] full actualization of the *ha* [phase] still linger. Therefore, the pace should be intensified in *kyū* with eye-catching action, such as fast dancing (*ranbu*)[25] or vigorous moves (*hataraki*). Intensifying the pace is the style called for at this point.[26]

The *ha* phase differs from the *jo* phase in that it is not straightforward, but detailed and more explicit, as well as being less rapid than the ensuing *kyū* phase of the program. Zeami does not provide concrete amplification of his characterizations of the three phases, but from this skeletal outline, several points do become clear. The dramatic effects of the detailed *ha* phase of a program are premised on a less detailed *jo* phase preceding it and establishing the foundation for the *ha* phase. He states that *jo* is the thing in its unaltered state, the only concrete information being that it should be based on chant and dance. *Ha* softens *jo*, adding explanation; the only concrete specifics provided are that the stage action should be more detailed, having more *monomane* elements.

What Zeami seems to be saying here is that writing plays for the *ha* phase of a program involves preserving the basics, chant and dance, but building on them by the insertion of more mimetic scenes. Whereas the two modes are accorded the central place in the straightforward foundation style that typifies the *jo* phase, representational elements (*monomane*) are aligned with the more detailed or involved structure that belongs to plays of the *ha* phase, typically plays in the feminine style. Moreover, with the addition of such mimetic elements, plays in the *ha* phase in the program would correspond to the standards that he argues noh of fine caliber should possess: novel stage action, climaxes, and "the artistic effect [*kakari*] of *yūgen*."

Zeami's reference to *ha* as a softened form of *jo* is a new note implying an integral structural relationship between plays in the *jo* and *ha* phases of a program. Implied is that the original dance and chant characteristic of the auspicious play are interpenetrated by *monomane* techniques, such that *ha* not only succeeds *jo* in temporal sequence, but also diversifies the basic structure of *jo* while building on it to create a composite of vocal, choreographic, and mimetic techniques. The *ha* play should build on the *jo* play. *Monomane*-based elements should build on a ground composed of the two modes of dance and chant.

The *Waki* Play: Training Ground for the Playwright

How, then, is the young playwright to be instructed in the writing of plays that promote the ideal *yūgen* resonance? If *Sandō* is any proof, Zeami saw that process, too, as incremental. The prerequisite for composing plays with complex action, or *monomane* scenes, was mastery of composition of the more basic style of play, in which dance and chant were the primary elements. We have already seen that in the realm of acting, the acquisition of techniques conducive to a *yūgen* atmosphere—that is, the acquisition of skill in the two modes and three styles—is treated as incremental. As noted in part 1 of this volume, *Shikadō* states that the actor's training should proceed in two major phases. First should come mastery of dance and chant, and only after that should training in the three styles of *monomane* ensue. The evidence points to a correlation between Zeami's pedagogical approach to composing in *Sandō* and to the training of the actor as described in *Shikadō*. Since dance and chant are the fundamental elements of noh plays of the *waki* type, it is *waki* noh that he introduces in the most detail. Once the playwright has grasped the means of composing texts that assure the centrality of the two modes, he may insert such *monomane* action as the fall of a Genpei warrior or "Lady Rokujō casting her curse on Lady Aoi" into that infrastructure. As his style of dramaturgy matures, he comes to treat the *waki* play as a prerequisite for cultivating skills in writing plays in other styles. Moreover, the ability to compose a *waki* play is a prerequisite for composing on more explicitly *yūgen* themes, such as plays about gentle characters.

Zeami's idea that the auspicious style of play should serve as the foundation on which other styles should build is corroborated by ideas that he later develops in such transmissions as *Go on* regarding the acquisition of skill in five basic styles of chanting. It will be recalled that these five styles correspond to five sorts of themes: auspiciousness *(shūgen)*, *yūkyoku* (a vocal piece expressly on the *yūgen* theme),[27] passionate longing *(renbo)*, lamentation *(aishō)*, and pieces of seasoned fluency *(rangyoku)*. In this paradigm, too, the foundation style is that of the auspicious mode. Moreover, each of the other four modes builds on the technical mastery of the preceding style of chant. We will concentrate on the two styles that concern us here, auspiciousness and *yūkyoku*, as well as on their interrelation. Zeami describes the most basic style in the following.

> Auspicious [chant] consists of tones that are tranquil and happy. It is straightforward, flows with ease, and the overtones *[kakari]* are those of a voice belonging to a well-managed [age].[28]

We have seen auspicious *waki* plays described as "straightforward" and smoothly flowing in the passage quoted above. What is new in this passage is Zeami's allusions to the definition of poetry offered in the "Great Preface" of the *Shijing*. In chapter 4 it was noted that Zeami alludes to the *Shijing* to bolster his definition of the themes of lamentation *(aishō)* and desolation *(bōoku)*: "The tones of a ruined state are filled with lament and brooding." Similarly, in his characterization of the auspiciousness theme, "Tones that are tranquil and happy *(anraku on)*" and "voice belonging to a well-managed [age]" *(chisei)* suggest the following line from the "Great Preface," which Zeami also quotes further on in *Go ongyoku jōjō*: "The tones of a well-managed age are at rest and happy; its government is balanced." Here, too, Zeami borrows the authority of the original discussion of the regulatory function of poetry.[29]

The *yūkyoku* mode, in turn, takes chant in the *shūgen* style as its foundation. This idea appears to originate with Zeami.

> In the *yūkyoku* mode, artistic effect *[kakari]* is added to the preexisting auspicious mode. Make the voice supple, bury [technical display of] the modulation, make the surface beautiful yet correct in how it flows. It is like viewing blossoms and moon in the evening and at dawn, all at once. In terms of substance and function, make the function your substance, and bury the [original] substance.[30]

Nose's exegesis of this passage is helpful. First, he reminds us of exemplars that Zeami uses elsewhere[31] to illustrate the relation between substance and function. Whereas the moon may be likened to substance, moonlight corresponds to function; a flower constitutes substance, whereas its fragrance is its function. Similarly, Nose says, in vocal music, the modulations on which the melodic line is based would constitute substance, whereas the artistic effect (*kakari*) produced by the melodic line would correspond to its function. Therefore, in the *yūkyoku* mode of chant, melodic modulation should remain the underlying foundation for the chant but should not appear to be so. The beauty of artistic effect (*kakari*)—that is, the overall effect of the flow of the chant—actually constitutes the function, but in the *yūkyoku* mode those elements should be brought to the fore such that they appear to be the substance of the chant.

At the level of training, both in the domains of chanting and acting, and as we are arguing here, in composing, Zeami advocates that the composite style replete with *yūgen* effects should not be the first step in the regimen. In *Go ongyoku jōjō*, he describes the auspicious style as the most basic and the style of seasoned fluency as the most advanced, requiring the skill of a master. At this level, the chanter has so internalized the requisite skills of the art that he can perform without conscious reference to them. Until he reaches that point, however, the training process is an incremental one. It is impossible to recapture the actual nature of these modes in performance, but one theoretical analogue with the dynamics of composing plays is clear: the *yūgen* style builds on that of *shūgen*, yet modifies or hones the original basic structure. In both domains, a *yūgen* style embodies a composite in which the foundation style of *shūgen* is tempered by additional elements that "soften," "beautify," and elicit artistic effect (*kakari*).

In his study titled *Nō no kenkyū*, Kanai notes that there are no extant plays attributed to Motoyoshi, Zeami's son and the recipient of *Sandō*, and on that basis speculates that Motoyoshi was not gifted as a playwright. For that reason, Kanai argues, Zeami deliberately restricted his instructions in *Sandō* to only the most rudimentary compositional principles, omitting some of his most outstanding works of the woman category, such as *Izutsu*, from his listing of sample plays.[32] There is one persuasive historical reason for this omission of *Izutsu* in particular from the *Sandō* listing, the fact that Zeami mentions the play only in the later transmission, *Sarugaku dangi*. This would seem to indicate that it had not been written when *Sandō* was composed in 1423. However, Kanai's general assertion that Zeami would not have written *Sandō* at all if Motoyoshi had already mastered the art of playwriting remains a plausible one. Although Kanai feels that Zeami abandoned all hope of inculcating the skills necessary for producing words of *yūgen* caliber in Motoyoshi, I think it equally likely that Zeami's detailed instructions on *waki* noh were intended as the first step in a carefully considered training program that guided the novice playwright toward a *yūgen* style of composition by increments.

The Three Techniques of Composition and the *Waki* Play *Takasago*

Just as the *waki* play offered the novice playwright a gateway for developing the basic skills for composing plays, it also offers us a laboratory for exploring Zeami's implementation of the *nikyoku santai* configuration at its incipient stages. Choosing *Takasago* over other works of the *waki* category follows the example of *Sandō*, for, as mentioned earlier, it is to *Takasago* that Zeami alludes in his description of plays featuring the venerable style (Segment 2.1). *Takasago* is generally considered to be the celebratory play par excellence and remains one of the most frequently performed of the *waki* plays.

In *Takasago*, Zeami provides the basic template on which to build in creating a *mugen* play in two acts. By examining the compositional principles in practice, a variety of points can be clarified. What, for instance, is meant by "straightforward structure"? What in the nature of the *waki* play lends itself to dance and chant? And how should text, music, and dance coexist in particular? The following analysis of *Takasago* is intended to provide the concreteness that is needed to address such questions.

We will begin with a short synopsis of the action of *Takasago* in accordance with Zeami's five-*dan* scheme. Stage directions in the following analysis are based on the contemporary ones. There are no extant directions contemporaneous with Zeami. I have not attempted to reconstruct past staging but have chosen to follow the modern stage directions as recorded in *Yōkyoku shū*, vol. 1, in Nihon Koten Bungaku Taikei 40. For a translation of *Takasago*, the reader is referred to appendix 2 of this volume.[33]

. . .

Dan I

The *waki* and *wakizure* (companions to the *waki*) enter down the bridgeway (*hashigakari*) and onto the stage. The *waki* is a Shintō priest from a prominent shrine in faraway Kyushu who is journeying to the capital of Kyoto to see the sights. The *wakizure*, who usually number two today, form his entourage. In the course of the traveling chant, they trace their route from Kyushu to the setting of the first act, Takasago Bay. Takasago Bay is located on the coast of the former province of Harima, which is now a part of Hyōgo Prefecture.

Dan II

The *shite*, an old man, and the *tsure* (companion to the *shite*), an old woman, enter down the bridgeway. The *shite* holds a rake and the *tsure* a broom.[34] They establish themselves as regular visitors to the Takasago shore and begin to sweep the needles from under a pine tree nearby.

Dan III

The *waki* questions the two about the famous legend of the wedded pine trees, one located on Takasago Bay and the other across the bay on the shore of Sumiyoshi, an area that was then part of Settsu Province and is now part of Osaka Prefecture. He wishes to know which pine corresponds to that of the legend and how the two pines came to be called the wedded pines. The old couple identify the very pine they are tending as the famed tree and explain that the story of the wedded pines hails from the "Kana Preface" (Kana jo) to the first imperial anthology of *waka* poems, the *Kokin shū*. The *waki* does not find it strange that pine trees should have spirits capable of mutual affection, but he does question the likelihood of such a union between two trees so distanced from each other. The *tsure* rebukes him with

How foolish	*Utate no*
what you say,	*ōsezōrō ya,*
may they be divided	*sansen banri o*
by mountains and rivers	*hedatsuredomo*
two caring hearts	*tagai ni kayou*
will make the passage,	*kokorozukai no*
for the path shared by man and wife	*imose no michi mo*
is never far.	*tōkarazu.*

Dan IV

Shite, tsure, and chorus extol the virtues of the pine tree and of *waka* poetry. Finally, when queried about their identities, the *shite* and *tsure* reveal that they are the spirits of the wedded pine trees, he the pine of Sumiyoshi, she the pine of Takasago.

Figure 9 The spirit of the Sumiyoshi pine tree, the *shite* of *Takasago* (Act 1). Rhythmic exchange *(rongi)* at the end of the act. The *shite* is pointing in the direction of Sumiyoshi Shrine and urging the *waki* to board a boat and follow him there. Actor: Sekine Tomotaka, Kanze school (performance variant: *Hachidan no mai*). (Courtesy of the photographer, Maejima Yoshihiro)

Urging the priest to follow them across the bay to Sumiyoshi, the two exit down the bridge way. Here the first act concludes.

[Interlude: a *kyōgen* performer (classical comedy) takes center stage. Cast as a resident of the place, he reiterates the legend of the two pines for the benefit of the *waki*, who has remained onstage.]

Dan V

The *waki* boards an imaginary boat, which bears him to Sumiyoshi. The *shite* of the second act, which is set at Sumiyoshi, is a deity of Sumiyoshi Shrine who enters alone down the bridgeway as a young male.[35] He praises the realm and performs a lively dance of celebration for the *waki*. Here the play ends.

. . .

Zeami exploits the imagery of the pine tree at multiple levels to achieve an auspicious message of considerable complexity. By itself, the pine tree is a traditional symbol of longevity, and the image of two wedded pines juxtaposes with this symbolism the theme of conjugal devotion. Moreover, the legend of the wedded pines of Takasago and Sumiyoshi springs from a famed reference to them by the poet Ki no Tsurayuki (868?–945?) in his "Kana Preface" to the *Kokin shū*. Zeami builds on that reference to weave the theme of the illustriousness of the Japanese poetic tradition into the play.

In *Sarugaku dangi*, Zeami compares *Takasago* to another of his *waki* plays, *Yumi Yawata*. Whereas he calls *Yumi Yawata* a straightforward work, he describes *Takasago* as a play "with fins," ostensibly a reference to embellishments beyond the absolute basics of the *waki* model. Since Zeami does not himself specify what he means by this singular metaphor, the "fins" remain a subject of perennial debate, but it is highly likely that the multiplicity of thematic material characteristic of *Takasago* accounts for at least one of them.[36] The remainder of this chapter will explore *Takasago* on the basis of the three techniques put forth in *Sandō*: the development of the play's material, its structure, and its lines.

TAKASAGO: THE WAY OF THE MATERIAL

Although Zeami's play is referred to as *Takasago* in records dating as far back as the 1450s, the title was not of his own making.[37] *Aioi* is the title that he chose and that appears in the listing of plays found in Segment 3.5 of

Sandō. No one knows why the play was renamed. Perhaps the revision was made in the spirit of one basic precept stated in Segment 1.4 of *Sandō*: "In noh, there should be a setting associated with the source material." Takasago Bay, the setting for the first act, was a site canonized by Ki no Tsurayuki's reference to it in the "*Kana* Preface" to the *Kokin shū*.[38] Yet Sumiyoshi, a still more familiar spot in the *waka* tradition, is the setting of the second act, and therefore Takasago makes up only half of the story.

The title *Aioi*, however, gets right to the thematic crux of the play and reproduces in a nutshell the complexity of its theme. *Aioi* is a play on words. As a sound unit it embraces two sets of homonyms and, consequently to the ear, a dual denotation. In their written forms, the meaning of the two homonyms is readily distinguishable, for each is customarily encoded in a different combination of Chinese characters. In both compounds *"ai"* constitutes the reading of the Chinese character meaning "union" or "conjunction." However, the characters for *"oi"* differ. In the first instance, *"oi"* denotes "growth" (相生) and in the second "aging" (相老). The combination of the characters for "union" and "growth" results in a compound denoting "growing together," whereas combining the character for "union" with the character for "aging" results in a compound meaning "growing old together."

The complex texture of imagery on which the play depends is encapsulated in Zeami's chosen title. The pine trees are united in their growth; a man and a woman are united in their lives. The two coexistent threads wind throughout the first act of the play until, in the rhythmic exchange (*rongi*) that closes the first act, they become intertwined as the *shite* and *tsure* chant in unison.

Now what have we	*Ima wa nani o ka*
to conceal?	*tsutsumu beki*
One of Takasago and	*Kore wa Takasago*
the other Sumiyoshi,	*Suminoe no*
we are the spirits	*Aioi no*
of the wedded pines	*matsu no sei*
come before you	*Fūfu to genji*
as man and wife.	*kitaritari.*

Zeami was aware that one layer of the *"aioi"* image would have literary associations for his audience. As noted above, the notion of the wedded pines of Takasago and Sumiyoshi may be traced to perhaps the most authentic of sources in the *waka* tradition, the "*Kana* Preface" to the *Kokin shū*.[39] This preface is sweeping in its scale. Much more than an introduction to a collection of poems, it is at once an account of the origins of the *waka* form and a critique of accomplished poets in that tradition. Moreover, the preface also represents an attempt to canonize the spirit behind the poetic impulse. It succeeds so well that it has been viewed by centuries of *waka* poets as the rhetorical fountainhead of Japanese poetry.

The "*Kana* Preface" opens with remarks on the cosmological significance of poetic expression.

> The seeds of Japanese poetry lie in the human heart and grow into leaves of ten thousand words. Many things happen to the people of this world, and all that they think and feel is given expression in description of things they see and hear. When we hear the warbling of the mountain thrush in the blossoms or the voice of the frog in the water, we know every living being has its song.
>
> It is poetry which, without effort, moves heaven and earth, stirs the feelings of the invisible gods and spirits, smooths the relations of men and women, and calms the hearts of fierce warriors.[40]

The act of poetic creation is the act of expressing through sensual images the myriad reflections that stir the mind. Moreover, all sentient beings, from the humblest insects to the deities, are susceptible to poetry. Implied is that poetry is more than an entertaining activity, for a poem is capable of purifying the spirit and of restoring the natural balance that pervades all beings.[41]

This idea of a fundamental well-being that informs all beings and that in its purest form is tantamount to poetic sensitivity is the underlying assumption of *Takasago*. Its most overt expression comes in the *kuse* section, which echoes Tsurayuki's idea.

Grass, trees, earth, and sand,	*Sōmoku dosha*
the voice of the wind,	*Fūsei*
the sound of the water,	*suion made*
all things are imbued	*Banbutsu no komoru*
with poetic feeling.	*kokoro ari.*

That two pine trees should have hearts does not strain belief, given such a premise. Moreover, such an idea was a familiar one to *sarugaku* audiences, since it was not unusual for plays to feature the spirits of plants.[42] In the second *dan*, the spirits go on to recite,

in the frosty spring night,	*okii ni mo*
the wind in the pines	*Matsukaze o nomi*
the sole accustomed sound.	*kikinarete*
Our hearts companions,	*Kokoro o tomo to*
on a mat of sedge	*sugamushiro no*
we share our thoughts,	*omoi o noburu*
that is all.	*bakari nari.*

The prevailing impression made by the ancient pair greeting dawn is their attunement with each other and their surroundings.

Of the many auspicious images recorded in the "*Kana* Preface," the pine tree is particularly replete with literary associations, and perhaps this is one reason Zeami chose the pines as the subject for a noh play. Along with Tsurayuki's "*Kana* Preface," he draws on a range of other sources, such as the Chinese classic *Shiji* (Historical records), compiled by Sima Qian (145?–86? B.C.E.), the imperial anthology of *waka* poems titled *Senzai waka shū* (Collection of waka poems of a thousand years; ca. 1188), and the Japanese anthology of poems in Japanese and Chinese titled *Wakan rōei shū* (Japanese and Chinese poems to sing; ca. 1013). Furthermore, the site of Sumiyoshi also had literary associations that were integral to the overall conception of the play. A place-name frequently quoted in *waka*, Sumiyoshi is also the location of the celebrated Sumiyoshi Shrine, whose deities were worshiped as the protectors of the entire *waka* tradition.[43] As we know, the apparition of a god in the second act of the *waki* play is an established convention, and the link with Sumiyoshi was a felicitous one in that regard. Although the spirit of the pine tree at Sumiyoshi has been canonized in Tsurayuki's "*Kana* Preface," nothing in that tract explicitly links the pine tree spirit to Sumiyoshi Shrine itself. Rather, the *shite's* transformation into the god of Sumiyoshi Shrine in the second act of *Takasago* is rendered credible by audience foreknowledge of the connection between the shrine and the *waka* tradition.[44]

Useful as the original "*Kana* Preface" was in the formulation of *Takasago*, several of the important elements of Zeami's version of the legend are notably lacking in that source. Zeami likens the Takasago pine to the eighth-century poetic anthology *Man'yō shū* (Collection of ten thousand leaves) and the Sumiyoshi pine to the *Kokin shū* of the tenth century; Tsurayuki is silent on this subject. Moreover, the notion of *aioi* in its meaning of "growing together" is redefined in *Takasago*. It is not the oneness between the poet and the pine trees that is stressed, but rather the oneness shared by the "wedded pines" themselves.

Although it is tempting to credit Zeami with these innovations, such was not the case. By Zeami's time, a body of critical commentaries of the Heian classics had come into being, and there is evidence that the prevailing conception of the "*Kana* Preface" held by Zeami's contemporaries owed more to such commentaries than to the preface itself. This is equally true for the content of *Takasago*. The following commentary is judged to be a work of the Kamakura period, titled *Kokin waka shū jo kikigaki (Sanryūshō)*.[45] (The author situates his persona in the imaginary time frame of the preceding Heian period.)

> Takasago stands for the creation in times past of the *Man'yō shū* by Emperor Kanmu and his court, which caused the path of the *waka* to flourish. Sumiyoshi stands for our own august emperor of the Engi era (901–923), commissioning Tsurayuki and other poets to create the *Kokin waka shū*, which caused the path of the *waka* to flourish. As for the pine tree, just as the needles of the pine are long enduring, so it is for the *waka*. "Growing together" means that in olden times and in the present reign of the Engi era alike, this path has been highly esteemed.

In the heightened exchange *(kakeai)* in the third *dan* of *Takasago*, the *shite* and *tsure* virtually echo these words.

> What men of old said is this, they exemplify an auspicious realm. The pine tree at Takasago stands for a past age when the *Man'yō shū* came into being. The pine of Sumiyoshi for the present age, the illustrious reign of the Engi emperor. Pine needles, like leaves of words, never run out, they prosper past and present ever the same, a metaphor in praise of this revered reign.

Zeami's specific source is unknown, but unquestionably his play was influenced by material from *Kokin waka shū jo kikigaki (Sanryūshō)* or a closely related member of this corpus of medieval commentaries.[46] As a result, his treatment of the legendary pine trees simultaneously fulfills two of his precepts on the technique of the material. By claiming the tenth-century poetic classic as his inspiration, he claims the most esteemed of authentic sources. Yet by implementing a medieval interpretation of this material, whether consciously or not, he also applies his precept that material should be previously familiar to audiences.

Although both the commentary and the play convey the same basic information, there is a shift in emphasis. Whereas the *Kokin waka shū jo kikigaki (Sanryūshō)* stresses the illustriousness of *waka* poetry itself, in *Takasago* the tone of praise of the realm and rejoicing dominates. In the latter it is thanks to the prosperity of the realm that pine trees and poetry flourish. Zeami's emphasis on celebration in the present is of course in keeping with the theme of auspiciousness that he ascribes to the *waki* play. The dramatic present of *Takasago* is the Engi era, a period viewed nostalgically by Muromachi literati as the golden age of Japanese letters. The dramatic past is the eighth century, a hazier period that was popularly credited with the first flowering of Japanese poetry in the form of the *Man'yō shū*. The image of the pine trees, constant and enduring, is used here as a device to fuse the dramatic past and present. Moreover, Zeami exploits that image to extend the time continuum by implication into the actual present of his audience as well. Although the play is ostensibly about the dramatic present of the Engi years, this notion of unending prosperity is equally applicable to the actual present—that is, the age of his Ashikaga patrons—elevating it to the same status as the two golden ages of the past. As Sanari has noted, to praise the poetic tradition amounted to revering the emperor and celebrating the realm.[47]

Zeami's most creative manipulation of the material has yet to be mentioned, however. He was confronted with the task of transforming the images of the two pine trees into three-dimensional figures for the stage, a problem he solves by using the technique of personification. The introduction of the spirit of the pines in the human form of an elderly couple appears to be his innovation on this tale. In *Kokin waka shū jo kikigaki (Sanryūshō)*, for instance, the exposition develops in a manner similar to the spoken exchange in the third *dan* of *Takasago*. In both cases, the "Kana

Preface" is first established as the source for the pine tree legend, and then the legend is challenged. In the commentary, the challenge goes as follows.

> **Question:** Takasago is in Harima, and Sumiyoshi is in the province of Settsu. There is a distance of three days between them. How can those pines be growing together? It does not make sense.

> **Answer:** In fact, the story is not true. It is a fictitious device for introducing an idea about which our school of poetry has an explanation.[48]

The discussion quoted earlier in this chapter concerning the relationship between the pine trees and the poetic anthologies then ensues. No mention is made of an elderly couple.

In *Takasago* as well the *waki* questions the *shite* about the plausibility of the "wedded pines," saying,

> The pines of Takasago and Sumiyoshi are known as the wedded pines. This place and Sumiyoshi are in separate provinces, so why are they named the wedded pines?

In the *shite*'s response, the information is given a new twist.

> It is stated in the "Preface" to the *Kokin shū* that the pines of Takasago and Sumiyoshi should be thought of as wedded pines. Be that as it may, this old man is from Sumiyoshi in Settsu Province; this old woman is a person of this place.

In midstream, the *shite* changes the subject to the elderly couple. The remainder of the spoken exchange (*mondō*) is devoted to their identities and their mutual devotion. It is only after the identities of the personified version of the pines have been introduced that Zeami moves to the heightened exchange in which he introduces the *Man'yō shū*/*Kokin shū* symbolism. Hence the twin pines symbolize the glories of the *waka* tradition and, by extension, the benevolence of the imperial house, an appropriately auspicious theme for a *waki* play and one that may boast the most revered of original sources. At the same time, the two new themes of conjugal devotion and human longevity are successfully introduced through the technique of personification.

In conclusion, it appears virtually certain that Zeami excerpted the analogy between the pine trees and the poetic anthologies from the *Kokin waka shū jo kikigaki (Sanryūshō)* or a similar poetic commentary. The similarities between the exposition of that commentary and *Takasago* are too close to be coincidental. That no mention of an old couple is made in any of the extant poetic commentaries of the age is also strong evidence that Zeami deliberately deviated from such material in order to add a more directly personal dimension to the pine tree legend. As Itō Masayoshi has noted, the absence of one source and the weaving together of several auspicious themes must be reasons that Zeami referred to this play as having "fins."[49] It should also be reiterated that despite his exhortations in his critical writings that a play have an original source or foundation story, the real inspiration for this play does not come from the original "*Kana* Preface" but from commentaries on it that are of medieval vintage.[50] Assuming that Zeami was aware of this difference, we may conclude that he set less stock in allusion to an authoritative text per se than he did to a story told in a way that was familiar to his audiences.

TAKASAGO: THE WAY OF STRUCTURING

In earlier chapters, the basic two-act, five-*dan* structure was introduced, and *Sandō*, Zeami's own primer on the subject, is provided in translation in appendix 1. But how do the principles of *waki* play structure apply to *Takasago*? We will next explore some of those structural attributes on a *dan-by-dan* basis. As is evident from the translation of the play in the appendix

First *Dan*

Component Part	Type of Chant	Performer(s)	Noh Action
Introductory Chant (*shidai*)	congruent (*hiranori*)	*waki* *wakizure*	announcement of departure from Kyushu
Name-Saying Speech (*nanori*)	intoned speech (*kotoba*)	*waki*	self-introduction
Traveling Chant (*michiyuki*)	congruent (*hiranori*)	*waki* *wakizure*	account of journey from Kyushu to Harima

of this volume, it faithfully follows the five-*dan* scheme that Zeami puts forth in Segment 2.2 of *Sandō*.

There are no discernible deviations from Zeami's *Sandō* model in the first *dan* of this play. Although in *Sandō* Zeami does not mention the presence of *wakizure*, they are normally cast in *waki* plays. Today there are usually two attendants, although four are also used on more formal occasions. In woman plays, the *waki* typically takes the identity of an itinerant Buddhist priest who enters alone, a presence conducive to the quieter, more introspective mood of plays in that category. In contrast, the *waki* play, coming at the head of the entire program, requires a stronger, more dignified atmosphere in keeping with the introductory *jo* phase. The *waki* play typically treats public themes, and the Shintō priest cast in the *waki* role is apt to be of illustrious social standing: one who identifies himself by name. This is the case in *Takasago*, in which the *waki* is a historical figure on record as having served in the Engi period as priest of the Aso Shrine in the province of Higo (present-day Kumamoto Prefecture) on the island of Kyushu.[51] This is in sharp contrast to the many itinerant Buddhist priests cast in the *waki* role of the woman plays, who remain nameless.

With the exception of the brief spoken passage of self-introduction (*nanori*), the entire *dan* progresses in passages of rhythmically congruent chant, or (as Zeami puts it) chant that progresses in syllables of 7-5-7-5. This emphasis on a fixed rhythmic scheme is consistent with his stipulation that the *jo* phase both of an entire program and of a given play should be direct and straightforward. Rhythmically congruent passages do not allow for as much individual vocal virtuosity on the part of the *shite* as do the non-congruent sections.

The section called the traveling chant (*michiyuki*) is particularly illustrative of the fluid use of imaginary space characteristic of the noh stage. According to the standard choreography of the play today, the *waki* and entourage enter wordlessly along the bridgeway to the instruments. They position themselves at the center of the bare stage, facing each other for the duration of the introductory chant. During the name-saying speech (*nanori*), the *waki* alone faces the audience, but turns back to face the *wakizure* for the traveling chant. Throughout the entire sequence, all figures remain stationary even as they accomplish their journey from the distant island of Kyushu to Takasago Bay. The transition is made through imaginary space by virtue of the telling. The traveling chant is in the high range and is perhaps the most vivid and developed of role chants performed by the *waki*.

Second *Dan*

Component Part	Type of Chant	Performer(s)	Noh Action
Entry Chant (*issei*)	noncongruent	*shite* *tsure*	description of Takasago Bay
Recitative (*sashi*)	noncongruent	*shite* *tsure*	reflections on themselves and their surroundings
Low-range Chant (*sageuta*)	congruent (*hiranori*)	*shite* *tsure*	preparation for task of sweeping needles
High-range Chant (*ageuta*)	congruent (*hiranori*)	*shite* *tsure*	*monomane* of sweeping needles, re-identification of site, praise of pine trees

In contrast to the introductory chant that opens the preceding *dan*, the *shite* and *tsure* enter on chant that is not rhythmically congruent. The entry chant (*issei*) starts and resolves in high tones and is replete with vocal embellishments that afford greater modulation than is typical in a chant that is bound to a fixed rhythm. In contemporary performance of *Takasago*, the *tsure* and the *shite* enter to the *shin-no-issei*, the instrumental music that is standard to the second *dan* of the *waki* play. The *shin-no-issei*, a variation on the standard entry music, is distinguishable by its extremely slow tempo. In today's staging, upon completing the entry chant, the couple remains motionless on the bridgeway to deliver the recitative (*sashi*), the low-range chant (*sageuta*), and the high-range chant (*ageuta*). The *shite* has appeared holding a rake, the *tsure* a broom. With the concluding lines of the high-range chant—" 'The Living Pines'/also from the distant past/a spot of renown"—the *shite* moves to stage center, the *tsure* to the front corner stage right, both gazing forward in the direction of the audience as they repeat the two final lines to bring closure to the *dan*.

In such fashion, the second *dan*, or the first of the three steps of the *ha* phase, is devoted entirely to the *shite* and *tsure*. The *dan* opens with the panoramic perspective of the whispering wind, the echoing bell, and the serenity of the Takasago shore on a spring evening. In the recitative, the tone grows more personal, to focus on the solitude and the gentle sensitivity of the aged couple who have passed so many years in that setting. Gradually, the perspective narrows to the shadows of the pine, as the two figures stand facing the audience, with rake and broom in hand while they chant.

In the shade of the pine,	*Ko no shitakage no*
the fallen needles	*ochiba*
we sweep	*kaku*
through lives	*Naru made inochi*
enduring	*nagaraete*

The shift from the panorama to the foreground consisting of the pine needles under the tree is effected on the bare stage. The poetic narration is much the verbal equivalent of a zoom lens. Such a progression from the large-scale to the small is characteristic of the narration in this portion of the play. The relation of the *shite* and *tsure* acting to the chanted line is a complex one. At the mimetic level, they continue their guise as an elderly couple at work clearing the pine needles from the shrine grounds. However, the poetic imagery that they have related in the chant prepares the spectator to see them metaphorically as well—as human emblems of the longevity of the pine tree and of the pristine natural setting in which the tree is enshrined.

In *Sandō*, Zeami addresses the importance of evoking visional affect (*kenpū*): the visual consummation of the import of the lines. He also stipulates that aural communication should precede visual. In *Sandō* he applies this principle to the infrastructure of the whole play, but he makes it clear elsewhere that it is equally applicable to smaller units, such as the *dan*. He reiterates this idea in more general terms in the fourth segment of his transmission titled *Kakyō*.

> If you appeal first to the ear of the audience and then time your visual expression to come slightly thereafter, that which has moved the ear will shift to the visual dimension, creating a sense of visional affect fulfilled.[52]

In the second *dan* of *Takasago*, the *shite* and *tsure*'s physical presence is contextualized by their chant in accordance with this principle. If it were not for that aural level of communication, then our sole visual impression would be that of two people readied to perform manual labor.

One further progression characteristic of Zeami's style of structuring a play is conspicuous in the second *dan*. Whereas in the opening sections of the *dan* the entry chant and the recitative are rhythmically noncongruent, the closing sections—the low-range chant and the high-range chant—are matched to the *hiranori* rhythmic scheme. We know that Zeami held that any unit of noh performance should embody the *jo-ha-kyū* progression. Within *Dan* II, the entry chant corresponds to the introductory *jo* phase, the recitative and the low-range chant to the developmental *ha* phase, and the more vivid chant in the high range to the climactic *kyū* phase of the dynamic. As the progression unfolds, the rhythmic tension builds. A device integral to sustaining that mounting tension is this progression from the noncongruent to the congruent rhythms. Moreover, this principle is manifested in each of the five *dan*. One important element of the interest of a noh in performance derives from such rhythmic transitions and the gradually strengthening tempos they induce.

Third *Dan*

Component Part	Type of Chant	Performer(s)	Noh Action
Spoken Exchange (*mondō*)	intoned speech (*kotoba*)	*waki*/*shite*	identification of legendary pine tree of Takasago
Heightened Exchange (*kakeai*)	noncongruent	*waki* *shite* *tsure*	account of legend of wedded pine trees and comparison with old couple
Heightened Exchange (*kakeai*)	noncongruent	*waki* *shite* *tsure*	establishment of correspondence between pine trees and poetic anthologies
High-range Chant (*ageuta*)	congruent (*hiranori*)	chorus	praise of the realm

The third *dan* is the one in which the *waki* and the old couple communicate for the first time. Again we see a progression from noncongruent to congruent chanting in the course of the development of the *dan*. The conversation between the *shite* and the *waki* commences in intoned speech (*kotoba*) and then shifts into a heightened exchange (*kakeai*: noncongruent chant of the recitative type). The *waki* breaks into this recitative (*sashi*) just at the point at which he reveals a deepening interest in the *shite* and *tsure*'s tale.

How strange indeed.	*Fushigi ya.*
You appear to be an elderly couple	*Mireba rōjin no*
together in this place	*fūfu to issho ni*

This noncongruent chant is then picked up by the *shite* and the *tsure* as well as they express their devotion and liken themselves to the ancient pines. The final passage rendered in unison by the *shite* and *tsure* comes to eight lines. The theme of this first of the heightened exchanges is succinctly summarized in its final lines.

Together with the pines are we	*matsu morotomo ni*
until this very age	*kono toshi made*
growing old together	*aioi no fūfu to*
as husband and wife.	*naru mono o.*

In Segment 2.1 of *Sandō*, Zeami allows for an extended exchange in which the aged couple "give the explanation of why something is the way it is." In *Takasago*, this section opens with the *waki*'s query about the pine trees and the setting.

About the wedded pines,	*aioi no matsu no*
isn't there more	*monogatari o*
to be told	*tokoro ni iioku*
in connection with this place?	*iware wa naki ka.*

Zeami cautions that this extended section should be relatively short. This final segment serves as the bridge from the *ha* to the *kyū* phase of the *dan*. As *shite* and *tsure* explain the imagery of the poetic anthologies, their exchanges grow increasingly brief, until with symphonic precision the tension mounts to the single line rendered in unison, "A metaphor in praise of this revered reign." The pattern of give-and-take goes as follows.

Shite	Tsure
A) two lines	———
B) ———	two lines
C) two lines	———
D) ———	one line
E) one line in unison	

The line in unison accomplishes a dual purpose: it signals a climax in the mounting dramatic and rhythmic tension and brings a momentary sense of resolution as the heightened exchange nears its close. That resolution is then fully realized through another sequence of exchanges, this time between the *waki* and the *shite*. The *waki* declares that he no longer doubts the word of the old couple and joins them in celebrating the scene. Again the give-and-take between the interlocutors grows briefer and more rhythmic.

WAKI:
Over there,   *Kashiko wa*
Sumiyoshi,   *Suminoe*

SHITE:
And here,   *koko wa*
Takasago   *Takasago*

WAKI:
their pines   *matsu mo*
blend in hue   *iro soi*

SHITE:
and spring too   *haru mo*
so tranquil.   *nodoka ni.*

The more discursive language that begins in the spoken exchange and continues through the first part of the first heightened exchange has grown gradually more condensed and prosodic as the relationship between *waki* and *shite* has transformed from one of mutual aloofness to one of mutual attunement with the larger surroundings. Moreover, the succinct language at the conclusion of this final exchange is destined as a bridge between the preceding noncongruent chant and the strictly congruent high-range chant that is to follow.

The chorus enters into the noh action for the first time in the ensuing high-range chant.[53] As Miyake Kōichi has pointed out, the chorus takes over when the preceding buildup of mutual emotional intensity has reached a climactic point.[54] It sustains that intensity and elaborates on it, but these goals are achieved not by further building of the already rapid tempo, but by tempering it. The pace is tempered by the weight of the choral voice and the balance inherent in the congruent *hiranori* scheme, such that both elements serve to deepen, not dilute, the emotional quality. In *Takasago* that quality is one of harmony and thanksgiving.

Upon the four seas	*Shikai nami*
the waves are serene,	*shizuka nite*
peace nurtured in the land	*Kuni mo osamaru*
by timely breezes	*tokitsukaze*
that rustle not the branches	*Eda o narasanu*
in so revered a reign.	*miyo nare ya*
And into such an age	*Ai ni aioi no*
the wedded pines	*matsu koso*
live on	*Medeta*
auspiciously.	*karikere.*

The scope at the close of *Dan* III is broad. It embraces all living things in the realm, and it treats the *shite* and the *tsure* as symbolic of all therein that is auspicious. As the chorus moves into the high-range chant, the *waki* seats himself and the *tsure* retreats to a spot upstage left in front of the chorus. At this point, *tsure* and *waki* characteristically fade into the background as the task of supporting the *shite* is shifted to the chorus.

The fourth *dan* of *Takasago* holds the *kuse* section, consisting of the *kuri*, the recitative (*sashi*), and the *kuse*. Although the *kuse* section is now an integral part of noh structure, coming characteristically in the third leg of the *ha* phase, it retains a highly integrated infrastructure. The content of the opening part of the *kuse* section, the *kuri*, is typically broad in scope and often rhetorically elevated in tone. This is the case in the *kuri* of *Takasago*,

Fourth *Dan*

Component Part	Type of Chant	Performer(s)	Noh Action
Kuri	noncongruent	chorus	reflection on nature of flora
Recitative (*sashi*)	noncongruent	chorus *shite*	praise of the pine tree and poetry
Kuse	congruent (*hiranori*)	chorus *shite*	development of Tsurayuki's idea that the spirit of poetry informs all beings
Rhythmic Exchange (*rongi*)	congruent (*hiranori*)	chorus *shite* *tsure*	old couple's admission of identity, invitation to Sumiyoshi

which celebrates the life cycle of all flora. Its general message both sustains the abstract level of discourse that predominated in the preceding high-range chant and serves as an introduction for the more concrete statements to come. Musically, however, the *kuri* and the subsequent *kuse* subpart differ entirely. The highly vivid music of the *kuri* has been likened to a waterfall, for it has a breathless, rushing quality that contrasts with the deliberate mood of the high-range chant. Typically the tempo quickens abruptly at its start, and, abundantly embellished, the choral chant soars into the highest range of the noh scale. For its duration, typically the *shite* silently stands facing the audience at center stage.

In the recitative, the scope narrows to the pine tree, which is singled out as exemplary among flora because of its constancy and long life. At the close, the pine image is again tied to poetry, the fusion of the two effected at the level of poetic word play. Tsurayuki opens his "*Kana* Preface" with, "The seeds of Japanese poetry lie in the human heart and grow into leaves of ten thousand words." "Leaves of words" (*koto no ha*) is a pun on the word *kotoba* (words/language). In the context of Tsurayuki's preface, *kotoba* (*koto no ha*) refers to "diction, rhetoric, imagery, syntax, and auditory effect,"[55] that is, the language used to express the poem. By itself, the mora "*ha*" means "leaf/leaves" and refers equally to deciduous leaves or pine needles.

Zeami exploits Tsurayuki's "leaf"/"word" metaphor in the closing passage of the recitative, which follows.

SHITE:

| pine tree branches | *matsu ga e no* |

CHORUS:

Laden with leaves of words	*koto no hagusa no*
on which beads of dew	*tsuyu no tama*
become as seeds	*kokoro o migaku*
to hone the heart,	*tane to narite*
for every living thing,	*iki to shi ikeru*
they say,	*mono goto ni*
is drawn to the shade cast	*Shikishima no kage ni*
by these Isles of poetry	*yoru to ka ya.*

Pine needles and dew take on the metaphoric significance. Whereas Tsurayuki speaks of "the leaves of words" as the outward expression of the poet's
conception or sensibility (*kokoro*), Zeami applies the metaphor somewhat
differently. The dew on the needles is a substance that literally "polishes the
heart" (*kokoro o migaku*), or hones poetic sensibility. The dew and the
needles/leaves of words are external elements that nurture the development
of inner sensibility.

It is customary for the *shite* to render the first line of the recitative,
whereupon the chant is passed to the chorus. Although the recitative also
opens in the high range and has a noncongruent rhythmic scheme, it lacks
the extremely high notes and the vocal embellishments of the *kuri*. The
recitative has been likened to a flowing stream, for it progresses smoothly,
with sheer musicality suppressed to shift the emphasis to the meaning of the
chanted line. Although the recitative is rendered for the most part by the
chorus, the *shite*, still remaining stationary, usually interjects a line or two,
as in *Takasago*. In Segment 2.1 of *Sandō*, Zeami suggests that the recitative
have five lines in the high range and an additional five from the lowering
to the close. Today it retains that melodic contour, opening in the high
range, then dropping to the middle range, and closing in the low range. The
final lines of the recitative of *Takasago* introduce the theme that is to be
developed in the ensuing *kuse*. In the opening portion of the *kuse*, Zeami
adumbrates the idea that all sentient beings are attuned to poetry.

CHORUS:

Thus was it also	*Shikaru ni*
stated in the words	*Nagayoshi ga*
of the poet Chōnō[56]	*kotoba ni mo*
that no voice,	*Ujō hijō no*
sentient or insentient,	*sono koe*
is excluded	*Mina uta ni moruru*
from song.	*koto nashi.*

The narrative ranges from grass to forests to insects crying out, until it focuses once again on the nature of the pine tree.

And among them all	*Naka ni mo*
this pine	*kono matsu wa*
surpasses	*Banboku ni*
ten thousand trees	*sugurete*

The ensuing *ageha* marks a structural turning point in the *kuse*. In *Sandō*, Zeami refers to the "high part" (*kō no mono*) of the *kuse*, that is, the final section in which the register of the chant shifts to the high range, beginning with the *ageha*. *Ageha* is the name for a component of chant consisting of the *shite*'s brief interjection of a line or two into the choral narrative. The *jo* and *ha* phases of the *kuse* precede the *ageha*, which marks the opening of the *kyū* phase of the play. The *kuse* combines a strong rhythmic scheme with colorful vocal modulation that grows increasingly elaborate, climaxing in the *kyū* portion. It opens in the low range and remains in the low and middle ranges until the *ageha*, whereupon the register shifts to the high range, dropping again to the low at the close. The dignified, rhythmic measures gradually build in tension and tempo. The *kuse* has been likened to a pool, its gripping rhythmicality indeed serving to deepen the overall musical effect.

In *Takasago*, the *ageha* is an allusion to the poem by Ōe no Masafusa that appears in the entry chant of *Dan* II. It serves to shift the narrative focus back to the scene at hand.[57]

At Takasago	*Takasago no*
there upon the hill above	*Onoe no kane no*
the bell sounds.	*oto su nari.*

The final section of the *kuse* reiterates the idea of the pine tree's symbolic longevity but intertwines that abstraction with the image of the *shite* raking the needles beneath the imaginary pine tree. One version of contemporary stage notations goes as follows.[58]

Though we sweep	
beneath the pine	*The shite moves upstage center*
morning and night,	*and rakes the (imaginary)*
that the fallen needles	*needles on the left and right.*
do not dwindle	
is true	*The shite gazes up at*
	(imaginary) branches.

This sense of timeless abundance underscores the celebratory mood.

The *shite*'s relation to the chanted lines has several levels. On the one hand, he may be viewed as facilitating the narrative. He becomes the visual focus for the chant that the chorus performs. At the same time, when he rakes the imaginary needles and gazes up at imaginary branches, he also takes on a mimetic relation to the object that the narrative describes—the pine tree. In such fashion, he plays a dual role as both participant in the narrative act and enactor of the story being narrated. One may argue that what he is enacting is not so much a dramatic scene per se as it is the narrative line itself.

In that capacity, the performer may also be said to embody narrative tropes. That is, he may take on a metaphoric relation to the scenery that goes beyond his dramatic role in the immediate scene. The pine needles are linked symbolically to Tsurayuki's "*Kana* Preface" and, by extension, to the Japanese poetic tradition in general. This is done at the level of word play that centers on the potential for a dual reading of the phrase *koto no ha*, as discussed above. The recitative passage quoted above ("laden with leaves of words") forges a link between Tsurayuki's image and the pine tree. That passage prepares the listener to appreciate the raking scene here in the *kuse* on two levels, as narration of the action and as metaphor. The "needles" stand for both the hardiness of the pine tree and the hardiness of the native poetic tradition. In turn, the visual presence of the *shite* as an elderly man raking pine needles may embrace both descriptive and metaphoric levels of meaning. The *shite*'s physical presence may be read as analogous to the longevity and auspiciousness of the pine tree; he, too, may be taken to be an entity that possesses the virtues under discussion.

The *shite* thus fulfills multiple roles in the exposition of the play. On the mimetic level, he is a character situated within the dramatic fiction. At the same time, he participates as a quasi-narrator in the telling of the story. As emblems of auspiciousness, he and his companion are in a symbolic relation with the wedded pines in the first act. However, by the second act of the play, we realize that the relationship between the couple and the pines is more than symbolic. With the transition from the first to the second act, the *shite's* identity shifts and he becomes more directly involved in acting out his own story. Yet in the second act, too, the *shite* is facilitator of a textual flow that introduces themes broader than the dramatic character he is playing. In his capacity as facilitator in enunciating those themes, he preserves a certain narrative distance even as he represents himself. His identity may take on different facets with the shifting perspectives of the text, but his physical presence remains the focal point for the intersection of all of these levels of the exposition: descriptive, mimetic, symbolic. Zeami's concept of *kenpū* (visional affect) involves the creation of such physical presence to which multiple meanings may be ascribed.

Although the *kuse* section is the unit of noh drama with the most complete internal integrity of structure, it should be evident that its organizational principles are the same as those that govern the play in its entirety. In fact, as noted above, the infrastructure of the *kuse* section may be viewed as a microcosm of noh structure: the *kuri* corresponds to the *jo* phase, the recitative and the first two-thirds of the *kuse* to the *ha* phase, and the remainder of the *kuse*, as well as the following rhythmic exchange, with the *kyū*. The narrative progresses from general to specific, the music from noncongruent to congruent, the performance from the aural to the visual.[59]

At the beginning of the ensuing rhythmic exchange (*rongi*), the *waki* is sufficiently mystified by the old couple to ask them their identities. The *shite* and *tsure* reveal that their relation to the pines is more than one of proximity. They *are* the spirits of the pine trees at Takasago and Sumiyoshi.

> We are the spirits
> of the wedded pines
> come before you
> as man and wife.

The suspense of revelation is fulfilled. Unlike the spoken exchange and heightened exchanges of *Dan* III, the rhythmic exchange that follows to close *Dan* IV is enacted exclusively by the chorus and the old couple, while the *waki* remains seated and silent. This section brings us back to the dramatic action. After they reveal themselves, the two step into an imaginary boat while urging the *waki* (indirectly through the chorus) to follow them to Sumiyoshi. They move upstage, step from the boat, and exit wordlessly down the bridgeway to conclude the first act. The final stage of this *dan*, the rhythmic exchange, abides by the *hiranori* pattern, and, as Zeami stipulates in *Sandō*, its pace is brisker than that of the preceding section.

A few words should be said about the fluidity of the choral perspective in this fourth *dan*. Whereas the *kuri*, the recitative, and the first two-thirds of the *kuse* are devoted to the objective narration praising the pine tree in the abstract, with the *shite*'s *ageha* the perspective swiftly changes to the subjective one of the *shite*. The chorus speaks on his behalf as he moves into the sweeping sequence.

Though we sweep	*Tachiyoru kage no*
beneath the pine,	*asayū ni*
morning and night,	*Kakedomo*
that the fallen needles	*ochiba no*
do not dwindle	*Tsukisenu wa*
is true.	*makoto nari.*

In the next lines, it just as swiftly reverts to an objective standpoint.

The needles of the pine	*Matsu no ha no*
undepleted,	*chiriusezu shite*
their hue deepening	*Iro wa nao*
as the laurel vine grows long,	*masaki no kazura*
a metaphor	*Nagaki yo no*
for this long reign,	*tatoe narikeru*

The rhythmic exchange opens with still another shift. The chorus chants

The past of two aged trees,
now revealed.
Do tell us please
your names.

The choral voice has effectively taken on what had been the task of the *waki* up to this point, to elicit information about the story from the *shite*. After the old couple aver their identities, the chorus devotes a few lines to the wonder of that revelation and then suddenly quotes the words of the exiting *shite* and *tsure*, followed by a narration of their action from a third-person vantage point.

First to Sumiyoshi,	*mazu yukite*
we'll go ahead,	*Are nite machi*
and there await you,	*mōsan to*
they said.	*Yūnami no*
They boarded	*migiwa naru*
a small	*Ama no*
fishing craft	*obune ni*
on the water's edge,	*uchinorite*
and trusting the winds	*Oikaze ni*
to guide them,	*makasetsutsu*
they sailed out	*Oki no kata ni*
toward the offing	*idenikeri ya*

During the interlude between *Dan* IV and *Dan* V, a *kyōgen* performer, cast as a resident of Takasago, reiterates the legend of the wedded pines and urges the *waki* to depart for Sumiyoshi. Although *kyōgen* (classical comedy) is an art distinct from noh, at least as early as Zeami's time, the two were performed on the same stage and ordinarily appeared on the same program. In addition to performing independent plays, *kyōgen* actors perform during the interludes between the acts of noh plays. The interlude has a dramatic reason as well as a practical one. First, the local resident narrates the background legend in a manner that is much simpler to grasp than the web of allusions composing the noh version. Second, his performance allows the actor playing the *shite* time to change costume backstage. Although some of the interludes hold dramatizations of some kind, the majority consist of this straightforward narration, with the local resident providing information to the *waki*.[60]

The second act of a Zeami play typically opens with a passage of high-range chant rendered by the *waki* and/or *waki* group, as is the case in *Takasago*. However, in most *mugen* plays, the setting of the two acts remains constant, and the chant is executed while the *waki* awaits the *shite*'s appearance

Figure 10 *Shite* of Act 2 of *Takasago*, deity of Sumiyoshi Shrine. The staging adheres to a special performance variant called *Hachidan no mai* (dance in eight sequences). The final god dance *(kami mai)* is performed in eight sequences rather than the normal five or three sequences and is danced at a quicker pace. The use of this mask *(mikazuki)* to represent the Sumiyoshi deity dates to the Muromachi period, but the mask is now usually reserved for special variant performances. The preferred mask since the sixteenth century has been the kinder, gentler *Kantan otoko*. Actor: Sekine Tomotaka, Kanze school. (Courtesy of the photographer, Maejima Yoshihiro.)

Figure 11 Finale of *Takasago*. The *shite* is about to exit. His raised arms accompany the lines, "The voice of the wind in the wedded pines, rushing clear and fresh ushers delight." Actor: Sekine Tomotaka, Kanze school (performance variant: *Hachidan no mai*). (Courtesy of the photographer, Maejima Yoshihiro.)

Fifth Dan

Component Part	Type of Chant	Performer(s)	Noh Action
High-range Chant (ageuta)	congruent (hiranori)	waki/wakizure	passage to Sumiyoshi
Recitative (sashi)	noncongruent	chorus/shite	pledge of devotion to sovereign; description of surroundings
Free Chant in High Range	noncongruent	chorus/shite	announcement of shite's apparition
Entry Chant (issei)	noncongruent	chorus/shite	description of scene, account of shite's movements
Rhythmic Exchange (rongi)	congruent (hiranori)	chorus/shite	praise of shite and surroundings, account of shite's movements

in his or her true identity. By contrast, in *Takasago*, the *waki* must travel from Takasago to Sumiyoshi in order to meet the *shite*. Today, the *waki* and *wakizure* move to center stage and face each other, whereupon we are to consider them aboard a boat bound for Sumiyoshi. On board this imaginary craft, they perform the traveling song describing their progress. This shift in the setting between the two acts of *Takasago* may be another "fin" in its structure.

The remainder of *Dan* V faithfully follows Zeami's model. The *shite*, cast now as the god of Sumiyoshi, enters in a male form that is youthful and vigorous, in stark contrast to the aged *shite* of the first act.[61] The *tsure* does not appear in the second act. The tempo here rushes forward, in keeping both with the youthfulness of the *shite* and the *kyū* phase of the play. The passages specified in the chart above as free chant in the high range and entry chant announce the god's apparition and prepare the way for the formal dance to follow. Whereas the *shite* of the first act was stationary most of the time, the young god is in perpetual motion. In today's staging, during the recitative he performs stamps and abstract dance moves on the bridgeway.

In the course of the free chant, he moves onto the main stage and stamps some more. During the entry chant, he whirls around the stage, stamps, and performs *monomane* moves intended to bring out the meaning of the lines. For instance, while chanting, "Breaking off a sprig of plum and arranging it in my hair," he imitates that gesture. To the choral line, "The snows of the second month sprinkle down on my robe," he flips his sleeve across his outstretched arms and gazes at the imaginary blossoms resting there.

It was noted that in *Dan* III the tension of the heightened exchange builds to a climax, whereupon it is carried over into a more structured high-range chant. The same pattern holds for the mounting tension of the recitative/free chant/entry chant sequence in *Dan* V, except that in this case the tension is caught and sustained in a more structured unit that is purely instrumental, known today as the *kami mai* (god dance). This instrumental dance seems to correspond to what Zeami prescribed for the eye-opening of the play. Although it is not known what this dance was like in Zeami's time, when it was probably still evolving, today it is the most rapid of the formal dance pieces, and the choreography is largely fixed. The instrumental ensemble for *Takasago* is composed of the flute, the shoulder drum, the hip drum, and the stick drum.[62] The overall tone of both dance and instrumentation is one of exhilaration and brisk rhythmicality.

When the dance nears completion, the chorus moves into the final rhythmic exchange, which, Zeami says, "should mount the rhythm, intensifying and flowing lightly to a close." The *shite* moves into another series of choreographed patterns intended to highlight the concluding lines. For instance, today at the choral line, "In robes pure we dance a prayer," he gazes fixedly at his sleeve. "To ward off evil spirits one arm be upraised" is accompanied by his raising his opened fan to the side and flapping it. He moves rapidly toward upstage right and matches two resounding stamps to the final lines, "Rushing clear and fresh ushers delight," whereupon he passes down the bridgeway and out of sight. In contrast to the carefully crafted verse of *Dan* IV, the lines of *Dan* V do not narrate a theme or story. Rather, they narrate the movements of the *shite*. The visual mode of presentation has become primary, and the flow coheres at the visual level.

TAKASAGO: THE WAY OF WRITING

In *Sandō*, Zeami devotes most of his discussion on the technique of writing to how prosodic techniques and themes already established in the *waka* tradition may be applied or expanded to suit the creation of a dramatic work. As introduced in chapter 4, his precepts center on the importance of borrowing and incorporating quotations from well-known poems that are thematically consistent with the material for the play. He exploits the kind of *honkadori* techniques already familiar in *waka* poetics. He also recommends that famous place-names rich in associations be incorporated into the script, also as a means of promoting associative linkages in the minds of the spectators. In chapter 4, such poetic devices were introduced in the abstract. Here we shall explore a bit further how they are used in *Takasago* and also touch on a sampling of compositional features that are important to the poetic diction, though not addressed specifically in *Sandō*.

Earlier, we examined one example of the *honkadori* (allusive variation) technique in *Takasago*. It consisted of the poem used for the entry chant at the opening of *Dan* II.

At Takasago	*Takasago no*
spring breezes in the pines	*matsu no harukaze*
deepen into dusk	*fukikurete*
The bell too is echoing	*Onoe no kane mo*
from the hill above.	*hibiku nari.*

The older poem by Ōe no Masafusa[63] to which Zeami is alluding was also introduced.

At Takasago	*Takasago no*
there upon the hill above	*onoe no kane no*
the bell sounds,	*oto su nari*
With the dawn	*Akatsuki kakete*
will frost have settled in?	*shimo ya okuran.*

We noted that this allusion to Masafusa's poem aided Zeami not only in establishing the setting and the *shite*'s link with it, but in adumbrating the lonely purity of his own poem. At the same time, we saw how subtle shifts in Zeami's own poem—from winter to spring, dawn to evening—work to soften the harshness of the older poem, in keeping with the mood of the play and the emotional qualities associated with the protagonist.

Masafusa's poem warrants reiteration here because in the course of the play Zeami exploits it in further ways that illustrate his poetics of the stage. In Segment 1.4 of *Sandō*, he stipulates the following.

In noh, there should be a setting associated with the source material.
If it is a place of poetic import—a renowned spot or a historic site—
then take words from well-known *waka* or phrases linked with it and
write them into what you judge to be the climax of the three *dan* of
ha. This will be a crucial juncture for expressiveness in the noh.[64]

In *Takasago*, Zeami adheres to his own advice. As has been noted, the *kuse*
falls in the third *dan* of *ha* and is one of the most musically brilliant of a
play's component parts. Moreover, the last third of the *kuse*, starting with
the *ageha*, is the climactic part of that section, what Miyake Kōichi calls the
phase in which the beauty of the music should be exploited to the fullest.[65]
Zeami seems to have considered this a climactic point, for he chooses to re-
allot Masafusa's well-known poem about the Takasago shoreline to the *shite's*
ageha and the choral lines following it. This time, the poem is repeated almost
unaltered and in its entirety, with the wintry image of the frost preserved.

SHITE:
At Takasago
there upon the hill above
the bell sounds,

Takasago no
Onoe no kane no
oto su nari,

CHORUS:
With the dawn
frost
has settled in

Akatsuki kakete
shimo wa
okedomo

Zeami makes one slight alteration in Masafusa's poem as alluded to in
the *kuse* section. Whereas the last two lines of the original express supposition, "With the dawn/will frost have settled in?" Zeami's lines in the *kuse*
are in the indicative present and are linked contrastively to the ensuing line.

CHORUS:
With the dawn
frost
has settled in
but the deep green hue
Of the pine needles
stays the same.

The result is a new combination of images, the frost from the original poem becoming the backdrop against which the deep green needles of the ensuing line are introduced.

Evergreen needles beneath frost is a stock poetic image for the strength of the pine tree. The image also works here to reinforce an allusion to a poem by Minamoto no Shitagō (911–983) positioned in the preceding recitative.

Its color of a thousand years	*issennen no iro*
stays deep in the snows,	*yuki no uchi ni fukaku*

When Zeami invokes Shitagō's poem in the recitative, he does not quote it in its entirety. In the *Wakan rōei shū* version, the poem goes

It is after the frost settles in
that the pine tree shines,
Its color of a thousand years
deepens in the snow.

Even though the frost image from Shitagō's poem is not explicit, surely Zeami assumed that the allusion would not be lost on the more literate members of his audiences. Moreover, the subsequent repetition of Masafusa's poem in the *ageha*, with its frost motif, seems calculated to echo this elliptical reference to frost, appearing in the preceding recitative. Through such allusive techniques, Zeami creates a juxtaposition of the images from Masafusa and Shitagō's poems (Takasago bay/deep green needles/frost/hardiness). As a result, the usage of Masafusa's poem in the *kuse* not only brings out the isolated serenity of the Takasago scene, but also the hardiness of its pine tree and, by extension, the hardiness of the Japanese poetic tradition, the realm itself, and the elderly couple.[66]

Zeami uses Masafusa's poem three times in *Takasago*. Along with its role in the entry chant (*Dan II*) and the *ageha* of the *kuse*, it also recurs in abbreviated and altered form at the opening of the high-range chant sung by the *shite* and *tsure* at the close of *Dan II*: "This place/is Takasago,/the pine on the hilltop too/is far along in years" (*Takasago no/Onoe no matsu mo/toshifurite*). In this instance, the "bell on the hill above" (*onoe no kane*) is replaced by the "pine on the hilltop" (*onoe no matsu*), reinforcing the tie between the aging pine and the aging couple. He uses the poem as a refrain or theme song throughout, each instance slightly different in context. By repeated reference to the same poem, this technique of the refrain is useful in strengthening the paradigmatic axis of the play—its network of associative images.

Although in *Sandō* Zeami exhorts the novice composer to draw on poems that articulate themes consistent with his own composition, he does not necessarily abide by that rule in *Takasago*. As his varied treatment of Masafusa's poem illustrates, he shows little concern for preserving the original poet's artistic intent and routinely manipulates allusions for his own artistic ends. For instance, he attributes the very famous *waka* by Fujiwara no Okikaze[67] to the *shite* in the recitative of *Dan* II.

Whom shall I regard	*Tare o ka mo*
as someone who knows me well?	*shiru hito ni sen*
Not even the Takasago pine	*Takasago no*
was here as company	*matsu mo mukashi no*
way back when.	*Tomo nara de*

This poem has been adopted almost unaltered, but in its new context its nuances shift. Okikaze had intended it as a lament on the part of the aged persona for friends who had died, hardly an auspicious subject. In Zeami's hands the poem retains its aura of loneliness, but in conjunction with the images that follow—the aged cranes nestled in their roost and the frosty dawn in early spring—it is the persona's venerable age in this serene moment that comes into the foreground.

There are numerous other poetic techniques at work in *Takasago* that are *not* mentioned in *Sandō*. Two of them are very basic to the text of a play: the *engo*, that is, words that form part of a web of associative links passed down across generations of poets, and the related technique of *kakekotoba* (pivot words/phrases). *Engo* literally means "related words." The relations are the paradigmatic ones premised on associative linkages that originate in poetic precedents from *waka* and *renga*. As Miner has discussed *engo* in his introductory study of Japanese *waka*, *engo* allow for the "relation of disparate elements in a poem by the use of a word that has or creates an 'association' with a preceding word or situation." He further points out that such invoking of *engo* often gives "an additional dimension of meaning . . . giving two expressions a secondary richness."[68]

Such associations were omnipresent in both *waka* and *renga*, and it is no exaggeration to say that they composed the parameters of poetic expression.

Without knowledge of these parameters, a poet had little basis for determining what was appropriate or original in the treatment of any poetic
theme in that tradition. Zeami's extensive use of such associative links is
evidence that he was mindful of such received poetics and that he assumed
certain members of his audiences would be as well.

Perhaps the best way to convey the nature of *engo* is to turn directly to
examples. They are numerous in the traveling chant (*michiyuki*) in the first
dan of *Takasago*, for instance. Although a full English translation of *engo*
would be impossible, and it would be equally unreasonable to present any
passage as having a set of such associative possibilities since the intertextual possibilities are truly limitless, I have attempted to convey part of
the word play of the original in the translation below.

In <u>traveling robes,</u>	*Tabigoromo*
On the road <u>fair and long</u>	*Sue <u>haru baru no</u>*
to the capital,	*miyakoji o*
on the road <u>fair and long</u>	*Sue <u>haru baru no</u>*
to the capital,	*miyakoji o*
Today our thoughts RISE UP	*Kyō omoiTATSU*
across shoreline WAVES,	*ura no NAMI*
our boat's path tranquil	*Funaji nodokeki*
with spring BREEZES,	*haruKAZE no*
How many days have passed?	*Iku ka <u>ki</u>nuran*
The course we have <u>come</u>	*ato sue mo*
the path ahead too	*Isa shirakumo no*
veiled in white clouds,	*<u>haru baru to</u>*
still <u>distant</u> we had thought	*Sashi mo omoishi*
<u>Hari</u>ma inlet,	*Harimagata*
but already we have reached	*Takasago no <u>URA</u> ni*
the BAY at Takasago,	*tsukinikeri*
but already we have reached	*Takasago no <u>URA</u> ni*
the BAY at Takasago.	*tsukinikeri.*

I will concentrate here on two sets of *engo* that are woven into this passage.
The first set of words has been underlined with a single line; the second is
in uppercase. The verbal "rise up" belongs to both sets. The first network
exists between *tabigoromo* (traveling robes), *haru baru* (lit. "afar, distant";
translated here as fair and long, or distant), *ki* (come), and *ura* (shore). The

original Japanese for "fair and long/distant" is *haru baru;* it consists of the repetition of the two-morae lexeme *haru* (with the "h" voiced upon repetition). *Haru* is homonymous with a verbal meaning "stretch" or "spread," as in stretching the wrinkles out of material. The word thus triggers an associative link with the image of the traveling robe of the first line. The next link in the chain is "rise" *(tatsu),* used in an idiom analogous to the English "thoughts arise." "Rise" may also refer here to the rising waves or to departing, as on a voyage. There is also a homonym for *tatsu* meaning "cut" (as in cloth). The verb *ki* translates as "come," and also puns with another verbal meaning "wear/put on." Moreover, the word translated as "shore" *(ura)* also refers to the reverse side of a piece of material. These relationships may be charted as follows.

Key Word: *koromo* (robe)

Japanese	Denotations	Associated Homonyms (*Engo*)
haru baru	distant	stretch taut (material)
tatsu	rise/depart	cut (cloth)
ki	come	put on, wear
ura	shore	reverse side (of material)

In addition, the *haru* of *haru baru* also puns with *haru* "spring" and "clear" (as in clear day), and it is linked phonologically to the place-name of Harima. There is a further *engo* in the line "Today our thoughts rise" *(kyō omoitatsu).* "Today" is *kyō* in the original Japanese and is homophonous with the medieval name for the capital city of Kyoto.

These word associations do not have direct bearing on the propositional meaning of the passage above. Rather, they are used to create a network of possibilities that enrich the texture of the narrative and play with it. Not all *engo* are predicated on homophonic linkages, however. Also possible are nonhomophonous associations based on semantic commonalities. The second set of *engo* in this passage is of that type, the elements being *tatsu* (rising), *nami* (waves), and *kaze* (wind). The connections between these three are comparatively obvious, "rising" alluding to "rising waves."

A number of *engo* employed by Zeami in *Takasago* are replicated in a *renga* manual titled *Renju gappeki shū* (Strings of linked jewels), composed by the court poet Ichijō Kanera to guide the novice poet. It is believed to have been composed in 1476, roughly a decade after Zeami's death, and therefore may be expected to contain material that overlaps with the poetic tastes of Zeami's day. The low-range chant situated in *Dan* II, for instance, contains two linkages that are listed in *Renju gappeki shū*. That section goes as follows.

> **Low-range Chant (*sageuta*), *Dan* II**
> SHITE: [and] TSURE:
>
> | | |
> |---|---|
> | The shoreline wind | *Otozure wa* |
> | whispers in the pine | *Matsu ni koto tou* |
> | and visits falling needles | *urakaze no* |
> | on our robes, | *ochibagoromo no* |
> | sleeve next to sleeve, | *sode soete* |
> | let's sweep clean the needles | *Kokage no chiri o* |
> | scattered beneath the pine. | *kakō yo* |

Renju gappeki shū lists *ura* (bay or shore) as having an association with *sode* (sleeve), and *matsu no ha* (pine needles) as an appropriate *engo* for the image of *chiri* (dust).[69] (As noted above, the original Japanese for "shore," *ura*, puns with the word for the inner lining of a garment.) The word "dust" (*chiri*) occurs in the final line of the passage quoted above: "*Kokage no chiri o kakō yo*," although it is not reproduced in the English translation. A more literal rendering of the line would be "Let's sweep away the dust in the shade of the tree." The connotation is one of purifying the space, or clearing it of any debris or impediments, namely the fallen needles. *Chiri* also puns with the verbal *chiru* (falling in a scattered way), as in the action of falling needles.

Renju gappeki shū also mentions *nezame* (wakefulness), *tomo* (companion), *matsu* (pine tree), *tsuru* (crane), *neburi* (slumber), and *toshinami* (age; lit. "waves of years") as likely links for *oi* (aging).[70] We noted earlier that Zeami's original title for this play (*Aioi*) puns on the word *oi*, denoting both "growing old together" and "growing together." Zeami seems to have similar guidelines in mind as those stated in *Renju gappeki shū*, for he employs all of the associative imagery listed above in that document in his depiction of this elderly couple in *Takasago*. It is also noteworthy that *Renju gappeki shū* goes to some length to point out that although it is commonly said that the pine tree does not lose its needles, needles do indeed fall. This is a point that the *renga* poet should be cognizant of when employing the image of the pine tree in composing, the author cautions. Zeami was clearly working within the parameters shared by the *renga* poets of the age and was applying poetic standards to the composing of *sarugaku* lines.

The second of the poetic techniques that Zeami uses extensively in *Takasago* but does not address expressly in *Sandō* is the *kakekotoba* (pivot word/phrase). A *kakekotoba* is any linguistic unit that serves to link two otherwise unrelated clauses. The *kakekotoba* may simply build on homophones, or it may also link at the syntagmatic level, in which such homophones can have dual meanings depending on how they are parsed. For his puns, Zeami draws on a core group of words connected to the themes of the play. One of those words is *matsu*, which means either "pine tree" or "await." The recitative of the *kuse* section has a pivot phrase that exploits those homonyms. In the English translation, an attempt has been made to preserve the pivot by substituting the verbal "pine" for the more literal translation of "await." The result goes as follows.

SHITE:

For such tidings we	*Kakaru tayori o*
pine	*matsu*
tree branches	*ga e no*

CHORUS:

| laden with leaves of words. | *koto no hagusa no* |

The place-name Sumiyoshi also has potential as a *kakekotoba*, as it can be broken down into *sumi*, meaning "live," and *yoshi*, meaning "good/well" or "auspicious." Zeami exploits those possibilities in the rhythmic exchange that concludes the first act.

CHORUS:

and forevermore	*Waga*
in this land	*Ōkimi no*
of our	*kuni nareba*
sovereign	*Itsu made mo*
wish their lives	*kimi ga yo ni*
to pass	*Sumiyoshi ni*
first to Sumiyoshi,	*mazu yukite*

The place-name Sumiyoshi works as a pivot here. When read in relation
to the preceding phrase (kimi ga yo ni/Sumiyoshi), the word may mean
"well to live," as in "well to live in this sovereign realm." When read in conjunction with the ensuing phrase (Sumiyoshi ni mazu yukite), it reads "go
first to Sumiyoshi," announcing the passage of the dramatic action to the
opposite shore for the second act. In these five brief syllables, then, Zeami
is able to bridge the gap between subjects as diverse as lauding the emperor
and narrating the stage action. Sumi also puns with the stem of the verbal
sumu, meaning "become bright, clear, lucid," a connotation also in keeping with the play's auspicious mood.[71]

In contrast to the use of the *honkadori* technique, which predominates
in high points of the action that concern the *shite*, both *engo* and *kakekotoba* permeate the poetic passages in the play. The traveling chant quoted
earlier, for instance, abounds in both techniques but has little to do with
telling the *shite*'s story. Where these techniques are sparsest is in the intoned
prose sections (*kotoba*), as might be expected. Whereas techniques of allusive variation or direct quotation of classical poems may be likened to
design patterns intended to attract attention to the play's material, *engo* and
kakekotoba resemble ground patterns that often enrich the poetic and prosodic possibilities of the text without having direct impact on the development of the story line. They are also integral to the narrative structure of
the chanted sections—that is, to the smooth linking of the 7-5-7-5.

Punning is the basis of still another technique that Zeami employs in
Takasago, the *monozukushi* (enumeration of things). This technique consists of the enumeration of a sequence of things that belong to some commonly recognized classification while incorporating as many puns and other
associative linkages as possible. This technique was not as favored by *waka*
poets of this period but was prominent in contemporaneous art forms such
as the *imayō* verse form and in *kyōgen*. The rhythmic exchange that constitutes the conclusion of *Takasago* is built on this technique. It enumerates
the titles of various pieces belonging to the repertoire of the court dance
genre called *bugaku* and of court orchestral music, or *gagaku*. Auspicious-
sounding titles such as *Seigaiha* (Sea-green waves), *Genjōraku* (Return to
the town), and *Senshūraku* (Music of a thousand autumns) are woven
into the final sequence of choreographed moves executed by the *shite*.
Since this play is devoted to celebrating the realm, it is also suitable that
the references should be to dances and music performed for the emperor and
his court.

Baba Akiko makes an interesting observation about this finale.[72] She notes that the *monozukushi* technique here works to defuse development of the story line. The play's final lines are open-ended; one might say the play concludes purely in the aural mode. The wind in the "wedded pines" is all that remains. She contrasts this style of closure with the type of ending that Kan'ami seems to have preferred. In *waki* plays attributed to Kan'ami, such as *Kinsatsu* (Golden talismans) and *Shirahige*, the concluding choral section is devoted to narrating the exit of the *shite*. Indeed, this is the closing preferred by all the authors of *waki* plays other than Zeami. The concluding choral passage, beginning with the line "To ward off evil spirits," has since been excerpted and reintroduced as an independent piece of chant that is often employed as *tsuke-shūgen*—to close a program of plays on an auspicious note. Baba suggests that the passage, now titled *Senshūraku*, has come down from the distant days before *sarugaku* crystallized into noh or *sarugaku* performers enjoyed the patronage of the Ashikaga.

She wonders if the chant was conceived by itinerant performers known as *shōmonji*, who performed *senzu manzai*, an art that specialized in such celebratory songs, which they performed in a variety of venues, including from door-to-door, at the New Year, and on other auspicious occasions. *Shōmonji* hailed from similar social contexts of outcast status, itinerancy, and dependency on patronage of religious institutions as *sarugaku* performers. Baba speculates that Zeami's choice of chant reminiscent of this heritage at the conclusion of *Takasago* might reflect a conscious rejection of his father's innovations and emphasis on dramatic *monomane* scenes, as well as a return to the more distant roots of *sarugaku*, dance, and song.

From Mimesis to Poiesis

Whether Zeami did have such a return to his forefathers in mind as he performed for Kyoto elites is a mystery. What can be said with more certainty is that he had grounds for enhancing the presence of dance and chant in his plays that had direct bearing on whether his troupe would continue to receive Ashikaga patronage. As we know from part 1 of this study, these were the elements most closely associated with the cachet of *yūgen*, for which the rival Ōmi troupe had enjoyed such success. Zeami, too, aspired to a *yūgen* mood by intensifying danced and chanted elements, while at the same time he struggled to preserve a place for the more mimetic scenes that were a hallmark of Yamato *sarugaku* passed down from his father.

Zeami's emphasis on dance and chant and his lesser emphasis on the representation of events for their own sake is clear from the description of the structure of *Takasago* found in Segment 2.1 of *Sandō*. Zeami discusses the component parts of each of the five *dan* in terms of their musical and prosodic structure, with only cursory reference to dramatic content. The result is a play whose infrastructure is built on chanted narrative as much as it is on a progression of events per se. *Takasago* also adheres to his precepts in *Sandō* on the climaxes of the play as moments having aural and visual appeal rather than as climactic points in the dramatic action. The sonic and semantic appeal of the lines should combine to bring home the import of the play, and that section should lead into the climactic dance at the end. The *kuse* section in the fourth *dan* of *Takasago* and the dance in the fifth *dan* assure such a progression.

The contrasts between Zeami's description of the nine character types in the second chapter of *Kaden* and of the three styles in *Sandō* underscore the reorientation of musical and choreographic elements with mimetic ones that had occurred over two decades. It will be recalled that his remarks on deities in the earlier document concentrate on the importance of costuming as well as on the delineation of two strains of deities, those who are demonic and those who are suited to dance. The old man is treated as a separate character type that should be dignified and graceful and should avoid bent posture. In *Sandō*, however, about the only reference to the representation of a venerable character or a deity occurs in Segment 2.1, on writing plays for characters in the venerable style. There he simply states that plays featuring old people generally lend themselves to the format of the *waki* (god) play. In *Sandō* he has merged these two characters into one style. This link that he has so forged between elderly characters and deities assures that his deities will have gentle natures that lend themselves to dance. *Takasago* reflects this clear preference for gentle, venerable deities and an eschewal of rough ones that holds for other of his *waki* plays as well. This preference makes sense if one understands that the intensification of chanted and danced elements was at the heart of his aspirations as both an actor and a playwright. For this reason, in *Sandō* little is said about representational techniques unless it is relevant to actualizing a dramatic prototype that ensures a sequence of chanted and danced moments.

Zeami did not abandon the mimetic scenes of the Yamato *sarugaku* of his father's generation. He reoriented them. The lines of the text rather than the behavior of characters became the object of representation.

Despite its "fins," *Takasago* is a *waki* play, which, according to his description, makes it relatively "straightforward." Mimetic stage business is kept to
a minimum. However, the five-*dan* prototype of *Takasago* provides the
basic, infrastructural model for a new rapprochement between musical and
mimetic elements. This model, or variations on it, holds for Zeami's plays
in the feminine or martial styles as well. Generally, his plays in the feminine or the martial styles have more mimetic scenes, but just as we have
seen in *Takasago*, those scenes are embedded in a larger fabric designed to
foster the elements of dance and chant. That is, scenes such as that in Act
1 of *Takasago*, in which the elderly couple sweep under the Takasago pine,
are not designed to represent events. The old couple becomes the embodied
counterpart to the chanted language of the text. Acting and text come to
coexist such that the performer's body may take on the tropes of language.

Though *Takasago* is only one instance of this five-*dan* prototype and its
expressive potential, it serves as a basic introduction to the dramatic model
that Zeami developed to accommodate his theory of the two modes and
three styles. The preceding analysis should also serve as a reminder that to
understand his dramaturgy, it is important to examine his plays within the
larger context of his performance theory. As the textual narrative became
more central to the experience of a performance, it nurtured a stage
dynamic in which the making of meaning was increasingly left to the imaginative powers of each spectator. We will now return to what Zeami has to
say in his treatises about why performances that followed the configuration
of *nikyoku santai* were best equipped to heighten attunement between
performers and audiences.

PART III

. . .

The Actor's Attunement and *Nikyoku Santai*

6

. . .

Actor and Audience

In part 1, we traced Zeami's development of a theory of acting in which chant, dance, and instrumental music become the most fundamental elements in the performance of a noh play. We retraced his efforts to reconcile the *monomane*-based acting style of the old Yamato *sarugaku* with the much admired *yūgen* style associated with Ōmi *sarugaku*. Whereas the *monomane* style emphasized the imitation of characters, the *yūgen* style was associated with singing and dancing. I have argued that Zeami's configuration of the two modes and three styles began as a means of reconciling and integrating these two strains of *sarugaku*. Drawing on precedents from Ōmi *sarugaku* and poetic theory, he developed an infrastructure of performance in which mimetic elements came to be mediated by poetic, sonic, and visual modalities. In this new style, the nature of the representational object had shifted from characters and their actions to the flow of a literary text itself. In turn, the spectator's role in the co-creation of meaning became a more active one, premised on his ability to "read" the performance text and synthesize its various levels of sensory input.

Part 2 traced the integration of the two modes and three styles in the domain of the playwright. It explored the strengthened role of poetic principles in the organization of the text, as well as Zeami's provisions for ensuring places for dancing and chanting in a play's progression of component parts. It was argued that the two modes and three styles had become central to Zeami's theory of acting and composing alike, an organizing principle that evolved in tandem with his deepening conception of how best to engage audiences. We noted that *Sandō* was as a set of working provisions designed to foster a certain chemistry between performers and spectators.

In the final phase of this volume the focus will be on what Zeami's critical treatises have to say about the principles of actor and audience interplay that the configuration of the two modes and three styles was designed to foster. As Yamazaki has noted in his study on the phenomenology of performance, "what stands out about Zeami is the emphasis he places at all levels on the spectator, and how this definitively colors his thinking at every turn."[1] As was noted in earlier chapters, Zeami's metaphor for moving stage effects throughout his theoretical writings is the "flower." As his ideas about the chemistry between actor and audience deepen, so does his concept of how the flower can come to bloom. The two modes and three styles are part of that larger project in his theory.

While the configuration of the two modes and three styles provides a set of guidelines for the articulation of danced, chanted, and mimetic elements, how the actor executes these elements in performance is an important issue that cannot be addressed solely by analyzing the guidelines in the abstract. This chapter will first turn to issues related to the *how* of the enactment. What kind of "actorly" intuitions does Zeami advocate for actualizing his precepts, and how can the actor best train to cultivate these intuitions? It will concentrate first on two principles of performance that assume the infrastructure provided by the two modes and three styles, but also depend on the actor's ability to react to his audience as he performs within those guidelines. These principles are the sequencing of auditory and visual modalities and the timing of the performance of those modalities. The discussion of sequencing will highlight visual manifestations of the actor's art, and timing will concentrate more on aural ones.

The final portion of this chapter will explore another dimension of the dynamics of actor-audience interaction to which Zeami pays increasing attention in his later critical writings: cultivation of the actor's "mind" (*kokoro*). Whereas the novice actor is guided by such techniques as the two modes and three styles, the seasoned actor, in part because of such training, ideally has come to enjoy an optimal attunement that informs all demonstrations of technique. Zeami's late criticism, along with reflecting a continued reliance on aesthetic domains such as that of *waka* criticism, draws increasingly on a range of terms and concepts from religious discourses to articulate the nature of this optimal attunement. Shinto myth and Buddhist and Daoist images are all enlisted in the service of this objective. This chapter will conclude with an overview of some of the ideas from such religious discourses that Zeami applies to develop his own theory of how an actor may cultivate ultimate attunement with audiences. Hopefully such an overview will in turn provide the groundwork for the concluding chapter, which returns to the central importance of the two modes and three styles in all facets of Zeami's drama theory. Concentrating on Zeami's late treatises, I will make the case that this configuration is not only integral to the development of skills, but also to the cultivation of the optimally attuned "mind" of the performer.

Before we begin, one brief disclaimer should be offered. Of course, a noh performance is a collaborative event among actors, chorus, musicians, and, ultimately, the audience. However, part 3 will concentrate on the acting of the *shite* and its relation to the audience. In Zeami's theory of the stage, it is the *shite* who provides the focal point for both the dramatic fiction and the dramatic diction. He treats the *shite* as the central enunciator of the two modes and three styles onstage, and enhancing the *shite*'s effectiveness is the primary motivation for writing critical treatises. For these reasons, it makes sense to take the *shite* as the starting point in this analysis, but with the awareness that he is one of numerous participants who co-create a performance.

Sequencing and Visual Fulfillment

"FIRST LET [THEM] LISTEN, THEN SHOW [THEM]"

Much has already been said in this study about Zeami's tendency to envision performance in terms of those modalities that appeal to the ear and those that appeal to the eye. It has been noted that he considered the sequencing of those elements to be important, in keeping with the principle that aural expression should precede visual expression. He addresses this most explicitly in *Kakyō* under the rubric "First Let [Them] Listen, Then Show [Them]" (*Mazu kikasete nochi ni mise yo*). Directing his remarks to the actor, he states that the visual and aural appeal of all styles of *monomane* ultimately depends on the purport of the spoken line. Then he broaches issues of delivery.

> If that part intended for the ear is made to go first, and then the bodily
> expression *(fuzei)* to follow slightly thereafter, then the selvedge at
> which the import of what is heard carries over into visualization
> should inspire a feeling of fulfillment arising from [the accruing of]
> the visual and the aural *(kenmon jōju)*.[2]

Sequencing of the auditory and visual elements in that order is important
to maximizing their total effect. Visualization of the story should be enacted
only after the audience has had the opportunity to become familiar with
that story through aural media. As Zeami states in Segment 3.3 of *Sandō*,
the two climactic points in the performance of a play are defined in terms
of the ear (ear-opening) and the eye (eye-opening). The ear-opening is that
point at which "the two aural dimensions of content and expressiveness
create one impression." Most of *Sandō* is devoted to the domain of the ear-
opening: thematic content and musical as well as structural organization of
the component parts of the play.[3] For this reason, the study of *Sandō* in part
2, as well as its sequel, the analysis of the *waki* play *Takasago*, has concentrated on those aspects as well.

However, the ear-opening is only the first part of the dynamic. Zeami
further explains that "the ear-opening is the responsibility of the playwright" and that the eye-opening is "an emanation of the *shite*'s power of
feeling." As noted in earlier portions of this volume, the eye-opening occurs
in the *kyū* phase of a play, typically the final dance of the *shite* in the fifth
dan. In *Takasago*, for instance, it corresponds to the *shite*'s dance. Since the
eye-opening is induced by the actor, it is not the center of attention in this
primer on composing, but at the same time it is clear that the eye-opening
is equally important to the stage event overall and ultimately depends on
the playwright as well as the performers. As Zeami states in *Sandō*, "[V]isual
expression cannot come into being if it is not assigned a place."[4]

He does not go into detail about the content of the eye-opening, but
focuses instead on those points of relevance to the playwright, such as
advice on where it should be planned for in the text. Yet he reserves his
highest praise for this moment, calling it "the instant that opens the eye to
the wondrous *(myō)*," a term that refers to the highest level of stage affect,
beyond all calculated intention. The eye-opening consists of visual
appeal that is predicated on the sonic and semantic content of the text but
is in itself beyond articulation in words. Zeami speaks of the eye-opening

in terms implying that the ultimate objective of the playwright should be to create the conditions that induce this climax in the minds of the audience.

This principle of progression from aural to visual modes applies to the organization of the two climactic points in the play overall, and also to smaller units of the exposition as well, such as the rendering of a single line. What is more, it should serve as the playwright's guide in the sequencing of the component parts of each *dan*. In Segment 3.1 of *Sandō*, Zeami offers an example of this principle in his discussion of the entry sequence appropriate for the character type of the *hōka* performer: "With this style in particular, the entrance along the bridgeway should evoke a sense of distant vision *(enken)*, and the vocal music should move both the ear and the heart." Although he does not refer explicitly to the principle of aural to visual here, it may be inferred from the description of this entry scene, in which the successful evocation of visual appeal is codependent with the chanting.

"Distant vision" is a term that Zeami uses throughout his transmissions to refer to the creation onstage of a sense of distance. As Smethurst has noted, *enken* is "a stylistic device whereby an author creates a geographical perspective."[5] At the same time, the *shite*'s enactment of a sense of distance is an integral part of the success of such a technique. The importance of synthesis between the aural and visual modalities is given concreteness in an anecdote about the play *Obasute* recorded in *Sarugaku dangi*. The *shite* of *Obasute* plays the part of the ghost of an elderly woman who, perceived as a burden because of her advanced age, has been left on a moonlit mountaintop to die. Zeami is discussing how the *shite* should match his performance to the line "I am ashamed even to be seen by the moon," advising that it has great potential for evoking a sense of "distant vision."

> As in *Sarugaku* the evocation of distance is fundamental, [this pose] should be deliberate and full. Therefore, to hide [one's face] with the fan from the person [playing] opposite at the words, "I am ashamed even to be seen by the moon," and bend forward, not looking at the moon at all, looks ugly. If one holds the fan high at "even to be seen by the moon," to hide oneself mainly from the moon, and just glances at the person, and finishes performing it in a subtle way, then it will look interesting.[6]

The gesticular elements having to do with the visual appeal clearly arise in conjunction with the chanted lines. The interpretation of this composite depends on the active, participatory role of the spectator. Neither the aural nor the visual component embodies a message complete in isolation. Rather, the full expressive potential of the two modes is realized as they blend in the mind of the spectator.

The emphasis that Zeami places on the synthesizing faculties of each spectator is a characteristic of his dramatic theory in general. In the ideal performance, the actor should refrain from trying to express everything he feels. As Zeami states in *Kakyō*, the actor should take care to physically demonstrate only seven-tenths of what he is feeling.[7] However, Zeami took care to provide signposts to guide the spectator's experience. First the playwright should lay the groundwork by choosing material that he assumes is familiar to his audiences. This includes a principal dramatis persona who is a type likely to perform dance and chant, a story that audiences will recognize, and poetic allusions that will be familiar to the ear. Furthermore, the playwright should structure the material so that the sequencing of aural to visual modes holds for all units of the play. This assures that the *shite's* performance will unfold against the background context, both sonic and linguistic, that the text provides.

Such an integral relation between chanted text and visual expression is congruent with the shift that Zeami implements away from a representational style that concentrates on depicting action toward the depiction of texts in which such tropes as metaphor and allusion play an important role. Such a shift implies that he placed a high level of trust in the spectator's ability to factor such tropes into his reading of the choreographed movements of the actor. The auditory-visual progression leaves it up to the spectator to synthesize these multiple layers of performance into a meaningful whole. When the auditory content is manifested in densely lyrical chanting and the visual content combines both *realis* and *irrealis* modalities as well, the challenges to the spectator are considerable.

Konishi has pointed out that it was common in the related domain of medieval poetics for composers of *waka* poems to deliberately leave their compositions open to interpretation with the expectation that certain interpretations would result. He notes that such a style implies a certain level of literacy: "The poet leaves things unsaid in the belief that his audience will supplement the poem within a Gestalt anticipated by the poet. This presupposes an audience whose cultural background is homogeneous with the poet's."[8] In Zeami's case also, a growing preference for densely allusive texts reflected his increased exposure to the cultural elite of the day, such as those who frequented the shogun's salons and who would presumably be well versed in the poetic tradition, or at least to have aspirations to be so.

FULFILLMENT OF "VISIONAL AFFECT" (KENPŪ JŌJU)

Over time Zeami's insights deepen into how the imagination of the spectator can be enlisted in the synthesis of aural and visual elements. The term that he uses for the full flowering or realization of the artistic intent is *jōju*. He employs a variation on this term in his definition of the eye-opening in *Sandō*, "*kenpū kan'ō no jōju.*" *Kenpū kan'ō* is translated below as "the feeling that the visional affect inspires" and *jōju* as "fulfillment": "As for the eye-opening, in the course of one play, there should be a revelatory point at which the feeling that the visional affect inspires is brought to fulfillment."[9] This fulfillment is the fruit of collaboration between performers and audience.

Zeami draws this connection between the aural-visual synthesis and fulfillment throughout his critical writings. In the *Kakyō* passage cited earlier, for instance, he refers to *kenmon jōju* (visual-aural fulfillment) as occurring when the material is arranged such that the aural elements slightly precede the visual ones. The term *jōju* also occurs as part of the compound *kenpū jōju* (fulfillment of visional affect). In the section of *Kakyō* titled "Dance Has Its Roots in the Voice" (*Mai wa koe o ne to nasu*),[10] Zeami introduces a paradigm consisting of five different methods of dance. The term *kenpū jōju* is situated at the heart of the paradigm.

The first method mentioned is called *shuchi*, "*shu*" meaning dance pattern and "*chi*" meaning "skill" or "method."[11] This method emphasizes the dancer's mastery of dance patterns and his ability to demonstrate technical expertise in realizing the *jo-ha-kyū* sequencing in his performance. Zeami uses the term *shu* (also read *te*) in particular to refer to those patterns that have to do with the movement of hands (pointing with one's fan, for instance) or feet (stamping, for instance). I will call *shuchi* the "gestural method."

The second method Zeami calls *buchi*, "*bu*" meaning dance and "*chi*" again meaning "skill" or "method." It contrasts with the gestural method in that the actor's physical presence is vested with appeal inspired by the overall atmosphere of his image (*sugata kakari*), rather than by specific, eye-catching dance patterns. In this second style, which I will call the "danced method," particular gestures are kept to a minimum in favor of a graceful stage presence arising from the overall flow of the movement.

The third method is the *sōkyokuchi* (synthetic method), which Zeami describes as a style that "introduces dance into the *jo-ha-kyū* progression of the preexisting gestural method."[12] The movement patterns of the gestural method are in an ornamented style *(umonfū)*, whereas the danced method is in an unornamented style *(mumonfū)*. This is the context for his reference to *kenpū jōju*, or "fulfillment of visional affect," of which he states, "It is the blending of the ornamented and the unornamented into the 'synthetic style' that makes for fulfillment of visional affect."[13]

The fourth and fifth methods build on this synthetic method. In both, gestural patterns and dance coexist but vary in their relative importance. The fourth method is called *shutaifūchi* (style in which gestural patterns are the substance). Of this he states, "Working within [the parameters of] the 'synthetic style,' in which the ornamented and the unornamented are blended, gestural patterns form the substance, and dance the function."[14] While both gestural patterns and dance coexist in this style, gestural patterns are placed in the foreground. Similarly, the fifth method, *butaifūchi* (lit. "style in which dance is the substance"), builds on the synthetic method and, beyond that, brings dance into the foreground over gesture.

The discussion next shifts to the relation between these five dance methods and the three styles of *monomane*. Zeami advises that the actor should choose which of the five methods to employ on the basis of the role he is playing. The fifth method is best for the feminine style of role, he adds, whereas the fourth method is appropriate for the martial style. The venerable style is not mentioned. The paradigm that Zeami is proposing may be diagrammed as shown on the facing page.

The fourth and fifth methods consist of variations that build on the third method for their effects. Zeami singles out this third method as having the potential for evoking *kenpū jōju*. Moreover, he adds that the key to the arousal of audience interest is such a combination of these first two styles.[15] Since the fourth and fifth methods are alternative modes of performance premised on the third method, it seems that the phenomenon of *kenpū jōju* must extend to them as well.

This combination of gestural method and danced method embodied in the synthetic style seems to reflect Zeami's efforts to combine the *monomane*-oriented style of Yamato with the *kakari*-oriented style of Ōmi. He uses the same metaphor to describe the danced method that he uses in

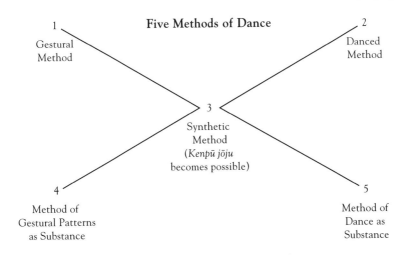

Five Methods of Dance

1
Gestural
Method

2
Danced
Method

3
Synthetic
Method
(*Kenpū jōju*
becomes possible)

4
Method of
Gestural Patterns
as Substance

5
Method of
Dance as
Substance

Sarugaku dangi to describe the *tennyo no mai* (celestial maiden dance): "a bird drifting in the wind."[16] Furthermore, he describes that method as relying on elements such as visual image *(sugata)* and *kakari* for its effects. These were qualities associated with Ōmi *sarugaku*. It is likely that the incorporation of the *tennyo no mai* into Yamato *sarugaku* added a new dimension that Zeami is attempting to articulate by introducing this category of the danced method. By contrast, the gestural method seems more reminiscent of the *monomane* traditions native to Yamato *sarugaku*.

Takemoto argues that these five methods are an early attempt by Zeami to forge a rapprochement between the Yamato and Ōmi strains that was a precursor to his configuration of the two modes and three styles.[17] Indeed, there is considerable overlap between the two paradigms. The five methods call to mind the kind of codependence of musical, choreographic, and mimetic elements that characterizes the two modes and three styles. However, in the case of the two modes and three styles, Zeami stipulates that the two modes should be the media through which *monomane* in the three styles is executed, whereas his discussion of the five methods fails to address how gestural patterns and dance might co-relate as substance *(tai)* and function *(yū)*. It seems that he had yet to map out a larger performative infrastructure in which such codependent elements might be integrated.

Although abstract, Zeami's reference to *kenpū jōju* provides an inkling of what kind of audience reception he was seeking by blending the gestural and the lyrical. He opens his description of the five methods by cautioning, "If the dance does not arise from the music, it cannot be moving."[18]

Here "music" (onjō) embraces both chanting and instrumentation on flute and drums.[19] It is clear that he envisioned the *shite's* stage presence in the larger context of musical elements that coexist with the visual modes of expression. Fulfillment was predicated on the affect inspired by the music, combined with affects inspired by the *shite's* physical presence onstage. The synthesis of these elements by the spectator into a meaningful whole was what Zeami termed *kenpū jōju*.

The term *kenpū jōju* comes up again in the transmission *Shūgyoku tokuka*. As previously introduced, this is a later work organized in a series of questions and answers, ostensibly between master and disciple. Zeami's discussion is a response to the following query: "It is said that *jōju* applies to all the arts. Is this as it seems on the surface? Or, is there a deeper meaning? What is the nature of it?"[20] His response represents the culmination of his thinking on the subject of *jōju*. Here, too, he asserts that a performance will have interest only if there is fulfillment of its visional affect. This, in turn, depends on a sense aroused in the audience that the performance has achieved resolution (*rakkyō*). He states,

> *Jōju* means to "become and settle into." In our art, this appears to be the heart of the interesting. *Jōju* corresponds to [the progression of] *jo-ha-kyū*. When you ask about the nature of this, becoming and settling into something constitutes a resolution. Without resolution, *jōju* cannot occur in the minds of the audience.[21]

He further observes that the fulfillment of visional affect (*kenpū jōju*) constitutes the threshold (*setsu*) at which a feeling of interest will be aroused.

Zeami's reference to the three phases of *jo-ha-kyū* as the constituents of *jōju* underscores the importance that this three-phased progression has come to hold in his ideas about the relation between an actor's timing and the arousal of interest in an audience. In the following segment, we will pursue some of those ideas.

Timing and Temporal Fulfillment

THE JO-HA-KYŪ PROGRESSION AND JŌJU

Zeami's implementation of the *jo-ha-kyū* principle in composing a play came relatively early in the development of his dramatic theory. By his later years, he comes to apply *jo-ha-kyū* to a growing range of variables in performance. As just noted, in *Shūgyoku tokuka* he identifies *jo-ha-kyū* as the guideline for nurturing the phenomenon of *jōju*. He stresses that it applies not only to the arrangement of the plays on the program and the internal organization of each play, but also to the single gesture of turning a sleeve or the resonance of a single stamp in a dance. His discussion of *jo-ha-kyū* even takes on an ontological nuance as he characterizes it as a life force that informs all phenomena.

> Upon careful reflection, it becomes clear that all things in the universe, good and bad, large and small, sentient and insentient, embody *jo-ha-kyū*. From the chirping of birds to the crying of insects . . . the singing of each in abidance with its own nature constitutes *jo-ha-kyū*.[22]

Each entity has its own nature and moves within its own inviolable proportions. To bolster his point, he alludes to the Chinese Daoist classic *Zhuangzi* (*Chuang-Tzu*; 369?– 286? B.C.E): "The duck's legs are short, but to stretch them out would worry him. The crane's legs are long, but to cut them would make him sad."[23] Similarly, it is the task of the playwright and performers to mutually grasp *jo-ha-kyū* as it applies to particular plays, performances, and audiences.

In an ensuing passage from *Shūgyoku tokuka*, Zeami further develops the connection between *jo-ha-kyū* and *jōju* at this most basic level.

> As Chōnō has stated, in spring, trees swaying in the eastern breezes, and in autumn, insects crying in chill dew brought by northern winds—all are the stuff of *waka* poems. This being so, all voices, sentient and insentient, are intoning poetry. The exquisite impression that they create is based on the fulfillment *[jōju]* of *jo-ha-kyū*. Plants and trees undergoing the rains and dews and reaching the stages of flowering and fruition—they too [embody] *jo-ha-kyū*. The same is true for the voice of the wind and the sound of water.[24]

All living beings are imbued with song. This is an idea familiar from Ki no Tsurayuki's "*Kana* Preface" to the *Kokin waka shū*, introduced in the context of the earlier analysis of *Takasago*. However, Zeami takes this idea one step further by ascribing a universal grammar to such song. The growth and maturation of a tree embodies *jo-ha-kyū*, as does a gust of wind. A fine performer, too, adjusts his overall performance to *jo-ha-kyū*, as well as his every breath and gesture. A poor performance on the part of the *shite* is like a tree that does not reach the *kyū* of fruition; it can inspire no sense of fulfillment, and therefore the audience will not be drawn in. On the other hand, fruition cannot take place without the preceding stages of nurturing and flowering. A fast-paced *kyū* section will bring no sense of resolution without the preceding *jo* and *ha* sections.

In such fashion, the actor's fostering of *jōju* depends on many factors in addition to those determined by the structure of a play, or by the two modes and three styles as an abstract paradigm. The same actor may judge it best to alter his rendering of the same play when performing for different audiences. The mood of the audience, too, is in accord with the rhythms of *jo-ha-kyū*, but it is up to the performer to sense what phase of that progression his audience is in. Zeami remarks,

> When, at one glance, the spectator experiences [a sensation of] interest, this means that *jo-ha-kyū* has been actualized. Enacting a style [that allows this to happen] constitutes *jo-ha-kyū* [as practiced by] the performer.[25]

ICHIZA JŌJU (FULFILLMENT [IN THE MINDS] OF ALL PRESENT)

In the opening passage of *Shūgyoku tokuka*, Zeami refers to the aura that surrounds a successful performance with the term *ichiza jōju* (fulfillment [in the minds] of all present). *Ichiza jōju* depends on the performer's technical skill and on how well he can adjust his performance to suit the atmosphere of the occasion. Performances should vary in accordance with an array of variables.

> Now then, the fact that the same expert [actor] can sustain the same superbly skilled style of expressiveness, but have varied reception from one performance to the next, may be due to a lack of attunement to [the balance of] yin and yang in the mood of the moment. If the actor's opening vocalization does not coincide with the tone on the scale that suits that moment, then it will not be in harmony with the prevailing mood.[26] This mood depends on [such variables as] the passing seasons, whether it is day or night, morning or dusk; the number of people, high or low, that have gathered; or whether the space is large or small.[27]

In other of his writings also, Zeami imparts instructions on how the *shite* should adapt his performance to the vicissitudes of particular performances. For instance, in *Kakyō* he notes that when an actor is summoned to perform before an audience having members somewhat flushed with liquor, a problem will arise because the mood of the audience is in a climactic *kyū* phase, whereas an opening performance is normally in the *jo* phase. In such a case, he cautions that the opening should be performed with *ha* overtones. He further qualifies this: "Taking a less sedate attitude, you should pass quickly over to a feeling proper to a noh of the middle developmental and ending climactic [portion of a total program]."[28] A technically brilliant performance will fail to engage audiences in real coproduction if the performer fails to intuit and adjust to the workings of the *jo-ha-kyū* dynamic, which will vary in each performance on the basis of such very local particulars.

Zeami's most microlevel application of *jo-ha-kyū* as the mechanism for creating *jōju* regards his recommended three steps in the process of initiating vocal expression. In *Shūgyoku tokuka*, he extrapolates on an earlier passage in *Kakyō* that first introduces the three. They consist of the actor listening to the wind instruments to determine pitch; internalizing that pitch on the basis of his own *ki* (vital energy flow); and, finally, performing the actual vocalization on that basis.[29] As Nearman notes in his commentary for this passage, *ki* (or pronounced in the Chinese style as "*qi* [*ch'i*]") is a "Taoist-derived term for the universal creative force responsible for the production of all phenomena."[30] Concerning what this highly precedented term denotes in Chinese sources, Owen provides a range of glosses: "breath," "air," "steam," "vapor," "humor," "pneuma," "vitality," "material force," or "psychophysical stuff."[31] He further notes that "at its most crassly empirical level, the role of *qi* in literature and poetry is the breath that comes out when one intones a text." However, this usage is closely related to its "primary function in Chinese physiology."

> It is a force in the body (coursing through the veins) as well as something appearing in the outer world. Ch'i has material (or pseudo-material) aspects, but it always carries other implications of "energy," "vitality," or "impelling force."[32]

Ki came to occupy an important place in numerous discourses of traditional Japan as well. In Zeami's application of the concept here to the specific context of *sarugaku*, the empirical meaning ascribed by Owen seems to remain. Zeami is referring to a vital energy harnessed in the lower abdomen that gives rise to breathing and the determination of tempos.[33] The passage in *Shūgyoku tokuka* reads,

> First, the tone; second, the *ki*; third, the voice. Internalizing the tone constitutes *jo*; projecting the *ki* constitutes *ha*; then the vocalization is *kyū*. When these three move the mind's ear and elicit [a feeling of] interest, then fulfillment has occurred.[34]

The actor should first absorb the external stimulus of the pitch of the wind instruments. He imports that information into his energy flow and concentration and regulates his breathing in preparation. Only after these preliminary stages are accomplished does he actually project his voice. This precept implies that the accomplished performer must have cultivated intuitions about vocalization as a total process. This is not to say that the three steps are the subject of conscious deliberation as he sings. Rather, he executes or embodies the progression, intuitively adjusting his rendering to suit the mood of his audience and the scene.

That which is evident to the actor, however, is not what stands to be consciously perceived by his audience. The audience, which in Zeami's time, of course, did not have access to his secret teachings, would most directly perceive the vocalization itself, that is, the *kyū* phase of the utterance. Whereas the vocalization is immediately recognizable, the audience will not be likely to become aware of the actor's preliminary determination of pitch or breath control until those elements find resolution in the final *kyū* phase. The vocalist's internalization of pitch and his focusing of energy flow and breath compose the *jo* and *ha* phases, both of which precede the conscious awareness of the listener. Although conscious interest is aroused only after the actual vocalization, this progression suggests that the audience, at a preconscious level, is also susceptible to the developmental *jo* and *ha* phases that precede it. That is, *jo* and *ha* would correlate with that part of the progression in which the spectator is attuned to a developing dynamic without necessarily being conscious of that dynamic.

This underlying assumption about the innate receptivity of all beings has interesting implications for understanding the phenomenon of performance. Far from vacuous, the silence before the sound is intense and expectant, accessible to the intuitive faculty but cognitively undecipherable. By virtue of the fact that the *jo-ha-kyū* principle captures a universal principle moving within us, we are sensible to its evocation onstage; we hear the silence. Something rivets our attention, although it has no form until it crystallizes in the completion of sound. Moreover, what is true at the microlevel of an utterance is equally true at every level of a performance. For Zeami, effective modulation of the three phases of *jo-ha-kyū* readies audiences to feel the stillness that contextualizes motion and to hear the silence that contextualizes sound.

THE WONDROUS, THE FLOWER, AND THE INTERESTING

In *Shūgyoku tokuka*, Zeami more fully develops his theory that the fulfillment occurring in the final *kyū* phase depends on earlier developmental phases. Although these earlier phases affect the audience, for them they are most probably preconscious variables. He states that a performance, to be effective, should induce a process of reception that has three phases: the wondrous (*myō*), the flower (*ka/hana*), and the interesting (*omoshiro/menbaku*).

> The wondrous is that which is ineffable and eludes the workings of the mind. That which looks to be wondrous is the flower. That which is apprehended [as form] is the interesting.[35]

To illustrate this process Zeami draws on the myth of the Sun deity, Amaterasu Ōmikami, recorded in the chronicle *Kojiki* (Record of ancient matters; 712). In the fourth chapter of *Kaden*, Zeami ascribes the origin of *sarugaku* to the singing and dancing of the deity in this most famous of myths.[36] Amaterasu barricades herself in a cave, plunging the world into darkness. The other deities assemble before the cave, where one among them performs a dance so boldly risqué that the others rock the cosmos with their laughter. Amaterasu becomes so curious when she hears the deity singing that she dislodges the rock at the mouth of the cave just enough to witness the scene. In that instant, her peers wrest her from it, restoring light to the world. Zeami compares the darkness that took hold while Amaterasu was in the cave to the wondrous. When she opens the door to the cave, there is a burst of light that he likens to the flower. The illumined faces of the attendant gods he calls the interesting.[37]

He further states, "From the perspective of our own deepest insights on this path, the [state of] 'no-mind' (*mushin*) is key to the arousal of interest in *sarugaku*."[38] He speculates that the state of mind of one who witnesses the sudden illumination that accompanies the opening of the cave may be described "simply as a feeling of joy" (*tada ureshiki kokoro nomi ka*) — a pre-conscious instant that brings a smile. Zeami is careful to emphasize that the interesting is not the moment when the faces become visible, but the moment when the forms in view are recognized as faces. The audience is first plunged into mystery. Then it is confronted with a burst of light, and finally comes to apperceive the form that the apparition takes. Without this final phrase of the process in which the spectator apprehends what it has perceived, interest will not be aroused. Whereas in earlier critical writings Zeami speaks of the flower and the interesting as the two facets of the principle of novelty,[39] the *Shūgyoku tokuka* tract adds this new element of the wondrous. This metaphorical burst of light is described as the first phase in arousal of spectator interest.

These ideas of the wondrous (*myō*) and the state of no-mind (*mushin*), which will be discussed in more detail in the following section of this chapter, are terms that Zeami appropriated from religious discourses to aid him in describing the ideal state of attunement between artists and audience. In his late writings, his precepts on how the performer can best cultivate such an optimal state of mind allude to such precedented terms and concepts with increasing frequency. In the following section, we will briefly explore how he comes to situate "performed mind" within a larger ontological framework tinged by Buddhist and Daoist ideas. This will be of use as we explore his developing concept of how the cultivation of spiritual attunement on the part of the actor is integral to his ability to evoke the "flower" in his performances.

Performed Mind

APPEAL TO THE EYE, THE EAR, AND THE MIND

Zeami devotes one segment of *Kakyō* to describing three primary modalities through which a noh performance may appeal to the audience: the visual (*ken*), the aural (*mon*), and the "mind" (*shin/kokoro*). Examining the three will be a useful starting point in investigating what he means here by "mind" and how it might be differentiated from the other two types of appeal. In the following passage from *Kakyō*, he describes a performance whose primary appeal is to the eye.

> As for noh that appeals based on visual [stimuli], from the start, the
> mood grows animated; the style of the dancing and singing is

captivating; audience members high and low give voice to their feelings; the occasion appears brilliant. This is noh that appeals based on visual [stimuli].[40]

He further remarks that a performer having such visual impact will appeal to all types of audiences. The second type of appeal is auditory.

As for noh that appeals based on auditory [stimuli], from the start, it is keenly poignant; right away the chanting [ongyoku] matches the tones [of the wind instruments], and is serenely graceful and captivating. This is above all an impression created by the chanting. It is an impression produced on the spot that involves skill that is the signature of the peerless master.[41]

He notes that performances emphasizing aural elements will demand a more discriminating audience than will the visually oriented performances. Moreover, when such a master performs a noh with strong auditory appeal, then "his inmost mind will naturally become manifest in the various acting styles, enhancing interest still more."[42] Slightly further on Zeami qualifies this statement.

When one is a consummate master, [traces of] the many things [mastered], and [traces of] the [cultivated] body, and of the [cultivated] mind, will of themselves emerge as a [composite] image produced in the dance and chant, and [the performance] will grow still more interesting as it unfolds.[43]

A superb performer will induce a type of cumulative affect attributable to a high level of cultivation of mind and body, arrived at through training and his own innate ability. Moreover, the traces of his accomplishment will be felt in his dancing and chanting.

The term *enken* (lit. "far, distant," and "view"), glossed here as "traces emerging in a composite," is a challenge to interpret because, at first glance, it does not seem congruent with Zeami's other usages of the term in his critical writings. As I noted earlier in this chapter, I translate its *Sandō* usages as "distant vision," to refer to a certain stage effect in which the actor strikes a pose of gazing off into the distance or makes the audience feel that they are viewing him from afar, or both. Such a reading does not seem to apply here, except when construed very loosely, as in Nose's annotation of the term, which takes *enken* to mean how the performance appears to the audience.[44]

NSTS and SNKBZ 88 interpret this particular usage in *Kakyō* to mean a foundation or background that exerts its influence indirectly to produce an effective "visional affect" *(kenpū)*, or a performance style that is visible to the eye. Tanaka glosses it persuasively as a "unified composite image" *(tōitsu sareta zentaizō)*, close to *kakari* in meaning."[45] Indeed, Zeami's description here suggests the same kind of multilayered configuration of performance that we have discussed in relation to the *kakari* dynamic. The images projected on the basis of the overall manipulation of these various elements are the co-creation of the modulating consciousness of the performers and the imaginative engagement of the spectators.

Zeami goes on to introduce a third type of appeal that is based on communication at the level of the "mind" *(shin/kokoro)*. This level is possible only for a superlative performer, who will inspire the following kind of effects.

> After a number of plays have already been performed, there is a type of noh that, in terms of the two modes, or *monomane*, or word play, does not have much, but there is a tranquil flow, in the course of which are spots that arouse interest for no apparent reason.[46]

There is nothing noteworthy about the play or the staging itself. The focal point of interest is not the music, dance, story, or language per se. He states that even discerning spectators may not be able to appreciate the subtlety of this type of performance because its effects are not attributable to a tangible source. Rather, they depend on the sensibility of the expert performer and the expert spectator.

MIND (KOKORO/SHIN), TECHNIQUE (WAZA), AND "NO-DOING"

Zeami employs the term "mind" in multiple contexts and at multiple levels.[47] On the one hand, he uses it in contradistinction to "technique" *(waza)*, which refers to all manner of stage action. Perhaps the most recognizable example in his critical writings of such a usage is the one that recurs in chapters three and seven of *Kaden*, in which he states, "The flower is the mind *(kokoro)*; the seed is technique *(waza)*."[48] More will be said about this precept in the ensuing chapter on the actor's training, but, briefly, it underscores the constitutive role that training in and mastering of techniques such as the *nikyoku santai* play in the cultivation of the actor's desired mental readiness. In terms of the actor's training, Zeami sees the mastery of techniques as a prerequisite to such cultivation. Yet in the case of the veteran actor who has previously mastered the requisite techniques, it is equally true that cultivated mind forms the sensibility that underlies and informs those techniques. Mind may be construed as a kind of ground out of which techniques may arise. In the passage above on auditory appeal, Zeami makes reference to such veteran acting in which the actor's "inmost mind will naturally become manifest in the various acting styles, enhancing interest still more."

Such a concept of "mind" shares similarities with the discussion in part 1 of this volume about how "mind" relates to *yūgen* effects. We centered the locus of such effects in the actor's sensibility. It was argued that this sensibility, or "mind," was the fundamental ground out of which all techniques became manifest. The first step in invoking a mood having *yūgen* depends on the performer's ability to manipulate the various layers of a performance in accordance with the occasion and the audience. It is the actor's sensibility that comes to bear in modulating the various elements in such a way that an overall impression of graceful beauty is fostered.

In a section of *Kakyō* titled "Concerning the One-Mindedness *(Isshin)* that Connects the Myriad Actions," Zeami makes what is perhaps his clearest statement on the relation between techniques and the mind of the actor that should ideally inform those techniques. More interesting than the techniques themselves, he says, are the intervals between them. He observes,

> When we ask why it is that intervals of "no-doing" should be so interesting, it is [the actor's] inmost nature connecting [the whole] by means of his unwavering concentration. This is [attributable] to the innermost workings of the mind, which remain vigilant so that concentration does not lapse during the pause after a dance, or at the point when chanting has ceased, or, for the rest, in the intervals between words, *monomane,* and all other elements.[49]

He adds that this inner mindfulness "gives off a fragrance" that will have interest for the spectator.[50]

Where does the mind described in the passage above come from? Here and elsewhere Zeami is averse to casting it solely as the outgrowth of an

actor's training. He reserves some autonomy for the mind of the actor independent of skill level. Take, for instance, the following disclaimer, found in
a segment of *Kakyō* that is devoted to the nature of the impression that an
accomplished performer will create onstage.

> There are times when [a *shite*] may have a poor voice and may not
> be very accomplished in the two modes, but he may enjoy a reputa-
> tion as a skilled performer. This is because dance and vigorous moves
> are techniques. That thing which controls is the mind.[51]

Zeami further explains that technical accomplishment is not necessarily a
prerequisite for moving an audience, and, by the same token, a technically
accomplished performance may lack interest. He postulates that interest
arises on the basis of the workings of the enlightened mind (*shōishin*)[52] and
the impression created by superb aptitude (*zuifū yori izuru kan*).[53] One gradually approaches the level of the accomplished through training, but inspiring interest is not the same thing, he adds. While on the one hand training
is constitutive of "performed mind," such training in itself is no guarantee
that a given actor's performances will necessarily appeal to audiences.

THE CHILL AND THE UNORNAMENTED

In *Kakyō*, Zeami describes performances that appeal primarily to the mind
as having a "tranquil flow in the course of which are spots that arouse
interest for no apparent reason."[54] In the ensuing sentence, he reflects further on the nature of this appeal. He remarks that performances such as this
may be said to have a quality of chill (*hietaru kyoku*), a term that will be
familiar from other aesthetic domains in medieval Japan.[55] In his note on
this passage, for instance, Tanaka likens Zeami's statement to a passage from
the critical treatise *Sasamegoto* (Whisperings; 1463) by the *renga* poet
Shinkei. The text of *Sasamegoto* follows a question-and-answer format.
The questioner asks about the import of the following.

> A poetic sage of the past, when asked, "How is it that poetry should
> be composed," answered, "Pampas grass on a withered field, a wan
> morning moon." The response: "This means you should concentrate
> on those spots in which nothing is said, and you should cultivate an
> understanding of the chill and desolate (*hiesabitaru*). Verses by those
> who have entered into the realm of mastery are all in this mode

alone. Such being the case, a verse [containing] "a withered field,"
could be followed only by a verse in the spirit of "a wan morning
moon."[56]

The headnote for this passage states that a phrase such as "a withered field,"
which is evocative of a deep, existential understanding, should not be
linked at the level of word play or technique.[57] The link should be guided
by the spirit, not the letter, of the preceding verse, the images of pampas
grass and morning moon linked on the level of the chill and desolate mood
that they project.

In her study of Shinkei's poetry, Ramirez-Christensen comments on the
nature of this understanding in ways that have relevance for our reading of
Zeami's sensibilities as well. At the level of poetic rhetoric, she argues that
Shinkei's preference for the aesthetic of " 'cold' and all its associated semes"
involved "a purified diction shorn of all ornament, all desire to impress or
seduce through the play of language alone, no matter how brilliant or
arresting."[58] Indeed, Zeami's valorization of the "chill" style of noh, which
appeals primarily to the mind over the more flowery, demonstrative style
appealing to the eye, suggests an analogous preference. Noh that appeals to
the mind also eschews all aspects that call attention to themselves, but in
the context of *sarugaku* performance, those aspects extend to all of the
visual and aural elements manifested on the stage.

In his critical writings, Zeami frequently writes of two contrasting styles,
umon (that having ornamentation) and *mumon* (that without ornamentation). By his late treatises, his valorization of the latter is explicit. In his
treatise *Yūgaku shudōfū ken*, an undated work believed to have been written
later than *Shikadō*, he turns to *waka* poetry for worthy exemplars of a style
that eschews all contrivance and ornamentation. The poem, by Fujiwara no
Teika, is one of the most famous in the tradition.

Stopping my horse,	*Koma tomete*
not even a shelter	*Sode uchi harau*
for brushing my sleeves—	*Kage mo nashi*
The crossing at Sano	*Sano no watari no*
In the snowy dusk	*Yuki no yūgure.*[59]

Although this is a poem whose excellence is universally recognized, Zeami
notes, it is impossible to pinpoint its appeal. It is a simple, unornamented

description without hidden meanings. Yet it elicits a feeling of depth or profundity that eludes articulation. He likens the *sarugaku* actor who has achieved the ultimate mastery belonging to the wondrous style of performance to this poem insofar as there is no "hint of artifice, or of intentionality in one's style, but an impression of no-mind is evidenced in detached seeing."[60]

There is agreement overall that Zeami seems to be referring to a style of stage presence in which the actor inspires a deep impression that eludes any vestige of conscious contrivance or striving for effects.[61] Such superb artistry leaves an imprint that cannot be traced to specific causes or calculations. His attribution of the highest accolade, the wondrous, both to Teika's poem and to an analogous style of *sarugaku* performance leaves little doubt about his own tendency at this late stage in his career to prefer unornamented styles of expression. Shinkei's statement above that "a poet should concentrate on those spots in which nothing is said" parallels Zeami's statement in the preceding section that the locus of interest in *sarugaku* performance should be the intervals of "no-doing." Such privileging of the tacit or the ineffable in their respective characterizations of mastery suggests that these two artists shared a certain horizon of expectations that reflected the intellectual climate of their time. Clearly for Zeami, the Buddhist concept of "the wondrous (*myō*)" was one such formative influence on his valorization of the unspoken. In the ensuing section, we return to this concept as he applied it to *sarugaku*.

"WONDROUS" ACTING

Along with employing *myō* to describe the most profound level of reception, Zeami uses it to characterize the supreme level of acting. This usage occurs in his late treatise *Kyūi*, which, it will be recalled, classifies nine such artistic levels or grades of ability. Whereas Zeami's discussion here of *myō* and audience reception in *Shūgyoku tokuka* unfolds with reference to a Shintō myth, in *Kyūi* it is clear that his usage of *myō* is also influenced by Mahayana Buddhism, for *myō* is introduced in relation to *chūdō* (the "Middle Way"), a fundamental tenet of the Mahayana teachings on emptiness (*śūnyatā*). Whereas Zeami describes the uppermost level of acting, *myōkafū* (style of the wondrous flower), as ineffable and beyond conceptualizing in words, the level just beneath this, *chōshinkafū* (style of the profound flower), is described as having visional affect that belongs to "the Middle Way."[62] More will be said in the following chapter about how this *Kyūi* typology applies more concretely to Zeami's ideas on *sarugaku* performance, but it will be useful here to briefly describe the concept of *chūdō* so that we may better understand how Zeami exploits the theory to articulate his ideas on performance.

The philosophy of the Indian scholar monk Nāgārjuna (ca. 150–250) is seminal to development of thought on the Middle Way.[63] In his treatise titled *Mūlamadhyamaka-kārikā* (Stanzas on the middle), he propounded a dialectical process by which one might come to grasp the nature of emptiness. The following passage from that writing is widely accepted as an encapsulation of the dialectic. It is based on a Chinese translation of *Mūlamadhyamaka-kārikā* by the Kuchean scholar Kumārajīva (344–413).

> Whatever dharma arises on the basis of the myriad causes and conditions, that I declare to be identical to inexistence *(wu)* [or, emptiness *(kong)*]. It is also provisional designation *(jia ming)*. This, furthermore, is the meaning of the middle way *(zhong dao)*.[64]

Nāgārjuna's process of discernments was embraced and further expounded on in a number of Mahayana sects. They became central to Tiantai (Jpn. Tendai) doctrine and were also important in the teachings of the Hossō (Skt. Yogācāra; Chn. Fa-xiang) school, which were promulgated at one of the temples—the Kōfukuji in Nara—that sponsored Zeami and his troupe. Although Zeami does not identify the teachings of a specific sect in his *Kyūi* reference to the Middle Way, elsewhere in his critical treatises he does forge an explicit link between his formulation of the "wondrous," the Middle Way, and the teachings of the Tendai sect.[65]

One of the most articulate discussions of the philosophy of the Middle Way is to be found in the commentary titled *Mohe zhi guan (Maka shikan,* Great cessation and insight) attributed to the Chinese Tiantai patriarch Zhiyi (Chih'i; 538–597).[66] Zhiyi, who takes Nāgārjuna's philosophy as a starting point, argues that there are three truths *(santai)* to be discerned in the precept cited above.[67] The following articulation of the three truths is based on Chih'i's characterization. First, one must grasp that all dharma ("phenomena, things, facts, existences, etc.")[68] are "dependently originated *(pratītya-samutpāda),* devoid of existence *(niḥsvabhāva),* and hence utterly incomprehensible *(anupalambha).*"[69] Having done this, one "enters emptiness from provisionality," whereby the discernment that all phenomena are codependent, relative, and devoid of absolute essence allows one to see into the illusory nature of one's own attachments and thus be liberated from them.

The second discernment is based on the negation of a negation. Donner and Stevenson describe that process: "By applying the same critique to the truth of emptiness itself, one severs biased attachment to emptiness . . . and reaffirms its fundamental identity with provisional existence."[70] The truth that all dharma are void of absolute essence applies equally to the concept of emptiness itself. One then reengages with the world, but with this new awareness of its provisionality and the pitfalls of essentialist thinking. Finally, the third discernment is a synthesis of the first two. Again, in the synopsis of Donner and Stevenson,

> From this point on both extremes of existence and emptiness are "simultaneously illumined and simultaneously eradicated" (shuang zhao shuang wang). When all vestiges of dualism (i.e., root nescience) vanish, the transcendent and unalloyed middle—the third and absolute truth—is revealed.[71]

It is very important to note that such insight could be cultivated only by means of meditative practices. In the Mohe zhi guan, Zhiyi advocated practicing "the threefold contemplation in a single mind (isshin sangan)." Stone characterizes its central aim as "to perceive, through contemplation of the thought-moment, that all phenomena manifest the three truths of emptiness, conventional existence, and the middle, that is, being simultaneously both empty and provisionally existing."[72] In Tendai doctrine, the term myōhō (wondrous dharma/law) is used to refer to this principle of making the myriad phenomena manifest in one mind (isshin) and thus perceiving the three truths (santai; the conventional, the ultimate, the middle) in one's own nature.[73]

Both Indian theorists on the Middle Way (the Mādhyamika school) and Tendai proponents share the fundamental premise that a nondual relation exists between mind and phenomena and that the Buddha nature interpenetrates them both. Stone points out that this premise stands in contrast with the philosophy of the Huayan (Jpn. Kegon) school, which holds that "mind is original, pure, and true, while phenomena are in contrast, unreal, arising only as the one mind is perceived through human ignorance.[74] The position held by Mādhyamika and Tendai proponents is that these two cannot be thus oriented chronologically, with mind antecedent to phenomena.

Rather, they are "reciprocally identical and simultaneous."[75] Tendai thought thus places emphasis on the "mutual inclusiveness of mind and all dharmas."

The Tendai *chūdō* paradigm came to influence other Buddhist sects, notably the Chan (Zen) sect, and it continued to be an important precept of Tendai thought in Japan as it further developed.[76] As Stone also points out, this "threefold contemplation in a single mind," which was "considered as Zhiyi's inner enlightenment,"[77] was transmitted to Saichō (767–822), the founding patriarch of Japanese Tendai, and remained central to medieval Tendai traditions as well. In medieval Japan, Stone notes that the threefold contemplation comes to be construed not only as a meditation method, but also as the "originally inherent nature of reality." As an instance of this view, she cites a passage from a medieval text in the Tendai tradition of *kuden* (oral transmission) titled *Ichijō shō* (One book of commentaries), which is of interest to us as we contemplate the intellectual climate of Zeami's time.

> Everything from our own speech to the sound of the waves rising or
> the wind blowing is the threefold contemplation in a single mind,
> the originally inherent three thousand realms [i.e., all dharmas].
> There is nothing to cultivate and nothing to attain. . . . The forms
> of all things exerting their functions and arising in dependence upon
> conditions is, without transformation, the threefold contemplation
> in its totality.[78]

Concerning this mutual encompassing of the mind and all dharmas, Zhiyi taught that "[t]he relationship is neither vertical nor horizontal, neither same nor different. It is obscure, subtle and profound in the extreme. Knowledge cannot know it, nor can words speak it. Herein lies the reason for its being called 'the realm of the inconceivable.' "[79]

Such a "realm of the inconceivable" is another way to refer to the realm of *myō*, the term that Zeami employs in his writings on the art of *sarugaku* to allude to ineffable effects on stage.[80] Zeami's description of the eighth highest of the nine grades listed in *Kyūi* singles it out as the level at which the "Middle Way between being and non-being *(umu chūdō)*" is characteristic. The style of the actor at this level embodies the interpenetration of "*u*" (being/substance) and "*mu*" (nonbeing/nonsubstance). He describes *myō* as situated above this style of the profound flower, represented in those "moments when [the actor's] mind is manifested as form in the nondual style of the wondrous" (*funi myōtai no ikei o arawasu tokoro*).[81] It is no longer possible to draw a distinction between the mind or intent (*i*) of the performer and its physical manifestation (*kei*; lit. "scenery") onstage. He states that this is the ultimate style, beyond which no further profound teachings exist.

Further hints as to what he means are provided in his discussion of "wondrous acting" in *Kakyō*: " 'Wondrous' (*myō*) means 'exquisite.' The 'exquisite' refers to an image that has no form (*katachi naki sugata*). That which has no form makes up the style of the wondrous (*myōtai*)."[82] Furthermore, in his treatise titled *Goi*, Zeami frames his description of the *myō* style in terms clearly reminiscent of the discernments of the conventional and the ultimate in the dialectic of the Middle Way.

> Myō is removed from "*u*" (being/substance) and "*mu*" (nonbeing/nonsubstance), yet embraces *u* and *mu*. The substance of "*mu*" becomes manifest in the visional affect (*kenpū*).[83]

Dualisms are resolved in this sphere in which the intangible is made manifest. In effect, when Zeami valorizes the "style of the wondrous flower" above all others, he assigns the greatest merit to acting whose effects cannot be described in terms of substance at all or transcend the being/nonbeing and substance/nonsubstance dualities altogether. In his later years, Zeami thus seems increasingly to allude to the Middle Way dialectic in articulating his own theory of *sarugaku* performance. He seems to be drawing an analogy between the ultimate insights that the Middle Way induces and the ultimate kind of stage affect, which similarly subsumes all vestiges of dualism.

NO-MIND (MUSHIN)

In *Kakyō* and subsequent treatises, Zeami frequently urges cultivation of a level of mind on the part of the actor that is beyond his discriminating consciousness. Moreover, as has been noted, in *Kakyō* he posits that noh appealing primarily to the mind arises from a state of *mushin* (no-mind), a term that was mentioned briefly in the earlier section on the timing of a performance, in which Zeami's paradigm of the wondrous, the flower, and the interesting was introduced. In this case, he attributes the state of *mushin* to the actor. As stated in the NSTS annotation, *mushin* refers here to effects that are not the result of the actor's conscious intention. It is a term that appears in both Buddhist and Daoist sources. Its appearance in this passage reflects this deepening of Zeami's views on the root causes of an actor's ability to move audiences, as well as his growing tendency to reach out to relevant religious terms and concepts as his interest in getting at the optimal qualities of the performing mind deepens.

In another *Kakyō* passage, he asserts that there is a kind of impact on audiences that surpasses the level that can be called interesting, or captivating (*omoshiroki kurai*), and he associates the performer who creates the impression of being in a state of *mushin* with this uppermost level.

> Also, there is a level above the level having interest in which one breathes, Ah!, without consciously knowing why. This is the [pre-reflective] impression. Since this impression does not appeal to the [discriminating] consciousness, interest will not be [consciously] ascribed to it. . . . This is because the true "impression" is in a sphere that does not involve the mind [discriminating consciousness].[84]
>
> It is this way with the levels of actors. One who develops by training in sequence from the beginning phase may be called a good actor. This is a level at which proficiency has already been reached. On top of this, when there is a degree of interest, then this is the level of the master of renown. On top of this, if the impression of no-mind *[mushin]* is present, then [the actor] is of the level to earn universal acclaim. You should train very, very well in these stages, adjust them as needed, and strive on the basis of your mind *[kokoro]* to attain the ultimate level of noh.[85]

Thus the most effective performers are capable of a nondiscriminatory consciousness that Zeami relates to the concept of *mushin*. This is a different order of mind from that to which Zeami refers in his final sentence above concerning *kokoro*, which the annotations concur regards the mindfulness that the performer should bring to bear in making judgments about how to perform most effectively—the "mind" as contrasted with *waza* (techniques).[86]

The occurrence of references to *mushin* in Zeami's critical writings suggests that Buddhist and Daoist ideas in circulation at that time had had an impact on his thinking about performance, or had at least aided him in articulating those ideas. In his study of Zen thought, Kasulis offers one characterization of *mushin* (no-mind, no-thought) as it is construed in Buddhist traditions.

> A state of consciousness in which the dichotomy between subject
> and object, experiencer and experienced, is overcome. Avoiding
> the usual categories imposed on experience (the flower is beautiful, a
> monk cannot have contact with a woman, or whatever), the function
> of no-mind is to respond immediately to present experiential data.[87]

Kasulis names two senses in which *mushin* is an active state. First, it involves
withdrawing from active intellectualization, which necessitates an act of
will. We all have habitual ways of thinking that characterize our subjective
views of the world and of ourselves. One must break the habit of "clutch-
ing at [such] dearly held thoughts."[88] Second, it involves "one's full participation in the present," the capacity to bear an "active, responsive awareness
of the contents of experience as directly experienced (before the intervention of complex intellectual activity)."[89]

Zeami uses the term *mushin* in isolation six times and in compounds nine
times in his treatises.[90] All of these usages occur in *Kakyō* or treatises
believed to have been written later than *Kakyō*. The term is also used in
the course of the section of *Kakyō* titled, "Concerning the One-Mindedness
That Connects the Myriad Actions." The relevant passage builds on the
one quoted earlier in this section. It goes,

> It will not be well for [the performer] to appear to have [some kind
> of] inner intent. If something is palpable, then it becomes a tech-
> nique. It will [cease to] be "no-doing." Having achieved a level of no-
> mind (*mushin*), you should connect the intervals with an ease of
> mind (*anshin*)[91] whereby even your own intent is hidden from your-
> self. This, in other words, is [the crux of] the spiritual force [capable
> of arousing feeling][92] that emerges in the connecting of myriad acts
> by means of the one mind (*isshin*).[93]

Zeami is describing a state of mind beyond the discriminating consciousness, an impression that is reinforced by his mention of personal
intent ("your own intent" in the translation above). This is a gloss for *waga
kokoro*, literally "my mind/heart." The Sino-Japanese reading of the character for "my" (*waga*), pronounced "*ga*," has strong Buddhist connotations.
"Ga" refers to "self" or "ego" (*ātman*), which, from a Buddhist standpoint,
does not exist. All sects of Buddhism share the premise of "non-self" (*muga*;
anātman), which may be characterized as the "principle of the nonexistence

of the ego, whereby the Buddha meant to say that an enduring personality or individual soul cannot be demonstrated to exist."[94] If one wrongly clings to a belief in "self" as a self-existing entity, then such an unreflexive stance will impede one's full attunement to one surroundings. Zeami seems to be employing the term here to state that the performer must tap into something more than his own personal intentions if he is to have the desired effect on his audience. As soon as an audience detects a willful intent on the part of the actor to impress them, this will have an alienating effect. To avoid such a pitfall, the actor must train until he reaches a level at which his innermost intent is beyond his own discriminating consciousness.

Zeami makes a statement in *Shūgyoku tokuka* that draws an explicit link between the state of *mushin*, evocation of the "wondrous flower," and the actor's ability to move beyond conscious intent in his acting. Such ability is linked to what he refers to as the true level of ease (*shinjitsu no an'i*).

> Though [the actor] play all manner of roles, not even the thought, "This is effortless," will occur to him inwardly. This is acting free of self-conscious effects or intent (*mukyoku mushin*). Might this be a level that may be called the wondrous flower of original nonbeing (*honmu myōka*)?[95]

Here his reference to "nonbeing" suggests that his framing of the topic of the actor's superlative mental conditioning was guided both by Buddhist and Daoist teachings on the subject (*mu* in Buddhist discourse, *wu* in Daoist). As Chang has pointed out in his study, from a Buddhist point of view, "conscious intention of attaining something" constitutes an impediment to achieving *śūnyatā*, the wisdom of the Middle Way.[96] To achieve such wisdom, all impediments must be removed. To do this, the Buddha advocated negation of "everything that could be conceived of as an object of thought." Regarding this point, Chang cites a teaching propounded by the fourth Ch'an patriarch, Daoxin.

> All the hindrances to the attainment of *bodhi* [wisdom] which arise from passions that generate karma are originally non-existent. Every cause and effect is but a dream. There is no triple world which one leaves, and no *bodhi* to search for. The inner reality and outer appearance of man and ten thousand things are identical. The great Tao is formless and boundless. It is free from thought and anxiety.[97]

The reference in the passage above to the Dao is a reminder that along with the Mādhyamika philosophy, Daoist philosophy had a profound impact on Mahayana schools that developed in China, such as Tiantai and Chan (Zen). Daoist teachings, too, warn against harboring a sense of self as a self-contained entity. Zeami also alludes to Daoist canonical works, such as the *Dao de jing*, in his treatises, and his reference in the passage above to the "wondrous flower of original nonbeing" also has a Daoist ring. His observation is reminiscent of a precept set forth in Book 38 of the *Dao de jing*, which reads,

> The highest attainment (Tē) [Jpn. *toku*] is free from attainment.
> Therefore, there is attainment.
> The lowest attainment is never free from attainment.
> Therefore, there is no attainment.[98]

In his exegesis of this passage, Chang explains that attainment involves the cultivation of "non-discrimination, non-differentiation, and above all, non-willing." He further cites the following precept of the *Zhuangzi*.

> When *Tē* is achieved, one is said to have returned to one's original nature. Thus, when the man of *Tē* stays inside, he is free from thoughts. When he acts, he has no worries. In the depths of his mind, nothing is contained.[99]

Such emptiness at the depths of mind is the product of a pre-ontological attunement that eschews dualisms. As stated in Book 16 of the *Dao de jing*,

> Reality is all-embracing.
> To be all-embracing is to be selfless.
> To be selfless is to be all-pervading.[100]

By letting go of the concept of self, one may come to experience the Dao, or the Way, the ultimate source of creativity. Again we turn to a passage from the *Dao de jing* for a characterization of such a reality.

> Ten thousand things in the universe are created from being.
> Being is created from non-being.[101]

Nonbeing for the Daoist is the wellspring out of which being becomes manifest. Kasulis characterizes the relation of personal creativity to the Dao as an "unselfconscious responsiveness."

> The Taoist's activity, like the operation of the Tao itself, arises natu-
> rally *in accordance with that which is*. To objectify the self, to consider
> it an agent of activity, is to overlook the Nonbeing at the source of
> all existence.[102]

Nonbeing "*precedes* and underlies the distinction between Being and its opposite, Nonbeing," Kasulis further notes. For this reason, he holds that "it is perhaps best to speak in terms of a *pre*-ontology of Nonbeing."[103] Zeami's discussions of nonbeing seem to make an analogous distinction. Whereas he characterizes the style of the profound flower in terms of the interpenetration of being and nonbeing, "the wondrous flower of original nonbeing *(honmu myōka)*" that he alludes to above seems to parallel the absolute, pre-ontological sense of the term.

The concept of *mushin* also seems to have assisted Zeami in establishing an argument for a pre-ontological basis for tacit communication between actor and audience. He not only allots the quality of *mushin* to the cultivated mind of the successful actor, but also to an uncultivated or pre-reflective state of nondiscriminating consciousness that characterizes sentient beings. It will be recalled that Zeami states in *Shūgyoku tokuka* that all beings are sensitive to the rhythms of *jo-ha-kyū*.

> Upon careful reflection, it becomes clear that all things in the universe,
> good and bad, large and small, sentient and insentient, embody *jo-ha-
> kyū*. From the chirping of birds to the crying of insects, . . . the sing-
> ing of each in abidance with its own nature constitutes *jo-ha-kyū*.[104]

After this passage, he inserts an explanatory note in the text stating, "In other words, these [phenomena] constitute the fulfillment of a gradeless *mushin (mui mushin no jōju)*."[105] He holds that all beings, whether consciously or not, embody the condition and are thus susceptible to the workings of this universal dynamic.

In an analysis of Zeami's understanding of *mushin*, Yusa addresses how it can be that *mushin* is equally present in the most cultivated and the most uncultivated of subjects from the perspective of "the Zen doctrine of the nature of the mind." She delineates a distinction between "the *satori*-mind" [the enlightened mind] and *"mushin."* The *satori*-mind is "possessed by only those people who have had the *satori* experience," whereas *mushin*, or "no-mind," refers to the "pure mind free of conceptualization and images (which is universally shared by all, but consciously apprehended by only those who have had the *satori* experience.)"[106] The difference between these two levels of understanding is the level of reflexivity that a person enjoys concerning his own embodiment of "no-mind."

It is also important to add that the belief that grasses and trees—in fact, all things in existence—could achieve enlightenment (*sōmoku jōbutsu*) was an established premise of Japanese Tendai and Shingon discourses and by Zeami's time had become a popular belief that extended well beyond ecclesiastic circles.[107] The understanding on Zeami's part of *mushin* as universally immanent in beings both sentient and insentient can be seen as consistent with this idea as well. The notion that all beings without exception were susceptible to the workings of *jo-ha-kyū* can be argued to be an extension of this basic idea. The passage quoted above from the Japanese Tendai commentary (*Ichijō shō*)—"Everything from our own speech to the sound of the waves rising or the wind blowing is the threefold contemplation in a single mind"—is a further expression of the widespread belief that all beings, sentient and insentient alike, possess the same Buddha nature.

ONE-MINDEDNESS (ISSHIN)

We will conclude this section on Zeami's appropriation of terms from religious discourses to describe the performing mind with a brief investigation into one more term having Buddhist antecedents. Zeami uses this term, *isshin* (one-mindedness/one mind), in the *Kakyō* passage above that reads,

> Having achieved a level of *mushin*, you should connect the intervals with an ease of mind (*anshin*) whereby even your own intent is hidden from yourself. "This, in other words, is [the crux of] the expressive power that emerges in the connecting of myriad acts by means of the one mind (*isshin*).[108]

As early as the third chapter of *Kaden* the term *isshin* appears, but in this *Kakyō* usage it refers more specifically to a certain type of mastery on the part of the actor.

To have reached the ultimate mastery at which the two concerns (lit. "two minds": *futatsu no kokoro*) of vocal music and stage business come to be of one mind (*isshin*) is the mark of peerless skill. This will be noh that is truly strong.[109]

Both the chanting and the acting ought to be unified in the "one mind" of the actor. That is, the actor's concentration forms the mutual basis for techniques appealing both to the auditory and visual faculties. Zeami reiterates this conception of "one-mindedness" as constituting the mutual ground for the various techniques in the much later transmission *Sarugaku dangi* as well. He draws an explicit link between such a dynamic and the fulfillment of the "wondrous flower": "Those spots in which acting and vocal music [both] adhere to the one mind will be where the wondrous flower of myriad virtues will open."[110] Maintaining mental concentration, or *isshin*, seems to be a prerequisite to eliciting optimal effects—that is, to making the "wondrous flower" open. Not only does this *isshin* provide the integrative basis for the various techniques, but, as stated in the quotation above from *Kakyō* concerning the "connecting of myriad acts by means of the one mind (*isshin*)," *isshin* should constitute an all-pervasive consciousness out of which moments of no-doing should arise.

While *isshin* thus has significance as a technical term specific to *sarugaku*, it also has Buddhist antecedents that offer reference points in exploring Zeami's usage of the term. As a Buddhist term, it denotes "the absolutely non-dual mind of suchness (*shinshō*) from which all worldly phenomena arise."[111] In his exegesis of this "connecting of the myriad acts" passage in *Kakyō*, Nearman argues that the *isshin* usage is especially reminiscent of the philosophy of consciousness promulgated in Hossō Buddhism. The Hossō school, which entered Japan in the seventh century, is sometimes referred to as the Consciousness-Only (Jpn. Yuishiki) school because it propounds that "all phenomena are produced from seeds (Skt. *bīja*; Jpn. *shūji*) stored in the *ālayavijñāna* (Jpn. *arayashiki*),"[112] or "store-consciousness." All antecedent experience comes to be stored as these seeds, which will affect future deeds. The store-consciousness may contain both defiled seeds and pure dharmas. As a person moves toward enlightenment, "the defilements are gradually eliminated and displaced by pure dharmas until finally there occurs a 'revolution of the personality-base.' "[113] This revolution occurs when the perceiver comes to realize that all "external things are shown by one's own mind."[114] That is to say, when an individual is able to cultivate consciousness of the illusory nature of the workings of the mind, realizing through meditation and discipline that the images that appear are "self-reflections of the mind" with no external reality of their own, then he can be said to have acquired an enlightened mind free from dualistic thinking.

According to Hossō doctrine, the store-consciousness is one of eight kinds of discernment or consciousness (vijñāna). The first five correspond to the senses of seeing, hearing, smell, taste, and touch. The sixth consciousness, "mind-consciousness," integrates the sensory perceptions of the first five senses and makes judgments about the external world. The seventh consciousness is "the thought center," which "judges, evaluates, and discriminates what the sixth has organized, and is identified as the source of feelings of 'self.' "[115] The eighth consciousness is the aforementioned "store-consciousness," in which reside the accumulated experiences of present and past lifetimes as seeds. The store-consciousness provides the karmic framework for a person's individual existence.[116] Nearman characterizes this eighth consciousness as "comprised of the innate, conditioned, or remembered contents of mind that come into play in response to the functioning of the other levels of mind." Together these eight centers "create what is subjectively experienced and defined as 'the world.' "[117] Nearman detects affinities between the Hossō theory of self-cultivation and Zeami's ideas on the actor's cultivation of mind.[118]

In Hossō teachings, the aforementioned "revolution" of one's personality is promulgated as the change of these eight states of consciousness into four states of mind "whose essence is the divine knowledge." For example, the seventh level of consciousness, which in the unenlightened consists of a sphere that differentiates phenomena and fosters deluded notions about self-consciousness and egotism, "changes into a state of mind which considers all creatures and things to be one and the same, thereby becoming the very source of sympathy for all animated beings."[119] The term that Nearman uses to describe the development of this "mind function" is "wisdom of equanimity," and he compares this condition to that point in an actor's training at which he has "gained mastery over his thoughts and feelings so that they do not unconsciously and inappropriately color his performance," and has "freed himself from self-conscious impulses."[120] He notes that this "wisdom of equanimity" would correspond "in Zeami's text to the 'assurance' that arises from the development of 'single-mindedness' [isshin]."[121]

As for the eighth consciousness, the "store-consciousness," it transforms from the receptacle for seeds—some of them deluded—to the receptacle of the "Buddha-body in the sphere of enlightenment." This enlightened condition is tantamount to the Great Mirror (Jpn. *daien kyōchi*), where "the storehouse of consciousness now functions to reflect the world as it is rather than to create an illusory 'world' that is taken for real."[122] Nearman explains that "one-mindedness" in relation to this eighth center is "designated paradoxically in both Hossō and Zeami texts as *mushin*, 'beyond mind,' referring to this mind as a mirror beyond the illusory imaginings produced by the discriminating seventh consciousness." Finally, he suggests that the title of Zeami's treatise, *Kakyō*, or "Mirror of the flower," was consciously inspired by this mirror imagery: "the mirror [that is the result] of the flower[ing of the actor's creativity]."[123] Nearman does not wish to suggest that Zeami was merely copying Hossō doctrine or promulgating his religious views. Rather, the parallels "derive primarily from a similarity of the psychological mechanisms that produce states of heightened awareness, insight, and creative freedom."[124]

It would seem that Nearman is correct that Zeami's title for his treatise was at least in part inspired by this mirror metaphor as it is used in Hossō precepts. This connection is especially intriguing because one major patron of Yamato *sarugaku*, the Kōfukuji, was the head temple of the Hossō sect in Japan.[125] At the same time, it is important also to emphasize the eclectic nature of Zeami's religious allusions. Already in this chapter we have noted parallels with Tendai, Zen, and Daoist sources as well as with Hossō ones. Zeami's usage of the mirror image is one example of his eclectic approach. In the ensuing chapter, for instance, I will introduce an allusion that Zeami makes to another famous mirror in a scripture at the heart of the Zen canon, *The Platform Sutra*. Specific sectarian differences aside, the mirror as metaphor for the psyche is widespread in both Buddhist and Daoist traditions.

"Mirror-knowledge," on the basis of which phenomena may be reflected indiscriminately, is a symbol of enlightenment that has antecedents going back to Pali and Sanskrit texts.[126] In Buddhist scriptures the mirror is also a stock image of impermanence,[127] one example of something that appears to have substance but is actually illusory. According to Mādhyamika philosophy, for instance, "it refers to all 'things' (dharmas) and entities without exception, since they are 'empty' (*śūnya*) of self-nature and are nothing but the product of the play of causes and conditions."[128] A reflection is a conditioned production that does not exist externally. So, too, is the mind. In Daoist writings also, the mind is frequently likened to a mirror that indiscriminately reflects the universe. This requires detachment and a serenity that is like a calm body of water. Take, for instance, the following passage from the *Zhuangzi*: "The mind (*xin* [Jpn. *kokoro*]) of the sage is quiet, it is the *mirror of heaven and earth*, and reflects the whole multiplicity of things."[129] For Daoists, a clear mirror is a metaphor for complete attunement undisturbed by arbitrary or partial views.

All of these examples of the mirror metaphor share a basic premise in keeping with Zeami's descriptions of utmost stage effects in *sarugaku* performance. Zeami seems to suggest that the supremely accomplished actor is like a mirror insofar as he can reflect phenomena in their suchness with a spontaneity unimpeded by discriminations between subject and object, actor and audience member.[130] The optimal training of the performer might be said to involve steps that induce him to shed subjectively based predilections that stand to impede such spontaneity.

The Actor's Path

It should be evident that Zeami was familiar with religious terms and ideas and not averse to employing then in his treatises. As mentioned above, *sarugaku* patrons at Kōfukuji belonged to the Hossō sect, hence a general knowledge on Zeami's part of Hossō teachings was to be expected. We do know that his critical writings that postdate the first three chapters of *Kaden* show a heightened frequency of terms that have Buddhist connotations or originate in Buddhist philosophy.[131] He took Buddhist vows by 1422, which means that he would have completed *Kakyō* within two years of having done so. We also know that he was affiliated with the Sōtō temple, Fuganji, in the Nara area.

We do know that Zeami came increasingly to explain the phenomenology of *sarugaku* with deliberate reference to religious beliefs and practices of his time. If we wish to understand his thinking on actor and audience relations, familiarity with contemporary intellectual and religious trends is obviously important. As Hoff has observed,

> It is helpful . . . to note how naturally, once he had begun to conceptualize the otherwise practical matters of theater, Zeami did so through terminology and ideas already at hand in the intellectual climate of the day. The importance of Buddhism at the time, especially of Zen, makes it understandable that its thought and practice would

provide him the clue, later in life, for an understanding of the joint experience of actor and audience.[132]

This point, that religious terminology and ideas may have become increasingly useful to articulate and guide Zeami's practical stage-derived insights, is an important one. At the same time, Hoff points out that Zeami's critical treatises are practical explanations of what works onstage, and his theoretical observations are the outgrowth of intuitions cultivated as an actor.

While adhering to the kind of balanced perspective that Hoff lays out, this chapter has aimed to track Zeami's references to several key religious concepts in order to suggest that they offered him both intellectual and experiential frameworks within which to articulate and develop his own ideas on the nature of *sarugaku* performance. We have seen that Zeami's treatises that postdate the early chapters of *Kaden* place increasing emphasis on postulating spiritual cultivation of the actor as integral to the elicitation of optimal effects onstage. He draws heavily on a range of religious terms and concepts to describe the ideal state of "mind," and he makes it quite clear that such a state is key to achieving optimal attunement with audiences. His precepts on *jōju* (fulfillment) and *jo-ha-kyū* assume an ontology in which the timing and sequencing of a performance must take into account the universal principles that motivate all beings. Moreover, he sees the non-discriminating state of *mushin* as instrumental to the achievement of a level of ease, which is a prerequisite to achieving such attunement with audiences.

Yet try as we might to grasp the nature of these effects, no amount of description of the accomplished actor once he "has arrived" will shed light on how he "got there." Moreover, concepts such as *mushin* and the wondrous cannot be expected to yield their meanings as concerns *sarugaku* practice without being resituated in that context. In the concluding chapter of this volume, we will return to Zeami's theories on training the actor. How does his training program foster the desired transformation in the actor from an ego-based sensibility to the detached sensibility on which he claims supreme effects depend? The analysis will concentrate on the stages of training as set down in a selection of Zeami's later treatises, and it will focus on their processual aspects, since Zeami's mature conception of how to instill the ability to connect with audiences is best explored from that developmental perspective.

Zeami's later writings suggest that he had come to consider the two modes of dance and chant as something much more than a delivery system for certain types of subject matter or even for promoting certain moods. They became the basis for implementing some fundamentally Buddhist and Daoist ideas about how a somatically driven transformation might be induced in the actor, a transformation that he had come to see as a prerequisite to achieving attunement with audiences. The two modes, and also the three styles, had become the fundamental program for bracketing the actor's subjectivity and thereby smoothing his progress toward the optimal state of no-mind.

7

·   ·   ·

Mind and Technique

THE TWO MODES IN TRAINING

This final chapter will return to issues related to Zeami's acting theory in his late critical writings, especially the training process that he advocates the novice actor undergo to optimize his ability to cultivate attunement with audiences. Particular attention will be paid to the views that Zeami articulates on the centrality of the performance configuration of *nikyoku santai* to the actor's training and development. Just as this configuration comes to be fundamental to his ideas about how the stage event is to be organized and how the play is to be composed, it also comes to serve as a set of guidelines for cultivating the optimal state of mind in the performer. I will argue that his incremental approach to training, with dancing and chanting to precede and then mediate acquisition of mimetic (*monomane*) techniques, was closely linked to the larger aim of honing the actor's ability to adjust spontaneously and fluently to all local variables in performance.

A central premise of this chapter is that the two modes of dance and chant not only came to be the guiding principles for how a noh performance was to be organized, but also came to be guidelines for a process of growth that the actor was to undergo in order to become capable of "the true flower" (*makoto no hana*), artistry that retains fresh appeal despite the passage of time. Zeami came to view the two modes to be just as central to the ideal process of maturation demanded of the actor as they were to the ideal performance by the mature actor. That is, they were just as important to "getting there" as they were to "being there." On the one hand, they are techniques that the actor must first absorb in order to cultivate the fluency and automaticity that he needs to react spontaneously on stage. Yet once the actor has reached the maturity of the uppermost levels of mastery, where such techniques have become second nature, then, paradoxically, following them is no longer an issue that requires his conscious attention.

Whereas the novice actor relies on such techniques to cultivate both body and mind, in the end the seasoned performer may achieve mastery only by internalizing such guidelines to the point that they are no longer part of his conscious awareness as he performs. Only then will he enjoy the spontaneity and attunement to his immediate surroundings that is needed for optimal effects onstage. The final segment will pursue Zeami's ideas about the actor who has reached the "level of seasoned fluency" (ran'i) and the stage of returning (kyakurai), both core concepts in his late treatises, whereby the actor may move audiences just as well by breaking away from the norms as by following them. In the final analysis, the actor's freedom depends on jettisoning conscious constraints imposed throughout the training process. At the same time, he must rely on intuitions that could not have been developed without such prior training.

"The Flower is the Mind; The Seed is Technique"

This section will begin with some further remarks on the famous precept introduced in the preceding chapter, "The flower is the mind; the seed is technique."[1] Zeami is employing the images of seed and flower to articulate his perceived interrelation of body and mind. The term "technique" (waza) here refers to all possible elements of acting, such as chanting, dancing, vigorous moves, and mimetic moves.[2] He explains that "flower" refers to that kind of stage effect that is attainable once the actor has mastered all the types of roles, internalized them, and come to understand how he can inspire his audience with a sense of novelty.[3]

As Nishio has noted, Zeami's use of the flower/seed imagery constitutes a significant departure from the canonized precedent of poet Ki no Tsurayuki as set down in his "Kana Preface" to the Kokin waka shū. In that document, Tsurayuki speaks of the human mind (kokoro) as the seed that gives birth to the "leaves of words." In contrast, Zeami's idea is that "[o]n the basis of training in the techniques, the flower that is expressive of the workings of the mind opens." Nishio further explains, "Training of the mind is made immanent in the training of the body; training by means of the mind is only possible when premised on training by means of the body."[4] Whereas in Tsurayuki's conception the mind is an a priori entity that expresses itself in words, Zeami's conception involves a cultivated "mind" that develops congruently with the body in the course of training.

For Zeami, the process of training is a lifelong one predicated first on mastering the technical aspects of the art through practice. When he wrote, "The flower is the mind; the seed is technique," he had not yet formulated the program of training represented in the *nikyoku santai*.[5] However, in the same chapter of *Kaden* that contains the initial instance of this precept, he does define training as a process of mastering basic models *(katagi)* involving vocal music, dance, vigorous moves, and *monomane*.[6] Mastery of technique depends on acquiring fluency in the established models of vocalization and movement. As a novice, the actor must engage in molding his physical being to this set of externally imposed standards. Zeami's most immediate concern in this discussion is that the learner gain mastery of all the various styles or techniques in order to become able to cater to the tastes of all kinds of audiences. The flower that creates a sense of novelty blossoms as a result of the actor's cultivation of mind. Such cultivation is possible on the basis of technical mastery of a variety of materials.

The idea that the *katagi* themselves may elicit new bodily modalities that may, in turn, create a new frame of "mind" becomes more focused in his later discussions of training in the paradigm of the *nikyoku santai*. As we have seen, this configuration was an innovation that had an impact on all aspects of Zeami's style of *sarugaku*. He was able to intensify the musical and choreographic modalities a) in the playing of all kinds of roles, and b) in the training of the actor. The process of training comes to be treated as incremental, with prescribed steps, the two modes first and the three styles and their derivatives only later.

Path to "A Style Having Mastery" (*Ushufū*)

Zeami's critical discussions of the relation of mind and technique from his middle works onward build on this training program. It will be recalled that in *Shikadō*, for instance, he calls for strict abidance to the *nikyoku santai* as a prerequisite for achieving a "style having mastery" *(ushufū)*. First the novice must learn by modeling himself after his teacher. Then he must make what he imitates his own. Then he must internalize it in "body and mind" (*shinjin*), and when he has reached a "level of ease" (*yasuki kurai/an'i*), then he can be said to be the master of his style (*nushi nari*). This, Zeami says, should make for "noh that is alive."[7]

While such training in the acquisition of bodily modalities is guided by external models, including both the teacher and the *katagi*, Zeami does not seem to be advocating that the actor shed all individual flavor in the process of acquiring skills. Rather, twice in the *Shikadō* passage he notes that natural talent is also part of the composite effect of training. For example,

> When, on the basis of his innate artistic potential, he quickly achieves the proficiency that training and study avail, and becomes "that thing" (*sono mono*), then he may be considered to possess a style having mastery.[8]

While annotators differ on the meaning of "that thing" (*sono mono*) in this passage, they concur that it involves the actor successfully appropriating and internalizing the various standards of *sarugaku* on the basis of his ability and training. The NSTS edition points the reader to a passage in *Kakyō* that defines *sono mono* as someone who has become an expert performer with the requisite level of artistry to be granted permission to teach.[9] Tanaka argues that *sono mono* refers to the art of the actor's teacher—that is, the learner has appropriated the art of his teacher and made it his own. Both of the older annotations, in NKBT 65 and Nose, state that it means that one's self and one's art have become as one.[10]

In any case, all interpretations agree that a personal transformation occurs on the part of the actor by means of training. At the same time, that training also serves to draw out and build on the talent or potential that the actor already enjoys individually. The importance that Zeami accords to the innate ability of the actor is reiterated in the subsequent section in *Shikadō* in which he introduces the metaphor of skin, muscle, and bone to explain the various levels of an actor's appeal. It will be recalled from chapter 3 that Zeami refers to the actor's expression of his native ability as "bone," whereas "muscle" corresponds to accomplishment in dancing and chanting and "skin" to the beauty and ease of the actor's image. Indeed, he seems to credit such innate ability with having potential for optimal effects. This passage also states that whereas the skin level corresponds to visual effects and the muscle level to aural effects, the bone level speaks to the mind (*kokoro*) of the spectator, the deepest level of reception.[11]

However, no matter how talented the novice actor, his talent can develop only if he submits to a rigorous training program. In part 1, Zeami's precepts in *Shikadō* on how the child actor should train were also introduced. He advocates that the two modes be inculcated prior to the three styles because this is the optimal approach for prolonging into adulthood the gracefulness (*yūgen*) that is natural to the childish form. Such inculcation of the two modes thus involves two quite different effects. On the one hand, it elicits a transformation of the novice actor's physical modes of being through the acquisition of forms, and a concurrent "bracketing" of his subjectivity. "Bracketing" is the term Nagatomo employs to underscore that at the beginning stages of training, "an actor *qua* subject cannot allow an interference of his subjective inclinations to influence the process of training."[12] At the same time, a second rationale underlying Zeami's advocacy of the two modes seems to have been perpetuation of the physical beauty particular to the youthful actor. He seems to be recognizing the actor's personhood—not as the extension of his original subjective mind, but rather as an extension of his youthful bodily presence.

The Two Modes as Vessel

The fundamental importance of the *nikyoku santai* in the education of the young actor is perhaps most graphically described in the treatise *Yūgaku shudōfū ken*, in which Zeami applies the metaphor of a vessel (*ki/utsuwa*) to characterize the actor who has thoroughly internalized dance and chant. For instance, he states,

> As for the performance of a very young child, the various types of
> *monomane* should not be taught that much. He should train entirely
> in the style of the two modes of dance and chant. These should be
> as a vessel.[13] The reason is that dance and chant are modes of expres-
> sion shared by all the arts of performance (*yūgei no shokyoku*). They
> are not techniques limited to this art alone. They constitute a style
> that is all-encompassing in musical entertainment (*yūgaku*).[14]

The two modes serve as a "vessel" that embraces all specific techniques, or, as the NKBT 65 annotation states, the two modes are "basic arts that 'blanket' or 'contain' (*hōkatsu suru*) all techniques in the art of *sarugaku*."[15] Unlike specific types of role-play, chanting and dancing are omnipresent elements. Therefore, training in these two arts should provide the actor with skills of a much broader applicability than those specific to *monomane* role types. Techniques of role-play should be developed only after the more elemental "vessel" is formed to contain them.

> Having thoroughly mastered these two modes, gradually, as [the young actor] approaches adulthood, what he can do will come together,[16] and already when he reaches the time to train in the three styles, no matter what [he performs], his chant will arouse feeling, and his dance will have interest. Is this not the reward for his virtue of having cultivated and sustained the vessel of dance and chant? I repeat, master fully the point that you should make the two modes the vessel that is all-encompassing, and make *monomane* your action (*waza*) [therein].[17]

Zeami warns that if the young performer masters *monomane* at a premature stage in his development, that is, prior to internalization of the two modes, then he may win provisional acclaim for his precocious acting. However, as he grows older, his style will cease to look precocious and will lose its novelty with audiences. Techniques of imitation in scale for a child actor will look too constricted when played by an adult. His precocious appeal will disappear because the beauty of the boy actor's figure and voice will no longer enhance his performance when he grows into manhood. Zeami reiterates that the way to preserve the gracefulness of youth is to train the body in danced and chanted modalities. Through acquisition of these techniques, the actor is undergoing guided transformation as his raw material is developed. The fact that chanting and dancing are not role specific in Zeami's mature conception of the *nikyoku santai* means that the actor who has mastered the two modes has a very broad and varied artistic base upon which to develop. The two modes form a framework within which enactment of the styles of *monomane* and their derivatives may unfold. More will be said about the vessel metaphor at the end of the chapter.

THE DEVELOPING ACTOR IS LIKE A RICE SEEDLING

In the same treatise, Zeami likens the actor's development to that of a rice seedling, and he warns that the seedlings should not be tampered with in the early stages of their development: "What should one do to cultivate a seedling? It seems that one should simply water it and let it grow on its own"[18] He further states,

> Concerning training in our art as well, when a very young child, [the actor] is like a seedling who, on the basis of the "moisture" provided by the two modes, will already come to flower. And even when his visional affect [stage presence] has reached its prime, to know what it is to come to fruition entails pondering and assimilating the established style[19] that will assure the longevity of his art; remaining mindful that there will be criticisms of his visional affect, good and bad, that are beyond his awareness; and engaging in training that will not allow him to forget that his ability to inspire a deep impression in his art should increase as the years go by, even when he grows old.[20]

Zeami's seedling metaphor underscores the idea that dance and chant nurture and bring out qualities that are nascent in the actor. What is more, it is better to delay specific acting techniques until the actor is past the age to outgrow them. On the other hand, the more basic and general skills of dancing and chanting do not pose this pitfall. Rather, they serve to extend the youthful grace of the actor's person into adulthood.

This lifelong process of training provides Zeami with another context within which to apply his *jo-ha-kyū* paradigm. Whereas the seedling corresponds to the *jo* phase and the flowering to the *ha* phase, the stage of fruition is *kyū*. The *jo* phase is characterized as the time to master the two modes, and the *ha* phase is the time to master skills in the "established style,"[21] but the final *kyū* phase is not defined in terms of the acquisition of technique. Rather, in this culminating phase, the cultivation of a reflexivity on the part of the seasoned actor that allows him to recognize his own weaknesses and strengths based on his receptivity to his audiences overrides any concerns about how to acquire or render specific techniques. Zeami concludes the section with a reiteration of the importance of the actor remaining vigilant concerning the likelihood that there are pitfalls in his own art beyond his ability to detect. The actor who adheres solely to his own limited perspective and ignores this likelihood is prone to experience deterioration in his art. This is akin to a rice seedling that has shot up only to be beaten down by the wind and rains, rotting without reaching fruition.

"MATTER IS NO DIFFERENT FROM VOIDNESS; VOIDNESS IS NO DIFFERENT FROM MATTER"

Zeami opens the ensuing segment of *Yūgaku shudōfū ken* with his own extrapolation of a much-quoted excerpt from the *Heart Sutra* (*Prajñā-pāramitā-hṛdaya-sūtra*; Jpn. *Hannya-haramita shin-gyō*): "Matter is no different from voidness; voidness is no different from matter" (*shiki soku ze kū, kū soku ze shiki*).[22] This is a foundational teaching on the nature of emptiness (*śūnyāta*) upon which Tiantai patriarch Zhiyi based his doctrines and meditational practices of the three truths (*santai*) and the Middle Way (*chūdō*) as broached in the previous chapter. "Matter is no different from voidness" refers to the existence of all phenomena as mutually conditioned and without permanent essence or substance. "Voidness is no different from matter" refers to the counter-premise that matter is not, therefore, altogether nonexistent. Rather, it exists provisionally through dependent origination. The Mādhyamika philosophy that Nāgārjuna first propounded took the teachings of this sutra as its basis. It teaches that "when all particular existence is reduced to *śūnyāta*, by the dialectic process of negation of negation, Supreme Enlightenment takes place and *prajñā-pāramitā*, or 'non-dual knowledge,' is fulfilled."[23]

As the NSTS annotators note, Zeami's application of this teaching to the domain of acting is a creative one. He states,

> In all artistic paths, there are the two: matter and voidness. The three stages of seedling, flower, and fruit come to a conclusion; the level of ease (*yasuki kurai/an'i*) is reached; and there is that point at which the myriad styles all find their fullest expression in accordance with the actor's artistic vision. This may be [a case of] "matter is no different from voidness."[24]

Seedling, flowering, and fruition correspond to the developmental stages in which the young actor acquires skill in the *nikyoku santai*. The level of ease is that stage in training in which the actor achieves fluency in these techniques. At this point, he has acquired the skill to freely actualize his artistic insights. Zeami enlists this line from the sutra to reinforce a point that he has consistently made since *Kaden*, that novelty and interest depend on the actor's ability to muster a wide range of performance styles. Out of the mind of the trained actor may spring a multiplicity of techniques.

However, Zeami warns, the actor who has mastered the expression of variety should not therefore assume that he need not develop further, for there is still the level that corresponds to the other part of the aphorism, "voidness is no different from matter." If the actor equates the pinnacle of his art purely with the ability to perform all manner of materials, then this is an indication that his own subjective viewpoint still limits him from grasping the nature of performance in toto. If one extends the analogy, such a limited understanding would involve the actor's failure to perceive that the forms he has mastered cannot suffice as the ultimate end of his training, for all material forms are by their nature provisional. Such a limited perception is a reminder that he should continue to practice vigilance concerning the existence of possible criticisms of his art on points that elude his own self-assessment.

Zeami's ensuing description of the performer who can rise to the level of "voidness is no different from matter" is qualitatively different from previous discussions of competence, which have centered on the acquisition of techniques. Whereas previously technique has been discussed as a set of guidelines instrumental to cultivating the optimal state of mind for a performer, in his statement below this idea is reversed. The actor has reached a plateau at which techniques are only grist for his performative intuitions, which not even he deliberates on consciously. He does not need to contrive to induce interesting effects; they emerge of their own.

> "Voidness is no different from matter" might correspond to [the case in which] there is no felt need for [self-]vigilance, and whatever is performed is done with seasoned fluency, and while clearly appearing to be an aberrant style, it arouses interest at a level in which no [distinctions can be drawn] between orthodox and unorthodox, or good and bad. If orthodox and unorthodox are together interesting, then they are beyond criticism of right or wrong. What is more, there should be no need to remain vigilant about that which is outside of one's awareness.[25]

The NSTS annotation for this level of artistry associated with "voidness is no different from matter" states, "It seems to be a metaphor for a sphere in which one's inner mind (*naishin*) is manifested in one's art without one's conscious awareness."[26] The NKBT 65 annotation states something similar: "A sphere in which one's inner mind, just as it is, is manifested in one's art." This state of mind is reminiscent of the enlightened state of *mushin* (no-mind) introduced in the previous chapter in some detail, wherein one's own intentions are hidden even from oneself. At this level, mind and body have achieved such a fluency that the actor need not attempt to monitor either. This allows him to concentrate fully on the immediate moment.

In his investigation into Zeami's uses for the term *kokoro* in his treatises, Pilgrim points out that this Buddhist phrase reflects Zeami's construal of a "hierarchy of two realms in the art." The lower is the "realm of form = void," and the higher is the "realm of void = form." Whereas in the lower realm the actor must still "use the distinction-making mind, and be aware of good and bad in his acting," in the higher realm such self-monitoring is no longer necessary. In this latter sphere, "one transcends all reason and distinctions, and acts from the basis of *mushin*."[27]

Again we encounter a paradox between Zeami's precepts on the cultivation of mind and those on acquisition of such techniques as the *nikyoku santai*. Although the actor is clearly in large part a product of intensive training in technique, ultimately he reaches a point at which he has outgrown the techniques themselves, or perhaps it is more accurate to propose that he is larger in scale than any one of them. He can freely employ them or break out of them for the purpose of creating optimal effects, but in either case he will do so with an artfulness that would not have been possible without his antecedent training. The phrase "done with seasoned fluency" in the passage above is a translation of the verbal *takekaeri*. It is a key concept in Zeami's late performance theory having to do with the issue of the mature performer's individual expressivity as his art emerges beyond techniques themselves. It will be addressed further in the context of the ensuing segment on his training program as he presents it in the late treatise *Kyūi*.

Kyūi: The Nine Levels of Artistry

Zeami's most systematic discussion about how the bodily modalities relate to the cultivation of mind in the process of training comes in *Kyūi*. This document is also especially clear on the pivotal role of the *nikyoku santai* in that overall process as he construed it in his late theory. As mentioned earlier, this is an undated treatise believed to have been composed relatively late in his career. He delineates nine levels of artistry and articulates where dance, chant, and *monomane* fit into that larger scheme. The nine levels cluster in three groupings, as follows.

Uppermost Three Levels (Phase 2)

Stage 6   Style of the wondrous flower (*myōkafū*)
Stage 5   Style of the profound flower (*chōshinkafū*)
Stage 4   Style of the serene flower (*kankafū*)

Middle Three Levels (Phase 1)

Stage 3   Style of the correct flower (*shōkafū*)
Stage 2   Style of breadth and detail (*kōshōfū*)
Entry Stage Style of early beauty (*senmonfū*)

Lowest Three Levels (Phase 3)

Style of strength and refinement (*gōsaifū*)
Style of strength and roughness (*gōsofū*)
Style of roughness and leadenness (*soenfū*)

PHASE 1, ENTRY STAGE: STYLE OF EARLY BEAUTY (SENMONFŪ)

The nine levels are not only a taxonomy, but a training program. To achieve the uppermost levels in the system, the actor must begin at the middle three levels, as marked in the listing above. Zeami's training method thus centers first on mastery of techniques. Of the three middle levels, the bottom rung, translated above as the "style of early beauty" (*senmonfū*), is where the actor should begin. At this level, the novice is expected to train exclusively in the two modes of dance and chant. Though his abilities are shallow, he is still capable of eliciting an impression of beauty.[28] Zeami's descriptive rubric for this entry style is the opening line from the *Dao de jing:* "The *Tao* [*Dao*] that can be spoken of is not the *Tao* itself."[29] He follows this with his own application of the adage to acting: "Once you have trod the true Way, then you should come to know the Way that can be spoken of [for what it is]."[30] The NSTS annotation comments that Zeami has removed this statement from its original context, in which "The *Tao* [the Way] that can be spoken of" was intended as a reference to Confucianism, which the author differentiated from the true, boundless way of the *Dao* itself.[31]

What Zeami intended by the attribution of this precept to *sarugaku* is not altogether clear. The NSTS, Tanaka, Nose, and NKBT 65 annotations and the Rimer and Yamazaki translation all agree that the true Way refers to the two modes of dance and chant. Nose, for instance, concurs that Zeami intended an analogy between the *Dao* as the true Way of the universe and the two modes of dance and chant as "the true Way" in *sarugaku*. Just as the *Dao* is viewed as a procreative force embracing all phenomena, Zeami perceived the two modes as the life force out of which all particular activities onstage should arise.[32] Interpretations of what he meant by "knowing the Way that can be spoken of [for what it is]" diverge, however. The NKBT 65 annotation speculates that this lesser Way is a reference to the aberrant styles classified in the bottom three rungs of the *Kyūi* classifications. Zeami felt that the novice actor should avoid those three at all costs, as he stresses in *Kyūi*.

In contrast, the NSTS note surmises that the "Way that is not the true Way" is a reference to training in the three styles.[33] Zeami is warning the novice actor not to consider *monomane* techniques as the most fundamental aspect of acting. Tanaka's annotation is in agreement, equating "the *Tao* itself" with the two modes and the "The *Tao* that can be spoken of" with the three styles of *monomane*. The annotation to the Rimer and Yamazaki translation also takes this position: "What the world calls the Way of nō is Role Playing, yet the True Way represents the Two Basic Arts" [the two modes].[34] These three interpretations are the best fit with what Zeami is advocating as the ideal program for growth in his late writings—that is, the two modes should serve as the all-embracing elements within which the actor might execute specific role types. As will become clear shortly, the three middle ranks of *Kyūi* provide three incremental phases for acquiring the two modes and the three styles, in that order.

The allusion to the *Dao de jing* seems a deliberate attempt on Zeami's part to underscore the fundamental significance that the two modes have come to have for all aspects of his style of *sarugaku*. As we saw in some detail in earlier segments of this volume, assigning the two modes a central place in the performance of all plays was Zeami's and Kan'ami's innovation on the mainstream style of performance in Yamato *sarugaku*. They reoriented this style of Yamato *sarugaku* from one that defined itself on the basis of its mimetic elements to one in which dance and chant came to form the underlying medium for those mimetic elements. It stands to reason that when Zeami wrote *Kyūi* he was still addressing peers whose preconceived ideas about *sarugaku* were based on traditional techniques of *monomane*. That is, through the Daoist allusion, he may have wanted to communicate that it was wrongheaded to construe techniques of imitation as the fundamental "Way" in *sarugaku*, when the "true Way" was actually composed of the more all-embracing elements of dancing and chanting.

PHASE 1, STAGE 2: STYLE OF BREADTH AND DETAIL *(KŌSHŌFŪ)*

At the next higher level, the style of breadth and detail *(kōshōfū)*, the actor solidifies his mastery of the two modes and moves on to the incremental acquisition of skills in playing specific roles, that is, the three styles and their derivatives. This is the level at which the actor acquires the techniques to actualize a wide range of styles so that he may "tell all about the spirit of the clouds on the mountains and the moon on the sea," an allusion to a phrase from the collection of Zen koans and commentaries titled *Fo guo Yuanwu chan shi Bi yan lu* (Jpn. *Bukka Engo zenji Hekigan roku,* Blue cliff record of the Zen master Engo; completed by 1125). The statement is a reference to exhaustively telling the nature of phenomena.[35] Whereas the Tanaka and NSTS annotations take this phrase to refer to all aspects of the art of *sarugaku,* Nose argues that Zeami is referring specifically to mastering all of the various representational styles in the *monomane* tradition. Given that the training actor does concentrate on internalizing the three *monomane* styles at this stage, Nose's interpretation seems plausible.[36] Zeami further states that many actors fail to rise above this level, but instead fall down into the lowest three levels because they have never sufficiently mastered the techniques.

PHASE 1, STAGE 3: STYLE OF THE CORRECT FLOWER *(SHŌKAFŪ)*

The uppermost of the three middle grades is called the style of the correct flower *(shōkafū).* At this level, the actor has trained in the entirety of the repertoire and has thoroughly internalized skills in the two modes and three styles. That is, the phase of growth involving the formal acquisition of techniques is over. Zeami describes the actor in this style as being further along than the style of breadth and detail, already at the entry stages of an artistry that is capable of eliciting the "flower."[37] Of the middle three grades, only the style of the correct flower bears the word "flower" in its name. The two lower of the entry levels pose technical challenges involving the acquisition of the *nikyoku santai.* Assumedly, the style of the correct flower is identified as being one that produces the flower because, for the first time, its practitioner can go beyond studying the techniques themselves to making artistic judgments on how those techniques should be applied in playing to specific audiences. Zeami offers two metaphors for the level of the correct flower, without offering an elucidation of them. Both seem to emphasize a bright and manifest presence of panoramic scale. The first is:

"In a bright haze, the sun sets, and all the mountains are crimson." The second is: "The bright sun alone in the blue sky, the many mountains, a bright and distant vista."[38]

From his earliest critical writings, Zeami predicates the true flower on the actor's capacity to perform multiple styles and roles. This ability allows the performer to adjust spontaneously to the moods and expectations of particular audiences. To be successful, he must be flexible enough to do this to suit all sorts of spectators. Zeami's discussion in *Kakyō* of three types of appeal in performance—the visual, the aural, and that rooted in the mind— does not simply describe the nature of audiences; it sets down the various standards that the actor must be ready to meet. The middle three grades set the foundation on which the actor can build, and they also set the scale, assuring that the actor's training will endow him with the breadth to cater to diverse tastes such as those described in *Kakyō*.

PHASE 2, STAGE 4: STYLE OF THE SERENE FLOWER *(KANKAFŪ)*

The three uppermost grades of this nine-grade scale are predicated on the technical mastery cultivated in the three middle grades. That is, achieving the style of the correct flower is a prerequisite to entry into the uppermost levels. Each of the three uppermost levels has the word "flower" in its title. The entry level of the three upper grades is *kankafū,* which I have translated as the "style of the serene flower." Zeami compares the *kankafū* style to snow piled in a silver bowl, an image that appears in a number of Buddhist texts. *Bao jing san mei ge* (Jpn. *Hōkyō zanmai ka,* Songs of meditation on the jewel mirror), a commentary by Dongshan Liangjie (807–869), a Ch'an priest of the Caodong (Jpn. Sōtō) sect, seems to be one of the earliest usages. The original phrase in *Hōkyō zanmai ka* is,

> As snow is contained in a silver bowl, and as a white heron hides in the bright moonlight, when you classify them they are different from each other, but when you unify them they are the same in the Source.[39]

In his commentary for this passage, Chang states that the images of snow and white heron are to be considered "symbols of Particularity, the objective events." On the other hand, the silver bowl and bright moonlight "refer to the Void, or universality. It is in this world of universality that the particularities join together." Another document in which this line is quoted was an influential one in Zen circles in Japan, the *Denkō roku* (Transmission of light; 1300), compiled by the Japanese Sōtō priest Keizan Jōkin (1268–1325). In his elucidation of this passage, Keizan emphasizes recognition of the existence of the particular within the universal: "Even if you understand that there is no duality, you are still carrying a one-sided view. When you examine and evaluate carefully, when a white heron stands in the snow they are not the same color, and white flowers and moonlight are not exactly like each other. Traveling in this way, you go on 'filling a silver bowl with snow, hiding a heron in the moonlight.' "[40]

In this segment of *Kyūi*, Zeami concentrates on the tactile beauty of the white snow against the silver bowl; he describes it as coloring that has white brightness and a pristine nature.[41] He also characterizes this level of acting as possessing a "truly gentle visual image." The original for "gentle" is *nyūwa*, the same word that he uses to describe the aristocratic presence having *yūgen* in the section of *Kakyō* titled "Entering the Realm of *Yūgen*." As the Tanaka annotation states, white snow was a staple image illustrative of the *yūgen* mood in medieval Japan (although Zeami does not explicitly equate the style of the serene flower with *yūgen* here).[42]

The style of the serene flower may be differentiated from the middle three levels before it because the actor is capable of a new reflexivity about his art.

> This is a critical stage at which your level of ease in each style should make a deep impression, and whether or not you have grasped the principle of the flower will become manifest. [At this point] you will be able to see effortlessly into the artistic stages that you have already [realized], and you will be firmly established in the upper levels of accomplishment in which a style having ease *[an'i]* has been reached.[43]

Thus an important attribute of this style is achievement of a level of ease (*an'i/yasuki kurai*). An'i (level of ease) was introduced in the previous chapter, in which it was described as a pivotal stage in the training of the actor. Moreover, in *Shikadō*, Zeami mentions it as one prerequisite to achieving a "style having mastery" (*ushufū*). In the passage cited above from *Yūgaku shudōfū ken*, it is also mentioned as the stage that ensues in the development of the child actor after he has undergone the stages of technical training. In *Kyūi*, this level of ease is described as a composure that comes with an unimpeded fluency in the techniques. Such fluency makes it possible for the first time to concentrate on something beyond the immediate execution of these techniques, giving the actor the leeway to look back on and assess the significance of his artistic training.

PHASE 2, STAGE 5: STYLE OF THE PROFOUND FLOWER
(CHŌSHINKAFŪ)

The second of the three upper levels in *Kyūi* is *chōshinkafū* (style of the profound flower). Zeami's metaphor describing this style is the view of one bare mountain peak that stands alone amongst snowy ones. He further likens it to the snowy peak of Mount Fuji that does not melt because the mountain "is deep"; height has its limits, but depth does not.[44] He characterizes this level as expressing the "ultimate form of *yūgen*" (*setsui no yūshi*). What is more, "the form of expression [involves] visional affect that [belongs to] the Middle Way of being and non-being (*umu chūdō*)." The annotation for this passage in NKBT 65 states that "Middle Way" may be construed as "an enlightened sphere in which the expression of being (*u*) and the expression of non-being (*mu*) are combined, but neither takes precedence."[45] As was noted in some detail in the previous chapter, Zeami is probably employing a Tendai precept in order to describe this artistic level. Such references to substance, or being, and its relation to nonsubstance, or nonbeing, are congruent with the Tendai worldview that all phenomena may be simultaneously perceived as both empty and provisionally existing. As stated under the entry for *umu* in the *Japanese-English Buddhist Dictionary*, "A dharma which is produced by causation is thought to exist; yet because it is the product of causation, it is lacking a real, permanent nature of its own; thus in an ultimate sense it is non-existent." Zeami's reference here to the Middle Way is congruent with his interest in the resolution of the particular and the universal as expressed elsewhere in his late treatises, such as his allusion to the precept from the *Heart Sutra*, "Matter is no different from voidness; voidness is no different from matter." Increasingly in his late period, he thus construes the chemistry of performance in relation to the teachings on *śūnyatā*.

MORE ON UMON/MUMON (ORNAMENTED/UNORNAMENTED)

In *Kyūi*, Zeami says nothing further about the actual application of the Middle Way paradigm to *sarugaku* performance. The NSTS, Tanaka, and Nose annotations all point out a parallel between his use of the terms "being" (*u*) and "nonbeing" (*mu*) in *Kyūi* and a discussion of distinctions between styles of vocalization recorded in his treatise *Fūgyoku shū*.[46] Zeami's usage in this treatise builds on the *u/mu* dualism, but he incorporates the two terms into the respective compounds *umon* and *mumon*, translated below as "ornamented" and "unornamented." *Mon* denotes embellishment, ornamentation, or design pattern, as in a raised design woven into a piece of fabric. *Umon* is used to refer to a vocal style that has ornamentation, whereas *mumon* refers to a style that has no obvious ornamentation. Since this latter discussion includes a number of basic parallels with Zeami's conception of mastery expressed in *Kyūi* and explains his thinking more in the context of actual performance, I include the entirety of the relevant segment below.

> Concerning the *kakari* mood [evoked by the progression of linkings] and the style of vocal music, there are two types.[47] People's tastes are of [different] types as well. There are people who enjoy a succession of measures with interesting modulation and colorful phrasing[48] and numerous spots that arouse an impression of musicality having ornamentation (*umon onkan*). Then again, there are those who like an unornamented style of vocalization that does not have much striking modulation, but simply sounds beautiful and ample. Neither should be considered superior to the other.
>
> However, there are types of non-ornamentation (*mumon*). The interesting impression that sounds as if it has no [calculated] expressivity and no ornamentation, but whose vocal mood [*kowagakari*] simply inspires interest, is an impression [created by virtue of] long experience. The performer, after having mastered the modulation and polished the accents, acquires a wondrous aural appeal [belonging to] the level of ease [*yasuki kurai*]. If the vocal music is simply [of a style] of non-ornamentation that is uncultivated [*mushin*], in which the non-ornamentation is untrained, and there is no reflection on the [mode of] expression, or mastery of the accenting, audiences will quickly tire of it.
>
> First, the level that has no ornamentation but has interest [shows] superior accomplishment. As for this [superior] level [of accomplishment], pursue the elements of training to their ultimate, master the accenting and the *ryo* and *ritsu* musical scales in executing the transitions between words and between verses, and then enter into the level of ease.[49] Internalize these various [elements] so

that they are second nature to you, and then a vocal style that elicits an impression of musicality without ornamentation will emerge. This will be unsurpassed [mujō]. When vocal music has reached this level, whether ornamented or unornamented, the substance of the expression will adhere to [the inclinations of] the mind.

Now then, as regards ornamented and unornamented [chanting], there is a distinction [to be made] in the aural expressivity. Concerning expression of the unornamented [strain], when the voice is only interesting, but upon listening very carefully, the impression is not that deep, then you may assume that it is non-ornamentation [resulting from] non-mastery. On the other hand, when chant seems to have no ornamentation, yet the impression it creates just seems more and more singular, and, at the same time, there is no limit to its interest, you will indeed know that this is non-ornamentation that has reached the ultimate [stage] of ornamentation and gone beyond it. This is the level of the wondrous voice of supreme accomplishment [jōka myōsei]. Therefore, the impression [arising from] unornamented musicality, since both ornamented and unornamented are subsumed in it, is of the first [merit]. Since there remain aspects that have not reached their ultimate in the impression [arising from] ornamented sound, it is of second [merit]. In one there are many; in two, there are only two.[50]

Both the ornamented and the unornamented styles of expression are thus premised on the acquisition of techniques and, through such training, the achievement of a level of ease. With the achievement of such fluency, the actor becomes capable of rendering techniques without reflection on those techniques per se. This constitutes a major step in the maturation process, analogous to entry into the three uppermost levels of the Kyūi system, in which the level of ease is one defining characteristic of the style of the serene flower and above.

Having reached such a level, the performer can concentrate on how to use the techniques rather than how to acquire them. For instance, he may choose to perform in either an ornamented or unornamented style. The ornamented style shows undisguised virtuosity. The unornamented style, on the other hand, channels the energy into a smooth vocal flow that does not call attention to itself. Zeami cautions that there is an inferior type of unornamented style that simply imitates the plain surface of the true unornamented style. When one listens carefully to this derivative style, it will lack depth of feeling. This is because the actor has not previously mastered the substance of the techniques or reflected on how he should render them.

The ideal style of non-ornamentation has greater complexity and depth because it subsumes and goes beyond ornamented styles. He concludes his analysis with an allusion to a line from a koan found in Case no. 2 of *Hekigan roku*: "In one there are many; in two there are only two."[51] One subsequent interpreter, the Japanese Sōtō priest Tenkei Denson (1648–1735), gives the following explanation of this phrase in *Hekigan roku*.

> If you postulate oneness, yet humans stand upright while animals stand on all fours, willows are green while flowers are red, all throughout the world; so you cannot say it is all one. Then again, if you postulate duality, still there is only one ultimate reality, the blessed ones of the ten directions all take the road to the door of nirvana, and all things return to one, so you cannot say they are dualistic. In any case, the point is that we are talking about the great way that is beyond all mundane measurements.[52]

Tenkei's statement echoes the precept embodied in the image of "snow in a silver bowl," the codependence of the particular and the universal. If we assume that Zeami interprets this aphorism from *Hekigan roku* similarly, then we may surmise that he is employing it to make the point that ornamented and non-ornamented chant, too, are codependent entities, yet they partake of a larger universal.

Yet it is difficult to explain how such a precept on codependence might suffice here to illustrate Zeami's point that the vocalist who masters a non-ornamented style has subsumed and moved beyond an ornamented style. Zeami's discussion assumes that non-ornamentation not only may be paired with ornamentation, but also somehow underlies such a dualism. In the preceding chapter, it was noted that Zeami's discussions of *u* (being/substance) and *mu* (nonbeing/nonsubstance) situate *mu* both in a dual relation with *u* (as in reference to the Middle Way [*umu chūdō*]), and in its own absolute, pre-ontological domain (as in reference to "the wondrous flower of nonbeing" (*honmu myōka*). This is a strategy that allows the notion of nonbeing or nonsubstance to be both discussed in a relative sense and also to remain "self-contained and ineffable."[53] Zeami's descriptions here of *umon* and *mumon* adopt an analogous strategy.

In *Sarugaku dangi*, Zeami further comments on the connection between technique and expressiveness in chanting, but he does so as it concerns the actual impact in performance. The passage addresses the various levels or grades of vocal music, and it opens by quoting the points on ornamented and unornamented vocalization made above in the earlier treatise *Fūgyoku shū*. To this he adds the following.

> Vocal music that simply has a beautiful melodic resonance has superior effects. Expressiveness is not [a thing]. When you become more and more advanced, and enter the level of ease, [expressiveness] naturally emerges from the modulation. It is like reflected light. So, when you find someone's expressiveness interesting, it is a preposterous thing to [try to] make it the substance [tai] of your training.[54]

Expressiveness is not itself a tangible technique and therefore cannot be imitated as such. Techniques serve to embody expression but are not tantamount to it. We have seen an analogous dynamic before in Zeami's descriptions of causal agent and effect (*tai/yū*) in *Shikadō*. He compares the causal agent to the moon, and the effect to the moonbeams, for instance. Extrapolating a bit, one cannot hope to produce a desired effect (moonbeam) without having emulated and mastered the causal agent (the moon). Techniques themselves may be viewed as design patterns (*u*) that arise out of the ground (*mu*) formed by the cultivated sensibility of the actor.

PHASE 2, STAGE 6: STYLE OF THE WONDROUS FLOWER (MYŌKAFŪ)

For Zeami, the pinnacle of stage affect comes with the accomplishment of the uppermost of the three highest grades of performance, *myōkafū*. The concept of *myō* (the wondrous or the ineffable) is another term with Buddhist connotations that is important to his conceptualization of his art, as has been seen. As mentioned in chapter 6, in the Tendai sect of Buddhism, *myōhō* (wondrous dharma) refers to "the principle of making the myriad phenomena manifest in one mind (*isshin*) and embracing the three truths (*santai*) in one's essential nature."[55] Zeami mentions the eye-opening in *Sandō* as that phase of a play in which the *shite* can open the mind's eye of the audience to the wondrous. *Myō* is also the term that he uses to describe the inspirational burst of light that occurs when Amaterasu Ōmikami opens the door of the cave, as described in *Shūgyoku tokuka*. Throughout his treatises he echoes the thought that this ultimate state cannot be captured in words and defies cognition.

In *Kyūi*, he reiterates the idea that the essence of *myō* is ineffable through citation of a phrase that pointedly defies logic: "In Silla, in the dead of night, the sun is bright."[56] After explaining that the quality of the wondrous resembles this phrase insofar as its meaning, too, is ineffable and eludes the discursive workings of the mind, he further states,

> The *yūgen* style [*yūfū*] of the supremely accomplished on this path is beyond [simple] praise. The impression of no-mind [*mushin no kan*], the detached seeing [*riken*][enabled by] a style that has no [ascribable] grade—these may be of what the Wondrous Flower consists.[57]

Thus Zeami avoids ascribing particular contents to such a style. The point seems to be that what moves audiences in the case of a performance of this caliber has little to do with particular thematic contents or moods. Rather, it has more to do with a mode of being onstage that is moving to audiences for reasons that cannot be pinpointed. It is impossible to define it in any one way. As introduced previously, Zeami's notion of *mushin* involves a mental state in which the actor transcends ego-based seeing (*gaken*) and experiences an attunement with the moment that not even he can explain in so many words. The meaning of "detached seeing [enabled by] a style that has no [ascribable] grade (*mui no ifū no riken*)" is subject to some interpretation. NSTS argues that when an actor becomes detached from consciousness of himself as performing, then a stage affect will naturally emerge that audiences will perceive as wondrous.[58]

To corroborate the same view, the NSTS annotators point out a very similar idea expressed in a segment of *Kakyō* devoted to explaining those elements of a performance that may be characterized as eliciting *myō* (the wondrous).[59] First, Zeami notes paradoxically that the substance of *myō* is "elements that have no form, or are not physically manifested (*katachi naki tokoro*)." In this earlier discussion, the effects of *myō* are not restricted to one grade of performance. Rather, they may be detectable in an actor from the very beginning of his training, although only the most discerning spectator will pick up on this fact, and the actor will not himself be conscious of it. Moreover, the average audience member will be unable to identify the specific inspiration for the interest he feels. When a superbly skilled performer elicits this sensation of *myō* in audiences, he will have a general awareness that he was able to foster that effect, but he, too, will be unable to ascribe it to particular factors. In short, if the nature of *myō* can be defined, then it is not truly *myō*, which is by its nature ineffable.

In the ensuing passage, Zeami again draws the connection between *myō* and the state of no-mind, as well as a style of performance that has no grade (*mushin mufū no kurai ni itaru kenpū*), stating,

> As concerns *myō* effects, when [a performer] has trained fully in the art and has arrived at the level of the master; when he has entered into the complete ease belonging to the level of seasoned fluency, and does not fixate on executing any particular technique; when he has arrived at visional affect at the level of no-mind/no-style [*mushin mufū*]—might this not approach *myō* effects? In general, when a *yūgen* style has been pursued to the point of seasoned fluency, might this not be a style that comes a bit close to *myō* effects?[60]

Although throughout this study I have glossed the term for visional affect (*kenpū*) as affects inspired by the performer's stage presence, especially his visual appeal, in the quotation above *kenpū* takes on a slightly more abstract nuance. Zeami is speaking of it as the manifestation onstage of intangible elements, such as a state of *mushin*, and a style unclassifiable as any particular style (*mufū*). As both annotators of the NSTS and NKBT 65 editions observe, the opening statements in the passage translated above offer a description of what is entailed in cultivating the ability to foster such an affect.[61] First, the actor must acquire the requisite techniques through thorough training. When he has mastered them fully, then he may move on to a "level of seasoned fluency" (*taketaru kurai*). The ease to which he refers has already been introduced in reference to the term "level of ease" (*yasuki kurai/an'i*) as the ability to perform easily, with a heightened reflexivity.

Although no style can replicate *myō* completely, since this is a quality that eludes tangible attributes, Zeami states that when a *yūgen* style reaches its ultimate maturity, it may come close. What he means by a *yūgen* style is not entirely clear, however. Whereas NSTS treats "*yūgen* style" (*yūgen no fūtei*) as a metonymy for "art that has reached the highest level" in general, the other annotations consulted frame this as a specific style that, when it reaches its full maturity, will approximate *myō*.[62] If we assume that this is a particular style that Zeami is referring to, what might the qualities of this style be?

Zeami does not attempt to articulate its specific qualities, nor do aforementioned annotators attempt to do so. What remains clear is that the style will be the outgrowth of a strictly prescribed training program. His words at the close of *Sandō* are a reminder that seeds of *yūgen* are the *nikyoku santai*.

> The style of expression will change over time, having old and contemporary versions, but from ages past, the master whose universal acclaim exceeds all the rest has ever been successful in capturing the atmosphere of *yūgen*. In the old style there was the *dengaku* player Itchū; in the middle years, the late master of our group, Kan'ami, and the Hie player, Inuō. All three made the *yūgen* elements of dance and chant the foundation of their styles and were masters of each of the three styles.[63]

The *Kyūi* taxonomy corroborates this, for the two modes and three styles are situated in the three middle ranks that make up the entry level. This training bears fruit in the upper echelons. Zeami makes explicit attributions of the *yūgen* quality in reference to the two uppermost levels of the *Kyūi* taxonomy. In the passage on the wondrous flower translated above, he speaks of a *yūgen* style as something subject to seasoned fluency, whereby it may approximate *myō* effects. To attempt an interpretation of this passage, it is important to next explore what is involved in this "level of seasoned fluency." Called *taketaru kurai* or also pronounced *"ran'i,"* it is another concept of key importance to understanding Zeami's late theory on an actor's training.

LETTING GO: THE LEVEL OF SEASONED FLUENCY (TAKETARU KURAI/RAN'I)

In his late drama theory, the concept of *taketaru kurai*, or *ran'i* (as it will be referred to hereafter), grows increasingly important. Whereas the *yūgen* quality is much discussed in treatises of Zeami's middle years, such as *Sandō*, *Nikyoku santai ningyō zu*, *Kakyō*, and *Shikadō*, in such late treatises as *Yūgaku shudōfū ken*, *Go on*, and *Go ongyoku jōjō*, it occupies an equally important place as *yūgen*. The *"ran"* of *ran'i* may mean "mature," "ripe," "at its peak"; or it may also mean "past its peak," "overripe." *"I"* again denotes "rank," "level," "grade." He uses *ran'i* interchangeably with the alternative reading for the term, *taketaru kurai*.

Zeami employs the term throughout his critical corpus to refer to an ideal state of maturity, in which the seasoned performer is completely in flow, beyond the constraints of conscious striving. A variation on *taketaru kurai* is used in the passage quoted earlier from *Yūgaku shudōfū ken*, which describes the acting style on a par with the precept from the *Heart Sutra*, "Voidness is not different from matter." The relevant passage goes: "there is no felt need for [self-]vigilance, and whatever is performed is done with seasoned fluency, and while clearly appearing to be an aberrant style, it arouses interest at a level in which no [distinctions can be drawn] between orthodox and unorthodox, or good and bad."[64] The term translated here as "done with seasoned fluency" is *takekaerite*, a compound verbal having the same root, *"take,"* with the verbal auxiliary suffix *"kaeri,"* which makes the statement more emphatic (having seasoned fluency to the ultimate degree). In the passage above from *Fūgyoku shū* also, Zeami speaks of seasoned fluency in connection with unornamented vocalization of the highest grade. "Singular" is the word I use for another variant consisting of the verbal stem *"take"* and the conjunctive particle *"te"* to form *takete*.

> When chant seems to have no ornamentation, yet the impression it creates just seems more and more singular, and, at the same time, there is no limit to its interest, you will indeed know that this is non-ornamentation that has reached the ultimate [stage] of ornamentation and gone beyond it. This is the level of the wondrous voice of supreme accomplishment.[65]

Zeami's first references to this concept occur in *Kakyō* and *Shikadō*. In the latter, he advises that the actor should work to eliminate unorthodox elements when in the early stages of internalizing techniques. Once he has completed such internalization, he may then occasionally mix an unorthodox style *(hifū)* with the orthodox style *(zefū)* as represented in the training program. (Elsewhere in the same treatise, Zeami describes the orthodox training program as the progression from acquisition of the two modes to that of the three styles.)[66] He states that the reason for mixing unorthodox with orthodox is the principle of novelty. Thus in this treatise, *ran'i* is treated as a style that the actor may consciously invoke by breaking away from the orthodox style and mixing in unorthodox elements.

This characterization of *ran'i* as embracing both the orthodox and the unorthodox has influenced numerous commentators' interpretations of the metaphors that Zeami employs to describe the uppermost levels of the *Kyūi* system. For instance, Nose cites the metaphor that he gives for the style of the profound flower, a bald peak among snowy ones, as evidence that he had *ran'i* in mind as an attribute of this grade of artistry. In Nose's view, the snowy peaks stand for the orthodox style of performance; the lone peak without snow is an anomaly suggestive of the unconventional *ran'i* style. The Middle Way embracing being and nonbeing (*umu chūdō*) that is mentioned in the description of this style stands for an artistic magnitude in which both orthodox and unorthodox aspects of performance are subsumed.

In his exegesis, Konishi concurs that such unorthodox elements correspond to the *ran'i* dynamic and that they coexist with orthodox *yūgen* elements in the style of the profound flower. Whereas Nose claims that *ran'i* is a style that is specific to the style of the profound flower, Konishi argues persuasively that the *ran'i* quality cannot be explained in terms of the objectified styles, but, rather, is a quality elicited by the master performer even when he chooses to perform in the style of strength and roughness or the style of strength and refinement. He states that "a non-*yūgen* style of expression is exactly [what is meant by] unorthodox, and it is just the [kind of] art that makes [the unorthodox] come alive as [seemingly] orthodox which must be the original meaning of [the term] *"ran'i."*[67] Indeed, Zeami elsewhere describes *ran'i* as a dimension that is not beholden to specific styles or techniques, but has gone beyond them. It will be recalled that in *Kakyō*, the *ran'i* concept is introduced in the larger discussion of those moments of performance that are evocative of *myō*: when the actor has "entered into the complete ease belonging to the level of seasoned fluency, and does not fixate on executing any particular technique,"[68] then his art will approach this level. This usage is similar to the usage cited above in *Yūgaku shudōfū ken*. The actor has gone beyond calculated effects. The substance of his expression may adhere to the free inclinations of his mind. At such a level, distinctions between orthodox and unorthodox become artificial.

The notion that the performer capable of *ran'i* enjoys a freedom and spontaneity that has as its prerequisite the internalization and mastery of techniques is also key to understanding a parallel concept that Zeami introduces in two of his late treatises, *Go ongyoku jōjō* and *Go on*. As previously noted, he sets down five classifications of vocal music, including the related term *rangyoku* (vocal music having seasoned fluency). In these two treatises, he describes the *rangyoku* style as a kind of vocal expression that is premised on mastery of the first four vocal styles (*shūgen* [auspiciousness], *yūkyoku* [yūgen], *renbō* [passionate longing], and *aishō* [lamentation]). It is a style more appropriate for the solo voice than for the choral voice. Just as in the case of *ran'i*, *rangyoku* assumes prior mastery of techniques and styles on the part of the performer. Such mastery allows him to trust to a highly cultivated set of intuitions in determining how to perform most effectively from one moment to the next. As Zeami notes about chanting in this modality, "having settled into the level of ease, all manner of expression arises spontaneously in accordance with one's intuitions about the moment *[sokuza no kiten]*."[69] It is the spontaneous nature of this *rangyoku* chanting that makes it technically difficult to perform in unison. We will come back to Zeami's precepts on *rangyoku* in the context of his bottommost levels of the *Kyūi* taxonomy introduced below.

THE BOTTOM THREE LEVELS OF *KYŪI*

The bottom three levels of the *Kyūi* are qualitatively different from the rest. The novice actor must not dabble in these levels unless he has already met the challenges of the middle and highest levels. The beginner must start with the style of early beauty and proceed up from there. This is because the middle three levels are his means of mastering the choreographic and vocal techniques that he will need to communicate onstage.

If an actor begins his training at these lowest levels, he will never achieve access to the uppermost levels. Starting from the bottom, the lowest three levels are the style of roughness and leadenness (*soenfū*), the style of strength and roughness (*gōsofū*), and the style of strength and refinement (*gōsaifū*). All three in this lowest grouping may be characterized as styles outside the orthodox training program that begins at the middle levels with inculcation of the *nikyoku santai*. Zeami warns that novices who begin training at these lowest levels run the risk of never even matriculating into the *Kyūi* system. Moreover, he notes that many of troupe heads train at the level of breadth and detail (*kōshōfū*) only to fail to achieve mastery at the next higher level, the correct flower (*shōkafū*). Such actors are destined to slip into the lowest three levels. One may conclude that because such actors were not able to master the two modes and three styles completely, they lacked the technical mastery needed to move upward in the system.

THE STYLE OF ROUGHNESS AND LEADENNESS (SOENFŪ)

This lowest level has little to redeem it. According to Zeami, performance that is rough and leaden will lack "detailed movement," that is, the quality of *saidō*. "Detailed movement" will be familiar as the same term that he uses in *Sandō* to refer to a breaking down of forceful expression. As he stated in that treatise, he advocated a *saidō* style for the execution of demonic roles, to better imbue an otherwise forceful facade with a "human heart."[70] He compares acting in the style of roughness and leadenness to the behavior of a flying squirrel: "A flying squirrel has five abilities: climbing trees, swimming, digging holes, flying, and running." All of these abilities are demonstrated in an unremarkable way that one would expect of a squirrel.[71] Although Zeami attributes this anecdote to *The Analects of Confucius*, in fact, the source appears to be a philosophical tract by the Confucian scholar Xunzi (313?–238? B.C.E.). That document states, "The squirrel has five talents, but cannot perform any one of them to perfection."[72] The purport of the statement in this context is that a squirrel will lack the concentrated focus that will allow it to excel in any one task. The term for "roughness" embraces that which is coarse, as well as having the nuance of being uncontrolled or wild. Whereas the word "strong" occurs in the two uppermost of the three low levels, the bottom level is not described as strong, but instead as rough or coarse.

In his exegesis of this passage, Nearman makes the point that Zeami's final statement in this segment, "When performing lacks refining, it is rough and leaden," may have multiple interpretations. Although in his rubric for the level of roughness and leadenness Zeami allots a Chinese character meaning "leaden" (pronounced "*en*" in its Sino-Japanese reading), the word for leaden is written elsewhere in this passage in a variant Japanese reading that is pronounced "*namaru*" and is written in phonetic symbols from the Japanese *kana* syllabary. This phonetic rendering of the orthography leaves open the possibility for alternate interpretations. Two further homonyms for *namaru* are possible, as Nearman points out. They are words meaning "dull or blunted" or "speak with a provincial accent or use a dialect speech pattern." Thus, here *namaru* may also be glossed as "When performing lacks refining, it is coarse and dulled" or as "it is coarse and sounds provincial." Nearman further observes that this second reading suggests that "acting in medieval Japan had reached a state of sophistication where the necessity for special vocal training for stage use was recognized and appreciated."[73] In any case, it is safe to conclude that acting at this bottommost level is unschooled and unrelated to the program of training that Zeami has developed.

THE STYLE OF STRENGTH AND ROUGHNESS (GŌSOFŪ)

The middle level of the bottom three is described as both strong and rough. Zeami compares this acting style to the behavior of a newborn tiger. His encapsulation resembles a phrase in a collection of Chinese poetry titled *Shihmen wen zi chan* (Jpn. *Sekimon moji zen*, The written word and [Zen] meditation at Shimen), composed by the southern Song priest Dehuang: "After a tiger is born and has lived three days, it will want to eat a cow."[74] While the actor in this category enjoys a formidable strength that is not present in the bottommost *soenfū*, he also lacks the refinement enjoyed by the actor occupying the next higher level. Zeami's differentiation between strong (*tsuyoki*) and rough (*araki*) is reminiscent of the distinction he makes between the same two qualities in chapter 6 of *Kaden*. His remarks in that earlier tract have to do with the apt imitation of subjects belonging to either of two groups, the strong or the *yugen*, that is, gentle characters.

> You should know that in all imitation (*monomane*), those spots that are untruthful will seem rough or weak. . . . First, if you play an inherently weak [or gentle] subject in a strong way, since [such imitation] is untruthful, it will seem rough. When you play an inherently strong subject in a strong way, this will seem strong. It will not seem rough. When you try to play an inherently strong subject in a *yūgen* style, since it will not be [truthful] *monomane*, it will not seem to have *yūgen*, it will seem weak. . . . Moreover, if you play [a strong subject] too strongly, it will seem particularly rough. If you try to play [in a style] even gentler than the *yūgen* style, that will seem particularly weak.[75]

Yet there is one important distinction to be made between Zeami's strong/rough categories in *Kaden* and the *Kyūi* references to those traits. Whereas the *Kaden* discussion precedes his formulation of the two-mode/three-style configuration, that configuration is at the heart of the *Kyūi* discussion. In *Kyūi*, distinctions between strong, weak, and "having *yūgen*" are not made on the basis of qualities taken to inhere in the subjects of imitation. Rather, the elicitation of these qualities has to do with the style of the performance. As Nose observes, the main distinction between the bottom three levels and the middle three levels of *Kyūi* is that the middle levels foster the requisite skills for eliciting *yūgen* effects, while the bottom three all belong to the strong/rough continuum, from which the quality *yūgen* is excluded.[76] In *Kyūi*, the elicitation of the *yūgen* quality is assumed to be enabled by training in the appropriate modalities and techniques of performance—that is, in the *nikyoku santai*. Because the bottom three levels are not premised on this foundation style, the seeds that will grow at the uppermost levels into *yūgen* are absent.

THE STYLE OF STRENGTH AND REFINEMENT (GŌSAIFŪ)

Zeami ranks the "style of strength and refinement" (*gōsaifū*) as the uppermost of the three lowest levels, describing it as follows.

> The gleam of the metal hammer moves. Cold is the glint of the sacred sword. The moving gleam of the metal hammer represents a style having strong movement. The cold glint of the sacred sword represents a chill *[hietaru]* style of expression. It appears to stand up to detailed scrutiny.[77]

The uppermost level of the three combines delicacy with strength, which suggests the presence of *saidō* elements. The distinction that Zeami draws between this kind of strength and that of the next lower level, which combines with roughness, is reminiscent of the distinction that he draws in *Sandō* and in *Nikyoku santai ningyō zu* between the *saidō* and the *rikidō* styles of movement. Whereas the *rikidō* style consists of unadulterated forcefulness, the *saidō* style breaks down the forcefulness into more detailed movement suggestive of more complex feeling. Moreover, Zeami labels the *rikidō* style as altogether aberrant, whereas the *saidō* style, when employed judiciously, may have its positive points (although he considers it, too, to be less desirable than the three styles). He avers that the "chill style of expression" that characterizes this level of strength and delicacy "appears to stand up to the detailed scrutiny" of audiences.

Whereas the image of the steel hammer invokes the quality of strength, the gleam of the sword blade elicits the quality of chill. Elsewhere in Zeami's treatises, his references to a "chill style of expression" (*hietaru kyoku*) are consistently in an approbatory vein. In chapter 6 it was pointed out that he mentions the same term, *hietaru*, in *Kakyō* in conjunction with the understated style of acting that appeals to audiences at the highest level of reception, that of the mind. He describes effects such as the following as evocative of this quality of "chill."

> There is a type of noh that, in terms of the two modes, or *monomane*, or word play, does not have much, but there is a tranquil flow, in the course of which are spots that arouse interest for no apparent reason.[78]

However, interpreters struggle to reconcile Zeami's use of *hietaru kyoku* in *Kakyō*, in which it is illustrative of supreme accomplishment, and his use of it in *Kyūi* to describe an acting style that is a detour from the true path that training should take. Nose points out that the chill beauty described in *Kakyō* differs markedly from that which is descriptive of the style of strength and roughness in *Kyūi* in one major way. Whereas in *Kakyō* Zeami advocates a training program in the two modes and three styles—the gateway to *yūgen* effects—as a prerequisite for reaching the ultimate developmental stage of "chill," the style of strength and delicacy in *Kyūi* has nothing to do with those modalities. It is what Nose calls a "non-*yūgen*" (*hi-yūgen*) style of art, as is also true for the two bottommost levels.

Tanaka merely states that the term as used in *Kyūi* does not refer to the kind of supreme artistry described in *Kakyō*, but rather to the ultimate expression of the quality of strength (*tsuyosa*), as befits the uppermost of the bottom three tiers, which all represent forceful styles. Nearman explores the Buddhist connotations of the image of the "precious sword" as "the double-edged Sword of Discernment and Discrimination, traditionally associated with Monju (Mañjuśrī), the Buddha's disciple who symbolizes All-Seeing Wisdom." He argues that the symbol of the precious sword is employed by Zeami to suggest that the actor has reached a level at which he is capable of "mental (spiritual) awareness, discernment, and creativity," the result of the actor's ability to concentrate more on detail. Nearman sees the "chill" quality described by Zeami here in *Kyūi* as consistent with his description of "chill" in reference to superb artistry in *Kakyō*, although he does recognize that the actor in the style of strength and refinement still lacks the self-control that comes with training.[79]

As was noted above, Konishi argues that a superb performer capable of eliciting the *ran'i* quality may actualize an impression of "chill" both at the uppermost levels and at the lower, non-*yūgen* level of strength and refinement; the central consideration is not the objective criteria of the levels themselves, but the ability of the individual actor to perform at multiple levels. Similarly, NSTS attempts to resolve the issue by ascribing the effects of an artistic style having chill awesomeness only to the superb performer who, after having mastered the upper levels, dips into the bottom ones for the sake of novelty.[80] Such an interpretation is persuasive because it is based on Zeami's discussion in *Kyūi* of the superb actor's returning from the higher levels to the lower ones, to which we will next turn.

RETURNING

When a performer has already mastered the middle and upper levels and then descends into the lowest three levels, he may create interesting effects. Zeami explains this in the following.

> When [an actor] enters at the middle three levels, and then reaches
> the upper three, achieves the Wondrous Flower belonging to the
> level of ease, and then returns to frequent the bottom three levels,
> performing those techniques [will result] in a softened form of expres-
> sion [*wafū no kyokutai*].[81]

His reference to returning in the above quotation represents a new element in his thinking about superlative effects onstage. The original Japanese is *kyakurai*, a Sōtō Zen term, according to Tanaka. In its entirety it reads *kōkyo kyakurai*, literally "to confront and pass on; to [then] turn and come back." It refers to the path of the bodhisattva, who, instead of passing into nirvana, chooses to return to this world in order to help all sentient beings to reach enlightenment.[82]

In the *Kyūi* system, Zeami employs *kyakurai* as a metaphor for the desired trajectory of the superbly accomplished performer. Once such a performer has achieved the uppermost levels in the system, it is appropriate for him to descend into the bottom levels. His reference to a softened style seems to refer to the effects derived when the consummate acting of the artist who is capable of the uppermost three levels is brought to bear on the un-schooled expression that characterizes the level of strength and delicacy. As Nose and others have noted, the result is a style in which the ultimate expression of the *yūgen* mood and the expression of strength traditional to Yamato are reconciled in the larger context of the master actor's sensibility.[83]

Zeami names only one exemplar for the *kyakurai* style of acting—his father, Kan'ami.

> From the beginning there have been artists of great ability who, while they have mastered the upper three levels of the Flower, have declined to descend to make use of the lowest three levels in their performances. Their choice might be likened to the old expression, "an elephant does not amuse himself by walking the path of a rabbit." I know of no one other than my late father Kan'ami who was able to perform in all styles from high to low.[84]

In *Sarugaku dangi*, Zeami offers critiques of some of the major actors of his time, and on that basis we may speculate concerning those actors who might have preferred not to descend from the uppermost heights. He mentions a contemporary of Kan'ami's, the *dengaku* performer Kiami, as one of the ancestors of the art (which includes *sarugaku* here) and as the father of vocal music. He credits Kiami with artistry at the level of the profound flower.[85] He also bestows accolades on a rival of his own generation, Zōami, who was a protege of Kiami. Zeami considered his strength to be vocal music, and he assigns him the rank of the serene flower. Zōami's chant was strongly evocative of the kind of chill beauty discussed above (*hie ni hietari*).[86] Then there was Inuō, the actor from the Hie troupe of Ōmi who found such favor with Yoshimitsu. Regarding Inuō, Zeami says,

> Inuō attained [the level of] the highest three flowers, and never dropped even to the highest of the middle [three levels]. He did not know the middle and lower [three levels].[87]

As we know, Zeami praises Inuō on many fronts: his dramatic rendering of plays, his skill at the *tennyo no mai* dance, and an acting style having *kakari*. The information that he did not even know the middle levels would seem to confirm that his style of art was distinct from the two modes/three style configuration developed by Zeami.

In *Sarugaku dangi*, Zeami reiterates that his father stood out from other performers because he "descended to the lowest three levels and mingled with the dust."[88] His account of Kan'ami's style singles him out as the most versatile, skilled both in female roles and demonic ones. Although he was a tall man, he could look slight in female roles. At middle age, he could look to be twelve. It is revealing that Zeami praises Kan'ami's skill in the demonic style. After a lifetime of denouncing demons, Zeami praises his father's performance of such a role.

It is tempting to ascribe a second interpretation to Zeami's usage of the term *kyakurai* in his *Kyūi* discussion above. Was Zeami also alluding to his own return to the style of his forefathers in Yamato *sarugaku*? Zeami calls both Kiami and Inuō his mentors and has only praise for his contemporary, Zōami. Yet he credits none of these masters with the ability to "return" to the strong/rough styles. What seems to have made Kan'ami different from the rest was his ability to play all kinds of roles, including those that were ostensibly lacking in the kind of *yūgen* atmosphere that seemed to attract shogunal patronage. Yet according to Zeami, when an actor who had mastered the uppermost levels played any role, no matter how rough, the results would be quite a different matter from an unskilled performance. Kan'ami could bring his expertise in the *yūgen* modalities—dance and chant—to bear in playing roles lacking in subject matter associated with *yūgen*. His personal atmosphere as expressed through those modalities could serve as an envelope for an ostensibly rough role, thereby lessening the impression of roughness and creating an elegant impression.

Softening the Unorthodox: Possible Analogues to *Kyakurai* in the Domain of *Waka* Pedagogy

As Konishi has pointed out, there is evidence that Zeami's formulation of the concept of *kyakurai* as it applied to *sarugaku* may have been influenced by pedagogical principles advocated by *waka* and *renga* poets such as Fujiwara no Teika and his interpreters.[89] Teika advocated that the novice poet start by learning four of ten poetic styles (*jittei*) that he characterized in his treatise *Maigetsushō* (Monthly notes; 1219) as "unaffected and gentle [*sunao ni yasashiki sugata*]." The four are the style of mystery and depth (*yūgen tei*), the style of appropriate statement (*kotoshikaru beki tei*), the style of elegant beauty (*uruwashiki tei*), and the style of deep feeling (*ushintei*). Once the poet has mastered these styles, he will be able to follow in the tradition of composing the native verse form of the thirty-one-syllable *waka* with "gentleness and sensibility" (*yasashiku monoaware ni*), across the various styles. Such training will ready him to handle even the demon-quelling style (*kiratsu no tei* or *oni hishigi tei*), which is most removed from the gentle styles and which is "marked by strong or even vulgar diction such as is found in some of the poems of *Man'yōshū*."[90] The novice poet should avoid this style at all costs, but it may be effective in the hands of a master poet. As Brower has noted, in *Maigetsushō*, Teika warned the novice poet away from this style until after he had mastered the more fundamental styles and developed his own voice as a poet. Such postponement is "not because the 'demon-quelling style' is superior to the others, but because it is more difficult, being at odds with the classical poetic values of beauty, elegance, and grace."[91]

The demon-quelling style continues to be discussed in poetic commentaries authored by Teika's successors, such as the *Sango ki* (Record of thrice five nights), a document traditionally attributed to Teika but now believed to have been written by Teika's grandson, Fujiwara no Tamezane (1266–1333).[92] It echoes Teika's teaching that the demon-quelling style must be postponed until mastery of the milder styles has been accomplished, but it departs from Teika's actual precepts by valorizing the demon-quelling style above all others. The author states,

> In my humble opinion, the caliber of any composition should be determined on the basis of its strength. Thus, the demon-quelling style may be rightly called the Middle Way of Japanese poetry *(uta [waka])*.[93]

The *renga* poet Shinkei, who was affiliated with the Reizei lineage of successors to Teika, echoes this sentiment in his treatise *Sasamegoto*. In the following passage, Shinkei assumes that he is quoting Teika's teaching, but he is actually following the precept set down later in *Sango ki* or a treatise of similar provenance.

> The honorable Teika called the demon-quelling style the Middle Way of Japanese poetry *(uta)*. Yet, he kept it a secret, for he said, "If this [style] were said to be peerless, then everyone would emulate it like no other. If an unaccomplished poet emulates it, it will go badly." What is more, he said that "many people have the general notion that a superior poem should be tranquil, gentle, and unadorned. This misses the mark."[94]

Both of these later interpretations of Teika's precepts diverge from them by singling out the demon-quelling style and an ancillary style of strong force *(gōriki no tei)* as tantamount to the Middle Way. Kidō Saizō, editor of *Sasamegoto* in the Nihon Koten Bungaku Taikei edition, asserts that the Middle Way refers to the Threefold Truth of Tendai, to which both Teika and his father Shunzei allude in their critical writings. However, Shinkei's observation also seems to suggest that the Middle Way may be construed here more concretely as the middle ground between styles erring on the side of roughness and styles that are too mild.

Where *Sango ki* and *Sasamegoto* do follow Teika's pedagogy is in advocating an incremental approach to composition that begins with certain fundamental styles and then branches off from them. The ability to handle the demon-quelling style depends on prior training in gentler styles. This is because the poet will thus be readied to contextualize the most unorthodox of materials in a supple linguistic flow that "softens" their impact. The mature poet will know how to handle such material by means of his treatment of it. In *Maigetsushō*, Teika states,

> Indeed, no matter how fearful a thing may be of itself, when it is put into a poem it is made to sound graceful and elegant [yū]. That being the case, what is to be gained by treating such things as cherry blossoms and the moon, which are by nature gentle, as if they were frightening?[95]

In chapter 3, it was noted that the poetics of Shunzei and Teika, foundation figures in Mikohidari poetic theory, were a major influence on Nijō Yoshimoto's conception of the transformational power of the aural dimension of *kakari*. All of these poets propounded the idea stated above that on the basis of the skillful linking of words that promote the sensation of a smooth linguistic flow, objects commonly thought fierce or incongruous in themselves may come across as gentle. Similarly, when linguistic treatment of ostensibly gentle or lyrical material is rough, it may come across as rough or frightening. As Teika put it, "In my view, there are no words that are intrinsically good or bad. Rather, it is from the effect of words when put together that such distinctions arise in poetic diction."[96] The master poet is thus able to move between different styles freely.

In Zeami's parlance, the artist capable of thus handling unorthodox subjects may be said to have reached the level of ease. In *Shūgyoku tokuka* also, he mentions descent into the bottom three rungs of *Kyūi*, and he describes the notion of "returning."

> When the actor has progressed from the three middle levels to full mastery of the uppermost three Flowers, then even if he descends to the bottom three levels, his grade [of artistry] will remain solidly in the uppermost three Flowers. . . . This is akin to gold mixed in sand,

a lotus blossom in the mud. Though he mix with [sand and mud], he will not take on their coloration. It is the accomplished actor of this grade who may be said to enjoy a true level of ease [*shinjitsu no an'i*].[97]

The superior performer who descends into the unorthodox realms of the bottom levels demonstrates a strength characteristic of these levels, but it is tempered by his "softening" effect. Though he mixes with these strong or unorthodox elements, they do not become defining features of his art. Zeami equates the ability to move between all nine *Kyūi* levels in this way with the ultimate level of ease.

Zeami's conception of the artist's freedom upon having reached the level of *kyakurai* shows fascinating parallels with these principles of *waka* pedagogy. First, the prerequisite for performing strong or unorthodox material effectively is prior mastery of the orthodox and gentler styles. Second, it is not the particular objects of representation that define artistic success, but how they are contextualized in performance. Third, the judgments of the master artist provide the ultimate ground for the contextualization of any given style. That is, the artist's own sensibility comes to bear and tempers whatever material he is working with. He will have a softening effect on the representation of demonic characters. Successful composition in the demon-quelling style in *waka*, successful incorporation of the unorthodox image of the demon in *renga*, and successful portrayal of the unorthodox style of strength and delicacy in the bottommost sector of the *Kyūi* system in *sarugaku*—all are predicated on having acquired a high level of skill and sensibility in the more orthodox styles.

These parallels are further evidence that Zeami discovered important clues in pedagogical writings on *waka* and *renga* in his quest to imbue his art with the kinds of elegance that would catch the eye of elite patrons. His two-mode/three-style training system began with training in vocalization and movement, skills that could be employed to instill grace in the representation of characters of all types. From there, the actor would proceed to the three styles with the precaution that the warrior style should be the last learned. Finally, representational techniques for the most unorthodox type of role, the *saidō* style of demon, should be learned only after that. By the time the actor embarks on portraying the unorthodox styles, he is previously schooled in the orthodox ones. Situating the two-mode/three style program as the foundation of the actor's training is Zeami's answer to Teika's principle of first inculcating poetic styles that are gentle and not idiosyncratic. It was

Zeami's strategy for ensuring that the first step in training the *sarugaku* actor would be to foster embodiment of "classical poetic values of beauty, elegance, and grace."

Unlike a number of earlier treatises, *Kyūi* does not topicalize the aesthetic quality of *yūgen*. Perhaps this is because it is no longer necessary to explicitly exhort actors to incorporate *yūgen* elements into *sarugaku* because the *nikyoku santai* was already so firmly established at the heart of his recommended training regimen, thereby assuring that the novice actor would follow a path that cultivated *yūgen* effects of itself.[98] Zeami had developed a style of performance designed to heighten *yūgen* effects, and by the composition of *Kyūi*, this already had been established as the orthodox style, at least among recipients of his treatises.

Perhaps because this orthodox style has become a given, in *Kyūi*, Zeami shows more interest in such unorthodox effects as *ran'i* and *kyakurai*, both dynamics that assume prior mastery of the orthodox styles but diverge from them. In the earlier *Shikadō*, he had shown an awareness of orthodox and unorthodox as two classifications of performance, and he wrote of how the two should interrelate. He urges the learner to pursue the two-mode/three-style configuration as the only possible way to acquire the orthodox style (*zefū*) in *sarugaku*. Achievement of the quality of *ran'i*, which he calls an unorthodox style (*hifū*), cannot be learned and is premised on prior mastery of the orthodox style, he warns. In contrast, *Kyūi* does not make explicit reference to an orthodox style per se. Rather, the narrative seems to assume it, as it concentrates on the potential for further breaks from the orthodox style, such as the *kyakurai* conception. The development of the *kyakurai* concept is evidence of a deepening interest on Zeami's part in getting the performer beyond the orthodox/unorthodox dualism to a level of cultivation of mind at which he is not guided by such discriminating consciousness. We will end this chapter by pursuing a bit further the role of *nikyoku santai* in helping the actor to achieve a level at which he may freely interact with his audiences without impediments.

The Role of *Nikyoku Santai* in the Cultivation of the Actor's Attunement

In the ensuing passage of *Shugyoku tokuka*, Zeami goes on to describe the level of ease enjoyed by the actor who can surf all the *Kyūi*. The passage will be familiar from chapter 6.

> Though [the actor] plays all manner of roles, not even the thought,
> "This is effortless," will occur to him inwardly. This is acting free of
> self-conscious effects or intent (*mukyoku mushin*). Might this be a
> level that may be called the wondrous flower of original nonbeing
> (*honmu myōka*)?[99]

In chapter 6, this passage was discussed in reference to the Daoist idea of
nonbeing as a realm of undifferentiated reality that is the wellspring of creativity. Also mentioned was the Prajñā-pāramitā and Tendai emphasis on
cultivation of the wisdom that allows one to discern phenomena simultaneously as both empty and provisionally existing. That is, wisdom entails
going beyond dualistic thinking. In both belief systems, too, to go beyond
dualistic thinking cannot be done on the basis of "conscious intention of
attaining something,"[100] which poses an obstacle to the attainment of such
wisdom.

In the same passage from *Shūgyoku tokuka*, Zeami remarks that when the
actor has exhausted all training and has learned all there is to learn and has
thereby achieved the level of ease, then "not a single thing will exist in his
mind. That not a thing exists is enabled by successful training." The line
"not a single thing will exist in the mind" (*shinjū ni ichimotsu mo nashi*)
comes from a famous accretion to the *Liuzu tan jin* (Jpn. *Rokuso dangyō*,
Platform sutra of the sixth patriarch), attributed to the sixth patriarch,
Huineng (638–713). In the following Song dynasty recension, the line in
italics below replaces the line that is bracketed right below it.

> Bodhi originally has no tree
> The mirror also has no stand
> *From the first not a thing is.*
> [Buddha nature is always clean and pure.]
> Where is there room for dust?

This verse is intended as a challenge to the premises of the verse below.

> The body is the Bodhi tree,
> The mind is like a clear mirror.
> At all times we must strive to polish it,
> And must not let the dust collect.[101]

As Demiéville has noted, the second verse to be composed (the first cited above) refuses to "recognize the existence of any impurity to be removed."

> Buddha-nature *(fo-hsing [fo xing]*; Skt. *buddhatā)*, the potentiality to become a Buddha, which is innate in all beings and by which they partake of the nature of Buddhas, itself absolutely pure in essence, is but another name for the absolute. If it is true that it is "eternally pure," this cannot be so in any sense which would have it differ from impurity, from dust—for it is completely identified with the latter.[102]

If Zeami was familiar with the original purport of this line, then he may be suggesting that the actor who practices "returning" has reached a condition in which his creativity assumes the *śūnyatā* precept that there are no dharmas that enjoy absolute essence, and he has thus gone beyond dualistic thinking.[103] Having mastered the various stages of training and levels of artistry, he should be able to move freely without such discriminations entering his conscious awareness.

In the concluding segment of *Yūgaku shudōfū ken*, Zeami describes with more concreteness how such a nondual state might apply to the mind and art of the actor. He illustrates his idea by returning to the metaphor of a vessel. In an earlier segment of *Yūgaku shudōfū ken*, he further amplifies the notion of the actor functioning as a vessel—here to describe the art of the master. He first identifies the locus classicus of the metaphor by citing the following passage from the third article of the fifth book of *The Analects of Confucius*: One of Confucius' disciples, Tzu-kung [Zigong], asked, " 'What do you think of me?' The Master said, 'You are a vessel.' Tzu-kung said, 'What sort of vessel?' The Master said, 'A sacrificial vase of jade!' "[104] As Nose has observed, Zeami takes this Confucian comparison of a man of capacity to a sacred vessel and recontextualizes it in a narrative with decidedly Buddhist overtones.[105] Zeami states,

> If one takes being *(u)* and nonbeing *(mu)* to be two paths, being is the manifested, nonbeing the vessel *(ki)*. That which makes being appear is nonbeing. For example, crystal is clear in substance, an object empty of colors or designs, but from it fire and water are born.[106] What kind of karma accounts for the production of differing elements such as fire and water from a clear substance empty of

color? It is said in a certain *waka:* "When one breaks up a tree and looks, there are no blossoms. Indeed, the flowers have bloomed in the spring sky." What brings the seeds that flower into the many styles of musical entertainment[107] into being is a quality of mind (*kokorone*) in which the expressive power of one's whole being is rooted.[108] Just as fire and water arise from the clear substance of crystal, and blossoms and fruit from the cherry tree, which does not itself have color, the supremely skilled expert who, on the basis of his inner mental imaging, can manifest the shadings (*kyokushiki*) of a piece in [the form of] visional affect, should be [considered] a vessel (*kibutsu*).[109]

The vessel metaphor corresponds to nonbeing (*mu*), as contrasted with the contents of the vessel (*u*). It is like a crystal (*mu*), which seems transparent yet gives birth to the elements of water and fire (*u*). A tree also is a vessel (*mu*) from which are born colorful blossoms (*u*). So, too, is the actor, whose capacity to express his power of feeling, something without tangible manifestations (*mu*), gives rise to "seeds that flower into many styles" (*u*). On the basis of the actor's inner mental imaging, or artistic vision (*mu*), visional affect is manifested onstage (*u*).

While annotators agree that *kokorone* here refers to the functioning of the mind, what exactly does that mean?[110] The term is sprinkled throughout Zeami's critical writings and seems to embrace a range of possible meanings, anything from taking precautions to judging the quality of the moment. One segment of *Sarugaku dangi*, which is devoted entirely to a discussion of *kokorone* in reference to *monomane* techniques, states,

> All manner of *monomane* is composed of the essential feeling content (*kokorone*). First, distinguish between the feeling content in each case, and then [decide] the staging (*fuzei*) and the mood (*kakari*).[111]

Whereas the NSTS annotation posits that the meaning of *kokorone* here is the meaning and intent expressed in the language, Nose suggests that it refers to a nuanced attentiveness (*bimyō na kokorozukai*). Tanaka offers an interpretation that seems most apropos to this passage and has efficacy for understanding the passage above from *Yūgaku shudōfū ken* as well. He suggests that *kokorone* refers to grasping the emotive core, referring both to the feelings experienced by the spectators and the emotive qualities suggested by the piece being performed.[112] I think the passage from *Yūgaku shudōfū ken* also uses *kokorone* in the manner that Tanaka suggests for the *Sarugaku dangi* passage: a cultivated mindfulness on the part of the performer that allows him to sense the feeling content produced by these multiple variables.

Returning to the discussion of what the vessel metaphor signifies in the final segment of *Yūgaku shudōfū ken*, Zeami next grants it cosmic proportions. He turns to a brief description of the wondrous flower as it applies to the arts of entertainment (*yūgaku*) and draws a clear analogy between the *kokoro* of the actor (*mu*) and the universe (*mu*) that forms the vessel within which all forms become manifest (*u*).

> Diverse is expression of the beauties of nature that adorns this elegant, life-prolonging art.[113] The universe is the vessel that gives birth to myriad things, sentient and insentient alike—flower and leaf, snow and moon, mountain and ocean, grass and tree—each at its time within the four passing seasons. You should concentrate on achieving the wondrous flower of musical entertainment by considering all things as fit imagery for it, by making your one mind (*isshin*) the vessel for all the universe, and situating [this] vessel with ease[114] on the boundless path of emptiness [nonbeing].[115]

The universe (*mu*) is the vessel that may hold all phenomena (*u*). The actor, too, becomes a vessel (*mu*) fit to contain all manifestations of material (*u*) in performance.

"Making your one-mind the vessel for all the universe" (*isshin o tenga no ki ni nashite*) employs the same term, *isshin* (one-mind/one-mindedness), that was explored in the concluding segment of chapter 6. It is clear that Zeami's usage of the term here is reminiscent of his *Kakyō* usage as discussed earlier—the segment about the performer achieving a level of *mushin* in which his intent is hidden even from himself. Concerning this consciousness, the *Kakyō* passage further states, "This, in other words, is [the crux of] the expressive power that emerges in the connecting of myriad acts by means of the one mind (*isshin*)."[116]

Nearman's insight that this usage of the term is reminiscent of the Yuishiki philosophy concerning the mind that has developed the "wisdom of equanimity" was also mentioned. In *sarugaku*, an actor who has attained such wisdom will enjoy "mastery over thoughts and feelings so that they do not consciously and inappropriately color his performance." Furthermore, the enlightened one-mind functions as a mirror beyond the illusory imaginings that are the product of discriminating consciousness.

Whether Yuishiki thought was the specific inspiration for Zeami's references to *isshin* or not, the term clearly has Buddhist connotations here. The more general definition cited in chapter 6, the "absolutely non-dual mind of suchness from which all worldly phenomena are manifested," seems equally apt in the context of this concluding passage of *Yūgaku shudōfū ken* also. This passage is focused on achieving *myō* effects onstage—that is, effects that are absolutely nondual. Zeami states here that an actor should make this one-mind his vessel and situate this vessel with ease on the path of emptiness or *śūnyatā* (*kūdō*), which he characterizes as a style of boundless nonbeing (*kōdai mufū no kūdō*). Clearly he is manipulating ideas rooted in Prajñā-pāramitā thought.

Zeami's reliance on such terms suggests that he intended an analogy between the nondual suchness of the enlightened consciousness and the cultivated no-mind of the master actor. His recurring references to the metaphor of the mirror also suggest that he perceived the ideal state of mind of the actor to be one in which his attunement frees him from such deluded distinctions as subject/object, self/other.

VESSEL VERSUS MIRROR

In his discussion in *Yūgaku shudōfū ken*, Zeami shows a preference for the metaphor of the vessel over that of the mirror. Perhaps this is because he treats the mirror elsewhere as an embodiment of the nondual (*myō*), whereas his precepts here are made with reference to the pre-*myō* realm of *u/mu* dualisms. The vessel image also proves a more promising tack for articulating the optimal training program from a developmental perspective. It allows him to bring that process more into the foreground. The process seems to entail emptying oneself of ego consciousness so as to become like the crystal that appears transparent but gives birth to diverse phenomena.

Prior to the two passages—translated above—from the final segment on the vessel metaphor, there is a short paragraph leading into them that encapsulates the incremental steps that the actor should follow in order to take on the qualities of this vessel. It states,

> Now then, as for the vessel, in our art, for the versatile adept to have [progressed] from the two modes and three styles to embody all the myriad styles[117]—this is to have capacity (*kiyō*).[118] Across the

diverse subject matter,[119] having the ability in one's person to manifest various styles, with visional affects arising from a wide range of
techniques—this is what I mean. Extending the visual and aural
affects [arising from] the two modes and three styles, and achieving
the meritorious level that never increases or diminishes, this is to be
a vessel.[120]

The prerequisite for proceeding to this full range of styles is first to have
mastered all three of the prototypical styles *(santai)*. In turn, as Zeami
reminds us at the beginning of *Yūgaku shudōfū ken*, the prerequisite for com-
mencing to learn the three styles is training in the two modes *(nikyoku)*.
The actor's ability to thus contain the full range of acting techniques in his
one body, whereupon he can give them full expression in a variety of manifestations in performance, is likened to being a vessel.

Zeami's reference to "extending the visual and aural affects" *(enkan o
nashite)* arising from the two modes and three styles is significant. Nose
takes this statement to mean that the "admirable artistic effects of which
the actor who has trained in and mastered the two modes and three styles
is capable . . . carry over and pervade his art when he performs other derivative styles as well."[121] It is important to note that the process of mastering
the myriad styles is not depicted simply as a linear progression from A to B.
B subsumes and builds on A. That is, the traces of A stand to be palpable
in B, and their cumulative affects in turn will emerge in the performance
of C. The term glossed as "never increases or diminishes" *(fuzō fugen)* has
Buddhist antecedents and a twofold interpretation, according to Nose. It
may either mean that because the myriad dharmas are empty, there is no
increasing or diminishing, or because the myriad dharmas are inexhaustible
and boundless, there is no increasing or diminishing. NSTS and NKBT 65
favor the latter reading but do not offer their reasons.[122] The former idea,
that the myriad dharmas are empty and therefore do not change, has its
locus classicus in the *Heart Sutra*, cited in this treatise.[123] It is worth considering how Zeami is applying the term in reference to stage effects. On
stage, the only way it would be possible to sustain an unchanging level of
effectiveness would be for the performer(s) to constantly adjust to inevitably
changing contexts. This ability is the crux of Zeami's flower, a concept that
remains unchanged from his earliest treatises.

It seems, then, that to take on his role as vessel effectively, the performer
must acquire the appropriate skills in the correct sequence. At the same

time, he must empty his mind of conscious striving. It also seems from Zeami's descriptions of the training process in *Yūgaku shudōfū ken*, and in others treatises such as *Kyūi*, that these two processes are one and the same. The way for the actor to suspend his subjective or arbitrary thoughts is to engage in a training program that disallows them. In the meantime, he is guided by his training to cultivate a new mode of mindfulness in which his cognitive activity is hidden even from himself. This is a condition that allows him heightened spontaneity and attunement with his audiences.

Such an idea of training as personal cultivation is of course far from unique in traditional pedagogies of East Asia. Yuasa explores this point in his book, which devotes one section to Zeami's ideas on performance and mind. Yuasa reminds us that Zeami's fundamental stance was that "true art cannot be mastered merely through the conceptual understanding, but must be acquired, as it were, through one's body. In other words, it is a bodily acquisition by means of a long, cumulative, difficult training."[124] He likens Zeami's approach to Zen cultivation, which "corrects the mode of one's mind by putting one's body into the correct postures," and he reminds us of a crucial point concerning such an approach to training—that it fosters practical rather than conceptual understanding. "What we acquire through our body can be unconsciously, naturally expressed in body movements fitting 'form.' "[125]

The body loses its "object-like weightiness, which resists the mind's function as subject." By the same token, the mind is "no longer a subject dominating the body as resistant object," and in this sense "the mind is made completely objective."[126] Yuasa refers to this condition as body-mind identity, with the result that "the bodily form dancing on stage signifies the *mind just as it is*."[127] At such a level, no consciousness distinguishing self and other exists. When the mind thus "becomes nothing," then "it freely expresses all beings, all that has a form."[128]

Yuasa's characterization of such a body-mind identity is congruent with my own position, that Zeami saw the two modes and then the three styles as playing a crucially constitutive role in fostering optimal attunement with audiences. This configuration offered physical models (such as those Zeami describes and sketches out in *Nikyoku santai ningyō zu*) that the actor was to embody through training. Analogous to Yuasa's characterization of the emulation of forms as a strategy for correcting deluded thinking in Zen practices, Zeami posited these modules of performance as a strategy for fostering the ability to reorient body-mind identity. A listing of those elements to which Zeami attributes the vessel metaphor in *Yūgaku shudōfū ken* goes as follows.

First Segment

Vessel

1. Two modes of dance and chant *(buga nikyoku)* (To be subsequently "filled" by the three styles when they are later learned)

Final Segment

Variant: "Having capacity" (kiyō; *punning on ki, which means vessel*)

2. The versatile adept who has progressed from the two modes and three styles on to execution of all the myriad styles
3. To possess the bodily capacity to produce a wide selection of techniques and styles

Vessel

4. The person who has expanded the visual and aural effects of the two modes and three styles to have an impact on all types of performance and has achieved a level that neither increases nor diminishes
5. Nonbeing *(mu)*
   A. As in a crystal that gives birth to fire and to water
   B. As a tree that produces blossoms and fruit
6. Inner mental imaging (resulting in visional affect)
7. Universe (manifesting myriad phenomena)
8. One mind *(isshin)* as vessel for the universe

While 5, 6, and 8 above concentrate on the inner workings of the actor's mind, 1 through 4 provide instructions on bodily training. At the core of that training are the two modes, to be learned in childhood. Zeami's conception seems to assume that the actor's development builds incrementally on the two modes—from them to the three styles to, ultimately, the entire range of performance styles. Once the actor has achieved such scale, his instructions shift to the workings of the mind. But this mind is of quite a different order from what the novice brings to the art. This mind corresponds to Yuasa's description of the mind free of ego consciousness—the mind that is formed through the long process of training; that is, the mind reformed in tandem with the body.

In his commentary on the final passage of *Yūgaku shudōfū ken*, Nose points out that Zeami's comparison of the master actor to a vessel whose manifestations are perfectly attuned to the passing seasons is reminiscent of his earliest and most fundamental teachings on the flower. At the heart of the flower concept is the ability to inspire a sense of freshness and novelty in audiences. To do this, the performer must have a broad and diverse repertoire, as well as attuned sensibilities about how to employ that repertoire in the larger context of interacting with audiences in the moment. By the time he composed Yūgaku shudōfū ken, Zeami had developed and deepened his philosophy concerning how to cultivate the ultimate attunement that will make such a flower bloom. It is interesting that he draws there on Buddhist terms such as fuzō fugen (never increases or diminishes) to suggest a standard of performance in which the flower might be routinely present despite the fact that it may be called, both literally and figuratively, one of the most evanescent of worldly things. And herein lies an irony of the flower that endures from the earliest of Zeami's treatises: to be successful at invoking it on a consistent basis, the actor must himself be constantly changing and adapting.

Over a lifetime, Zeami develops a training program with the nikyoku santai configuration at its core to provide guidelines for cultivating this adaptability. Even this configuration is not a permanent fixture, however, and must be jettisoned when the formative stages of bodily training are achieved and it is no longer needed. Whereas nikyoku santai comes to be the orthodox training program for the novice, in the realms of ran'i and kyakurai, conscious adherence to it becomes an obstacle. The actor must let go and move on.

But throughout his pedagogical writings, what remains constant is Zeami's insistence that the actor remain open and adaptive vis-à-vis his audiences and his surroundings. There is little doubt that contemporary philosophical thinking and belief systems aided Zeami in his understanding of how such optimal adaptability might be fostered and guided him in articulating underlying principles of the flower. However, Zeami's final reference to the metaphor of the changing seasons in Yūgaku shudōfū ken is a reminder that what mattered most in his enterprise had not changed very much. As he had stated it in chapter 7 of Kaden,

> The actor who has pursued all the options to the fullest is like one who bears seeds that will flower the year through—from the plum blossoms of early spring to the chrysanthemums blooming to their close in autumn.[129]

Coda

◆   ◆   ◆

If one were to query the average spectator of noh today as to what Zeami's legacy to the art might be, it is likely the reply would somehow link Zeami with the aesthetic quality of *yūgen*. If one were to then ask what "the legacy of *yūgen*" might refer to, replies would probably vary considerably, for today it is a very fuzzy concept. The nonspecialist might be hard put to answer with any clarity, which is hardly surprising. As this volume has tried to demonstrate, the aesthetic concept was originally closely constrained by the social and artistic aspirations of a particular time and place. Certainly neither the tension between the Ōmi and Yamato styles nor the pressures to conform to shogunal vicissitudes has much relevance to how the art is perceived or responded to today.

Obviously much has changed, and on multiple levels, since Zeami's time. In an essay titled "Tradition and Transformation in Nō Theatre," Omote disputes what he sees as a general predisposition to perceive noh as "a form of theatre still being performed today in exactly the same way as it was six hundred years ago." He continues, "I find it difficult to imagine that a stage art performed by living people could not have changed at all through the ages."[1] He also makes a very basic point about noh that applies as well to other traditional performing arts—the score may remain the same, but "the performance itself changes according to the changing views of directors and performers, and as a result of technological changes in the instruments."[2] He goes on to make a persuasive case by describing changes in the repertoire, the plays and their performance, the structure of the stage, and the tempo of performing. Hence one must tread carefully when attempting to ascribe lasting influence on the part of a figure such as Zeami, who lived so long ago. Nonetheless, it would be equally inaccurate to deny his legacy.

To return to our imaginary survey of present-day audience opinions on the relation between Zeami and *yūgen*, one likely response would refer to the elegant beauty of the spectacle. Indeed, the rich costumes (which mostly postdate Zeami) and the priceless masks are works of art in their own right. Performers, too, seem to be highly conscious of these elements and to cherish them. Yet I can recall occasions in the course of my own training as an amateur learner of dance and chant when I heard professional actors complain that it is not very satisfying to be told that their performances were "pretty" (*kirei*). In his critique of audiences in *Kakyō*, Zeami tells us about spectators who are predisposed to respond foremost to the visual appeal of performances. As we know, he ranks them as the least perceptive of his three types of spectators.

One major constituency of spectators at almost any performance today is amateur learners. Many of them are primarily interested in one element of the art, and often it is the chant (*utai*). Records of amateurs learning *utai* go back to the Muromachi period.[3] It was also enormously popular throughout the Edo period, when the general populace could have access to *utai* texts even though there were few opportunities for those of humble social standing to see full-fledged performances. Zeami's play *Takasago*, for instance, continues to be staged today, both as a performed play and as a chanted piece. He might be surprised to learn that excerpts of his play are still performed occasionally at wedding receptions because of the thematic aptness of the text.

Today, amateur learners routinely purchase chant books (*utaibon*), in which the modulation of the lines is notated. A lesson normally entails chanting with book open, while the teacher, a professional, listens and corrects. Learners will typically bring their chant books to performances, and a certain number will be guilty of losing track entirely of what is transpiring onstage because of the familiar allure of the chant notations on the printed page. "Spectators" thus preoccupied have been dubbed in noh parlance *kubi-hon-tō* (the "neck [nose]-in-the-book contingent")[4] and are notorious for trying the patience of the performers onstage. Then there are the amateur learners of an instrument such as the shoulder drum (*kot-suzumi*), some of whom get so caught up in the drumming patterns that they will start to tap them out by hand as they sit and watch the play. If the reader will forgive another anecdote, I once heard an actor grumble that he lost his concentration because one such spectator in the front row was enthusiastically drumming her knees to the beat. Perhaps these types of spectators are the modern counterparts to those in the audience whom Zeami described as most sensitive to auditory stimuli.

One may rest assured that such behavior was not quite what Zeami had in mind when he wrote of those among the spectators who are most attracted to the aural dimension. But still, the *kubi-hon-tō* and the knee-slappers are actively appreciating the performance, and they are doing so with primacy given to the auditory mode. If anyone in an audience today were to explain the evocation of *yūgen* in terms of the aural modalities that a performance has to offer, he or she would likely come from among this group, whose ears (at least) are engaged in the flow of performance.

There is still another level of Zeami's original ranking of types of appreciation introduced in chapter 6. It is an appreciation experienced at the level of the mind (*kokoro*). As I cast about for a possible modern analogue, a rumination over a successful performance written by Yashima Masaharu comes to mind. It goes as follows.

> The excitement that we feel when we've seen really fine noh has something that is hard to get in other kinds of drama. I don't mean effects like "being enveloped in an atmosphere of elegance" and so on. Rather, it is as if the cosmos is right there. The *shite*'s image seems like a withered, ancient tree, or a fossil that appears to stand firm against the wear of time. While there is a vivid sense of his body's material presence, at the same time, [that presence] is quite abstract and spiritual too. What is more, when you are there facing the stage, you get sleepy and follow the *shite*'s progress with eyes half closed; intoxicated by the rhythms of the *hayashi*, you slip into a languid state. Yet as you tread your path homeward, or when in your car, you've probably had the eerie experience of feeling that the *shite*'s image is burned into the back of your mind and continues to be felt as a vivid presence in your psyche (*seishin*).[5]

Yashima is a scholar of Zeami, well acquainted with what Zeami had to say about the ideal effects of a performance. At the same time, he is a knowledgeable spectator of the modern noh and a regular author of performance reviews. He brings these two dimensions together in the description above of what he considers a successful performance today to consist. Yashima's reference to "the atmosphere of elegance" seems a conscious attempt to dispel any notion that pretty pageantry (an adorned style) is the locus of ultimate effects. "The cosmos is right there" immediately suggests the image of actor as vessel, invoked by Zeami in *Yūgaku shudōfū ken*. Therein Zeami calls the actor who has mastered the two modes and the three styles—and thus attained the means to play all roles—a vessel *(ki)*. As we know, he then went so far as to compare such an actor to the universe.[6] The withered, ancient tree and the fossil, Yashima's images for the *shite*, are surely reminiscent of the cold style *(hietar[i])* that Zeami ascribes to the mature actor. Dance, rhythm, and chant have an intoxicating effect. These are, of course, the elements corresponding to Zeami's two modes, to which he quite purposely assigned a central function in the exposition of a play, thereby creating a sense of flow that sustains all the other elements. The idea of the *shite* as an object of memory, branded in the mind after the performance is over, also recalls the phenomenon of visual consummation *(kenpū jōju)* that Zeami stresses in his treatises—the eye-opening phase.[7]

Experienced practitioners of the stage art speak of similar intuitions. In fact, it seems to me that Brook's description of the true test of theatre is not so different from Zeami's. He asks what the acid test is in theatre—what remains with the spectator after the production has ended.

> Fun can be forgotten, but powerful emotion also disappears and good arguments lose their thread. When emotion and argument are harnessed to a wish from the audience to see more clearly into itself—then something in the mind burns. The event scorches onto the memory an outline, a taste, a trace, a smell—a picture.[8]

Brook further observes that what remains after the play is over is its central image—he describes as its "silhouette"—which when done right will shape the "essence" of what the play "has to say." He continues, "When years later I think of a striking theatrical experience I find a kernel engraved on my memory: two tramps under a tree, an old woman dragging a cart, a sergeant dancing, three people on a sofa in hell—or occasionally a trace deeper than any imagery." He further qualifies what he means by memory. It is not about "remembering the meanings precisely," but rather having the kernel in memory from which to "reconstruct a set of meanings."[9]

Brook seems to be describing the performance that leads to such core images as part of a process that ideally fosters a co-creative role on the part of the spectator. Core images seed the creation of memories that accrue meaning as they live in the imagination. This dynamic recalls the kind of echo chamber of allusion and memory—the open theatre—that Zeami's *nikyoku santai* set into motion and that he has described in his treatises in terms of *kenpū jōju* (consummation of visional affect). Perhaps both Brook and Zeami, through their extensive experience interacting with audiences, came to some similar insights on the nature of audience interest and response.

And what of Zeami's precepts for cultivating the actor's attunement, the focus in part 3 of this volume? Are concepts that have been influenced by religious discourses of traditional Japan, such as *mushin*, a continuing legacy felt by actors today? Of course, it is very difficult to know or judge what a noh performer might feel without being one. One thing is certain: performers' opinions about the meaning of a performance can differ dramatically from one individual to the next. A few years back at a conference, I witnessed a professional noh actor in his forties state emphatically, in response to a question about the role of religion in noh, that noh has no deities or buddhas, because it is drama (*engeki*). What came to mind when I heard this was a counterexample—another noh actor of my acquaintance, a navy veteran of World War II, who in 1995 performed Zeami's warrior play *Yashima* on board a Japanese destroyer escort ship in the hope of appeasing the spirits of the war dead. Secretly I marveled at the fact that those two actors might perform successfully on the same stage despite such seeming contrasts in their views on the expressive function of their art.[10] But the discursive level is not the primary one on which they must connect. Attunement becomes possible in practice.

It seems to me that the place to look for Zeami's most lasting legacy for performers and spectators alike is probably something even more basic than specific systems or beliefs like the seemingly contrasting ones held by the two performers mentioned above. It has more to do with a design for a performance that Zeami and Kan'ami were seminal in developing that—and this is crucial—ensured room for the imagination of each performer and spectator. That is, the aim was to make room for diversity of interpretation.

Kagaya has noted the emergent orientation of noh in later times, in particular the Meiji period (1868–1912), during which it struggled for new patrons upon the collapse of the Edo *bakufu*. She sees a key to the vitality of the art and its capacity to induce diverse interpretations as being rooted in its quality of reaching the viewer as "not quite complete."[11] She points out that it "therefore requires of the viewer active, constructive participation," and she further observes, "Due to the reflexivity of a *nō* performance, it is often the case that commentary on it says much about the commentator's constructive faculties."[12]

Kagaya's points are well taken. At the same time, one can add that the capacity of the art to induce diverse responses is not random, but the outgrowth of careful design, especially as articulated in the parameters that are imposed by *nikyoku santai*. Happily, there have been many styles of plays and varying interpretations exercised in particular performances, but without being reductionist about it, I think it is fair to say that all styles have unfolded in the coexistence of musical, poetic, and representational elements first joined with one another in the formulation of the *nikyoku santai*.

On the website of Hinoki Shoten, one of the major booksellers specializing in noh-related materials, there is a page in English titled "A quick definition of noh." It is quick enough to quote in full.

> Noh is a composite art based on the elements of song, dance, and drama. It is the oldest living drama form in the world today which [*sic*] makes use of masks.[13]

While Zeami cannot be given credit for the second sentence in this characterization, his legacy has a lot to do with the first. Not only does *nikyoku santai* assure that the elements listed coexist in any performance, but as we have seen, it assures a tension between the mimetic and poetic dimensions that indeed demands interpretation. Thus did Zeami do his part to assure that the focal point of interest in a noh performance would continue to be what emerges when minds meet by means of an interaction of music, dance, and story.

Appendix 1

. . .

An Annotated Translation of *Sandō*

THE THREE TECHNIQUES OF NOH COMPOSITION

by Zeami Motokiyo

F irst a few words on the variant manuscripts of *Sandō*. To briefly review what was mentioned in the introduction, Zeami's critical treatises started to be published only in 1908 and 1909 by Yoshida Tōgo. *Sandō* was one of fifteen treatises published by Yoshida in 1909.[1] He took the subtitle for the first four sections—"Nōsakusho" (Noh composition)— to be the title of the entire treatise, and that error was corrected by subsequent annotators, but *Sandō* is sometimes still referred to as *Nōsakusho*.

Zeami's original handwritten manuscript of the treatise has been lost. My translation is based on the Yoshida recension. The Yoshida text is a transcription of the Matsunoya Bunko manuscript of *Sandō*, which was destroyed in the Great Kantō earthquake of 1923. The copyist and the circumstances of the transcription of the lost Matsunoya Bunko manuscript are unknown, but it is thought to have dated to the early seventeenth century. The oldest extant manuscript, the Sōsetsu text, is believed to have been copied by the seventh head of the Kanze troupe, Kanze Sōsetsu (1509–1583), and is thought to have been passed down among successive generations of Kanze troupe heads (*sōke*). However, it is now in the holdings of the National Diet Library in Tokyo, and I will refer to it as the Diet text. The fourth extant manuscript is a copy of the text now in the Diet holdings that was done in the late Edo period by Tokugawa Munetake. It is owned by the Tayasu branch of the Tokugawa family. All of these texts are basically similar, variations amounting to errors in copying or differences in layout, and it is surmised that all descend from a manuscript now lost. Those spots in which the import differs significantly across manuscripts are mentioned in the annotations of the *Sandō* translation.

The annotated text that I adhered to most closely in the translation is the Yoshida recension as presented in Omote Akira and Katō Shūichi, eds., *Zeami, Zenchiku, Gei no Shisō, Michi no Shisō 1*, which Iwanami Shoten published in 1995. This is a revised edition of a volume of the same title by the same editors: volume 24 of the Nihon Shisō Taikei series, originally published by Iwanami in 1974. I have also been guided by the annotated editions of *Sandō* in volume 88 of the Shinpen Nihon Koten Bungaku Zenshū series, published by Shōgakukan in 2001, and in volume 1 of Nose Asaji's *Zeami jūrokubu shū hyōshaku*, first published by Iwanami in 1940. The text published in Shinpen Nihon Koten Bungaku Zenshū is annotated by Omote Akira and originally appeared in volume 51 of the Nihon Koten Bungaku Zenshū edition (Shōgakukan) in 1973. Both the Shōgakukan editions and the Nose edition adhere to the Yoshida recension as well. I have also referred to the Diet text as published and annotated in volume 65 of the Nihon Koten Bungaku Taikei series, edited by Nishio Minoru and published by Iwanami in 1961, and to the traced reproduction of the Matsunoya Bunko manuscript recently discovered by Takemoto Mikio, director of the Tsubouchi Memorial Theatre Museum. I am most grateful for his willingness to share a copy of the manuscript along with related materials.

1. Points on Composing Noh

(1.1) To start with, the three techniques, material, structuring, and writing, form the basis.[2] First is understanding the material; second, structuring the play; third, writing the play. Grasp the nature of the material in the source,[3] work the three phases of *jo-ha-kyū* into five *dan;* then, gather the words, adding the modulation and writing line by line.

(1.2) **Material:** Make sure you understand that the personage [featured] in the original story for the play, the one who performs, has a crucial bearing on the dance and chant.[4] Generally speaking, the art of musical entertainment[5] takes form in dance and chant. However celebrated an ancient or

artist, if the personage is not the type to perform these two modes of acting, then visional affect[6] cannot materialize. Make sure you ponder and
appreciate this well.

For example, among the types of characters in the *monomane* repertoire,
the celestial maiden, female deity, and shrine maiden do the dance and
chant of *kagura*. Among male figures[7] are gentlemen of artistic accomplishment such as Narihira, Kuronushi, and Genji.[8] Among female personages
there are Ise, Komachi, Giō, Gijo, Shizuka, Hyakuman; women such as
these are accomplished artists.[9] Since each of these personages is
renowned[10] for his or her ability in the entertainments of dance and chant,
making any of them into the core figure[11] of a noh ought naturally to work
to good effect. Also, among the wandering entertainers called *hōka*, there
are players of the *yūkyō* type like Jinen Koji, Kagetsu, Tōgan Koji, and
Seigan Koji,[12] as well as personages who have no legendary stature, male
and female, young and old; only upon shaping any one of these into a root
style[13] conducive to dance and chant should you compose the play. Finding the figure fit for the important foundation style[14] is called [the technique
of] the material.

Also, for what is called made-up noh,[15] which has no source but is
newly conceived and formed in connection with a noted place or historical site, there are times when the visional affect of the performer alone can
move an audience. This task demands the skill of the consummate master.

(1.3) Structure: Once the material has been found in this way, determine
well how the action will unfold.

First of all, there are five *dan* in the *jo-ha-kyū* progression. *Jo* forms one
dan; ha, three *dan; kyū,* one *dan.* The opening player enters,[16] and the portion from his recitative and introductory chant through the long segment
of chant constitutes one *dan.*[17] *Ha* begins here. Now the *shite* enters, and
the portion from his entry chant through the long segment of chant forms
one *dan.*[18] After that, the spoken exchange with the *waki* and the long passage of choral chant form one *dan.*[19] And then after that, one section of
vocal music, whether the *kuse* section or plain chant, forms one *dan.*[20] *Kyū*
begins here. A formal dance or vigorous moves, and the *hayabushi* match
or the *kiribyōshi* match form one *dan.*[21] The above comes to five *dan.* However, depending on the magnitude of the source, six *dan* are possible. Or,
depending on the type, there may be a four-*dan* play, lacking one *dan.* But
primarily, the foundation style is determined in five *dan.*

Set down these five *dan;* ask yourself, "How much vocal music is right for *jo,* how much for the three types of vocal music in the three steps of *ha,* and how much in the musical style fitting for *kyū,*" thus determining the number of lines[22] of vocal music; set up your play—this is what I call structuring a noh. The musical modulation[23] in each phase of *jo-ha-kyū* should vary in accordance with the type and tone of the noh.[24] The length of one play should be measured by the number of lines of vocal music in the five *dan.*

(1.4) Writing: Make sure you ask yourself and answer the question, "What kind of words would it be best to write for this style of personage," from the opening line of the play and for all the types of characters that appear.[25] In your writing, you should allot words from poems in Chinese or Japanese[26] that invoke various associations, such as auspiciousness, *yūgen,* passionate love, personal grievance, and desolation, in accord with the style of the noh.[27] In noh, there should be a setting associated with the source material.[28] If it is a place of poetic import[29]—a renowned spot or a historic site—then take words from well-known *waka* or phrases linked with it and write them into what you judge to be the climax of the three *dan* of *ha.*[30] This will be a crucial spot for expressiveness[31] in the noh. For the rest, fine words, well-known verses, and such must be written in for the *shite* to render.[32] Applying these points in this way is what is called writing a noh.

—Conclusion of "Material, Structuring, and Writing: The Three Techniques"[33]

2. Points on Composing for the Three Styles

THE THREE STYLES ARE THE OLD MAN, THE WOMAN, AND THE WARRIOR.

(2.1) The style of the old man: This is generally in the style of the *waki* play.[34] In the auspicious scheme, the opening player[35] enters for the first *dan*—the introductory chant through the long section of chant[36]—chanting 5-7-5, and then continuing the mora count of 7-5 for seven or eight lines. Count "7-5" as one line, a *waka* poem as two lines.[37]

Now the *shite* enters (the first *dan* of *ha* begins here)[38] [along with a companion] in the guise of an old couple or the like[39] for the entry chant of 5-7-5-7-5 and the second verse of 7-5-7-5,[40] followed by the recitative, which continues in 7-5 for about ten lines. The one passage of chant, lasting from the chanting in the low range to the part in the high range,[41] goes for about ten lines. The second *dan* of *ha* starts here.[42] Next comes the spoken exchange[43] between the *waki* and the *shite*, in which [the utterances] should not exceed four or five apiece.[44] In this spoken exchange, the old couple or the like may give the explanation of why something is the way it is in further conversation. This should not exceed two or three [utterances] apiece. Next comes the part in the high range, and from opening to close (position for the ear-opening?),[45] that choral chant should be about ten lines, chanted in two parts.[46] The third *dan* of *ha* starts here.[47] After that, if there is a *kuse* section,[48] the voice in the raised register forms about five lines, the [high-range part of the] recitative *[sashi]* about five lines, and the lowering to the close about five lines. The [first part of the] *kuse* is about twelve or thirteen lines. The high part is about twelve or thirteen lines. After that, a rhythmic exchange of two or three [utterances] apiece is chanted; it should come to a close briskly and lightly.

Kyū starts here.[49] Now the *shite* who enters—whether a celestial maiden or a male personage[50]—delivers a high-range passage[51] and a recitative from the bridgeway, and then intones an entry chant, the latter portion delivered in unison with lingering fullness, to resolve in the low range.[52] Next a rapid exchange[53] of two or three lines apiece is chanted; the chant should mount the rhythm, intensifying and flowing lightly to a close. Depending on [the nature of] the character who dances[54] (position for the eye-opening, but not fixed),[55] it may be preferable to exit on the *kiribyōshi* match.[56] For either one or the other, lengthiness is ill-advised. The length should be judged by the number of lines of chant.

This is the contour of noh in the *jo* style.[57] Since the casting of an old man suits this style, the way of structuring the play for the style of the old man has been singled out. The play having the style of the old man may take other contours as well, depending on the type [of character].[58] Also, for auspicious noh that features a female personage, the five-*dan* scheme remains the same.

(2.2) The noh image of the woman: Write it in such a way as to embellish its style. Dance and chant are fundamental to this style of performance in particular. Within it, there should be a very elevated style of personage. For the gentlewoman, whether a junior consort, an imperial concubine, Lady Aoi, Yūgao, or Ukifune, be mindful of the noble image, the uncommon aristocratic presence and appearance, when you write.[59] Accordingly, pay careful heed to the vocal music and fine *kakari*⁶⁰ music, for they must not resemble those of professional *kusemai* entertainers or the like. That refined *kakari* must have beauty, its grade that of ultimate *yūgen*; the [vocal] music, too, must [inspire a feeling of] wonder;⁶¹ gesture and bearing must be unsurpassed. Not the slightest flaw may be countenanced.

Within material in the style that is to have this kind of personage, it is possible on occasion to discover something akin to a gem among gems. A rare find indeed is material of the *yūgen* flower which, beyond the exquisite visional affect of the gentlewoman's person,⁶² bears such visional affect as Lady Rokujō casting her curse on Lady Aoi, Yūgao succumbing to the evil spirit, and Ukifune possessed.⁶³ Such seeds that flower⁶⁴ are even more precious than [what is described] in an old *waka* poem: "Let's infuse the cherry blossom with the fragrance of the plum, and make it bloom on the willow branch."⁶⁵ Accordingly, it may be the artist equal to this style who is worthy to be called master of the ultimate impression of the wondrous.⁶⁶

Among the other female types are Shizuka, Giō, Gijo, and the like. Since they are *shirabyōshi* dancers they should recite a *waka*, intone the entry chant with lingering fullness, mount the rhythm of the eight-beat measure, chant up into the third range, and stamp the rapid pattern, exiting with the dance.⁶⁷ For such as this, the serene mood of the *kiribyōshi* match should be suitable for just before the exit. Then there are Hyakuman, Yamamba, and the like, who are *kusemai* performers;⁶⁸ hence they should by and large be easy [to adapt]. Within the five *dan*, make *jo* and *kyū* short, making *ha* the [main] body; put the *kuse* section in the central position and divide it into two parts, with the latter part building to a rapid tempo; write with detailed attention to the authentic *kusemai* style, concluding the dance on the introductory chant pattern.⁶⁹

As for the style of the madwoman, since it is a question of madness, by all means craft the style with special care, and develop the music with detail in keeping with the comportment; if the figure has *yūgen*, then whatever is done will have interest. When you compose, make the costumes beautiful; arrange the *kakari* of the musical phrases with skill; pursue each aspect fully, and add color.⁷⁰

He who distinguishes in such a manner between the varieties, from the ultimate style⁷¹ to the gentlewoman, the *shirabyōshi*, the *kusemai* dancer, and the madwoman, composing noh true to the artistry of each, may be called a composer who knows the Way of Noh.

(2.3) The image of the warrior: If, for instance, your source material is about a famous commander of the Genji or the Heike clans, take special care to write as it is told in the *Tale of the Heike*.

Here also the proportions of the five *dan* and the length of the vocal music must be considered. If there is an interlude, the *kuse* section should appear in the latter act. In that case, *ha* will carry over into *kyū*.[72] Such a play may come to six *dan* or so. Or, if there is no interlude, four *dan* may result. It should depend on the play. Condense the first act, and write it with all brevity.

Since the image of the warrior depends on the source material, the mode of writing cannot be uniformly prescribed. Make the vocal passages brief and, in *kyū*, close on the *hayabushi* match as suits the warrior style.[73] Depending on the personage, a show of fierceness may at times be called for. Put to heroic phrases, it should be gripping.

The warrior apparition[74] should always have a name-saying speech.[75] Keep this in mind as you write.

—Conclusion of "Composing Noh in the Three Styles"

(3.1) The *hōka* entertainer: This is a derivative of the martial style, and the acting is in the *saidō* style.[76] Whether for Jinen Koji or Kagetsu, for a male behaving madly, or a female behaving madly, for that matter, the nature of the noh[77] should determine the mode of *saidō* movement to use.

Once the opening player[78] has completed the *jo dan* and the instruments play in readiness, [the *shite*], costumed as a *hōka* entertainer, intones a full and flowing recitative[79] from the bridgeway. Whether *waka* of old or other well-known lines, the expressions should be familiar but interesting, and [this] recitative, interspersed with straight prose, should flow to a close after seven or eight lines, whereupon the entry chant should ensue. With this style of *monomane* in particular, the entrance along the bridgeway should evoke a sense of distant vision,[80] and the vocal music should stir both the ear and the mind.[81] Keep these points in mind, find the right words, follow through with the type[82]—this is how you should compose. Now then, the section of chant opening with the recitative[83] should be brief, chanted smoothly and cleanly.[84] It should be the standard length for chant in the introductory portion [of *ha*].[85] Next comes the spoken exchange with the *waki*, in which the content is pursued in conversation that culminates in a heightened exchange[86] of about four or five lines apiece, followed by ten lines of chant in the high range,[87] to be composed to have all lightness and buoyancy. The portion from the dance to the *kusemai*[88] should be detailed and intense. In *kyū*, embellish the style by contriving various touches to add color, such as the *hayabushi* match,[89] the *otoshibushi*,[90] or the like.

This type of play may have the chance recovery of a child by a parent, or the sought-after reunion of a couple or of siblings or the like, upon which the play is made to conclude. For such a noh, write a *kyū*-style climax[91] into the third *dan* of *ha* and make the concluding *dan* a rhythmic exchange; if it is a reunion between parent and child, or sibling and sibling, then a touch of the affective appeal[92] of tearful noh[93] should color the exit scene. This style of play should have roughly the same visional affect[94] as the style of madness.

(3.2) Composing noh for the demon in the style of *saidō* movement: This is a variant derived from the style of the warrior.[95] It has the form of a demon and the heart of a human.[96]

The majority of plays such as this are in two acts. The first act, whether three *dan* or two, should be written with all brevity, and the apparition [featured] in the second act[97] should definitely be a demon of the ghost type.[98] From the bridgeway he should deliver four or five lively lines of recitative, and after the entry chant,[99] bound to the edge of the stage,[100] employ body and feet with minuteness; address the words in rapid succession, and there should be *otoshibushi*.[101] Next there may be about ten choral lines chanted rapidly and lightly in the high range,[102] or a rapid exchange of about three or four lines apiece may be all right as well.[103] The conclusion[104] should build in a sequence of musical phrases such as the *hayabushi, kiru fushi*,[105] and the like. On the basis of the musical phrasing,[106] visional affect of a style [conducive to] the flower[107] may emerge in the vigorous movement.[108] You should ponder the style of musical expression[109] carefully before you compose.

Also, besides this [type], there is the demon in the style of forceful movement.[110] The demon in the style of forceful movement has the force, the form, and the heart of a demon.[111] The angry aspect of that figure belongs to an aberrant style. Our group does not recognize this style of image. Only the demon in the style of *saidō* movement is to be portrayed on stage.

(3.3) Only upon gaining complete insight into these points should you compose.

Moreover, in this regard, there exist what are called the ear-opening and the eye-opening, which, in the course of one play, are positioned somewhere in *ha* and *kyū*.[112] The ear-opening is that instant in which the two aural dimensions form one impression.[113] Write down the important content from the original source material[114] for the play into words that open the mind's ear[115] of the listener, and [this] one auditory dimension[116]—that is, the written word that conveys the import—should blend with the vocal expressiveness[117] and foster an aural impression in which content and expressiveness are as one sound; this is the site for [actualizing] a deep impression[118] [of the type] to instantly stir the admiration of all. The sphere in which the two aural dimensions of content and expressiveness create one impression is named the ear-opening.

As for the eye-opening, in the course of one play, there should be a revelatory point at which the feeling aroused in the visional affect is brought to fulfillment.[119] Positioned somewhere in the dancing or vigorous movement,[120] it is the instant that moves all present to feel the wondrous.[121] This is a style manifested[122] on the basis of the actor's power to inspire an impression.[123] Though it might seem unrelated to the playwright's composing, a place in the play for such [eye-opening] visual expressiveness as this[124] should not be neglected. Therefore, you should compose having taken great care to determine that [climactic] point in the action[125] to which danced expression belongs. Since this is the wondrous moment in the play in which the eye opens, it is named the eye-opening.[126]

Thus, the ear-opening is the work of the playwright, the eye-opening the [outgrowth] of the actor's technique.[127] When one master is capable of both of these tasks,[128] no problems should arise. Moreover, there may be an instant that opens ear and eye as one to the wondrous.[129] Oral transmission; see me in person.[130]

(3.4) When you compose plays for a juvenile actor,[131] there are certain things that you must understand. When a juvenile plays a supporting role,[132] as a child of another actor or a daughter, for instance, there should be no difficulty since he looks the part. If he plays the main role in the noh,[133] do not cast him in a style that is unsuitable. In a play [composed for] a juvenile actor, it is unsuitable to cast a juvenile as a father or mother or some such[134] who is searching and grieving for a missing offspring, while a still younger child is cast in the part of [that] son or daughter, and then on the grounds of a chance reunion, [the two] act in a style of clinging, embracing, and tearful sighing that is absolutely sure to arouse distaste.[135] The fact that spectators may respond negatively, saying, "In the case of noh [performed] by young people, they perform well enough, but there is a keenly pathetic quality to the visional affect,"[136] is the fault of this style of noh. When a juvenile plays the lead in a play, he should be someone's child or younger brother who is reunited with the parent, or consumed by the grief of parting with the elder brother,[137] or some such. This is a style suitable for his person. Even if it concerns [scenes] not a part of parent-child enactments,[138] *monomane* in the venerable style[139] will ill suit the acting of a juvenile.

Furthermore, there are points for an actor of advanced years to understand.[140] To be sure, putting on a mask and making one's appearance look [the part] are integral to [the art of] *monomane*, but when you are of advanced age and [appear] in a style that is unsuitable, you will fail to be credible in other's eyes.[141] For example, when a young actor imitates old age, there should be no problem. However, when an actor well on in years plays the part of someone's daughter, or of a famed young commander and warrior-aristocrat,[142] such as Atsumori or Kiyotsune,[143] the audience will definitely not perceive his image to be like those.[144] Mark this well.

Accordingly, when you write a noh, consideration of what is suitable and realistic for the style of the actor [in question]—this is of the first importance. You must discern the natural talents of the actor; it is not possible without a thorough understanding of noh.[145] The most important thing for the playwright is this.

(3.5) From the noh [repertoire] spanning the three styles [and their derivatives],[146] a number of the styles [of works] that enjoy widespread popularity in recent times:[147]

> *Yawata, Aioi, Yōrō, Oimatsu, Shiogama, Aridōshi*—this group
> featuring the venerable style;[148]
> *Hakozaki, Unoha, Mekurauchi, Shizuka, Matsukaze Murasame,*
> *Hyakuman, Ukifune, Higaki no onna, Komachi*—featuring the
> feminine style;[149]
> *Michimori, Satsuma no kami, Sanemori, Yorimasa, Kiyotsune,*
> *Atsumori*—featuring the martial style;[150]

> *Tango monogurui, Jinen Koji, Kōya, Ōsaka*—featuring the player of
> the *yūkyō* type;[151]
> *Koi no omoni, Sano no funabashi, Shii no Shōshō, Taisan moku*—
> featuring the style of *saidō* movement.[152]

New compositions should be patterned on plays such as these.

As a rule, the compositions of recent years have consisted of new styles that are slight variations on old styles. The madwoman from the work of old, *Saga monogurui*, is the *Hyakuman* of today. *Shizuka* has an original style as well. *Tango monogurui* goes back to *Fue no monogurui*, and *Matsukaze Murasame* to *Shiokumi*. *Koi no omoni* goes back to *Aya no taiko*. *Jinen Koji* has past and present styles. *Sano no funabashi* has an old style. Each and every one has a revised style of composition based on the original style. In abidance with each age, the words are slightly altered and the expression[153] reworked to assure that the material continues to flower over the years.[154] Throughout the years to come, the same guidelines as these should remain unchanged.

(3.6) Generally speaking, discrimination between good and poor in noh is not up to one individual. Since it is a type of art that gains acclaim by exposure in the capital and the provinces, far and near, it cannot be hidden from the world. Accordingly, styles and pieces[155] will change over time, having old and contemporary versions, but from ages past, the master whose universal acclaim exceeds all the rest has ever been successful in capturing the atmosphere (*kakari*) of *yūgen*.[156] In the old style there was the *dengaku* player Itchū; in the middle years, the late master of our group, Kan'ami, and the Hie player, Inuō.[157] All three made the *yūgen* elements of dance and chant the foundation of their styles[158] and were masters of each of the three styles. As for others, artists who perform only the style of the warrior and the style of *saidō* movement may well achieve instant notice, but their reputations will not endure with the public. Judging from this, when it comes to the grade of supreme effect in the style having a true foundation of *yūgen*,[159] the visional affect appears to remain unchanged no matter what the era.[160]

Hence, you should make [material that has] the seeds to flower into *yūgen* the foundation of your style when you compose.[161] I repeat, from the past on into the future, the passing years produce artists of various accomplishments, but only the *shite* who performs in the style of *yūgen* can win

acclaim[162] that is supreme and lasting. Having heard word of the old masters and observed the distinctions between the new, I know that the mark
of the artist who has won a name both in the capital and the provinces is
a style that does not depart from the flowering style of *yūgen*.[163]

The above covers most of the major points of understanding I have
gained from what I have seen and heard in recent years. I believe that the
various plays I have composed during the Ōei years will hold their own in
the future. Study these various points with care.

This document is to be passed on to my son, Motoyoshi, and is to remain
secret instruction.

—Sixth day of the second month of Ōei 30[164]

Zea[mi](*kao*)[165]

Appendix 2

. . .

An Annotated Translation of *Takasago*

By Zeami Motokiyo

Persons

WAKI: a Shintō priest
WAKIZURE: attendants to Shintō priest (2 or 4)
KYŌGEN ACTOR: a resident of Takasago[1]
CHORUS
SHITE of first act *(maejite):* an old man (spirit of Sumiyoshi pine tree)
TSURE: an old woman (spirit of Takasago pine tree)
SHITE of second act *(nochijite):* the god of Sumiyoshi Shrine
(young male figure)

Act 1

FIRST DAN

Introductory Chant *(shidai)*

WAKI [and] WAKIZURE:
Now for the first time we start   *Ima o hajime no*
dressed in traveling robes,   *tabigoromo*

now for the first time we start
dressed in traveling robes,
the days and journey too
are long lasting.[2]

Ima o hajime no
tabigoromo
Hi mo yuku sue zo
hisashiki.

Name-saying Speech (nanori)

WAKI:

I am the priest of Aso Shrine in Kyushu,[3]
Tomonari by name. Since I have not
yet seen the capital, I have
resolved to go there, taking in the
famous sites along the way.

Somo somo kore wa Kyūshū
Asonomiya no kannushi
Tomonari to wa waga koto
nari. Ware imada miyako o
mizu sōrō hodo ni, kono
tabi omoitachi miyako ni
nobori, michisugara no
meisho o mo ikken sebaya
to zonji sōrō.

Traveling Chant (michiyuki)

WAKI [and] WAKIZURE:

In traveling robes,
on the road fair and long
to the capital,
on the road fair and long
to the capital,
today our thoughts rise up
across shoreline waves,
our boat's path tranquil
with spring breezes.
How many days have passed?
The course we have come,
the path ahead too
    veiled in white clouds,[4]
still distant we had thought
Harima inlet,[5]
yet already we have reached
the bay at Takasago,
already we have reached
the bay at Takasago.[6]

Tabigoromo
Sue haru baru no
miyakoji o
Sue haru baru no
miyakoji o
Kyō omoitatsu
ura no nami
Funaji nodokeki
harukaze no
Iku ka kinuran
ato sue mo
Isa shirakumo no
haru baru to
Sashi mo omoishi
Harimagata
Takasago no ura ni
tsukinikeri
Takasago no ura ni
tsukinikeri.

SECOND *DAN*

Entry Chant (*issei*)

SHITE [and] TSURE:

At Takasago	*Takasago no*
spring breezes in the pines	*matsu no harukaze*
deepen into dusk,	*fukikurete*
The bell too is echoing	*Onoe no kane mo*
from the hill above.[7]	*hibiku nari.*

Second Verse (*ni-no-ku*)

TSURE:

The waves are hidden	*Nami wa kasumi no*
in shoreline mists,	*isogakure*

SHITE [and] TSURE:

sound alone marks ebb and flow	*Oto koso shio no*
of the tides.	*michihi nare.*

Recitative (*sashi*)

SHITE:

Whom shall I regard	*Tare o ka mo*
as someone who knows me well?	*shiru hito ni sen*
In Takasago	*Takasago no*
even this pine is not	*matsu mo mukashi no*
a friend of the past.[8]	*tomo nara de.*

SHITE [and] TSURE:

Year after passing year,	*Sugikoshi yoyo wa*
unknown the snowy number[9]	*shirayuki no*
Piling, piling up,	*Tsumori tsumorite*
As hoary cranes[10]	*oi no tsuru no*
Remain in their roost	*Negura ni nokoru*
beneath the dawn moon,	*ariyake no*
oft awakening	*Haru no shimoyo no*
in the frosty spring night,	*okii ni mo*
the wind in the pines	*Matsukaze o nomi*
the sole accustomed sound.	*kikinarete*

Our hearts companions,	*Kokoro o tomo to*
on a mat of sedge	*sugamushiro no*
we share our thoughts,	*Omoi o noburu*
that is all.	*bakari nari.*

Low-range Chant (sageuta)

SHITE [and] TSURE:

The shoreline wind	*Otozure wa*
whispers in the pine	*Matsu ni koto tou*
and visits falling needles	*urakaze no*
on our robes,	*Ochibagoromo no*
sleeve next to sleeve,	*sode soete*
let's sweep clean the needles	*Kokage no chiri o*
scattered beneath the pine,	*kakō yo*
let's sweep clean the needles	*Kokage no chiri o*
scattered beneath the pine.	*kakō yo.*

High-range Chant

SHITE [and] TSURE:

The place	*Tokoro wa*
is Takasago,	*Takasago no*
the place	*Tokoro wa*
is Takasago,	*Takasago no*
the pine on the hilltop too	*Onoe no matsu mo*
is far along in years,	*toshifurite*
and waves of aging	*Oi no nami mo*
wash up to our shores.	*yorikuru ya*
In the shade of the pine,	*Ko no shitakage no*
the fallen needles	*ochiba*
we sweep	*kaku*
through lives	*Naru made inochi*
enduring	*nagaraete*
until what unknown time	*Nao itsu made ka*
"The Living Pines"[11]	*iki no matsu*
also from the distant past	*Sore mo hisashiki*
a spot of renown,	*meisho ka na*
also from the distant past	*Sore mo hisashiki*
a spot of renown.	*meisho ka na.*

THIRD *DAN*

Spoken Exchange (*mondō*)

WAKI:
While I await a resident of this place, an elderly couple has come. You there, old man. I have something to ask you.

Satobito o aimatsu
tokoro ni, rōjin fūfu
kitareri. Ika ni kore
naru rōjin ni tazunubeki
koto no sōrō.

SHITE:
Do you mean me? What might it be?

Konata no koto nite
sōrō ka. Nanigoto nite
sōrō zo.

WAKI:
Which tree is the famed Takasago pine?

Takasago no matsu to wa
izure no ki o mōshisōrō zo.

SHITE:
The one whose shade this old man has just swept clean, this is the Takasago pine.

Tadaima kono jō ga
kokage o kiyomesōrō
koso, Takasago no matsu
nite sōrae.

WAKI:
The pines of Takasago and Sumiyoshi are known as the wedded pines. This place and Sumiyoshi[12] are in separate provinces, so why are they named the wedded pines?

Takasago Suminoe no
matsu ni aioi no na
ari. Tōsho to Sumiyoshi
to wa kuni o hedatetaru
ni, nani tote aioi no
matsu to wa mōshisōrō zo.

SHITE:
It is stated in the "Preface" to the *Kokin shu*[13] that the pines of Takasago and Sumiyoshi should be thought of as wedded pines. Be that as it may,

Kokin no jo ni iwaku,
Takasago Suminoe no
matsu mo aioi no yō ni
oboe to ari. Sarinagara,

this old man is from Sumiyoshi in
Settsu Province; this old woman is
a person of this place. (To TSURE.)
If you know something more,
speak out.

*kono jō wa ano Tsu no
kuni Sumiyoshi no mono,
kore naru nba koso tōsho
no hito nare. Shiru
koto araba mōsatamae.*

Heightened Exchange (kakeai)

WAKI:

How strange indeed.
You appear to be an elderly couple
together in this place
yet you claim to live
in distant Sumiyoshi
and Takasago,
lands divided
by mountain and ocean,
how can what you say
possibly be true?

*Fushigi ya
mireba rōjin no
fūfu to issho ni
arinagara
tōki Suminoe
Takasago no
urayama kuni o
hedatete sumu to
iu wa ika naru
koto yaran.*

TSURE:

How foolish
what you say,
may they be divided
by mountains and rivers,
two caring hearts
will make the passage,
for the path shared by man and wife
is never far.

*Utate no
ōsezōrō ya,
sansen banri o
hedatsuredomo
tagai ni kayou
kokorozukai no
imose no michi mo
tōkarazu.*

SHITE:

Reflect, if you will,
on our words.

*Mazu anjite mo
goranze yo.*

SHITE [and] TSURE:

Insensate may be
the pine trees
at Takasago
and Sumiyoshi,

*Takasago
Suminoe no
matsu wa hijō no
mono da ni mo*

but they are known nonetheless
as the wedded pines.
How much more should we
of human feeling
throughout the many years
from Sumiyoshi
cross back and forth,
an old man and woman,
together with the pines are we
until this very age
growing old together
as husband and wife.[14]

aioi no na wa
aru zo kashi.
Mashite ya shō aru
hito to shite
toshi hisashiku mo
Sumiyoshi yori
kayoinaretaru
jō to nba wa
matsu morotomo ni
kono toshi made
aioi no fūfu to
naru mono o.

Heightened Exchange II (kakeai)

WAKI:
Hearing your account,
how interesting!
Well then, back to the story
we asked you to tell
about the wedded pines,
isn't there more
to be told
in connection with this place?

Iware o kikeba
omoshiro ya
satesate saki ni
kikoetsuru
aioi no matsu no
monogatari o
tokoro ni iioku
iware wa naki ka.

SHITE:
What men of old said
is this,
they exemplify
an auspicious realm.

Mukashi no hito no
mōshishi wa
kore wa medetaki
yo no tameshi nari.

TSURE:
The pine tree at Takasago
stands for a past age
when the *Man'yō shū*
came into being.[15]

Takasago to iu wa
jōdai no
Man'yō shū no
inishie no gi.

SHITE:
The pine of Sumiyoshi

Sumiyoshi

for the present age,
the illustrious reign
of the Engi emperor.[16]

to mōsu wa
ima kono miyo ni
sumitamō
Engi no on-koto.

TSURE:
Pine needles, like leaves of poetry,
never run out,

Matsu to wa tsukinu
koto no ha no

SHITE:
they prosper past and present
ever the same,

sakae wa kokin
aionaji to

SHITE [and] TSURE:
a metaphor in praise
of this revered reign.

Miyo o agamuru
tatoe nari.

WAKI:
When I truly listen,
how wondrous it seems.
At last all doubts come clear
as the light this spring day

Yokuyoku kikeba
arigata ya
ima koso fushin haru
no hi no

SHITE:
softly shimmering
on the western sea.

hikari yawaragu
nishi no umi no

WAKI:
Over there,
Sumiyoshi,

Kashiko wa
Suminoe

SHITE:
And here,
Takasago

koko wa
Takasago

WAKI:
their pines
blend in hue

matsu mo
iro soi

SHITE:

| and spring too | *haru mo* |
| so tranquil. | *nodoka ni.* |

High-range Chant

CHORUS:

Upon the four seas	*Shikai nami*
the waves are serene,[17]	*shizuka nite*
peace nurtured in the land	*Kuni mo osamaru*
by timely breezes	*tokitsukaze*
that rustle not the branches	*Eda o narasanu*
in so revered a reign.	*miyo nare ya*
And into such an age	*Ai ni aioi no*
the wedded pines	*matsu koso*
live on	*Medeta*
auspiciously.	*karikere.*
Try as we may,	*Ge ni ya*
truly vain our efforts	*aogite mo*
to justly voice our praises,	*Koto mo oroka ya*
for in this realm	*kakaru yo ni*
our people enjoy	*Sumeru tami tote*
a state so bountiful	*yutaka naru*
the blessings of our sovereign,	*Kimi no megumi zo*
are rare indeed.	*arigataki.*

FOURTH *DAN*

***Kuse* Section**

Kuri

CHORUS:

Although it is said	*Sore sōmoku*
that plants have no feeling	*kokoro nashi to mōsedomo*
they never miss their time	*kajitsu no toki o*
to flower or bear fruit.	*tagaezu.*
Basking in the goodness	*Yōshun no*
of the spring sun,	*toku o sonaete*
from the southernmost branches	*nanshi hana*
the blossoms start to open.[18]	*hajimete hiraku.*

Recitative

SHITE:
Yet for all of that
the image of this pine
stays constant,
heedless of the time
for blossoms or leaves.

Shikaredomo
kono matsu wa
sono keshiki to koshinae
ni shite
kayou toki o wakazu.

CHORUS:
Though four seasons pass
its color of a thousand years
stays deep in the snows,[19]
The pine tree blooms
but once in a thousand years—
ten times this occurs, it is claimed.[20]

Yotsu no toki
itarite mo
issennen no iro
yuki no uchi ni fukaku
mata wa shōka no iro
tokaeri to mo ieri.

SHITE:
For such tidings we
    pine
tree branches

Kakaru tayori o
    matsu
ga e no

CHORUS:
laden with leaves of words
on which beads of dew
become as seeds
to hone the heart,
for every living thing
they say
is drawn to the shade cast
by these Isles of poetry.[21]

koto no hagusa no
tsuyu no tama
kokoro o migaku
tane to narite
iki to shi ikeru
mono goto ni
Shikishima no kage ni
yoru to ka ya.

Kuse

CHORUS:
Thus was it also
stated in the words
of the poet Chōnō[22]
that no voice,

Shikaru ni
Chōnō ga
kotoba ni mo
Ujō hijō no

sentient or insentient,	*sono koe*
is excluded	*Mina uta ni moruru*
from song.	*koto nashi.*
Grass, trees, earth, and sand,	*Sōmoku dosha*
the voice of the wind,	*Fūsei*
the sound of the water,	*suion made*
all things are imbued	*Banbutsu no komoru*
with poetic feeling.	*kokoro ari.*
The forests	*Haru no*
at springtime	*hayashi no*
swaying	*Tō*
in the eastern winds,	*fū ni ugoki*
the autumn insects	*aki no mushi no*
crying out	*hokuro ni*
in the northern dews,	*naku mo*
do not all things reveal themselves	*Mina waka no sugata*
in lyric form?	*narazu ya.*
And among them all	*Naka ni mo*
this pine	*kono matsu wa*
surpasses	*Banboku ni*
ten thousand trees,	*sugurete*
The verdure of the pine tree[23]	*Shūhakkō no*
does endure	*yosooi*
A thousand autumns	*Senshū no*
past and present	*midori o nashite*
remaining	*Kokon no*
ever green,	*iro o mizu*
A tree so worthy	*Shikō no*
that the First Emperor[24]	*onshaku ni*
bestowed upon it	*Azukaru hodo no*
rank in his court.	*ki nari tote*
In foreign lands	*Ikoku ni mo*
and in our realm alike	*honchō ni mo*
praised	*Banmin kore o*
by all the people.	*shōkan su.*

SHITE (AGEHA):
At Takasago   *Takasago no*

there upon the hill above	*Onoe no kane no*
the bell sounds.	*oto su nari.*

CHORUS:

With the dawn	*Akatsuki kakete*
frost	*Shimo wa*
has settled in	*okedomo*
but the deep green hue	*matsu ga e no*
of the pine branches	*Ha iro wa onaji*
stays the same.	*fukamidori*
Though we sweep	*Tachiyoru kage no*
beneath the pine,	*asayū ni*
morning and night,	*Kakedomo*
that the fallen needles	*ochiba no*
do not dwindle	*Tsukisenu wa*
is true.	*makoto nari*
The needles of the pine	*Matsu no ha no*
undepleted,	*chiriusezu shite*
their hue deepening	*Iro wa nao*
as the laurel vine grows long,[25]	*masaki no kazura*
a metaphor	*Nagaki yo no*
for this long reign,	*tatoe narikeru*
forever green,	*tokiwagi no*
among its kind,	*Naka ni mo na wa*
the Takasago pine,	*Takasago no*
hereafter too	*Matsudai no*
singled out	*tameshi ni mo*
auspiciously	*Aioi no matsu zo*
as the wedded pine.	*medetaki.*

Rhythmic Exchange

CHORUS:

Indeed the pine branches	*Ge ni na o etaru*
have earned wide renown,	*matsu ga e no*
the past of two ancient trees	*Oiki no mukashi*
now revealed.	*arawashite*
Do tell us please	*Sono na o*
your names.	*nanoritamae ya*

SHITE [and] TSURE:
Now what have we
to conceal?
One of Takasago and
the other Sumiyoshi,
we are the spirits
of the wedded pines
come before you
as man and wife.

Ima wa nani o ka
tsutsumu beki
Kore wa Takasago
Suminoe no
Aioi no
matsu no sei
Fūfu to genji
kitaritari.

CHORUS:
How wondrous, then
the miracle of the pines
for which this place is known
is before us.

Fushigi ya sate wa
nadokoro no
　　Matsu no kidoku o
arawashite.

SHITE [and] TSURE:
It is said that plants and trees
do not possess feeling,

Sōmoku kokoro
nakeredomo

CHORUS:
yet earth and trees alike[26]

Kashikoki yo tote

SHITE [and] TSURE:
revere this realm,

tsuchi mo ki mo

CHORUS:
and forevermore
in this land
of our
sovereign
wish their lives
　　to pass
first to Sumiyoshi,
we'll go ahead,
and there await you,
they said.
They boarded

　　Waga
Ōkimi no
kuni nareba
Itsu made mo
kimi ga yo ni
　　Sumiyoshi ni
mazu yukite
Are nite machi
mōsan to
Yūnami no
migiwa naru

a small	*Ama no*
fishing craft	*obune ni*
on the water's edge,	*uchinorite*
and trusting the winds	*Oikaze ni*
to guide them,	*makasetsutsu*
they sailed out	*Oki no kata ni*
toward the offing,	*idenikeri ya*
they sailed out	*Oki no kata ni*
toward the offing.[27]	*idenikeri.*

Act 2

FIFTH *DAN*

High-range Chant

WAKI [and] WAKIZURE:

At Takasago	*Takasago ya*
we hoist the sail	*Kono urabune ni*
on this small fishing craft	*ho o agete*
we hoist the sail	*Kono urabune ni*
on this small fishing craft,	*ho o agete*
the tide rises	*Tsuki morotomo ni*
together with the moon,	*ideshio no*
the waves bring Awaji Isle	*Nami no Awaji no*
into view,	*shimakage ya*
then past the offing	*Tōku Naruo no*
of distant Naruo,	*oki sugite*
And swiftly we have come	*Haya Suminoe ni*
to Sumiyoshi,	*tsukinikeri*
and swiftly we have come	*Haya Suminoe ni*
to Sumiyoshi.	*tsukinikeri.*

Recitative

SHITE:

Even one as I,	*Ware mite mo*
long familiar with the pine	*hisashiku narinu*
on Sumiyoshi's shore,	*Sumiyoshi no*
wonder how many ages	*Kishi no himematsu*

it has known.
Know you not, my lord,
our intimacy,
unseen the sacred fence
round your realm
from distant ages?[28]
A dance by the god,
beat the evening drums,
soothe my spirits,
shrine attendants.[29]

ikuyo henuran.
Mutsumashi to
kimi wa shirazu ya
mizugaki no
Hisashiki yoyo no
kami kagura
Yoru no tsuzumi no
hyōshi o soroete
Suzushimetamae
miyazukotachi.

Free Chant in High Range

CHORUS:
On the western sea
of Aokigahara
from amidst the waves

Nishi no umi
Aokigahara no
namima yori

SHITE:
the god of Sumiyoshi
has risen.[30]

Araware ideshi
Sumiyoshi no

Entry Chant

SHITE:
The season is spring
on Asaka strand[31]
where snow scarce remains.

Haru nare ya
Nokon no yuki no
Asakagata.

CHORUS:
In the shade along shore
where seaweed is gathered,

Tamamo karu naru
kishikage no

SHITE:
Sitting down on the pine roots
and rubbing my waist against them,

Shōkon ni yotte
koshi o sureba

CHORUS:
My hand is filled
with the green of a thousand years.

Sennen no midori
te ni miteri.

SHITE:

Breaking off a sprig of plum
and arranging it in my hair,

Baika o otte
kōbe ni saseba

CHORUS:

The snows of the second month
sprinkle down on my robe.[32]

Jigetsu no yuki
koromo ni otsu.

GOD DANCE *(KAMI MAI)*

Rhythmic Exchange

CHORUS:

How wondrous is this
divine appearance,
How wondrous is this
divine appearance,
Beneath the Sumiyoshi moon
the god dance unfolds,
A vision so truly rare
moves us to prayer.

Arigata no
yōgō ya
Arigata no
yōgō ya
Tsuki Sumiyoshi no
kami asobi
Mikage o ogamu
aratasa yo.

SHITE:

Indeed a great host
of maidens dancing,
their voices, too, ringing clear
through Sumiyoshi
Where the pine tree also
casts its reflection
Upon the
     "Sea Green Waves"[33]
must come from such a scene.

Ge ni samazama no
maibime no
Koe mo sumu nari
Suminoe no
Matsukage mo
utsuru naru
     Seigaiha
to wa
kore yaran.

CHORUS:

God and sovereign alike
must tread the straight path,
When leading to springtime
in the capital

Kami to kimi to no
michi sugu ni
Miyako no haru ni
yukubeku wa

SHITE:

Fitting is the dance of old	*Sore zo Genjō*
"Return to the Town."	*raku no mai*

CHORUS:

In robes pure we dance a prayer	*Sate banzei no*

SHITE:

that our lord live long	*omigoromo.*

CHORUS:

To ward off evil spirits	*Sasu kaina ni wa*
one arm be upraised,	*akuma o harai*
To grasp life and well-being	*Osamuru te ni wa*
one arm be lowered,	*jufuku o idaki*
"The Dance of a Thousand Autumns"[34]	*Senshūraku wa*
sustains the people	*tami o nade*
"The Dance of Ten Thousand Years"	*Manzairaku ni wa*
brings longevity,	*inochi o nobu*
The voice of the wind	*Aioi no*
in the wedded pines	*matsukaze*
Rushing clear and fresh	*Sassatsu no koe zo*
ushers delight,	*tanoshimu*
Rushing clear and fresh	*Sassatsu no koe zo*
ushers delight.	*tanoshimu.*

Notes

．　　◆　　．

Introduction

1. Daniel Gerould, "Zeami the Theorist in the Context of World Theatre," in Benito Ortolani and Samuel L. Leiter, eds., *Zeami and the Nō Theatre in the World* (New York: Center for Advanced Studies in Theatre Arts, The City University of New York, 1998), 13.

2. Michael Huxley and Noel Witts, "Twentieth-Century Performance: The Case for a New Approach," in Michael Huxley and Noel Witts, eds., *The Twentieth-Century Performance Reader* (London: Routledge, 1996), 2.

3. *Kaden* (also known as *Fūshikaden*), in Omote Akira and Katō Shūichi, eds., *Zeami, Zenchiku, Gei no shisō, Michi no shisō* 1. Nihon Shisō Taikei Shinsōhan (Tokyo: Iwanami, 1974; 2nd ed., 1995), 56. Citations are to the 1995 ed. This edition of Zeami and Zenchiku's treatises will hereafter be referred to as NSTS. More will be said about the composition of the parts of *Kaden*, as well as the titles of those parts, in chapter 1.

4. *Kaden*, NSTS, 57.

5. Ibid., 55.

6. *Kakyō*, NSTS, 100. The marionette metaphor is taken from a fourteenth-century work by a Rinzai Zen priest titled *Gettan Oshō hōgo* (Priest Gettan's Buddhist precepts). Nearman offers a detailed analysis of Zeami's usage of the metaphor in "*Kakyō*: Zeami's Fundamental Principles of Acting, Part Two," *Monumenta Nipponica* 37.4 (winter 1982): 490–494.

7. The "*tai*" in "*santai*" has also been glossed variously (three role types, three modes, three bodies). I believe that "styles" is most faithful to the spirit in which Zeami uses the term in that he had been influenced by its pervasive use in pedagogical writings on Japanese poetry, such as Fujiwara no Teika's usage, *waka jittei* (ten styles of *waka* composing). I am grateful to Professor Omote Akira, emeritus professor of Hōsei University, for pointing this parallel out during a consultation there in 1994.

8. The text of Yoshimoto's letter is available in Fukuda Hideichi, "Zeami no yōshō jidai o shimesu Yoshimoto no shojō," in Nihon Bungaku Kenkyū Shiryō Kankōkai, ed., *Yōkyoku, kyōgen*, Nihon Bungaku Kenkyū Shiryō Sōsho (Tokyo: Yūseidō, 1981), 33–40. It is dated the seventeenth day of the fourth month of 1376. More will be said about this in chapter 1.

9. Hans-Georg Gadamer, *Truth and Method* (New York: Crossroad, 1982), 350.

10. Elin Diamond, "Brechtian Theory/Feminist Theory: Toward a Gestic Feminist Criticism," in Carol Martin, ed., *A Sourcebook of Feminist Theatre and Performance: On and Beyond the Stage* (London: Routledge, 1996), 129. To be sure, Brechtian and noh dramas are worlds apart, yet in both styles the use of narrative modes of exposition tends to undermine any claims to realistic depiction.

11. Hoff has pointed to a tendency in the mid-twentieth century for Japanese scholars and performers to oversubscribe to the idea that narrative recitation (*katarimono*) is fundamental to noh. He argues that this grew out of a felt need to differentiate noh from Western forms of drama. While there is truth to his observation, to overlook the importance of the narrative mode in the exposition of noh would be equally misrepresentative. Hoff's observation has specifically to do with the 1960s in Japan. Frank Hoff, "Killing the Self: How the Narrator Acts," *Asian Theatre Journal* 2.1 (1985): 1–27.

12. Hayden White, *Figural Realism: Studies in the Mimesis Effect* (Baltimore, Md.: The Johns Hopkins University Press, 1999), 5.

13. The Matsunoya Bunko manuscript was previously in the holdings of a former daimyō family by the name of Hori, and they are believed to date to a copy transcribed in the sixteenth century. It is also thought that the original manuscript had been passed down in the Ochi Kanze line, Zeami's direct descendants, about whom there are no genealogical records after the mid-sixteenth century. For more general information on the Matsunoya manuscripts, see Erika de Poorter, *Zeami's Talks on Sarugaku: An Annotated Translation of the 'Sarugaku Dangi'* (Amsterdam: J. C. Gieben, 1986), 47–48.

14. Yoshida Tōgo, *Nōgaku koten Zeami jūrokubu shū* (Tokyo: Nōgakkai, 1909). (This collection actually includes fifteen writings rather than sixteen.) Subsequent print editions that rely primarily on the Yoshida *bon* recension include that in volume one of Nose Asaji's collection of Zeami's treatises, *Zeami jūrokubu shū hyōshaku*, first published in 1940, and that in the Nihon Shisō Taikei series, edited by Omote Akira

and first published in 1974 (see selected bibliography for details). These are two sources that have been very influential in modern Zeami scholarship.

15. Takemoto Mikio, "Yoshida Bunko Zeami nōgakuron shiryō shōkai," *Bungaku* 4.4 (2003): 199–206.

16. I would like to express my gratitude to Professor Takemoto for generously sharing a digital reproduction of the newly discovered text along with related materials, and also to Professor Shinko Kagaya for taking the time to apprise me of and send me the information. A photographic reproduction of this text has since been published in Takemoto, "Yoshida Bunko zō shinshutsu bon Sandō ni tsuite," in *Waseda Daigaku 21 seiki COE puroguramu, engeki no sōgōteki kenkyū to engekigaku no kakuritsu*, Engeki Kenkyū Sentā kiyō III (2004): ten plates (pages unnumbered) preceding Takemoto's article, 1–7.

17. Tashiro Keiichirō, *Mugen nō* Asahi Sensho 500 (Tokyo: Asahi Shinbunsha, 1994), 170.

18. Ibid.

19. Kenneth K. Yasuda, *Masterworks of the Nō Theater* (Bloomington: Indiana University Press, 1989), 2.

20. A letter from William to Henry, dated 4 May 1907, congratulating him on *The American Scene*. Quoted in Denis Donoghue, "Introduction," in Henry James, *The Golden Bowl*. Everyman's Library no. 117 (New York: Alfred A. Knopf, 1992), xiv.

21. Ibid., xvi.

22. According to Tashiro, the term *mugen nō* was first coined in a radio broadcast in 1926 by the scholar Sanari Kentarō (1890–1966). In 1930–1931, Sanari published the seven-volume annotated collection of plays titled *Yōkyoku taikan*, which allotted all the plays in the repertoire to either a *mugen* category, or what he called "*geki nō*," or "dramatic noh." Tashiro argues that the impetus for the formulation of the categories *mugen* and *genzai* was a generally heightened awareness regarding the noh tradition as something distinct from the Western realistic theatre, which was having a major impact on the Japanese theatre scene throughout the Taishō years. He speculates that Sanari's inspiration for the term was the Japanese term *mugen geki* (dream drama), which was coined in this period to refer to dramatic works by European playwrights such as August Strindberg (1849–1912) who were interested in portraying the fantastic or hallucinatory in their plays. Tashiro, *Mugen nō*, 12–14.

23. Yuasa Yasuo, *The Body: Toward an Eastern Mind-Body Theory*, ed. T. P. Kasulis, trans. Nagatomo Shigenori and T. P. Kasulis (Albany: State University of New York Press, 1987), 106.

24. These are Nagatomo's words in a chapter that develops Yuasa's views on self-cultivation as transformative practice. Nagatomo Shigenori, *Attunement through the Body* (Albany: State University of New York Press, 1992), 75.

25. Hare's study of Zeami's dramaturgy comes immediately to mind; Thomas Blenman

Hare, *Zeami's Style: The Noh Plays of Zeami Motokiyo* (Stanford, Calif: Stanford University Press), 1986. Also Masaru Sekine, *Ze-ami and His Theories of Noh Drama* (Gerrards Cross, England: Colin Smythe, 1985).

26. Makoto Ueda, *Literary and Art Theories in Japan* (Cleveland: Western Reserve University, 1967), 60.

27. Andrew T. Tsubaki, "Zeami and the Transition of the Concept of *Yūgen*: A Note on Japanese Aesthetics," *The Journal of Aesthetics and Art Criticism* 30.1 (1971): 57, 63.

28. Mark J. Nearman, "Zeami's *Kyūi*: A Pedagogical Guide for Teachers of Acting, *Monumenta Nipponica* 33.3 (1978): 324, note 92.

29. Janet Goff, *Noh Drama and The Tale of Genji: The Art of Allusion in Fifteen Classical Plays* (Princeton, N.J.: Princeton University Press, 1991), 34.

30. William R. LaFleur, *The Karma of Words: Buddhism and the Literary Arts in Medieval Japan* (Berkeley: University of California Press, 1986), 130–131.

31. Arthur H. Thornhill III, "*Yūgen* after Zeami," in James R. Brandon, ed., *Nō and Kyōgen in the Contemporary World* (Honolulu: University of Hawai'i Press, 1997), 43.

32. Steven T. Brown, *Theatricalities of Power: The Cultural Politics of Noh* (Stanford: Stanford University Press, 2001), 31–32.

33. Donald Keene, *Nō and Bunraku* (New York: Columbia University Press, 1990), 24.

Chapter 1: The Social Context of Zeami's Secret Treatises

To my knowledge, there are presently at least three well-rounded biographical studies of Zeami. Therefore, the contents of this chapter will concentrate on information needed to follow issues immediately relevant to this volume, such as patronage, literacy, and other social factors that contextualize the production of secret treatises. I will also introduce new information that has become available since the following recommended sources were published. See De Poorter, *Zeami's Talks*; Hare, *Zeami's Style*; and P. G. O'Neill, *Early Nō Drama: Its Background, Character, and Development, 1300–1450* (London: Lund Humphries, 1958).

1. He inherited his father's surname, Kanze, and went by the common name *(tsūshō)* Saburō; he was often referred to as Kanze Saburō. As a child he also went by Fujiwaka, a name bestowed on him by the poet Nijō Yoshimoto. His real name *(jitsumei)* was Motokiyo. The name that is most widely recognizable today, Zeami, is an abbreviation of his artistic name, Zeamidabutsu, which he took in middle age. In his writings, he also refers to himself as Zea or Ze. Moreover, he was also referred to respectfully, with a polite title (Master) appended, as Ze-shi. Later in life he took a Buddhist name as well, Shiō or Shiō Zenbō.

2. After the court aristocrat Sanjō Kintada (1324–1383) spotted the young Zeami sitting beside Ashikaga Yoshimitsu in the viewing stands at the Gion Festival in Kyoto, he recorded this famous reaction in his diary. He referred to Zeami's calling as "an occupation for beggars" *(kojiki no shogyō)*. Diary entry for 7 VI Eiwa 4 in his

personal diary, *Gogumaiki*. Quoted in Omote Akira and Amano Fumio, *Nōgaku no rekishi*, Iwanami Kōza Nō Kyōgen (Tokyo: Iwanami, 1987), 1:43. Hereafter referred to as Iwanami Kōza, vol. 1. Stanca Scholz-Cionca discusses Zeami's outcast status in more detail in "Outcast Imagery in Zeami's Plays," in Ortolani and Leiter, eds., *Zeami and the Nō Theatre*, 29–39.

3. Saburō Kiyotsugu. His common name was Saburō and his real name Kiyotsugu. His artistic name was Kanze. Omote and Amano surmise that he took Buddhist vows late in life, whereupon he assumed the Buddhist name Kan'amidabutsu, often abbreviated to Kan'a or Kan'ami. They also believe that he returned to lay status at the end of his life. The name Kanze became a surname for his lineage as of his generation. Iwanami Kōza, 1:33. He became the first official head of the Kanze troupe, and his son Zeami was designated the second.

4. Zeami's birth date has been narrowed down to either 1363 or 1364 based on statements that he makes in his critical treatises. De Poorter goes into some detail on the reasoning of several of the major hypotheses on this in *Zeami's Talks*, 29–32. I am going by the 1363 birth date.

5. Today *Shikisanban* is titled *Okina*. Originally the piece featured a series of three venerable males dancing in sequence to bless peace and prosperity in the realm. In Zeami's time, the sequence involved an opening dance by a young male figure, Senzai, followed by two venerable figures, Okina and Sanbasō, dancing in sequence. Not much is known about the origins of the piece, but records of its performance may be traced to the late Heian and early Kamakura periods. It seems to have been connected with Buddhist temple attendants called *shushi* or *sushi*, who would perform song and dance (called *hashiri*) at festivals and temple services for purposes of warding off or appeasing pestilent spirits. These practices are believed to have been the basis for the formation of a group of performers that specialized in *Okina sarugaku*, which was performed as a kind of blessing (*shukutō*) at temple- and shrine-based events. From the earliest records, the elders of the four Yamato *za* (*yoza no osa*) would signal the opening of *takigi sarugaku* (firelight *sarugaku*) by performing *Okina sarugaku* in front of the shrine, Kasuga Ōmiya; this performance was called *shushi hashiri*. It is not clear whether *Okina sarugaku* players were originally active as *shushi* or whether they incorporated the *shushi hashiri* into their own art. Based on Iwanami Kōza 1:21–23 and 1:329–331. Coexisting with *Okina sarugaku* during this same time frame was a miscellany of entertainment arts also referred to as *sarugaku*, which embraced humorous skits, dancing, singing, acrobatics, etc. Until the early Kamakura period this second stream of *sarugaku* was treated as strictly subsidiary to *Okina sarugaku*. According to Omote and Amano, this relation started to be reversed in the mid-Kamakura period and had shifted decisively by Kan'ami's lifetime. Iwanami Kōza, 1:21–22. For more on this topic, see Amano Fumio, *Okina sarugaku kenkyū* (Osaka: Izumi Shoin, 1995).

6. Omote has pointed out that the performance at Imagumano appears nowhere in extant contemporary records and that, in fact, both the date and exact location are

products of speculation. It is surmised that it refers to Imagumano Shrine, located in Higashiyama Ward, Imagumano, Naginomori-cho, Kyoto. All we know is what Zeami himself states in *Sarugaku dangi*, "It occurred at a place called Imagumano when Zeami was twelve." See Omote, "Kan'ami Kiyotsugu to Yūzaki-za," *Bungaku* 51.7 (1983): 43–46. Also NSTS, 498–499, appendix note 168.

7. In the medieval period, the *za*, often translated as "guild," was the core unit of commercial activity in general. A groundbreaking study of the *za* unit and a detailed discussion of its function within the performing arts is provided in Hayashiya Tatsusaburo, *Chūsei geinōshi no kenkyū* (Tokyo: Iwanami Shoten, 1960), 417–490. For an introduction in English, see Toyoda Takeshi and Sugiyama Hiroshi with V. Dixon Morris, "The Growth of Commerce and the Trades," in John Whitney Hall and Toyoda Takeshi, eds., *Japan in the Muromachi Age* (Berkeley: University of California Press, 1977), 129–144.

8. The other three *za* of the Yamato region are Tobi, Sakado, and Enman'i, which evolved respectively into the Hōshō, Kongō, and Konparu schools.

9. Iwanami Kōza, 1:37.

10. For more on the festivals in which members of Zeami's *za* were committed to appear, see De Poorter, *Zeami's Talks*, 22–24. For more on Kasuga Shrine and Kōfukuji in this period, see Royall Tyler, *The Miracles of the Kasuga Deity* (New York: Columbia University Press, 1990).

11. They were the Yamashina, Shimosaka, and Hie, who were affiliated with Hie Shrine, and the Mimaji, Ōmori, and Sakōdo, whose affiliations are not clear. By the early Edo period, the *za* of Ōmi had been eclipsed by the Yamato *za*, however, and were reduced to assisting Yamato productions in subsidiary roles as musicians and companions to the main actors. Amano Fumio, "Ōmi sarugaku," in Nishino Haruo and Hata Hisashi, eds., *Shintei zōho nō, kyōgen jiten*, rev. and exp. ed. (Tokyo: Heibonsha, 1999), 234–235.

12. According to Katagiri Noboru in the entry on "Kanjin nō" in Nishino and Hata, eds., *Nō, kyōgen jiten*, 238–239.

13. De Poorter, *Zeami's Talks*, 24–25.

14. Iwanami Kōza, 1:331. This source also points out that Okina *sarugaku* (*Shikisanban*) bore resemblances to performances by a type of attendant (*shushi*; also read *jushi* or *sushi*) at religious services whose role was to pray for peace and protection from demonic forces. For more on earlier phases of Okina *sarugaku*, see Iwanami Kōza, 333–336.

15. Omote, "Kan'ami Kiyotsugu," 43–46.

16. Ibid.

17. The description in *Gogumaiki* of Zeami's presence at Yoshimitsu's side during the Gion Festival suggests that such a relationship might have existed.

18. Fukuda, "Zeami no yōshō jidai," 34. Since the discovery and initial publication of this document by Fukuda in *Geinōshi kenkyū* no. 10 (July 1965), its authenticity has

been contested by Omote and others. One reason is its fulsome tone, which Omote suggests is unlikely on the part of a member of a regental family toward someone in Zeami's marginalized calling. He hypothesizes that Yoshimoto must have written the letter, which praises Yoshimitsu's discriminating taste in dancers, in the hope that it would come to Yoshimitsu's attention. Omote Akira, " 'Yoshimoto shōsokushi' shōkō," in his *Nōgakushi shinkō* (Tokyo: Wan'ya Shoten, 1986), 2:132–133.

More recently, Momose has questioned the style of the letter. Among his reasons is that it was written in vernacular *kana*, whereas one would expect a court aristocrat of this period to compose a missive such as this in *kanbun*. (It is addressed to a Buddhist cleric identified only by the high-ranking title "Sonshōin.") However, Momose concludes that such an unconventional choice might not be atypical of Yoshimoto, whose idiosyncratic stylistic choices may be attested elsewhere in his corpus. Momose Kesao, "Nijō Yoshimoto to Zeami, shojō o chūshin ni shite," *Nōgaku kenkyū* no. 23 (1998): 5–6. For a translation of the text of Yoshimoto's letter, see Hare, *Zeami's Style*, 17–18.

19. Based on an entry in *Fuchiki*, the diary of retired emperor Sukō (1334–1398). I have based my information on Omote Akira, " 'Kanze' chūshin no nōgakushi nenpyō (1)," *Kaden*, Zaidan hōjin Kanze Bunko Nenpō (1996), 3:15. See Hare, *Zeami's Style*, 19, for a translation of the journal entry.

20. Takemoto Mikio, *Kan'ami, Zeami jidai no nō* (Tokyo: Daitōkyū Kinen Bunko, 1992), 3.

21. Takemoto Mikio, *Kan'ami, Zeami jidai no nōgaku* (Tokyo: Meiji Shoin, 1999), 25.

22. Ibid., 42.

23. Iwanami Kōza, 1:25.

24. Ibid., 26. The titles of the two *dengaku* pieces on the program are "Sadatoshi, retainer of Emperor Murakami, goes to China and brings back a famous lute to the Japanese court" and "Prince Hanzoku captures King Fumyō." Both titles suggest that these *dengaku* pieces, too, had dramatic content.

25. All of these plays are mentioned in Zeami's *Sandō*, which is translated in appendix 1. *Aoi no Ue* continues to be a popular play today. The Ōmi *sarugaku* player Inuō's staging of this play is described in *Sarugaku dangi*, NSTS, 263; De Poorter, *Zeami's Talks*, 83. In *Sandō*, Zeami says that its material has the potential for *yūgen* appeal; NSTS, 137. Also in *Sandō*, Zeami writes that *Shiokumi* is an earlier version of the extant play *Matsukaze* (*Matsukaze, Murasame* in Zeami's time; it appears to have undergone multiple revisions to reach its present form). Zeami merely mentions that *Sano no Funabashi* also underwent revisions; *Sandō*, NSTS, 143. In *Sarugaku dangi*, Zeami speaks of the *dengaku* player Kiami's style of rendering of lines from *Matsukaze, Murasame*, so it is speculated that he may have written *Shiokumi*. *Sarugaku dangi*, NSTS, 285; De Poorter, *Zeami's Talks*, 105–106.

26. Yashima first published her discovery, "*Jimu kata shokaishō* shihai monjoshō, I," in her institute's publication, *Kita no maru, Kokuritsu Komonjo kanpō*, no. 32 (October

1999). She subsequently published another article about it: " 'Ōei sanjūyonen ennō kiroku' ni tsuite," *Kanze* 67.8 (2000): 50–56. For more on the circumstances of composition, see her article in *Kanze*. Two months following, Omote also wrote on the significance of this new discovery in the same source: Omote Akira, " 'Kanze ryū shi sankyū (sono jūni), Zeami shukke chokugo no Kanze za, Ōei sanjūyonen ennō kiroku o megutte," *Kanze* 67.10 (2000): 27–32.

27. This new information challenges some of the established assumptions among scholars concerning the state of Zeami's troupe at this time. Zeami had stepped down as head of the troupe and Motomasa had already succeeded him, so one would expect that Motomasa would receive top billing in the program, but the lead roles of the fifteen plays are divided quite evenly between the three actors. Because this is unconventional casting, it is cause for speculation about whether Motomasa was up to fulfilling his duties. Takemoto Mikio wonders this, for instance, in a recent article about the contents of this program: "Zeami bannenki nō to nō sakusha," *Nō to kyōgen* no. 1 (2003): 127. Moreover, it is assumed that a rivalry existed between Motomasa and his cousin, On'ami, both possibly contending for the headship of the troupe, but this program suggests that they were quite capable of cooperating.

28. This performance was called *bettōbō sarugaku*, or *sarugaku* held at the quarters of the superintendent upon his invitation. This would be one part of the *takigi sarugaku* held annually as part of the religious services of the Shunigatsu-e at Kasuga Shrine, from the first to the fourteenth of the second month. (The *bettōbō sarugaku* was not necessarily held every year, though.) For more details, see De Poorter, *Zeami's Talks*, 23.

29. For an English translation of Ōeyama, see H. Mark Horton, trans., "Ōeyama (The Demon of Ōeyama)," in Karen Brazell with J. Philip Gabriel, eds., *Twelve Plays of the Noh and Kyōgen Theaters*, Cornell University East Asia Papers no. 50 (Ithaca, N.Y.: Cornell University East Asia Program, 1988), 147–167. For the Japanese, see Sanari Kentarō, ed., *Yōkyoku taikan* (Tokyo: Meiji Shoin, 1930–1931), 1:553–571. For a translation of *Shōjō*, see Ezra Pound and Ernest Fenollosa, *The Classic Noh Theatre of Japan* (New York: New Directions, 1959), 46–48. For the Japanese, see Sanari, ed., *Yōkyoku taikan*, 2:1347–1353. Also in SNKS, 2:169–173.

30. Omote Akira, "Nō no rekishi," *Bessatsu Taiyō: Nihon no kokoro, nō*, no. 25 (winter 1978): 64.

31. Ibid., 66. Takemoto is in basic accord with Omote's assessment and has written about the characteristics of Rin'ami's style in some detail. See his *Kan'ami, Zeami jidai no nōgaku*, 69–70.

32. *Go on*, part 2, NSTS, 223. More will be said about this composition later in this study.

33. NSTS, 291; De Poorter, *Zeami's Talks*, 114. *Sarugaku dangi* also states that it was performed at Tōnomine by Konparu Gon no kami, an actor roughly contemporary with Kan'ami, and then later revised. For an English translation of the play, see Eileen

Kato, trans., "Komachi and the Hundred Nights," in Donald Keene, ed., *Twenty Plays of the Nō Theatre* (New York: Columbia University Press, 1970), 51–63. For the Japanese, see SNKS, 1:341–349.

34. De Poorter, *Zeami's Talks*, 25. She quotes O'Neill, *Early Nō Drama*, 96–97. She also points out two examples in *Sarugaku dangi* of seemingly unlettered performers, the Kanze affiliated actor Jūnigorō Yasutsugu in section 167 (who must dictate a letter to Zeami rather than write it down himself), and in section 219 the *dengaku* contemporary of Kan'ami, Kiami. The original passages are found in NSTS, 313 and 299–300; they are translated in De Poorter, *Zeami's Talks*, 136–137 and 121–122, respectively.

35. Nine of Zeami's holographs have come down to us (*Zeami jihitsu nōhon*). They are the texts of the plays *Naniwa no ume, Morihisa, Tadatsu no Saemon, Eguchi, Unrin'in, Matsura, Akoya no matsu, Furu,* and *Kashiwazaki. Kashiwazaki* is undated. The other plays are dated from 1413 (actually existed in 1412) to 1428. Two further texts from this time are extant, for the plays *Tomoakira* and *Yoroboshi*. Their colophons date them as 1427 and 1429, respectively, although the *Yoroboshi* manuscript is a transcription done early in the Edo period (1600–1867). Based on Getsuyōkai, eds., *Zeami jihitsu nōhon shū* (Tokyo: Iwanami, 1997), 2:1–2. All of these texts are included in that volume.

36. Iwanami Kōza, 1:54.

37. Walter J. Ong, *Orality and Literacy: The Technologizing of the Word* (London: Methuen, 1982), 43.

38. Ibid., 42.

39. This tally includes two documents that, strictly speaking, are not critical treatises. They are *Museki isshi* (One page on the remains of a dream; 1432), a brief lament about the sudden death of his elder son, Jūrō Motomasa, and *Kintōsho* (Writings of the Golden Isle; 1436), eight pieces of chant composed while in exile on Sado Island. In addition to the twenty-one documents, there are two letters addressed from exile to his son-in-law, Komparu Zenchiku (dated the fourteenth day of the fifth month and the eighth day of the sixth month; on neither is the year specified). *Zeshi rokujū igo sarugaku dangi* certainly qualifies as a discourse on the art of *sarugaku*, and I have included it in the tally of twenty-one, but it should be recalled that it was set down by Zeami's second son, Shichirō Motoyoshi. For a translation of *Kintōsho*, see Susan Matisoff, trans., "Kintōsho: Zeami's Song of Exile," *Monumenta Nipponica* 32.4 (1977): 441–458. Annotated editions of the originals of all of these texts may be found in NSTS.

40. Omote has written a useful summary of these periodizations as proposed by various scholars in his "Zeami: Sono nōgaku tenkai no jikiteki kubun o chūshin ni," *Nōgakushi shinkō*, 2:143–170. The article was first published in Zenkoku Daigaku Kokugo Bungakkai, Kōza Nihon Bungaku 6, *Chūsei hen II* (Tokyo: Sanseidō, 1969), 165–192. In the article, Omote advocates that the analysis of Zeami's ideas in

treatises from *Shikadō* (1420) onward should be based on subject matter groupings rather than on a blanket chronological ordering.

41. Kōsai Tsutomu argues the case for On'ami being Zeami's adoptive son in his *Zoku Zeami shinkō* (Tokyo: Wan'ya shoten, 1970), 82–97. More later in this chapter on the circumstances of On'ami's succession to the headship of the Kanze.

42. According to *Kitano jinja kokiroku* (Ancient records of Kitano Shrine). Based on entry in Omote, ed., " 'Kanze' chūshin no nōgakushi nenpyō (1)," 15.

43. For more on this expedition, see Ochiai Hiroshi, "Inuō no jidai, '*Rokuon'in saikoku gekō ki*' no kiji o shōkai shi tsutsu," *Nōgaku kenkyū* no. 18 (1993): 101–144.

44. Based on Omote, ed. " 'Kanze' chūshin no nōgakushi nenpyō (1)," 15.

45. The evolution of this treatise in a compilation of seven books or chapters, as it appears in the NSTS edition, is very complex. I am following Omote's assessments of the probable provenance of the seven chapters that have been compiled in NSTS as he sets it down in "*Kaden* no shomei to henmei o megutte," *Nō to Kyōgen* no. 1 (2003): 8–16. This is the inaugural issue of the recently founded Nōgaku Gakkai, a research group on noh and *kyōgen* based in Japan. Omote's arguments on the history of Zeami's treatises in that article are largely consistent with those that he set down in NSTS, which he edited and published in 1974 (republished in 1995), although the article includes minor updates on his findings and interpretations. NSTS is widely considered to be the authoritative source on the history of these texts and provides the most comprehensive compendium of information on this subject.

According to Omote, some versions of *Kaden* consist of the first four chapters, others of the first five chapters. Multiple compilations exist, ranging from four or five to seven chapters. What can be said with certainty is that the first three chapters were written by 1400. We know this because the colophon of the third chapter is dated as such.

46. I am following Omote's positions on the correct names of the chapters of this treatise, which number seven in the NSTS edition. Omote holds that only the first five chapters of the seven are correctly referred to as *Fūshikaden*. His argument is that Zeami subsequently assigned them that title when he revised them and added chapter 5 to them.

There is strong evidence that chapters 6 and 7 of this treatise predate Zeami's revised compilation of the first five chapters under the title *Fūshikaden*. We know, for instance, that both of these existed as independent manuscripts prior to their incorporation into the larger treatise. Moreover, Zeami uses *Kaden* rather than *Fūshikaden* in referring to these chapters by name. For these reasons, Omote argues that any compilation of multiple chapters that includes the manuscripts of chapters 6 and 7 is more aptly named *Kaden* than *Fūshikaden*. This seems reasonable to me, and I will follow his nomenclature despite the fact that the treatise in seven parts has been more consistently referred to by specialists as *Fūshikaden* in the postwar years. I will therefore refer to all seven chapters of the NSTS compilation of the treatise as *Kaden* and will identify each part therein by specifying its chapter number. I will also refer to chapter 6 by name as *Kaden dairoku*, "Kashu" (Transmission of the flower, chapter 6, "Training in the flower") and chapter 7 as *Kaden daishichi*, "Besshi kuden" (Transmission of the flower, chapter 7, "Special oral transmissions"). For more on the complexities of naming *Kaden* and its parts, see Omote, "*Kaden* no shomei," 8–16.

47. NSTS, 38.

48. Annotators also have titled this chapter *Ōgi hen* (Section on initiation into the secrets), or *Ōgi ni iwaku* (As it says in initiation into the secrets). I am following Omote's recommended nomenclature here. Omote, "*Kaden* no shomei," 16.

49. For a detailed discussion, see Omote, *Nōgakushi shinkō*, 2:148–151.

50. *Kaden*, chapter 5, NSTS, 46.

51. Kitagawa Tadahiko, *Zeami*, Chūō Shinsho 292 (Tokyo: Chūō Kōronsha, 1980), 38–39.

52. Based on Omote, ed. " 'Kanze' chūshin no nōgakushi nenpyō (1)," 15.

53. Iwanami Kōza, 2:21.

54. We know that the first fourteen of the eighteen segments comprising *Kakyō* existed as of 1418 because Zeami makes reference to them in his treatise *Kashu no uchinukigaki* (Excerpt from "Training in the flower"; 1418). Portions of the first fourteen segments also appear to have been subsequently added to the manuscript. The intended recipient of *Kakyō* was Zeami's son, Motomasa, or so his other son, Motoyoshi, states in *Shiki shūgen* (Celebratory pieces for the four seasons), a collection of chant pieces in the holdings of the head of the Kanze school (Kanze Bunko collection). Iwanami Kōza, 2:78.

The manuscript was shared with Konparu Zenchiku subsequent to the death of Motomasa. In a postscript to the Konparu manuscript, a person who we assume to be the young Zenchiku (signed Tsurauji) acknowledges that he has made a copy of the manuscript. *Kakyō*, NSTS, 109. In his study on Zenchiku, Itō Masayoshi also takes the name that is signed, Tsurauji, to be the same person as Konparu Ujinobu (Zenchiku): *Konparu Zenchiku no kenkyū* (Kyoto: Akao Shōbundō, 1970), 22.

55. Based on De Poorter, *Zeami's Talks*, 22.

56. These two performances are mentioned in *Manzai jugō nikki*. Based on Omote, ed., " 'Kanze' chūshin no nōgakushi nenpyō (1)," 16.

57. Ibid., 17.

58. *Sarugaku dangi*, De Poorter, *Zeami's Talks*, 134; for original, see NSTS, 310.

59. *Kyakuraika*, trans. Mark J. Nearman as "Zeami's Final Legacy for the Master Actor," *Monumenta Nipponica* 35.2 (1980): 195.

60. Based on Omote's assessment in " 'Kanze' chūshin no nōgakushi nenpyō (1)," 17.

61. See De Poorter, *Zeami's Talks*, 42–43, for an interesting overview of the multiple theories on why Yoshinori might have exiled Zeami.

62. Kōsai Tsutomu first published the information about the discovery of this register in 1960; see his "Zeami no shukke to ie, Fuganji monjo ni terashite," *Bungaku* no. 3 (1960). It was he who discovered the entry for Zeami's wife, which helped dispel doubts that the person listed with the posthumous name of Shiō was indeed Zeami. Zeami is listed as having donated a rice paddy to the temple. Omote surmises he did so as payment for memorial masses in perpetuity. Omote Akira, " 'Fuganji nōchō' tsuikō, in *Nōgakushi shinkō*, 2:511.

63. Ōtomo Taishi, "Zeami and Zen," in Ortolani and Leiter, eds., *Zeami and the Nō Theatre*, 47–52.

Chapter 2: Developing Zeami's Representational Style

1. *Kaden*, NSTS, 20. Translations are my own unless otherwise indicated. The original Japanese for "should take utmost care to train" is *tashinamu beshi*. I have followed the NSTS interpretation: *"kokorogake keiko suru"*; ibid. Nose Asaji has *"jūbun kenkyū gakushū shinakereba naranai"* (must investigate and learn fully); Nose, 1:36. Tanaka Yutaka glosses it as *"doko made mo fukaku ginmi suru ga yoi"* (should investigate as deeply as possible). Tanaka, 24.

2. *Kaden*, NSTS, 20.

3. It will be recalled that of the three most authoritative manuscripts of this fifth chapter of *Kaden* (the Sōsetsu shomei *bon*, the Yoshida *bon*, and the Konparu *bon*), only the Sōsetsu shomei *bon* is dated (1402). For that reason, the accuracy of the date is held in question. Omote and Takemoto hold that Zeami probably composed this tract sometime between 1400 and 1408. Iwanami Kōza, 2:33–34.

4. *Kaden*, NSTS, 46.

5. Ibid., 42.

6. *Kakyō*, NSTS, 97.

7. *Shikadō*, NSTS, 119.

8. Nose, 1:146.

9. NKBT 65, 373, note 38. *Fuzei no bi* may also be rendered as "beauty of atmosphere." In Zeami's treatises, however, it refers more often to the visual impact of the acting.

10. *Kaden*, Tanaka, 15, note 15.

11. Ibid., NSTS, 42.

12. SNKBZ 88, 254, note 4.

13. De Poorter, *Zeami's Talks*, 84. Original in NSTS, 264.

14. De Poorter, *Zeami's Talks*, 83; NSTS, 263.

15. *Kyakuraika*, NSTS, 247.

16. De Poorter, *Zeami's Talks*,136; NSTS, 312.

17. Takemoto Mikio, *Tennyo no mai no kenkyū, Nōgaku kenkyū* no. 4 (July 1978): 153–154. Also in Takemoto, *Kan'ami, Zeami jidai no nōgaku*, 331.

18. For a more detailed account of the origins of the *kusemai*, see O'Neill, *Early Nō Drama*, 42–52.

19. The drawings of the *shirabyoshi* and *kusemai* performers from *Shichijūichiban shokunin uta awase* are pictured in ibid., 47. It is one of a genre of fictional poetry contests staged between two teams of artisans, each of whom supposedly submits a poem on a set topic in competition with peers on the other team. (The topics assigned in this work are love and the moon.) This *uta awase* is believed to be a collaborative effort on the part of courts aristocrats, among them Sanjō Nishisanetaka (1455–1537) and Asukai Masayasu (1436–1509). For an illustrated text in full, see Iwasaki Kae et al., *Shichijū ichinin uta awase, Shinsen kyōka shū, Kokin hinaburi shū*, Shin Nihon Koten Bungaku Taikei 65 (Tokyo: Iwanami, 1993).

20. Whereas the NSTS annotation surmises that these are the names of troupes of *kusemai* performers, Nose surmises that they are the names of individual performers. NSTS, 223; Nose, 2:234.

21. *Go on*, II, NSTS, 223.

22. It is not clear what significance Zeami saw in the attribution of the character "*kyoku*" to be read "*kuse*" in *kusemai*. He could have intended it to simply mean "tune" or "music" or to mean "unorthodox" (lit. crooked), or to embrace both meanings. In any case, the character read "*mai*" and meaning "dance" is added to "*kuse*," suggesting that this was an art form in which the musical line was closely linked to dance.

23. *Ongyoku kuden*, NSTS, 77.

24. *Sarugaku dangi*, De Poorter, *Zeami's Talks*, 97; NSTS, 276. *Tada utai* is equated here with the style of singing called *kouta*.

25. *Go on*, II, NSTS, 223. In this volume, Tamarin is referred to by the alternative name Rin'ami.

26. *Ongyoku kuden*, NSTS, 77.

27. Omote discusses the role of *sarugaku* performers as entertainers at private residences in "*Kan'ami, Zeami jidai no 'utai,*' " *Zeami shinkō*, I (Tokyo: Wan'ya shoten, 1979), 279–285.

28. This *kusemai* was later embedded in a full-length play by the same name, *Shirahige*. The *shite* plays the deity of Shirahige Shrine in Ōmi Province. This deity, Shirahige Myōjin, appears in the original legend (and in the play) as a fisherman and ostensible owner of the Mount Hiei area. The Buddha Śākyamuni approaches him to request rights to Mount Hiei so that the Tendai sect headquarters may be established there. The fisherman initially refuses to give up the land because fishing will then be disallowed since it violates the Buddhist prohibition against taking life. The conflict is resolved when the Buddha Yakushi arrives to claim proprietorship of the mountain. He overrules the fisherman-cum-deity and invites Śākyamuni to use Mount Hiei. In the noh version, the fisherman then admits that he is actually the deity of Shirahige Shrine and disappears into its sanctuary. This is the conclusion of the first act. In the second act, the deity appears in his true form and dances, whereupon a celestial maiden and a dragon deity also appear and dance in honor

of the deity. The play in its current form is thought to postdate Kan'ami and Zeami. The text of the play, including the *kusemai* section, which is in the first act, is included in Sanari Kentarō, ed., *Yōkyoku taikan* (Tokyo: Meiji Shoin, 1964), 3:1461–1476.

29. For text, see *Go on*, II, in NSTS, 224–225. Omote surmises that this *kusemai* was originally composed as an independent piece to be chanted. NSTS, 487, appendix note 136. Later it was worked into a full-length noh play titled *Yura monogurui* (The madwoman of Yura), which ends on a happier note. The woman's husband searches for the wife and finds her at the brothel in Kakegawa. He recognizes her by the song that she performs telling the story of her life. They are reconciled and spend the remainder of their time following the path of the Buddha together. *Yura monogurui* is of unknown authorship and is not currently performed. For the text, see Tanaka Makoto, *Mikan yōkyoku shū*, III, Koten Bunko 212 (Tokyo: Koten Bunko, 1965), 103–107.

30. Takemoto Mikio, "*Nō no buntai o tsukutta mono,*" in Kunisaki Fumimaro, ed., *Chūsei setsuwa to sono shūhen* (Tokyo: Meiji Shoin, 1987), 474–475. While Takemoto's assessment seems plausible, other interpretations seem equally possible.

31. Goff writes, "Contemporary records describe him as a member of the circle led by Gusai (Kyūsei; c. 1284–c. 1378), Nijō Yoshimoto's *renga* mentor, while a poetry treatise by Imagawa Ryōshun (1326–ca. 1414) states that Nijō Yoshimoto considered him the second rank of *renga* poets." Janet Goff, "Noh and Its Antecedents: 'Journey to the Western Provinces,' " in Thomas Hare, Robert Borgen, and Sharalyn Orbaugh, eds., *The Distant Isle: Studies and Translations of Japanese Literature in Honor of Robert H. Brower* (Ann Arbor: The University of Michigan, Center for Japanese Studies), 166. Quoted from *Rokusho roken*, cited in Kidō Saizō, *Renga shi ronkō* (Meiji Shoin, 1971–1973), 1:316. Goff, "Noh and Its Antecedents," 177, note 5. Goff's article is a critical study and translation of *Saikoku kudari*.

　　Kaidō kudari is connected to an interesting anecdote. According to *Sarugaku dangi*, Rin'ami incurred Yoshimitsu's displeasure and was exiled to eastern Japan. That document also states that when Zeami was a young boy he performed *Kaidō kudari* for Yoshimitsu, which moved the shogun to pardon its exiled author.

32. For the text, see *Go on* in NSTS, 226–228. The *Sarugaku dangi* anecdote is found in NSTS, 277.

33. The text is in *Go on*, NSTS, 228–229.

34. Ibid., 225.

35. Omote postulates that this technique of embedding a *kusemai* in a play was Kan'ami's innovation. See Omote Akira, "Zeami izen," *Kokubungaku, kaishaku to kyōzai no kenkyū* 25.1 (1980): 54. On the other hand, Itō Masayoshi, the editor of the three-volume collection of noh libretti published by Shinchōsha, postulates that this technique was Zeami's innovation; SNKS, 3:468.

36. *Sarugaku dangi*, NSTS, 291. In *Sandō*, Zeami notes that there were earlier versions

of *Hyakuman*, but he does not mention who the original author of the play might have been. *Sandō*, NSTS, 143. For the text of *Hyakuman*, see Yokomichi Mario and Omote Akira, eds., *Yōkyoku shū*, Nihon Koten Bungaku Taikei 40–41 (Tokyo: Iwanami, 1960 and 1963), 1:193–200.

37. In *Utaura*, the *shite* plays a male shaman who, in a state of possession, dances to the lines of *Jigoku no kusemai*. It functions as a discrete narrative with no direct role in the development of the action. For the text, see Yokomichi and Omote, eds., *Yōkyoku shū*, 1:395–403.

38. SNKS, 3:469.

39. Omote "Zeami izen," 54.

40. *Fūgyoku shū*, NSTS, 158.

41. *Giri*, which I have translated as "lively language" following the NSTS annotation (42), is glossed by Nose as "plot"; Nose, 1:146–147.

42. *Kaden*, NSTS, 42–43. There is a passage in *Sarugaku dangi* that paraphrases this statement in *Kaden*: "Our forefather, Kan'a. He gained renown especially on the basis of *Shizuka ga mai no nō* and *Saga no dainenbutsu no onna monogurui*, and the like. His was a style of peerless *yūgen*." *Sarugaki dangi*, NSTS, 264. This statement seems to confirm that Zeami is making a connection between his father playing female roles and his invoking of the *yūgen* quality.

43. The text for *Yoshino Shizuka* is found in Yokomichi and Omote, eds., *Yokyōku shū*, 1:89–95, 1:193–200. It is also possible that Zeami is referring here to the play known today as *Futari Shizuka*.

44. *Go on*, NSTS, 224, 226. *Yūkyoku* is one of five musical themes (*go on*) that Zeami comes to posit in such late theoretical writings as the treatise *Go on*. The character for "*yū*" is the same as the first character in the compound *yūgen*. *Yūkyoku* refers to music that possesses the *yūgen* mood.

45. *Fushizuke shidai*, NSTS, 150. The term *kakari* is used in two senses in this passage. First, it occurs in phrases such as *yūgen no kakari* (style that . . . has *yūgen*) or *tada utai no kakari* (style of plain chant), in which it has a generic meaning that I have glossed as "style." It is also used more specifically to refer to the affect created by the flow of the words and lines (*moji utsuri, ku utsuri no kakari*). In this instance, I have translated *kakari* as "artistic effect."

46. The NSTS annotators speculate that *Fushizuke shidai* was composed prior to *Sandō* (1423) or *Kakyō* (1424), but after Zeami's treatise *Ongyoku kuden* (1419). NSTS, 560–561.

47. *Kaden*, NSTS, 47–54. The sixth chapter of *Kaden* is undated. The NSTS edition argues that its style and cohesiveness suggest it was an independent tract originally. Zeami's original manuscript (*Zeami jihitsu bon*) is preserved in the holdings of the Kanze House (Kanze Bunko). The lineage of the Kanze head (*iemoto*) descends from Zeami's younger brother Shirō, and the NSTS annotators thus surmise that Zeami may have intended this document for him; NSTS, 552.

48. *Kaden*, NSTS, 51.
49. Ibid.
50. Ibid. The original Japanese for "elegant" is *yasashi*.
51. *Sandō*, NSTS, 137–138.
52. Ibid., 134.
53. *Sarugaku dangi*, in De Poorter, *Zeami's Talks*, 80; NSTS, 260.
54. Ibid.
55. Tanaka's annotation cites the poetic commentary titled *Kokin jo shō [Kokin waka shū jo kikigaki (Sanryūshō)]* by Fujiwara no Tameie (1198–1275) as a possible source for this quotation derivative of the *Shijing*. Tanaka, 173. The idea from the *Shijing* was already a familiar one in Japanese *waka* poetics, and indeed it is quite likely that Zeami's exposure to it was mediated by such a commentary in Japanese.
56. Ibid. For the original passage in *Sandō*, see NSTS, 143.
57. *Sarugaku dangi*, De Poorter, *Zeami's Talks*, 80–81; NSTS, 260.
58. Ibid., De Poorter, *Zeami's Talks*, 81; NSTS, 261.
59. The original for De Poorter's "illusion" is *omokage: "sono omokage omokage o ima suru nari"* (NSTS, 261). *Omokage* has a range of meanings. It may refer to an image that appears to be real but isn't, such as a picture in one's memory, or an image in a mirror. It may also mean an image that bears a resemblance to something else: a semblance, vestige, or flavor of some other thing. Ōno Susumu, Satake Akihiro, and Maeda Kingorō, eds., *Iwanami kogo jiten*, rev. ed. (Tokyo: Iwanami, 1990), 252. De Poorter's rendering adheres to the former sense of the word. Rimer and Yamazaki's translation of *omokage* is "slight flavor," which adheres to the latter sense. J. Thomas Rimer and Yamazaki Masakazu, trans., *On the Art of the Nō Drama: The Major Treatises of Zeami* (Princeton, N.J.: Princeton University Press, 1984), 173. The NSTS and Tanaka Yutaka annotations concur that Zeami is saying that he performs only a semblance of a demon, a rendering that is "demon-like"; NSTS, 260; Tanaka, 174. Nose interprets this to mean that he performed only a semblance of what his own predecessors had performed. Nose, 2:296. Nose does not explain his interpretation, but it may have been influenced by a statement that Zeami makes about performing demonic roles in a letter to Konparu Zenchiku, written late in the former's life from his place of exile on Sado Island: "The demon in the style of forceful movement is practiced by other schools. However, my late father would occasionally perform the demon insofar as he would make his vocalization powerful, so I also learned it"; NSTS, 318.
60. *Shikadō* is dated 1420; *Nikyoku santai ningyō zu*, 1421; *Kakyō*, 1424; *Shūgyoku tokuka*, 1428.
61. *Kakyō*, NSTS, 86.
62. SNKBZ 88, 298.
63. *Kashu no uchinukigaki*, NSTS, 71.
64. *Nikyoku santai ningyō zu*, NSTS, 124.

65. Ibid., 126.
66. Ibid., 127.
67. Ōno, Satake, and Maeda, eds., *Iwanami kogo jiten* (Iwanami dictionary of classical Japanese), 411.
68. *Nikyoku santai ningyō zu*, NSTS, 126–127.
69. Ibid., 127. One is reminded of Charlie Chaplin's idea that humor depends on contradictory forces. For Chaplin, such contradiction could be expressed physically, as in, " 'I wanted everything a contradiction,' he said of his initial invention of the tramp costume for a Mack Sennett film. 'The pants baggy, the coat tight, the hat small and the shoes large. I was undecided whether to look young or old, but remembering Sennett had expected me to be a much older man, I added a small moustache.' " Michael Wood, "Charlie Chaplin and His Times by Kenneth S. Lynn," *The New York Review of Books* 44.12 (1997): 8.
70. *Nikyoku santai ningyō zu*, NSTS, 128.
71. Ibid.
72. *Kakyō*, Mark J. Nearman, trans., "*Kakyō:* A Mirror of the Flower (Part 1)," *Monumenta Nipponica* 37.3 (August 1982): 352; NSTS, 85. Square brackets in this translation are the translator's. As Nearman himself points out, "harmony between the two principles" may also be taken more specifically to mean the two principles of movement of the body and stamping. Nearman, trans., *Kakyō*, *Monumenta Nipponica* 37.3 (1982): 353. This second interpretation is preferred by Nose; Nose, 1:290. NSTS also follows such an interpretation; NSTS, 85. However, the modern gloss in the SNKBZ 88 edition equates the two principles with what is seen and what is heard; SNKBZ 88, 297. Tanaka Yutaka synthesizes these two possible interpretations: "movement of the upper torso, which is visible to the eye, and movement of the feet, which the ear can hear"; Tanaka, 119.
73. *Nikyoku santai ningyō zu*, NSTS, 129. The NSTS notation for this passage points out that "the final phase" (*kyūfū*) might also refer to the final phase of an actor's training, after mastery of all the basic roles of the repertoire has been accomplished. NSTS, ibid. The original for "images" in the phrase "interesting images" is *yosōi*, which Nose interprets to mean *omomuki* or *fuzei*, here meaning "mood"; Nose, 1:499–500. NSTS interprets it to mean *fūshi* (image) or *arisama* (state [of being]).
74. *Nikyoku santai ningyō zu*, NSTS, 130.
75. Ibid. The phrase "*kyokufū o taikō ni ategaite*" is ambiguous because "*kō*" in the compound *taikō* is written in *kana* syllabary. (The Chinese character used to write "*tai*" means "large.") The Yoshida text attributes characters meaning "large" and "volume/magnitude." Nose's annotation of the term is based on the Yoshida text annotation, which results in Nose's gloss, "make the overall style of the dance big in scale." Nose, 1:502. The NSTS annotation reads *taikō* as "foundation," which is the basis for my gloss, "concentrate on the musical style." Moreover, NSTS interprets *kyokufū* (or *kyokufu*) to mean the rhythm of the musical accompaniment, which the dancer

should make the foundation of his dance. However, the original term is much less explicit, with a range of possible meanings depending on the context, e.g., style of expression, style of vocal music, style of piece. For instance, in his discussion of the adaptation of the *kusemai* into Yamato *sarugaku* in the treatise *Fushizuke shidai*, Zeami explains that the *kusemai* is a style of musical expression (*kyokufū*) in which chant is matched to dance: "*mai nite utau kyokufū nar[i].*" NSTS, 151.

76. *Shikadō*, NSTS, 113.

77. *Nikyoku santai ningyō zu*, NSTS, 124. The passage here takes as its starting point a passage in *Shikadō* that reads, "You should understand that the initial *yūgen* [effect] of the childish form will remain [when playing] the three styles, and the myriad [techniques] derived from the three styles will also enjoy expressive impact. NSTS, 113. The *Shikadō* passage provides an interesting example of the complexity of Zeami's conception of *yūgen*, applying both to how an actor should conduct himself in all roles and to attributes expressly allotted to only certain character types. On the one hand, he argues for a transferal of the *yūgen* grace that a child enjoys to his later execution of all styles of acting. On the other hand, the same passage credits the feminine style as the seminal one for the projection of grace (*yūgen*) and courtly elegance (*yūgen miyabitaru yoshikakari*); NSTS, 113.

78. *Shūgyoku tokuka*, NSTS, 192.

79. Ibid.

80. Ibid., 193.

81. Ibid.

82. Ibid.

83. Ibid., 193–194.

84. Ibid., 194.

85. Ibid.

86. *Shikadō*, NSTS, 113–114.

87. Kitagawa Tadahiko, " 'Monomane jōjō' kara 'santai' ron e," *Bungaku* 51.7 (July 1983): 55–56.

88. *Shūgyoku tokuka*, NSTS, 194.

89. Ibid., 194–195.

90. Ibid., 195. Zeami's attribution of this proverb to the *Mengzi* is incorrect. According to the appendix of the NSTS edition, the original source is the Confucian classic *Shujing* (*Shu Ching*, The book of documents; ca. 90 B.C.E.). In Zeami's time it was a proverb with wide circulation. It, or variants on it, are found, for instance, in the thirteenth-century collection of tales *Shaseki shū*, compiled by Mujū Ichien; Dōgen's theoretical work on Buddhism of the thirteenth-century, *Shōbōgenzō zuimonki*; and the fourteenth-century primer on *renga* poetics *Renri hishō*, by Nijō Yoshimoto. NSTS, 455, appendix note 51.

91. The opening section of the *Shūgyoku tokuka* passage under discussion here states, "If you do not enter into true *monomane*, then it is unlikely that you will acquire

this personal magnitude" (*Makoto no monomane ni irifusazu ba, kono gaibun o uru koto aru majiki nari*). NSTS, 192.

Chapter 3. Fierce Moons, Gentle Demons: From Ends to Means

Epigraph. *Kaden*, NSTS, 20.

1. *Kakyō*, NSTS, 97.

2. Ibid., 96–97. "[C]ommonly" is my translation for *ōkata*, and "seen" is a translation of *mokuzen*, lit. "before one's eyes." The NSTS annotators point out that Zeami uses *ōkata* (ordinary, common) in contrast to the flavor of *yūgen* as truly understood. Nose glosses *ōkata* in its adverbial usage, meaning "generally," and gives *mokuzen* a more literal interpretation: "First, generally speaking, in noh the *yūgen* style is one that appears before one's eyes *[ganzen ni arawareru mono]*, and spectators prize this *yūgen* aspect exclusively, but an actor who [truly] possesses *yūgen* is not easy to come by"; Nose, 1:360. Nose's reading suggests that Zeami's intended meaning was that the run-of-the-mill style of *yūgen* was that which appealed to the visual faculties, but that there were other *yūgen* modalities as well.

3. As in the other commentaries cited above, Nearman also makes a distinction between the "look of *yūgen*," as something considered foremost by Zeami's contemporaries, and "*yūgen* per se." His interpretation then diverges, however, when he concludes that "*yūgen* is but one aspect of his [Zeami's] theatre and by no means the ultimate." Mark J. Nearman, trans., "*Kakyō*: Zeami's Fundamental Principles of Acting (Part 2)," *Monumenta Nipponica* 37.4 (winter 1982): 480. Nearman's suggestion that this passage reveals a diffident attitude on Zeami's part toward *yūgen* needs substantiation.

4. I have followed Nose's annotation in translating the phrase *jinbō* as "facial features." In the manuscript versions, no Chinese characters are attributed to "*bō*" in the compound *jinbō* (*jinbau*), so more than one reading is possible. The character read in the Japanese *kun'yomi* style as *nozomi* has also been attributed to "*bō*," meaning "an appearance that commands respect." NSTS, SNKBZ 88, and Tanaka annotate it in this way. NSTS, 97; SNKBZ 88, 316–317; Tanaka, 139. As Nose notes in his commentary, one manuscript dating to the mid-Edo period, the Tanaka *bon*, allots the Chinese character for person followed by "*sou*" in *kana* symbols. Nose, 1:361. This may be read as *ninsō*, meaning "facial features." While this may be a later copyist's embellishment, I agree that this reading best suits the context of the passage, which concentrates on the physical presence of a person.

5. *Kakyō*, NSTS, 97–98.

6. The original for "linking of the musical phrases proceeds beautifully" (*fushikakari utsukushiku kudarite*) has multiple interpretations. Tanaka glosses it as the linking or the flow of the musical phrases (*fushi no tsuzukegara, nagare*); NSTS and SNKBZ 88 equate *fushikakari* with melody (*senritsu*); Nose glosses it as the atmosphere of the musical phrases (*fushi no omomuki*). Tanaka, 140; NSTS, 97; SNKBZ 88, 317; Nose, 1:360. The word *fushi* by itself refers here to a melodic phrase; *kakari* may be

interpreted to mean "linking" or "spanning." Tanaka's gloss of the compound *fushi-kakari* seems aptest in this context since the overall effect of the flow of the utterances is under discussion. The term *ongyoku*, translated here as "music," may refer to both vocal and instrumental music in Zeami's writings. Here it is likely it refers to vocal music, although three of the four editions consulted are noncommittal on this point. SNKBZ 88 glosses the term as *utai*, or "noh chant"; SNKBZ 88, 323.

7. The original for "supple," *nabi nabi*, is glossed by NSTS as *mi ni kokoro yoku* (pleasant, agreeable); NSTS, 97. SNKBZ 88 has *nabiyaka ni kokoro yoku* (supple and pleasant); SNKBZ 88, 317. Nose defines it as *ryūrei ni, shinayaka ni* (flowingly, in a supple way); Nose, 1:360. Tanaka has *miyabiyaka* (elegant, graceful); Tanaka, 140. The term refers to a quality of supple polish or smoothness connotative of courtly elegance.

8. *Yosooi*, which I have translated as having "a feeling [of composure] about you," is closest to Nose's gloss, *kehai yōsu* (a feeling of, a look of); Nose, 1:361. Tanaka interprets it as *shigusa* (acting, gestures, bearing); Tanaka, 140. The SNKBZ 88 gloss is *shitai* (figure, as in "cut a figure"); SNKBZ 88, 317.

9. "[P]oints of interest to the eye" is a translation of two characters (*midokoro, kenjo*) that may be interpreted either as "points visible to the eye" or "spectator" or "place where the spectators are seated." NSTS, SNKBZ 88, NKBT 65, and Tanaka all assign the former interpretation here, whereas Nose reads it as "spectator." NSTS, 97; SNKBZ 88, 317; NKBT 65, 425; Tanaka, 140; Nose, 1:360.

10. The original term for "bearing" is *minari*. NSTS and SNKBZ 88 interpret this as *karada no kamae* (bodily posture, pose); NSTS, 97, and SNKBZ 88, 317. Tanaka is more specific, glossing this as *jōtai* (the upper part of the body); Tanaka, 140.

11. The rubrics are quoted from Nearman's translation. Nearman, trans., *Kakyō*, *Monumenta Nipponica* 37.3 (1982): 350, 352.

12. *Kakyō*, NSTS, 97.

13. Ibid., NSTS, 98.

14. Based on ibid., NSTS, 98.

15. Nijō Yoshimoto, *Kyūshū mondō* (*Nijō Yoshimoto rengaron*) *hyōshaku*, in Nose Asaji chosaku shū henshū iinkai, ed., *Nose Asaji chosaku shū* (Kyoto: Shinbunkaku, 1982), 7:308. This treatise is in a question-and-answer format, and the passage quoted here is the response to the query "What should the poet bear in mind concerning *iji* in *renga*?" Ibid.

16. For instance, in *Kyūshū mondō*, Yoshimoto also claims that though poets may compose in various styles, if they are *renga* masters, they will not differ in sensibility (*iji*) concerning the words (*kotoba*). *Kyūshū mondō*, 314.

17. Nose also notes that Yoshimoto more typically refers to the "mind" of the poet as *iji*, which he states is synonymous with this second reading of *kokoro*. Nose Asaji, *Yūgenron*, in Nose Asaji chosaku shū henshū iinkai, ed., *Nose Asaji chosaku shū* (Kyoto: Shibunkaku, 1981), 2:296–300. Citing Nose's opinion, Mizukami qualifies

it further, arguing that *iji* refers to the workings of the poetic mind (*kokoro*)—the cultivated poetic sensibility in action. He also makes the point that Yoshimoto's conception of *iji* is close to the poetic principle of *hon'i* (the essential nature of things)—the idea shared by both *waka* and *renga* poets that poetic composition involves fathoming the true nature of phenomena and capturing that nature in verse. Mizukami Kashizō, *Chūsei karon to renga* (Tokyo: Zentsū Kikaku Shuppan, 1977), 21, 25. Yoshimoto's exhortation in the opening section of the passage cited from *Kyūshū mondō* to strive for personal images that are truthful seems to corroborate Mizukami's interpretation.

18. *Kyūshū mondō*, 308.

19. Nijō Yoshimoto, *Hekirenshō* (Some warped ideas on linked verse; 1345), ed. Ijichi Tetsuo, in NKBZ 51, 19–20. Just prior to the passage quoted, Yoshimoto states, "Language having *yūgen* is something that one is born with." Whereas Ijichi takes this statement to mean literally that this is an innate talent, Nose's commentary of the same passage attributes this ability to the poet's social background. An individual of aristocratic upbringing will have naturally acquired the grace and elegance associated with aristocratic speech. Nose Asaji, *Hekirenshō (Nijō Yoshimoto rengaron) hyōshaku, Nose Asaji chosaku shū*, 7:166. I have adopted Steven D. Carter's English translation for the title of this treatise.

20. Nijō Yoshimoto, *Jūmon saihishō*, NKBT 66, 111. "Fresh and smooth" is my translation of *sawasawa subesube to*.

21. Ibid., 110–111. Headnote 14 of NKBT 66 cites a very similar passage from *Maigetsushō* (Monthly notes, 1219) by the influential *waka* poet Fujiwara no Teika: "one should not ascribe goodness and badness entirely to the words. The quality of the language of *uta* will be determined solely by the transitions between the words [*tsuzukegara*]." Ibid., 110. More will be said about this parallel in chapter 7.

22. Ibid., 114.

23. Nijō Yoshimoto, *Renrihishō*, NKBT 66, 51–52. "Moons and blossoms" is a literal gloss of the term *kagetsu*, which also is a synecdoche for all received images associated with elegance in the poetic tradition.

24. Yoshimoto's *Renga shinshiki* (New rules on renga), a rulebook composed in 1372, states that the image of the demon should appear only once in a *renga* composition in one hundred verses. Nijō Yoshimoto, *Renga shinshiki*, in Okami Masao, ed., *Rengaron shū*, Koten Bunko 63 (Tokyo: Koten Bunko, 1952), 1:9. For an English translation of *Renga shinshiki*, see Steven D. Carter, *The Road to Komatsubara: A Classical Reading of the Renga Hyakuin*, Harvard East Asian Monographs 124 (Cambridge, Mass.: Harvard University Press, 1987), 41–72. The translation of the passage cited here is on 43. In Zeami's theory, of course, the *rikidō* style of demon is off-limits. In an undated letter to his son-in-law, Konparu Zenchiku, Zeami cautions that only seasoned actors at the end of their careers should attempt to perform demon roles; NSTS, 318–319.

25. Nijō Yoshimoto, *Renga jūyō*, in Okami Masao, ed., *Rengaron shū*, Koten Bunko 92 (Tokyo: Koten Bunko, 1955), 3:4.

26. Nose, *Yūgenron*, 309.

27. Yoshimoto, *Kyūshū mondō*, 314.

28. NKBT 66, 6.

29. *Ongyoku kuden*, NSTS, 74. The same passage appears in *Kakyō*, NSTS, 104.

30. *Kakyō*, NSTS, 104; *Ongyoku kuden*, NSTS, 74. The original term for "modulation" is *fushi*; "affixing the modulation" corresponds to *fushi o tsukeru*. To affix the modulation involves deciding the basic melodic patterns for the phrases. I have chosen *fushi* as "modulation" rather than "melody" to underscore the idea that the melodic aspects of the lines are determined in conjunction with the wording. Melody is not considered an entity autonomous from the words.

The original Japanese for "make distinctions between the words clear" is *monji* (also *moji*) *o wakatsu*. The NSTS annotation for this states, "to sing in a way that clearly distinguishes the meaning of the words"; NSTS, 75. However, the Nose annotation has "to sing in a way that makes the pronunciation of the words clear"; Nose, 2:10.

31. "Each sound" is my rendering of *goin/goon* (lit. five sounds). This may refer to the five basic pitches of the musical scale. Nose and the Nearman translations follow this interpretation; Nose, 2:10–11; Nearman, trans. with commentary, "*Kakyō*: Zeami's Fundamental Principles of Acting (Part 3)," *Monumenta Nipponica* 38.1(1983): 59. NSTS, Tanaka, and SNKBZ 88 concur that the term refers to the set of sounds comprising the Japanese syllabary (*gojū on*). With one exception, all of its moras contain one of the five primary vowel sounds (a, i, u, e, and, in Zeami's time, wo). NSTS, 75; Tanaka, 152; SNKBZ 88, 328.

32. *Ongyoku kuden*, NSTS, 74. Also in *Kakyō*, NSTS, 104. Annotators disagree on how the opening clause about *kakari* relates to the rest of the sentence. Nose's gloss takes it as one in a sequence of steps forming part of the compositional process, i.e., the composer should make sure that the words and phrasing will be conducive to *kakari* and in addition should pay attention to correct vocalization and smooth transitions; Nose, 1:9–10. On the other hand, Tanaka's gloss makes all of the activities listed part of the step-by-step program for creating *kakari*, i.e., since *kakari* is based on words and phrasing, the words and phrasing should be thus and thus; Tanaka, 152. Grammatically, either interpretation is possible. It seems to me that contextually Tanaka's interpretation is more apt, given that Zeami considers *kakari* to be a property that emerges on the basis of the overall flow of the lines.

33. Miyake Akiko, "Zeami no kiiwaado, 'kakari,' " *Kokubungaku, kaishaku to kyōzai no kenkyū* 35.3 (1990): 118.

34. Nose, 2:10.

35. *Ongyoku kuden*, NSTS, 75.

36. "A skilled [performer] is one who, though [rendering] the standard pattern of mod-

ulation, understands [how to be] expressive. Expressiveness is the flower above [and beyond] the modulation." Chapter 7 of *Kaden*, NSTS, 57. Although this treatise is dated 1418, one year earlier than *Ongyoku kuden*, one manuscript of it is believed to have existed as early as 1408. It is therefore possible that Zeami had not yet developed the triad consisting of *fushi*, *kakari*, and *kyoku* introduced in *Ongyoku kuden*.

37. Ibid., NSTS, 75.

38. Nose, 2:11.

39. *Sarugaku dangi*, De Poorter, *Zeami's Talks*, 99; NSTS, 277–278.

40. *Sarugaku dangi*, NSTS, 278. What is called *fushi* in the first place also means something hard, like in bamboo.

41. *Sarugaku dangi*, De Poorter, *Zeami's Talks*, 99–100; NSTS, 279.

42. In *Kakyō*, too, Zeami gives this example, but there he adds the following explanation: "In the Analects of Confucius it is said: 'Bear, tiger and leopard are skins used as targets for the bow: tiger is for the Emperor, leopard for the dukes, bear for the great officers.' Therefore, one should say tiger-leopard-bear, but for euphony's sake one says it in the other order." DePoorter, *Zeami's Talks*, 192. The sentence in question does not appear in the *Lunyu* as Zeami contends, but resembles a passage in *Zhouli* (*Chou-li*, Book of rites, chap. 2, 22b). DePoorter, *Zeami's Talks*, 192. Cf. NSTS, 105.

43. Nose Asaji, " 'Kakari' " no geijutsuteki seikaku," *Nose Asaji chosaku shū* (Kyoto: Shibunkaku Shuppan, 1985), 1:270.

44. *Kaden*, Tanaka, 15, note 15.

45. *Kaden*, NSTS, 52.

46. Ibid. Nose interprets *giri* as "dramatic story line"; Nose, 1:201. The NSTS, Tanaka, and SNKBZ 88 exegeses take *giri* to mean "effects that depend on the meaning of the words"; NSTS, 52, 437–438; Tanaka, 77, 61; SNKBZ 88, 271.

47. *Kaden*, NSTS, 52. The NSTS annotation glosses "if the aural effects of the chant are solid" as "if the mood of the chant is staunchly aligned with the character"; NSTS, 52. The Tanaka annotation has "If the modulation is solid overall, and it is supple and smooth"; Tanaka, 78. The SNKBZ gloss is "If the flow of the modulation is solid"; SNKBZ 88, 271; the Nose annotation is "If the musical progress is solid"; Nose, 1:201.

48. In later transmissions, Zeami cites plays on celebratory themes (*shūgen*) as examples of straightforward plays, a point that will be discussed in more detail in chapter 5 of this volume.

49. *Kaden*, NSTS, 52. "Basic nature" is my translation of *hon'yō*. NSTS and Tanaka gloss *"hon"* as *honrai* (original, essential, natural); NSTS, 52; Tanaka, 78. The SNKBZ 88 annotation suggests *honkakuteki* (orthodox, full-scale) or *risōteki* (ideal); SNKBZ 88, 271. Nose gives *honkakuteki* or *kihonteki* (fundamental); Nose, 1:201.

50. *Kaden*, NSTS, 51.

51. The NSTS and Tanaka editions interpret *jintai* (or *nintai*), translated as "human form," to refer to the dramatic character; NSTS, 48; Tanaka, 70. The SNKBZ 88

annotation allows for two possibilities, the dramatic character or the actor's image; SNKBZ 88, 263. Nose does not comment. My translation embraces both of these readings.

52. The original for "air" is *fuzei*. Tanaka interprets this as stage action (*shigusa*); Tanaka, 70. SNKBZ 88 glosses it as "image" (*sugata*) or "behavior" (*furumai*); SNKBZ 88, 263. NSTS reads it as "atmosphere" (*omomuki*); NSTS, 48. Although Zeami often uses *fuzei* to refer to the visual impression created by the acting, in this instance it seems to mean something closer to "stage presence."

53. *Kaden*, NSTS, 47–48.

54. Ibid., NSTS, 34–35.

55. One type of short passage of chant most frequently sung by the lead actor upon his entrance, or, as in this case, immediately prior to a dance.

56. *Kakyō*, NSTS, 85–86.

57. *Sarugaku dangi*, De Poorter, *Zeami's Talks*, 89: NSTS, 268.

58. Ibid.

59. The original for "meaning [of the words]" is *kokorone*. The translator has followed the NSTS gloss here. De Poorter, *Zeami's Talks*, 177; NSTS, 269. Tanaka glosses this as "the character's feeling as evidenced by the lines." Tanaka, 188. Nose interprets it as "the feeling expressed through the chant" (*utai no kokoromochi*); Nose, 2:350. "Acting" is the translation for *fuzei*. Zeami frequently uses the term in this way throughout his treatises, although it may occasionally correspond more closely to "atmosphere."

60. *Sarugaku dangi*, De Poorter, *Zeami's Talks*, 89–90; NSTS, 268–269. For the original text of *Matsukaze*, see Yokomichi and Omote, eds., *Yōkyoku shū*, 1:57–65.

61. *Shikadō*, NSTS, 116.

62. Ibid.

63. Ibid. The referent for "have been developed" is *kono shinajina*, which the NSTS, Nose, and Tanaka annotations agree refers to the other two elements, bone and flesh. Nose, 1:461; Tanaka, 108.

64. Tanaka Yutaka, "Karon to nōgakuron," *nō, chūsei geinō no kaika*, ed. Geinōshi kenkyūkai, Nihon no Koten Geinō 3 (Tokyo: Heibonsha, 1970), 167.

65. Ibid., 167–168.

66. Tanaka argues that the muscle level refers broadly to all choreographed movement. I am in accord with his interpretation here.

67. See chapter 2, note 72.

68. Nearman, trans., "Mirror of the Flower," 350. For original, see NSTS, 85. "Causal agent" (*tai*) is also sometimes translated as "substance," "effect," (*yū*) as "function."

69. Ibid., 351.

70. *Kaden*, NSTS, 60–61.

71. *Kaden*, NSTS, 51–52.

72. *Sandō*, NSTS, 140.

73. NSTS, 318. The letter closes with the month and day of composition (eighth day of the sixth month) but does not affix the year. The NSTS annotation estimates that it was written around 1435, one year after Zeami was exiled to Sado Island.

74. Yashima Masaharu, *Zeami no nō to geiron* (Tokyo: Miyai Shoten, 1985), 285–286.

75. Dōmoto Masaki, *Nō, kyōgen no gei* (Tokyo: Tōkyō Shoseki, 1983), 197.

Chapter 4. Composing the Text

1. Nose, Tanaka, and SNKBZ 88 state that having "a good number of plays" refers to having an ample variety in one's repertoire. Nose, 1:83; Tanaka, 41; SNKBZ 88, 234. NSTS specifies that these should be plays of the actor's own composing; NSTS, 30.

2. This passage is taken from the introduction to *Kaden*, which goes, "Those who wish to advance on this path should not pursue other paths. However, because the path of composing *waka* avails one of refined attunement to [the beauties of] nature and of long life, it alone may be followed [without objection]." *Kaden*, NSTS, 14. The NSTS annotation points out that *kadō*, translated as "path of composing *waka*," would embrace both the thirty-one-mora verse form called the *uta*, and *renga*, the linked verse form. It is also possible to construe *kadō* here more loosely to refer to poetry or versifying in general, as does the Rimer translation; Rimer and Yamazaki, trans., *On the Art of the Nō Drama*, 3.

   Annotators diverge on the meaning of one phrase, *fugetsu ennen no kazari*, translated here as "avails one of refined attunement to [the beauties of] nature and of long life." This follows the NSTS interpretation; NSTS, 428. NKBT 65, Tanaka, and Nose interpret this passage to mean that *waka* (with its attunement to the beauties of nature) provides an additional attraction that enhances noh. The confusion arises from the ambiguities of the term *ennen*, which may be taken literally to mean "long life" or may be read as a metonymy for the *sarugaku* art, or for the performing arts in general. NKBT, 342; Tanaka, 14; Nose, 1:9–10.

3. *Kaden*, NSTS, 30.

4. *Kakyō*, NSTS, 85. "The nature of the utterances" is *iigoto no shina* in the original. NSTS and SNKBZ 88 interpret *shina* as the content of the lines. NSTS, 85; SNKBZ 88, 297 (modern gloss). Tanaka interprets it as the mood of the lines (*omomuki*). This seems preferable to the NSTS and SNKBZ 88 readings because it is inclusive of the sonic appeal of the language as well as its referential content. Tanaka, 119. Contrastively, Nose interprets *shina* as stage action or gestures that serve to mediate the lines; Nose, 1:293. Zeami's main point here, that the stage action should be informed by the utterance, is brought out more aptly in the NSTS, SNKBZ 88, and Tanaka readings.

5. *Kaden*, NSTS, 49.

6. Ibid.

7. An elderly couple is featured in the first act. Today, the protagonist of the

second act is a young male figure, the deity of Sumiyoshi Shrine. It is not known whether this is the original casting for the second act. Some scholars surmise that Zeami cast the Sumiyoshi deity as an elderly figure. See SNKS, 2:475–476.

8. More than 90 plays of the present noh repertoire belong to the "living-time" category; Matsuda Tamotsu, *Nō, kyōgen nyūmon*, Bunken no Geinō Kanshō Shirīzu (Tokyo: Bunken Shuppan, 1976), 61. There are roughly 230 plays in the present repertoire, although the number varies somewhat according to the particular school of noh.

9. Etsuko Terasaki, *Figures of Desire: Wordplay, Spirit Possession, Fantasy, Madness, and Mourning in Japanese Noh Plays*, Michigan Monograph Series in Japanese Studies 38 (Ann Arbor: The University of Michigan Center for Japanese Studies, 2002).

10. Esperanza Ramirez-Christensen, *Heart's Flower: The Life and Poetry of Shinkei* (Stanford: Stanford University Press, 1994), 269.

11. The sparsity of mimetic elements allows for still another reading of the couple's function onstage: as that of narrators describing the scene in a linguistic style that makes no explicit reference to their own involvement in it. In this early phase of the play, the two exist simultaneously as partakers in the action and narrators of it.

12. Morita Yoshinori, *Chūsei senmin zatsugeinō no kenkyū* (Tokyo: Yuzankaku Shuppan, 1974), 204.

13. Ibid., 205.

14. Annotated translations of all three of these plays, *Higaki*, *Izutsu*, and *Tadanori*, are found in Yasuda, *Masterworks of the Nō Theater*, 303–324, 186–226, and 253–276, respectively.

15. *Ama* and *Sanemori* are found in Yokomichi and Omote, eds., *Yōkyoku shū*, 1:157–165 and 265–273, respectively. For an English translation of *Ama*, see Nippon Gakujutsu Shinkōkai, ed. and trans., *Japanese Noh Drama: Ten Plays Selected and Translated from the Japanese* (Tokyo: Nippon Gakujutsu Shinkōkai, 1960), 3:173–192; or Royall Tyler, ed. and trans., *Japanese Nō Dramas* (London: Penguin, 1992), 22–36. For an English translation of *Sanemori*, see Nippon Gakujutsu Shinkōkai, ed. and trans., *The Noh Drama: Ten Plays from the Japanese*, 8th printing (Rutland, Vt.: Charles E. Tuttle, 1955), 37–56. Also, Mae J. Smethurst, *The Artistry of Aeschylus and Zeami: A Comparative Study of Greek Tragedy and Nō* (Princeton, N.J.: Princeton University Press, 1989).

16. *Sarugaku dangi*, NSTS, 288.

17. Itō Masayoshi holds that noh playwrights drew as much from medieval poetic commentaries on Heian literary classics as from those works themselves in formulating the stories for plays; see his studies on Ariwara no Narihira: "Yōkyoku to *Ise monogatari* no hiden: *Izutsu* no baai o chūshin to shite," in Nihon Bungaku Kenkyū Shiryō Kankōkai, ed., *Yōkyoku, kyōgen*, 106–114; and "Yōkyoku

Kakitsubata kō: Sono shudai o tōshite mita chūsei no *Ise monogatari* kyōju to Narihira-zō ni tsuite," *Bunrin*, no. 2 (1967): 61–83.

18. The reader is referred to Janet Goff's study, *Noh Drama and* The Tale of Genji.

19. See, for instance, Omote Akira, *Nōgaku shi shinkō* (Tokyo: Wan'ya Shoten, 1979), 1:492–493; Kitagawa, *Zeami*, 52–53; or Takemoto, *Kan'ami, Zeami jidai no nō*, 19–24.

20. Konishi Jin'ichi, "Nō to *Genji monogatari*," in Nihon Bungaku Kenkyū Shiryō Kankōkai, ed., *Yōkyoku, kyōgen*, 101–105.

21. Tadanori's identity as a poet is introduced in Book 7 and his death in Book 9 of the Kakuichi manuscript of *Heike monogatari*; see Takagi Ichinosuke et al., eds., *Heike monogatari*, Nihon Koten Bungaku Taikei 33 (Tokyo: Iwanami, 1960), 2:61–117 and 2:164–236. For the text of the play *Tadanori*, see Yokomichi and Omote, eds., *Yōkyoku shū*, 1:241–248.

22. Yonekura Toshiaki, "Nō no sozai to kōzō: *Sanemori* no nō o chūshin ni," *Bungaku* 31.1 (1963): 57–65. The diary entry that Yonekura cites is dated the eleventh day of the fifth month of Ōei 21 in the *Mansai jugō nikki*; found in Zoku Gunsho Ruijū Kansei Kai, ed., *Zoku Gunsho ruijū*, Book 870, Supplement 1 (Tokyo: Zoku Gunsho Ruijū Kai, 1928), 46.

23. Nogami Toyoichirō, *Nō, kenkyū to hakken* (Tokyo: Iwanami Shoten, 1930), 144.

24. Nihon Daijiten Kankōkai, ed., *Nihon Kokugo Daijiten*, vol. 6, reduced-size ed., 2nd printing (Tokyo: Shōgakukan, 1981), s.v. "jo ha kyū."

25. However, Zeami does mention the names of *gagaku* pieces in some of his plays, such as *Takasago*, which will be introduced in the ensuing chapter of this volume.

26. Nijō Yoshimoto, *Tsukuba mondō*, NKBT 66, 86.

27. *Kaden*, NSTS, 29; *Kashu no uchinukigaki*, NSTS, 68–71; *Kakyō*, NSTS, 90–93.

28. *Kakyō*: NSTS, 91.

29. *Shūgyoku tokuka*, NSTS, 191.

30. Zeami distinguishes between the main actor *(tōryō no shite)* and all other actors, whom he assigns to one group labeled *waki no shite* (secondary actors). For instance, see *Shudōsho*, NSTS, 234–236. For an interesting analysis of the role of the *waki*, especially how it has been construed by modern scholars, see Ruxandra Marginean, "Naturalizing Nō: Interpreting the *Waki* as 'The Representative of the Audience,'" in Stanca Scholz-Cionca and Samuel L. Leiter, eds., *Japanese Theatre and the International Stage*, Brill's Japanese Studies Library 12 (Leiden: Brill, 2000), 133–147.

31. Yasuda, *Masterworks of the Nō Theater*, 152. Yasuda provides a useful introduction to the major structural components of a play.

32. Ibid.

33. *Nanori* (name-saying speech) is the term for this segment today. In Zeami's day, its opening portion was probably sung in recitative *(sashigoe)* rather than intoned

prose. The NSTS annotators surmise that this is the reason that in *Sandō* Zeami refers to this segment as *sashigoe*. Today its entirety is generally performed in intoned prose; NSTS, 462, appendix note 69.

34. The pause for alteration of the *shite's* costume that characteristically occurs in the course of the one-act play is called the *monogi*. There are only a few two-act plays, such as *Funa Benkei*, in which the *shite* of the first and second acts are completely different characters, although the two roles are usually played by the same actor today.

    It should be pointed out that not all scholars agree that those instrumental in creating this dramatic prototype intended that the *shite* of the first and second acts be seen as the same person. For instance, Tokue maintains that it makes more sense to interpret the protagonist of the first act as an innocent bystander who becomes possessed by the spirit of the character that the play is about and serves as his or her medium. That spirit then appears overtly in the second act. Tokue draws on the theories of Honda Yasuji. Tokue Gensei, *Muromachi geinōshi ronkō* (Tokyo: Miyai Shoten, 1984), 216.

35. Miyake Kōichi, *Yōgeiko no kihonjishiki* (Tokyo: Hinoki Shoten, 1979), 128.

36. The practice of casting the *waki* as choral leader continued until the late sixteenth century. Iwanami Kōza, 1:220. In the Kanze school, whose records are most complete, it was not until the late eighteenth century that the names of *waki* actors ceased to appear in performance records as chorus members together with the names of actors specializing in *shite* roles. Iwanami Kōza, 1:222.

37. Miyake Kōichi, *Yōgeiko no kihonjishiki*, 140–141.

38. For a detailed study of the structure of the noh *kuse* section and its performance today, see Monica Bethe and Karen Brazell, *Nō as Performance: An Analysis of the 'Kuse' Scene of 'Yamamba,'* Cornell University East Asia Papers, no. 16 (Ithaca, N.Y.: Cornell China-Japan Program, 1978).

39. Hayashiya, *Chūsei geinōshi no kenkyū*, 397.

40. Nishino and Hata, eds., *Shintei zōho nō, kyōgen jiten,* s.v. "Kouta," 307. For an analysis and translation of a collection of *kouta* titled *Kangin shū* (1518), see Frank Hoff, *Song, Dance, Storytelling: Aspects of the Performing Arts in Japan,* Cornell University East Asia Papers, no. 15 (Ithaca, N.Y.: Cornell China-Japan Program, 1978).

41. Takemoto Mikio, "Kan'ami jidai no nō," *Bungaku* 51.7 (1983): 157.

42. Miyake Akiko, *Kabu nō no kakuritsu to tenkai* (Tokyo: Perikansha, 2001), 6.

43. *Ongyoku kuden*, NSTS, 77.

44. In *Kakyō*, for instance, Zeami states the following: "In *sarugaku*, the *waki* play corresponds to the *jo* phase [of a program]. The play should be straightforward without too much detail; it should be celebratory, and should have overtones [*kakari*] that flow correctly. NSTS, 90.

45. According to the tabulations of Kenneth Yasuda, the *kuse* section occurs in the first act of all the *waki* plays in the present repertoire. On the other hand, it occurs in

the second act of 83 percent of the warrior plays of the repertoire; Yasuda, *Masterworks of the Nō Theater*, 157.

46. *Shudōsho*, NSTS, 236–239. (Although the first ideograph is the character for *narau/shū*, the medieval reading was "*shu*." NSTS, 234.)

47. Ibid., NSTS, 236.

48. Ibid., NSTS, 237.

49. Zeami's used *hataraki* to refer broadly to choreographed moves suitable for strong characters and not suitable for gentle ones. Since his time, various types of such movement sequences have evolved under the rubric *hatarakigoto*. Examples of *hatarakigoto* today are *kakeri*, typically performed by a mad person or the ghost of a warrior, or *maibataraki*, performed by demons or other strong beings. For more on *hatarakigoto*, see the entry for it in Nishino and Hata, eds., *Shintei zōho nō, kyōgen jiten*, 324.

50. The translation of "congruent" for *hyōshi ai* and "noncongruent" for *hyōshi awazu* adheres to the terminology that Bethe and Brazell use. They define "non-congruent count, *hyōshi awazu*" as "the rhythm of the vocal line when it does not keep the same count as the drums." See their *Nō as Performance*, 189.

51. Zeami did not use the term *hiranori*. The closest corresponding terms are *tada utai* and *tada ongyoku*. The term was coined by Umewaka Manju in a piece titled *Yōyō shū*, composed in 1856. Although the exact matching of syllables to beats has fluctuated over time, it is believed that this category of chant does date back to Zeami. Nishino and Hata, eds., *Shintei zōho nō, kyōgen jiten*, s.v. "Hiranori," 327–328. This is true for the other two rhythm patterns, *ōnori (kiribyōshi)* and *chūnori (hayabushi)* as well.

52. All three matching patterns are subject to variation. Those variations are one major source of musical interest. Not only are a large number of instrumental combinations possible, but the number of morae in each line of the text may vary as well. In the *hiranori* scheme, for example, the number of syllables in one line may range from five to eighteen. The rhythmic structure of noh music is introduced in Tamba Akira, *La structure musicale du nō* (Paris: Klincksieck, 1974), 207–215. There is also an English translation: Tamba Akira, *The Musical Structure of Nō*, trans. Patricia Matoré (Tokyo: Tokai University Press, 1981).

Though Zeami states in Segment 1.1 of *Sandō* that setting the musical modulation of the lines is an integral part of the technique of writing, he devotes very little of this treatise to that subject. Presumably, the musical aspects of composition were more familiar to his target reader, a *sarugaku* practitioner, than were the techniques of poetic composition discussed in *Sandō*—techniques that gave *sarugaku* an unprecedentedly literary turn. He does address questions of musical phrasing in detail in another treatise believed to have been written at some point in his middle years, *Fushizuke shidai*. In NSTS, 145–154.

53. Robert H. Brower, trans., *Fujiwara Teika's Hundred-Poem Sequence of the Shōji Era*,

1200, Monumenta Nipponica Monograph 55 (Tokyo: Sophia University Press, 1978), 21.

54. Haruo Shirane, "Lyricism and Intertextuality: An Approach to Shunzei's Poetics," *Harvard Journal of Asiatic Studies* 50.1 (1990): 73.

55. Takemoto, *Kan'ami, Zeami jidai no nōgaku* 50.

56. Yokomichi and Omote, eds., *Yōkyoku shū,* 1:220.

57. Poem 398 in the book of winter poems in the seventh imperial anthology, the *Senzai waka shū;* Shinpen Kokka Taikan, ed. Henshū Iin Kai (Tokyo: Kadokawa Shoten, 1983), vol. 1, pt. 1:193.

58. Baba Akiko, "*Takasago:* Kamimai to senzu manzai," *Kokubungaku* 25.1 (1980): 78.

59. It is also customary to end a day's full program on an auspicious note by either performing a portion of a *waki* play or by chanting a celebratory passage. This practice was the established norm as of the Edo period. This type of passage is called *tsuke-shūgen.*

60. It is unclear what the original title of this treatise was or whether one actually existed. The extant manuscripts are all copies. Yoshida Tōgo coined this title. The document is not dated, but according to Omote's analysis in NSTS, its content and terminology suggest that Zeami composed it later in his career. The same five themes are also introduced in *Sarugaku dangi,* which dates to 1430. NSTS, 566.

61. This characterization is based on the headnote in Ozawa Masao, ed., *Kokin waka shū,* Nihon Koten Bungaku Zenshū 7 (Tokyo: Shōgakukan, 1971), 168.

62. Laura Raspica Rodd, trans., with Mary Catherine Henkenius, *Kokin shū: A Collection of Poems Ancient and Modern* (Princeton, N.J.: Princeton University Press, 1984), 149. The poem in Japanese is found in Ozawa, ed., *Kokin waka shū,* 172, poem 356. Priest Sosei was a ninth-century poet. This poem contains three *kakekotoba* (pivot words): *matsu* (pine tree/wait), *tsuru* (crane/perfective auxiliary suffix), and *kage* (shade, protection.) The headnote states that he composed the poem on behalf of the daughter of Yoshimine no Tsunenari, although the annotation in Ozawa, ed., *Kokin waka shū,* indicates that it is believed it was actually composed for Yoshimine no Tsuneyo; ibid. The Go ongyoku jōjō citation is found in NSTS, 200. The poem is also found in Shinpen Kokka Taikan, vol. 1, pt. 1:17.

63. *Ongyoku kuden,* NSTS, 76.

64. Translation by Stephen Owen in *Readings in Chinese Literary Thought,* Harvard-Yenching Institute Monograph Series 30. (Cambridge, Mass.: Council on East Asian Studies, Harvard University, 1992), 43.

65. NSTS, 80–81. This is corroborated in Nihon Daijiten Kankōkai, ed., *Nihon kokugo daijiten,* vol. 9, s.v. *bōoku.* (Also the reduced-size ed.)

66. *Ongyoku kuden,* NSTS, 81.

67. For *Sekidera Komachi,* see Sanari, ed., *Yōkyoku taikan,* 3:1609–1623. For an English translation, see Donald Keene, ed., *Twenty Plays of the Nō Theatre* (New York: Columbia University Press, 1970), 65–80.

68. Karen Brazell, trans., *Komachi at Sekidera (Sekidera Komachi)*, in Keene, ed., *Twenty Plays of the Nō Theatre*, 70.

69. Brower, trans., *Fujiwara Teika's Hundred-Poem Sequence*, 30.

70. For *Kinuta* and *Kayoi Komachi*, see Yokomichi and Omote, eds., *Yōkyoku shū*, 1:331–339 and 1:75–80. For an English translation of *Kayoi Komachi*, see Keene ed., *Twenty Plays of the Nō Theatre*, 51–63; for an English translation of *Kinuta*, see Tyler, ed. and trans., *Japanese Nō Dramas*, 156–170; or Nippon Gakujutsu Shinkōkai, *Japanese Noh Drama*, 3:113–131.

71. In the late treatise *Go ongyoku jōjō*, Zeami introduces *yūkyoku* (piece of chant in the *yūgen* style) as one of five chanting styles. He qualifies each of the five in turn. His characterization of *yūkyoku* has the following note affixed to it: "*Yūkyoku* is a style of expression (*kyokufū*) that all five types of vocal music should share." NSTS, 201. I believe that Zeami is here trying to compensate for his own tendency to conflate his characterizations of the *yūgen* quality as both an emergent property of performance and as a referential content assumed to inhere in certain materials.

72. *Go ongyoku jōjō*, NSTS, 200. This poem is included in the second book of the *Haru* (Spring) poems in the eighth imperial anthology *Shinkokin waka shū*; poem 114, Shinpen Kokka Taikan, vol. 1, pt. 1:219.

73. Poem 437, second book of autumn poems in the *Shinkokin waka shū*; Shinpen Kokka Taikan, vol. 1, pt. 1:225. The poem exploits the fall motif of a deer calling out in search of its mate.

74. NSTS, 201. *Hanjo* is the story of a young woman who is employed in a brothel. She falls in love with a guest. They exchange fans as a pledge of their feelings. She is driven from her place of employ because she cannot concentrate on her work for the love of this man. When he comes back to be with her, she has disappeared. She turns up at a festival in Kyoto where she has gone out of her mind pining for him. They are reunited there, their tie reconfirmed when each returns the other's fan. The play is by Zeami. Yokomichi and Omote, eds., *Yōkyoku shū*, 1:350–347. For an English translation, see Tyler, ed. and trans., *Japanese Nō Dramas*, 108–119.

75. For a listing of the *waka* poems most frequently quoted in noh plays, see Minegishi Yoshiaki, "Yōkyoku to waka," in Nogami Toyoichirō, ed., *Nōgaku zensho*, rev. ed. (Tokyo: Sōgensha, 1980), 3:126–127.

76. Edward Kamens, *Utamakura, Allusion, and Intertextuality in Traditional Japanese Poetry* (New Haven: Yale University Press, 1997), 8.

77. *Kaden*, NSTS, 47. Zeami goes on to state that the reason for this is that audiences are primarily interested in watching and listening to the star actor of the troupe (*tōryō*) perform in the *shite* role.

78. *Kaden*, NSTS, 47–50; for an English translation, see Rimer and Yamazaki, trans., *On the Art of the Nō Drama*, 43–46. *Sarugaku dangi*, NSTS, 287–292; De Poorter, *Zeami's Talks*, 112–114.

351

79. *Sandō*, NSTS, 143.
80. Ibid.

Chapter 5. Zeami's Theory in Practice:
An Analysis of the *Waki* Play *Takasago*

1. Zeami's preference for aged characters in *waki* plays was by no means the norm in his time. It will be recalled that the second chapter of *Kaden* mentions two types of deities, strong ones not suited for dancing and gentle ones who were. Zeami's preference for gentle deities was in keeping with his program to promote the centrality of music and dance. For a detailed account of the formation of plays in the *waki* classification, see Gerry Yokota-Murakami, *The Formation of the Canon of Nō: The Literary Tradition of Divine Authority* (Osaka: Osaka University Press, 1997).

2. His opinion about the lack of *yūgen* potential in *waki* plays does not seem to change much over time, for that matter. In the late transmission *Sarugaku dangi*, for instance, he states the following about the auspicious mode (*shūgen*) in relation to chanting: "the auspicious [piece] should be straightforward and correct, with an absence of captivating modulation (*omoshiroki fushi*). If one applies the nine-grade [scale], it would belong to the Style of the Correct Flower" (*shōkafū*); NSTS, 275. The "nine grades" (*kyūi*) is a reference to the typology of nine levels of acting skill that Zeami delineates in his late treatise titled *Kyūi*; NSTS, 173–177. The style of the correct flower is the uppermost of the three middle grades, which Zeami introduces as the grouping of entry-level grades for the training actor. At this level of the correct flower the actor should have mastered the techniques involving the two modes and the three styles but will not yet have reached the uppermost three levels at which a *yūgen* style becomes characteristic.

   In the passage from *Sarugaku dangi* quoted here, *shūgen* (auspicious piece) refers to a piece of chant in the auspicious mode. The original context for the passage is a discussion of chanting styles, not plays in their entirety. However, further along in this passage, Zeami observes that the *dengaku* actor Kiami sang in a style that had a kind of interest not appropriate for *waki* plays or celebratory chants (*Waki no nō, shūgen ni aru majiki fushi nari*), in effect lumping the chanting styles and plays together. Moreover, in Segment 2.1 of *Sandō*, Zeami refers to composition for a protagonist in the venerable style, which he states will generally apply to the *waki* play, as following an auspicious scheme (*shūgen no fūtei*); NSTS, 136. Since Zeami linked the *shūgen* style of chant to the *waki* play, his description of it is relevant to our discussion of how a *waki* play should be composed.

3. Zeami's transmission titled *Kashu no uchinukigaki* is dated Ōei 25 (1418), so it was written eighteen years after the passage quoted above from the third chapter of *Kaden*. It is thought to be an earlier draft of the passage in *Kakyō* that is devoted to articulation of the principle of *jo-ha-kyū* (NSTS, 90–93). The passages

from *Kashu no uchinukigaki* and *Kakyō* are virtually identical, but there are a few variations. One of them is the sentence "*Saruhodo ni tadashiku omote naru sugata nari*" (As such, it has a configuration that is correct and 'up front'), which is omitted from the *Kakyō* version. "Up front" (*omote naru*): lit., being the outside surface; being the front. I think it likely that Zeami borrowed this term from the discourse of *renga*, in which it refers to the front side of a folded sheet of paper having poems on both sides. When the term is not modified, it usually refers to the first group of poems in an entire *renga* sequence. However, NSTS states only that the term means "full-scale" or "orthodox" (*honkakuteki*), or "representative" (*daihyōteki*); NSTS, 68.

4. Whereas *Kashu no uchinukigaki* states that it should be *sugu naru nō* (a straightforward noh), the *Kakyō* text states it should be *sugu naru honzetsu* (a straightforward foundation story); NSTS, 68 and 90, respectively.

5. *Kakari* is used here in its aural aspect, referring to the mood elicited by the flow of the lines.

6. Most basic elements (*hontai*: in *Kakyō*, this term changes to *hontaifū* (most basic/elemental style); *Kashu no uchinukigaki* and *Kakyō*, NSTS, 68 and 90, respectively.

7. *Kashu no uchinukigaki*, NSTS, 68. In *Kakyō*, this last sentence is omitted.

8. "Authentic" (*tadashiki*): recognizable to audiences as an established source in literature and/or legend. NSTS states that *tadashiki* applies to material that "is based on an authoritative classic or a widely known story [*setsuwa*]" (29). Tanaka basically concurs and also specifies two examples, *Ise monogatari* and *Genji monogatari*; Tanaka, 40.

9. "The vocal music and movement should be staged in the usual way, and should be done with smoothness and ease" (*ongyoku hataraki mo ōkata no fūtei ni te, surusuru to yasuku su beshi*): this phrase comes from the Konparu manuscript, the text introduced in the NSTS edition. (However, NSTS substitutes *fūtei* for the original term in the Konparu manuscript, *fusei* [pronounced "*fuzei*"]; NSTS, 29. According to NSTS, the two terms are roughly synonymous in this instance, referring to movement or action onstage. See appendix, 430–431, note 8.) The Yoshida manuscript has *ongyoku mo mai mo tadashiku sugu naru kakari ni su beshi* (the chant and the dance should be made to flow with a mood [*kakari*] of correctness and directness); Nose, 1:79. According to NSTS, appendix note 8, the Yoshida manuscript has evidence of later revisions (553).

10. The term used to mean the last play in the program is *ageku*. It is borrowed from the terminology of *renga*, in which it means the last verse in a linked-verse sequence.

11. *Kaden*, NSTS, 29.

12. *Kashu no uchinukigaki*, NSTS, 68.

13. Tanaka glosses this usage of *kakari* as "the overall image of a piece based on the synthesis of [such elements as] language and stage style (*fūtei*)"; Tanaka, 70. Nose's

modern translation: "the mood of the entirety" (*zentai no fūshu*); Nose, 1:174. SNKBZ 88 has "the overall image" (*zentaiteki na sugata*); SNKBZ 88, 263.

14. *Kaden*, NSTS, 48.

15. Stage action (*fuzei*): in *Kashu no uchinukigaki*, the original term is *fuzei*; in the *Kakyō* variant it is *fūtei*. NSTS, 68 and 90, respectively.

16. "Since it is not [yet] the time to exert all of your skill, this too is still part of the jo [phase]" (*te o kudaku jibun ni te nakereba, kore mo mada jo no bun nari*); in *Kakyō* this reads, *te o mo itaku kudaku jibun ni te nakereba, kore mo imada jo no nagori no fūtei nari* (since it is not [yet] the time to go all out to exert your skill, this is still stage action that has lingering jo elements); NSTS, 68 and 90, respectively.

17. *Kashu no uchinukigaki*, NSTS, 68. This sentence is missing from the *Kakyō* variant; NSTS, 90.

18. *Kashu no uchinukigaki*, NSTS, 68.

19. *Kakyō*, NSTS, 91. The phrase under scrutiny here appears both in *Kakyō* and *Kashu no uchinukigaki*; NSTS, 68. (The annotation of this passage in the NSTS edition of *Kashu no uchinukigaki* is cross-referenced to the *Kakyō* annotation.)

20. *giri nō*: NSTS argues that the term refers to noh plays that rely for their interest largely on the appeal of verbal dexterity and repartee. It is also suggested that a reliance on interesting words and expressions was probably a traditional hallmark of the Yamato *sarugaku* style. As examples, NSTS mentions the *mondō* sequences in the plays *Sotoba Komachi*, *Hōkazō*, and *Miidera*, as well as the discussion of the "wedded trees" in the third *dan* of *Takasago*; NSTS, 438, appendix note 21. This sentence is lacking in *Kakyō*.

21. "tearful *sarugaku*" (*naki sarugaku*): NSTS interprets this as a play having a tragic denouement, but no examples are provided; NSTS, 68. In an article that explores the meaning of this term, Amano argues that *naki sarugaku* refers to an older type of play that fell out of favor with Zeami after he had developed his own dramatic prototype. Amano suggests that Zeami had older living-time plays in mind, such as *Kamuro Kōya* (*Karukaya*), attributed to the *dengaku* actor Kiami, in which a tearful reunion between a father and son is enacted. See Amano Fumio, " 'Naki sarugaku' kō, genryū to shiteki ichizuke," *Kokugakuin zasshi* 82.3 (1981): 27–42.

22. I have followed Nose's interpretation of this sentence, included in his annotations of the *Kakyō* version of the passage; Nose, 1:323, 325. The interpretation given in NSTS may be translated as "Since this is the parting phase, it should have an atmosphere appropriate for an ending"; NSTS, 69.

23. "the detailed rendering of various elements" (*komaka ni iroiro o tsukushite*): NSTS takes this to mean to "exhaust all kinds of devices" (*kakushu no shukō o shitsukushite*); NSTS, 69.

24. "the full showing of things" (*kuwashiku koto o arawasu*): this phrase is omitted from the *Kakyō* text; NSTS, 69 and 91.

25. "fast dancing" (*ranbu*): lit., wild or unorthodox dance. NSTS, Nose, and Tanaka

annotations concur that in this context the term refers to a fast-paced dance; NSTS, 69; Nose, 1:325; Tanaka, 129. (The Nose and Tanaka annotations are of the identical text in *Kakyō*.) Tanaka ventures to add that it may correspond to fast-paced dances in today's staging, such as the *otokomai* or *hayamai* dances; Tanaka, ibid. The term was also used generically to refer to *sarugaku*.

26. *Kashu no uchinukigaki*, NSTS, 68–69.

27. As previously noted, in *Go ongyoku jōjō*, Zeami also states that *yūkyoku* is a style that should run through all five modes of vocalization. NSTS, 201. The usage of *yūkyoku* here seems analogous to Zeami's usage of the term *yūgen* in *Sandō*, to delineate both a theme that treats subject matter considered to have *yūgen* effects and, in its broader usage, as an atmosphere that should emerge in performance.

28. *Go ongyoku jōjō*, NSTS, 198. Similar to note 5 above, *kakari* is used here in its aural aspect, referring to the mood elicited by the flow of the lines.

29. The passage from the *Shijing* is quoted from Owen, *Readings in Chinese Literary Thought*, 43.

30. *Go ongyoku jōjō*, NSTS, 198.

31. These exemplars are found in *Shikadō*, NSTS, 117.

32. Kanai Kiyomitsu, *Nō no kenkyū* (Tokyo: Ōfūsha, 1969), 884.

33. Other English translations of *Takasago* are also available. For instance, see Richard A. Gardner, "Takasago: The Symbolism of the Pine," Monumenta Nipponica 47.2 (1992): 203–240; Hare, *Zeami's Style*, 65–128; and Tyler, trans., *Japanese Nō Dramas*, 277–292; For an English translation of the *kyōgen* interlude *(ai)*, see Hare, *Zeami's Style*, 96–97; or Tyler, trans., *Japanese Nō Dramas*, 287–289. A Japanese version may be found in SNKS 2:289–290. There are no extant texts of the *ai* that date to Zeami's time. All those cited here date to the Edo period.

34. Today in the Kanze and Hōshō schools, the *shite* enters carrying a rake. In the Kongō, Kita, and Konparu schools, however, he carries a broom. Which prop is the original one is unknown. Kanai, *Nō no kenkyū*, 294.

35. Today the Hōshō and Kanze schools cast the *shite* of the second act as a god of Sumiyoshi Shrine appearing as the spirit of the pine tree there. NSTS, 444, appendix note 128.

36. *Sarugaku dangi*, NSTS, 286. For a summary of recognized interpretations of the "fins" of *Takasago*, see Kanai, *Nō no kenkyū*, 292–293.

37. The Kasuga Shrine in Nara refers to the play as *Takasago* in a record dated 1452; Kōsai Tsutomu, "Takasago: Sakusha to honsetsu," *Kanze*, no. 1 (1964): 10.

38. According to Kōsai, Takasago Shrine was not a particularly illustrious institution with a long history. It is not mentioned, for instance, in the fifty-volume *Engi shiki*, commissioned in 905. Kōsai surmises that the shrine was built to honor a famous pine tree in the area. For that reason, it is not at all strange for the spirit of the pine tree to also serve as the deity of Takasago Shrine. Ibid., 12–13.

39. *Kokin waka shū*, ed. Saeki Umetomo, Nihon Koten Bungaku Taikei 8 (Tokyo:

Iwanami, 1958), 93–104. For an English translation, see Rodd and Henkenius, trans., *Collection of Poems Ancient and Modern;* or Helen Craig McCullough, trans., Kokin waka shū: *The First Imperial Anthology of Japanese Poetry with Tosa Nikki and Shinsen waka* (Stanford, Calif.: Stanford University Press, 1985).

40. Rodd and Henkenius, *Collection of Poems Ancient and Modern,* 35; or McCullough, *First Imperial Anthology,* 3.

41. Although Tsurayuki's "*Kana* Preface" was ostensibly a manifesto intended to hold up the validity of *waka,* a native Japanese form vis-à-vis Chinese poetic forms, he borrows heavily from Chinese philosophical and poetic precedents to make his case. The idea that poetry soothes the hearts of gods, spirits, and fierce warriors comes directly from the "Great Preface" to the *Shijing.* See Helen Craig McCullough, *Brocade by Night: "Kokin Waka shū" and the Court Style in Japanese Classical Poetry* (Stanford, Calif.: Stanford University Press, 1985), 303–305. McCullough also has done an English translation of *Kokin shū* in her *First Imperial Anthology.*

42. Records of *shite* cast as plant spirits go back at least as far as Zeami, e.g., *Saigyōzakura* (Saigyō and the cherry tree). On a related topic, the relation of such spirits to Buddhist thought, see Donald Shively, "Buddhahood for the Nonsentient: A Theme in Nō Plays," *Harvard Journal of Asiatic Studies* 20 (1957): 135–161. For an English translation of *Saigyōzakura,* see Eileen Katō, trans., "*Saigyōzakura* and the Cherry Tree," in *Twelve Plays of the Noh and Kyōgen Theaters,* rev. ed., Cornell East Asian Papers 50 (Ithaca, N.Y.: East Asia Program, Cornell University, 1988), 81–97.

43. The principal deities of worship at the Sumiyoshi Shrine complex number three: Sokozutsunoo no Mikoto, Nakazutsunoo no Mikoto, and Uwazutsunoo no Mikoto. Okinagatarashihime no mikoto (the Empress Jingū) is also worshiped there. All are revered as protectors of the *waka* tradition. Zeami does not assign a specific identity to the deity that appears in the second act of *Takasago.*

44. As a rule, the *shite* of the first act of a *waki* play is an avatar of the god himself, who appears as himself in the second act. The more complex transformation of the spirit of the pine to the god of Sumiyoshi Shrine is unusual and is considered to be another "fin" of the structure of *Takasago.* The Kanze and Hōshō schools cast the *shite* of the second act also as the spirit of the pine tree, a revision thought to have been made for consistency.

45. The complete text of the *Kokin waka shū jo kikigaki (Sanryūshō)* is found in Katagiri Yōichi, ed., *Chūsei* Kokin shū *chūshakusho kaidai* (Kyoto: Akao Shōbundō, 1973), 2:260–263; quotation from 262. Katagiri has coined the subtitle *Sanryūshō* to identify a corpus of sixteen variant manuscripts, some of whose titles differ slightly; ibid., 21–24. For a detailed study of this text, see Susan Blakely Klein, *Allegories of Desire: Esoteric Literary Commentaries of Medieval Japan,* Harvard-Yenching Institute Monograph Series 55 (Cambridge, Mass.: Harvard University Asia Center, 2002).

46. For more on the relation between *Takasago* and medieval commentaries, see Itō

Masayoshi, "Yōkyoku *Takasago* zakkō, "*Bunrin*, no. 6 (March 1972): 111–125. Itō
also makes note of the connection between *Takasago* and *Kokin waka shū jo kikigaki*
(*Sanryūshō*) at relevant points in his annotation of *Takasago* in SNKS, 2:282–292.
Also Klein, *Allegories of Desire*.

47. Sanari, ed., *Yōkyoku taikan*, 3:1858.

48. *Kokin waka shū jo kikigaki* (*Sanryūshō*), 261.

49. SNKS, 2:475.

50. For a study of how medieval commentaries came to bear in the composing of noh
    plays, especially plays drawing on material from *Genji monogatari* and *renga* hand-
    books, see Goff, *Noh Drama and* The Tale of Genji.

51. Tomonari is listed in a document titled *Aso-shi keifu* (Geneology of the Aso clan),
    cited in SNKS 2:283, note 3.

52. NSTS, 85.

53. In Zeami's day, the chorus was in its formative stages. Whether there was actually
    a separate choral group or a group of players in role as *wakizure* onstage is unclear.
    Dōon, the term for choral singing that Zeami uses, encompasses chant in which
    players in role, such as the *waki*, *shite*, and *tsure*, all participated as well. Iwanami
    Kōza, 1:219–220.

54. Miyake Kōichi, *Yōgeiko no kihonjishiki*, 140–141.

55. McCullough, *Brocade by Night*, 326. McCullough defines *kokoro*, the other impor-
    tant category posited by Tsurayuki, as that which embraces "topic, theme, tone, and
    conception." Ibid.

56. This passage at the opening of the *kuse* is attributed to *Nagayoshi shiki* (Nagayoshi's
    personal chronicle), the diary of the Heian poet Chōnō, or Fujiwara no Nagayoshi
    (also read Nagatō; fl. tenth century). The same passage is attributed to Nagayoshi
    in *Yōkyoku shūyōshō*, a critical exegesis of noh librettos by the poet Inui Teijo
    (d. 1703); Inui Teijo, *Yōkyoku shūyōshō*, in Muromatsu Iwao, ed., Kokubun Chū-
    shaku Zensho, rev. ed., 1968 (Tokyo Sumiya Shobō, 1907), 6:12. However, the
    whereabouts of such a diary by Nagayoshi are unknown today; NSTS, 443, appen-
    dix note 125. As Klein has noted, recent scholars are inclined to think that the diary
    was spuriously cited by medieval commentators to bolster their own authority.
    Zeami may have chosen to allude to the document here because it was widely
    thought to contain a narrative about a revelation that the poet Narihira received
    from the Sumiyoshi deity. For more on the significance of Nagayoshi's putative diary,
    see Klein, *Allegories of Desire*, 182–185.

    In his annotation of this passage in SNKS, vol. 2, Itō Masayoshi points out that
    the medieval commentary *Kokin waka shū jo kikigaki* (*Sanryūshō*) contains the same
    passage as that attributed to Nagayoshi in the *Takasago* passage. It is likely that
    Zeami drew this material from the commentary. SNKS, 2:287–288.

57. Masafusa's poem is no. 398, in the *Senzai waka shū; Shinpen Kokka Taikan*, vol. 1,
    pt. 1:193.

58. I have followed the notation in SNKS, 2:223. In the *waki* play, the *shite* usually remains in a stationary, kneeling position at stage center throughout the *kuse*, allowing the chorus to voice his emotions. Today this type of stationary *kuse* (*iguse*) is one of two major types of *kuse*, the other being the danced *kuse* (*maiguse*). *Takasago* is an exception to the rule of the *waki* play. This choreographed segment at the conclusion of the *Takasago kuse* is therefore surmised to be another "fin" in the anatomy of this play.

59. For a detailed study of the infrastructure of the *kuse* section of a noh play, see Bethe and Brazell, *Nō as Performance*.

60. For more on the *kyōgen* texts, see note 33 above.

61. Some scholars speculate that the *shite* of the second act was originally cast as an old man, arguing that such casting would be more consistent with the mood of the first act and the preconceived image of the god of Sumiyoshi as an old man figure. See Kanai, *Nō no kenkyū*, 303–304; and Omote Akira et al., "Zeami no nō, I," *Kanze*, no. 6 (1963): 34. However, there is no concrete evidence for such a supposition. Yashima Masaharu, for instance, argues that Segment 2.1 of *Sandō*, which describes the finale of *Takasago* as having a male figure or celestial being chanting with lightness and perhaps performing *kiribyōshi* moves, is evidence that the *shite* of Act II had always been a young male. Yashima Masaharu, *Zeami no nō to geiron*, 351.

  Today the Hōshō and Kanze schools cast the *shite* of the second act as a god of Sumiyoshi Shrine appearing as the spirit of the Sumiyoshi pine tree. NSTS, 444, appendix note 128.

62. Although we know from Zeami's critical treatises that the flute, the stick drum, and the "*tsuzumi*" drum existed in his time, it is not known with certainty whether *tsuzumi* referred to both the shoulder drum (*kotsuzumi*) and the hip drum (*ōtsuzumi*) or one of the two. In a document from Zeami's late years, reference is made to a *kotsuzumi*, which leads some scholars to infer that there must have been an *ōtsuzumi* as well. Omote Akira, "Tradition and Transformation in Nō Theatre," trans. Erika De Poorter, *Maske und Kothurn* 35 (1989): 12.

63. Poem 398, the *Senzai waka shū*; Shinpen Kokka Taikan, vol. 1, pt. 1:193.

64. *Sandō*, NSTS, 135–136.

65. Miyake Kōichi, *Yōgeiko no kihonjishiki*, 151.

66. Rimer and Chaves offer an alternate translation to this poem that opens up another possible reading in the context of this play. The translation goes as follows.

> The glory of the Duke Eighteen—
>   revealed after the frost!
> The colors of a thousand years
>   deepen in the snow.

"The glory of the Duke Eighteen" is the translation of an alternate term for pine tree used in the first line of this poem: *shūhakkō* (or *jūhakkō*). J. Thomas Rimer and

Jonathan Chaves, eds. and trans., *Japanese and Chinese Poems to Sing: The* Wakan rōei shū (New York: Columbia University Press, 1997), 130. The original is in Ōsone Shōsuke and Horiuchi Hideaki, eds., *Wakan rōei shū*, Shinchō Nihon Koten Shūsei 61 (Tokyo: Shinchōsha, 1983), no. 425: 163.

Shūhakkō is derived by breaking the Chinese character for *matsu* into three component radicals and ordering them in sequence, their meanings being "ten-eight-Duke." See appendix 2, note 23. The word has a Chinese folk etymology in which a man dreams of a pine tree growing out of his stomach. This is interpreted to mean that the man would become a duke in eighteen years. Perhaps the ultimate targets for Zeami's praise were not pine trees. Zeami also weaves the term into the *kuse* passage preceding the *ageha*, *Shūhakkō no yosooi/Senshū no midori o nashite* ("the verdure of the pine tree does endure a thousand autumns past and present"; or, alternatively, "the glory of the duke eighteen does endure a thousand autumns past and present").

67. Poem no. 909 in *Kokin waka shū*; Shinpen Kokka Taikan, vol. 1, pt. 1:28.
68. Earl Miner, *An Introduction to Japanese Court Poetry* (Stanford, Calif.: Stanford University Press, 1968), 161.
69. Kidō Saizō and Shigematsu Hiromi, eds., *Rengaronshū*, vol. 1, Chūsei no Bungaku 880-04 (Tokyo: Miyai Shoten, 1972), 62.
70. Ibid., 141.
71. Zeami exploits this further nuance in passages such as that found in the second act in which the *shite*, the deity of Sumiyoshi, remarks on the scene.

Indeed a great host	*Ge ni samazama no*
of maidens dancing,	*maibime no*
their voices too ringing clear	*Koe mo sumu nari*
through Sumiyoshi*	*Suminoe no*

*According to Klein, Suminoe is the name of a small inlet below Sumiyoshi Shrine. As she also states, the place-names Suminoe and Sumiyoshi are nearly interchangeable. Klein, *Allegories of Desire*, 228, note 32. For simplicity, I have used Sumiyoshi only in my English translation of *Takasago*.

72. Baba, " 'Takasago' ": Kamimai to senzu manzai," 81.

Chapter 6. Actor and Audience

1. Yamazaki Masakazu, *Engi suru seishin* (Tokyo: Chūō kōronsha, 1983), 47.
2. NSTS, 85. "Fulfillment arising from [the accruing of] the visual and the aural" is a translation of the term *kenmon jōju*. The NSTS interpretation of this term is, "Upon hearing the words chanted, interest will shift to the stage action *(shosa)* that immediately follows, appealing to the visual faculty. In this instant in which the focus of interest shifts, the expressive appeal of movement and chanting will be jointly realized, creating a deep impression" (85). Tanaka similarly interprets it as a deep impression created when "the visual and the auditory together are fulfilled";

Tanaka, 120. The Nose gloss for the term states, "The chant and the patterned movements *(kata)* are well blended and arouse feeling in the spectators"; Nose, 1:293. Nearman's translation of *kenmon jōju* is "the full realization of the visual and the auditory [elements]; Nearman, "Mirror of the Flower," pt. 1, 354. The Rimer translation reads, "satisfying sensation of a genuine union between the two images;" Rimer and Yamazaki, trans., *On the Art of the Nō Drama*, 76.

3. For more on the techniques of vocalization, see Zeami's secret transmission titled *Ongyoku kuden* in NSTS, 73–81.

4. *Sandō*, NSTS, 141.

5. Smethurst, *Artistry of Aeschylus and Zeami*, 152.

6. De Poorter, *Zeami's Talks*, 90. Original in NSTS, 269.

7. *Kakyō*, NSTS, 84–85.

8. In this case, it is the poet Fujiwara no Shunzei's ideas on the aesthetic quality of "refined charm" *(en)* that are under discussion. *A History of Japanese Literature. The High Middle Ages*, trans. Aileen Gatten and Mark Harbison, ed. Earl Miner (Princeton, N.J.: Princeton University Press, 1991), 3:60. For Japanese original, see Konishi Jin'ichi, *Nihon bungeishi* (Tokyo: Kōdansha, 1986), 3:69.

9. *Sandō*, NSTS, 141.

10. *Kakyō*, NSTS, 86–88.

11. Based on Nose, 1:305.

12. *Kakyō*, NSTS, 88.

13. Ibid.

14. Ibid.

15. Ibid.

16. Ibid.

17. Takemoto, *Kan'ami, Zeami jidai no nōgaku*, 382. Takemoto gives three reasons for this thesis. The first is the absence of any reference to an unornamented style whose magnitude includes an unornamented style but surpasses it. This concept is first introduced in Zeami's treatise *Fūgyokushū*, an undated work thought to have been composed around the same time as *Sandō*. Takemoto surmises that the five methods were formulated prior to the composition of *Fūgyokushū*, since the five methods assume that the ornamented and unornamented are contrasting categories of the same order. He also notes that Zeami uses the term *nantai* (masculine style) instead of the terms *rōtai* (venerable style) or *guntai* (martial style) in his designation of the *monomane* styles. This seems to suggest that the three styles had not yet crystallized as such. Finally, Takemoto points out that the discussion of the five methods does not address issues related to the training of the actor, a prevailing concern in Zeami's late treatises.

18. *Kakyō*, NSTS, 87.

19. According to both the Tanaka and NSTS annotations, here *onjō* (lit. "musical voice") refers to auditory elements broadly construed. Tanaka, 121; NSTS, 86.

20. *Shūgyoku tokuka,* NSTS, 190.

21. Ibid.

22. Ibid., 191.

23. Ibid., 92. An English translation of the entire passage from the *Zhuangzi* may be found in Burton Watson, trans., *The Complete Works of Chuang Tzu,* Book 8 (New York: Columbia University Press, 1968), 99–100.

24. *Shūgyoku tokuka,* NSTS, 191.

25. Ibid.

26. The sole extant manuscript of *Shūgyoku tokuka,* the Hachizaemon *bon,* on which the NSTS edition is based, has a note affixed to the left of the words *tōki wagō* (in harmony with the prevailing mood) that directs the reader to the precept recorded in *Kakyō* on the desirable steps for the performer to follow when starting to vocalize; ibid., 84. (See the ensuing passage of this chapter for more on this concept.) NSTS annotators hold that the note most likely is a faithful copy of a note in the original manuscript (no longer extant), which was in Zeami's or, perhaps, Zenchiku's hand; ibid., 474–475, appendix note 99, and commentary on 565.

27. Ibid., 184–185.

28. Yasuda, *Masterworks of the Nō Theater,* 136. For original, see *Kakyō,* NSTS, 91–92.

29. *Kakyō,* NSTS, 84.

30. For an English translation and detailed exegesis of this passage, see Nearman, "Mirror of the Flower," pt. 1, 343–349. The Chinese character that Zeami actually allots to write *ki* is not the character meaning "breath" or "life energy," but another character, also pronounced *"ki"* in Japanese, meaning "the right timing" or "the right moment." Based on Zeami's consistent use of the second character in contexts in which breath is under discussion, annotators concur that his choice of the other character is idiosyncratic and does not reflect his message. See Nose's analysis, 1:282–283. Basically, I concur, although Zeami may have consciously misallotted the timing character to add a nuance of meaning.

31. Owen, *Readings in Chinese Literary Thought,* 584.

32. Ibid.

33. Tanaka, 117, note 3.

34. *Shūgyoku tokuka,* NSTS, 191–192.

35. Ibid., 188.

36. *Kaden,* NSTS, 38.

37. It should be noted that *omoshiro,* translated here as "the interesting," puns on one putative derivation of the word, which breaks it down into the components *omo* (face or surface) and *shiro* (lit. "white" or "bright"). One interpretation of its earliest usages seems to correspond to Zeami's usage here: "the feeling aroused by something bright suddenly appearing before one's eyes." Nakada Norio et al., *Kogo daijiten* (Tokyo: Shōgakukan, 1983), 299.

38. *Shūgyoku tokuka,* NSTS, 188.

39. For instance, see *"Besshi kuden,"* NSTS, 64.
40. *Kakyō*, NSTS, 102.
41. Ibid., 102. Annotators diverge on the meaning of the phrase translated here as "right away the chanting matches the tones [of the wind instruments]." This translation is in accordance with Tanaka's gloss of the phrase; Tanaka, 149. Nose, SNKBZ 88, and NKBT 65 all hold that *chōshi*, here translated as "tones" ("matches the tones," or *chōshi ni aite*), is an abbreviated reference to the phrase *toki no chōshi*, which would result in the alternative interpretation that the chanting matches the overall mood appropriate to that particular time and place. Nose, 1:395; SNKBZ 88, 299; NKBT 65, 431. The Rimer translation states, "The music and text are chosen in accord with the season [and the time of day]"; Rimer and Yamazaki, trans., *On the Art of the Nō Drama*, 100.
42. *Kakyō*, NSTS, 103. "Inmost mind" is *naishin* in the original. NSTS, Tanaka, and Nose provide no annotation for this term. NKBT 65 glosses it as "a vigilance in the depths of the mind" *(kokoro no oku no kokorozukai)* and "the mind in the depths of consciousness" *(ishiki no soko no kokoro)*; NKBT 65, 428. Rimer translates it as "spiritual resources," Nearman simply as "by his own mind," which he annotates as "a personal creation as distinct from a learned model." Rimer and Yamazaki, trans., *On the Art of the Nō Drama*, 100; Nearman, "Zeami's Fundamental Principles of Acting," pt. 3, 54. More will be said about this term in what follows.

    "Acting styles" is a translation of *fūtei*, which Tanaka glosses as *geitai* (artistic forms) and NSTS as *me ni uttaeru . . . engi* (acting/performing that appeals to the eye). Tanaka, 149; NSTS, 103. Nose interprets this statement to mean that such a performer will possess a loftiness of mind *(shin'i ga takai)* that will naturally be felt in his *fūtei* as "various shadings and fragrances"; Nose, 1:395–396.
43. *Kakyō*, NSTS, 103. "Many items" is my translation of *monokazu*, which may mean something closer to "the given number of items," i.e., an entire grouping of items comprising some kind of set. It may also mean an "abundance of items." Zeami does not specify what items he means. The annotations in NKBT 65, SNKBZ 88, and the modern translation in Nose take this to refer to the abundant number of plays that the superb performer has mastered. NKBT 65, 431; SNBZ 88, 326; Nose, 1:395. NSTS glosses it as "abundance of artistic expression *(geigyoku)* mastered"; NSTS, 103. Tanaka broadens the scope to all manner of pieces and techniques spanning dance, chant, and *monomane*; Tanaka, 150. Indeed, Zeami uses *monokazu* quite often to refer globally to techniques and materials external to the learner that he must absorb as part of the process of training.
44. Nose, 1:396.
45. NSTS, 103; SNKBZ 88, 326; Tanaka, 150.
46. *Kakyō*, NSTS, 103.
47. Pilgrim discusses the *kokoro* of the art as Zeami depicts it in his treatises as embracing four aspects: 1) "The *kokoro* of emotion and feeling"; 2) "The *kokoro* of the

knowing, conscious, intending self"; 3) "The *kokoro* of the unconscious, void, spontaneous, instinctual, *a priori* mind"; and 4) "The all-encompassing, deep, and spiritual *kokoro.*" The reader is referred to Richard B. Pilgrim, "Some Aspects of *Kokoro* in Zeami," *Monumenta Nipponica* 24.4 (1969): 393–401.

48. *Kaden*, NSTS, 37 and 56.

49. *Kakyō*, NSTS, 100.

50. Ibid.

51. Ibid., 95.

52. Both the Nose and Tanaka glosses for this term stay close to its original meaning, "the enlightened Buddhist mind"; NSTS and SNKBZ 88 gloss it more metaphorically as a "firmly established level of artistry." NKBT 65 combines the two meanings as having a level of artistry firmly established and resulting from an enlightened mind. However, the appendix of the same speculates that Zeami is using the term metaphorically. Nose, 1:350; Tanaka, 136; NSTS, 94; SNKBZ 88, 313; NKBT 65, 422 and 557.

53. Tanaka's gloss of this sentence differs some. Whereas all the other annotations consulted interpret *zuifū* as "innate ability," Tanaka glosses it as "superb artistic form (*sugureta geitai*)" and states that such form is predicated on the actor having an enlightened mind; Tanaka, 136. Though Zeami does not say this explicitly, I agree with Tanaka that this is his gist. The term *zuifū* is believed to have been coined by Zeami; Nose, 1:351.

54. *Kakyō*, NSTS, 103.

55. Ibid.

56. Shinkei, *Sasamegoto*, NKBT 66, 175.

57. Ibid.

58. Ramirez-Christensen, *Heart's Flower*, 194.

59. *Yūgaku shudōfū ken*, NSTS, 166.

60. Ibid. It is interesting that Heidegger employs a similar image of snow to invoke ineffability: "When in the winter nights snowstorms tear at the cabin and one morning the landscape is hushed in its blanket of snow . . . Thinking's saying would be stilled in its being only by becoming unable to say that which must remain unspoken." Martin Heidegger, *Poetry, Language, Thought*, trans. Alfred Hofstadter (New York: Harper and Row, 1975), 56. Quoted in Chang Chung-yuan, trans., with introduction and commentaries, *Tao: A New Way of Thinking* (New York: Harper & Row, 1975), xxi–xxii.

61. Interpreting the meaning of the last clause in this statement is a challenge. "Impression of no-mind" is my translation of *mukan no kan*, lit. "impression (or feeling) of no-impression/no-feeling." NSTS reads this as synonymous with *mushin no kan*, or "impression/feeling of no-mind." On the other hand, Nose and NKBT 65 conclude that the term refers to a wondrous impression that eludes words. Nose also speculates that such a wondrous impression (*myō*) and the impression of *mushin* are one

and the same. Annotators also diverge on who the subject of the "detached seeing" might be. For Nose, "detached seeing" refers to the spectator's vantage point, from which he experiences an impression of the performer as wondrous. On the other hand, both NSTS and NKBZ 65 argue that in this case it is the actor who enjoys a detached perspective—detached from his own conscious awareness of self. The sense of such detachment, or egolessness, emerges in the actor's performance, becoming discernible to the audience. Nose, 1:532; NSTS, 166; NKBT 65, 445.

62. *Kyūi*, NSTS, 176.
63. Gadjin M. Nagao, *Mādhyamika and Yogācāra, A Study of Mahayana Philosophies: Collected Papers of G. M. Nagao*, ed. and trans. L. S. Kawamura with G. M. Nagao (Albany: State University of New York Press, 1991), 211.
64. Verse eighteen from the twenty-fourth chapter of the *Middle Treatise (Zhong-lun)*, in *Taishō shinshū daizōkyō* 30.33b11–12, no. 1564. I have quoted the English translation provided by Neal Donner and Daniel B. Stevenson, ed. and trans., in *The Great Calming and Contemplation: A Study and Annotated Translation of the First Chapter of Chih'i's Mo-ho chih-kuan* (Honolulu: University of Hawai'i Press, 1993), 11. The bracketed portion of the translation was inserted by Donner and Stevenson.
65. Zeami draws an explicit link between the Middle Way, the wondrous, and Tendai teachings in his treatise *Goi*; NSTS, 170. He links the wondrous with Tendai precepts in *Yūgaku shudōfū ken* as well; NSTS, 166. Both of these undated treatises are believed to have been written late in Zeami's career.
66. Recorded and rearranged by disciple Guan-ding. *Japanese-English Buddhist Dictionary*, rev. ed. (Tokyo: Daitō Shuppansha, 1991), 215.
67. Donner and Stevenson observe in their introductory commentary to their English translation of the *Mo-ho chi-kuan* (pinyin *Mohe zhi guan*) that the "three truths" system "introduces the middle truth as a third, absolute truth that transcends and unifies the conventional and ultimate truths." Donner and Stevenson, ed. and trans., *Great Calming and Contemplation*, 12. They also point out that modern scholars agree that Nāgārjuna had two truths in mind, the ultimate and the conventional truths. Zhiyi and other Tiantai thinkers saw Nāgārjuna's statement as containing three truths: the ultimate, the conventional, and the middle. Ibid., 11.
68. Nichiren Shoshu International Center, ed., *A Dictionary of Buddhist Terms and Concepts*, 2nd printing (Tokyo: Nichiren Shoshu International Center), 65.
69. Donner and Stevenson, ed. and trans., *Great Calming and Contemplation*, 12.
70. Ibid.
71. Ibid.
72. Jacqueline I. Stone, *Original Enlightenment and the Transformation of Medieval Japanese Buddhism*. Studies in East Asian Buddhism 12, Kuroda Institute (Honolulu: University of Hawai'i Press, 1999), 120.
73. Kawamura Yoshiteru, ed., *Tendaigaku jiten* (Tokyo: Kokusho Kankōkai, 1990), 317.
74. Stone, *Original Enlightenment*, 8.

75. Nagao, *Mādhyamika and Yogācāra*, 191.
76. The doctrine of the Middle Way as articulated in the Mādhyamika Buddhism propounded by Nāgārjuna and followers evolves into what is known in Japan as the Sanron, or Three-Treatises philosophy. Chang provides a useful overview of the evolution of the philosophy of the Middle Way in his introduction to *Original Teachings of Ch'an Buddhism Selected from* The Transmission of the Lamp (New York: Pantheon Books, 1969), 3–38.
77. Stone, *Original Enlightenment*, 178.
78. Ibid. The full title given is *Ichijō shō (Eshin-ryū naishō sōjō hōmon shū)*.
79. Stone, *Original Enlightenment*, 179. Stone slightly modified the English translation of the passage attributed to Chih'i, which she cites from Wm. Theodore de Bary et al., eds., *Sources of Chinese Tradition* (New York: Columbia University Press, 1960), 1:328. The original passage is found in *Taishō shinshū daizōkyō* 46:54a9–10, a13–18 in Takakusu Junjirō et al., eds., 85 vols. (Tokyo: Taishō Issaikyō Kankōkai, 1924–1934).
80. For instance, *myō* is glossed as *fukashigi*, along with Sanskrit readings *su, sat, mañju*, and *sūksma* in *Sōgō bukkyō daijiten*, (Comprehensive dictionary on Buddhism), ed. Sōgō bukkyō daijiten henshū iinkai (Kyoto: Hōzōkan, 1987), 2:1372.
81. *Kyūi*, NSTS, 176. In his treatise *Goi*, Zeami states the following concerning what he means by "*i*" (mind, intent): "*I* refers to manifesting one's inner mindfulness outwardly, invoking an impression of unsurpassed wonder *(shimyō)*"; NSTS, 170–171.
82. *Kakyō*, NSTS, 101.
83. *Goi*, NSTS, 170.
84. I have omitted a sentence prior to this one in which Zeami likens this preconscious awareness to the emotion denoted by the thirty-first hexagram *hsien* (咸) in the *Yijing* (*I Ching*, Book of changes). In that context, it refers to "a time when Natural Influences prevail in Forming Relationships without Designs or Schemes"; Barry R. Trosper and Gin-hua Leu (Ken C. Yang, illus.), I Ching: *The Illustrated Primer* (San Jose: KGI Publications, 1986), 143. The note in NSTS points out that here Zeami construes the hexagram to refer to the state of *mushin*, perhaps influenced by neo-Confucian thought; NSTS, 95. Zeami further describes this state of mind as pure, or unadulterated *(konzenu)*; the NSTS annotation points out that in the later treatise *Shugyoku tokuka*, Zeami comes to employ the term *tae naru* (wondrous, exquisite) to describe this state; ibid. According to Kōsai Tsutomu, the locus classicus for *konzenu* is the Sōtō Zen work by the priest Gasan Jōseki titled *San'un kaigetsu* (Clouds on the mountain, moonlight on the sea); *Zeami shinkō* (Tokyo: Wan'ya Shoten, 1962), 25.
85. *Kakyō*, NSTS, 95–96.
86. Ibid., 96; Tanaka, 137; Nose, 1:351; NKBT 65, 423; SNKBZ 88, 314.
87. Thomas P. Kasulis, *Zen Action Zen Person* (Honolulu: University of Hawai'i Press, 1981), 47.

88. Ibid.

89. Ibid., 47–48.

90. According to a concordance done by Nakamura Itaru, *Zeami densho yōgo sakuin*, Kasama Sakuin Sōkan 86 (Tokyo: Kasama Shoin, 1985), 346. *Mushin* occurs in the following treatises.

> ◆ *Kakyō* (1424): *mushin* (2x); *mushin no kan* (1x); *mushin mufū* (1x)
> ◆ *Fūgyokushū* (undated): *mushin* (1x)
> ◆ *Kyūi* (undated): *mushin* (1x)
> ◆ *Shūgyoku tokuka* (1428): *mushin* (3x); *mushin no kan* (4x); *mushinkan* (2x)

91. Zeami's term for "ease of mind" *(anshin)* is open to more than one interpretation. "*Shin*" clearly denotes "mind," but the meaning of "*an*" is disputed. The NSTS, Nose, NKBT 65, and SNKBZ 88 annotations take the position that it denotes a state of mind in which the actor is contemplating how to perform effectively. This reading is based on the notion that Zeami allotted a character for "*an*" that did not reflect his intended meaning. He chose to write it with a character meaning "ease" or "serenity." However, these annotators concur that Zeami's intended meaning was "plan" or "scheme," the character for which is also pronounced "*an*." Tanaka's interpretation takes Zeami's allocation more literally, glossing *anshin* as a "calm, unfettered [state of] mind." My own translation adheres more closely to Tanaka's interpretation. NSTS, 100; Nose, 1:377; NKBT 65, 562; SNKBZ 88, 321; Tanaka, 144.

92. The term for "spiritual force [capable of arousing feeling]" is *kanriki*. NSTS holds that it refers to the "effects produced by one's inner mindfulness" *(naishin no kan no kōka)*; NSTS, 100. This is in agreement with the NKBT 65 note, but that earlier source adds the gloss *shinriki*, "power of the heart/mind"; NKBT 65, 428. Tanaka glosses the phrase as "workings of the mind in its intensity" *(kinchō shita kokoro no hataraki)*; Tanaka, 145. Nose points out that Zeami normally uses the graph "*kan*" when he is referring to feeling quality that involves the audience. He concurs that *shinriki*, "power of the heart/mind" is involved here, but as it impresses the audience; Nose, 1:378. I am in agreement with Nose's interpretation.

93. *Kakyō*, NSTS, 100.

94. Bruno Petzold, with Shinshō Hanayama, *The Classification of Buddhism, Bukkyō kyōhan*, ed. Shohei Ichimura (Wiesbaden, Germany: Otto Harrassowitz, 1995), 299. Petzold's characterization continues, "[the Buddha] vested this idea in the formula of 'the five Skandhas or Aggregates' (i.e. body, sensation, conception, volitional and dispositional forces, and consciousness) that do not constitute any ego" (299). We will be returning to this concept of the Aggregates at the end of this chapter.

95. *Shūgyoku tokuka*, NSTS, 190. Whereas NSTS annotators hold that *honmu myōka* alludes to "the wondrous flower that has reached [the level of] true nothingness

(*makoto no mu*)," NKBZ 65 annotates the phrase as "the wondrous flower among wondrous flowers; the original wondrous flower." NSTS, 190; NKBT 65, 460.

96. Chang, trans., *Original Teachings of Ch'an Buddhism*, 5.

97. Ibid., 5–6.

98. Chang, trans., *Tao: A New Way of Thinking*, 97. Chang traces the meaning of Tē (pinyin *de;* Jpn. *toku*) and concludes that in this context it is close to "Tao" in meaning (97).

99. Ibid.

100. Ibid., 42.

101. Ibid., 102.

102. Kasulis, *Zen Action Zen Person*, 36.

103. Ibid, 32. Kasulis further points out that the pairing of the terms "Being" and "Nonbeing" has the effect of relativizing the term and concludes,

> Only by understanding Nonbeing as *both* absolute and relative can we understand how it is the source of Being. If we think of Nonbeing only in its relative sense, it is the mere contrary of Being. If we think of it only in its absolute sense, it is self-contained and ineffable. (35)

104. *Shūgyoku tokuka*, NSTS, 191.

105. Ibid.

106. Michiko Yusa, "*Riken no Ken:* Zeami's Theory of Acting and Theatrical Appreciation," *Monumenta Nipponica* 42.3 (1987): 340.

107. Stone, *Original Enlightenment*, 30.

108. *Kakyō*, NSTS, 100.

109. *Kaden*, NSTS, 35.

110. *Sarugaku dangi*, NSTS, 275.

111. Nakamura Yoshihiko, Okami Masao, and Itakura Atsuyoshi, eds., *Kadokawa kogo daijiten* (Tokyo: Kadokawa Shoten, 1982), 278. The term translated here as "mind" is *shinshō*.

112. *Japanese-English Buddhist Dictionary*, 11.

113. Richard H. Robinson, *The Buddhist Religion* (Belmont, Calif.: Dickenson Publishing Company, 1970), 71.

114. Ibid.

115. Nearman's discussion of Hossō ideas on *isshin* is from "*Kakyō*, Zeami's Fundamental Principles of Acting, Part 2," *Monumenta Nipponica* 37.4 (1982): 459, 460–496. (The second of three installments.) Nearman's note at the bottom of page 492 states that his account of Hossō thought is based on the twelfth-century text *Hossō nikan shō* (A summary of Hossō [thought] in two volumes) by Ryōhen.

116. Based on *A Dictionary of Buddhist Terms and Concepts*, 313–314.

117. Nearman, "Zeami's Fundamental Principles of Acting," pt. 2, 492.

118. Nearman is not alone in detecting affinities with Hossō doctrine and images. For instance, see Okano Moriya, *Nō to yuishiki* (Tokyo: Seidosha, 1994).
119. Petzold, *Classification of Buddhism*, 345.
120. Nearman, "Zeami's Fundamental Principles of Acting," pt. 2, 493.
121. Ibid.
122. Ibid., 494.
123. Ibid.
124. Ibid., 492.
125. Okano Moriya has written a book exploring connections between the noh of Kan'ami and Zeami and Hossō philosophy: *Nō to yuishiki*.
126. Robinson, *Buddhist Religion*, 91.
127. The *Vimalakīrti-nirdeśa-sūtra* is a commonly cited source on metaphors of impermanence. The holy man Vimalakirti says, "A bodhisattva should regard all living beings as a wise man regards the reflection of the moon in water or as magicians regard men created by magic. He should regard them as being like a face in a mirror; like the water of a mirage; like the sound of an echo; like a mass of clouds in the sky; like the previous moment of a ball of foam; like the appearance and disappearance of a bubble of water; like the core of a plantain tree; like a flash of lightning . . . like a sprout from a rotten seed." Robert A. F. Thurman, trans., *The Holy Teaching of Vimalakirti: A Mahayana Scripture* (University Park: Penn State University Press, 1976), 57.
128. Paul Demiéville, "The Mirror of the Mind," in Peter N. Gregory, ed., *Sudden and Gradual Approaches to Enlightenment in Chinese Thought*. Kuroda Institute Studies in East Asian Buddhism 5 (Honolulu: University of Hawai'i Press, 1987), 23.
129. Quoted in ibid., 18. Quoted from Burton Watson, trans., *The Complete Works of Chuang Tzu* (New York: Columbia University Press, 1968), 97.
130. The notion of "one mind" *(isshin)* is integral to the beliefs and practices of other Buddhist sects as well. As we have seen, *isshin* is important to one of the most fundamental meditational practices in Tendai, *isshin sangan* (the threefold contemplation in a single mind), first taught by the Chinese Tiantai patriarch Zhiyi. In the Kegon school of Buddhism, the "one mind *(isshin)*" refers to one manifestation of the cosmic mind. For a discussion of Kegon doctrine in relation to the critical writings of Zeami's son-in-law, Konparu Zenchiku, see Thornhill, *Six Circles, One Dewdrop*, 92–98. It is likely that Zeami, too, was familiar with Kegon usages of the term.
131. For a compendium of Zen-related usages and references in Zeami's critical writings, see Tai Shōnosuke, *Chūsei geinō no kenkyū* (Tokyo: Ōfūsha, 1976), 59–138. Tai points out the seeming correlation between Zeami's proliferation of Zen-related usages and his taking of the tonsure on 59–60.
132. Frank Hoff, "Seeing and Being Seen: The Mirror of Performance," in James H. Sanford, William R. LaFleur, and Masatoshi Nagatomi, eds., *Flowing Traces:*

Buddhism in the Literary and Visual Arts of Japan (Princeton, N.J.: Princeton University Press, 1992), 131.

Nishio Minoru makes a similar point in his study when contrasting Zeami and his son-in-law Zenchiku's use of Buddhist references in their respective treatises: "In Zeami's treatises, Buddhism, more specifically a Zen-like knack or touch, is rather striking. But none of these is any more than a means to an end, whether as the logic of his personal artistic transmissions, or employed as categories. With Zenchiku's transmissions, however, Buddhist thought takes center stage, and the art is then elucidated in those terms." Nishio, *Dōgen to Zeami* (Tokyo: Iwanami Shoten, 1965), 291. This remark by Nishio is emblematic of the ambiguities involved in attributing Buddhist influence to Zeami. Obviously that influence is considerable, or Nishio would not have written a book that links Zeami with Dōgen, founder of the Sōtō Zen sect in Japan.

Chapter 7. Mind and Technique: The Two Modes in Training

1. *Kaden*, NSTS, 37 and 56.
2. Ibid., 37.
3. Ibid., 56.
4. Nishio Minoru, "Zeami no geijutsuron no tokushitsu to Dōgen no eikyō," in Kawamura Kōdō and Ishikawa Rikizan, eds., *Dōgen zenshi to Sōtōshū*, Nihon Bukkyōshū Shi Ronshū 8 (Tokyo: Yoshikawa Kōbunkan, 1985), 344–345.
5. Zeami introduces this adage initially in Chapter 3 of *Kaden*, which is dated 1400. He makes a second reference to it in chapter 7 of *Kaden*; it is a quotation of the initial usage with a brief reiteration of its import. NSTS, 37 and 56.
6. *Kaden*, NSTS, 34.
7. *Shikadō*, NSTS, 114.
8. Ibid. The NKBT 65 annotation differs from all the others consulted on the meaning of the term *geiriki*, translated here as "innate artistic potential." NKBT 65 holds that *geiriki* refers to "artistic skill level that has previously been acquired"; NKBT 65, 402.
9. *Kakyō*, NSTS, 94. The Nihon no Meicho edition, which contains a modern Japanese translation of *Shikadō*, offers a still different reading, interpreting *sono mono ni naru koto* to mean that the actor becomes one with his role (*jiko to yaku to ga ittai to natte*); Yamazaki Masakazu, ed., *Zeami*, Nihon no Meicho 18 (Tokyo: Chūō Kōronsha, 1977), 205.
10. Tanaka, 104; NKBT 65, 402; Nose, 1:446.
11. *Shikadō*, NSTS, 116.
12. Shigenori Nagatomo, "Zeami's Conception of Freedom," *Philosophy East and West* 31.4 (1981): 404.
13. Zeami cites the third article of the fifth book of *The Analects of Confucius* as his source for this metaphor of a vessel. One of the disciples of Confucius asks him how he should be characterized, and Confucius compares him to a sacred vessel. Zeami

also cites two Confucian commentaries for the passage. One of those, by Kong An Guo (d. ca. 100 B.C.E.), instructs us that characterizing this man as a "vessel" *(ki)* is a reference to him being "clever" or "skillful" *(kiyō)*. This interpretation would seem to be based on the fact that one of the two characters used to write *kiyō* is the same "vessel" *(ki)* character. The original passage from the *Analects* may be found in James Legge, *Confucius:* Confucian Analects, The Great Learning *and* The Doctrine of the Mean. Repub. 2nd rev. ed. (New York: Dover, 1971), 173.

14. *Yūgaku shudōfū ken,* NSTS, 162–163. Annotators' opinions divide somewhat on the meaning of *yūgaku,* translated here as "musical entertainment." The NSTS annotation glosses it with the phrase "in the entirety of *sarugaku,* which has musical entertainment as its objective." NKBT treats *yūgaku* as a synecdoche for *sarugaku.* NSTS, p. 163; NKBT 65, 441. As both editions point out, Zeami's usage of *yūgaku* in his critical writings includes instances in which its use as such a synecdoche is clearly intended. NSTS, 457–458; NKBT 65, 559–560. Nose's modern translation leaves the term as is. Nose, 1:514. Although I have opted for the more literal translation of the term, it is likely that Zeami is actually referring to his own art of *sarugaku* here.

15. *Yūgaku shudōfū ken,* NKBT 65, 440.

16. "What he can do will have come together" is a translation for *monokazu soroite. Monokazu,* lit. "number of items," is cryptic. NSTS and NKBT 65 offer no annotation. Nose holds that in this context it refers to the various elements such as the chanting, dancing, and vigorous moves, which start to come together in maturity. When the actor is still preadolescent, it is likely that his dancing may have matured more quickly than his chanting or his mimetic techniques, for instance. As he approaches adulthood, he may be expected to enjoy a skill level at which inadequacies have been erased and all skills are on the same par. Nose, 1:515–516.

17. *Yūgaku shudōfū ken,* NSTS, 163.

18. Ibid., 164. Zeami borrows his image of seedlings from the twenty-first section of the ninth book of *The Analects of Confucius:* "The Master said, 'There are cases in which the blade springs, but the plant does not go on to flower! There are cases where it flowers, but no fruit is subsequently produced!' " Legge, *Confucius,* 223. As Hare has noted, Zeami by no means restricted his allusions to one religious tradition: "Commentators have frequently and plausibly demonstrated the presence of an element of Zen in these ideas, but there are other elements from the intellectual traditions of East Asia that may have an equally important share in such thought." Hare illustrates his statement with reference to the Confucian analects, the *Heart Sutra,* and the *Classic of Poetry.* Hare, *Zeami's Style,* 233.

19. What the "established style" *(jōfū)* refers to is not spelled out here. Whereas Nose and NKBT 65 simply indicate that it refers to the foundational or fundamental style, NSTS posits that it refers to the foundational style of the *santai* (three styles: the old person, the woman, and the warrior). Nose, 1:525; NKBT 65, 443; NSTS, 164.

I believe that the referent for *jōfū* is the two modes and three styles. In *Shikadō*, Zeami employs the character *"jō"* (translated above as "established") similarly in the compound *jōi honpū chitai*, glossed in the NSTS annotation as the "original foundational style that serves as the standard for assuring a correct level of artistry" (*tadashii gei'i o kakuritsu suru kiso to naru kihonteki hontai*). In the passage in question in *Shikadō*, Zeami is defining the two modes and three styles as constituents of this original foundational style; NSTS, 113.

20. *Yūgaku shudōfū ken*, NSTS, 164.
21. "Established style": see note 19.
22. The Tang priest Xuanzang's (Jpn. Genjō; 660–664) translation of *Prajñā-pāramitā-hṛdaya-sūtra* (Jpn. *Hannya haramitta shin-gyō*, Sutra of the Heart of Wisdom [*Heart Sutra*]). With the exception of the Amidist schools, this sutra has been treated with importance in almost all Japanese Buddhist sects, the frequent subject of exegesis and recitation. Nakamura Hajime and Kino Kazuyoshi, eds., *Hannya shingyō, Kongō Hannya kyō*, Iwanami Bunko 360 (Tokyo: Iwanami, 1960), 162.
23. Chang, *Original Teachings of Ch'an Buddhism*, 4.
24. *Yūgaku shudōfū ken*, NSTS, 165. The Sanskrit term for "voidness" (*kū*) is *śūnyatā*. The *Japanese-English Buddhist Dictionary* gives "Sunyata is identical with matter" as a translation for *Kū soku ze shiki* and states, "*Śūnyatā* is not nothingness, as is sometimes misunderstood." Rather, "it is in no way different from the matter which constitutes our world." *Japanese-English Buddhist Dictionary*, 210.
25. *Yūgaku shudōfū ken*, NSTS, 165.
26. Ibid.
27. Pilgrim, "Some Aspects of *Kokoro* in Zeami," 397.
28. I have based this on Yamazaki's interpretation. Yamazaki Masakazu, ed. and trans., *Zeami*, Nihon no Meicho 10, 2nd ed. (Tokyo: Chūō Kōronsha, 1969), 228. Nearman avoids the notion of beauty in his translation of the rubric for this level: "The Mark of Surface Design." He argues that it promotes the misleading impression that Zeami is more "concerned with aesthetic appreciation of performance than with the practice of acting." Mark J. Nearman, "Zeami's *Kyūi*: A Pedagogical Guide for Teachers of Acting," *Monumenta Nipponica* 33.3 (autumn 1978): 314, note 51. However, I believe that the term is appropriate here because one function of the two modes is to amplify the physical grace of a person.
29. *Kyūi*, NSTS, 175. One translation of the full statement from the *Dao de jing* reads, "The Tao [Dao] that can be spoken of is not the Tao itself. The name that can be given is not the name itself." Quoted from Kasulis, *Zen Action Zen Person*, 30. Kasulis explains, "This passage points to an ineffable ground of all existence—to that which eludes our grasp as soon as we point it out or give it a name." The Chinese term for "Tao itself" is *chang dao*; the *chang* signifies permanence and constancy. The translation that Kasulis quotes is from Chang, trans., *Tao: A New Way of Thinking*.
30. *Kyūi*, NSTS, 175.

31. The NSTS exegesis concludes that the original meaning of the lines is lost in Zeami's usage. Whereas the "true way" seems to correspond to the trajectory through the middle levels into the upper ones, "that which is thought to be the way" seems to correspond to the bottom three levels. However, Zeami's exegesis of the original adage states that after having "trod the path of the true way," then one should come to understand that which is thought to be the way. Since the bottommost three levels are clearly undesirable in Zeami's mind, the annotators conclude that "[t]he *Tao* that cannot be spoken of" cannot correspond to the bottom levels after all. Finally, they surmise that "[t]he *Tao* that cannot be spoken of" must refer to "some phase coming after, which constitutes a higher level." NSTS, 473, appendix note 96.

    The NKBT annotation, on the other hand, surmises that "the true way" refers to the training process that begins with the acquisition of the two modes; "that which is thought" to be the way to the unorthodox style of the bottom three levels. NKBT 65, 561, *Kyūi* appendix note 5.

32. Nose, 1:559–560. Nose's interpretation of the second "Way," the one that can be spoken of, diverges considerably from those of the other annotators. First, about the "True Way" (*tsune no michi*), he says, "The True Way has standards, rules, norms. To absolutely follow those standards or norms in the proper order; to accumulate expertise by studying and training in compliance with those specifications; and, finally, to emerge from these norms and move away from them—progressing [in this way] to a realm of absolute freedom is a training method characteristically East Asian." Then he identifies the "Way that can be spoken of" as something that the training actor will link up with not long after he has embarked on the "True Way," whereupon he will realize that the two Ways are in accord. Nose does not explain further how he gets this interpretation. It is interesting that he mentions a dynamic of acquiring techniques only to shed them as being typically East Asian. Although this statement may be criticized by readers today as a gross overgeneralization, it is a just description of the crux of Zeami's training program. Nose, 1:560.

33. NSTS, 175.

34. Rimer and Yamazaki, trans., *On the Art of the Nō Drama*, 122. Nearman interprets the reference to mean that the phenomenal should not be confused with the underlying principle of the universe, but Zeami is suggesting that one may reach the latter through the former. Nearman, "Zeami's *Kyūi*," 314, note 52.

35. This is a ten-fascicle collection of koans with annotations. Hereafter referred to as *Hekigan roku*. The phrase appears in Case no. 53 and may be found in Iriya Yoshitaka et al., eds., *Hekigan roku*, Iwanami Bunko 720 (Tokyo: Iwanami, 1994), 2:212. The anecdote concerns a Zen master who speaks exhaustively to a disciple, but the disciple still does not understand. For an English translation with commentary, see Thomas Cleary, *Secrets of the Blue Cliff Record: Zen Comments by Hakuin and Tenkei* (Boston: Shambhala, 2000), 176–178. Also see Nearman's exegesis of the *Hekigan roku* anecdote in "Zeami's *Kyūi*," 315, note 55.

36. NSTS, 175; Tanaka, 166; Nose, 1:559.
37. *Kyūi*, NSTS, 174.
38. Ibid. The source of the first metaphor is unknown, although the annotators assume some Zen Buddhist source. One phrase of the second statement, "The bright sun alone in the blue sky" (*seitenhakujitsu no itten*), appears in Case no. 15 of *Hekigan roku*; Iriya Yoshitaka et al., eds., *Hekigan roku*, Iwanami Bunko 670 (Tokyo: Iwanami, 1992), 1:212.
39. Translation by Chang in *Original Teachings of Ch'an Buddhism*, 47. The phrase "snow in a silver bowl" is also alluded to in Case no. 13 of *Hekigan roku*, 1:194; Cleary, *Secrets of the Blue Cliff Record*, 44–46.
40. Thomas Cleary, trans., *Transmission of Light: Zen in the Art of Enlightenment by Zen Master Keizan* (San Francisco: North Point Press, 1990), 117.
41. *Kyūi*, NSTS, 174.
42. Tanaka, 166.
43. *Kyūi*, NSTS, 176.
44. Ibid., 174.
45. *Kyūi*, NKBT 65, 450. The annotation also points out that this concept is basic to Buddhism teachings in general, although there are different nuances depending on the sect. Nose is of the opinion that the Tendai conception corresponds to Zeami's usage here. He says that it is based on the Tendai idea of the "three truths" (*santai*) and echoes the Tendai teaching (see chap. 6). In Nose's assessment of it, "The middle way is neither provisionally real nor non-substantial. Then again, it is provisionally real and also non-substantial." This is supposed to be suggestive of the state of *myō*, the wondrous, he adds. Nose, 1:575–576.

    Nose also draws the analogy between the Buddhist terms *u* (provisionally real) and *mu* (nonsubstantial), and Zeami's terms, *umon* (ornamented) and *mumon* (unornamented). Nose, 1:576.
46. *Kyūi*, NSTS, 176; Tanaka, 169; Nose, 1:576.
47. I have followed the NSTS annotation for "mood and style of the vocal music" (*ongyoku no kakari, fūtei*). The annotation glosses *kakari* as *omomuki* and *fūtei* as *yōshiki*. NSTS, 159. Nose, on the other hand, treats the two words as synonymous, both meaning "mood" or "atmosphere" (*fūshu*). Nose, 2:123.
48. My translation of *ku o irodorite* as "colorful phrasing" follows the gist of Nose's gloss for the phrase: *ku utsuri ya moji utsuri no hanayaka ni kikoeru koto* (transitions within and between phrases sounding colorful); Nose, 2:124. NSTS interprets *ku o irodorite* as *ku utsuri nado no henka o ōku shite* (give the phrasing and such lots of variety).
49. For more on *ritsu* and *ryo* musical scales, see Rimer and Yamazaki, trans., *On the Art of the Nō Drama*, 77–78, note 2.
50. *Fūgyoku shū*, NSTS, 159–160. This treatise is undated. Omote points out that a section of this document that discusses how to affix the musical modulation to the chanted phrases concludes with, "Items concerning the fixing of the modulation

appear in a separate writing." He surmises that this is a reference to Zeami's treatise *Fushizuke shidai*, also undated. (NSTS, 561. Original text in *Fūgyoku shū*, NSTS, 158.) Passages from *Fūgyoku shū* are referred to in *Sarugaku dangi*, so we know *Fūgyoku shū* was written prior to 1430.

51. *Hekigan roku*, 1:60. It is available in English in Cleary, trans., *Secrets of the Blue Cliff Record*, 8–9.

52. Cleary, trans., *Secrets of the Blue Cliff Record*, 9.

53. See chap. 6, note 103.

54. *Sarugaku dangi*, NSTS, 285.

55. Kawamura Yoshiteru, ed., *Tendaigaku jiten*, 317. *Japanese-English Buddhist Dictionary*, 260.

56. According to Nose, this phrase occurs in Zen Buddhist sources in circulation in medieval Kyoto. He mentions a thirteenth-century sutra titled *Chūshinkyō* (Sutra of commentary on mind) and the commentary titled *Muchū mondō* (Dreamlike dialogues) by the Rinzai Zen priest Musō Soseki (1275–1351). The sun's brightness in this aphorism refers to the revelation of the primal ground of the mind. For more details, see Nose, 1:549–550; and Nearman, "Zeami's *Kyūi*," 323–324, note 90.

57. *Kyūi*, NSTS, 174.

58. Zeami uses the term *riken* (detached seeing) in contradistinction to the term *gaken* (subjective seeing) in his writings. *Riken* also appears in the compound *riken no ken*, lit. "vision of detached seeing." Tanaka explains that this is "to truly view things objectively, vision based on [a condition of] so-called *mushin*" (Tanaka, 109). Whereas in some instances Zeami's usage seems to apply to objective seeing on the part of the audience, in other instances the term is clearly used to refer to the actor's ability to see himself as the audience members see him. Nagatomo notes that "detached seeing" is contrasted with "ego's seeing," and "hence it is an elimination of the ego-consciousness." Movements become "spontaneous, independent of the striving consciousness of the actor." Shigenori Nagatomo, "Zeami's Conception of Freedom," *Philosophy East and West* 31.4 (1981): 410–11. This interpretation, like the NSTS gloss, seems apt for this particular usage of the term.

　　Both the Nose and Tanaka annotations disagree somewhat with the NSTS note. Nose sees *riken* as referring to the image of the performer as seen through the eyes of the spectators. Tanaka interprets the term as referring to a "peerless visional affect that is removed from the average visional affect." NSTS, 174; Nose, 1:550; Tanaka, 165.

59. *Kakyō*, NSTS, 101.

60. Ibid.

61. NSTS, 101; NKBT 65, 429.

62. NSTS, 101; NKBT 65, 429; SNKBZ 88, 323; Tanaka, 147.

63. *Sandō*, NSTS, 143.

64. *Yūgaku shūdōfū ken*, NSTS, 165.

65. *Fūgyoku shū*, NSTS, 160.
66. For a discussion of *hifū* and *zefū*, see *Shikadō*, NSTS, 114–115. The opening section of *Shikadō* is devoted to the centrality of the *nikyoku santai*; NSTS, 112–113.
67. Konishi Jin'ichi, *Nōgakuron kenkyū*, Hanawa Sensho 10, 2nd ed. (Tokyo: Hanawa Shobō, 1964), 221.
68. *Kakyō*, NSTS, 101.
69. *Go ongyoku jōjō*, NSTS, 202.
70. Tanaka interprets the term *saidō* less specifically as a descriptive term for techniques that lack nimble execution because of the actor's rough, leaden style; Tanaka, 168.
71. *Kyūi*, NSTS, 175.
72. Hsun Ch'ing, *The Works of Hsüntze*, trans. Homer H. Dubs (London: Arthur Probsthain, 1928), 35.
73. Nearman, "Zeami's *Kyūi*," 309. Nearman's comments are based on what is known as the Yoshida manuscript (Yoshida *bon*). The whereabouts of Zeami's original manuscript are unknown, but scholars do not question that the Yoshida transcription is in the lineage of that document. Nearman's translation of the final sentence goes, "When performance lacks refining, it is coarse and dulled."
74. Shimen (lit. "stone gate") is a place-name, so I have chosen not to translate it here. The term in the title, *wen zi chan* (Jpn. *monji zen*, the written word and [Zen] meditation), refers to the idea that the written word can be a form of meditative practice.
75. *Kaden*, NSTS, 50.
76. Nose, 1:570.
77. *Kyūi*, NSTS, 175. The reference to hammer and sacred sword resembles a statement in Case no. 12 of *Hekigan roku*, 1:182; Cleary, trans., *Secrets of the Blue Cliff Record*, 41. See Nearman, "Zeami's *Kyūi*," 310–312, for more details.
78. *Kakyō*, NSTS, 103.
79. Tanaka, 167; Nearman, "Zeami's *Kyūi*," 312–313.
80. Nose, 1:570; Tanaka, 167; NSTS, 175.
81. *Kyūi*, NSTS, 176.
82. Tanaka, 169.
83. Nose, 1:580–582.
84. Rimer and Yamazaki, trans., *On the Art of the Nō Drama*, 124; for original, see NSTS, 176–177. The note in the English translation cites the source for the aphorism as "*Zheng dao ge* (Cheng-tao ke; Jpn. *Shōdōka* [The Song of Enlightenment]) by the Chinese priest Yongjia (Yung-chia; A.D. 665–713; Jpn. Yōka) of the Tiantai sect" (124). According to Nose, the aphorism was in familiar use. Nose, 1:579.
85. *Sarugaku dangi*, NSTS, 261–262.
86. Ibid., 262–263.
87. *Sarugaku dangi*, De Poorter, *Zeami's Talks*, 83; for the original, see NSTS, 263.
88. *Sarugaku dangi*, De Poorter, *Zeami's Talks*, 85; for the original, see NSTS, 264.

89. Konishi, *Nōgakuron kenkyū*, 218–220. Konishi credits Minemura Fumito with the initial insights that the *kyakurai* pattern has analogues in Teika's *Maigetsushō* and in *Guhishō* (Selection of my humble secrets; undated), a poetic commentary produced by one of Teika's successors. Konishi himself then points out the parallel with *Sasamegoto*.

According to Klein, the author of *Guhishō* is thought to have been sympathetic to the Nijō poetic faction and may have been Fujiwara no Tamezane (1266–1333); Klein, *Allegories of Desire*, 97.

90. Robert H. Brower, "Fujiwara Teika's *Maigetsushō*," *Monumenta Nipponica* 40.4 (winter 1985): 406. The poem that Brower proffers as an exemplar of this style is included in the *Man'yō shū* (4:503) as well as the *Shinkokin shū* (10:911).

Breaking off the reeds	*Kamikaze ya*
That grow along the beach at Ise	*Ise no hamaogi*
Of the Divine Wind,	*Orishikite*
Does he spread them for his traveler's bed	*Tabine ya suran*
There on the rough sea strand?	*Araki hamabe ni*

Brower, "Fujiwara Teika's *Maigetsushō*,"407, note 19. Brower's translation is based on the annotated edition of *Maigetsushō* in Hashimoto Fumio, Ariyoshi Tamotsu, and Fujihira Haruo, eds., *Karon shū*, Nihon Koten Bungaku Zenshū 50 (Tokyo: Shōgakukan, 1975).

91. Brower, "Fujiwara Teika's *Maigetsushō*," 406–407.

92. Klein, *Allegories of Desire*, 97. Klein estimates that *Sango ki* was written sometime between 1312 and 1317. It is thought to favor the Nijō strain of the Mikohidari poetic tradition. Ibid.

93. Sasaki Nobutsuna, ed., *Nihon kagaku taikei* (Tokyo: Kazama Shobō, 1956), 4:328–329.

94. Shinkei, *Sasamegoto*, in NKBT 66, 132–133.

95. Brower, "Fujiwara Teika's *Maigetsushō*," 412.

96. Ibid., 414.

97. *Shūgyoku tokuka*, NSTS, 190.

98. Both *Sandō* and *Shikadō* conclude by providing exemplars of the *yūgen* mood, for instance. In the former, it claims that the quality is key to successful performances past and present, and in *Shikadō*, a description of the quality is offered: "A swan with a flower in its bill, might this be the image of *yūgen*?" NSTS, 143 and 119. The term does not appear at all in *Kyūi*, although the related terms *yūfū* (style having *yūgen*) and *yūshi* (image having *yūgen*) are used to refer to the style of the wondrous flower and style of the profound flower, respectively. However, they are used as descriptive terms that are not central to his arguments in this treatise. NSTS, 174 and 176.

99. *Shūgyoku tokuka*, NSTS, 190.

100. Chang, *Original Teachings of Ch'an Buddhism*, 5.
101. Philip B. Yampolsky, *The Platform Sutra of the Sixth Patriarch* (N.Y.: Columbia University Press, 1967), 94 and 130.
102. Demiéville, "Mirror of the Mind," 15–16.
103. The gloss in the *Japanese-English Buddhist Dictionary* for *mu ichimotsu* (not a single thing) reads, "Nothing to cling to. A term used by Hui-nēng (Enō) to indicate the lack of substance in all things; it stems from the sūnyatā concept in the *Prajñāpā-ramitā-sūtra.*" *Japanese-English Buddhist Dictionary*, 225.
104. *Yūgaku shudōfū ken*, NSTS, 166. The original passage from the *Analects* may be found in Arthur Waley, trans. and annot., *The Analects of Confucius* (New York: Vintage Books, 1938), 107. Zeami further cites two Confucian commentators on the passage, Kong An Guo (d. ca. 100 B.C.E.) and Buozi (6 B.C.E.– A.D 65). The passage attributed to Kong An Guo instructs us that characterizing this man as a sacred "vessel" *(ki)* is a reference to him being clever or skillful *(kiyō)*, i.e., a man of capacity. This interpretation would seem to be based on the fact that one of the two characters used to write *kiyō* is the same "vessel" *(ki)* character. Zeami seems to have been influenced by this idea. Buozi's passage explains that a vessel made of jade is a sacred object worthy to be used for ritual offerings of food. According to the NSTS annotation, both of these commentaries trace to a Han-dynasty work titled *Lunyu ji jie* (Jpn. *Rongo shikkai*, Collected commentaries on the "Analects"), or a similar collection. NSTS, 166.
105. Nose, 1:540.
106. In a note to his *Kyūi* translation, Nearman suggests that Zeami's ideas on the nature of crystals "may have derived from Chinese sources as his terminology and its use are the same as that found in Chinese works on the subject." He directs the reader to Joseph Needham, *Science and Civilisation in China* (Cambridge: Cambridge University Press, 1962), 4:pt. 1, 100 and 114. On 114, it states, "There was a persistent theory in China, probably of Buddhist origin, that ice turned into rock-crystal after thousands of years." On 100 it is mentioned that "another Chinese name for rock-crystal seems to have been *huo ching* ('fire-essence')." Nearman, "Zeami's *Kyūi*," 321, note 80. NSTS cites a note in Konishi's *Zeami shū* that points out a similar idea in the treatise on *waka* composition titled *Nomori no kagami*. In a discussion of *honkadori* (technique of allusive variation), this text refers to a "crystal that can emit fire or water droplets when exposed to the sun or the moon," the gist being that a crystal may serve as the common medium for the production of two very contrastive elements. NSTS, 472, appendix note 93. The original passage is found in Sasaki, ed., *Nihon kagaku taikei*, 80.
107. "Seeds that flower into the many styles": this gloss is in concord with Nose's interpretation of *kashu* (whose original meaning is cryptic; lit. "blossoms and seeds"). NSTS and NKBT 65 interpret this to refer to parallel actions, flowers blossoming and seeds sprouting. Nose, 1:539; NSTS, 167; NKBT 65, 446.

108. "Quality of mind in which the expressive power of one's whole being is rooted" *(isshin kanriki no kokorone):* NSTS and NKBT 65 gloss *kokorone,* translated here as "quality of mind," as *kokoro no hataraki,* "the workings of the mind." NSTS, 167; NKBT 65, 446.
109. *Yūgaku shudōfū ken,* NSTS, 166.
110. NSTS and NKBT 65: "the workings of the mind, which is the root of one's power of artistic expression"; 446 and 167, respectively.
111. *Sarugaku dangi,* NSTS, 270.
112. Ibid.; Nose, 1:359; Tanaka, 190.
113. It is also possible to interpret the term *fūgetsu ennen* (translated as "elegant, life-prolonging art") as denoting the art of *sarugaku.* "Ennen" is also the proper name for an art that was performed at temples from the mid-Heian to the Muromachi period by monks or temple pages as entertainment after Buddhist masses. However, its appearance in the compound *fūgetsu ennen,* in which *fūgetsu* refers to the beauties of nature, makes it more probable that we are to read *ennen* in its literal meaning, "prolongation of life," and to interpret the entire phrase as a metonymy for *sarugaku;* NSTS, 427–428, appendix note 1.
114. *Anki shite,* "situate with ease": *"an"* is written with the character glossed here as "ease," as in "level of ease" *(an'i); "ki"* is written with the character for "vessel"; NSTS, 167.
115. Ibid.
116. *Kakyō,* NSTS, 100.
117. I interpret *bankyoku,* translated above as "myriad styles," to mean all the various styles of performance that the actor has available. It is possible to also gloss *bankyoku* as "myriad pieces," although none of the annotations consulted do so; ibid.
118. *Kiyō,* "have capacity": meaning clever or skillful; ibid. The first character in *kiyō (ki)* may also be read to mean "vessel" (Jpn. *utsuwa*) and is the same character used for vessel in the *Analects.* Zeami is punning on this usage in the classical canon.
119. *Shotei,* "diverse subject matter": probably a reference to the *monomane* subjects deemed fit for the *sarugaku* repertoire; ibid.
120. *Yūgaku shudōfū ken,* NSTS, 166.
121. Nose, 1:438–439.
122. Ibid., 539; NSTS, 167; NKBT 65, 445.
123. Nihon Daijiten Kankōkai, eds., *Nihon Kokugo daijiten* (Tokyo: Shōgakukan, 1975), 9:396.
124. Yasuo Yuasa, *The Body: Toward an Eastern Mind-Body Theory,* ed. T. P. Kasulis, trans. Nagatomo Shigenori and T. P. Kasulis (Albany: State University of New York Press, 1987), 105.
125. Ibid.
126. Ibid., 108.
127. Ibid., 109.

128. Ibid.
129. *Kaden*, NSTS, 56.

Coda

1. Omote Akira, "Tradition and Transformation in Nō Theatre," trans. Erika de Poorter. *Maske und Kothurn: Internationale Beitrage zur Theaterwissenschaft* 35.2–3 (January 1989): 11.
2. Ibid.
3. Omote Akira, "Muromachi ki no utai," in his *Nōgakushi shinkō*, 1:86–287.
4. According to Horigami Ken, chief editor of *Nōgaku jānaru*, the term *kubi-hon-tō*, also pronounced *"shu-hon-tō,"* is a term specific to noh. Nowadays one does not hear the word much. It was used much more in the 1960s, a time when amateur learners proliferated. Horigami Ken, "Kubi-hon-tō to nō no kankyaku," *Shōin* 8.33 (2003): 1. I would like to thank Professor Reiko Yamanaka for bringing this article to my attention.
5. Yashima Masaharu, *Zeami no nō to geiron*, 324.
6. "The universe is the vessel that gives birth to myriad things, sentient and insentient alike—flower and leaf, snow and moon, mountain and ocean, grass and tree—each at its time within the four passing seasons. You should concentrate on achieving the wondrous flower of musical entertainment by considering all things as fit imagery for it, by making your one mind *(isshin)* the vessel for all the universe, and situating [this] vessel with ease on the boundless path of emptiness [nonbeing]." *Anki shite* (situate with ease): *an* refers to "ease," as in "level of ease" *(an'i)*; *ki* means "vessel." *Yūgaku shudōfū ken*, NSTS, 167.
7. Yashima himself equates the impact of this lingering image to the detached seeing of *riken no ken*. This use of *riken no ken* parallels a usage by Zeami in *Shikadō* in which he describes the artistry at the bone level (in the skin-muscle-bone metaphor) as that which, when viewed in retrospect *(riken no ken)*, has no weaknesses.
8. Peter Brook, *The Empty Space* (N.Y.: Atheneum, 1968), 136.
9. Ibid.
10. It should also be noted, as Rath does, that Zeami's legacy is ongoing and very much subject to reinvention, especially among his descendents in the Kanze school, who tend to present him as a founding figure to be revered. Rath points out the existence of Kanze troupe heads as far back as the eighteenth century who have invoked Zeami's name to legitimize their own art and that of the school. He also introduces one very serious student of Zeami among noh performers, the gifted actor Kanze Hisao (1925–1978), whose art was assuredly colored by his understanding of Zeami's ideas and who wrote quite extensively about them; Eric C. Rath, "Remembering Zeami: The Kanze School and Its Patriarch," *Asian Theatre Journal*, 20.2 (fall 2003): 191–208. For Kanze Hisao's writings on Zeami, see Kanze

Hisao, *Kanze Hisao, Zeami o yomu,* ed. Ogihara Tatsuko, Heibonsha Raiburarii (Tokyo: Heibonsha, 2001). But one should keep in mind that Zeami's writings were not available to most noh actors until the last century, when they entered the public domain. Nor do traditional modes of noh training give much credence to the discussion of secret writings at the practice space, even if they are accessible. So Hisao must be viewed as somewhat of an exception among noh performers.

11. Shinko Kagaya, "Western Audiences and the Emergent Reorientation of Meiji Nō," in Stanca Scholz-Cionca and Samuel L. Leiter, eds., *Japanese Theatre and the International Stage* (Leiden: Brill, 2001), 174.

12. Ibid.

13. www.hinoki-shoten.co.jp/english/english_3.html. Sept. 9, 2004.

Appendix 1: An Annotated Translation of *Sandō*

1. Yoshida Tōgo, *Nōgaku koten Zeami jūrokubu shū* (Tokyo: Nōgakkai, 1909). The 1908 publication was based on the Kosugi manuscript of *Sarugaku dangi:* ibid., Yoshida, *Zeshi rokujū igo Sarugaku dangi kōi narabi hoketsu* (Tokyo: Nōgakkan, 1908).

2. Whereas the Diet text and the Matsunoya manuscript reproduction treat the phrase "Points on Composing Noh" as a heading set off from the body of the text, in the Yoshida manuscript it forms the opening line of the text itself. I have followed the Diet and Matsunoya manuscript reproduction texts because they are thought to preserve Zeami's original format.

   Three techniques, lit. "three ways" (*sandō*): 1) material (*shu/tane*), the material drawn by the playwright from the source (*honzetsu*); 2) structuring (*saku/tsukuru*), the overall musical structure; 3) writing (*sho/kaku*), the composition in both the poetic and musical sense.

3. Original story (*honzetsu*): prior source from which the playwright may draw his material. While some interpreters hold that Zeami intends this to refer to classical sources, his plays draw on popular materials and legend as well. See chapter 4 for details.

4. The Yoshida text identifies what the *shu* (seed; material) consists of as "*sono waza o nasu jintai ni shite, buga no tame taiyō nar[i]*" ([It] is the person who performs, and this is crucial for dance and chant). The traditional interpretation for this reading is that material may be defined as a character already associated with performing in a well-known source, who is then imported into a noh play as its lead, and the choice of this character has important bearing on dance and chant in the play; Nose, 1:593–594; NSTS, 462, appendix note 68. In the Diet and Matsunoya reproduction texts the opening clause is predicated with the verbal *yoru* (depend), "*sono waza o nasu jintai ni yot[t]e*" (depending on the personage that performs). This variance influences possible interpretations of the sentence-final clause. Takemoto suggests that it means "the effectiveness of the dance and chant will be dependent on the

personage performing" (*sono waza o nasu jintai ni yot[t]e buga no tame taiyō nar[i]*). As Takemoto has observed, the newly discovered Matsunoya manuscript reproduction corroborates the Diet text, increasing the likelihood that the two are closer to Zeami's original text; Takemoto, "Yoshido Bunko zō shinshutsu bon *Sandō* ni tsuite," in Engeki Kenkyū Sentā kiyō III, 2–3. For more on varying interpretations of this passage, see NSTS, 462, appendix note 68.

5. "art of musical entertainment" (*yūgaku*): I have glossed the term quite literally. Zeami also uses it on occasion as a metonymy for the art of *sarugaku*. The NSTS annotation takes the latter interpretation; NSTS, 134.

6. "visional affect" (*kenpū*): "That art which the eye can see," Nose, 1:594; "stage effect," NSTS, 134; and NKBT 65, 470; "the impact of the outwardly manifest aspect of the performance," SNKBZ 88, 353. In *Yūgaku shūdōfū ken*, the term is used in contradistinction to the inner mental state of the *shite*: " Just as fire and water arise from the clear substance of crystal, and blossoms and fruit from the cherry tree, which does not itself have color, the supremely skilled expert who, on the basis of his inner mental imaging, can manifest the shadings (*kyokushiki*) of a piece in [the form of] visional affect, should be [considered] a vessel (*kibutsu*)"; NSTS, 167. In *Shūgyoku tokuka*, the term is used in contradistinction to the aural mode of expression, the process of moving an audience depending on successfully transferring the impression made on the auditory faculties to the visional affect (*kenpū*); NSTS, 185.

   To embrace both meanings I have coined the term "visional affect." Whereas the use of "visual" would exclude all other modes of expression such as the aural mode of chant, "visional," allows for a more metaphorical type of sight that is the cumulative effect of all those factors that combine onstage to produce a vision in the minds of the audience. Moreover, I have opted for "affect" over "effect" because *kenpū* goes beyond projection on the part of the performer to encompass the impression made on the responding audience by that projection.

7. Whereas the Yoshida text has *nantai* (男体; male figure), the Diet and Matsunoya manuscript reproductions have *jintai* (人体; human figure). Takemoto suggests that Yoshida Tōgo substituted *nantai* in his recension to correct an error that had existed in the lost *Sandō* manuscript from which the extant manuscripts all are believed to descend. Takemoto observes that *jintai* also can mean a person of high social standing, which might be apt in the context of this passage, but since none of the other instances of the word in *Sandō* adhere to such a usage, it probably does not apply here either. He points out that this may well be a case in which Yoshida deliberately altered a reading in the Matsunoya Bunko manuscript (on which his recension is based), which is significant because it puts into question the prevailing assumption among scholars that the Yoshida recension consists of transcriptions of older manuscripts with minimal editorial intervention; Takemoto, "Yoshida Bunko zō shinshutsu bon *Sandō* ni tsuite," in Engeki Kenkyū Sentā kiyō III, 3.

8. Ariwara no Narihira (825–880): famed poet and putative hero of *The Tales of Ise* (*Ise monogatari*); one of the "six poetic geniuses" (*rokkasen*) designated in the "*Kana* Preface" to the *Kokin waka shū*; Ōtomo no Kuronushi (ninth century): another of the six poetic geniuses; Hikaru Genji: fictional protagonist of the eleventh-century classic *The Tale of Genji* (*Genji monogatari*) by Murasaki Shikibu.

9. "women such as these are accomplished artists" (*kaku no gotoki yūjo*): the word *yūjo* may also mean "women of pleasure," although the court poets among them would not normally be classified as such. NSTS glosses this as "refined women with a connection to singing and dancing"; NSTS, 134. While this definition seems quite secular, the *yūjo* identity is not that one-dimensional. The character for "*yū*" in *yūjo*, meaning "play" or "amuse," is also used to write the word *asobi*, referring to ritual entertainment for the Shintō deities or for the comfort of humans as well, in which music and dance were customary media. It is likely that use of the word *yūjo* would also have had this connotation. In the Diet text and the Matsunoya manuscript reproduction, this sentence is treated as a note, whereas it is part of the main text in the Yoshida manuscript. The Diet text and Matsunoya reproduction are believed to more accurately replicate the layout of the original manuscript.

   Ise: also known as Ise no Go; court poetess of the late ninth to early tenth century; Ono no Komachi (ninth century): one of the six poetic geniuses, a legendary beauty, and the *shite* of four plays in the current repertoire—*Ōmu Komachi*, *Sekidera Komachi*, *Sōshi arai Komachi*, and *Sotoba Komachi*; also cast in the companion role in *Kayoi Komachi*; Giō and Gijo: fictional *shirabyōshi* dancers in *The Tale of the Heike* (*Heike monogatari*) who were patronized by the head of the Taira house, Taira no Kiyomori; Shizuka: also known as Shizuka Gozen (twelfth century); famed *shirabyōshi* dancer and concubine to Minamoto no Yoshitsune; Hyakuman: legendary *kusemai* performer of the fourteenth century.

10. In the Yoshida text, the *kanji* compound glossed here as "renowned personages" is *meibō* (名望); the compound that occurs in the Diet text and Matsunoya reproduction has a different second character (名輩). The meaning of this second compound is not clear, but literally the characters would mean "famous companion." Annotators concur that Zeami (or a subsequent copyist) probably meant to write the word *meibō*, since its meaning fits the context perfectly, but his idiosyncratic choice of the second character created ambiguity. Takemoto points out that Yoshida Tōgo probably altered the second character accordingly, which is significant because it provides further evidence that Yoshida took a more active editorial hand than commonly thought. Takemoto, "Yoshida Bunko zō shinshutsu bon *Sandō* ni tsuite," in Engeki Kenkyū Sentā kiyō III, 2.

11. "core figure" (*konpontei*): *shite* of the play.

12. *Hōka*: type of itinerant performer who often dressed as a lay Buddhist priest; active from the Muromachi into the Edo period. Their art was a miscellany, including

juggling, acrobatics, singing *kouta* as well as dancing, and playing instruments such as a bamboo rattle *(kokiriko)* and a small stick drum *(kakko)*.

Three of the four *hōka* entertainers that Zeami mentions—Jinen Koji, Kagetsu, Tōgan Koji, and Seigan Koji—figure as the *shite* of extant noh plays named after them. Seigan Koji is not featured in any extant plays. Zeami also assigns these *hōka* to a subgroup that he labels *yūkyō*, which may be defined as professional entertainers who are motivated to perform—and to perhaps forget themselves—as part of their calling, in contrast with deranged characters *(monogurui)*, for instance, who perform as a result of some shock to their mental equilibrium. Noh *hōka* are typically affiliated with Buddhist institutions. In the three extant plays named above, the *shite* typically wears the *kasshiki* mask, which reproduces the features of a young male such as the type that commonly served as a temple page. Nakamura describes what he calls the trademark of the *kasshiki* mask, "The bangs on the forehead [of the *kasshiki* mask] were probably intended to emphasize the gentle, girlish beauty of a beautiful young boy"; Nakamura Yasuo, *Nō no men*, 4th printing, Nihon no Bi to Kyōyō 22 (Kyoto: Kawara Shoten, 1969), 190.

As a style of performance, *yūkyō* (lit. "playful madness") suggests an altered state of consciousness in which the performer seems to have forgotten himself as he becomes swept up in the moment. Miyake Kōichi, in his primer on the basics of noh performance today, has characterized it as "behavior that is completely artless, such as delighting in the moon and flowers, singing and dancing, or accosting people in fantastical witticisms. It is not the brand of madness associated with the mental patient, but poetic behavior purified of all worldly calculation. Therein lies its airy, elegant tone." *Yōgeiko no kihonjishiki*, 216.

13. "root style conducive to dance and chant" *(buga ni yoroshiki fūkon)*: the Yoshida text uses *fūtei* (style of figure). The Diet text and the Matsunoya manuscript reproduction have *fūkon* (lit. "root style").

14. "foundation style" *(honpūtai)*: the most basic style, that is, premised on danced and chanted elements.

15. "made-up noh" *(tsukuri nō)*: a play that is not based on a preexisting source or story material.

16. "opening player" *(kaikonin)*: according to the NSTS annotation, this refers to the first character to perform chanting, normally the *waki*; NSTS, 135. In Zeami's dramatic prototype, the *waki* conventionally enters (with or without an entourage) to open the play.

17. "recitative" *(sashigoe)*: today also referred to as *sashi*. Section of recitative; characterized by simple modulation and incongruent rhythmic scheme. Whereas today the *waki* typically enters on the introductory chant and then moves into a short prose self-introduction called the name-saying speech *(nanori)*, here Zeami specifies that the introductory chant should follow the *sashigoe*. NSTS notes that in Zeami's

time, the opening section of the name-saying speech was evidently in recitative rather than intoned prose *(kotoba)*, judging from notations in extant chant books. Moreover, the order of the introductory chant and the name-saying speech was reversed whenever preceded by what was called the *kaiko* (opening utterance).

The *kaiko*, which consisted of a passage of recitative celebrating the auspiciousness of the realm, would precede the opening play in a program. Although usually performed by the *waki*, it was a ritual opener not directly related to the dramatic content of the ensuing noh play. NSTS speculates that the order was reversed in order to effect a smooth musical transition from the recitative of the opening ceremony to that at the commencement of the name-saying speech. See NSTS, 462–463, appendix note 69. Throughout the Edo period, the *kaiko* continued to be performed on formal occasions, such as events sponsored by the bakufu or the imperial court, for instance, but it is rarely performed today; Nishino and Hata, eds., *Shintei zōho nō, kyōgen jiten,* s.v. "Kaikō," 237. (*Kaikō* would be a modern pronunciation; read *kaiko* in the annotated editions of *Sandō* consulted.)

"Introductory chant" *(shidai):* segment of chanted verse composed of three lines having hemistichs of 7-5, 7-5, and 7-4 morae, the second line a repetition of the first. It adheres to the *hiranori* match. Conventional entry chant for the *waki*.

"Long segment" *(hitoutai):* lit. "one [passage of] chant"; the term is very general and embraces several different types of chanted passages. Here (in the first *dan*) it usually corresponds to a traveling chant *(michiyuki).* Rendered mostly in the high range, adhering to the *hiranori* match. It describes the journey of the *waki* to the locale of the story to unfold.

18. "entry chant" *(issei):* verse in five lines of alternating five and seven morae sung in the high range; incongruent rhythmic scheme. Conventional entry pattern for the *shite*. In the second *dan* of a *waki* play, the passage of chant called "long segment" *(hitoutai)* often consists of two phases, what are known today as a low-range chant *(sageuta)* and a high-range chant *(ageuta).* The terms *ageuta* and *sageuta* appear to have come into use only later—as of the late Muromachi period of thereafter; NSTS, 468, appendix note 82.

19. "spoken exchange" *(mondō/mondai):* lit. "question and answer." In its narrow sense, it is a section of prose dialogue. In its more general usage, it is a section of prose dialogue that builds into recitative exchange (today called the *kakeai).* Zeami here means the latter.

"Long passage of choral chant" *(dōon hitoutai):* the first choral passage of the play; today called the *shodō.* It is most often sung in the high range.

20. Refers to a series of components that make up what is known today as the *kuse.* Adapted into noh by Zeami's father, Kan'ami, from the contemporaneous form of musical entertainment, the *kusemai.* The noh *kuse* section consists of three parts: the *kuri,* the *sashi,* and the *kuse.* The fully developed *kuse* prototype begins with a passage of *shidai* (introductory chant) and repeats the passage at the close; this is

thought to emulate the original *kusemai* most faithfully. Nishino and Hata, eds., *Shintei zōho nō, kyōgen jiten*, s.v. "*Kuse*," 304. For more on the *kuse* section, see Segments 2.1 and 2.2 below.

"Plain chant" (*tada utai*): the original vocal music of *sarugaku*. Called *kouta bushi*. According to Zeami, it is more melodious than *kuse* music, with less stress on the beat. The noh music that has evolved as of Kan'ami and Zeami's time blends the *kusemai* and *kouta bushi* styles.

21. "formal dance" (*mai*): in its broad sense, the term "dance" may apply to various types of choreographed movement positioned throughout the play. The *kuse* section, for instance, often features a dance by the *shite* supported both by the chorus and the instruments. Zeami's usage here more narrowly delineates *mai* in contradistinction to *hataraki*, translated as "vigorous moves." In other words, *mai* was the preferred type of choreography for gentle, lyrical types of characters, whereas *hataraki* was more appropriate for strong characters. In this latter sense, *mai* refers to a dance section typically positioned in the final portion of a play. Most of it is performed without chanting, but with instrumentation.

A set of dances forming a classification called *mai* was just beginning to develop in Zeami's generation, and the different types of *mai* had not yet been clearly established, at least not as a taxonomy that was written down. As a classification of formal dances today, *mai* may be characterized as extended, choreographed sequences patterned in congruence with each instrumental measure. For more on the types of *mai* as currently classified, see Konparu Kunio, *The Noh Theater: Principles and Perspectives*, trans. Jane Corddry and Stephen Comee, rev. and exp. ed. (New York: Weatherhill, 1983), 206.

"Vigorous moves" (*hataraki*): the other set of options mentioned by Zeami for choreographed sequences performed to instrumental backup (with a minimum of chanting). Frequently positioned in the final *dan*. Brief in duration and rugged in tone, they are typically assigned to less gentle characters such as warriors or demons. For more on the classification today, see Konparu Kunio, *Noh Theater*, 205.

"*Hayabushi* match": believed to correspond to the *chūnori* rhythm pattern of today, in which one prototypical measure has sixteen morae matched to eight beats (with variations). It typically is employed in the finale of plays featuring warriors or demons. For "*Kiribyōshi* match," see n. 56.

22. "number of lines" (*kukazu*): the prototypical metric line in a noh libretto consists of an upper hemistich of seven morae and a lower hemistich of five morae (with abundant variation).

23. "modulation" (*fushizuke*): modulation of the vocal line, which includes matching it to the instrumental line and assigning relative (not absolute) pitches, as well as vocal ornamentation.

24. "type and tone of the noh": *nō no shina-kakari*.

25. "all the types of characters that appear" (*demono no shinajina*): the NSTS appendix

points out that Zeami in his critical writings frequently uses the term *demono* (lit. "appearing/entering entity") in reference to the character appearing in his or her true identity in the second act of a play, as is the case further on in Segment 2.3 (see note 50 below); NSTS, 432, appendix note 12. In this case, however, he seems to refer to all of the dramatis personae who enter.

26. "poems in Chinese or Japanese" (*shiika/shika*): poems in Chinese would include both compositions in Chinese from the continent and poems written in Chinese by Japanese poets.

27. "the style of the noh": *nō no fūtei*.

28. "setting associated with the source material": *honzetsu no zaisho*. Literally, *zaisho* means "existing place." It may be taken to refer to a position existing in the noh text in which the setting of the source material (*honzetsu*) is designated, which is Nose's interpretation; Nose, 1:602. It may also simply refer to the existence of a locale associated with the source material (*honzetsu*); NSTS, 135; SNKBZ 88, 356. Also see NSTS, 71–72, appendix note 71.

29. "place of poetic import" (*kyokusho*): Nose surmises that *kyokusho* means the same as *zaisho* (see preceding note), i.e., a position in the text (featuring a place-name replete with poetic connotations); Nose, 1:602. NSTS and SNKBZ 88 hold that the term refers to a locale of repute that has potential to arouse interest; NSTS, 135; SNKBZ 88, 356.

30. "climax" (*tsume*): the word generally means finale or closing portion. Here, it applies to the climactic point or points in the *ha* phase, although it is not altogether clear where Zeami is stating this should occur. It may be interpreted as either the climactic points in the three *dan* making up the *ha* phase, or as the climactic point of the three *dan* sequence that makes up the *ha* phase. Nose holds that it refers to the section toward the end of the third *dan* of the *ha* phase, probably the *rongi*; Nose, 1:602. SNKBZ 88 points out the existence of the two possible interpretations but does not commit to either, although the fact that it is typical for the setting to be referred to in the context of the *shite's* entry in the first *dan* of *ha* is also pointed out; SNKBZ 88, 356. The NSTS and NKBT 65 editions do not comment. I think Zeami probably has the climax of the entire sequence of the three *dan* in mind here, which often corresponds to one highlight in the action, the *kuse* section.

31. "crucial spot for expressiveness" (*kyokusho*): this same word is glossed differently above as "place of poetic import" (see note 29). In contrast to their glosses of the term above, NSTS and SNKBZ 88 interpret it here as a portion of the play in which the acting should reach a climax (*wazadokoro*); NSTS, 136; SNKBZ 88, 356. NKBT 65: an important point in the play (472). Nose: the most important spot for expression in the play (1:602, 603). The Diet text and the reproduction of the Matsunoya Bunko manuscript both have a Chinese compound, *shōsho*, written with the character "*shō*," meaning correct or true, and the same character for place or point (*sho*)

that occurs in *kyokusho*. The precise meaning is not clear. My translation adheres to the Yoshida text.

32. As Nose states in his exegesis of this sentence, Zeami's point is that familiar, precedented language should be allotted to the protagonist and not to secondary characters; Nose, 1:603.

33. Conclusion of the opening portion of the treatise with its general introduction to the three techniques. In the Yoshida text and the Matsunoya reproduction, this statement is recorded in smaller characters that set it off from the preceding text. In the Diet text, the characters are the same size as what has preceded.

34. "*waki* play" (*waki nō*), also called the god play (*kami nō*): typically the *shite* takes the identity of an old man in the first act to reenter in his true identity as a Shintō deity in the second act. Auspicious themes predominate. The *waki* play was at the heart of the *jo* phase of Zeami's prototypical program. In his time, it was the first classification of play to be performed after the ritual opener, *Shikisanban*. This is how the term is derived. *Waki* literally means "side." The *waki* play was the first play to follow *Shikisanban*, i.e., it was *beside* it on the program. The statement translated as "this is generally in the style of the *waki* play" is formatted as a note in the Diet and Matsunoya reproduction texts.

35. "opening player" (*kaikonin*): see note 16.

36. Positioned as it is here in the first *dan*, this extended passage of chant would correspond to the traveling song (*michiyuki*). See note 17.

37. "one line" (*ku*): the standard format of a line of chant in noh, composed of an upper hemistich of seven morae and a lower one of five. The *waka* is the major verse form of classical Japanese poetry, composed of two lines of 5-7-5 and 7-5 morae, respectively. Zeami is stipulating that the two hemistichs of a *waka* poem be worked into a noh script as two lines of chant.

38. In the Diet text and the Matsunoya text reproduction, the phrase enclosed in parentheses in this translation is treated as a note to the side of the main line of text.

39. It is standard in *waki* noh for the *shite* to enter with a personage cast in the role of the companion (*tsure*). The companion aids the *shite* in exposition of the story. Zeami seems to have the play *Takasago* (*Aioi*) in mind here. In *Takasago*, the *shite* and companion are both Shintō deities, who appear in the guise of an elderly couple in the first act. Plays featuring other types of *shite* may or may not have the companion role, depending on the nature of the source material and the classification of the play in the repertoire. The *waki* may also enter with a companion or companions.

40. "second verse" (*ni no ku*): the most fully elaborated format for the entry chant (*issei*) has two lines of 7-5 that follow the standard 5-7-5-7-5. Today, as a rule, the *tsure* of a *waki* noh sings the first line, and the *shite* and *tsure* sing the second line of the *ni no ku* in unison.

41. "one passage of chant" (*hitoutai*): one passage of low-range chant (*sageuta*) and an ensuing passage of high-range chant (*ageuta*), as these passages are referred to today.

42. In the Diet text and the Matsunoya manuscript reproduction, this sentence is formatted as a note (in smaller script) to the right side of the main line.

43. "spoken exchange" (*mondō*/*mondai*): see note 19.

44. Whereas the Yoshida text treats this sentence as part of the main text, it is inscribed in smaller characters as a note in the Diet text and Matsunoya text reproduction.

45. The question enclosed in parentheses—(position for the ear-opening?)—is formatted as a note in the Yoshida text but is absent from the Diet text. In the traced copy of the Matsunoya Bunko text, the note is inserted to the right of the main text where it states, "*Mina doōn ni utaidasu koto yori*" (From the beginning of the choral chant).

46. Zeami's reference to "two parts" appears to correspond to the performance of the *ageuta* today. It is usually divided into two parts by the insertion of a momentary pause in the chanting about midway through the segment. This pause is called the *uchikiri*; SNKBZ 88, 357.

47. In both the Diet text and the Matsunoya reproduction, this is formatted as a note that reads, "*Kore yori ha*" (from here, *ha*).

48. Zeami refers here to the entire *kuse* section, which is normally composed of three main structural parts, the *kuri*, the *sashi* (recitative), and the *kuse*. The *kuri* (referred to by Zeami as *aguru koe* [raised voice]) is chanted primarily in the high range, dropping to the low range at the close. The rhythm is incongruent and the modulation lavishly ornamented. The ensuing recitative opens in the high range and then moves to the low range, totaling about ten lines altogether. In Zeami's time, it seems that the recitative (*sashigoe*) was construed more narrowly as the opening high-range section of what is now considered recitative, or *sashi*. Today, the "lowering to the close" portion is considered *sashi* as well.

   The *kuse* that follows is most frequently structured in one cycle of three phases. The first twelve or thirteen lines, which Zeami refers to more narrowly as the *kuse*, make up the first two phases of the *kuse* as it is known today. This two-phase sequence moves between the low and middle ranges to close in the low range. The third phase opens with a short passage in the high range, the *ageha*, which is interjected by the *shite*. The rest of the phase is performed in the high range by the chorus, dropping to the low range at the close. The *kuse* adheres to the *hiranori* match. It is frequently followed by a rhythmic exchange (*utai rongi*) that unfolds primarily between the *shite* and the chorus. It also adheres to the *hiranori* match. Whereas the Diet text has *utai rongi*, the Yoshida text and the Matsunoya text reproduction have *kotoba rongi*, which is puzzling, since the *utai rongi* is much more apt to follow the *kuse*. NSTS suggest that it was a copyist's error; NSTS, 464, appendix note 72.

49. I have translated the Diet text and the Matsunoya reproduction (which format this phrase as a note). The Yoshida text merely states, "*Kore yori*" (From here).

50. This time, the *shite* reentering for the second act *(demono no jintai)* is in his true identity. The companion *(tsure)* frequently reenters as a celestial maiden, the *shite* as a male deity.

51. The "high-range passage" *(kō no mono)* referred to here is rhythmically incongruent. The SNKBZ 88 annotation equates it with a segment that modern critics have classified as *jō no ei* (recitation in the high register); SNKBZ 88, 358. This classification gained wide recognition when proposed by Yokomichi Mario in the introductory matter to a collection of librettos coedited with Omote Akira in the Nihon Koten Bungaku Taikei series (See Yokomichi and Omote, eds., *Yokyoku shū*, 1:5–28). It is characterized as a classification of vocal components in which "the rhythm does not follow a beat and which are recited like traditional Japanese poetry *(waka)*." This quotation is from the translation and analysis of the Yokomichi material in Frank Hoff and Willi Flindt, eds. and trans., "The Life Structure of Noh: An English Version of Yokomichi Mario's Analysis of the Structure of Noh," excerpt from vol. 2, nos. 3 and 4, of *Concerned Theatre Japan* (1973): 225.

52. "latter portion" *(goku)*: the *ni no ku* (see note 40). In plays of the *waki* classification, the *ni no ku* of the unabridged entry chant *(issei)* in plays of the *waki* classification, the *shite* often exchanges lines with the chorus in a *kakeai* (heightened exchange) format. Today, in the case of *Takasago*, a rapidly paced dance of the *kami mai* (god dance) type follows.

53. "rapid exchange" *(seme rongi)*: in *Sandō*, Zeami mentions three types of *rongi* (exchanges): the *utai rongi*, which corresponds to the modern *rongi* (rhythmic exchange); the *kotoba rongi*, which appears to correspond to the *kakeai* (heightened exchange), which does not abide by a congruent rhythmic scheme; and the *seme rongi*. It is not clear how the *seme rongi* differs from the other two types. Elsewhere Zeami uses the verbal of the same derivation, *semu*, to refer to speeding up the tempo. For instance, in *Sarugaku dangi*, it states, "To [dance] first quickly, then composedly is all determined." "Quickly" is the gloss for this verbal; NSTS, 267; translation from De Poorter, *Zeami's Talks*, 88. SNKBZ 88 surmises that it refers to a rapid-paced passage coming after the final dance; SNKBZ 88, 358. Note 72 of the appendix to NSTS speculates that the verbal *semu* may be used here to mean "pursue," as in pursuing the truth of a matter fully *(kotowari o seme)* through further question and answer. Such a *seme rongi* would continue the momentum of a preceding *kakeai*; NSTS, 464.

54. "[the nature of] the character who dances": *demono no bugaku no jintai*.

55. The phrase in parentheses is written to the side of the main line in the form of a note in the Yoshida text and the Matsunoya text reproduction; it is missing from the Diet text.

56. "*kiribyōshi* match": corresponds to what is today called the *ōnori* match. SNKBZ 88 notes that *ōnori* frequently follows formal dances of the *chū-no-mai* and *gaku* types, as well as the *maibataraki*, a type of vigorous move. On the other end, the *kami mai*,

the kind of dance featured in *Takasago*, tends to lead into a rhythmic exchange, which is in the *hiranori* rhythmic scheme; SNKBZ 88, 358.

57. That is, the style of the play that opens the program; usually a *waki* play.

58. "the type [of character]": *shinajina*.

59. "gentlewoman" (*kinin no nyotai*): a subtype belonging to the style of the woman. Lady Aoi: principal wife of Hikaru Genji in the early chapters of *Genji monogatari*; does not figure as a *shite* in the present repertoire, although allusion is made to her in the play *Aoi no Ue*. Yūgao: character from *Genji monogatari* and *shite* of the play *Yūgao*. Ukifune: also a character from *Genji monogatari* and *shite* of the play *Ukifune*.

60. "vocal music and fine *kakari*" (*ongyoku, yoshikakari*): the Yoshida text has *ongyoku, yorikakari*, but the Diet text and the Matsunoya reproduction have *ongyoku, yoshikakari*. Nose keeps the Yoshida reading, whereas NSTS and SNKBZ 88 adopt *yoshikakari*; Nose, 1:614; NSTS, 137; SNKBZ 88, 359. The term *yoshikakari* occurs three times in Zeami's treatises; SNKBZ 88, 341, note 23. For instance, in *Shikadō*, Zeami states that training in *nikyoku santai* will provide the substance for a *yoshikakari* having *yūgen* and courtly elegance. Annotators concur that the term refers to an elegant atmosphere, although SNKBZ 88 does comment that in this context in *Sandō* it seems to relate to the music; SNKBZ 88, 359, note 27. It seems to me that Zeami is making reference to the two modes here, *ongyoku* embracing the aural and *yoshikakari* the overall visual image or stage presence of the character. In the next line, he also exhorts the actor to strive for refined *kakari* having the beauty of *yūgen*. Here, too, *kakari* seems to refer to the overall stage presence that a character projects.

61. "the [vocal] music, too, must [inspire a feeling of] wonder" (*kyoku mo myōsei*): the modern Japanese translation of this phrase in SNKBZ 88 is "the vocal music (*ongyoku*) too must be of superb composition (*zetsumyō no sakkyoku*) (359). Nose's note construes this as the caliber of the vocal music itself; it should be unexcelled; Nose, 1:618. The meaning of the word *kyoku* may vary in Zeami's treatises, from music (primarily vocal) to expressiveness in general. Clearly Zeami is referring here to the auditory level, but it is possible to read *kyoku* more generally as expressiveness at the auditory level. A more literal gloss of *myōsei* (*sei* meaning sound, voice) might be "wondrous voice." Therefore, an alternate gloss for this phrase might be "vocal expressiveness [of the caliber that inspires a sense of] wonder."

62. Here, visional affect refers to the physical presence of the gentlewoman, who Zeami is introducing as the case study for penultimate gracefulness of person.

63. Here visional affect seems to extend to the affective impact of material that preserves the elegant tone while also providing dramatic stage action. The spirit of one of Genji's lovers, the Rokujō lady, attacks his principal wife, Aoi no Ue; chap. 9 of *Genji monogatari*. Briefly, Genji's lover, Yūgao, dies mysteriously in a nocturnal tryst with him, probably a victim of spirit possession on the part of the Rokujō lady;

chap. 4 of *Genji monogatari*. Caught between two lovers, Ukifune is moved by a mysterious force to attempt suicide; chap. 53 of *Genji monogatari*.

64. "seeds that flower" (*kashu*): lit. the character for flower (*ka*) and for seed (*shu*). "Seed" connotes source material in Zeami's usage throughout this treatise. It reads well here as material with promise to induce the "flower." The defining characteristics for *kashu* seem to be materials having both courtly polish and dramatic content.

65. *Ume ga ka o sakura no hana ni niowasete, yanagi ga eda ni sakasemu: waka* attributed to Nakahara no Munetoki; *Goshūi waka shū*; Shinpen Kokka Taikan, vol. 1, pt. 1:111, note 82 (Spring 1). Zeami replaces the original optative/exclamatory suffix *shigana* with the inflecting auxiliary *mu* in its volitional usage, which creates a slightly different nuance. The original goes more like, "Would that one might infuse the cherry blossom with the fragrance of the plum, and make it bloom on the willow branch" (*Ume ga ka o sakura no hana ni niowasete, yanagi ga eda ni sakasete shigana*).

66. "ultimate impression of the wondrous" (*mujō myōkan*): in Zeami's parlance, the highest grade of performance, evocative of a sense of unfathomable wonder that cannot be traced to any specific acting technique or calculated stage effect.

67. *Waka*: section of high-range chanting loosely modeled on the 5-7-5-7-7 of the *waka* verse form; rhythmically incongruent. Entry chant (*issei*): along with its primary use as an entry chant, this pattern is sometimes used to lead into the dance section. Measure of eight beats (*yahyōshi/yatsubyōshi*): thought to correspond to the *hiranori* match with its prototype of twelve morae matched to eight beats (plus a plethora of variations). In this section of a play, the rhythmicality of the eight-beat phrase mounts in intensity, in part because of growing tension in the drumming patterns; "mount" refers to the *shite*'s matching his performance to that intensified rhythmic sense. Third range (*sanjū*): highest octave on the noh scale. This term was also used to refer to the highest octave in rival art forms such as *Heikyoku* (Heike recitation), *sōga* (type of popular song), and the *shirabyōshi*. Rapid pattern (*seme*): appears to be a term borrowed from the *shirabyōshi* form referring to a pattern of intensified stamping accompanied by rapid-paced drumming near the conclusion of the dance performance; NSTS, 138.

68. *Kusemai* performers (practitioners of the art of the *kusemai*): Hyakuman: *shite* of the play *Hyakuman*; modeled on a legendary performer of the *kusemai*. The play is about Hyakuman's search for her lost child. Her grief drives her to madness, which, in turn, prompts her to perform with uncharacteristic abandon. She recovers her child at the end of the play. Yamamba: *shite* of the play *Yamamba*. A *kusemai* entertainer (*tsure*) takes the name of a legendary old crone-cum-mountain spirit, Yamamba (*shite*), to be confronted with her namesake deep in the mountains.

69. "the latter part" (*nochi no dan*): Zeami is describing the type of *kuse* section known today as the *ni dan guse* (two-step *kuse*). Instead of the one cycle standard to the noh

kuse, it has two cycles of three phases each. The second cycle is usually shortened to two phases, divided by a second *ageha* (high-range interjection by the *shite*). Based on Zeami's description of the *kuse* structure in *Sarugaku dangi,* the section that should build to a rapid tempo seems to come between the two *ageha*; NSTS, 276–277.

Along with its function as an entry pattern, the introductory chant *(shidai)* appears at the beginning and the close of the formal, unabridged *kuse* section, as is thought to have been the case in the original *kusemai* form. The full-scale *kuse* section is preserved in *Hyakuman* and *Yamamba.*

70. Another subtype of the woman category is the style of the madwoman *(onna monogurui).* In contrast with the earlier three subtypes of the woman category (the gentlewoman, *shirabyōshi* dancer, and *kusemai* entertainer), the madwoman is distinguished by her behavior. Therefore, it is crucial to make that madness felt in performance.

"Comportment" *(tachi furumai):* I have followed the Diet text and and the Matsunoya Bunko reproduction copy. The Yoshida text has *ii furumai* (manner of speaking).

"Skillfully arrange the *kakari* of the musical phrases" *(fushi no kakari o taku-miyosete):* Nose and NKBT 65 gloss *kakari* as the atmosphere of the musical phrases; Nose, 1:617; NKBT 65. SNKBZ 88 interprets this same phrase as "apply all one's skill to composing the musical lines"; SNKBZ 88, 360. Here *kakari* seems to refer to the smooth linking of the musical phrases *(fushi).*

71. "ultimate style" *(jōkafū):* the style whose material Zeami refers to earlier as "a gem among gems"; that is, material that holds both a personage of aristocratic refinement and a dramatic story. Nose interprets this differently, equating the "ultimate style" with the character having aristocratic presence; Nose, 1:617.

72. In a two-act play there is an interlude between the acts. The *shite* exits at the end of the first act to change costume; he reenters in his "true" identity, here as a warrior, to open the second act. The second act *(nochi no kire):* I have followed the Diet and Matsunoya reproduction texts; the Yoshida text has *nochi no kiwa.* The *kuse* section is normally positioned in the third *dan* of the *ha* phase; shifting the *kuse* section to the second act results in the *ha* phase flowing over into the *kyū* phase with no break in between.

73. The *hayabushi* rhythmic scheme; see note 21.

74. "warrior apparition" *(guntai no demono):* the *shite* of the second act appearing in his original identity.

75. "name-saying speech" *(nanorigoe):* it was customary for a warrior to announce him-self (name, rank, station, etc.) to his opponent prior to engaging in battle with him. Zeami appears to have this precedent in mind. (*Nanori* is also the name of a com-ponent part of a noh play, normally allotted to the *waki* when he enters in the first *dan* to introduce himself. Not what is being referred to here.)

76. "the acting is in the *saidō* style" *(saidō no taifū nari)*: in contradistinction to the acting style of forceful movement *(rikidō)* typified in the performance of the angry demon; lit. translates as "pulverized/broken-down movement." The unified force field projected by the angry movement is "broken" or "scattered" into minuter movement, with the effect that the movements retain a show of vigor but no longer project one front of demonic force. By minute movement, Zeami means, for instance, that the actor's torso should remain motionless when he performs a pattern of stamps, or, when he moves the upper half of his body, his lower limbs should remain still. See *Kakyō*, NSTS, 85. Such contrasts serve to soften the overall effect and give it increased complexity in keeping with the human heart.

77. Noh *(nō)*: may refer to the play, the characters doing the acting, or the performance more generally; NSTS, 139. The Rimer and Yamazaki translation interprets it as the "style of the characters." In his treatise *Ninkyoku santai ningyō zu*, Zeami makes a similar statement specifying that the style of pulverized movement should depend on whether the character performing is "old or young, child or adult, or a madwoman"; NSTS, 128.

      "Male behaving madly" *(otoko monogurui)*; "female behaving madly" *(onna monogurui)*: plays about characters who lose their mental equilibrium out of personal suffering, often separation from a lover or child. The *shite* of *Hyakuman*, or plays by Zeami such as *Hanjo* or *Hanagatami*, would be examples of *onna monogurui*. Plays featuring *otoko monogurui* have proved to be less popular over time and are fewer in number. Examples might be *Utaura* by Motomasa and *Kōya monogurui* by Zeami and revised by Motomasa.

78. "opening player" *(kaikonin)*: normally the *waki*. See note 16.

79. "recitative": *sashigoe*.

80. "distant vision" *(enken)*: the NSTS interpretation for *enken* here is that the *shite* strikes a pose of gazing off into the distance and thereby invokes a distant vista in the spectators' imaginations; NSTS, 497, appendix note 164. SNKBZ 88 is in agreement (363); Nose glosses it as the image of the *shite* onstage as perceived by the spectators (1:633).

81. "stir both the ear and the mind" *seimon ikyoku (o) furuite*: the term *seimon ikyoku* appears to originate with Zeami. In the Diet and Matsunoya texts, the particle *"o"* marks the compound *seimon ikyoku*, which makes the construction a transitive one; it undergoes the action of a here unspecified agent. Without the particle, the phrase may be read as intransitive. NSTS adheres to the transitive construction and interprets the phrase to mean that the actor appears on the bridgeway, and while creating the effect of "distant vision," he gives his chanting mounting interest; NSTS, 139. The SNKBZ 88 note interprets this as the performer employing his own "heart and mind to build musical interest"; SNKBZ 88, 363. Nose follows the Yoshida text, which adheres to the intransitive construction. He holds that the compound refers to both the musical interest and the interest of the import of the lines combined;

this interest should mount steadily until it "reaches the state of overflowing"; Nose, 1:633.

82. "the type" (*shina*). Zeami frequently refers to figure types suitable for imitation, or *monomane*, with the plural of this term, *shinajina*, e.g., *monomane no jintai no shinajina*, in *Sandō* (Segment 1.2). While it is not clear what "type" refers to in this instance, it likely refers to the type of character.

83. "recitative" (*sashigoto*): according to NSTS, *sashigoto* is the same thing as *sashigoe*.

84. NSTS notes that the section opening with recitative (*sashigoto no jo yori utau koto*) seems to correspond to the section often following the *kakeri* dance in madness plays, which begins with recitative, followed by a low-range chant and a high-range chant; NSTS, 139.

85. "chant in the introductory portion [of *ha*]" (*jobun no ongyoku*): *jo* is the name of the first of the five *dan* of Zeami's dramatic prototype, but its usage here in the compound *jobun* seems to refer to the opening portion of the *shite*'s performance, i.e., that portion of *ha* that precedes the spoken exchange (*mondō*). This would correspond to the first *dan* of *ha*; NSTS, 469, appendix note 83. Nose makes the same assessment; Nose, 1:634. However, NKBT 65 and SNKBZ 88 differ, equating *jobun* with the first *dan* of the play; NKBT 65, 476; and SNKBZ 88, 363.

86. "heightened exchange" (*kotoba rongi*): according to appendix note 72 of NSTS, this corresponds to what today is referred to as *kakeai*; NSTS, 464. For more on *kakeai*, see notes 19, 52, and 53 above.

87. "chant in the high range" (*kō no mono no utai*): refers to high-range chant of the congruent type; now called *ageuta*; NSTS, 139.

88. "[The portion] from the dance to the *kusemai*" (*mai yori kusemai ni itaru made*): I have followed the Diet text; the Yoshida text and Matsunoya reproduction have "[portion] up to the dance" (*mai ni itaru made*). As NSTS notes, in the plays *Jinen Koji* and *Tōgan Koji*, featuring *hōka* figures, the *kuse* follows a formal dance of the *chū no mai* type. This is a reversal of the more common sequence of *kuse* section and then final dance; NSTS, 140.

89. One of three basic rhythmic schemes; see note 21.

90. *Otoshibushi*: meaning unclear; seems to refer to a pattern of modulation in which there is an abrupt shift from the high range to the low range; NSTS, 140.

91. "*kyū*-style climax" (*tsumedokoro no kyūfū*): according to NSTS, a scene reminiscent of the climactic *kyū* phase of a play; NSTS, 140. This would seem to correspond to the climax that Zeami refers to as the eye-opening (*kaigen*) in Segment 3.3 of *Sandō*.

92. "affective appeal" (*ifū*): a term that appears to have been coined by Zeami referring to affective quality as manifested onstage. When a play has such a reunion scene, Zeami advocates that the fast-paced tempos typical of the *kyū* phase of his prototypical play be situated instead in the third phase of *ha*, and that the final *kyū* phase be instead made melancholy (and assumedly more measured in pace), in a manner eliciting tears.

93. "tearful noh" *(naki nō)*: the precise meaning is not clear. NSTS and SNKBZ 88 maintain that it involves the manifestation onstage of a tragic mood; NSTS, 140; and SNKBZ 88, 364. NKBT 65 and Nose concur that this is a play having a melancholy mood, but state more specifically that it refers to the actual performance of tears on stage; NKBT 65, 477; and Nose, 1:635.
94. "visional affect" *(kenpū)*: see note 6.
95. "This is a variant derived from the style of the warrior" *(guntai no matsuryū no binpū nari)*: the Matsunoya and Diet texts format this statement as a note beside the main text. (Matsunoya version: *guntai matsuryū no binpū nari*.)
96. "the form of a demon and the heart of a human" *(kyōkishinnin/kyōkishinjin)*: in *Kaden*, Zeami specifies that there are two types of demons: angry ghosts or victims of possession and true demons of hell; NSTS, 25–26. The acting style of *saidō* movement is appropriate for the first type. The demon in the style of *saidō* movement makes a demonic appearance but has a human heart; he retains the bluster of the forceful demon, but that ferocity is compromised by his susceptibility to more complex human emotions. In the Yoshida and Matsunoya texts, this sentence is transcribed as part of the body of the text. In the Diet text, it is formatted as a note, in smaller script.
97. "apparition [featured] in the second act" *(nochi no demono)*: see note 25.
98. "demon of the ghost type" *(ryōki)*: Zeami, in specifying that the demon be of the ghost type, is expressing his preference for the kind of demon figure that has a human heart; SNKBZ 88, 364. A ghost is the spirit of a dead human, in contrast to a hell-dwelling demon, who has no human attributes.
99. "entry chant" *(issei)*: see notes 18, 40, 52, and 67.
100. "the edge of the stage" *(butai giwa)*: the area upstage where the bridgeway and the main stage meet.
101. *Otoshibushi*: see note 90.
102. "the high range" *(kō no mono)*: Zeami uses this term generally to refer to high-range chant of the *ageuta* type, but few noh plays featuring the *saidō* style have an *ageuta* situated right after such an entry pattern for the *shite* (recitative and entry chant). However, many plays have a choral *ageuta* that follows a heightened exchange *(kakeai)*. Therefore, the NSTS interpretation of this passage is, "An *ageuta* is chanted, and it may be appropriate, depending on the context, to position a rapid exchange *(seme rongi)*, or the like, prior to it"; NSTS, 465, appendix note 75.
103. "rapid exchange" *(seme rongi)*: see notes 53 and 102.
104. "conclusion" *(kyū)*: *kyū* does not refer to the fifth *dan* in its entirety in this case. Zeami uses it rather to refer to the final portion of the fifth *dan*, the part right before the exit; NSTS, 140. SNKBZ 88 speculates that *kyū* here refers to the final portion that comes after the vigorous moves *(hataraki)* or other related choreography; SNKBZ 88, 364. In his rendering of this passage into modern Japanese,

however, Nose equates *kyū* with the final *dan* in its entirety; Nose, 1:639. In NKBT 65, no annotation is offered.

105. *"hayabushi, kiru fushi"*: *hayabushi* corresponds to the *chūnori* rhythmic scheme; see note 21. The exact meaning of *kiru fushi* is not clear. Nose holds that it is likely the same as *kiribyōshi*, corresponding to the *ōnori* rhythmic scheme (see note 56 above); Nose, 1:640. NSTS and SNKBZ 88 surmise that it refers to one particular rhythmic pattern belonging to the basic *kiribyōshi* rhythmic scheme. The point is also made that plays about demons commonly conclude on the *chūnori* and *ōnori* rhythms today as well; NSTS, 140; and SNKBZ 88, 364.

106. "musical phrasing" *(fushigakari)*: in Zeami's treatises, the meaning of this term may range from the mood elicited on the basis of the sequencing of the musical phrases to the musical mood more generally. NSTS glosses it here as the mood arising from the vocal music *(ongyoku no jōshu)*; NSTS, 140. SNKBZ 88 attributes it to the effectiveness of the musical phrasing *(fushizuke no guai)*; SNKBZ 88, 364. Nose glosses it as the mood arising from the musical phrasing *(kyokusetsu no jōshu)*; Nose, 1:639. The NKBT 65 note is essentially the same as the Nose gloss *(fushizuke no omomuki)*.

107. "style [conducive to] the flower" *(katei)*: the underlying musical elements play the vital function of softening and embellishing the rough, strong style of *monomane* appropriate to the demon. The NSTS, Nose, and NKBT 65 annotations all construe *katei*, which literally translates as "the form/style of the flower," along the lines of the English adjective "flowery" *(hanayaka na)*, to indicate a quality of beauty having color and a touch of gaiety. In *Kaden*, Zeami likens the demon's performance ideally to a flower blossoming on a rock; NSTS, 26. The idea of flowery beauty is consistent with that image. However, in translation, "flowery" fails to suggest the more dynamic implications of the flower image in the context of Zeami's overall aesthetic. The SNKBZ 88 annotation avoids this pitfall with the gloss "stage effects having a style that appears to possess the flower" (364). I think this interpretation is aptest for the following reasons.

Generally, Zeami uses the metaphor of the flower to refer to any outgrowth of the performer's art that has the effect of moving the audience. In *Kakyō* he likens the beauty of *yūgen* to a flower, saying, "Although the types of personages [noh *shite*] may vary, when any of them looks like a beautiful flower, it is always the same flower"; NSTS, 98. This metaphorical flower encompasses more than "flowery." Indeed, Zeami's purpose for including the description of the demon's performance is to describe how the impression of *yūgen* may flower in it. I have translated *katei* as "style [conducive to] the flower" in the hope of retaining this more dynamic connotation of a form that holds within it the seeds of *yūgen*.

108. "vigorous movement" *(hataraki)*: rather than referring to a piece of choreographed movement positioned in one specific point in the play (typically the fifth *dan* finale), Zeami seems to be using the term here to refer more broadly to the general

type of movement performed by strong characters, in contradistinction to the more lyrical type of movement of gentle characters, classified as *mai*. Also see note 21. He is saying that in general, for the movement of a demonic character to have the ultimate appeal of the flower, the composition of the music is vitally important.

109. "style of musical expression" (*kyokufū*): the style of the vocal music; SNKBZ 88, 364; and NSTS, 140. "One should compose upon having carefully designed and thoroughly grasped the [right scheme for the] vocal music and the stage style (*fūtei*)"; NKBT 65, 477. The NKBT 65 interpretation also seems viable. *Shikadō* employs *kyokufū* in reference to the training of a child actor. When still a young child, he should not yet be trained in the three styles, but should perform "all styles of expression" (*shotei no kyokufū*) as himself. It is clear that *kyokufū* is not limited to the auditory in this context, but seems to refer to going through the motions of performing all styles of plays without masks or *monomane*; *Shikadō*, NSTS, 112. Since the child must make no pretensions to representation of characters, then the two styles of expression open to him would be the entry level ones, the two modes of dance and chant. Extrapolating from this example, I think it likely that Zeami's advice in *Sandō* refers to carefully mapping out the appropriate uses of both modes.

110. "demon in the style of forceful movement" (*rikidōfūki*): the true demon, whose heart is as ferociously and uncompromisingly demonic as his form; his movements are broad, forceful strokes, impervious to complication. In *Kaden*, Zeami rejects this style because the fear inspired by unrestrained force precludes the possibility of audience empathy. In deemphasizing the style of the forceful demon, the Zeami group was breaking away from the mainstream of Yamato *sarugaku*, which had traditionally specialized in demon *monomane*. In *Nikyoku santai ningyō zu*, Zeami allows for an occasional performance in the forceful style for the sake of novelty; NSTS, 129.

What follows in this paragraph is formatted as a note in both the Diet text and the Matsunoya text reproduction.

111. "the force, the form, and the heart of a demon": *seikyōshinki*.

112. Zeami's description of the positioning appropriate for the ear-opening (*kaimon*) and eye-opening (*kaigen*) is vague, perhaps to allow for individual variation. The ear-opening would logically occur toward the end of the *ha* phase and is particularly suitable for the *kuse* section, which, characteristically, holds the greatest musical complexity and the most condensed recapitulation of the *shite*'s story. The eye-opening occurs in the dance or vigorous modes, which are ordinarily positioned in the *kyū* phase. *Kaigen* is a term of Buddhist provenance. When the eyes were carved into a new Buddhist statue, this was thought to also infuse it with life (*tamashii o komeru*). This moment was referred to as *kaigen*. *Kaimon* appears to be a word that originates with Zeami; SNKBZ 88, 365.

113. "instant in which the two aural dimensions form one impression" (*nimon ikkan o nasu kiwa*): ideally the two levels of communication of the chanting—the message

of the words and the musicality—merge into one overall impression in the mind of the listener. "Instant" *(kiwa):* NSTS and SNKBZ 88 gloss this word as *shunkan* (instant, moment); NSTS, 140; and SNKBZ 88, 365. Nose prefers to gloss it as *sakai* (boundary, domain); 1:645.

114. "important content from the original source" *(honzetsu no kotowari): honzetsu* refers to the source for the story material. *Kotowari:* the main points from, or the gist of, the original source; NSTS, 141; Nose, 1:646.

115. "open the mind's ear" *(shinni o hiraku):* a literal rendering of the Japanese. *Shinni* (mind/ear) refers to one's heart/mind doing the listening—the capacity to perceive at a deeper level than the senses. The expression is used here to indicate that the important content of the material, conveyed by means of the words, strikes a chord of understanding in the listeners.

116. "one auditory dimension" *(ichimon):* this follows the Diet text. The Yoshida text has *issei* (one voice, one sound). No such phrase explicitly identifying what precedes as "one auditory dimension" or "one voice" appears in the Matsunoya text reproduction.

117. "vocal expressiveness" *(kyokusei):* the sonic appeal of the voice, the second auditory track in Zeami's total concept of auditory appeal, encompassing the affixing of the musical modulation *(fushizuke)* and the impact of the chanting *(utai);* NSTS, 141; SNKBZ 88, 365. NKBT 65 glosses the term as "the feeling of the vocal music" *(ongyoku no kanji);* NKBT 65, 478. Nose glosses it as the "atmosphere possessed by the vocal music" *(ongyoku no motsu jōshu);* 1:647. Such musical elements must blend nicely with the first auditory track, i.e., communication of the import of the lines.

118. "the site for [actualizing] a deep impression" *(kansho):* Zeami tends to use *kan* (impression) to refer to the feelings aroused in the audience; *sho* (lit. "place") has polyvalent possibilities. On the one hand, it seems to refer here to the underlying basis or crux of such an impression, as suggested in the NSTS gloss of *kandokoro* (vital point, crux); NSTS, 141. At the same time, it may also refer to the actual position in the text in which the ear-opening should occur, as in the NKBT 65 note, for instance, which glosses *kansho* as *kandō no ba,* which may mean the place or the scene that [creates] a deep impression; NKBT 65, 478.

119. "a revelatory point at which the feeling aroused in the visional affect is brought to fulfillment" *(kenpū kan'ō no jōju no manako o arawasu zaisho):* here *zaisho* (lit. "existing place") refers to a position in the dramatic action; also see note 28. For the details on *kenpū* (visional affect), see note 6. Whereas *kenpū* may refer to the affects that all kinds of stage action foster, here it seems to refer more narrowly to the affects inspired on the basis of visual media. This usage of *kenpū* resembles one in the later treatise *Shūgyoku tokuka,* in which Zeami describes fulfillment *(jōju)* as a domain in which the impression aroused by the music *(onkan)* is transferred to *kenpū;* NSTS, 185.

Fulfillment (jōju) is the same term that Zeami uses frequently in his critical corpus in reference to bringing audience interest to fruition. It is often discussed as a process governed by the principal of jo-ha-kyū. See the first four sections of chapter 6.

120. "dancing or vigorous movement" (maihataraku fūtei no kan ni): "in the course of acting that involves dancing or [other] choreographed movement (shosa); NSTS, 141. Normally near or in the fifth and final dan of the prototype.

121. "instant that moves all present to feel the wondrous" (sokuza ichidō no myōkan o nasu tokoro): myō (the wondrous) is the highest level of stage affect, according to Zeami. The term occurs here in the compound myōkan, which might be translated as "impression of wonder" or "wondrous impression." For more on the experience of the wondrous, see notes 61 and 66, as well as the discussions of it in chapters 6 and 7.

122. "style manifested" (shuppū): Zeami appears to have coined this term, which annotators concur refers to a manifest style of performance—what the actor can actually deliver onstage.

123. "actor's power to inspire an impression" (shite no kanriki): the artistic and spiritual power that the actor is capable of bringing to bear in order to move audiences; SNKBZ 88, 366. NSTS and NKBT 65 are in basic agreement, though they omit reference to spiritual power or, more literally, "power of the heart/mind" (shinriki); NSTS, 141; and NKBT 65, 478. Nose holds that it is the most fundamental spiritual power (konponteki na shinriki) of which the actor is capable, viewed from the perspective of the impression that it makes on the audience; Nose, 1:648. The overall gist of this statement seems to be that representation of the material visually onstage is the actor's bailiwick, and its successful execution depends on him, not on the composer.

124. "such [eye-opening] visual expressiveness as this" (kayō no genkyoku): Nose and NSTS suggest that this refers to the spot that holds the climactic kaigen acting; Nose, 1:648; and NSTS, 141. NKBT 65: the superb expression (kyoku) of the kaigen (478). SNKBZ 88: the most important acting (ganmoku no engi). It is the responsibility of the playwright to allow a place for such highlights as he maps out the overall contours of the action.

125. "[climactic] point in the action" (wazadokoro): an important scene in a play for demonstrating technique, in this case for the performance of the dance or vigorous moves aimed at inducing the eye-opening.

126. Zeami is playing on the metaphor of the Buddhist statue coming to life when the third eye is carved into it to make the point that the play is like an organism that comes fully to life when the eye-opening segment occurs. The eye-opening constitutes the final touch that brings the entire play to fruition.

127. "the actor's technique" (shite no waza): waza refers to outwardly manifested techniques in general—what the actor does onstage. Here the actor's skill level is connoted as well.

128. "one master is capable of both of these tasks" (ryōjō issaku no tatsujin): the ideal situation is for one person to be capable of handling both the composing and the performing.

129. The meaning of the original sentence, kaigen ikkai (no) myōsho aru beshi, is obscure. The Yoshida text has kaigen itsu ni kaigen, the genitive particle (no) replaced by a kanji for the nominal gen, meaning "base" (pronunciation of the resulting kanji phrase based on Nose's gloss; Nose, 1:644). Nose avers that the meaning of the phrase is unclear; ibid., 645. The genitive particle no in kaigen ikkai (no) myōsho adheres to the Diet manuscript and the Matsunoya text reproduction. My translation follows them.

   NSTS, NKBT 65, and SNKBZ 88 surmise from the overall meaning of the passage that the compound kaigen (with two characters meaning "open" and "eye," i.e., eye-opening) is a copyist's error and that Zeami originally wrote mongen (a compound combining characters with the meanings of "listen" or "ear" and "eye"). Mongen would refer to the phenomenon of the ear-opening and the eye-opening occurring together. NSTS, 141; NKBT 65, 478; SNKBZ 88, 366. The Matsunoya manuscript tracing seems to confirm at least one copyist's error, that of Yoshida Tōgō. The Matsunoya text, on which Yoshida based his recension, does indeed read mongen ikkai (no) myōsho, or the "wondrous spot in which the ear and the eye open at once." Apparently, the copyist of the Diet text made the same error, which Takemoto thinks was a coincidence; Takemoto, "Yoshida bunko Zeami nōgakuron shiryō shōkai," 203.

   I have followed the Matsunoya text. A photographic reproduction of this passage may be found in frontispiece 7 of the matter preceding Takemoto's article, "Yoshida Bunko zō shinshutsu bon Sandō ni tsuite," in Engeki Kenkyū Sentā kiyō III.

130. The Diet text and Matsunoya Bunko reproduction reverse the order of these two statements and format "Oral transmission" as a note.

131. Zeami does not specify the age of the juvenile (waranbe). SNKBZ 88 states that it refers to someone who has not yet experienced genpuku (the coming-of-age ceremony); SNKBZ 88, 366. That age could vary from around eleven to seventeen.

132. "supporting role" (waki no shite): lit. "side doer," i.e., not the main "doer" or actor. Although shite now refers exclusively to the role of the protagonist, it was used more generically to indicate "actor" in Zeami's time. Shite came to refer to the protagonist specifically from the late Muromachi period; SNKBZ 88, 216. For that reason, I have translated shite simply as "actor" throughout this segment. Waki no shite could refer to any type of supporting role, including those that are now formally differentiated, as the waki (lit. side [person]), and the companion roles. Today, a prepubescent child would ordinarily be cast in the dedicated role type for children, called kokata.

133. "main role in the noh" (hitori nō): the juvenile himself plays the role of protagonist.

134. "father or mother" (*oya ka haha nado*): lit. "parent or mother." It adheres to the Yoshida recension. In the Diet text, the *kana* character *so* replaces the *kana* for *ka*. This is also true for the recently discovered Matsunoya text reproduction. All the annotated texts consulted follow the Yoshida text variant: NKBT 65, 479; Nose, 1:651; NSTS, 141; SNKBZ 88, 366. However, recently Omote has suggested that the attribution of the character for *so* in the Diet text and Matsunoya reproduction may be correct after all. He observes that when *so* is pronounced in combination with the *on'yomi* reading of the character for mother (*bo*), one gets *sobo* (grandmother), and the resulting phrase (*oya, sobo nado*) would translate as "parent [or mother], grandmother, or the like." Based on a copy of the NSTS edition of this passage with Omote's notes inscribed in the margins to indicate where the NSTS recension and Matsunoya text reproduction differ. Received courtesy of Professor Takemoto.

135. In plays that feature mad characters, loss or parting with a child is a common cause of such madness, and in most extant plays a reunion occurs as the final sequence. Zeami is cautioning that casting two children in the roles of parent and child in a play of this type will strike audiences as being in bad taste. "Bad taste" is my translation of *shoku*, also pronounced "*zoku*," whose meanings range from vulgar and unrefined to unorthodox. Nijō Yoshimoto, whose influence on Zeami was unquestionable, frequently uses the term in opposition to the quality of *yūgen* in his critical treatises on *renga* (see chap. 3).

136. "keenly pathetic quality to the visional affect" (*mugoki tokoro no kenpū aru*): *mugoi* may also mean cruel, or unfeeling, or lacking in compassion. I am guided here by Nose's gloss, *mugoku ijirashii* (cruelly touching/pathetic); also, *kao o somuketa* (makes one want to avert one's eyes); Nose, 1:652, 654, respectively. Visional affect (*kenpū*): here meaning the overall stage affect. See note 6 for more on this term.

137. The Diet text and Matsunoya copy have "older brother, sibling" (*ani, kyōdai*).

138. "even if it concerns [scenes] not a part of parent-child enactments" (*tatoi oyako no monomane ni nashi tomo*): even in the enactment of other types of scenes unrelated to those between parents and children that have been previously described, it will not seem suitable for young actors to play the roles of elderly characters.

139. "*monomane* in the venerable style" (*rōtai no monomane*): style of the old person (*rōtai*), one of Zeami's three prototypical styles of representation (*santai*).

140. May be read both as points that an older *shite* needs to bear in mind and, by extension, as points that a playwright composing a play for an older *shite* needs to bear in mind; NSTS, 142.

141. There are certain roles that the elderly actor will not be able to play credibly, regardless of how well he has disguised his age by use of mask and costume, the tools of his trade.

142. "famed young commander and warrior-aristocrat: (*meishō no waka tenjōbito*): lit. "famous commander and young, high-ranking court aristocrat." In the late twelfth

century, many members of the Taira clan, a warrior clan, had also been successful at garnering rank in the imperial court bureaucracy. Apparently Zeami felt that an elderly person was unsuited to either of these role types.

143. Atsumori: *shite* of the warrior play *Atsumori* by Zeami; the ghost of the young warrior of the Taira clan, Atsumori, returns to make peace with his assassin, the Minamoto warrior Kumagai no Jirō Naozane (the *waki*). Kiyotsune: *shite* of the warrior play *Kiyotsune* by Zeami; the ghost of the young warrior of the Taira clan, Kiyotsune, appears to his wife in order to ease her resentment over his decision to drown himself rather than accept defeat by the Minamoto clan. Atsumori (1169–1184) was the nephew of the powerful clan head Taira no Kiyomori. However, he never rose above lower fifth rank, junior grade. Kiyotsune (d. 1183) was the third son of Shigemori. He reached lower fourth rank, senior grade. Both men were acclaimed for their courtly sensibilities and artistic accomplishments, and their lives were cut short by the Genpei War.

144. "the audience will definitely not perceive his image to be like those" (*kenjo no omoinashi, sara ni sore ni narazu*): it will be impossible for an elderly actor to create an impression that is congruent with the images that audience members are already likely to possess for such well-known figures who contrast so starkly from himself. *Sara ni* (definitely [not]) is replaced by *sō ni* in the Yoshida text, altering the import to, "The audience will not easily perceive . . ."

145. "it is not possible without a thorough understanding of noh" (*nō o shirade wa kanō bekarazu*): the referent is not clear. It could refer to a thorough understanding of actors' natural talents. However, in *Sarugaku dangi*, there is one segment devoted to the composition of plays, and it quotes, or actually paraphrases, this passage from *Sandō* in the following fashion: "Being able to distinguish between the nature of each type of figure is not possible without an understanding of noh" (*Sono jintai jintai no hodo o miwaku beki koto, nō o shirade wa kanō bekarazu*); NSTS, 286. This seems to be evidence that Zeami intended the referent in the *Sandō* also to be the types of roles.

146. "three styles [and their derivatives]" (*santai no nō gakari*): *gakari* is interpreted by NKBT 65 and NSTS as "applied styles" (*ōyōfū*); NKBT 65, 480; and NSTS, 142. *Gakari* appears only in the Diet text.

147. Of the twenty-nine plays listed, only the text of *Mekurauchi* is no longer extant. However, the titles of a good number of these plays have changed over time. They are as follows, and there is more about these plays in the ensuing notes.

Yawata	*Yumi Yawata**
Aioi	*Takasago*
Shiogama	*Tōru*
Shizuka	*Yoshino Shizuka**
Matsukaze Murasame	*Matsukaze*
Higaki no onna	*Higaki*

Komachi	*Sotoba Komachi**
Satsuma no kami	*Tadanori*
Kōya	*Kōya monogurui**
Ōsaka	*Ōsaka monogurui**
Sano no funabashi	*Funabashi*
Shii no Shōshō	*Kayoi Komachi*
Taisan moku	*Taisan pukun*

* Probably the same plays (or revised versions), but there is no definitive proof.

148. *Yawata* (present title *Yumi Yawata*): *waki* play in two acts by Zeami; the *shite* is a deity of Iwashimizu Hachimangū Shrine who appears in the first act as an elderly shrine attendant and asks a retainer of retired Emperor Go-Uda to present the emperor with his gift, a bow contained in a brocade pouch. The old man explains that the bow symbolizes the strength that the Iwashimizu deities—patron deities of war—provided in the unification of Japan. Now that the bow is enclosed in the brocade pouch, it becomes a symbol of peace in a unified realm. The old man reveals his identity and dances, promising continued protection. In *Sarugaku dangi*, Zeami calls this a very "straightforward" play (*sugu naru*), in contrast to *Aioi*, which has "fins." He also mentions that *Yawata* was written to commemorate the beginning of the present shogun's rule (but does not specify which shogun he means); *Sarugaku dangi*, NSTS, 286. The principal deity of the shrine is Hachiman, patron of war and of the Ashikaga clan.

   Aioi (presently titled *Takasago*): *waki* play in two acts by Zeami; see chapter 5 and appendix 2 of this volume.

   Yōrō (Longevity springs): *waki* play in two acts by Zeami. The play celebrates the magical powers of the waters of a spring in Mino Province (southern part of Gifu Prefecture), as well as the theme of filial piety. The *shite* in the first act is an old man of the place who appears in the company of his son (*tsure*). The *waki* is a retainer of the emperor who has been sent to inquire whether there is truly a spring whose waters have rejuvenating effects. The *shite* avers that he and his wife have been rejuvenated by the water, which they have enjoyed thanks to their filial son. In the second act, the *shite* plays a deity of the spring who appears as a young male to dance and to celebrate the auspiciousness of the spring and, by extension, the realm.

   Oimatsu (The pine tree that followed [its master]): *waki* play by Zeami. In the background is the legend of the plum tree and pine tree from the garden of the Heian courtier Sugawara no Michizane (845–903). The trees are said to have joined him in exile in Dazaifu, Kyushu. The play is set on a spring day at the site of Michizane's grave, Anrakuji Temple in Dazaifu, and the *shite* in the first act appears as an old man in charge of caring for the trees; the *tsure* is a young man in charge of the blossoms. The *waki* is a Kyoto resident who arrives during his pilgrimage to the shrine and inquires about the famous trees. The *shite* explains that they are auspicious symbols of learning and longevity. In the second act, the *shite* returns as the spirit of the pine tree, dances, and blesses the sovereign and the realm.

Shiogama: the original title of the play currently titled *Tōru;* it now belongs to the fifth classification. Zeami claims authorship in *Sarugaku dangi.* The *shite* is the Heian courtier Minamoto no Tōru (822–895), and the play is about his legendary love for his mansion, the Kawara no In, and its garden, which was constructed from sand brought from the scenic beach at Shiogama (present-day Miyagi Prefecture). After Tōru's death, the mansion and the garden declined, and there were rumors that his outraged spirit frequented the site. In the play, the *shite* of the first act is an old man, a salt gatherer, who tells the *waki*, a visitor to Kyoto, the story of Kawara no In. The *shite* appears as the ghost of Tōru in the second act to express his longing and frustration, as well as his love for the beauty of the setting through his dance. Kan'ami was said to have performed a play, no longer extant, titled *Tōru no otodo,* which featured a demon. It is possible that *Shiogama* is a revision of this earlier play.

Aridōshi: this is now a fourth-category play. Its authorship is claimed by Zeami in *Sarugaku dangi;* he also mentions that the music was in the style of the *dengaku* artist Kiami. The *waki* is the celebrated poet and author of the "*Kana* Preface," Ki no Tsurayuki, who is on a pilgrimage with an attendant (*wakitzure*) in Kii Province (present-day Wakayama Prefecture). He passes by Aridōshi Shrine without dismounting from his horse and thereby risks offending the deity of the shrine, Aridōshi *myōjin.* Indeed, Tsurayuki's horse collapses and cannot move. An elderly shrine attendant (*shite*) appears and urges Tsurayuki to compose a verse to appease the deity, which is successful. As it turns out, the shrine attendant is actually the deity, who then says a Shintō prayer and does a short dance to celebrate the virtues of *waka* poetry.

149. *Hakozaki:* a *waki* play featuring a female character; attributed to Zeami. The *waki* is Mibu no Tadamine, a courtier and respected poet of the early Heian period. He takes an autumn pilgrimage to Hakozaki Shrine in Chikuzen Province (present-day Fukuoka), Kyushu. A young woman of the locale (*shite*) appears to him under a pine tree on the grounds. He asks her to tell him about the renowned Hakozaki pine. She identifies it as the one near her and tells him that it marks the place where a box containing the miraculous triyium—writings on the three kinds of Buddhist enlightenment—is buried. She offers to show him the box to reward him for his piety. In the second act, the *shite* appears as the spirit of Empress Jingū, the mythical unifier of Japan, who dances for Tadamine. Takemoto points out that this and the next play in Zeami's *Sandō* listing, *Unoha,* mark the early stages of Zeami's efforts to import elements from the *tennyo no mai* (dance of the celestial maiden) from Ōmi *sarugaku* into Yamato *sarugaku* and to recast them as highlights in plays

about Shintō deities in accordance with Zeami's own instructions in Segment 1.2 of Sandō: "[T]he celestial maiden, female deity, and shrine maiden do the dance and chant of *kagura*." Takemoto, *Kan'ami, Zeami jidai no nōgaku*, 304–305. The play ceased to be performed in the Edo period.

Unoha (Cormorant feathers): also a *waki* play by Zeami featuring a female character. Like *Hakozaki*, it ceased to be performed in the Edo period. The play is set on the shoreline in Hyūga Province (present-day Miyazaki Prefecture, Kyushu) and retells the myth of the birth there of the Shintō deity Unoha fuki awasezu no mikoto (deity of the hut partially thatched with cormorant feathers). His father was the Shintō deity Hiko hohodemi no mikoto, and his mother the dragon princess Toyotamahime (princess of abundant jewels) from the dragon palace under the sea. Through this union, Hiko hohodemi no mikoto came into possession of the precious jewels that controlled the waxing and waning of the tides. The couple came to earth when she became pregnant, and Hiko hohodemi no mikoto managed to thatch only part of the parturition hut before the birth occurred, which is how the child received his name.

Toyotamahime's image intersects with that of the revered dragon princess of the twelfth book of the *Lotus Sutra*. Barely eight years of age, she shows such religious insight that despite the fact that as a woman she was considered defiled and unqualified for buddhahood, she manages to reach enlightenment. When she presents a priceless jewel to one of Buddha's disciples, she is transformed into a man on the spot, which clears the way for her spiritual progress.

Toyotamahime is the *shite* of the second act of *Unoha*. The play is set on the birthday of the child. The *shite* of the first act appears as a young woman who makes her living from the sea; she appears with a young female cohort (*tsure*). They encounter the *waki*, a retainer of the emperor, and his attendant (*wakitsure*), who are there to pay their respects at this famous spot. (There is evidence that the *waki* was originally cast as a historical personage, the illustrious Tendai priest Genshin; SNKS, 2:412.) The women retell the myth of the birth and go through the motions of thatching the hut. In the second act, Toyotamahime reappears to reveal her identity and to dance. (The original dance was probably a *tennyo no mai*.) The play ends with the intertwining of the jewel imagery of the Shintō myth and the Buddhist parable. Toyotamahime says to the *waki*, "The jewels of ebb and flow *(raises fan and circles stage)* are wondrous treasures and yet, my heart desires the true jewel of enlightenment." Jeanne Paik Kaufman, trans., *Unoha* (Cormorant plumes), in Brazell with Gabriel, eds., *Twelve Plays of the Noh and Kyōgen Theaters*, 20.

Mekurauchi (Blind person strikes): a play by Zeami with no extant script. The title suggests that the *shite* may have disguised herself as a blind person in order to carry out a revenge killing; the NSTS note surmises that it may be an earlier version of the play *Mochizuki*, a revenge piece in which a woman disguises herself as a blind female minstrel to carry out the deed; NSTS, 142. Zeami mentions the same title in *Go on* under the *yūkyoku* classification and attributes the musical composition to his father. It is not clear what the relation might be between the work named in *Go on* and that listed in *Sandō*. Takemoto surmises that Zeami imported Kan'ami's older composition into his play; Takemoto, *Kan'ami, Zeami jidai no nōgaku*, 9.

Shizuka: generally believed to correspond to the play now titled *Yoshino Shizuka*, currently classified as a third-category woman play. In *Sarugaku dangi*, Zeami attributes this work to Seiami; NSTS, 291. Seiami was an actor affiliated with the Kanze group, but little is known about him except that he seems to have been somewhere between Kan'ami and Zeami in age; Miyake, *Kabu nō no kaku-ritsu to tenkai*, 118–119. It is thought that the play might be a revision of an earlier work by Kan'ami that Zeami refers to as *Shizuka ga mai no nō*. See chapter 2 for the basic story of *Yoshino Shizuka*. It has also been argued that *Shizuka* may be an earlier version of the current play *Futari Shizuka*. Also see note 9 above.

Matsukaze, Murasame: a play now classified in the third group, the woman plays. The current title is *Matsukaze*. A favorite in the repertoire, it is about the ghosts of two fisher girls who had fallen in love with the Heian courtier Ariwara no Yukihira when he was exiled to their shore. One of the two, Matsukaze (*shite*), in a fit of longing, mistakes a shoreline pine for him as she broods over his memory. (For an introduction to the play, also see chap. 3.) In *Sarugaku dangi* the play is attributed to Zeami, but other treatises suggest that there were earlier versions. *Go on* mentions that Kiami, the *dengaku* actor, composed passages of an earlier avatar titled *Shiokumi*. *Go on* also indicates that Kan'ami had a hand in an earlier version; for more on the history of the play, see Takemoto, *Kan'ami, Zeami jidai no nōgaku*, 165–172.

Hyakuman: the play about the *kusemai* performer Hyakuman who loses her wits as she wanders in desperation, searching for her lost child. She is reunited with the child at the Dainenbutsu ceremonies at Seiryōji Temple on the western outskirts of the capital. This fourth-category piece, built on the *monogurui* theme, continues to be popular today. For more on its history, see chapter 2.

Ukifune: the story from the final chapters of *Genji monogatari* about the ghost of the gentlewoman Ukifune, whose feelings are torn between two suitors, Kaoru and Niou. In the play, her ghost returns to tell her story—how, unable to resolve her confict, she wandered in a daze until she became the seeming victim of spirit possession. She was discovered by a priest who brought her back to her senses. Subsequently, she becomes a nun. In the play, the *waki*'s identity is also that of a Buddhist priest who listens to her recapitulation of her story, which culminates in a short, choreographed sequence. Ukifune is one of the characters that Zeami credits with the most *yūgen* appeal in Segment 2.2 of *Sandō*. In *Sarugaku dangi*, he specifies that the script was composed by Yokoo Motohisa, someone he calls an amateur; nothing is known about him; NSTS, 291. Zeami claims credit for musical composition. The play now belongs to the fourth group, miscellaneous plays.

Higaki no onna (Woman of the cypress hedge): now titled *Higaki*. Zeami claims authorship of this play. The setting is Unganji Temple in Higo Province (Kumamoto Prefecture). Every day an elderly woman (*shite*) (actually a ghost) appears to draw holy water. A priest (*waki*) asks her to identify herself. She explains that she was once a *shirabyōshi* dancer who lived "in a cottage with a fence made of cypress hedge"; Yasuda, *Masterworks of the Nō Theater*, 304. She reveals that she had been too proud and misbehaved, so now she is punished for her past sins, for she must shoulder red-hot pails of fire when she draws water. She asks the priest to pray for her. She also admits her longing for her lost splendor, especially on the occasion when she composed a poem and danced for the courtier Fujiwara no Okinori. In the second act of the play, she performs an extended dance (*jo-no-mai*) expressive of her longing. Today *Higaki* is at the heart of the third classification (woman plays). It is also designated as one of the "three old-woman" pieces (*san rōjo*), which are considered the most challenging to perform in the entire repertoire.

Komachi (Komachi on the stupa): in which the *shite* takes the identity of Komachi as an ancient crone who wanders, homeless. She is accosted by priests of Kongōbuji Temple on Mount Kōya, the headquarters of the Shingon sect of Buddhism, when they see her resting on a stupa along the path they are traveling. An argument ensues in which Komachi bests them on the subject of the true nature of the dharma. In the second act, she is possessed by the spirit of her spurned suitor, Shii no shōshō. In *Sarugaku dangi,* Zeami says that the play used to be longer; he attributes it to Kan'ami; NSTS, 287 and 291. *Sotoba Komachi* is a fourth-category play and, as an old-woman piece, is considered very demanding.

150. All the plays listed under the style of the warrior are based on material in *Heike monogatari* about the epic battle between the Taira and the Minamoto clans. They are all by Zeami except for one, *Michimori*. All of the plays belong to the second classification, which features the ghosts of warriors.

Michimori is the creation of the Kanze group actor Seiami. In *Sarugaku dangi,* Zeami states that it was originally a very wordy play that he streamlined some; NSTS, 287. *Michimori*, though a warrior piece, is a love story. It relates the death of Taira no Michimori at the Battle of Ichinotani (1184), one of the final battles in the Genpei War, and the suicide of his wife, Kozaishō, who could not endure the prospect of life without him. She plunges into the sea and drowns.

Satsuma no kami (presently titled *Tadanori*) is introduced in chapter 4.

For more on the *shite* of the plays *Atsumori* and *Kiyotsune,* see note 143 above.

Sanemori is the story of an old warrior, Saitō Sanemori, who insists on going to battle for the Taira despite his advanced age. He dyes his hair black to conceal his age and then dies in battle. The play reenacts a scene in which the dye is washed out of the hair on his decapitated head and his identity is ascertained.

Sanemori is also introduced in chapter 4. *Yorimasa* tells the story of the death of the Minamoto warrior Yorimasa by ritual suicide on the grounds of Byōdōin Temple on the outskirts of Kyoto when a coup in which he is involved against the Taira fails.

All of these are two-act plays in which the warrior spirit appears in his true identity in the second act to relive the end of his life. They all continue to be performed today. It is interesting that Zeami's list of plays features only warriors who lose in battle.

151. Player of the *yūkyō* type: plays about *hōka* (see note 12) or similar young males who perform. The plays listed feature either characters who perform as part of their métier (*Jinen Koji*) or males who lose their mental composure due to emotional duress (*otoko monogurui*): *Tango monogurui*, *Kōya*, and *Ōsaka monogurui*.

Tango monogurui is attributed to Seiami. A young boy is disowned by his father for failing to apply himself at a temple where he has been sent to study. The boy then tries to drown himself but is rescued by a passerby. Years later they return to see the boy's family after he has become an erudite Buddhist monk. They learn that the parents are still wandering in a crazed state (*monogurui*) over the loss of their son, and the young man determines that he will hold a prayer service for them. He is reunited there with his father. This play is full of dialogue and dramatic action, an interesting counterexample to Zeami's style, with its emphasis on musical modes of depiction. It is a fourth-category piece that fell out of the repertoire in the Edo period.

Zeami attributes the play *Jinen Koji* to his father, Kan'ami. It is the story of a *hōka* by that name who was well known for his skills as a Buddhist preacher. A young girl presents him with a robe at a prayer service and asks him to pray for the souls of her dead parents in return for her offering. Jinen Koji realizes that she has sold herself into slavery to pay for the robe. He pursues the slave traders and persuades them to release the girl in return for entertaining them with a miscellany, including the performance of a *kusemai* piece and dancing to the *kakko* stick drum. This is a fourth-category play that continues to be performed. It is representative of an older pattern in Yamato *sarugaku* of staging musical performance as part of the plot action—as a performance within a performance.

Kōya (presently called *Kōya monogurui*) is the story of a young boy who resolves to become a monk after his father dies. A family retainer who is opposed to this decision searches until he finds the boy in the company of a priest from Mount Kōya. Moved by the eloquence of the priest, the retainer gives himself up to a dance in praise of the Mount Kōya complex. He is reunited with the boy and resolves to take the tonsure and join him. This is a fourth-category play. In the Kanze school, it was rewritten in the eighteenth century so that the boy is persuaded to return to the secular world in order to carry on the family line in the way befitting a warrior; *Shintei zōho nō, kyōgen jiten*, s.v. "*Kōya monogurui* [61]. In

Go on, Zeami attributes the *kuse* section of this play to Motomasa; NSTS, 216–217. This play is still performed today, but infrequently.

Ōsaka (probably the original title for the play now known as *Ōsaka monogurui*): Zeami claims authorship of this play. Like *Jinen Koji*, it treats the kidnapping of a child by slave traders. When his child is kidnapped by them, a father takes to the road to try to find him. When he finds lodging for the night, he learns that there is a blind person in the vicinity who performs as a *monogurui* (deranged person) and who has a child with him. When the father seeks them out, he is reunited with his child thanks to the good offices of the blind person. As it turns out, the blind performer is actually the deity of the Osaka barricade, a famous spot in Japanese poetry, known as a site for reunions. The deity identifies himself and disappears. This fourth-category play is not part of the current standardized repertoire and is rarely performed.

152. Featuring demon *shite* in the style having "the form of a demon, but a human heart." The first in Zeami's list is *Koi no omoni* (Heavy weight of passion). The play is by Zeami. It is not classified in the fourth group (miscellaneous plays). In the first act, the *shite* is an elderly gardener who has fallen passionately in love with a gentlewoman, consort to an emperor. When she gets wind of his feelings for her, she has a brocade-wrapped package delivered to him and agrees to see him if he proves able to lift the package. He takes the bait and tries desperately to lift it, but this is an impossible charge, he discovers, for it contains a large stone. The *shite* realizes that he has been duped and commits suicide, vowing vengeance. He appears in the second act in demonic form to punish the woman, but relents when he realizes her regret. In the end he becomes her guardian spirit. As Zeami states in the ensuing passage of *Sandō*, this play had an earlier avatar titled *Aya no taiko* in which the *shite*, also an old gardener, tries desperately to beat a drum that a high-ranking gentlewoman, the object of his infatuation, has given him to taunt him. If the drum sounds, she will appear to him. However, as it turns out, the drumheads are made of damask, which, of course, will not make a sound. The old man drowns himself and comes back as a demon to inflict his vengeance, forcing the court lady to try to make the drum sound. This play ends without the demon's forgiveness. It is probably the same as the play now titled *Aya no tsuzumi*. The authorship of this older work is not known.

Sano no funabashi (Floating bridge at Sano; now known as *Funabashi*): the story of two young lovers who were accustomed to meeting on a bridge between their homes. Their parents disapproved of the union and removed planks in the bridge to foil their meetings, whereupon the couple leap into the water and drown. In the play a traveling mountain ascetic comes to their village. A young man and woman appear to ask him to make a contribution toward building a bridge. They relate the story of the two lovers, revealing that they are indeed the ghosts of the two, who have become demons and cannot find release from their obsessive attach-

ment. They ask the ascetic to pray for them, and he helps them find enlightenment. Zeami lists this as his revision of an older play from the *dengaku* repertoire.
Shii no shōshō (now named *Kayoi Komachi*) is a fourth-category play. In *Sarugaku dangi*, Zeami attributes authorship to Kan'ami, but he also says that it was a
revision of a play composed by a preacher *(shōdōshi)* from the Yamato area and first
performed by Konparu Gon no kami, grandfather of Konparu Zenchiku; NSTS,
291. For more on the play, see chapter 1.

Taisan moku (presently titled *Taisan pukun*): a play now classified in the miscellaneous group, it is named after its *shite*, one of the ten kings *(jūō)*, originally
Chinese deities believed to "reside in the world of the dead and give consecutive
sentences to the departed as they pass through their respective judgment areas";
Alicia Matsunaga, *The Buddhist Philosophy of Assimilation: The Historical Development of the* Honji-Suijaku *Theory* (Tokyo: *Monumenta Nipponica* and Charles E.
Tuttle, 1969), 37. A Heian courtier renowned for his love of cherry blossoms
prays to Taisan pukun that the life of the blossoms might be prolonged. A *tennyo*
descends and breaks off a branch of the blossoms, whereupon Taisan pukun appears
to reprimand her and to grant the courtier his wish.

For information on where the above texts may be found in Japanese, as well
as critical articles on them in Japanese, see Takemoto Mikio and Hashimoto Asao,
eds. *Nō, kyōgen hikkei. Bessatsu Kokubungaku*, no. 48 (1995). For a useful list of
what English translations of noh plays are available, see www.meijigakuin.ac.jp/
~watson/no/utai_checklist.html.

153. "expression": *kyoku*.

154. "the material continues to flower over the years" *(nennen kyorai no kashu)*: the
exact meaning of *kashu*, a phrase written with the characters for "flower" and
"seed," is unclear. I have translated is as "material that flowers." *Kashu* is used elsewhere in *Sandō* in reference to material from which the playwright may draw to
induce the flower; see note 64. However, NSTS states that it should mean "art [as
in that of the performer] that flowers over the years"; NSTS, 143. The annotation
in SNKBZ 88 points out that a similar phrase is used in chapter 7 of *Kaden* in reference to the actor's ability to continue to possess the flower as his age progresses:
nennen kyorai no hana (art that flowers over the years); SNKBZ 88, 480; citation
from NSTS, 59. However, the compound *kashu* does not appear in that passage.
Throughout *Sandō* Zeami quite consciously uses the Chinese character for *shu* to
refer to the material that the playwright draws from in composing, so I think it is
consistent to gloss *kashu* as "material that elicits the flower."

155. "styles and pieces" *(fūkyoku)*: NSTS and SNKBZ 88 gloss this as "artistic style"
(geifū); NSTS, 143; and SNKBZ 88, 369. Nose equates it with "style of figure
[onstage]" *(fūtei)* and "piece" as in a number performed on a program *(kyokumoku)*;
1:668. NKBT 65 has "style" or "technique" *(fūtei, gikō)*; NKBT 65, 481. The two

characters for *fūkyoku* often appear in reverse order in Zeami's critical writings (*kyokufū*), in which case they can have a range of meanings related to style of expression. However, the word *fūkyoku* does not occur as frequently. I think Nose's reading may be the closest. Given the context of this passage, it is likely that Zeami is referring to both styles of performance and compositional styles. After all, one may expect both to be subject to the vicissitudes of time. I think it is also possible that *fūkyoku* refers to "style of piece or play" here, analogous to Zeami's usage of the term *fūtei*, which may be translated literally as "style of figure [cut by the actor onstage]."

156. "atmosphere of *yūgen*": *yūgen no kakari*.

157. Itchū, the famed *dengaku* performer and mentor of Kan'ami, is mentioned in *Kaden* and *Sarugaku dangi*; NSTS, 43, 261, respectively. Inuō, also known as Dōami, was the famed performer in the style of Ōmi *sarugaku*, in the same generation as Kan'ami; mentioned in *Sarugaku dangi*; NSTS, 263.

158. "made the *yūgen* elements of dance and chant the foundation of their styles": *buga yūgen o honpū to shite*.

159. "the grade of supreme effect in the style having a true foundation of *yūgen*": *makoto no yūgen honpū no jōka no kurai*.

160. The style having the true *yūgen* foundation never loses its power to move audiences. Such a style has the *nikyoku santai* at its foundation. Elsewhere, Zeami defines the grade of supreme effect (*jōka no kurai*) as that stage in an actor's mastery at which he has the ability to perform the dance and chant of a play interestingly, but without conscious deliberation—as if by second nature; see *Fūgyoku shū*, NSTS, 159.

161. "[material that has] the seeds to flower into *yūgen* (*yūgen no kashu*): NSTS and SNKBZ 88 gloss *kashu* in this instance as "the seeds of the flower that is called *yūgen*"; NSTS, 144; and SNKBZ 88, 370. Nose maintains that here *kashu* refers generally to any factor that makes the flower of *yūgen* bloom; 1:669. Although it is true that this concluding segment concerns the overall importance of the *yūgen* atmosphere in performance, these final remarks are added in order to stress the underlying importance of compositional style. Moreover, this particular sentence concerns the writing process and is consistent with Zeami's other uses of the word *kashu* throughout this treatise. For these reasons I have again chosen the more specific gloss of "material" for *shu*.

162. "acclaim" (*meibō*): in the Diet text and Matsunoya text reproduction, a different Chinese character is allotted as the second in the compound. See note 10.

163. "flowering style of *yūgen*": *yūgen no kafū*.

164. 1423. The Ōei period lasted from 1394 to 1428.

165. The Diet text lacks Zeami's signature and his written seal (*kao*).

Appendix 2. An Annotated Translation of *Takasago*

This translation is based on a manuscript dated 1713 that is believed to be a faithful copy of a handwritten copy by Kanze Kojirō Nobumitsu (1435–1516), son of Zeami's nephew, On'ami. I have adhered to the annotated edition in Yokomichi Mario and Omote Akira, eds., *Yōkyoku shū*, I, NKBT 40 (Tokyo: Iwanami Shoten, 1960): 219–225. I have also consulted the following annotated editions of *Takasago*: SNKS, vol. 2: 281–292; Koyama Hiroshi, Satō Kikuo, and Satō Ken'ichirō, eds. *Yōkyoku shū*, I, Nihon Koten Bungaku Zenshū 33 (Tokyo: Shōgakukan, 1973): 53–65; and Sanari Kentarō, ed. *Yōkyoku taikan*, vol. 3: 1857–1874.

1. The *kyōgen* actor, who plays a person from the locale of Takasago, has lines only in the interlude between the two acts, which is not translated here. He retells the story of the pine trees in response to the *waki*'s query and then suggests that they cross over to Sumiyoshi together in his boat. For English translations, see chap. 5, note 33.

2. "long lasting": translation of *hisashiki*; refers to the journey ahead and also connotes the idea of longevity, setting an appropriate tone for an auspicious play of the *waki* classification.

3. Aso Shrine is located in what is now Ichinomiya-machi, Kumamoto Prefecture, Kyushu. Their destination is the capital, Kyoto.

4. In the original, "white cloud" (*shirakumo*) is a pun on "not know," which is suggested by "*shira-*," the *mizenkei* inflection of the verbal *shiru*.

5. Harima is the name of a former province, now the southwestern part of Hyōgo Prefecture. Takasago is located on the southern coast, west of the present-day city of Akashi.

6. In performance today, the following lines are added by the *waki* after the traveling chant: "Before we know it, we have arrived at Takasago Bay in Harima. Let us linger here a bit and inquire into the nature of the place." These lines form one component part called the *tsukizerifu* (arrival lines).

7. There is an allusion to a poem by Oe no Masafusa: poem 398 in the book of Winter poems in the seventh imperial anthology the *Senzai waka shū*; Shinpen Kokka Taikan, vol. 1, pt. 1:193. *Onoe* (lit. "top of a mountain") may also be interpreted as a place-name. Onoe is located on the eastern shore of an estuary letting out onto Takasago Bay. Onoe Shrine was celebrated in *waka* as the location of the Takasago pine.

8. Citation of a poem by Fujiwara no Okikaze, *Kokin waka shū*, no. 909; Shinpen Kokka Taikan, vol. 1, pt. 1:18.

9. *Shirayuki*, translated as "white snows," puns on the *mizenkei* inflection of the verbal *shiru*, connoting "not know."

10. Zeami draws on two poems in Chinese from the *Wakan rōei shū* collection to give the crane image added depth. Both are written on the theme of the crane, a symbol of longevity, auspiciousness, and tranquil grace. The following is by the Chinese poet Bai Juyi (Po Chüi-i; 772–846), poem no. 445.

Its voice approaches my pillow—
the crane of a thousand years;
Its reflection slips into my wine cup—
the Peak of the Five Ancients.

The second is by the Heian poet Miyako no Yoshika (834–879), poem no. 449.

A hungry squirrel will be restive,
Flurried when it nurses its young;
An aged crane is peaceful at heart,
and will sleep serenely.

Kawaguchi Hisao and Shida Nobuyoshi, eds., *Wakan rōei shu, Ryōjin hishō*. Nihon Koten Bungaku Taikei 73 (Tokyo: Iwanami, 1965), 163–164.

11. "The Living Pines" (Iki no matsu): a pun on the place-name Iki no Matsubara. Located in Kyushu, it is a place name frequently cited in *waka*.

12. Sumiyoshi is located across the bay from Takasago in Settsu Province, now part of Osaka Prefecture.

13. *Kokin waka shū (Kokin shū)*, first imperial poetic anthology, completed in the early tenth century (commissioned ca. 905).

14. *Aioi*, translated as "wedded," is a pun meaning both "growing together," as in the two trees, and "growing old together," as in the elderly couple.

15. The *Man'yō shū* is the first and largest of the Japanese poetic anthologies, compiled in the eighth century.

16. Engi emperor: Emperor Daigo (885–930), who reigned from 897 to 930. Daigo was an enthusiastic patron and participant of *waka* composition, and one period of his reign, the Engi years (901–923), subsequently came to be heralded as the heyday of *waka* composition. Daigo commissioned the *Kokin waka shū*.

17. "Upon the four seas/the waves are serene" (*Shikai nami shizuka nite*): an established metaphor in *waka* for peace in the realm.

18. "Basking in the goodness/of the spring sun/from the southernmost branches/the blossoms start to open": invocation of poem written in Chinese by Sugawara no Fumitoki; Kawaguchi and Shida, eds., *Wakan rōei shū*, 70, no. 92.

19. "Though four seasons pass/its color of a thousand years/stays deep in the snows": invocation of poem written in Chinese by Minamoto no Shitagō; ibid., 157, no. 425.

20. "The pine tree blooms/but once in a thousand years—/ten times this occurs, it is claimed": The pine tree was said to bloom once every thousand years throughout its life span of ten thousand years; a familiar motif in Chinese and Japanese letters.

21. This entire choral passage echoes the "*Kana* Preface" of the *Kokin waka shū*. Shikishima, translated as "isles of poetry," is a poetic epithet for the land of Japan.

22. The opening passage of the *kuse* is attributed to the diary of the Heian poet Fujiwara no Nagayoshi (Chōnō). For more on the diary, see chapter 5, note 56.

23. The standard word in Japanese for "pine tree" is *matsu* (松). In this instance, how-ever, a second word is used: *shūhakkō* (or *jūhakkō*). *Shūhakkō* is derived by breaking up the component radicals in the Chinese character for *matsu* and ordering them in the following sequence:

$$(十) \, sh\bar{u}/ju + (八) \, hak\text{-} + (公) \, k\bar{o} = (十 \, 八 \, 公) \, sh\bar{u}hakk\bar{o}.$$

24. *Shikō*: the Japanese pronunciation of the Chinese title Shihuang, the name assumed by the "First Most Sublime Ruler of the Qin," who founded the Qin Dynasty of China (221–207 B.C.E.). The *Shiji* contains an anecdote about Shihuang awarding court rank to a pine tree that sheltered him from the rain in a hunting expedition. The pine suddenly grew large and spread its branches. Ssu-ma Ch'ien (Sima Qian), *Shih chi*, I (Peking: Chung Hua Shu Chu, 1959), Book 6, 242.

25. "laurel vine" (*masaki no kazura*): an evergreen shrub with a vining habit; cited as a metaphor for the longevity of the *Kokin waka shū* collection in Tsurayuki's "*Kana* Preface": "*Matsu no ha no chiriusezu shite, masaki no kazura, nagaku tsutawari*" (The needles of the pine do not all fall; the laurel vine trails long); *Kokin waka shū*, ed. Saeki Umetomo, 103.

26. "earth and trees alike": allusion to the following passage in the fourteenth-century martial chronicle *Taiheiki*: "Be it earth or trees, all things belong to this land of our sovereign, so where could there be a corner left to harbor a demon?"; Gotō Tanji and Kamata Kisaburō, eds., *Taiheiki*, II. Nihon Koten Bungaku Taikei 35 (Tokyo: Iwanami, 1961), Book 16, 168.

27. The *shite* and *tsure* board an imaginary boat and depart for Sumiyoshi, entreating the *waki* to join them there. The two exit down the bridgeway to end the act, while the *waki* remains seated.

28. "Even one as I/long familiar with the pine/on Sumiyoshi's shore/wonder how many ages/it has known": citation of poem found in episode 117 of *Ise monogatari*. In the original, the emperor visits the Sumiyoshi shore, where he composes the poem as a tribute to the god of Sumiyoshi. In the *Takasago* version, the poem is attributed to the *shite*, who is himself the god. "Know you not, my lord/our in-timacy,/unseen the sacred fence round your realm/from distant ages?": allusive variation on a poem in *Ise monogatari*, composed by the Sumiyoshi deity in response to the emperor's poem. The original poem: *Mutsumashi to kimi wa shiranami/mizu-gaki no hisashiki yo yori/iwaisometeki* (Our intimacy, my lord/like white waves, don't you know?/A sacred fence/from ancient times/protects your realm). Sakakura Shigeyoshi et al., eds., *Taketori monogatari, Ise monogatari, Yamato monogatari*. Nihon Koten Bungaku Taikei 9 (Tokyo: Iwanami Shoten, 1957), 178. In this play, the deity chants the two poems in sequence. Whereas in its original context "*Mutsu-mashi to*" (Our intimacy) refers to the relation between deity and sovereign, in the

noh libretto, it can be read as the intimacy between the two pines of Takasago and Sumiyoshi.

29. In the original, the phrase *hisashiki yoyo* (from distant ages) forms a pivot: *mizugaki no hisashiki yoyo* (sacred fence/round your realm/from distant ages) and *mizugaki no kamikagura* (from distant ages, the dance of the gods). The deity is announcing his intention to perform the "dance of the gods," and he is instructing the shrine ritualists to beat the drums in accompaniment to propitiate his spirit.

30. On the western sea/of Aokigahara/from amidst the waves/the god of Sumiyoshi/has risen": citation of poem by Urabe no Kanenao: *Shoku Kokin waka shū*, no. 732; Shinpen Kokka Taikan, vol. 1, pt. 11:332. Zeami alters *shioji* (sea route) to *namima*, meaning "amidst the waves." Aokigahara is a famous Kyushu place-name in *waka*. The librettos in use in the Kanze and Hōshō schools substitute *kami matsu* (the spirit of the pine) for *Sumiyoshi no kami* (the god of Sumiyoshi). Although this translation is based on a Kanze text, in this instance I have followed the text of the Kongō, Kita, and Konparu schools because it is closer to Kanenao's poem and is thought to preserve Zeami's original line; Yokomichi and Omote, eds., *Yōkyoku shū* 1:444, appendix note 129.

31. Asaka is an old place-name for the eastern section of coastline of Sakai City in southern Osaka Prefecture; it was part of the Sumiyoshi district *(gun)*. Asaka no ura (Asaka Bay) is a famous place-name in *waka*. The gathering of seaweed and the place-name of Asaka are an allusion to poem 121 of the *Man'yō shū*: "When the evening falls/the ocean tide will come in/at Sumiyoshi/along Asaka inlet/let's gather seaweed quickly." Kojima Noriyuki et al., eds., *Man'yō shū*, Nihon Koten Bungaku Zenshū 2 (Tokyo: Shōgakukan, 1971), 1:129. The syllables *asa* also mean "shallow" and function here as a pun, the second meaning being "shallow snow."

32. Based on a poem originally in Chinese by Tachibana no Aritsura (ca. early tenth century), no. 30 in *Wakan rōei shū*. Transliterated into Japanese, it reads: *Shōkon ni yotte koshi o sureba/sennen no midori te ni miteri/baika o otte kōbe ni sashihasameba jigetsu no yuki koromo ni otsu.* Ōsone Shōsuke and Horiguchi Hideaki, eds., *Wakan rōei shū*, Shinchō Nihon Koten Shūsei (Tokyo: Shinchōsha, 1983), 21. As the editors of the edition above note, this poem seems to be arranged as the sequel to the preceding poem in the collection by Sugawara no Michizane, which, in translation, reads, "We recline on pine trees, rubbing waists against them,/to absorb their immunity to encroaching wind and frost./We concoct vegetable broth and sip it with our mouths, in hopes our inner humors will be well tempered now." Rimer and Chaves, eds. and trans., *Japanese and Chinese Poems to Sing*, 35. The image of the falling plum petals likened to snow also seems to trace to a line in a poem by Bai Juyi titled "A Composition under the Blossoms on the Fifth Day of the Second Month," in the twentieth book of his collection of poems known in Japanese as *Hakushi monjū*. The plum blossom is also a symbol of hardiness.

33. *Seigaiha* (Sea green waves), *Genjōraku* (Return to the town), and *Senshūraku* (The dance of ten thousand years): all titles of court dances belonging to the *bugaku* genre. *Senshūraku* is also the title of a piece of court orchestral music *(gagaku)*.

34. Today the remainder of this passage is frequently performed as an independent piece of chant to end a day's program on an auspicious note *(tsuke-shūgen)*.

Character Glossary

• • •

ageha 上ゲ端

ageku 挙句

ageuta 上歌

aguru koe 上声

Aioi 相生・相老

aishō 哀傷

Akashi 明石

Akoya no matsu 阿古屋松

Ama 海人・海士

Amaterasu Ōmikami 天照大神

Amida 阿弥陀

an 安・案

an'i 安位

ani, kyōdai 兄・兄弟

anki 安器

anraku on 安楽音

Anrakuji 安楽寺

anshin 安心

Aoi 葵

Aoi no Ue 葵上

Aokigahara 檍が原

araki 荒き

arayashiki 阿頼耶識

Aridōshi 蟻通

Aridōshi *myōjin* 蟻通明神

Ariwara no Narihira 在原業平

Ariwara no Yukihira 在原行平

Asaka 浅香

Asaka no ura 浅香の浦

Asukai Masayasu 飛鳥井雅康

Ashikaga Takauji 足利尊氏

Ashikaga Yoshimitsu 足利義満

Ashikaga Yoshimochi 足利義持

Ashikaga Yoshinori 足利義教

Aso 阿蘇

Aso-shi keifu 阿蘇氏系譜

Atsumori/Atsumori 敦盛

Aya no taiko 綾の大鼓

Aya no tsuzumi 綾鼓

ayakashi 怪士

417

Baba Akiko　馬場あき子

Bai Juyi (Po Chü-i)　白居易

bakufu　幕府

bankyoku　万曲

Bao jing san mei ge (Pao-ching san-mei ke)　宝鏡三昧歌

bettō　別当

bettōbō sarugaku　別当坊猿楽

Biwa (ko)　琵琶（湖）

bōkoku　亡国

bōoku　ぼうをく・ばうおく

buchi　舞智

buga ni yoroshiki fūkon　舞歌によろしき風根

buga nikyoku　舞歌二曲

buga yūgen o honpū to shite　舞歌幽玄を本風として

bugaku　舞楽

Bukka Engo zenji Hekigan roku　仏果圜悟禅師碧巖録

Buozi (Pao Hsien)　苞子

butai giwa　舞台際

butaifūchi　舞体風智

Byōdōin　平等院

Caodong　曹洞

Chan　禅

chang dao　常道

chi　智

ch'i　気

Chigusa　千種

Chikuzen　筑前

chiri　塵・散り

chiru　散る

chisei　治声

Chōnō/Nagayoshi/Nagatō　長能

chōshinkafū　籠深花風

chū no mai　中ノ舞

Chuang-Tzu　荘子

chūdō　中道

chūjō　中将

chūnori　中ノリ

Chūshinkyō　注心経

daien kyōchi　大円鏡智

Daigo *tennō*　醍醐天皇

Daigoji　醍醐寺

daimyō　大名

Dainenbutsu　大念仏

dan　段

Danzan jinja　談山神社

Dao de jing (Tao tē ching)　道徳経

Daoxin　灌頂

Dazaifu　太宰府

Dehuang　徳洪

demono no bugaku no jintai　出物の舞楽の人体

demono no jintai　出物の人体

demono no shinajina　出物の品々

dengaku　田楽

Denkō roku　伝光録

Dōami　道阿弥

Dōgen　道元

Dōmoto Masaki　堂本正樹

Dongshan Liangjie　洞山良价

dōon　同音

dōon hitoutai　同音一歌・同音一謡

Ebina no Naamidabutsu　海老名の南阿弥陀仏

eboshi　烏帽子

Eguchi　江口

Eiwa　永和

en　鉛

en　艶

Enami Saemon Gorō　榎並左衛門五郎

engeki　演劇

Engi　延喜

Engi shiki 延喜式

engo 縁語

enkan o nashite 延感を成て

enken 遠見

enken no fūtei 遠見の風体

enkin 遠近

enkyō 遠郷

Enman'i (Emai) *za* 円満井座

Enryakuji 延暦寺

Fa xiang 法相

Fo guo Yuanwu chan shi Bi Yan lu (Fo-kuo Yüan-wu-ch'an-shih Pi-yen-lu) 仏果圜悟禅師碧巌禄

fo xing 仏性

Fuchiki 不知記

Fue no monogurui 笛物狂

Fuganji 補厳寺

fūgetsu ennen 風月延年

fūgetsu ennen no kazari 風月延年のかざり

Fūgyoku shū 風曲集

Fujiwaka 藤若

Fujiwara no Ietaka 藤原家隆

Fujiwara no Nagayoshi 藤原長能

Fujiwara no Okikaze 藤原興風

Fujiwara no Okinori 藤原興範

Fujiwara no Shunzei 藤原俊成

Fujiwara no Tameie 藤原為家

Fujiwara no Tamezane 藤原為実

Fujiwara no Teika 藤原定家

fukashigi 不可思議

Fukakusa Shii no Shōshō 深草四位少将

fūkon 風根

Fukuoka 福岡

fūkyoku 風曲

Fumyōō 普明王

Funabashi 船橋

Funa Benkei 船弁慶

funi myōtai no ikei o arawasu tokoro 不二妙体の意景をあらはす処

Furu 布留

fushi 節

fūshi fuzei no utsukushisa 風姿風情の美しさ

fushi no omomuki 節の趣

fushi no tsuzukegara, nagare 節のつづけがら、流れ

Fūshikaden 風姿花伝

Fūshikaden daiichi, "Nenrai keiko jōjō" 風姿花伝第一、『年来稽古条々』

Fūshikaden daini, "Monomane jōjō" 風姿花伝第二、『物学条々』

Fūshikaden daisan, "Mondō jōjō" 風姿花伝第三、『問答条々』

Fūshikaden daishi "Shingi" 風姿花伝第四、『神儀』

fushikakari 節かかり

fushikakari utsukushiku kudarite 節かかり美しく下りて

fushizuke 曲付

fushizuke no guai 曲付のぐあい

fushizuke no omomuki 曲付の趣

Fushizuke shidai 曲付次第

Futari Shizuka 二人静

futatsu no kokoro 二の心

fūtei 風体

fuzei · fūzei 風情

fuzei no bi 風情の美

fuzō fugen 不増不減

ga 我

ga no uta 賀歌

gagaku 雅楽

gaibun 我意分

gaken 我見

gaku 樂

gakutō 樂頭

Gasan Jōseki 峨山韶碩

geifū 芸風

geiriki 芸力

geki nō 劇能

Genji 源氏

Genji monogatari 源氏物語

Genjō 玄奘

Genjōraku 還城楽

genkyoku 眼曲

Genpei 源平

Genshin 源信

genzai nō 現在能

Gettan Oshō hōgo 月庵和尚法語

Gijo · Ginyo 祇女

Gikeiki 義経記

Giō 祇王

Gion 祇園

giri 義理

giri nō 義理能

Go on 五音

Go ongyoku jōjō 五音曲条々

Gogumaiki 御愚妹記

Goi 五位

goin 五音

Go-Komatsu 後小松

goku 後句

gōriki no tei 強力体

Goshūi wakashū 後拾遺和歌集

gōsofū 強麁風

Guanding 灌頂

Guhishō 愚秘抄

guntai 軍体

guntai no demono 軍体の出物

ha 破

Hachidan no mai 八段の舞

Hachiman 八幡

Hachizaemon-bon 八左衛門本

hakama 袴

Hakozaki 箱崎

Hakushi monjū 白氏文集

hana 花

Hanagatami 花筐

hanayaka na 花やかな

Hanjo 班女

Hannya haramita shin gyō 般若破
羅蜜多心経

Hanzoku taishi 斑足太子

Harima 播磨

haru 張る・春・晴る

harubaru はるばる

hashigakari 橋懸り

hashiri 走り

hataraki 働キ・はたらき

hatarakigoto 働事

hayabushi 早節・早曲

hayamai 早舞

hayashi 囃子

Heian 平安

Heike monogatari 平家物語

Heikyoku 平曲

Hekigan roku 碧巌録

Hekirenshō 僻連抄

hie ni hietari 冷えに冷えたり

Hie za 日吉座

Hiei 比叡

hiesabitaru 冷え寂びたる

hietaru 冷たる

hietaru kyokufū 冷たる曲風

hifū 非風

Higaki 檜垣

Higaki no onna 檜垣の女

Higashiyama　東山

Higo　肥後

Hikaru Genji　光源氏

Hiko hohodemi no mikoto　彦火
　火出見尊

Hinoki Shoten　檜書店

hiranori　平ノリ

Hiroshima　広島

hisashiki　久しき

hitokakari　一かかり

hitori nō　独り能

hitoutai　一謡・一歌

hiyūgen　非幽玄

hōka　放下

hōkatsu suru　包括する

Hōkazō　放下僧

hokku　発句

Hōkyō zanmai ka　法鏡三昧歌

hon'i　本位

honka　本歌

honkadori　本歌取り

honmu myōka　本無妙花

hontai　本体

hontaifū　本体風

hon'yō　本様

honzetsu　本説

honzetsu no zaisho　本説の在所

Hori　堀

Hōsei [Daigaku Nōgaku Kenkyūjo]
　法政（大学能楽研究所）

Hōshō　宝生

Hossō　法相

Hossō Nikan Shō　法相二巻鈔

Huayan　華厳

Huineng　慧能

Hyakuman/Hyakuman　百万

Hyōgo　兵庫

hyōshi ai　拍子合

hyōshi awazu　拍子不合

Hyūga　日向

i　意

I chū ni kei ari.　意中に景あり。

Ichijō Kanera　一条兼良

*Ichijō shō (Eshin-ryū naishō sōjō
　hōmon shū)*　一帖抄（恵心流内
　證相承法門集）

Ichijōin　一乗院

ichimon　一聞

Ichinomiya-machi　一宮町

Ichinotani　一谷

ichiza jōju　一座成就

iemoto　家元

ifū　意風

iguse　居グセ

ii furumai　言振舞

iigoto no shina　云事の品

iji　意地

ikareru koto　怒れる事

Iki no Matsu　生の松

Iki no Matsubara　生の松原

Imagawa Ryōshun　今川了俊

Imagumano　今熊野

imayō　今様

Inuō　犬王

Ise　伊勢

Ise no Go　伊勢の御

Ise monogatari　伊勢物語

issei　一声・一セイ

isshin　一心

isshin kanriki no kokorone　一身感力
　の心根

isshin o tenga no ki ni nashite　一心
　を天下の器になして

isshin sangan　一心三観

Itchū　一忠

Itsukushima　厳島

Iwanami kogo jiten　岩波古語辞典

Iwanami Kōza　岩波講座

Iwanami Shoten　岩波書店

Iwashimizu Hachimangū　石清水
八幡宮

Izumi Shikibu　和泉式部

*Izumi Shikibu no itawari o Murasaki
Shikibu no toburaitaru koto*　和
泉式部ノ病ヲ紫式部ノ訪ヒタル
コト

Izutsu　井筒

ji　機

jia ming　假名

Jigoku no kusemai　地獄の曲舞

Jimu kata shokaishō　寺務方諸廻請

jinbō　人望

Jinen Koji　自然居士

Jingū kōgō　神功皇后

Jinson　尋尊

jintai　人体

jitsumei　実名

jo dan　序段

jobun　序分

jōfū　定風

jōgakushin　乗樂心

jo-ha-kyū　序破急

jōju　成就

jōka myōsei　上果妙声

jōka no kurai　上果の位

jōkafū　上果風

jo-no-mai　序の舞

Jōwa　貞和

Juchin　寿椿

Jūmon saihishō　十問最秘抄

Jūnigorō Yasutsugu　十二五郎康次

Jūnijirō　十二次郎

Jūō　十王

Jūrō Motomasa　十郎元雅

ka　花

*Kabu wa kono michi no hontai naru
beshi.*　歌舞ワコノ道ノ本体ナ
ルベシ。

Kaden　花伝

Kaden daishichi, "Besshi kuden"
花伝第七、「別紙口伝」

kadō　歌道

kaeru　帰る

Kagajo　加賀女

kage　蔭・陰

Kagetsu　花月

kagura　神楽

Kaidō kudari　海道下

kaigen　開眼

kaigen ikkai (no) myōsho aru beshi.
開眼一開（之）妙所可有。

kaigen itsu ni kaigen　開眼一開元

kaiko/kaikō　開口

kaikonin　開口人

kaimon　開聞

kakari　カカリ・かかり

kakeai　掛ケ合・掛合

Kakegawa　掛川

kakekotoba　掛詞

kakeri　カケリ

kakko　羯皷

kaku　書く

Kaku no gotoki yūjo.　此如遊女。

Kakuichi　覚一

Kakyō　花鏡

Kamakura　鎌倉

kami　神

kami mai　神舞

kami nō　神能

Kamidō　上道

Kamuro Kōya (Karukaya)　禿高野（苅萱）

Kan'a　観阿

kana　仮名

Kana jo　仮名序

Kanai Kiyomitsu　金井清光

Kan'ami Kiyotsugu　観阿弥清次

Kan'amidabutsu　観阿弥陀仏

kanbun　漢文

Kangin shū　閑吟集

kanjin nō　勧進能

kanjin sarugaku　勧進猿楽

kankafū　閑花風

Kanmu　桓武

kanriki　感力

kansho　感所

Kantan otoko　邯鄲男

Kantō　関東

Kanze　観世

Kanze Hisao　観世寿夫

Kanze Kojirō Nobumitsu　観世小次郎信光

Kanze Motomasa　観世元雅

Kanze Saburō　観世三郎

Kanze *za*　観世座

Kaoru [daishō]　薫（大将）

Kashiwazaki　柏崎

kashu　花種

Kashu no uchinukigaki　花習内抜書

Kasuga　春日

Kasuga jinja　春日神社

Kasuga Ōmiya　春日大宮

Kasuga Wakamiya　春日若宮

katachi naki sugata　形なき姿

katagi　形木

Katō Shūichi　加藤周一

Kawachi　河内

Kawara no in　河原院

kayō no genkyoku　かやうの眼曲

Kayoi Komachi　通小町

Kegon　華厳

Keizan Jōkin　瑩山紹瑾

Keizan Oshō Denkō roku　瑩山和尚伝光録

kemari　蹴鞠

ken　見

kenjo　見所

kenjo no omoinashi, sara ni sore ni narazu.　見所の思ひなし、更にそれにならず。

kenmon jōju　見聞成就

kenpū　見風

kenpū jōju　見風成就

kenpū kan'ō no jōju　見風感応の成就

kenpū kan'ō no jōju no manako o arawasu zaisho　見風感応の成就の眼をあらはす在所

ki　来・着

ki　機

ki　気

Ki no Tsurayuki　紀貫之

Kiami　喜阿弥

kibutsu　器物

Kidō Saizō　木藤才蔵

Kii　紀伊

kimi ga yo ni/Sumiyoshi　君が代に／すみよし（住吉・住良）

kinin no nyotai　貴人の女体

Kinsatsu　金札

Kintōsho　金島書

Kinuta　砧

kirei　きれい

kiribyōshi　切拍子

kiru fushi　切る曲

Kita　喜多

Kitagawa Tadahiko　北川忠彦

Kitano jinja kokiroku　北野神社古記録

Kitano Tenmangū　北野天満宮

Kitayama　北山

kiyō　器用

Kiyomori　清盛

Kiyotsune/Kiyotsune　清経

kō no mono　甲の物・甲物

kō no mono no utai　甲物の謡

kobeshimi　小癋見

kōdai mufū no kūdō　広大無風の空道

Kōfukuji　興福寺

koi　恋

Koi no netori　恋の音取り

Koi no omoni　恋重荷

Kokage no chiri o kakō yo.　木陰のちり(塵・散り)を掻かうよ。

kokata　子方

Kokin jo shō　古今序抄

Kokin waka shū　古今和歌集

Kokin waka shū jo kikigaki
(*Sanryūshō*)　古今和歌集序聞書：三流抄

kokiriko　コキリコ

kōko kyakurai　向去却来

kokoro　心

kokoro no mama narazu　心のままならず

kokoro o kudaku　心を砕く

kokoro o migaku　心を磨く

kokorone　心根

komaka ni iroiro o tsukushite　細カ二色々ヲ尽クシテ

kong　空

Kong'an guo (K'ung An-kuo)　孔安国

Kongō　金剛

Kongōbuji　金剛峯寺

Konishi Jin'ichi　小西甚一

kono shinajina　この品々

Konparu　金春

Konparu *bon*　金春本

Konparu dayū Ujinobu　金春太夫氏信

Konparu Gon no kami　金春権守

Konparu *za*　金春座

Konparu Zenchiku　金春禅竹

konpontei　根本体

konponteki na shinriki　根本的な心力

konzenu　混ぜぬ

Kore yori ha.　是自破。

kōshōfū　広精風

koto no ha　言の葉

kotoba　言葉・詞

kotoshikaru beki tei　事可然体

kotsu　骨

kotsujiki (kojiki) no shogyō　乞食の所行

kotsuzumi　小鼓

kouta　小歌

kouta bushi　小歌節

kouta bushi kusemai　小歌節曲舞

koutai　小謡

kowagakari　声がかり

Kōya　高野

Kōya (monogurui)　高野(物狂)

Kozaishō　小宰相

ku o irodorite　句を色どりて

kuden　口伝

kūdō　空道

Kumamoto　熊本

kun'yomi　訓読み

kuri　クリ

kuse クセ

kusemai 曲舞

kuwashiku koto o arawasu クワシク事ヲアラワス

kuzururu 崩るる

kyakurai 却来

Kyakuraika 却来華

Kyōgaku 経覚

kyōgen 狂言

kyoku 曲

kyokufū/kyokufu 曲風

kyokufū o taikō ni ategaite 曲風を大かうに宛てがひて

kyokushiki 曲色

Kyoto 京都

kyūfū 急風

kyūi (Kyūi) 九位

Kyūsei (Gusai) 救済

Kyūshū mondō 九州問答

Liuzu tan jing (Liu-tsu T'an-ching) 六祖壇経

Lunyu ji jie (Lun yü chi chieh) 論語集解

Maejima Yoshihiro 前島吉裕

mai 舞

mai nite utau kyokufū 舞にて謡ふ曲風

Mai wa koe o ne to nasu. 舞声為根。

maibataraki 舞働

Maigetsushō 毎月抄

maiguse 舞グセ

maihataraku fūtei no kan ni 舞動風体の間に

Maka Shikan 摩訶止観

makoto no hana 真の花

makoto no monomane 誠の物まね

Makoto no monomane ni irifusazu

ba, kono gaibun o uru koto aru majiki nari. 誠の物まねに入りふさずば、この我意分を得ることあるまじきなり。

Mansai jugō nikki 満済准后日記

Man'yō shū 万葉集

marubu 転ぶ

masaki no kazura 真折の葛

Masuda Shōzō 増田正造

matsu 松・待つ

matsu no ha 松の葉

Matsukaze 松風

Matsukaze, Murasame 松風、村雨

Matsunoya Bunko *bon* 松迺舎文庫本

Matsunoya Bunko *eisha bon* 松迺舎文庫影写本

Matsura 松浦

Mazu kikasete nochi ni mise yo. 先聞後見

meishō no waka tenjōbito 名将の若殿上人

Mekurauchi 盲打

menbaku 面白

Mengzi (Meng-tzu) 孟子

Mibu no Tadamine 壬生忠岑

Michimori 通盛

michiyuki 道行

Miidera 三井寺

mikazuki 三日月

miko 巫女

Mikohidari 御子左

Mimaji 敏満寺

Minamoto 源

Minamoto no Shitagō 源順

Minamoto no Tōru 源融

Minamoto no Yorimitsu (Raikō) 源頼光

minari 身なり

Mitsui Bunko 三井文庫

Miyake Akiko 三宅晶子

Miyake Kōichi 三宅祝一

Miyako no Yoshika 都良香

Miyazaki 宮崎

mizenkei 未然形

mizugaki no hisashiki yoyo 瑞垣の久しき代々

mizugaki no kamikagura 瑞垣の神神楽

Mochizuki 望月

Mohe zhi guan (Mo-ho chi-kuan) 摩訶止観

moji utsuri, ku utsuri no kakari 文字移り、句移りのかかり

mokuzen 目前

mon 聞

mondō/mondai 問答

mongen 聞眼

Mongen ikkai (no) myōsho 聞眼一開（之）妙所

monji 文字

Monju 文殊

monoaware na wabizumai 物哀れな侘住い

monogi 物着

monogurui 物狂

monokazu soroite 物数そろひて

monomane 物まね

monozukushi 物尽し

monzeki 門跡

Morihisa 盛久

Motokiyo 元清

Motomasa 元雅

Mototsugu 元次

mu 無

mu ichimotsu 無一物

Muchū mondō 夢中問答

mufū 無風

muga 無我

mugen geki 夢幻劇

mugen noh 夢幻能

mugoki tokoro no kenpū 酷き所の見風

mui mushin no jōju 無位無心の成就

mujō 無上

Mujū Ichien 無住一円

mukan no kan 無感の感

mukyoku mushin 無曲無心

mumon 無文

mumonfū 無文風

Murasaki Shikibu 紫式部

Muromachi 室町

Muromachi-dono 室町殿

Museki isshi 夢跡一紙

mushin 無心

mushin mufū no kurai ni itaru kenpū 無心無風の位に至る見風

mushufū 無主風

Musō Soseki 夢窓疎石

myō 妙

myōhō 妙法

myōka 妙花

myōkafū 妙花風

Myōrakuji 妙樂寺

myōtai 妙体

Naami 南阿弥

nabi nabi なびなび

nabiki 靡き

Nagayoshi shiki 長能私記

Naginomori-chō 梛の森町

naishin 内心

naishin no kan no kōka 内心の感の効果

Nakazutsunoo no Mikoto　中筒男命

naki sarugaku　泣キ申樂

namaru　鉛る・訛る・鈍る

namima　波間

Naniwa no ume　難波梅

nanori　名ノリ

nantai　男体

Nara　奈良

narau/shū　習う・習

neburi　眠り

nezame　寝覚め

Nihon Koten Bungaku Taikei　日本古典文学大系

Nihon Koten Bungaku Zenshū　日本古典文学全集

Nihon Shisō Taikei　日本思想大系

Nijō Yoshimoto　二条良基

nikutai gengo　肉体言語

nikyoku　二曲

nikyoku santai　二曲三体

Nikyoku santai ningyō zu　二曲三体人形図

ninnai no kakari　人ないのかかり

ninsō　人相

Niō[miya]　匂（宮）

Nishi no umi Aokigahara no namima yori araware ideshi Sumiyoshi no.　西の海檍が原の波間より現はれ出でし住吉の

Nishinotake　西岳

Nishio Minoru　西尾実

nō　能

Nō, kyōgen no gei　能・狂言の芸

Nō no kenkyū　能の研究

[N]ō o shirade wa kanō bekarazu.　能を知らではかなふべからず。

Nogami Toyoichirō　野上豊一郎

nōkan　能管

Nomori no kagami　野守の鏡

Nonomiya　野宮

Norikiyo　憲清

Norikiyo ga Toba-dono nite jisshu no uta yomite aru tokoro　憲清ガ鳥羽殿ニテ十首ノ歌詠ミテアルトコロ

Nōsakusho　能作書

Nose Asaji　能勢朝次

nozomi　望み

Nushi nari　主也

nyotai　女体

nyūwa　柔和

Obasute　伯母捨・姨捨

Ochi Kanze　越智観世

Ōe no Masafusa　大江匡房

Ōei　応永

Ōeyama　大江山

Ōgi　奥義

oi　老

Oimatsu　老松

ōkata　大方

Okina (*Okina*)　翁

Okina sarugaku　翁猿楽

Okinagatarashihime no Mikoto　息長足姫命

Ōmi　近江

omo　面

omokage　面影

omomuki　趣

Ōmori　大森

omoshiro　面白

omoshiroki fushi　面白き曲

omoshiroki kurai　面白き位

Omote Akira　表章

omote naru　面ナル

On'ami　音阿弥

ongyoku　音曲

Ongyoku kuden　音曲口伝

Ongyoku hataraki mo ōkata no fūtei ni te, surusuru to yasuku su beshi.　音曲、はたらきも大方の風体にて、するすると、安くすべし。

Ongyoku mo mai mo tadashiku sugu naru kakari ni su beshi.　音曲も舞もただしくすぐなるかかりにすべし。

ongyoku no kakari, fūtei　音曲の懸、風体

onjō　音声

onkan　音感

Ono no Komachi　小野小町

Onoe/onoe　尾上・尾の上

onoe no kane　尾の上の鐘

onoe no matsu　尾の上の松

ōnori　大ノリ

osa　長

Ōsaka　逢坂

Ōsaka (monogurui)　逢坂（物狂）

otokomai　男舞

Ōtomo no Kuronishi　大友黒主

Ōtomo Taishi　大友泰司

Otozuru　乙鶴

otsuru　落つる

ōtsuzumi　大鼓

oya ka haha nado　親か母など

oya, sobo nado　親、そ母（祖母）など

qi　気

Qin　秦

rakkyo　落居

ranbu　乱舞

rangyoku　闌曲

ran'i　闌位

Reizei　冷泉

renbo　恋慕

renga　連歌

Renga jūyō　連歌十様

Renga shinshiki　連歌新式

Renju gappeki shū　連珠合壁集

Renrihishō　連理秘抄

riken　離見

riken no ken　離見の見

rikidō　力動

rikidōfū　力動風

Rikugi　六義

Rin'ami　琳阿弥

Rinzai shū　臨済宗

ritsu　律

rokkasen　六歌仙

Rokujō　六条

Rokujō no miyasudokoro　六条御息所

Rokuso dangyō　六祖壇経

rongi　論議・ロンギ

Rongo shikkai　論語集解

rōtai　老体

rōtai no monomane　老体の物まね

ryo　呂

ryo-chū-kan keishiki　呂中干形式

Ryōdō Shinkaku　了堂真覚

ryōjō issaku no tatsujin　両条一作の達人

Saburō　三郎

Saburō Kiyotsugu　三郎清次

Saburō Motoshige　三郎元重

Sado　佐渡

Saga monogurui　嵯峨物狂

sageuta　下歌

Saichō　最澄

saidō　砕動

saidōfū 砕動風

Saigyō 西行

Saigyōzakura 西行桜

Saikoku kudari 西国下

Saitō Sanemori 斉藤実盛

Sakado 坂戸

sakai 境

Sakōdo 酒人

saku 作

san rōjo 三老女

Sanari Kentarō 佐成謙太郎

Sanbasō 三番叟

Sandō 三道

Sanemori 実盛

Sango ki 三五記

Sanjō Kintada 三条公忠

Sano no funabashi 佐野船橋

santai (sandai) 三諦

santai no nō gakari 三体の能懸り

San'un kaigetsu 山雲海月

sarugaku 猿楽・申楽

Sarugaku dangi 申楽談儀

sarugaku za 猿楽座

*Saruhodo ni, tadashiku, omote naru
    sugata nari.* サルホドニ、正シ
    ク、面ナル姿ナリ。

Sasamegoto ささめごと

sashi サシ

sashigoe さし声

sawasawa subesube to さはさはす
    べすべと

Seiami 井阿弥

Seigaiha 青海波

Seiryōji 清涼寺

seitenhakujitsu no itten 晴天白日の
    一点

Sekidera Komachi 関寺小町

Sekimon moji zen 石門文字禅

Sekine Tomotaka 関根知孝

senmonfū 浅文風

senritsu 旋律

Senshūraku 千秋楽

Senzai 千歳

Senzai waka shū 千載和歌集

Senzu manzai 千秋万歳

setsui no yūshi 切位の幽姿

Settsu 摂津

Shaseki shū 沙石集

Shichijūichiban shokunin utaawase
    七十一番職人歌合

Shichirō Motoyoshi 七郎元能

shidai 次第・シダイ

Shiga 滋賀

Shigemori 重盛

Shih-men wen-tzu ch'an 石門文字
    禅

Shihuang (Shih Huang) 始皇

Shii no Shōshō 四位の少将

shiika 詩歌

Shiji (Shih-chi) 史記

Shijing (Shih-ching) 詩経

Shikadō 至花道

Shikai nami shizuka nite 四海波静
    かにて

Shiki soku ze kū, kū soku ze shiki.
    色即是空、空即是色。

Shikisanban 式三番

Shikishima 敷島

Shikō 始皇

Shimodō 下道

Shimosaka 下坂

shimyō 至妙

shin 心

shina-kakari 品かかり

Shingon 真言

shinjin 身心

shinjitsu no an'i 真実の安位

Shinjū ni ichimotsu mo nashi. 心中 に一物もなし。

Shinkei 心敬

shin no issei 真ノ一声

Shinpen Nihon Koten Bungaku Zenshū 新編日本古典文学全集

shinriki 心力

shinshō 心性

Shintō 神道

Shiō 至翁

Shiō Zenbō 至翁善芳

Shiogama 塩竈

shioji 潮路

Shiokumi 汐汲

shirabyōshi 白拍子

Shirahige 白髭

Shirahige Myōjin 白髭明神

shirakumo 白雲

shiro 白

Shirō 四郎

shiru 知る

shite シテ・為手・仕手

shite no kanriki 為手の感力

Shizuka 静

Shizuka Gozen 静御前

Shizuoka 静岡

sho 書

Shōbōgenzō zuimonki 正法眼蔵随聞記

Shōdōka 証道歌

shōdōshi 唱導師

shōishin 正位心

Shōjō 猩々

shōkafū 正花風

shōmonji 唱門師

shōsho 正所

shotei 諸体

shu 手

shu 種

shuang-chao shuang-wang 雙照雙亡

shuchi 手智

Shudōsho 習道書

shūgen 祝言

shūgen no fūtei 祝言の風体

Shūgyoku tokuka 拾玉得花

shūhakkō (jūhakkō) 十八公

Shūhakkō no yosooi/Senshū no midori o nashite 十八公のよそほい／千秋の緑をなして

shuji 種子

Shujing (Shu-ching) 書経

shukkai・jukkai 述懐

shukutō 祝濤

Shunigatsu-e 修二月会

shuppū 出風

shura 修羅

shuradō 修羅道

shushi・jushi・sushi 呪師

shushi hashiri 呪師走

shutaifūchi 手体風智

Shuten dōji 酒呑童子

Sima Qian (Ssu-ma Ch'ien) 司馬遷

soenfū 奄鉛風

sōke 宗家

Sokozutsunoo no mikoto 底筒男命

sokuza ichidō no myōkan o nasu tokoro 即座一同の妙感をなす所

sokuza no kiten 即座ノ気転

sōkyokuchi 相曲智

sōmoku jōbutsu 草木成仏

Sono jintai no hodo o miwaku beki koto, nō o shirade wa kanō bekarazu. 其人体の程を見分べきこと、能を知らではかなふべからず。

sono mono その物

sono mono ni naru koto その物に成る事

sono omokage omokage o ima suru nari. 其面影面影を今する也。

Sonshōin 尊勝院

Sosei 素性

Sōsetsu- bon 宗節本

Sōsetsu shomei bon 宗節本署名本

Sōshi arai (Komachi) 草紙洗(小町)

Sōtō shū 曹洞宗

Sotoba Komachi 卒塔婆小町

sugata 姿

sugata-kakari 姿かかり

Sugawara no Fumitoki 菅原文時

Sugawara no Michizane 菅原道真

sugu naru 直なる

sugu naru nō 直ぐナル能

sugureta geitai すぐれた芸態

suikan 水干

Sukō 崇光

sukoshi monomane ni hazururu tomo 少し物まねにはづるるとも

Suma 須磨

sumi 住み・澄み

Suminoe 住吉

Sumiyoshi 住吉

Sumiyoshi ni mazu yukite 住吉にまづ行きて

Sung 宋

tabigoromo 旅衣

tachiai 立合

Tachibana no Aritsura 橘在列

tada ongyoku 只音曲

tada ureshiki kokoro nomi ka ただうれしき心のみか。

tada utai 只謡

tada utai no kakari 只謡のかかり

Tada utai wa, fushi o hon ni su. 只謡は、節を本にす。

Tadanori 忠度

tadashiki 正しき

Tadatsu no Saemon 多度津左衛門

tai 体

Taiheiki 太平記

taiko 太鼓

taikō 大かう

Taira 平

Taisan moku 泰山もく

Taisan pukun 泰山府君

Taishō 大正

Takasago 高砂

Takasago no/Onoe no matsu mo/ toshifurite 高砂の／尾の上の松も年古りて

takekaerite/takekaeri 闌かへりて・闌かへり

Takemoto Mikio 竹本幹夫

taketaru kurai 闌けたる位

takete 闌けて

takigi sarugaku 薪猿楽

Tamarin 玉林

Tanba 丹波

Tanaka-bon 田中本

tane 種

T'ang 唐

Tango monogurui 丹後物狂

Tashinamu beshi. たしなむべし。

Tashiro Keiichirō 田代慶一郎

tatsu 立つ・裁つ

Tatoi, oyako no monomane ni nashi tomo　たとひ、親子の物まねになしとも

Tayasu　田安

tē　特

Te o kudaku jibun ni te nakereba, kore mo mada jo no bun nari.　手ヲ砕ク時分ニテナケレバ、コレモマダ序ノ分ナリ。

Te o mo itaku kudaku jibun ni te nakereba, kore mo, imada jo no nagori no fūtei nari.　手をもいたく砕く自分にてなければ、是もいまだ序の名残の風体也。

Teiwa　貞和

Tendai　天台

Tenjiku　天竺

Tenkei Denson　天桂伝尊

tennyo no mai　天女の舞

Tiantai (T'ien t'ai)　天台

Toba　鳥羽

Tobi　外山

Tōgoku kudari　東国下

tōitsu sareta zentaizō　統一された全体像

tōki wagō　当気和合

toku　特

Tokugawa　徳川

Tokugawa Munetake　徳川宗賢

tomo　友

Tomoakira　知章

Tomonari　友成

Tōnomine　多武峰

Tōru no otodo　融の大臣

tōryō no shite　棟梁のシテ

Tosa Mitsunobu　土佐光信

toshinami　年波

Toyotamahime　豊玉姫

tsuchi mo ki mo　土も木も

tsuke-shūgen　付祝言

tsukizerifu　着キゼリフ

Tsukuba mondō　筑波問答

tsure　ツレ

tsuru　鶴

tsūshō　通称

tsuyoki　強き

tsuyosa　強さ

Tzu-kung　子貢

tsuzukegara　つづけがら

u　有

uchikiri　打切

Ukai　鵜飼

Ukifune/*Ukifune*　浮舟

Umewaka Manju　梅若満寿

umon　有文

umon onkan　有文音感

umonfū　有文風

umu chūdō　有無中道

Unoha　鵜羽

Unoha fuki awasezu no Mikoto　鵜羽葺不合尊

Unrin'in　雲林院

ura　浦・裏

Urabe Kanenao　卜部兼直

uruwashiki tei　麗体

ushufū　有主風

uta　歌

utaawase　歌合

utai　謡

utaimono　謡物

utamakura　歌枕

Utaura　歌占

Uwazutsunoo no Mikoto　表筒男命

wa shite chū suru shaku no gi 和シ
テ注スル釈ノ義

wafū no kyokutai 和風の曲体

waga kokoro 我心

waka 和歌

Wakan rōei shū 和漢朗詠集

Wakayama 和歌山

waki ワキ

waki nō 脇能

*Waki no nō, shūgen ni aru majiki
fushi nari* 脇の能、祝言に有る
まじき節也。

waki no shite 脇の為手

wakizure ワキヅレ

waranbe 童

Waseda Daigaku 早稲田大学

waza わざ・態

wazadokoro 能所・態所

wu 無

xian 咸

xin 心

Xuanzang (Hsüan-tsang) 玄奘

Xunzi (Hsün-tzu) 荀子

yaburu 破る

Yakushi nyorai 薬師如来

Yamashina 山階

Yamato 大和

Yamato *za* 大和座

Yamazaki Masakazu 山崎正和

yasashi 優し

Yashima Sachiko 八嶋幸子

Yasuda Zenjirō 安田善次郎

yasuki kurai 安き位

Yawata (Yumi Yawata) 八幡(弓八
幡)

yojō 余情

Yōka 永嘉

Yōkyoku shū 謡曲集

Yōkyoku shūyōshō 謡曲拾葉抄

Yonekura Toshiaki 米倉利昭

Yongjia (Yung-chia) 永嘉

Yorimasa 頼政

Yōrō 養老

Yoroboshi 弱法師

yoru 寄る

yoshi 吉・良し

yoshikakari よしかかり・由懸り

Yoshida *bon* 吉田本

Yoshida Bunko 吉田文庫

Yoshida Tōgo 吉田東伍

yōshiki 様式

Yoshikoshi Ken 吉越研

Yoshikoshi Tatsuo 吉越立雄

Yoshimine no Tsunenari
良岑経也

Yoshimine no Tsuneyo 良岑経世

Yoshino Shizuka 吉野静

*Yōshun no toku o sonaete nanshi
hana hajimete hiraku.* 陽春の徳
を備へて南枝花初めて開く。

yosooi よそほひ

Yōyō shū 洋々集

yoza 四座

yū 用

yū 優

yūfū 幽風

yūgaku 遊樂

Yūgaku shudōfū ken 遊樂習道風見

Yūgao/Yūgao 夕顔

yūgei no shokyoku 遊芸の諸曲

yūgen 幽玄

yūgen no fūtei 幽玄の風体

yūgen no kafū 幽玄の花風

yūgen no kakari 幽玄のかかり

yūgen no kashu 幽玄の花種

yūgen miyabitaru yoshikakari 幽玄
みやびたるよしかかり

Yūgen no sakai ni iru koto 幽玄之境
入事

yūgen tei 幽玄体

Yuima-e 維摩会

Yuishiki 唯識

yūkyō 遊狂

yūkyoku 幽曲

Yura monogurui 由良物狂

Yura no minato 由良湊

Yūzaki 結崎

Yūzaki *za* 結崎座

za 座

Ze 世

Zea 世阿

Zeami 世阿弥

Zeami jihitsu bon 世阿弥自筆本

Zeami jūrokubushū hyōshaku 世阿
弥十六部集評釈

Zeami kankei no shoshiryō 世阿弥
関係の諸資料

Zeami Motokiyo 世阿弥元清

Zen 禅

Zeshi rokujū igo Sarugaku dangi 世
子六十以後申樂談儀

Zheng dao ge (Cheng-tao ke) 証道
歌

Zhiyi (Chih'i) 智顗

zhong dao 中道

Zhong-lun (Chung lun) 中論

Zhuangzi (Chuang Tzu) 荘子

Zigong (Tzu kung) 子貢

zō onna 増女

Zōami 増阿弥

zoku/shoku nari 俗なり

zoku/shoku naru kotoba 俗なる言
葉

zuifū 瑞風

zuifū yori izuru kan 瑞風より出る
感

Selected Bibliography

. . .

Sources in Japanese

Amano Fumio. " 'Heike monogatari' to nō, kyōgen." *Kokubungaku, kaishaku to kanshō* 47.7 (1982): 125–131.

———. "Keiseiki no nō, monogurui nō no baai." *Kokubungaku* 31.10 (1986): 56–62.

———. " 'Naki sarugaku' kō: Genryū to shiteki ichizuke." *Kokugakuin zasshi* 82.3 (1981): 27–42.

———. "Nō ni okeru katarimono no sesshu: Chokusetsu taikensha no katari o megutte." *Geinōshi kenkyū*, no. 66 (1979): 16–34.

———. "Nō to katarimono, nō no kusemai sesshu o megutte." *Kokubungaku, kaishaku to kanshō* 51.4 (1986): 87–92.

———. *Okina sarugaku kenkyū.* Osaka: Izumi Shoin, 1995.

———. "Okina sarugaku no seiritsu: jōgyōdō shushōe to no kanren." *Bungaku* 51.7 (1983): 166–178.

———. "Zeami to Zen, *Rokuso dangyō* o megutte." *Kokubungaku kaishaku to kanshō* 65.10 (2000): 163–173.

Baba Akiko, ed. *Nihon meika shōjiten.* Tokyo: Sanseidō, 1984.

———. *Oni no kenkyū.* Kadokawa Bunko 3517. Tokyo: Kadokawa Shoten, 1980.

———. *Shura to en.* Tokyo: Kōdansha, 1975.

———. "*Takasago:* Kamimai to senzu manzai." *Kokubungaku* 25.1 (1980): 76–81.

Dōmoto Masaki. *Nō, kyōgen no gei.* Tokyo: Tokyo Shoseki, 1983.

———. *Zeami.* Tokyo: Geki Shobō, 1986.

Enoki Katsurō, ed. *Ryōjin hishō.* Shinchō Nihon Koten Shūsei. Tokyo: Shinchōsha, 1979.

Fukuda Akira. *Chūsei katarimono bungei, sono keifu to tenkai.* Miyai Sensho 8. Tokyo: Miyai Shoten, 1981.

Fukuda Hideichi, Shimazu Tadao, and Itō Masayoshi, eds. *Chūsei hyōron shū: Karon, rengaron, nōgakuron.* Kanshō Nihon Koten Bungaku 24. Tokyo: Kadokawa Shoten, 1976.

Fukui Kyūzō. *Kōhon Tsukuba shū shinshaku.* Tokyo: Kokusho Kankōkai, 1981.

Geinōshi kenkyūkai, ed. Nihon Geinōshi. 7 vols. Tokyo: Hōsei Daigaku Shuppankyoku, 1981–1990.

————, ed. Nihon no Koten Geinō. 10 vols. Tokyo: Heibonsha, 1969–1971.

————, ed. Nihon Shomin Bunka Shiryō Shūsei. 16 vols. Tokyo: San'ichi Shobō, 1973–1978.

Getsuyōkai, eds. *Zeami jihitsu nōhonshū,* vol. 2 (Tokyo: Iwanami, 1997).

Gondō Yoshikazu. *Nōgaku techō.* Kyoto: Shinshindō, 1979.

Gondō Yoshikazu, Nakagawa Akira, and Tsuyuno Gorō. *Nihon no yūrei, nō kabuki rakugo.* Asahi Karuchā Bukkusu 24. Osaka: Ōsaka Shoseki, 1983.

Gotō Hajime. *Kaitei Nihon geinōshi nyūmon.* Rev. ed. Gendai Kyōyō Bunko 494. Tokyo: Shakai Shisōsha, 1978.

————. *Nō no keisei to Zeami.* Tokyo: Mokujisha, 1989.

————. *Nōgaku no kigen.* Tokyo: Mokujisha, 1975.

————. *Zoku Nōgaku no kigen.* Tokyo: Mokujisha, 1981.

Gotō Tanji and Kamata Kisaburō, eds. Taiheiki, II. Nihon Koten Bungaku Taikei 35. Tokyo: Iwanami, 1961.

Haga Yaichi and Sasaki Nobutsuna, eds. *Kōchū Yōkyoku sōsho.* 3 vols. Tokyo: Hakubunkan, 1914.

Hama Kazue. *Nihon geinō no genryū, sangaku kō.* Tokyo: Kadokawa Shoten, 1968.

Hashimoto Asao. *Chūsei shigeki to shite no kyōgen.* Tokyo: Wakakusa Shobō, 1997.

Hashimoto Fumio, Ariyoshi Tamotsu, and Fujihira Haruo, eds. *Karon shū.* Nihon Koten Bungaku Zenshū 50. Tokyo: Shōgakukan, 1975.

Hata Hisashi. "Nō, kyōgen, kōwaka no 'katari.' " *Gekkan bunkazai,* no. 204 (1980): 18–25.

Hayashiya Tatsusaburō. *Chūsei geinōshi no kenkyū.* Tokyo: Iwanami Shoten, 1960.

————. *Kabuki izen.* Iwanami Shinsho 184. Tokyo: Iwanami, 1979.

Hayashiya Tatsusaburō et al, eds. *Kodai chūsei geijutsuron.* Nihon Shisō Taikei 23. Tokyo: Iwanami, 1973.

Hirakawa Sukehirō. *Yōkyoku no shi to seiyō no shi.* Asahi Sensho 49. Tokyo: Asahi Shinbunsha, 1975.

Hisamatsu Sen'ichi, ed. *Nihon Bungaku Hyōronshi 3: Kodai chūsei hen.* Rev. ed. Tokyo: Shibundō, 1976.

————. *Nihon karonshi no kenkyū.* Tokyo: Kasama Shobō, 1963.

Hisamatsu Sen'ichi et al., eds. *Chūsei*. Shinpan Nihon Bungakushi 3:. Tokyo: Shibundo, 1971.

Hisamatsu Sen'ichi and Nishio Minoru, eds. *Karon shū, nōgakuron shū*. Nihon Koten Bungaku Taikei 65. Tokyo: Iwanami Shoten, 1961.

Honda Yasuji. *Nō oyobi kyōgen kō*. Tokyo: Maruoka Shuppansha, 1943.

Horiguchi Yasuo. " 'Oimatsu' kō; tsuketari tobiume, oimatsu no koto." *Kanze*, no. 1 (1977): 6–12.

———. *Sarugaku nō no kenkyū*. Tokyo: Ōfūsha, 1987.

———. "Yōkyoku ni miru katarite no omokage." *Geinōshi kenkyū*, no. 36 (1972): 46–53.

Hōshō Fusao et al., eds. *Hōshō-ryū: Mai no hayashi*. Recording, 4 discs. Tokyo: Victor, 1978.

Hyōdō Hiromi. *Heike monogatari no rekishi to geinō*. Tokyo: Yoshikawa Kōbunkan, 2000.

Ijichi Tetsuo. *Renga no sekai*. Nihon Rekishi Sōsho 15. Tokyo: Yoshikawa Kōbunkan, 1967.

Ijichi Tetsuo, Omote Akira, and Kuriyama Riichi, eds. *Rengaron shū nōgakuron shū hairon shū*. Nihon Koten Bungaku Zenshū 51. Tokyo: Shōgakukan, 1973.

Ikeuchi Nobuhiro. *Nō no mikata, utai no kikikata*. Tokyo: Isobe Kōyōdō, 1918.

Inui Teijo. *Yōkyoku shūyōshō*. Ed. Muromatsu Iwao. Kokubun Chūshaku Zensho. Rev. ed., 1968. Tokyo: Sumiya Shobō, 1907.

Iriya Yoshitaka et al., eds. *Hekigan roku*. 3 vols. Iwanami Bunko. Tokyo: Iwanami, 1992, 1994, 1996.

Ishii Tomoko. "Ōsaka monogurui ni tsuite no ikkōsatsu, *Sandō* kihankyoku to shite no igi o megutte." *Nō, kenkyū to hyōron*, no. 18 (1991): 11–22.

Itō Hiroyuki, Imanari Genshō, and Yamada Shōzen, eds. Bukkyō Bungaku Kōza. 9 vols. Tokyo: Benseisha, 1994–1996.

Itō Masayoshi. "Buga yūgen no hatsugen, Zeami o tōshite mita Zenchiku." *Bungaku* 31.1 (1963): 44–56.

———. *Konparu Zenchiku no kenkyū*. Kyoto: Akao Shōbundō, 1970.

———. "Yōkyoku chūshaku to geinōshi kenkyū, kaishakushi to shite no nō katazuke." *Geinōshi kenkyū*, no. 108 (1990): 1–9.

———. "Yōkyoku *Kakitsubata* kō, sono shudai o tōshite mita chūsei no *Ise monogatari* kyōju to Narihira-zō ni tsuite." *Bunrin*, no. 2 (1967): 61–83.

———. "Yōkyoku *Takasago* zakkō." *Bunrin*, no. 6 (1972): 111–125.

———, ed. *Yōkyoku shū*. 3 vols. Shinchō Nihon Koten Shūsei. Tokyo: Shinchōsha, 1983, 1986, 1988.

Iwanami Kōza Nihon Bungakushi. Vol. 16. *Kōshō bungaku, I*. Tokyo: Iwanami, 1997.

Iwasaki Kae et al. *Shichijū ichinin utaawase, Shinsen kyōka shū, Kokin hinaburi shū*. Shin Nihon Koten Bungaku Taikei 65 (Tokyo: Iwanami, 1993).

Iwasaki Kikuo, ed. *Banbayashi tezuke taisei*, vol. 1. Osaka, Yoshida Yōkyoku Shoten, 1934.

Iwasaki Masahiko. "Ashirai ai no tenkai." *Nō, kenkyū to hyōron*, no. 18 (1991): 38–49.

———. "Sarugaku no setsuwa to oni." *Nōgaku kenkyū*, no. 26 (2001): 37–82.

Kanai Kiyomitsu. *Nō no kenkyū*. Tokyo: Ōfūsha, 1969.

Kaneko Genshin. *"Kokinshū" to yōkyoku*. Tokyo: Yōkyoku Daikōza Kankōkai, 1934.

Kanze Hisao. *Kanze Hisao chosaku shū*. 4 vols. Ed. Yokomichi Mario and Ogihara Tatsuko. Tokyo: Heibonsha, 1981. (Four vols. of Kanze Hisao's writings compiled and published posthumously.)

———. *Kanze Hisao, Zeami o yomu*. Ed. Ogihara Tatsuko. Heibonsha Raiburarii 411. Tokyo: Heibonsha, 2001.

———. *Kokoro yori kokoro ni tsutōru hana*. Tokyo: Hakusuisha, 1991.

Kanze Sakon, ed. *Kanze-ryū shimai katazuke*. Tokyo: Hinoki Shoten, 1977.

———, ed. *Kanze-ryū yōkyoku hyakuban shū*. Tokyo: Hinoki Shoten, 1976.

———, ed. *Kanze-ryū yōkyoku zoku hyakuban shū*. Tokyo: Hinoki Shoten, 1939.

Katagiri Noboru. " 'Manzai jugō nikki shihai bunsho' o megutte, Ashikaga Yoshinori no Zeami fushi Sentō shutsuen soshi to Kanze mōshijō." *Nōgaku kenkyū*, no. 22 (1997): 59–78.

Katagiri Yōichi. *Chūsei "Kokinshū" chūshakusho kaidai*. 6 vols. Kyoto: Akao Shōbundō, 1971–1987.

Katō Shūichi et al., eds. *Nihon bunka no kakureta kata*. Tokyo: Iwanami, 1984.

Kawaguchi Hisao and Shida Nobuyoshi, eds. *Wakan rōei shū, Ryōjin hishō*. Nihon Koten Bungaku Taikei 73. Tokyo: Iwanami, 1965.

Kawamura Kōdō and Ishikawa Rikizan, eds. *Dōgen zenji to Sōtō shū*. Nihon Bukkyōshūshi Ronshū 8. Tokyo: Yoshikawa Kōbunkan, 1985.

Kawamura Yoshiteru, ed. *Tendaigaku jiten*. Tokyo: Kokusho Kankōkai, 1990.

Kawase Kazuma, ed. *Kōchū "Nōsakusho," "Fushizuke shidai," "Yūgaku shudōfū ken," "Shudōsho."* Tokyo: Wan'ya Shoten, 1965.

———. *Nō to wa nani ka: Nō geijutsu no hyōgen no honshitsu*. Kōdansha Bunko 180. Tokyo: Kōdansha, 1976.

———. *Nōgakuron zuisō*. Tokyo: Wan'ya Shoten, 1968.

Kidō Saizō and Imoto Kōichi, eds. *Rengaron shū, hairon shū*. Nihon Koten Bungaku Taikei 56. Tokyo: Iwanami Shoten, 1961.

Kidō Saizō and Shigematsu Hiromi, eds. *Rengaron shū*, vol. 1. Chūsei no Bungaku 880-04. Tokyo: Miyai Shoten, 1972.

Kita Roppeita. *Roppeita geidan*. Shimin Bunko 115. Tokyo: Kawade Shobō, 1952.

Kitagawa Tadahiko. *Kan'ami no geiryū*. Miyai Sensho 4. Tokyo: Miyai Shoten, 1978.

———, ed. *"Kangin shū," "Sōan kouta shū."* Shinchō Nihon Koten Shūsei. Tokyo: Shinchōsha, 1982.

———. " 'Monomane jōjō' kara 'santai' ron e." *Bungaku* 51.7 (1983): 47–56.

———. *Zeami*. Chūkō Shinsho 292. Tokyo: Chūō Kōronsha, 1980.

———. "Zeami to fukushiki mugen nō no tenkai." *Geinōshi kenkyū*, no. 34 (1971): 1–12.

Kitagawa Tadahiko and Yasuda Akira, eds. *Kyōgen shū*. Nihon Koten Bungaku Zenshū 35. Tokyo: Shōgakukan, 1972.

Kō Yoshimitsu. *Kō-ryū kotsuzumi shōfu*. 2 vols. Tokyo: Nōgaku Shorin, 1956, 1961.

Kobayashi Seki. *Nō: Honsetsu to tenkai*. Tokyo: Ōfūsha, 1977.

Kobayashi Shizuo. *Yōkyoku sakusha no kenkyū*. Kyoto: Nōgaku Shorin, 1974. (1st ed.,
1942.)

———. *Seami*. Rev. ed. Tokyo: Hinoki Shoten, 1958.

Kojima Hideyuki. *Yōkyoku no ongakuteki tokusei*. Kojima Hideyuki Taikan Kinen
Shuppan Kai. Tokyo: Ongaku no Tomo Sha, 1985.

Kojima Tomiko. *Ongaku kara mita Nihonjin*. NHK Ningen Daigaku (Jan.–Mar. 1994).
Tokyo: Nippon Hōsō Shuppan Kyōkai, 1994.

[Shinpen] Kokka Taikan. Ed. Shinpen Kokka Taikan Henshū Iin Kai. 10 vols. with
separate indexes. Tokyo: Kadokawa Shoten, 1983–1992.

Konishi Jin'ichi. *"Michi," chūsei no rinen*. Nihon no Koten 3. Kōdansha Gendai
Shinsho 393. Tokyo: Kōdansha, 1975.

———. *Nihon bungeishi*. 5 vols. Tokyo: Kōdansha, 1986–1992.

———. *Nōgakuron kenkyū*. Hanawa Sensho 10. 2nd ed. Tokyo: Hanawa Shobō, 1964.

———. "Sakuhin kenkyū: Yūgao." *Kanze*, no. 10 (1980): 4–9.

———. "Shunzei no yūgenfū to shikan." *Bungaku* 20.2 (1952): 12–20.

———. "Ushintai shiken." *Nihon gakushiin kiyō* 9.2 (1951): 115–142.

Konparu Anshō. *Konparu Anshō denshō shū*. Ed. Hōsei Daigaku Nōgaku Kenkyūjo,
comp. Omote Akira and Oda Sachiko. Nōgaku Shiryō Shūsei 9. Tokyo: Wan'ya
Shoten, 1978.

———. *Konparu Anshō katazuke shū*. Ed. Hōsei Daigaku Nōgaku Kenkyūjo, comp.
Oda Sachiko. Nōgaku Shiryō Shūsei 14. Tokyo: Wan'ya Shoten, 1984.

Konparu Kunio. *Nō e no izanai: Jo-ha-kyū to ma no saiensu*. Kyoto: Tankōsha, 1980.

———. *Zoku Nō e no izanai*. Kyoto: Tankōsha, 1984.

Konparu Sōichi. *Konparu-ryū taiko zensho*. Tokyo: Nōgaku Shorin, 1953.

Koyama Hiroshi. "Yōkyoku o yomu tame ni." *Kokubungaku, kaishaku to kanshō* 42.2
(1983): 240–264.

Kōsai Tsutomu. *Nōyō shinkō, Zeami ni terasu*. Tokyo: Hinoki Shoten, 1972.

———. *Zeami shinkō*. Tokyo: Wan'ya Shoten, 1962.

———. *Zoku Zeami shinkō*. Tokyo: Wan'ya Shoten, 1970.

Kubota Jun. *Chūsei waka shi no kenkyū*. Tokyo: Meiji Shoin, 1993.

Kubota Jun and Kitagawa Tadahiko, eds. *Chūsei no bungaku*. Nihon Bungakushi 3.
Tokyo: Yūhikaku, 1976.

Kugimoto Hisaharu. *Chūsei karon no seikaku*. Tokyo: Kokugo o Aisuru Kai, 1969.

Kunisaki Fumimaro, ed. *Chūsei setsuwa to sono shūhen*. Tokyo: Meiji Shoin, 1987.

Maruoka Akira. *Nōgaku kanshō jiten*. Tokyo: Kawade Shobō Shinsha, 1961.

Masuda Shōzō. *Nō no dezain*. Kara Shinsho 55. Tokyo: Heibonsha, 1978.

———. *Nō no hyōgen*. Chūkō Shinsho 260. Tokyo: Chūō Kōronsha, 1971.

Matsuda Tamotsu. *Nō, genkō yōkyoku kaidai*. Tokyo: Kinseisha, 1984.

———. *Nō, kyōgen nyūmon*. Bunken no Geinō Kanshō Shiriizu. Tokyo: Bunken Shuppan, 1976.

———. "Zeshi hen nenkō." Excerpted from *Zeshi, sarugaku nō no kenkyū*. Tokyo: Shindokushosha, 1991, 10–37, 451–488.

Matsuoka Shimpei. "Enron, kairaku no in'yō ni tsuite." In *Chadō bunkaron*. Chadō-gaku taikei 1. Kyoto: Tankōsha, 1999.

———. "Genji nō no shintai to kankaku." *Genji kenkyū*, no. 2 (1997): 140–163.

———. *Nō, chūsei kara no hibiki*. Tokyo: Kadokawa Shoten, 1998.

———. "Staging Noh." *Acta Asiatica*, no. 73 (1997): 1–15.

———. *Utage no shintai*. Tokyo: Iwanami, 1991.

———. "Yūgen ga enjaku suru toki, Ikkyū, Zenchiku no sekai." *Bungaku* 7.2 (1996): 32–40.

———. "Zeami no hana, hana kara fū e." *Kokubungaku* 42.5 (1997): 92–99.

Mikata Ken. " 'Kagura' " yori 'yūgaku' e, iwayuru 'chū no mai' no isō ni tsuite." *Geinōshi kenkyū*, no. 19 (1967): 19–33.

———. *Nō no rinen to sakuhin*. Osaka: Izumi Shoin, 1999.

Minemura Fumito, ed. *Shinkokin waka shū*. Nihon Koten Bungaku Zenshū 26. Tokyo: Shōgakukan, 1974.

Mitoma Keiko. "Zeami no yūgenkan no hensen, 'Kurai no dan' ni miru zōho no kanō-sei o megutte." *Nō, kenkyū to hyōron*, no. 18 (1991): 1–10.

Mitsui Bunko, ed. *Mitsui Bunko bekkan zō hinzuroku nōmen*. Tokyo: Benridō, 1989.

Miyake Akiko. "Fukushiki mugen nō no seiritsu." *Kokubungaku* 31.10 (1986): 64–69.

———. *Kabu nō no kakuritsu to tenkai*. Tokyo: Perikansha, 2001.

———. "Kaden shūhitsu ka no saku nō jōkyō." *Bungaku* (bimonthly issue) 1.6 (2000): 2–14.

———. "Motomasa no sakushi hō, *Sumidagawa* to *Morihisa* ni mirareru shinjō hyō-gen." *Kokugo kokubun* 49.4 (1980): 44–60.

———. "Nō no shikon: Zeami no jokei." *No, kyōgen hikkei. Bessatsu kokubungaku* 48 (1995): 21–26.

———. "*Sandō*-ki no Zeami to *Matsukaze* no mai." *Chūsei bungaku* 35 (1990): 115–124.

———. "Shinrigeki to shite no nō." Ed. Waseda Daigaku Kokubungakkai. *Kokubun-gaku kenkyū*, no. 100 (1990): 78–87.

———. *Taiyaku de tanoshimu, Izutsu*. Tokyo: Hinoki Shoten, 2000.

———. "Uchū o kanjiru, *Yashima* no ikusa-gatari." Shin Nihon Koten Bungaku Taikei 45, Geppō 48: 1–4. Tokyo: Iwanami Shoten, 1993.

———. "Zeami no kiiwaado, 'kakari.' " *Kokubungaku* 35.3 (1990): 118–119.

———. "Zeami no monomane ron, *Kayoi Komachi* to *Sotoba Komachi*." Ed. Mejiro Gakuen Joshi Tanki Daigaku Kokugo/Kokubun-ka Kenkyūshitsu. *Kokugo kokubungaku* 2 (1993): 15–27.

———. "Zeami no monomane ron, kohon *Besshi kuden* no ichi." Ed. Mejiro Gakuen
Joshi Tanki Daigaku Kokugo/Kokubun-ka Kenkyūshitsu. *Kokugo kokubungaku* 1
(1992): 17–27.

———. "Zeami no monomane ron, mai kusemai no seiritsu." *Chūsei bungaku*, no. 42
(1997): 85–93.

———. *Zeami wa tensai de aru, nō to deau tame no isshu no tebikisho.* Tokyo: Sōshisha,
1995.

———. "Zenchiku no nōgakuron ni okeru kokoro no mondai." *Kokubungaku kenkyū*
91 (1987): 24–36.

Miyake Kōichi. *Hyōshi no seikai.* Rev. ed. Tokyo: Hinoki Shoten, 1979.

———. *Kanze-ryū zōho fushi no seikai.* Rev. ed. Tokyo: Hinoki Shoten, 1960.

———. *Utaikata hyakugojūban.* Tokyo: Hinoki Shoten, 1981.

———. *Yōgeiko no kihonjishiki.* Tokyo: Hinoki Shoten, 1979.

Miyake Noboru. *Nō enshutsu no kenkyū.* Tokyo: Nōgaku Shorin, 1948.

———. "*Takasago*: Utaikata to kanshō." *Kanze*, no. 2 (1964): 7–17.

Mizukami Kashizō. *Chūsei karon to renga.* Tokyo: Zentsū Kikaku Shuppan, 1977.

Momose Kesao. "Nijō Yoshimoto to Zeami, shojō o chūshin ni shite." *Nōgaku kenkyū*,
no. 23 (1998): 1–11.

Morita Mitsuharu. *Morita ryū ōgi roku.* Tokyo: Nōgaku Shorin, 1980.

Morita Yoshinori. *Chūsei senmin zatsugeinō no kenkyū.* Tokyo: Yūzankaku Shuppan, 1974.

Moriya Takeshi. *Chūsei no genzō.* Kyoto, Tankōsha, 1985.

———. "Kinsei shoki no hōka to kabuki." *Geinōshi kenkyū*, no. 34 (1971): 31–44.

Musō Kokushi. *Muchū mondō.* In Satō Taishun, ed. Iwanami Bunko, no. 1046–1047.
Tokyo: Iwanami, 1934.

Nagazumi Yasuaki. "Shura-nō to Heike no monogatari, Zeami no *Tadanori* o
megutte." *Kanze*, no. 8 (1970) 3–9.

Nakada Norio et al., eds. *Kogo daijiten.* Tokyo: Shōgakukan, 1983.

Nakamura Hajime and Kino Kazuyoshi, eds. *Hannya shingyō, Kongō hannya kyō.*
Iwanami Bunko 360. Tokyo: Iwanami, 1960.

Nakamura Itaru, ed. *Zeami densho yōgo sakuin.* Kasama Sakuin Sōkan 86. Tokyo:
Kasama Shoin, 1985.

Nakamura Yasuo. *Nō no men: Butai ni miru.* Nihon no Bi to Kyōyō 22. 4th printing.
Kyoto: Kawara Shoten, 1980.

Nihon Bungaku Kenkyū Shiryō Kankōkai, ed. *Yōkyoku, kyōgen.* Nihon Bungaku
Kenkyū Shiryō Sōsho. Tokyo: Yūseidō Shuppan, 1981.

Nihon kagaku taikei. Ed. Sasaki Nobutsuna and Kyūsojin Hitaku. 15 vols. Tokyo:
Kazama Shobō, 1977–1981.

Nihon kokuko daijiten. Ed. Nihon Daijiten Kankōkai. 10 vols. Reduced size ed. Tokyo:
Shōgakukan, 1979–1981.

Nippon Meichō Zenshū Kankōkai, ed. *Yōkyoku sanbyakugojūban shū.* Comp. Nonomura
Kaizō. Nihon Meicho Zenshū 29. Tokyo: Nippon Meichō Zenshū Kankōkai, 1928.

Nishi Kazuyoshi. "Zeami hiun no ichiyōin, Ashikaga Yoshinori to On'ami to o meguru mondai." Nihon Daigaku Kokubungakukai, ed. *Gobun* 12 (1962): 21–32.

———. *Zeami kenkyū*. Tokyo: Sanseidō, 1977.

Nishino Haruo. "Sakuhin kenkyū: *Unrin'in* shokō." *Kanze*, no. 4 (1975): 4–10.

———, ed. *Yōkyoku hyakuban*. Shin Nihon Koten Bungaku Taikei 57. Tokyo: Iwanami, 1998.

———. "Zeami bannen no nō, *Nōhon sanjūgoban mokuroku* o megutte." *Bungaku* 39.5 (1971): 37–48.

———. "Zeami kaden, Zeami no geiron ha ika ni gokai sarete kita ka." *Kokubungaku* 35.3 (1990): 68–75.

———. "Zeami no nō gaikan." *Kokubungaku, kaishaku to kanshō* 42.2 (February 1977):103–111.

———. "Zeami no sakugeki hō: Nōsaku no nagare no naka de." *Kokubungaku* 25.1 (1980): 63–69.

Nishino Haruo and Hata Hisashi, eds. *Nō, kyōgen jiten*. Tokyo: Heibonsha, 1987.

———, eds. *Shintei zōho nō, kyōgen jiten*. Rev. and exp. Tokyo: Heibonsha, 1999.

Nishio Minoru. *Dōgen to Zeami*. Tokyo: Iwanami Shoten, 1965.

Nishio Minoru et al., eds. *Yōkyoku, kyōgen*. Exp. ed. Zōho Kokugo Kokubungaku Kenkyūshi Taisei 8. Tokyo: Sanseidō, 1977.

Nogami Toyoichirō, ed. *Kaichū Yōkyoku zenshū*. Rev. ed. 6 vols. Tokyo: Chūō Kōronsha, 1949–1951.

———. *Nō, kenkyū to hakken*. Tokyo: Iwanami Shoten, 1930.

———. *Nō no saisei*. Tokyo: Iwanami, 1935.

———, ed. *Nōgaku zensho*. Rev. ed. 7 vols. Tokyo: Sōgensha, 1979–1981.

Nonomura Kaizō, ed. *Kōchū Zeami jūrokubu shū*. Tokyo: Shun'yōdō, 1916.

———, ed. *Yōkyoku sanbyakugojūban shū*. Nihon Meicho Zenshū. Tokyo: Nihon Meicho Zenshū Kankōkai, 1928. (Unnumbered vol. in series.)

Nose Asaji. *Nōgaku genryū kō*. Tokyo: Iwanami Shoten, 1938.

———. *Nose Asaji chosakushū*. Ed. Nose Asaji Chosaku Shū Henshū Iinkai. 10 vols. Kyoto: Shibunkaku Shuppan, 1981–1982.

———, ed. *Zeami jūrokubushū hyōshaku*. 2 vols. Tokyo: Iwanami, 1940–1944.

Ochiai Hiroshi. "Inuō no jidai, '*Rokuon'in saikoku gekō ki*' no kiji o shōkai shi tsutsu." *Nōgaku kenkyū*, no. 18 (1993): 101–144.

———. " '*Kaden*' Ōgi hen saikō." *Bungaku* (bimonthly edition) 1.6 (2000): 77–87.

Oda Sachiko. "Nō no engi to enshutsu, shōzokuzuke, katazuke o meguru shomondai." *Nōgaku kenkyū*, no. 10 (1984): 63–108.

———. "Nō no kata, nō no shōzoku, kijo idetachi no hensen." *Kokubungaku* 31.10 (1986): 76–82.

———. "Saidōfūki no nō: *Sandō* no reikyoku o chūshin ni." *Nō: Kenkyū to hyōron*, no. 6 (1975): 16–26.

———. "Sakuhin kenkyū: *Funabashi*." *Kanze*, no. 1 (1977): 3–10.

————. "Zeami no shūgen nō." *Geinōshi kenkyū*, no. 80 (1983): 25–38.

Ogasawara Kyōko. *Geinō no shiza, Nihon geinō no hassō*. Tokyo: Ōfūsha, 1976.

Okami Masao, ed. *Yoshimoto Rengaron shū*. 3 vols. Koten Bunko 63, 78, 92. Tokyo: Koten Bunko, 1952, 1954, 1955.

Okamoto Akira. "Nō to shintairon, 'mizu no kagami' no engi isō," *Kokubungaku* 28.13 (1983): 20–27.

Omote Akira, ed. *Bessatsu Taiyō: Nihon no kokoro, nō*, no. 25 (winter 1978).

————. "*Kaden* kara *Fūshikaden* e no honbun kaitei." Osaka Daigaku Kokubungaku Kenkyūshitsu, ed. *Gobun* 38 (1981): 49–61.

————. "*Kaden* no shomei to henmei o megutte." *Nō to kyōgen*, no. 1 (2003): 8–16.

————. "Kan'ami Kiyotsugu to Yūzaki-za." *Bungaku* 51.7 (1983): 35–46.

————, ed. *Kanze Bunko zō Muromachi jidai yōhon shū*. 2 vols. Tokyo: Zaidan hōnin Kanze Bunko, 1997.

————, ed. " 'Kanze' chūshin no nōgakushi nenpyō (1)." *Kaden* 3, Zaidan hōnin Kanze Bunko Nenpō (1996): 13–22.

————. " 'Kanze-ryū shi sankyū (sono jūni), Zeami shukke chokugo no Kanze za, Ōei sanjūyonen ennō kiroku o megutte." *Kanze*, no. 10 (2000): 27–32.

————. *Nōgakushi shinkō*. 2 vols. Tokyo: Wan'ya Shoten, 1979, 1986.

————. "Sakuhin kenkyū: *Aoi no Ue*." *Kanze*, no. 8 (1973): 5–11.

————. "Sakuhin kenkyū: *Tōru*." *Kanze*, no. 8 (1980): 20–28.

————. "Zeami izen." *Kokubungaku*, 25.1 (1980): 48–55.

————, ed. *Zeami jihitsu nōhon shū*. Tokyo: Iwanami, 1997.

————. "Zeami oyobi yōkyoku no 'yūgaku' no go o megutte." *Nōgaku kenkyū*, no. 22 (1997): 1–58.

————, ed. *Zeami, "Sarugaku dangi."* Iwanami Bunko 33-001-2. Tokyo: Iwanami, 1960.

————. "Zeami seitan wa Jōji sannen ka: 'Zeami jūni no toshi' kō." *Bungaku* 31.10 (1963): 60–71.

Omote Akira and Amano Fumio. *Nōgaku no rekishi*. Iwanami Kōza Nō Kyōgen, vol. 1. Tokyo: Iwanami, 1987.

Omote Akira and Itō Masayoshi, eds. *Konparu kodensho shūsei*. Tokyo: Wan'ya Shoten, 1969.

Omote Akira and Katō Shūichi, eds. *Zeami, Zenchiku*. Nihon Shisō Taikei 24. Tokyo: Iwanami, 1974.

————. *Zeami, Zenchiku*. New Printing. Gei no Shisō, Michi no Shisō 1. Nihon Shisō Taikei Shinsōhan. Tokyo: Iwanami, 1995.

Omote Akira and Takemoto Mikio. *Nōgaku no densho to geiron*. Iwanami Kōza Nō Kyōgen, vol. 2. Tokyo: Iwanami, 1988.

Ōno Susumu, Satake Akihiro, and Maeda Kingorō, eds. *Iwanami kogo jiten*. Tokyo: Iwanami, 1974.

Ōtani Setsuko. "Zeami to Zen oboegaki." *Bungaku* (bimonthly edition) 1.6 (2000): 51–65.

Ozawa Masao, ed. *Kokin waka shū.* Nihon Koten Bungaku Zenshū 7. Tokyo: Shōgakukan, 1971.

Saeki Junko. "Yūjo no imayō, sono hikaku bunkateki hirogari." *Chūsei bungaku,*
no. 46 (2001): 15–25.

Saeki Umetomo, ed. *Kokin waka shū.* Nihon Koten Bungaku Taikei 8. Tokyo:
Iwanami, 1958.

Sagara Tōru. *Zeami no uchū.* Tokyo: Perikansha, 1990.

Sahashi Hōryū. *Zenyaku* Hekigan roku. 2 vols. Tokyo: San'ichi Shobō, 1984–1985.

Sakakura Shigeyoshi et al., eds. *Taketori monogatari, Ise monogatari, Yamato monogatari.* Nihon Koten Bungaku Taikei 9. Tokyo: Iwanami Shoten, 1957.

Sakamoto Setchō. *Sakamoto Setchō nōhyō zenshū.* 2 vols. Tokyo: Unebi Shobō, 1943.

Sanari Kentarō, ed. *Yōkyoku taikan.* 7 vols. Tokyo: Meiji Shoin, 1930–1931. Reprints:
1964, 1983–1984.

Sanekata Kiyoshi. *Nihon bungei riron.* Sanekata Kiyoshi Chosakushū 3. Tokyo:
Ōfūsha, 1985.

Sasamoto Masaharu. "Kami to hito o tsunagu oto, chūsei no oto to koe." *Chūsei bungaku,* no. 46 (2001): 27–35.

Satoi Rokurō. *Yōkyoku hyakusen: Sono shi to dorama.* 2 vols. Tokyo: Kasama Shoin,
1979, 1982.

Sekiyama Kazuo. *Bukkyō to minkan geinō.* Tokyo: Hakusuisha, 1986.

Shimotsuma Shōshin. *Shimotsuma Shōshin shū.* 3 vols. Ed. Hōsei Daigaku Nōgaku
Kenkyūjo. Nōgaku Shiryō Shūsei 1 (comp. Nishino Haruo); 3 (comp. Furukawa
Hisashi); 6 (comp. Katagiri Noboru). Tokyo: Wan'ya Shoten, 1973–1976.

Suganuma Akira. *Dōgen jiten.* Tokyo: Tōkyōdō Shuppan, 1977.

Suzuki Keiun. *Nō no omote.* Tokyo: Wan'ya Shoten, 1960.

Suzuki Tadashi. *Engeki ron, ekkyo suru chikara.* Tokyo: Parco, 1984.

Tada Kōryū et al, eds. *Tendai hongaku ron.* Nihon Shisō Taikei 9. Tokyo: Iwanami,
1973.

Tai Shōnosuke. *Chūsei geinō no kenkyū.* Tokyo: Ōfūsha, 1976.

———. "Zeami no geifū o meguru ni san no mondai." *Geinōshi kenkyū,* no. 10
(1965): 15–26.

Takashima Motohiro. "Nō ni okeru takaikan to jujutsu no imi." In Sagara Tōru and
Satō Masahide, eds., Tokushū, Yōkyoku no shisō. *Kikan Nihon shisōshi,* no. 24
(1984): 24–41.

Takei Kazuto. "Kochūshaku to dokkai no kanōsei." *Kokubungaku,* 40.10 (1995):
70–76.

Takemoto Mikio. "Fūtei keisei shiron." *Nō, kenkyū to hyōron,* no. 13 (1985): 1–12.

———. "Kaden no seiritsu o meguru shomondai." *Bungaku* (bimonthly edition) 1.6
(2000): 66–76.

———. "Kan'ami jidai no nō." *Bungaku* 51.7 (1983): 155–165.

———. *Kan'ami, Zeami jidai no nō.* Tokyo: Daitōkyū Kinen Bunko, 1992.

————. *Kan'ami, Zeami jidai no nōgaku.* Tokyo: Meiji Shoin, 1999.

————. "Nō ni okeru kanshibun no juyō." In Wakan Hikaku Bungakukai, ed., *Chūsei bungaku to kanbungaku* 2. Wakan Hikaku Bungaku Sōsho 6. Tokyo: Kyūko Shoin, 1987, 263–282.

————, ed. *Nōgaku shiryō shū.* Waseda Daigaku Zō Shiryō Eiin Sōsho 21. Tokyo: Waseda Daigaku Shuppanbu, 1988.

————. " 'Oyako monogurui' kō." *Nōgaku kenkyū,* no. 6 (1980): 81–122.

————. "*Sandō* no kaisaku reikyoku o meguru shomondai." *Jissen kokubungaku,* no. 19 (1981): 19–35.

————. " 'Sandō' shippitsu igo no Zeami no sakufū." *Chūsei bungaku,* no. 42 (1997): 94–105.

————. "Shirabayashi kō." *Kokubungaku kenkyū,* no. 65 (1978): 24–34.

————. "Tennyo no mai no kenkyū." *Nōgaku kenkyū,* no. 4 (1980): 93–158.

————. "Yoshida Bunko Zeami nōgakuron shiryō shōkai." *Bungaku* 4.4 (2003): 199–206.

————. "Yoshida Bunko zō shinshutsu bon *Sandō* ni tsuite." *Waseda Daigaku 21 seiki COE puroguramu, engeki no sōgōteki kenkyū to engekigaku no kakuritsu.* Engeki Kenkyū Sentā kiyō III (2004): 1–7.

————. "Zeami jidai no kabu nō, utaimai no keisei zakkō." *Nōgaku kenkyū,* no. 22 (1997): 99–123.

Takemoto Mikio and Hashimoto Asao, eds. *Nō, kyōgen hikkei. Bessatsu Kokubungaku,* no. 48 (1995).

Takemoto Mikio, Omote Kiyoshi, and Miyake Akiko, eds. "Nōgaku shiryō shū ni, kaidai." *Waseda Daigaku Zō Shiryō Eiin Sōsho 37* (excerpt). Tokyo: Waseda Daigaku Shuppanbu, 1994.

————. *Taiyaku de tanoshimu,* Takasago. Tokyo: Hinoku Shoten, 2000.

Takemura Shōhō, ed. *Bukkyō shisō jiten.* Tokyo: Kyōiku Shinchōsha, 1982.

Taki Kōji and Matsuoka Shimpei. "Zeami no shintaisei, taidan." *Kokubungaku,* tokushū 35.3 (1990): 26–47.

Tanaka Makoto. "*Hakozaki monogurui* ni tsuite." *Kanze,* no. 4 (1978): 3–10.

————. "Yōkyoku no ongakuteki kenkyū: kagakuteki kenchi kara no." *Kanze,* no. 10 (1973): 5–9.

————, ed. *Mikan yōkyoku shū.* 31 vols. Koten Bunko. Tokyo: Koten Bunko, 1963–1980.

Tanaka Masako. "Zeami no oni." *Geinōshi kenkyū,* no. 65 (1979): 25–38.

Tanaka Yutaka. *Chūsei bungakuron kenkyū.* Tokyo: Hanawa Shobō, 1969.

————, ed. *Zeami geijutsuron shū.* Shinchō Nihon Koten Shūsei. Tokyo: Shinchōsha, 1976.

Tani Hiroshi. *Chūsei bungaku no tassei.* Tokyo: San'ichi Shobō, 1962.

Tashiro Keiichirō. *Mugen nō.* Tokyo: Asahi Shinbunsha, 1994.

————. *Yōkyoku o yomu.* Tokyo: Asahi Shinbunsha, 1987.

Toita Michizō. "Hyōgen kara mita Zeami no tokushoku." *Kokubungaku* 8.1: 43–49 (1963).

———. *Kan'ami to Zeami.* Iwanami Shinsho 719. Tokyo, Iwanami Shoten, 1979.

———. "Zeami to shura-nō." *Bungaku* 22.9 (1954): 60–68.

Tokita, Alison, and Komoda Haruko, eds. *Nihon no katarimono, kōtōsei, kōzō, igi.* Nichibunken Sōsho 26. Kyoto: International Research Center for Japanese Studies (Nichibunken), 2002.

Tokue Gensei. *Geinō, nōgei.* Miyai sensho 2. Tokyo, Miyai Shoten, 1983.

———. "Hōka zō ron." *Kokugakuin zasshi,* no. 72 (1971): 1–16.

———. "Mukoiri Jinen Koji kō." *Kokugo to kokubungaku* 45.7 (1968): 27–41.

———. *Muromachi geinōshi ronkō.* Tokyo, Miyai shoten, 1984.

———. "Sakuhin kenkyū: Yōrō." *Kanze,* no. 1 (1978): 5–11.

Tomiyama Yasuo. "Zeami ni okeru 'kakari' no kōzō, ge." *Geinōshi kenkyū,* no. 108 (1990): 10–26.

———. "Zeami ni okeru 'kakari' no kōzō, jō." *Geinōshi kenkyū,* no. 107 (1989): 34–50.

Torii Akio. *Chinkon no chūsei, nō denshō bungaku no seishinshi.* Tokyo, Perikansha, 1989.

Ueki Yukinobu. "Ennen furyū to sono keisei." *Geinōshi kenkyū,* no. 11 (1965): 1–19.

Umehara Takeshi. *Jigoku no shisō. Umehara Takeshi chosaku shū,* vol. 4. Tokyo, Shūeisha, 1981.

Usui Nobuyoshi. *Ashikaga Yoshimitsu.* Jinbutsu Sōsho 38. Tokyo: Yoshikawa Kōbunkan, 1960.

Utaishō, Fūkashō. Ed. Munemasa Isoo. 3 vols. Kyoto: Shibunkaku Shuppan, 1981.

Wakita Haruko. *Josei geinō no genryū, kugutsu, kusemai, shirabyōshi.* Kadokawa Sensho 326. Tokyo: Kadokawa Shoten, 2001.

———. "Kami nō no ichi, sarugaku nō no jujukusei to zaichi kyōdōtai." *Geinōshi kenkyū,* no. 144 (1999): 1–16.

———, ed. *Nihon joseishi,* vol. 2 (*Chūsei*). Tokyo: Joseishi Sōgō Kenkyūkai, 1982.

Watanabe Moriaki. "Utsukushiki mono no keifu, hana to yūgen." In Sagara Tōru, Bitō Masahide, and Akiyama Ken, eds., *Kōza Nihon shisō,* vol. 5. Tokyo: Tōkyō Daigaku Shuppankai, 1984.

Watanabe Moriaki, Watanabe Tamotsu, and Asada Akira, eds. *Engeki o yomu.* Tokyo: Hōsō Daigaku Kyōiku Shinkō Kai, 1997.

Watanabe Tamotsu. *Nihon no buyō.* Iwanami Shinsho (new red ed.) 175. Tokyo: Iwanami, 1991.

Yamanaka Reiko. "Kanze Motoakira no kogaki o megutte." *Nōgaku kenkyū,* no. 22 (1997): 125–150.

———. *Nō no enshutsu, sono keisei to henyō.* Chūsei Bungaku Kenkyū Sōsho 6. Tokyo: Wakakusa Shobō, 1998.

———. "Nyotai nō ni okeru 'Zeami-fū' no kakuritsu, *Matsukaze* no hatashita yakuwari." *Nō: Kenkyū to hyōron* 14 (1986): 1–11.

————. "*Shōjō midare* no enshutsu no rekishi (1), *Ran* seiritsu made no shosō." *Nōgaku kenkyū*, no. 23 (1998): 99–122.

————. "Shoki *Kaden* jidai no shite tōjō dan." *Bungaku* (bimonthly edition) 1.6 (2000): 15–21.

————. "*Ukifune* o megutte, *Go on* (ge), shoshū fumei utai to no kanren nado." *Nōgaku kenkyū*, no. 27 (2002): 1–23.

Yamane Kiyotaka, ed. Tsukuba shū *sōsakuin*. Tokyo: Kazama Shobō, 1983.

Yamashita Hiroaki. "*Heike monogatari* no katari to sono kyokufushi." *Bungaku* 47.11 (1979): 12–23.

————. *Katari to shite no* Heike monogatari. Tokyo: Iwanami, 1994.

————. "Muromachi jidai no heikyoku ni kansuru ikkōsatsu." *Kokugo to kokubungaku* 36.11 (1968): 39–50.

————. "Nō to Heike no ikusa monogatari, *Shigehira* o megutte." *Bungaku* (bimonthly ed.) 1.6 (2000): 112–124.

Yamazaki Masakazu. *Engi suru seishin*. Tokyo: Chūō kōronsha, 1984.

————. *Geijutsu, henshin, yūgi*. Chūō Kōronsha, 1975.

————, ed. and trans. *Zeami*. Nihon no Meicho 10. 2nd ed. Tokyo: Chūō Kōronsha, 1969.

Yashima Masaharu. "Chūsei shijin to shite no Zeami." *Nō: Kenkyū to hyōron*, no. 2 (1973) 1–9.

————. "*Nōsakusho* ni okeru onna no nō tasseiten ni tsuite (shozen): *Izutsu* e no michi." *Bungei to hihyō*, no. 3 (1966): 36–56.

————. "Sakuhin kenkyū: *Yumi Yawata*." *Kanze*, no. 1 (1978): 5–11.

————. "Shura to aishō." *Kanze*, no. 12: (1973) 4–8.

————. "Zeami ni okeru monogurui nō no kiseki." *Nōgaku shichō*, no. 2 (1973): 18–27.

————. "Zeami ni okeru *Obasute* no ichi, *Sarugaku dangi* kaishaku o tōshite." *Nōgaku shichō*, no. 1 (1972): 22–41.

————. *Zeami no nō to geiron*. Tokyo: Miyai Shoten, 1985.

Yashima Sachiko. " 'Ōei sanjūyonen ennō kiroku' ni tsuite." *Kanze*, no. 8 (2000): 50–56.

Yokomichi Mario. *Nōgeki shōyō*. Tokyo: Chikuma Shobō, 1984.

Yokomichi Mario, Nishino Haruo, and Hata Hisashi, eds. *Nō no sakusha to sakuhin*. Iwanami Kōza Nō Kyōgen 3. Tokyo: Iwanami, 1987.

Yokomichi Mario and Omote Akira, eds. *Yōkyoku shū*. 2 vols. Nihon Koten Bungaku Taikei 40–41. Tokyo: Iwanami, 1960, 1963.

Yonekura Toshiaki. "Nō no sozai to kōsō: *Sanemori* no nō o chūshin ni." *Bungaku* 31.1 (1963): 57–65.

Yoshida Tōgo. *Nōgaku koten Zeami jūrokubu shū*. Tokyo: Nōgakkai, 1909.

Yūseidō henshūbu, ed. *Nihon bungakushi o yomu 3: Chūsei*. Tokyo: Yūseidō, 1992.

Zaidan Hōjin Kanze Bunko. *Kaden*, no. 2. Zaidan Hōjin Kanze Bunko Nenpō, vol. 2 (1995).

―――. *Kaden*, no. 3. Zaidan Hōjin Kanze Bunko Nenpō, vol. 3 (1996).

Zenkoku Daigaku Kokugo Bungakkai. *Kōza Nihon Bungaku 6. Chūsei hen II*. Tokyo: Sanseidō, 1969.

Sources in Western Languages

Arntzen, Sonja. "The *Wakan rōeishū*: Cannibalization or Singing in Harmony?" In Rebecca Copeland, Elizabeth Oyler, and Marvin Marcus, eds., *Proceedings of the Association for Japanese Literary Studies, Acts of Writing*, vol. 2. Association for Japanese Literary Studies, 2001, 155–171.

Araki, James T. *The Ballad-Drama of Medieval Japan*. Rutland, Vt.: Charles E. Tuttle, 1964.

Atkins, Paul S. "Fabricating Teika: The *Usagi* Forgeries and Their Authentic Influence." In Stephen D. Miller, ed., *Proceedings of the Association for Japanese Literary Studies, Issues of Canonicity and Canon Formation in Japanese Literary Studies*, vol. 1. Association for Japanese Literary Studies, 2000, 249–258.

Auerbach, Eric. *Mimesis: The Representation of Reality in Western Literature*. Trans. Willard R. Trask. Princeton, N.J.: Princeton University Press, 1953.

Averbuch, Irit. *The Gods Come Dancing: A Study of the Japanese Ritual Dance of Yamabushi Kagura*. Ithaca, N.Y.: Cornell University East Asia Program, 1995.

Bachnik, Jane M., and Charles J. Quinn, Jr., eds. *Situated Meaning: Inside and Outside in Japanese Self and Language*. Princeton, N.J.: Princeton University Press, 1994.

Baker, G. P., and P. M. S. Hacker. *Wittgenstein, Understanding and Meaning*, vol. 1. Oxford: University of Chicago Press, 1980.

Bakhtin, M. M. *Speech Genres and Other Late Essays*. Trans. Vern W. McGee, ed. Caryl Emerson and Michael Holquist. Austin: University of Texas Press, 1986.

Bargen, Doris G. *A Woman's Weapon: Spirit Possession in* The Tale of Genji. Honolulu: University of Hawai'i Press, 1997.

Bauman, Richard, ed. *Folklore, Cultural Performances, and Popular Entertainment: A Communications-centered Handbook*. New York: Oxford University Press, 1992.

―――. *Story, Performance, and Event: Contextual Studies of Narrative*. New York: Cambridge University Press, 1986.

―――. *Verbal Art as Performance*. Rowley, Mass.: Newbury House Publishers, 1977.

Benjamin, Andrew. *Art, Mimesis and the Avant-garde: Aspects of a Philosophy of Difference*. London: Routledge, 1991.

Bethe, Monica, and Karen Brazell. *Dance in the Nō Theater*. 3 vols. Cornell University East Asia Papers no. 29. Ithaca, N.Y.: Cornell China-Japan Program, 1982.

―――. *Nō as Performance: An Analysis of the "Kuse" Scene of "Yamamba."* Cornell University East Asia Papers no. 16. Ithaca, N.Y.: Cornell China-Japan Program, 1978.

Bethe, Monica, and Richard Emmert. *Noh Performance Guides*. Tokyo: National Noh

Theater: *Matsukaze*, with Royall Tyler, 1992; *Atsumori*, with Karen Brazell, 1995; *Aoi no ue*, 1997.

Blacker, Carmen. *The Catalpa Bow: A Study of Shamanistic Practices in Japan*. London: Mandala (Allen and Unwin), 1975.

Bloor, David. *Wittgenstein: A Social Theory of Knowledge*. New York: Columbia University Press, 1983.

Bodiford, William M. *Sōtō Zen in Medieval Japan*. Kuroda Institute Studies in East Asian Buddhism 8. Honolulu: University of Hawaiʻi Press, 1993.

Brandon, James R. *Nō and Kyōgen in the Contemporary World*. Honolulu: University of Hawaiʻi Press, 1997.

———. "Zeami on Acting: Values for the Western Actor." In Benito Ortolani and Samuel L. Leiter, eds., *Zeami and the Nō Theatre in the World*. New York: Casta, 1998, 101–108.

Brazell, Karen. "Enacting Allusions: A Technique of the Nō Theater." In *International Symposium on the Conservation and Restoration of Cultural Property: Nō, Its Transmission and Regeneration*. Tokyo: Tokyo National Research Institute of Cultural Properties, 1991, 43–54.

———, ed. *Traditional Japanese Theater: An Anthology of Plays*. New York: Columbia University Press, 1998.

Brazell, Karen, with J. Philip Gabriel, eds. *Twelve Plays of the Noh and Kyōgen Theaters*. Cornell University East Asia Papers no. 50. Ithaca, N.Y.: Cornell University East Asia Program, 1988. Rev. ed. 1990.

Brook, Peter. *The Empty Space*. New York: Atheneum, 1968.

Brower, Robert H. "The Foremost Style of Poetic Composition: Fujiwara Tameie's *Eiga no Ittei*." *Monumenta Nipponica* 42.4 (1987): 391–429.

———. *Fujiwara Teika's Hundred-Poem Sequence of the Shōji Era, 1200*. Monumenta Nipponica Monograph no. 55. Tokyo: Sophia University Press, 1978.

———. "Fujiwara Teika's *Maigetsushō*." *Monumenta Nipponica* 40.4 (winter 1985): 399–425.

Brower, Robert H., and Earl Miner. *Fujiwara Teika's Superior Poems of Our Time*. Stanford, Calif.: Stanford University Press, 1967.

———. *Japanese Court Poetry*. Stanford, Calif.: Stanford University Press, 1961.

Brown, Steven T. *Theatricalities of Power: The Cultural Politics of Noh*. Stanford, Calif.: Stanford University Press, 2001.

Carlson, Marvin A. *The Haunted Stage: The Theatre as Memory Machine*. Ann Arbor: The University of Michigan Press, 2001.

———. *Performance: A Critical Introduction*. London: Routledge, 1996.

———. *Theories of the Theatre: A Historical and Critical Survey from the Greeks to the Present*. Ithaca, N.Y.: Cornell University Press, 1984.

Carter, Steven D., ed. and trans. *Just Living: Poems and Prose by the Japanese Monk Tonna*. New York: Columbia University Press, 2003.

————, ed. *Literary Patronage in Medieval Japan*. Ann Arbor: The University of Michigan Center for Japanese Studies, 1993.

————. *The Road to Komatsubara: A Classical Reading of the* Renga Hyakuin. Harvard East Asian Monographs 124. Cambridge, Mass.: Harvard University Press, 1987.

————. " 'Seeking What the Masters Sought': Masters, Disciples, and Poetic Enlightenment in Medieval Japan." In Thomas Hare, Robert Borgen, and Sharalyn Orbaugh, eds., *The Distant Isle: Studies and Translations of Japanese Literature in Honor of Robert H. Brower*. Ann Arbor: The University of Michigan Center for Japanese Studies, 1996, 35–58.

————, trans., with introduction. *Traditional Japanese Poetry: An Anthology*. Stanford, Calif.: Stanford University Press, 1991.

————. *Unforgotten Dreams: Poems by the Zen Monk Shōtetsu*. New York: Columbia University Press, 1997.

Chaitin, Gilbert D. *Rhetoric and Culture in Lacan*. Literature, Culture, Theory 19. Cambridge: Cambridge University Press, 1996.

Chance, Linda H. *Formless in Form: Kenkō,"Tsurezuregusa," and the Rhetoric of Japanese Fragmentary Prose*. Stanford, Calif.: Stanford University Press, 1997.

Chang Chung-yuan, trans. *Original Teachings of Chan Buddhism Selected from* The Transmission of the Lamp. New York: Pantheon Books, 1969.

————, trans. *Tao: A New Way of Thinking*. New York: Harper & Row, 1975.

Chatman, Seymour. *Coming to Terms: The Rhetoric of Narrative in Fiction and Film*. Ithaca, N.Y.: Cornell University Press, 1990.

————. *Story and Discourse: Narrative Structure in Fiction and Film*. Ithaca, N.Y.: Cornell University Press, 1978.

Clark, Timothy T. "*Mitate-e*: Some Thoughts, and a Summary of Recent Writings." In *Impressions: The Journal of the Ukiyo-e Society of America, Inc.* no. 19 (1997): 7–27.

Cleary, Thomas, trans. *Secrets of the Blue Cliff Record: Zen Comments by Hakuin and Tenkei*. Boston: Shambhala, 2000.

————. *Transmission of Light: Zen in the Art of Enlightenment by Zen Master Keizan*. San Francisco: North Point Press, 1990.

Clifford, James, and George E. Marcus, eds. *Writing Culture: The Poetics and Politics of Ethnography*. Berkeley: University of California Press, 1986.

Cohen, Tom. *Anti-mimesis from Plato to Hitchcock*. New York: Cambridge University Press, 1994.

Collcutt, Martin. *Five Mountains: The Rinzai Zen Monastic Institution in Medieval Japan*. Harvard East Asian Monographs no. 85. Cambridge, Mass.: Harvard University Press, 1981.

Cranston, Edwin A. " 'Mystery and Depth' in Japanese Court Poetry." In Thomas Hare, Robert Borgen, and Sharalyn Orbaugh, eds., *The Distant Isle: Studies and*

Translations of Japanese Literature in Honor of Robert H. Brower. Ann Arbor: The University of Michigan Center for Japanese Studies, 1996, 65–104.

Crites, Stephen. "Angels We Have Heard." In James B. Wiggins, ed., *Religion as Story.* New York: Harper & Row, 1975.

de Bary, Wm. Theodore, Donald Keene, George Tanabe, and Paul Varley, eds. *Sources of Japanese Tradition from Earliest Times to 1600.* 2nd ed. Vol. 1. New York: Columbia University Press, 2001.

DeCoker, Gary. "Traditional Approaches to Learning in Japan: *Michi* and the Practice of Calligraphy in Japan's Middle Ages." In Thomas Hare, Robert Borgen, and Sharalyn Orbaugh, eds., *The Distant Isle: Studies and Translations of Japanese Literature in Honor of Robert H. Brower.* Ann Arbor: The University of Michigan Center for Japanese Studies, 1996, 105–124.

De Marinis, Marco. *The Semiotics of Performance.* Trans. Áine O'Healy. Bloomington: Indiana University Press, 1993.

De Poorter, Erika. *Zeami's Talks on Sarugaku: An Annotated Translation of the* Sarugaku Dangi. Amsterdam: J. C. Gieben, 1986.

Derrida, Jacques. *Writing and Difference.* Trans., with introduction, Alan Bass. Chicago: University of Chicago Press, 1978.

Donald, Merlin. *Origins of the Modern Mind: Three Stages in the Evolution of Culture and Cognition.* Cambridge, Mass.: Harvard University Press, 1991.

Donner, Neal, and Daniel B. Stevenson, eds. and trans. *The Great Calming and Contemplation: A Study and Annotated Translation of the First Chapter of Chih-i's* Mo-ho chih-kuan. Honolulu: University of Hawai'i Press, 1993.

Dreyfus, Hubert L. *Being-in-the-World: A Commentary on Heidegger's* Being and Time, *Division 1.* Cambridge, Mass.: MIT Press, 1992.

Duranti, Alessandro, and Charles Goodwin, eds. *Rethinking Context: Language as an Interactive Phenomenon.* Cambridge: Cambridge University Press, 1992.

Elison, George, and Bardwell L. Smith, eds. *Warlords, Artists, and Commoners: Japan in the Sixteenth Century.* Honolulu: University of Hawai'i Press, 1982.

Ferris, Leslie, ed. *Crossing the Stage: Controversies on Cross-dressing.* London: Routledge, 1993.

Field, Norma M. "*Yūgen* and Zeami: The Eternal Flower." Master's thesis, Indiana University, 1974.

Fischer-Lichte, Erika. *The Show and the Gaze of Theatre: A European Perspective.* Iowa City: University of Iowa Press, 1997.

Foley, John Miles. *Immanent Art: From Structure to Meaning in Traditional Oral Epic.* Bloomington: Indiana University Press, 1991.

———. *The Singer of Tales in Performance.* Bloomington: Indiana University Press, 1995.

———, ed. *Teaching Oral Traditions.* Approaches to Teaching World Literature Series. New York: MLA of America, 1998.

———. *The Theory of Oral Composition: History and Methodology.* Bloomington: Indiana University Press, 1988.

Fukumori, Naomi. "Chinese Learning as Performative Power in *Makura no sōshi* and *Murasaki Shikibu nikki.*" In Rebecca Copeland, Elizabeth Oyler, and Marvin Marcus, eds., *Proceedings of the Association for Japanese Literary Studies, Acts of Writing,* vol. 2. Association for Japanese Literary Studies, 2001, 101–119.

Gadamer, Hans-Georg. *Truth and Method.* New York: Crossroad, 1982.

Gardner, Richard A. "*Takasago:* The Symbolism of the Pine." *Monumenta Nipponica* 47.2 (1992): 203–240.

Garfield, Jay L. *Empty Words: Buddhist Philosophy and Cross-Cultural Interpretation.* New York: Oxford University Press, 2002.

Gebauer, Gunter, and Christoph Wulf. *Mimesis: Culture, Art, Society.* Trans. Don Reneau. Berkeley: University of California Press, 1995.

Genette, Gèrard. *Figures III.* Paris: Éditions du Seuil, 1972.

———. *Narrative Discourse: An Essay in Method.* Trans. Jane E. Lewin. Ithaca, N.Y.: Cornell University Press, 1980.

Gerould, Daniel. *Doubles, Demons, and Dreamers: An International Collection.* New York: Performing Arts Journal Publications, 1985.

———, ed. *Theatre/Theory/Theatre.* New York: Applause Books, 2000.

———. "Zeami the Theorist in the Context of World Theatre." In Benito Ortolani and Samuel L. Leiter, eds., *Zeami and the Nō Theatre in the World.* New York: Casta, 1998. 11–18.

Goff, Janet. *Noh Drama and* The Tale of Genji: *The Art of Allusion in Fifteen Classical Plays.* Princeton, N.J.: Princeton University Press, 1991.

———. "Noh and Its Antecedents: 'Journey to the Western Provinces.' " In Thomas Hare, Robert Borgen, and Sharalyn Orbaugh, eds., *The Distant Isle: Studies and Translations of Japanese Literature in Honor of Robert H. Brower.* Ann Arbor: The University of Michigan Center for Japanese Studies, 1996, 165–181.

———. "The Role of the Audience in Noh." *Acta Asiatica,* no. 73 (1997): 16–38.

Goldman, Michael. *On Drama: Boundaries of Genre, Borders of Self.* Ann Arbor: The University of Michigan Press, 2000.

Goodman, Lizbeth, with Jane de Gay, eds. *The Routledge Reader in Gender and Performance.* London and New York: Routledge, 1998.

Gregory, Peter N., ed. *Sudden and Gradual Approaches to Enlightenment in Chinese Thought.* Kuroda Institute Studies in East Asian Buddhism no. 5. Honolulu: University of Hawai'i Press, 1987.

Hall, John Whitney, and Toyoda Takeshi, eds. *Japan in the Muromachi Age.* Berkeley: University of California Press, 1977.

Hare, Thomas Blenman. "A Separate Piece: Proprietary Claims and Intertextuality in the Rokujō Plays." In Thomas Hare, Robert Borgen, and Sharalyn Orbaugh, eds., *The Distant Isle: Studies and Translations of Japanese Literature in Honor of Robert*

H. Brower. Ann Arbor: The University of Michigan Center for Japanese Studies, 1996, 183–203.

———. *Zeami's Style: The Noh Plays of Zeami Motokiyo*. Stanford, Calif: Stanford University Press, 1986.

Harich-Schneider, Eta. *A History of Japanese Music*. London: Oxford University Press, 1973.

Heinrich, Amy Vladeck, ed. *Currents in Japanese Culture*. New York: Columbia University Press, 1997.

Hoff, Frank. "Killing the Self: How the Narrator Acts." *Asian Theatre Journal* 2.1 (1985): 1–27.

———. "Seeing and Being Seen: The Mirror of Performance." In James H. Sanford, William R. LaFleur, and Masatoshi Nagatomi, eds., *Flowing Traces: Buddhism in the Literary and Visual Arts of Japan*. Princeton: Princeton University Press, 1992, 131–148.

———. *Song, Dance, Storytelling: Aspects of the Performing Arts in Japan*. Cornell University East Asia Papers no. 15. Ithaca, N.Y.: Cornell China-Japan Program, 1978.

Hoff, Frank, and Willi Flindt, eds. "The Life Structure of Noh" (Adapted from the Japanese of Yokomichi Mario). *Concerned Theatre Japan*, no. 2 (1973): 209–256.

———, eds. and trans. *The Life Structure of Noh: An English Version of Yokomichi Mario's Analysis of the Structure of Noh*. Excerpt from vol. 2, nos. 3 and 4, of *Concerned Theatre Japan*. Racine, Wis.: *Concerned Theatre Japan*, 1987, 1973.

Holquist, Michael. *Dialogism:Bakhtin and His World*. New Accents. New York: Routledge, 1990.

Horiguchi, Yasuo. "Literature and Performing Arts in the Medieval Age: Kan'ami's Dramaturgy." *Acta Asiatica*, no. 33 (1977): 15–31.

Horton, H. Mack. "*Renga* Unbound: Performative Aspects of Japanese Linked Verse." *Harvard Journal of Asiatic Studies* 53.2 (1993): 443–512.

Hsueh-tou. *The Blue Cliff Record* (Chinese *Pi yen lu*). Trans. Thomas Cleary and J. C. Cleary. Boulder, Colo.: Shambhala, 1977.

Hsun, Ch'ing. *The Works of Hsüntze*. Trans. H. H. Dubs. London: Arthur Probsthain, 1928.

Hubbard, Jamie, and Paul L. Swanson, eds. *Pruning the Bodhi Tree: The Storm over Critical Buddhism*. Honolulu: University of Hawai'i Press, 1997.

Huey, Robert N. *Kyōgoku Tamekane: Poetry and Politics in Late Kamakura Japan*. Stanford, Calif.: Stanford University Press, 1989.

———. *The Making of* Shinkokinshū. Harvard East Asian Monographs no. 208. Cambridge, Mass.: Harvard University Press, 2002.

———, trans. "*Sakuragawa*, Cherry River." *Monumenta Nipponica* 38.3 (1983): 295–312.

Huxley, Michael, and Noel Witts, eds. *The Twentieth-Century Performance Reader*. London: Routledge, 1996.

Hurwitz, Leon, trans. *Scripture of the Lotus Blossom of the Fine Dharma*. New York: Columbia University Press, 1976.

IJsseling, Samuel. *Mimesis: On Appearing and Being*. Trans. Hester IJsseling and Jeffrey Bloechl. The Netherlands: Kok Pharos, 1997.

James, Henry. *The Golden Bowl*. Intro. by Denis Donoghue. Everyman's Library. New York and Toronto: Alfred Al Knopf, 1992.

Japanese-English Buddhist Dictionary. Rev. ed. Tokyo: Daitō Shuppansha, 1991.

Jauss, Hans Robert. *Toward an Aesthetic of Reception*. Trans. Timothy Bahti. Theory and History of Literature 2. Minneapolis: University of Minnesota Press, 1982.

Jones, Sumie. "Sex, Art, and Edo Culture, An Introduction." In *Imaging Reading Eros*. Proceedings for the Conference on Sexuality and Edo culture, 1750–1850. Indiana University, Bloomington, Aug. 17–20, 1995, 1–13.

Kagaya, Shinko. "Nō, the Emergent Orientation of a Traditional Theater in Cross-cultural Settings." Ph.D. dissertation, The Ohio State University, 2000.

———. "Western Audiences and the Emergent Reorientation of Meiji Nō." In Stanca Scholz-Cionca and Samuel L. Leiter, eds., *Japanese Theatre and the International Stage*. Brill's Japanese Studies Library. Leiden: Brill, 2000, 12:161–175.

Kamens, Edward. *The Buddhist Poetry of the Great Kamo Priestess: Daisaiin Senshi*. Michigan Monographs Series in Japanese no. 5. Ann Arbor: The University of Michigan Center for Japanese Studies, 1990.

———. "Dragon-girl, Maidenflower, Buddha: The Transformation of a *Waka* Topos, 'The Five Obstructions.' " *Harvard Journal of Asiatic Studies* 54.2 (1993): 389–444.

———. *Utamakura, Allusion and Intertextuality in Traditional Japanese Poetry*. New Haven Conn.: Yale University Press, 1997.

Kasulis, Thomas P. "Reality as Embodiment: An Analysis of Kūkai's *Sokushinjōbutsu* and *Hosshin Seppō*." In Jane Marie Law, ed., *Religious Reflections on the Human Body*. Bloomington: Indiana University Press, 1995, 166–185.

———. *Zen Action Zen Person*. Honolulu, University of Hawai'i Press, 1981.

Kasulis, Thomas P., ed., with Roger T. Ames and Wimal Dissanayake. *Self as Body in Asian Theory and Practice*. Albany: State University of New York Press, 1993.

Keene, Donald. *Essays in Idleness: The Tsurezuregusa of Kenkō*. New York: Columbia University Press, 1967.

———. *Nō and Bunraku*. New York: Columbia University Press, 1990.

———. *Nō: The Classical Theatre of Japan*. Rev. paperback ed. Tokyo: Kodansha International, 1973.

———. *Seeds in the Heart: Japanese Literature from Earliest Times to the Late Sixteenth Century*. A History of Japanese Literature, vol. 1. New York: Henry Holt, 1993.

———, ed. *Twenty Plays of the Nō Theatre*. New York, Columbia University Press, 1970.

Kerman, Joseph. *Opera as Drama*. New York: Vintage Books, 1956.

Klein, Susan Blakely. *Allegories of Desire: Esoteric Literary Commentaries of Medieval*

Japan. Harvard-Yenching Institute Monograph Series no. 55. Cambridge, Mass.: Harvard University Asia Center, 2002.

Konparu, Kunio. *The Noh Theater: Principles and Perspectives*. Trans. Jane Corddry and Stephen Comee. Rev. and exp. ed. New York: Weatherhill, 1983.

Kwon, Yung-Hee K. *Songs to Make the Dust Dance: The "Ryōjin hishō" of Twelfth-century Japan*. Berkeley: University of California Press, 1994.

LaFleur, William R. *The Karma of Words: Buddhism and the Literary Arts in Medieval Japan*. Berkeley: University of California Press, 1986.

———, trans., with introduction. *Mirror for the Moon: A Selection of Poems by Saigyō (1118–1190)*. New York, New Directions, 1977, 1978.

———. "Symbol and *Yūgen*: Shunzei's Use of Tendai Buddhism." In James H. Sanford, William R. LaFleur, and Masatoshi Nagatomi, eds., *Flowing Traces: Buddhism in the Literary and Visual Arts of Japan*. Princeton, N.J.: Princeton University Press, 1992,16–46.

Lakoff, George. *Women, Fire, and Dangerous Things: What Categories Reveal about the Mind*. Chicago: University of Chicago Press, 1987.

Langer, Susanne K. *Feeling and Form: A Theory of Art*. New York, Charles Scribner's Sons, 1953.

———, ed. *Reflections on Art*. Baltimore, Md.: Johns Hopkins University Press, 1957.

Law, Jane Marie, ed. *Religious Reflections on the Human Body*. Bloomington: Indiana University Press, 1995.

Legge, James. *Confucius: Confucian Analects, The Great Learning and The Doctrine of the Mean*. Repub. 2nd rev. ed. New York: Dover, 1971.

Ley, Graham. *From Mimesis to Interculturalism: Readings of Theatrical Theory Before and After "Modernism."* Exeter: University of Exeter Press, 1999.

Malm, William P. *Japanese Music and Musical Instruments*. Rutland, Vt.: Charles E. Tuttle, 1959.

———. *Nagauta, the Heart of Kabuki Music*. Rutland, Vt.: Charles E. Tuttle, 1963.

———. "The Rhythmic Orientation of Two Drums in the Japanese Nō Drama." *Ethnomusicology*, no. 11 (1958): 89–95.

Marginean, Ruxandra. "Naturalizing *Nō*: Interpreting the *Waki* as the Representative of the Audience." In Stanca Scholz-Cionca and Samuel L. Leiter, eds. *Japanese Theatre and the International Stage*. Brill's Japanese Studies Library. Leiden: Brill, 2000, 12:133–147.

Marra, Michele. *The Aesthetics of Discontent: Politics and Reclusion in Medieval Japanese Literature*. Honolulu, University of Hawai'i Press, 1991.

———. *Representations of Power: The Literary Politics of Medieval Japan*. Honolulu: University of Hawai'i Press, 1993.

Mass, Jeffrey P., ed. *The Origins of Japan's Medieval World: Courtiers, Clerics, Warriors, and Peasants in the Fourteenth Century*. Stanford, Calif.: Stanford University Press, 1997.

Matisoff, Susan, trans. "*Kintōsho*: Zeami's Song of Exile." *Monumenta Nipponica* 32.4 (1977): 441–458.

———. *The Legend of Semimaru, Blind Musician of Japan*. New York: Columbia University Press, 1978.

Matsunaga, Alicia. *The Buddhist Philosophy of Assimilation: The Historical Development of the* Honji-Suijaku *Theory*. Tokyo: Monumenta Nipponica and Charles E. Tuttle Co., 1969.

McCullough, Helen Craig. *Brocade by Night: 'Kokin Wakashū' and the Court Style in Japanese Classical Poetry*. Stanford, Calif.: Stanford University Press, 1985.

———, trans. "*Kokin wakashū*": *The First Imperial Anthology of Japanese Poetry with* "*Tosa Nikki*" *and* "*Shinsen waka*." Stanford, Calif.: Stanford University Press, 1985.

McKinnon, Richard N. "Zeami on the Art of Training." *Harvard Journal of Asiatic Studies*, no. 16 (1953): 200–224.

Miller, Stephen D. "Religious Boundaries in Aesthetic Domains: The Formation of a Buddhist Category (*Shakkyō-ka*) in the Imperial Poetry Anthologies." In Eiji Sekine, ed., *Proceedings of the Midwest Association for Japanese Literary Studies, Ga/Zoku Dynamics in Japanese Literature*, vol. 3. Midwest Association for Japanese Literary Studies, 1997, 100–120.

Miner, Earl. *An Introduction to Japanese Court Poetry*. Stanford, Calif.: Stanford University Press, 1968.

Miner, Earl, Hiroko Odagiri, and Robert E. Morrell, eds. *The Princeton Companion to Classical Japanese Literature*. Princeton, N.J.: Princeton University Press, 1985.

Morrell, Robert E. "The *Shinkokinshū*: 'Poems on Śākyamuni's Teachings. (*Shakkyōka*).' " In Thomas Hare, Robert Borgen, and Sharalyn Orbaugh, eds., *The Distant Isle: Studies and Translations of Japanese Literature in Honor of Robert H. Brower*. Ann Arbor: The University of Michigan Center for Japanese Studies, 1996, 281–320.

Mueller, Jacqueline. "The Two Shizukas, Zeami's *Futari Shizuka*." *Monumenta Nipponica* 36.3 (1981): 285–298.

Murray, Timothy, ed. *Mimesis, Masochism, & Mime: The Politics of Theatricality in Contemporary French Thought*. Ann Arbor: The University of Michigan Press, 1997.

Nagao, Gadjin M. *Mādhyamika and Yogācāra, A Study of Mahayana Philosophies: Collected Papers of G. M. Nagao*. Ed. and trans. L. S. Kawamura with G. M. Nagao. Albany: State University of New York Press, 1991.

Nagatomo, Shigenori. *Attunement through the Body*. Albany: State University of New York Press, 1992.

———. "Zeami's Conception of Freedom." *Philosophy East and West* 31.4 (1981): 401–416.

Nearman, Mark J. "Feeling in Relation to Acting: An Outline of Zeami's Views." *Asian Theatre Journal*, no. 1 (1984): 40–45.

———. "*Kakyō*: Zeami's Fundamental Principles of Acting." *Monumenta Nipponica* 37.3 (1982): 333–374; 37.4 (1982): 459–496; and 38.1 (1983): 49–71.

———. "The Visions of a Creative Artist: Zeami's *Rokurin Ichiro* Treatises." *Monumenta Nipponica* 50.2 (1995): 235–261; 50.3 (1995): 281–303; 50.4 (1995): 485–522; and 51.1 (1996): 17–52.

———. "Zeami's Final Legacy for the Master Actor" (incl. trans. of *Kyakuraika*, "The Flower of Returning"), *Monumenta Nipponica* 35.2 (1980): 153–197.

———. "Zeami's *Kyūi*: A Pedagogical Guide for Teachers of Acting." *Monumenta Nipponica* 33.3 (autumn 1978): 299–332.

Needham, Joseph. *Science and Civilisation in China*, vol. 4, part 1. Cambridge: Cambridge University Press, 1962.

Ng, Yu-Kwan. *T'ien-t'ai Buddhism and Early Mādhyamika*. Tendai Institute of Hawai'i Buddhist Studies Program, University of Hawai'i, 1993.

Nichiren Shoshu International Center, ed. *A Dictionary of Buddhist Terms and Concepts*. 2nd printing. Tokyo: Nichiren Shoshu International Center, 1983.

Nippon Gakujutsu Shinkōkai, ed. and trans. *Japanese Noh Drama: Ten Plays Selected and Translated from the Japanese*. 3 vols. Tokyo: The Nippon Gakujutsu Shinkōkai, 1955–1960.

Nishino, Haruo. "Twofold Structure in Nō Expression." In Stanca Scholz-Cionca and Samuel L. Leiter, eds., *Japanese Theatre and the International Stage*. Brill's Japanese Studies Library. Leiden: Brill, 2000, 12:149–160.

Ochi, Reiko. "Buddhism and Poetic Theory: An Analysis of Zeami's *Higaki* and *Takasago*." Ph.D. dissertation, Cornell University, 1984. Ann Arbor, Mich.: University Microfilms, 1984.

Omote, Akira. "Tradition and Transformation in Nō Theatre." Trans. Erika De Poorter. *Maske und Kothurn: Internationale Beitrage zur Theaterwissenschaft* 35 (January 1989): 11–20.

Ong, Walter J. *Orality and Literacy: The Technologizing of the Word*. London: Methuen, 1982.

O'Neill, P. G. *Early Nō Drama: Its Background, Character, and Development, 1300–1450*. London: Lund Humphries, 1958.

Ortolani, Benito. *The Japanese Theatre:From Shamanistic Ritual to Contemporary Pluralism*. Princeton, N.J.: Princeton University Press, 1995.

———. "Zeami's Mysterious Flower: The Challenge of Interpreting it in Western Terms." In Stanca Scholz-Cionca and Samuel L. Leiter, eds., *Japanese Theatre and the International Stage*. Brill's Japanese Studies Library. Leiden: Brill, 2000, 12:113–132.

Ortolani, Benito, and Kazuyoshi Nishi. "The Year of Zeami's Birth with a Translation of the *Museki Isshi*." *Monumenta Nipponica* 20.3–4 (1965): 319–334.

Ortolani, Benito, and Samuel L. Leiter. *Zeami and the Nō Theatre in the World*. New York: Casta, 1998.

457

Owen, Stephen. *The Poetry of the Early T'ang.* New Haven, Conn.: Yale University Press, 1977.

———. *Readings in Chinese Literary Thought.* Harvard-Yenching Institute Monograph Series no. 30. Cambridge, Mass.: Harvard University, Council on East Asian Studies, 1992.

Pavis, Patrice, ed. *The Intercultural Performance Reader.* London: Routledge, 1996.

Petzold, Bruno, with Shinshō Hanayama. *The Classification of Buddhism, Bukkyō kyōhan.* Ed. Shohei Ichimura. Wiesbaden, Germany: Otto Harrassowitz, 1995.

Pilgrim, Richard B. "Intervals *(Ma)* in Space and Time: Foundations for a Religio-Aesthetic Paradigm in Japan." *History of Religions* 25.3 (1986): 255–277.

———. "Six Circles, One Dewdrop: The Religio-Aesthetic of Komparu Zenchiku." *Chanoyu Quarterly*, no. 33 (1983): 7–23.

———. "Some Aspects of *Kokoro* in Zeami." *Monumenta Nipponica* 24.4 (1969): 136–148.

———. "Zeami and the Way of Nō." *History of Religions* 12.2 (1972): 136–148.

Pinnington, Noel J. "Crossed Paths: Zeami's Transmission to Zenchiku." *Monumenta Nipponica* 52.2 (1997): 201–234.

Plutschow, Herbert E. *Chaos and Cosmos: Ritual in Early and Medieval Japanese Literature.* Leiden: E. J. Brill, 1990.

Postlewait, Thomas. "History, Hermeneutics, and Narrativity." In Janelle G. Reinelt and Joseph R. Roach, eds., *Critical Theory and Performance.* Ann Arbor: University of Michigan Press, 1992, 356–368.

Pronko, Leonard. *Guide to Japanese Drama.* Boston: G. K. Hall, 1984.

———. *Theater East and West: Perspectives toward a Total Theater.* Berkeley: University of California Press, 1967.

Quinn, Charles J., Jr. "Point of View in the Clause: A Rhetorical Look at *Kakari-Musubi*." In Thomas Hare, Robert Borgen, and Sharalyn Orbaugh, eds., *The Distant Isle: Studies and Translations of Japanese Literature in Honor of Robert H. Brower.* Ann Arbor: The University of Michigan Center for Japanese Studies, 1996, 371–407.

Quinn, Shelley Fenno. "How to Write a Noh Play: Zeami's *Sandō*." *Monumenta Nipponica* 48.1 (1993): 53–88.

———. "Oral and Vocal Traditions of Japan." In John Miles Foley, ed., *Teaching Oral Traditions.* New York: Modern Language Association, 1998, 258–265.

Ramirez-Christensen, Esperanza. *Heart's Flower: The Life and Poetry of Shinkei.* Stanford, Calif.: Stanford University Press, 1994.

Rath, Eric C. "Remembering Zeami: The Kanze School and Its Patriarch." *Asian Theatre Journal* 20.2 (2003): 191–208.

Raz, Jacob. "The Actor and His Audience. Zeami's Views on the Audience of the Noh." *Monumenta Nipponica* 31.3 (1976): 251–274.

————. *Audience and Actors: A Study of Their Interaction in the Japanese Traditional Theatre*. Leiden: E. J. Brill, 1983.

Reider, Noriko T. *Tales of the Supernatural in Early Modern Japan, Kaidan, Akinari, Ugetsu Monogatari*. Japanese Studies, vol. 16. Lampeter, Wales: Edwin Mellen, 2002.

Riffaterre, Michael. *Fictional Truth*. Baltimore, Md.: Johns Hopkins University Press, 1990.

————. *Semiotics of Poetry*. Bloomington: Indiana University Press, 1978.

Rimer, J. Thomas, trans. *"Taema." Monumenta Nipponica* 25.3–4 (1970): 431–445.

Rimer, J. Thomas, and Jonathan Chaves, eds. and trans. *Japanese and Chinese Poems to Sing: The* Wakan rōei shū. New York: Columbia University Press, 1997.

Rimer, J. Thomas, and Yamazaki Masakazu, trans. *On the Art of the Nō Drama: The Major Treatises of Zeami*. Princeton, N.J.: Princeton University Press, 1984.

Rodd, Laurel Rasplica, trans., with Mary Catherine Henkenius. *Kokinshū: A Collection of Poems Ancient and Modern*. Princeton, N.J.: Princeton University Press, 1984.

Rubin, Jay. "The Art of the Flower of Mumbo Jumbo." *Harvard Journal of Asiatic Studies* 53.2 (1993): 513–541.

Sakabe, Megumi. "Text: '*Modoki*: The Mimetic Tradition in Japan.'" In Michele Marra, *Modern Japanese Aesthetics: A Reader*. Honolulu: University of Hawai'i Press, 1999, 251–262.

Sakurai Chūichi et al., trans. *The Secret of Nō Plays: Zeami's "Kadensho."* Kyoto: Sumiya-Shinobe Publishing Institute, 1968.

Sanford, James H., William R. LaFleur, and Masatoshi Nagatomi. *Flowing Traces: Buddhism in the Literary and Visual Arts of Japan*. Princeton, N.J., Princeton University Press, 1992.

Sarra, Edith. "Women, Readerly Response, and the Problem of Imitation: Mumyōzōshi and the Vexed Beginnings of the *Monogatari* Canon." In Stephen D. Miller, ed., *Proceedings of the Association for Japanese Literary Studies, Issues of Canonicity and Canon Formation in Japanese Literary Studies*, vol. 1. Association for Japanese Literary Studies, 2000, 447–469.

Schechner, Richard. *Between Theater and Anthropology*. Philadelphia: University of Pennsylvania Press, 1985.

————. *Essays on Performance Theory, 1970–1976*. New York: Drama Book Specialists, 1977.

————. *The Future of Ritual: Writings on Culture and Performance*. New York: Routledge, 1993.

————. *Performance Theory*. New York: Routledge, 1988.

Schechner, Richard, and Willa Appel, eds. *By Means of Performance: Intercultural Studies of Theatre and Ritual*. New York: Cambridge University Press, 1990.

Scholz-Cionca, Stanca. *Entstehung und Morphologie des klassichen Kyogen im 17. Jahrhundert: vom mittelalterlichen Theater der Aussenseiter zum Kammerspiel des Shogunats*. Munchen: Iudicium, 1998.

———. "Outcast Imagery in Zeami's Plays." In Benito Ortolani and Samuel L. Leiter, eds., *Zeami and the Nō Theatre in the World*. New York: Casta, 1998, 29–39.

Scholz-Cionca, Stanca, and Samuel L. Leiter, eds. *Japanese Theatre and the International Stage*. Brill's Japanese Studies Library, vol. 12. Leiden: Brill, 2000.

Seiffert, Renè. *La tradition secrète du Nō suivie de une journèe de Nō*. Paris: Èditions Gallimard, 1960.

Sekine, Masaru. *Ze-ami and His Theories of Noh Drama*. Gerrards Cross, England: C. Smythe, 1985.

Sellers-Young, Barbara. *Breath, Mask and Character: A Movement Guide for Actors*. Davis, Calif.: Navins, 1997.

Senelick, Laurence, ed. *Gender in Performance: The Presentation of Difference in the Performing Arts*. Hanover, N.H.: Tufts University, University Press of New England, 1992.

Serper, Zvika. "An Experiment in Fusion: Traditional Japanese Theatre and Modern Productions of *Agamemnon* and *Macbeth*." In Stanca Scholz-Cionca and Samuel L. Leiter, eds., *Japanese Theatre and the International Stage*. Brill's Japanese Studies Library. Leiden: Brill, 2000, 12:385–395.

Shevtsova, Maria. "Interculturalism, Aestheticism, Orientalism: Starting from Peter Brook's Mahabharata." *Theatre Research International* 22.2: 98–104.

Shidehara, Michitaro, and Wilfrid Whitehouse, trans. "*Seami Jūrokubushū*: Seami's Sixteen Treatises." *Monumenta Nipponica* 4.2 (1941): 204–239; and 5.2 (1942): 180–214.

Shirane, Haruo. *The Bridge of Dreams: A Poetics of the* Tale of Genji. Stanford, Calif.: Stanford University Press, 1987.

———. "Lyricism and Intertextuality: An Approach to Shunzei's Poetics." *Harvard Journal of Asiatic Studies* 50.1 (1990): 71–85.

———. "Poetic Essence (*Hon'i*) as Japanese Literary Canon." In Stephen D. Miller, ed., *Proceedings of the Association for Japanese Literary Studies, Issues of Canonicity and Canon Formation in Japanese Literary Studies*, vol. 1. Association for Japanese Literary Studies, 2000, 153–164.

Shirane, Haruo, and Tomi Suzuki, eds. *Inventing the Classics: Modernity, National Identity, and Japanese Literature*. Stanford, Calif.: Stanford University Press, 2000.

Shōtetsu. *Conversations with Shōtetsu [Shōtetsu monogatari]*. Trans. Robert H. Brower, with an introduction and notes by Steve D. Carter. Ann Arbor: The University of Michigan Center for Japanese Studies, 1992.

Slawson, David A. *Secret Teachings in the Art of Japanese Gardens: Design Principles, Aesthetic Values*. Tokyo: Kodansha Intl., 1987.

Smethurst, Mae J. *The Artistry of Aeschylus and Zeami: A Comparative Study of Greek Tragedy and Nō*. Princeton, N.J.: Princeton University Press, 1989.

———. *Dramatic Representations of Filial Piety: Five Noh in Translation, with an Introduction*. Ithaca, N.Y.: Cornell University East Asia Program, 1998.

States, Bert O. *Dreaming and Storytelling*. Ithaca, N.Y.: Cornell University Press, 1993.

———. *Great Reckonings in Little Rooms: On the Phenomenology of Theater*. Berkeley: University of California Press, 1985.

Stone, Jacqueline I. *Original Enlightenment and the Transformation of Medieval Japanese Buddhism*. Kuroda Institute Studies in East Asian Buddhism 12. Honolulu: University of Hawai'i Press, 1999.

Strong, Sarah M. "Komachi at the Crossroads: Elements of Popular Female Performance in Two Nō Plays." In Eiji Sekine, ed., *Proceedings of the Midwest Association for Japanese Literary Studies*, Ga/Zoku *Dynamics in Japanese Literature*, vol. 3. Midwest Association for Japanese Literary Studies, 1997, 122–140.

Swanson, Paul L. *Foundations of T'ien-t'ai Philosopy: The Flowering of the Two Truths Theory in Chinese Buddhism*. Berkeley: Asian Humanities Press, 1989.

Tamba Akira. *The Musical Structure of Nō*. Trans. Patricia Matoré. Tokyo: Tokai University Press, 1981.

———. *La structure musicale du nō*. Paris: Klincksieck, 1974.

Tao-yüan Shih. *Ching-te ch'uan teng lu*. Trans. Chang Chung-yuan. New York: Pantheon Books, 1969.

Teele, Roy E., Nicholas J. Teele, and H. Rebecca Teele, trans. *Poems, Stories, Nō Plays: Ono no Komachi*. World Literature in Translation. New York: Garland Publishers, 1993.

Terasaki, Etsuko. *Figures of Desire: Wordplay, Spirit Possession, Fantasy, Madness and Mourning in Japanese Noh Plays*. Michigan Monography Series in Japanese Studies 38. Ann Arbor: The University of Michigan, Center for Japanese Studies, 2002.

———. "Images and Symbols in *Sotoba Komachi*: A Critical Analysis of a Nō Play." *Harvard Journal of Asiatic Studies* 44.1 (1984): 155–184.

———. " 'Wild Words and Specious Phrases': *Kyōgen Kigo* in the Nō Play *Jinen Koji*." *Harvard Journal of Asiatic Studies* 49.2 (1989): 515–552.

Thornhill, Arthur H. III. *Six Circles, One Dewdrop: The Religio-Aesthetic World of Komparu Zenchiku*. Princeton, N.J.: Princeton University Press, 1993.

———. "*Yūgen* after Zeami." In James R. Brandon, ed., *Nō and Kyōgen in the Contemporary World*. Honolulu: University of Hawai'i Press, 1997, 36–64.

Thurman, Robert A. F., trans. *The Holy Teaching of Vimalakirti: A Mahayana Scripture*. University Park: Penn State University Press, 1976.

Tōgasaki, Fumiko. "*Ga-Zoku* and Verbal-Visual Dynamics in the 'Picture Contest' Chapter of *The Tale of Genji*." In Eiji Sekine, ed., *Proceedings of the Midwest*

Association for Japanese Literary Studies, Ga/Zoku Dynamics in Japanese Literature, vol. 3. Midwest Association for Japanese Literary Studies, 1997, 89–99.

Trosper, Barry R., and Giu-hua Leu (Ken C. Yang, illus.). I Ching: *The Illustrated Primer*. San Jose: KGI Publications, 1986.

Tsubaki, Andrew A. "Zeami and the Transition of the Concept of *Yūgen*: A Note on Japanese Aesthetics." *Journal of Aesthetics and Art Criticism* 30.1 (1971): 55–67.

Tsunoda, Ryusaku, Wm. Theodore de Bary, and Donald Keene, eds. *Sources of Japanese Tradition*. 2 vols. New York: Columbia University Press, 1958.

Turner, Frederick. *Natural Classicism: Essays on Literature and Science*. New York: Paragon House Publishers, 1985.

Turner, Victor. *The Anthropology of Performance*. New York: Performing Arts Journal Publications, 1986.

————. *From Ritual to Theatre: The Human Seriousness of Play*. New York: Performing Arts Journal Publications, 1982.

Tyler, Royall. "Buddhism in Noh." *Japanese Journal of Religious Studies* 14.1 (1987): 19–52.

————, ed. and trans. *Japanese Nō Dramas*. London, Penguin, 1992.

————. *The Miracles of the Kasuga Deity*. New York: Columbia University Press, 1990.

————. "The Nō Play *Matsukaze* as a Transformation of *Genji monogatari*." *Journal of Japanese Studies* 20.2 (1994): 377–422.

————. " 'The Path of My Mountain': Buddhism in Nō." In James H. Sanford, William R. LaFleur, and Masatoshi Nagatomi, eds., *Flowing Traces: Buddhism in the Literary and Visual Arts of Japan*. Princeton, N.J.: Princeton University Press, 1992, 149–179.

————. "The *Waki-Shite* Relationship in Nō." In James R. Brandon, ed., *Nō and Kyōgen in the Contemporary World*. Honolulu: University of Hawai'i Press, 1997, 65–90.

Ueda, Makoto. *Literary and Art Theories in Japan*. Cleveland: Western Reserve University Press, 1967.

Varela, Francisco J., Evan Thompson, and Eleanor Rosch. *The Embodied Mind: Cognitive Science and Human Experience*. Cambridge, Mass.: MIT Press, 1991.

Vitz, Evelyn Birge. *Orality and Performance in Early French Romance*. Cambridge: D. S. Brewer, 1999.

Waley, Arthur. *Japanese Poetry: The "Uta."* London: Lund Humphries, 1965.

————, trans. *The Nō Plays of Japan*. New York: Grove Press, 1957.

Walton, Kendall L. *Mimesis as Make-Believe: On the Foundations of the Representational Arts*. Cambridge, Mass.: Harvard University Press, 1990.

Wang Sook Young. "Rengashi Sōgi no koten kenkyū, *Kokinshū* denju to chūshaku. In Stephen D. Miller, ed., *Proceedings of the Association for Japanese Literary Studies, Issues of Canonicity and Canon Formation in Japanese Literary Studies*, vol. 1. Association for Japanese Literary Studies, 2000, 471–485.

Watanabe, Moriaki. "Zéami ou le souci du langage." *Représentation*, no. 1 (1991): 8–16.

Weisstein, Ulrich, ed. *The Essence of Opera*. New York: Norton Library, 1964.

White, Hayden. *Figural Realism: Studies in the Mimesis Effect*. Baltimore, Md.: John Hopkins University Press, 1999.

Wittgenstein, Ludwig. *Philosophical Investigations*. Trans. G. E. M. Anscombe. 3rd ed. New York: Macmillan, 1958.

Wylie-Marques, Kathryn. "Zeami Motokiyo and Etienne Decroux: Twin Reformers of the Art of Mime." In Benito Ortolani and Samuel L. Leiter, eds., *Zeami and the Nō Theatre in the World*. New York: Casta, 1998, 109–126.

Yamazaki, Masakazu. "The Aesthetics of Transformation: Zeami's Dramatic Theories." Trans., with introduction, by Susan Matisoff. *Journal of Japanese Studies* 7.2 (1981): 215–257.

Yampolsky, Philip B. *The Platform Sutra of the Sixth Patriarch*. New York: Columbia University Press, 1967.

Yasuda, Kenneth K. "The Dramatic Structure of *Ataka*, a Nō Play." *Monumenta Nipponica* 27.4 (1972): 359–398.

———. *Masterworks of the Nō Theater*. Bloomington: Indiana University Press, 1989.

———. "A Prototypical Nō Wig Play: *Izutsu*." *Harvard Journal of Asiatic Studies* 40 (1980): 399–464.

———. "The Structure of *Hagoromo*, a Nō Play." *Harvard Journal of Asiatic Studies* 33 (1973): 5–89.

Yip, Leo Shing Chi. "Reinventing China: Cultural Adaptation in Medieval Japanese Nō Theatre." Ph.D. dissertation, The Ohio State University, 2004.

Yokota-Murakami, Gerry. *The Formation of the Canon of Nō: The Literary Tradition of Divine Authority*. Osaka: Osaka University Press, 1997.

Young, J. Z. *Philosophy and the Brain*. Oxford: Oxford University Press, 1986.

Yuasa, Yasuo. *The Body: Toward an Eastern Mind-Body Theory*. Ed. T. P. Kasulis, trans. Nagatomo Shigenori and T. P. Kasulis. Albany: State University of New York Press, 1987.

Yusa, Michiko. "*Riken no Ken*: Zeami's Theory of Acting and Theatrical Appreciation." *Monumenta Nipponica* 42.3 (1987): 331–345.

Index

• • •

210; and the interesting, 212; and
jōju (fulfillment), 210–212, 213,
299, 398n119; in *kuse* section, 179;
ontology of, 130, 211–212, 214–215,
231–232; in programs, 129–130,
150–154; in structure of play,
130, 144–145, 152–153, 171–173,
293–295, 296, 298, 394nn85, 91, 92;
and vocal expression, 213–214,
361n26
jōju (fulfillment), 207, 210; *ichiza jōju*
(fulfillment in the minds of all present), 212–215; *kenmon* (visual and
aural), 207, 359n2; *kenpū* (visional
affect), 207–210, 288, 299, 398n119;
and *rakkyō* (resolution), 210
Jūnigorō Yasutsugu, 32, 329n34
Jūnijirō, 32
Jūrō Motomasa. *See* Kanze Motomasa

Kaden (Transmission of the flower), 3,
36–37, 330nn45–46; I: "Items concerning training over the years", 37,
330n45; II: "Items concerning imitation," 37, 44–46, 83; III: "Question and answer on various matters,"
37, 99–100, 115, 129, 150–151,
218, 232–233, 240, 330n45, 369n5;
IV: "Divine matters," 37, 215,
330n45; V: "Initiation into the
secrets," 37, 60, 330n46; VI: "Training in the flower," 63, 97, 98–99,
107, 116, 144, 151, 266, 330n46,
335n47; VII: "Special oral transmissions," 38, 106, 218, 240, 284,
330n46, 369n5
Kagaya, Shinko, 289–290
Kaidō kudari, 33, 56, 57
kaiko/kaikō (opening utterance) 383n17
kaikonin (opening player). *See waki*

kakari (mood, overtones), 10, 110; aural
dimension, 50–51, 61–62, 89–90,
93–96, 150, 155–156, 255–256, 296,
335n45, 355n28, 392n70; and chant
and dance, 10, 50–51, 96–97, 101,
117, 296; as emergent property, 95,
96–100, 102–104, 108, 151, 353n13;
and 5 dance methods, 207–208; and
monomane, 95, 100–101, 102, 151,
153, 208–209, 278; and *nikyoku*, 95,
301; and Ōmi *sarugaku*, 95, 209; and
poetics, 95, 273; and Skin, muscle,
and bone, 103–104; and visional
affect *(kenpū)*, 218, 390n60
kakeai (heightened exchange), 132,
133, 171, 172–173, 298, 390n60;
in *Takasago*, 164, 172, 308–311
kakekotoba (pivot word/phrase),
193–194
Kakyō (Mirror of the flower), 50, 67,
69, 95, 96, 102, 104–105, 129, 135,
170, 206, 213, 217, 218, 219–220,
226, 227, 235, 260, 270; on *monomane*, 95; on, sequencing, 203–207,
207–210; title, 235
Kamens, Edward, 143
Kanai Kiyomitsu, 156–157
Kan'ami Kiyotsugu, 9, 27, 55–56, 57,
60, 66, 145, 195, 261, 301, 325n3,
408n151, 409n152
Kanze Hisao, cover, 79f, 125f
Kanze Motomasa, 32, 41, 57, 58,
327n26, 328n29, 331n54, 408n151
Kanze Motoyoshi, 33, 34, 41, 51,
156–157, 302, 331n54
Kanze Sōsetsu, 291
Kashu no uchinukigaki (Excerpt from
"Training in the Flower"), 67, 129,
150, 152–153, 331n54, 352n3
Kasuga-Kōfukuji complex, 28, 31, 32,

About the Author

. . .

SHELLEY FENNO QUINN (Ph.D., Indiana University) is associate professor of Japanese in the Department of East Asian Languages and Literatures at The Ohio State University, where she teaches Japanese literature, theatre, and classical language. She has studied noh dance and chant and the noh flute with teachers in Japan and performed the play *Hagoromo*. Prof. Quinn has twice been visiting researcher at Hōsei University's Institute for Nōgaku Studies and, in addition to a multimedia introduction to the noh, is at work on a study of the life and art of the late influential actor and writer Kanze Hisao.

PRODUCTION NOTES
Quinn / *Developing Zeami*

Book and cover design and composition by Diane Gleba Hall
Text set in Goudy Old Style
Printing and binding by The Maple-Vail Book Manufacturing Group
Printed on 60 lb. Text White Opaque, 426 ppi